Tensions in
Contemporary
Theology

Tensions in Contemporary Theology

Second Edition

Stanley N. Gundry
and Alan F. Johnson, *Editors*

Foreword by Roger Nicole

BAKER BOOK HOUSE
Grand Rapids, Michigan 49506

CONTENTS

FOREWORD

At the threshold of a volume like this one, some people may wonder why evangelicals need be concerned with many modern thinkers whose approach is far remote from the evangelical point of view. Can we not safely leave them to their own speculations and devices and carry our task as evangelical thinkers without reference to them? I would like in this preface to address myself briefly to this outlook.

1. Evangelicals need to be acquainted with the major theological thinkers of our time. We cannot expect to commend our own outlook if we show ourselves completely ignorant of the position held by others. In a certain sense we need to earn our right to disagree, and part of this earning lies in an accurate understanding and appraisal of the position of those with whom we differ. One charge which evangelicals have often leveled at others is that they have presented criticism of the conservative stance that manifested very inadequate information, often based on second-hand materials and reflecting a biased approach and a caricature of what the evangelical view is. We cannot afford to emulate this kind of onesidedness. Since we want to be treated fairly, we owe it to ourselves and to others to treat others fairly. This involves achieving a proper understanding of our opponents' points of view, of their statements, and of their aims. This volume attempts to provide a beginning in this direction in that it seeks in every case to make a fair representation of the position of the men discussed. Obviously, it will not be an appropriate substitute for reading the works of these men themselves, but it will provide guidelines developed in the spirit of fairness which will assist the evangelical in securing a sense of orientation in the midst of a variety of opinions which could otherwise appear bewildering.

2. The evangelical needs to learn many important lessons, even from those with whom he disagrees. They often have managed to

7

make their voices heard in a more effective way than we have. They sometimes have related themselves to problems and aspirations which may have been neglected in evangelical circles. Thus, even in places where faithfulness to the biblical message demands that we should disagree, we may cull valuable insights into the mood and spirit of our age. Furthermore, we ought not to reason that, because certain positions are subject to criticism, they contain no element of truth whatsoever. In most cases views which command a wide support do embody substantial elements of truth. We must ever remain teachable and be prepared to find valuable insights, even in places where at first we might not have been inclined to seek teaching for ourselves. By broadening the range of our horizon we may be in a better position to understand our own faith and commend it to others.

It is therefore a happy development that a volume like the present one should be issued, written from a strictly evangelical point of view by authors who have made a proper study from primary sources of the men and movements they describe and with an attitude of generosity and candor that ought at all times to characterize a servant of the Lord.

ROGER NICOLE

Gordon-Conwell Theological Seminary

PREFACE

Modern theology appears to be in a virtual labyrinth. So complex is this maze that only a few have successfully penetrated its intricate passageways. Especially for the uninitiated, the task of understanding the many schools of contemporary Christian theology seems bewildering, to say the least. Yet it is essential for a strong evangelical Christian faith to be able to both understand these current theologies and to offer sound criticism which leads to the building of a positive theology.

But do we not already have many volumes on modern theology? How does this book differ from those already in print? These are appropriate questions. Two features of the present work distinguish it from comparable books in print. In the first place it addresses itself to the theologies of the sixties and seventies in a concise yet comprehensive manner in the span of a single volume. Other treatments tend to be either superficial, if they are comprehensive, or too detailed and limited in scope to serve as introductions, such as whole volumes dealing with theology of hope or process theology.

Another distinguishing feature of this work is that each of the contemporary alternatives in theology is analyzed and evaluated from a conservative orientation by evangelical scholars who are experts in their areas. We are aware of more liberally committed books, but this volume is intended to meet the need for an evangelical analysis and response to the recent theological scene. The chapters which follow have been written by people who are teachers of philosophy and theology and who represent a wide variety of theological backgrounds and traditions, thus insuring an absence of more narrow theological divisions. Included are both seasoned, senior scholars as well as younger scholars emerging as evangelical spokesmen. They not only are evangelical in commitment, but are also distinguished scholars in their fields and recognized as specialists in certain areas. We, the editors, have chosen a secon-

9

dary role. Instead of contributing ourselves, we wanted to be learners. Having conceived the plan for the book, we contacted those
people who, in our and others' judgments, were the best qualified in
each special area. To our surprise and joy, they each enthusiasti-
cally consented to be a part of the total project.

The writers of this book were invited by the editors to prepare
an original contribution dealing with one aspect of the theologies of
the sixties and seventies. Each author was in possession of the
complete outline of the book and a thumbnail sketch of not only their
own assignment but also each of the others. Thus, the volume is
more than a symposium of essays on a common theme. Though
multiple in authorship, we believe there is also a strong unity that
binds the material together and creates the impression of a singular
development. Within the broad guidelines which we laid down, each
author was free to develop his approach as seemed best to him. The
contributors were instructed to write for students in upper division
college and introductory seminary courses, with the hope that pas-
tors and others concerned to maintain an awareness of recent
theological developments would also be attracted to the book. The
major portion of each chapter was to analyze and explain the option,
attempting to capture the genius of the position and its major representatives. Finally, each chapter was to contain a critique of the
viewpoint from a conservative, evangelical perspective. The treatment was to be scholarly but aimed at the student rather than the
academician. Whether these goals were achieved the reader will
have to decide.

The specific focus of the book is found in chapters three through
nine, where six major phenomena related to understanding the current theological picture are discussed. Chapters one and two are
introductory and set the stage for properly viewing the current
scene; chapter ten sets forth the conservative option and points in
a positive fashion to the future of evangelical theology. Dr. Ramm's
opening chapter traces the historical background for the present
maze of views showing how most of the alternatives of the previous
centuries had run into dead-ends by the mid twentieth century.
From this impasse sprang the alternatives of the sixties and seventies, which are touched on by Dr. Ramm and further elaborated
in chapters three to nine.

In chapter two, Dr. Grounds further sets the stage for succeeding chapters by discussing four pacesetters of the current scene:
Bultmann, Bonhoeffer, Tillich, and Teilhard. While these men did

not produce theologies in the sixties and seventies, certain motifs in their thought were picked up and developed more radically by their successors, that is, Bultmann's demythologizing, Bonhoeffer's man come of age and religionless Christianity, Tillich's view of God, and Teilhard's cosmic evolution.

As a first step, we also considered it essential to have a competent philosopher discuss the whole bearing of recent trends in religious language analysis. Chapter three, by Dr. Obitts, does this job well, though understandably some without philosophical background may find this chapter somewhat more difficult than the others. The remaining chapters on secular theology, theology of hope, process theology, contemporary Roman Catholic theology, and liberation theologies are self-explanatory.

One may wonder why no treatment is given of some of the more standard modern theologians as Barth, Brunner, and Reinhold Niebuhr. Our reasons for these omissions are twofold: first, they did not produce theologies in the sixties and seventies; and second, there is an abundance of helpful material already in print discussing thoroughly their views.

Our hope as editors is that this project will stimulate conservative theological students toward a more careful understanding of modern theology; its evangelical assessment; and the present crucial need for a positive, scholarly, world-related and evangelical theology. We agree with the recent lament of Dr. Harold Lindsell, editor of *Christianity Today,* when he remarked:

> I do not now see among young evangelicals any large number of bright minds articulating and defending the Christian faith in the arena of biblical and systematic theology. In a recent issue of *Christianity Today* (December 20, 1974), Klaus Bockmuhl said: "The great teachers of a past generation have gone, and it is not yet decided which turn theology will take. . . . There could come indeed a renaissance of evangelical theology. But it will certainly take hard work and the combined efforts of all who see the task set before them." . . . I would love to see a Luther, Calvin, Knox, or Edwards rise among you to do for your age what some of the keenest minds I know did for mine.[1]

This also is our hope in sending forth the following pages.

STANLEY N. GUNDRY
ALAN F. JOHNSON

1. Harold Lindsell, "Think on These Things," *The Other Side,* March-April 1975, pp. 20-21.

THE FORTUNES OF THEOLOGY FROM SCHLEIERMACHER TO BARTH AND BULTMANN

1

The Fortunes of Theology from Schleiermacher to Barth and Bultmann

by
BERNARD RAMM

This book specifically focuses on the theological tensions of the last two decades; nevertheless it is appropriate, indeed absolutely necessary, to survey the theological landscape of the preceding years. The theological trends which emerged as the neoorthodox theology of Barth and Brunner and the existential theology of Bultmann and began to wane in the 1950s must be seen against the panorama of the intellectual and theological climate of the preceding years. Because Friedrich Schleiermacher's *Addresses on Religion to Its Cultured Despisers* (1799) was the first book in the tradition of modern religious liberalism, we have chosen to begin our survey with the early nineteenth century. In general, our method will be to focus on topics or themes rather than individual theologians, countries, or types of theology.

THE IMPACT OF THE ENLIGHTENMENT

While we propose to survey modern theology since Schleiermacher, we dare not ignore the climate of opinion out of which it emerged and in which it developed, and that climate was the

BERNARD RAMM, A.B., B.D., M.A., Ph.D., is professor of Christian theology at American Baptist Seminary of the West, Berkeley, California. He is the author of numerous books and articles, including his recent ones, *The God Who Makes a Difference* (Word, 1972) and *The Evangelical Heritage* (Word, 1973).

15

Enlightenment.[1] It was during the seventeenth and eighteenth centuries that the characteristic modern approach to most of the sciences and university disciplines emerged. It was a time of intense
self-awareness of methodology for all subject matters. There was a
general distrust of tradition, custom, antiquity, and authority, with a
premium placed upon skepticism, reason, and analysis.

The impact of the Enlightenment on the modern mind and
hence on theology can be discerned in many areas, but most significantly in those following.

HISTORICISM

The canons of scientific history (often called historiography)
were refined during the Enlightenment along with the highest standards for historical accuracy and objectivity. This led to a continuous questioning of the historical integrity and believability of the
historical materials in sacred Scripture.

SCIENTISM

Modern science from Galileo to the present has been a success
story. Consequently, it is no longer considered the task of
philosophers to tell us about the world at large or the world in the
small. Science is considered capable of giving solid answers. In
addition to piecemeal information, it gives a scientific vision, or
picture of reality, which replaces what men have thought in the past.
For the Enlightenment mentality, this in turn means that wherever
the ancient Scriptures conflict with modern science—geology, as-
tronomy, and biology in particular—then Scripture must give way to
science. Wherever Scripture pictures the universe in a way contrary
to the world view of scientism or describes events which are supernatural, modern man is to choose science over Scripture.

CRITICISM

Studies in manuscripts from the medieval and classical periods
revealed that many documents which claimed to be authentic and
trustworthy were actually not. Consequently, all documents from
the past must be carefully checked for authenticity, accuracy, and
factuality. No longer can documents be accepted at face value.

Holy Scripture is subjected to the same scrutiny. It is claimed
that the Pentateuch is a series of literary fragments stitched together, rather than one book, and that it was composed late in
Israel's history, not early. The gospels were not written by the men
the Church has claimed. Rather, they were productions of unknown

men in the Christian Church in its earliest history. The book of Isaiah was written by two hands, and perhaps three. This type of criticism has been codified under the title "higher criticism."[2]

RATIONALISM

The Deists were pioneers in theology who espoused the dictum that reason is the test of all truth, including religious truth. They had been anticipated by the founders of modern philosophy, who went a secular route in philosophical methodology even though they still believed in God. This trust in reason was summarized by Kant in his three great "critiques," in which he argued that reason is queen in science, or knowledge; in ethics and religion; and in beauty, or aesthetics.

If this be the case, then Christian theologians must subject irrational or mysterious elements in the Christian faith to reason. Doctrines that offend reason—in any of its functions—must then be eliminated as viable topics of theology.

TOLERATIONISM

Explorers from the time of Columbus until now have discovered great cultures and their religions all around the world. We may now speak of the great religions of the world. And, as Gotthold Lessing asserted in his famous drama, *Nathan the Wise* (1779), no one religion is to claim absolute truth in the presence of other great religions. Toleration is the supreme virtue in matters of religion, and dogmatism is the most reprehensible attitude. The implication tends toward an ecumenism not only of Christian communions but of world religions. Indeed, a natural religion composed of the best elements of many religions is to be preferred. This means the end of strong, vigorous Christian theology.

OPTIMISM

The Enlightenment mentality no longer believes in the black doctrine of original sin. The progress of man realized from the advances in all the sciences as well as better knowledge of psychology and sociology means that the race is on the upward curve. Condorcet and the other French encyclopedists projected man's upward direction. Given time, given more and more scientific knowledge of all sorts, the inevitable result is upward progress. Gloomy doctrines of man and of this life as a burden, a cross-bearing, gave way to more optimistic views of man's powers and of the joy and vitality of life here and now.

KANTIANISM

In addition to these significant Enlightenment emphases, the matrix out of which modern theology grew, the philosophy of Immanuel Kant (1724-1804) demands special mention. In many ways he was the theoretical founder of religious liberalism, because so many liberal theologians built directly upon Kant's philosophy or upon some alternate version of it. He created a new apology for the Christian religion (as he understood it) by showing in his *Critique of Pure Reason* (1781) that science was mute about religion. Science by its very nature could say nothing for or against it. Then in his *Critique of Practical Reason* (1788) he attempted to found upon reason and reason alone the validity of the concepts of God, freedom, and immortality. In so doing he gave religion a strong ethical interpretation, which has been a characteristic of the theology of religious liberalism from that time until the present. His theses propounded in the *Critique of Pure Reason* were very similar to David Hume's and did much to discredit the apologetics of orthodox theology as well the possibility of supernatural religion.

THE RISE OF RELIGIOUS LIBERALISM

In the broadest definition possible, religious liberalism was the effort to restate the Christian faith in harmony with the Enlightenment, or from the perspectives of the Enlightenment. For our purposes we shall use the terms *modernist* or *liberal* as synonyms, although some writers prefer to use the word *liberal* for theologians who still accept some normative status for Jesus and Holy Scripture, whereas modernists are strictly philosophers of religion who may or may not give allegiance to the Christian faith.

The basic assumption with which most theologians of religious liberalism worked was that some form of philosophical idealism was the best basis for reconstructing the Christian faith for the mentality of the Enlightenment.

The pioneer in reconstructing theology by using an articulate philosophical base was Schleiermacher.[3] He worked with different aspects of German philosophical idealism to create a theology acceptable to Enlightenment mentality. Examination of three basic philosophical concepts will show how philosophy is at work in his theology.

1. Religion is essentially about feeling (*Gefühl*). This is feeling philosophically understood as that sense within man of his

continuity with the Spirit of the universe and his oneness with God. It is not mere emotion. German identity philosophy, namely, that at bottom all the differences of the universe stem from one root and are at that root identical, is behind this. Although usually called *panentheism,* it approaches pantheism; and to some interpreters of Schleiermacher, it is pantheism.

2. In terms of man's response to God, or as this feeling comes to consciousness, it is a feeling of absolute dependence upon God. There is some debate about the translation of *schlechthinnigen* (absolute, or unconditional), but the point is, it is something man can give only to God.

3. This can also be expressed in levels of consciousness. Sin is essentially sensuous consciousness, by which is meant any kind of total preoccupation with this world to the exclusion of man's real total dependence upon God and God consciousness, the feeling or the sense of the feeling of being unconditionally dependent upon God.

The implications of Schleiermacher's understanding of religion are far-reaching. First, it is an attack upon dogmatic, creedal orthodoxy. Vigorous assent to Christian dogma as part of the vitality of faith is excluded. Indeed, in his *Addresses* he commends the cultured despisers of religion for rejecting "the dogmas and propositions of religion." "They are not in any case the essence of religion itself."[4]

Second, all Christian doctrines either are reconstructed so as to conform to these philosophical criteria or are eliminated. The locus of faith is no longer in what God says (divine revelation) or in what God does (redemption in history) but primarily in what man experiences. The hope was that these cultured despisers of religion in Germany who rejected orthodoxy would now be willing to accept this retooled version of Christianity.

Third, the center of gravity of Christianity is now in the experience of the Christian and not in those sovereign acts of grace and revelation which God does in history. The essence of all religion, including Christianity, is experience; its seat is not reason, conscience, or volition but *feeling.* Christ is Redeemer in that He creates the change of consciousness within us through the preaching in the church.

Schleiermacher did not start a school as such but was an inspiration in many schools. One of these was known as the mediating theology school *(Vermittlungstheologie,* for example, Flücke, Neander, Nitzsch, Tholuck, Lange, Dorner, Rothe, Martensen, Beyschlag). This group filled the gap between Schleiermacher and Ritschl. It was guided by three principles:

1. The general intellectual advances of the Enlightenment were not to be denied.
2. The centrality of Christ and the importance of a profound Christian experience as taught by Schleiermacher were positive gains.
3. But the severe reduction of theology by Schleiermacher was wrong, and a more positive attitude toward historic theology should be pursued. A number of the great doctrines Schleiermacher had rejected still had validity in the Christian church.

After Kant, philosophy came to be dominated by Georg Hegel (1770-1831), a contemporary of Schleiermacher who served on the same university faculty. Hegel's unique contribution to philosophy was that history carried its own meaning. History itself was going through an evolutionary process, although of a cultural and rational kind, not biological as Darwin was later to say. Furthermore, this evolution of culture went through a process from the simple to the complex, and by reason of pushes and pulls (the dialectic) which forced all the elements of culture forwards and upwards.

Hegel's influence extended to biblical criticism and theology. In the field of biblical criticism, Wellhausen and followers in the Old Testament and Baur and followers in the New Testament attempted to reconstruct biblical history and documents using as their point of leverage the Hegelian philosophy of history. As for theology, Hegel subsumed it under his philosophical theology, or better, under philosophy itself. Although Hegel had his own version of Christianity, it did not seem to play any important part in the development of theology except obliquely.[5]

One of the better known of the Hegelian theologians was A. E. Biedermann (1819-1885). Common to Hegelians, he made a distinction between the "Christ principle" and the "Jesus of history." The "Christ principle" was the union of God and man, or the God-man union. The "Jesus principle" is that this consciousness of the God-man union reached its highest manifestation in Jesus; but we do not absolutely need the historical Jesus, for humanity can live on the

Christ principle. The infiltration of a philosophy totally corrupting the New Testament witness is obvious to an evangelical reader.

Another Hegelian, P. K. Marheineke (1780-1846), is somewhat important in that some scholars believe that Karl Barth derived from him the notion that revelation is an encounter or experience and not the communication of divinely revealed truth. Overall, the impact of Hegel was greater among the Old and New Testament critics than among the theologians.*

It should be mentioned that there was a strong apologetical element in Hegel's philosophy, which had its strongest impact in Denmark and to which Sören Kierkegaard (1813-55) made such a vigorous rebuttal. Philosophy said literally what theology said metaphorically or symbolically. All the doctrines of theology were capable of philosophical defense if they were translated into literal philosophical language. Hence the historic doctrine of the God-man became in philosophy symbolic of the continuity of the divine and the human. Traces of such philosophical retranslations of theology may be found in the theology of Paul Tillich in the twentieth century.

Another theologian showing the distinct influence of philosophy upon his thought was Samuel Taylor Coleridge (1772-1834). Technically he was a poet and man of letters and not a theologian, yet his influence on theology in England and America was enormous. He studied in Germany and brought to England the philosophical idealism reigning in Germany at that time, with its liberal interpretation of Christianity. This he summarized in his book, *Aids to Reflection* (1825), which became the carrier of German idealism and German liberalism to England and America. President James Marsh (1794-1847) of the University of Vermont edited and published an edition of *Aids to Reflection* in 1829, which marked one of the earliest importations from Germany to America of liberal theology.

The name Albrecht Ritschl (1822-89) is also written large across the face of liberal theology. The religious liberalism which spread to England, America, and eventually to the mission fields of the world bore the imprint of the theology of Ritschl. Although he repudiated the role of metaphysical philosophy in theology and claimed to have a theology founded on a historical religion—namely, the historical

*We are bypassing a discussion of Ludwig Feuerbach (1804-72) because his views of Christianity are mainly critical. He is the supposed link between Hegel and Marx. His most famous book is *The Essence of Christianity* (1854), the recent edition of which has a foreword by Karl Barth. Barth felt that Feuerbach's attack on Christianity sank liberal theology.

Jesus—we find in fact another philosophical theology. Philosophically Ritschl was indebted to Kant, but with variations adapted from
the German philosopher Hermann Lotze (1817-81), who had done
much to develop value theory. He had a great impact on Ritschl. So
instead of the split of matters of science and matters of ethics which
characterized Kant's philosophy, Ritschl substituted matters of
value for matters of ethics, even though ethics still played a major
part in his theology.

Based on his philosophical presuppositions, Ritschl divided all
sentences into those which expressed judgments of fact and judgments of value—*judgment* being a Kantian expression. Hence, that
Jesus died on the cross is a factual, historical judgment; but that in
some sense Jesus died for me is a value judgment. Theology is then
concerned with value judgments.

Ritschl seems to have meant that value judgments were just as
much part of reality as historical judgments. But in the advancement
of the modern approach to science and history, it became more and
more difficult to assert that a value judgment had as much "reality"
to it as a historical judgment. This was one of the reasons liberal
theology eventually began to pull apart, and rightly so. The resurrection of Christ, for example, is to the evangelical both a historical and
a value judgment. Similarly, revelation, to the evangelical, is something which happens in history per se, as well as inside of the
prophets; and it is therefore both a value judgment and a historical
judgment—to use Ritschl's terms. But in liberal Ritschlian theology,
it became decreasingly evident that value judgments denoted reality
per se, and in many cases they did not.

Although Ritschlian themes permeated liberal theology, we will
mention only two of the more prominent Ritschlian theologians,
Wilhelm Herrmann (1846-1922) and Ernst Troeltsch (1865-1923).
Herrmann's significance derived from the wide influence he exercised. He exerted the greatest theological influence upon Bultmann
and Barth in their student days. Bultmann found it easy to move
from the personalism of Herrmann into the existentialism of
Heidegger, and Barth said that he began his first assignment after
university days in Geneva with no other theology than that of
Herrmann.

Herrmann was a disciple of Kant and Ritschl. He was very
Kantian in that Christianity was reduced to the moral teachings of
the historical Jesus. That which cannot be acted upon (morally?)
cannot be a matter of Christian faith. Hence such matters as the

preexistence of Christ or His session at the right hand of God could not be matters of saving faith. Again, this is typical liberal reductionism.

Troeltsch was a more diluted Ritschlian. Other philosophers besides Kant had influenced him, such as Windelband, Rickert, and Dilthey. He worked hard at a new synthesis, but it was never compelling. He tried to develop a theory of man being natively religious by his doctrine of the religious a priori. On the positive side, he attempted to relate Christianity more to history than other Kantians and was famous for his work, *The Social Teaching of the Christian Churches* (1921).[6]

Liberalism took root and grew in the United States in the nineteenth century. It was not immune to the European currents we have been discussing. American Unitarianism and Romanticism were soils especially receptive to radical theological change; but the general erosion that had been occurring in American theology was conducive to further and even more destructive changes in more orthodox circles.

The story of American liberal theology in this century is complex, but the name Horace Bushnell (1802-76) stands above all others. He was a pastor-theologian who kept moving and shifting with the theological moods. He was influenced by Coleridge's famous *Aids to Reflection* through the Marsh edition of 1829, by German idealism, and by Schleiermacher's view of the Trinity. Early in his career he expounded a type of moral-influence theory of the atonement, similar to that of later liberals. Because he so strenuously objected to the stylized conversions of the evangelists of his time and taught that children ought to be nurtured into Christianity rather than evangelized into it, he is called the father of religious education. Ahlstrom also sees him as the real founder of liberalism in American theology.[7]

Another facet of liberal theology especially typical of American liberalism needs to be delineated—the so-called Social Gospel. Ritschl had redefined the Church and the Kingdom of God in strongly ethical terms. The supreme maxim was the ethic of love as taught by Jesus, and the church was composed of those who accepted this ethic. To spread this ethic in all of society was to extend the Kingdom of God.[8] In these theses lay the seeds of what later was to be called the Social Gospel.

Christian Socialism existed as movements in Germany, Switzerland, and England before the Social Gospel emerged in America.

It was in America that the expressions *Social Gospel* and *liberalism* became practically synonymous. Although the pioneering work was S. Colwell's *New Themes for the Protestant Clergy* (1851), Washington Gladden *(The Christian Way, 1887)* is reckoned as the father of the Social Gospel and Walter Rauschenbusch (*Christianity and the Social Gospel,* 1907) its most famous theologian. Instead of thinking of salvation as bringing the reconciliation of individuals with God and effecting eternal life in heaven, Social Gospellers tended to preach societal salvation in the here and now in an attempt to ameliorate the social evils of the times. This would be effected by spreading Jesus' ethic of love, bringing reconciliation of individuals to one another, and restructuring of societal institutions.

The evangelicals and fundamentalists thought the Social Gospel was a betrayal of and a misrepresentation of the Gospel as found in the New Testament. While there is a social ethic, to speak of a Social Gospel is to use a misnomer. The liberals replied with an exposition of the concept of the Kingdom of God and with their keen awareness of sociological problems. To redeem a man and not his society was an abstraction. Many stormy sermons were preached on both sides of this issue. Because of the practical identity between liberal theology and the Social Gospel, an understandable yet extreme reaction settled upon many evangelicals, in which they feared to work out the social ethic implicit in their own theology lest they betray the New Testament Gospel as the liberals had done.

THE CONFRONTATION WITH EVOLUTION

The main importance of Charles Darwin's *The Origin of Species* was its attempt to formulate the theory of evolution into an empirical law. That the world and its population had gone through some sort of change from the simple to the complex was an idea as old as the pre-Socratic philosophers. That there was a philosophical evolution of all things had been taught by the philosopher Hegel. But to formulate an empirical, somewhat testable biological theory was the achievement of Charles Darwin.

To many evangelical theologians this seemed to conflict with the Genesis record, especially when combined with the uniformitarian theory of geology announced by Sir Charles Lyell (1797-1875) in his famous text, *Elements of Geology* (first edition, 1838; six editions published in his lifetime). To this he added a work on *The Antiquity of Man* (1863).[9]

Uniformitarian geology and biological evolution seemed to contradict orthodox theology on such matters as creation, an original Adam, an historical Fall, original sin, and total depravity. We mention only two incidents somewhat typical of the confrontations which occurred.

First, in Oxford, England Bishop Samuel Wilberforce (1805-73) debated in 1860 with T. H. Huxley (1825-95), Darwin's public defender and popular spokesman. It was a contest between the oratory of Soapy Sam (as Wilberforce was called, among other such names) and the sturdy, scientific mentality of Huxley. In a famous encounter, Wilberforce asked Huxley whether he was a descendant from the monkeys on his mother's or father's side. Huxley replied in so many words that he would sooner be the descendant of an ape than a dishonest theologian. Huxley clearly won the honors of that debate, though the issue was far from settled.

Second, we cite the famous Scopes trial in Dayton, Tennessee (July 1925). Tennessee had passed a law forbiding the teaching of evolution in its school system. Scopes was a high school teacher in Dayton who challenged the law. The case became famous when the greatest political orator of the time and outspoken fundamentalist, William Jennings Bryan, undertook the prosecution, and the famous defense lawyer Clarence Darrow undertook the defense. Although Bryan formally won the case, in the popular mind the weight of evidence was with the losing side.

Another aspect of the theory of evolution was significant for theology and biblical studies. Liberal theologians used the theory of evolution not only for the explanation of biological phenomena but as part of their world view. They saw religion as well as Holy Scripture going through a process of development from the simple to the complex, in direct analogy to biological evolution. This was reflected in their higher critical theories and reconstructions of biblical history. Naturally the conflict between fundamentalists and liberals became even sharper when evolution was expanded beyond biology and became part of the philosophical platform of liberalism.[10]

As an example, the results of accepting the evolutionary world view become evident when one examines the liberals' view of the Fall and original sin. Liberal theology rejected the historic doctrines of a Fall in Adam, original sin, and total depravity; yet it did not hesitate to develop ideas similar to these concepts.[11] For example, the doctrine of original sin was said to mean really that society itself had enough corruption in it that children born into a corrupt society became corrupt people. If we could ever have a perfect society, so-called original sin and total depravity would disappear.

Others took an unusual ethical approach to the problem: man fell "upward." Beasts have no conscience; but when in the course of evolution some prehuman creature felt guilty about something it did, it had progressed morally. Although from our moralistic prudishness it looks like a fall down, it was actually a fall up, because finally a creature had registered a moral experience.

Still others took evolution in a different direction, saying there is always a lag in evolution. There was a time when aggression and ferocity were necessary for survival. But for a human being with a more highly developed brain and a sense of morality, such attitudes or behavior patterns are wrong. But we still carry along some of our evolutionary attitudes as a drag, and it is that which makes us sinful.

The problem of evil also was treated as an evolutionary lag, an irrational surd, a sort of sludge in the universe, a cosmic fall, a part of the ·necessary resistance in soul making, or as just part of the world order inherent in an evolving universe. One of the reasons why neoorthodoxy was later to pound liberal theology so hard was liberalism's light view of sin and evil. Even its theory of "dis-value" or "dys-teleology" was not adequate to meet the raw edge of evil as men experience it.†

THE QUESTION OF THE BIBLE

The Enlightenment not only pressured theologians to seek a new basis for Christian faith in a philosophical rootage, it also forced theologians to face up to the critical studies which had occurred in historical research in the secular disciplines.

The application of critical literary methods to Scripture along with critical historical studies—the two cannot be separated—led to what was dubbed "higher criticism." Lower criticism was the study of the text of Scripture and the problem of variant readings; higher criticism was the study of the authorship, date, reason for composition, literary unity of the book, and whatever other problems the book posed.

Because higher criticism became so critical of traditional views

†Edgar Sheffield Brightman (1884-1953) did the most to solve the problem of evil with his concept of a finite God. For a survey of his thought see William Robert Miller, *Contemporary American Protestant Thought* (New York: Bobbs Merrill, 1973), chap. 9. In that Miller includes no evangelicals in his book, one comes to the very odd conclusion that according to Miller no orthodox or evangelical theologians were doing any thinking. What a strange concept of ecumenicity.

of Holy Scripture, it became known as a special activity of liberal theologians. To this day the expression *higher criticism* is taken in a negative sense by many evangelicals. Our concern is not with criticism as such but with the way higher criticism was used to undermine the integrity of Scripture and, with that, the entire orthodox program in theology.

What brought higher criticism to the attention of more than the university and seminary scholars were the famous cases of ecclesiastical trial for heresy and the accompanying publicity in the popular press. For example, Bishop J. W. Colenson wrote *The Pentateuch and the Book of Joshua Critically Examined* (1862-1879). Here he followed the growing conviction that the Pentateuch was composed from a series of sources and that the history recorded in the Pentateuch was not exactly the way the events must have taken place. He was excommunicated by the Church of England (1866), although he was able to continue as bishop of Natal.

In Great Britain, William Robertson Smith (1846-94) was tried for the advanced views he expressed in the ninth edition of the *Encyclopaedia Britannica*. His articles on the Old Testament seemed too far afield for orthodox views of Holy Scripture, so he was removed from his professorial chair in Aberdeen in 1881. However, the University of Cambridge picked him up, and there he finished his academic career.

In America a controversy erupted over the views of C. A. Briggs (1841-1913). Because he held to higher criticism in his views of the Old Testament, he was suspended from the Presbyterian church by the General Assembly (1893). His seminary, Union Theological Seminary of New York, stood by him, however, and became an interdenominational school. *Neo Orthodoxy*

As liberalism grew and as fundamentalism became a more unified and articulate movement, the conflicts and skirmishes, large and small, kept following the course of biblical studies. The liberals argued that Scripture as a human document was subject to ordinary human forces in its composition. The fundamentalists argued that the divine inspiration of Scripture exempted it from many such purely human factors. Perhaps the differences would not have been so magnified had not the liberals used the theories of higher criticism to declare the impossibility of deriving orthodox theology from Holy Scripture. That put the fat into the fire.

From debates over the literary integrity of the Pentateuch, the battles over literary criticism spread to other parts of the Bible, such as the gospels. Strong views had been expressed against the historical integrity of the gospels by Reimarus in the *Wolfenbüttel Fragments* as early as 1774-78. The classic summary of these skeptical lives of Christ is Albert Schweitzer's *The Quest for the Historical Jesus* (1910). The more famous of them, which received much public attention, were those of D. F. Strauss (*Leben Jesu,* 1835-36) and J. E. Renan *(Vie de Jésus,* 1860). Of course, the solid Christology of past orthodoxy could not be sustained on such skeptical views of the historical integrity of the gospels. Further, the historic views of revelation, inspiration, and canon could also not be defended if such skeptical attitudes were correct.

It is not that liberal theology rejected Holy Scripture. It relocated its authority. One of the pioneers in this was S. T. Coleridge, who said that the Bible was the Word of God because it reached him more deeply than any other book. The power of Scripture was, then, in its spiritual effect upon man and not in its objective inspiration. Although Harry Emerson Fosdick (1878-1969) was not among the theologians, he did much to popularize liberal views in America. His book, *The Modern Use of the Bible* (1924), accepted the critical reconstruction of the Bible and biblical history. It is a classic in showing how the liberal mind found the authority of Holy Scripture in the religious experiences the Bible inspired and not in its dogmatic content, its divine inspiration, nor in its nature as a special revelation from God.

But not everyone in the nineteenth century produced attacks upon Holy Scripture. Efforts were made to save it for theology. One of the more significant efforts was the work of J. C. K. von Hofmann (1810-77) and the Erlangen University school. Von Hofmann operated from two theses: (1) the Bible was essentially a record of holy history, or salvation history *(Heilsgeschichte);* and (2) man appropriated this holy history (following Schleiermacher) by a living faith in Christ and regeneration. The bedrock of Scripture was the line from creation to redemption in Christ to consummation in Christ. The holy history is more fundamental than the apparent record of Scripture itself, so that a certain amount of biblical criticism was not considered fatal to the authority of Scripture. His *Interpreting the Bible* (1880) has been translated into English. The general notion of a holy history has had a pervasive influence in twentieth-century theology. Recent representatives of this approach have been Otto Piper and Oscar Cullmann.

A second movement which attempted to preserve the theological worth of Scripture while admitting a measure of biblical criticism is known as "biblical realism."[12] Although its propounders were mainly German, it had representatives in England (C. H. Dodd, James Denney, W. Manson, T. W. Manson) and America (Moses Stuart, John A. Broadus, Sampey, A. T. Robertson). A biblical realist was a scholar who believed that regardless of how the different books of the Scriptures had been composed and regardless of the critical problems associated with them, they still were the Word of God to the Church. Therefore, serious exegesis was still in order. These men kept alive real exegesis in the church, and some of them exerted a great influence on neoorthodox theologians and even on Paul Tillich (although that is sometimes hard to see!). The greatest heritage of biblical realism in the twentieth century is the massive, nine-volume *Theological Dictionary of the New Testament* edited by Gerhard Kittel and G. Friedrich.

The problem facing orthodox theologians of the nineteenth century was, At what point should the orthodox faith be defended? By recourse to older creeds? By recourse to the Reformers? A very important strategy was adopted by what came to be called "the old Princeton school," referring to the days of Princeton Theological Seminary from its foundation in 1812 to its reorganization in 1929. A. A. Hodge and Benjamin Warfield wrote a famous essay on the inspiration of the Bible ("Inspiration," *Presbyterian Review,* 1881) in which they argued that the doctrine of inspiration was the dividing line between orthodox and liberal theology. They defended an inerrant Scripture (but with many qualifications which some of their followers have ignored) which was verbally inspired (again with qualifications often subsequently ignored). This strategy was eventually adopted by a wide circle of men outside the Presbyterian camp, including such variant groups as Lutherans and fundamentalists. In England a similar position was taken by J. W. Burgon (1813-88), famous for his position which seemed to lead logically to the supernatural character and therefore the infallibility of even the spelling of words in Scripture.

Although the writings of Warfield on inspiration have been the most authoritative among fundamentalists and evangelicals in America, the work of the Swiss theologian L. Gaussen (1790-1863) has also been of great influence.[13] Other men, like James Orr of Scotland and Abraham Kuyper of Holland, preferred to take a wider view of revelation and God's action in history for their point of defense rather than a very strict view of inspiration, although both were very strong in their view of the absolute authority of Scripture in matters of faith and morals.

The Christology of Liberalism

One of the results of the historical undermining of the gospels was the undermining of historic Christology. This created the "Jesus or Christ" problem, namely, to what degree is the Christ of systematic theology really the Jesus of history? Or, has synoptic criticism so undermined the historical reliability of the gospels that no Christological materials can be obtained from them? Furthermore, Ritschlians especially regarded affirmations of Christ's preexistence, deity, and incarnation as reflections of Greek metaphysical concepts having no justified place in Christian theology. Consequently, liberalism's Christology usually involved the denial of the historic doctrines of the deity of Christ (as affirmed in the creed of Nicea) and of the incarnation (two natures in one Person, as affirmed at Chalcedon). In their place, liberalism suggested that Christ was the *Urbild* (the master copy, the archetype) and Christians were the *Abbild* (that which is struck off from the *Urbild*, the copy). Each liberal theologian elaborated the particulars of this theory for himself. So far as conservatives could see, liberals were saying that Christ was only the great Example, and we are Christians because we "walk in His steps."

The great reduction in Christology is seen in the famous lectures of Adolf von Harnack (1851-1930). He was the world's leading church-historian and one of the most erudite theologians of modern times. In the winter of 1899-1900 he lectured in Berlin, expounding his Ritschlian view of Christianity. These lectures, reconstructed from the notes of the listeners, were published eventually in English under the title, *What is Christianity?* (1901). In it he said the Gospel was about the Father and not about the Son. That is to say, Christ was not the unique Son of God, incarnate for man's salvation, and dying once for all the sins of the world; but rather He was the One whose pure spirituality and filial piety showed us what it meant to be a true son of God. Later dogmas about Christ were perversions of Christianity, the work of the Greek spirit on the soil of the Gospel. Christianity was a practical, not a theoretical, affair.

Another species of Christology which came in for much discussion was kenotic Christology, based on the Greek verb of Philippians 2:7 (*kenoō*). In simplest terms, the question was whether Christ emptied Himself of His so-called natural attributes (like omnipotence and omnipresence) but not His so-called spiritual or personal attributes (like love and justice). Those who defended a kenotic Christology defended the view that our Lord did empty Himself of His natural attributes. The issue is very complicated and the details are spelled out in Donald G. Dawe, *The Form of a Servant*.[14] Thomasius and Gess are usually associated with this view, and in England Charles Gore (1853-1932) was defending a kenotic Christology in order to relieve problems connected with biblical criticism.[15] It was being argued that if Christ were omniscient then all He said about Old Testament matters was the absolute truth. But if He had emptied himself of His omniscience, then Jesus knew no more than the ordinary Jew of the time about biblical criticism, and so His words cannot be appealed to settle such matters.

One of the most famous books on Christology was Martin Kähler's *The So-Called Historical [historische] Jesus and the Historic [geschichtliche] Biblical Christ* (1892 and 1896). In it he claimed that the Christ of the gospels, the Christ of theology, and the Christ of preaching were the one and same Christ. The book has had a positive hearing among later neoorthodox and evangelical scholars. It is used against the modern Bultmannians who would wish to clearly separate the Christ of the gospels as unsifted by criticism and the sifted Christ of their existential kerygma.[16]

THE DOCTRINE OF GOD

As the orthodox doctrine of God and the Trinity eroded in liberal theology, new efforts were made to restate the doctrine of God. Liberal theology really started out with pantheism in the theology of Schleiermacher—so claims H. R. Mackintosh.[17] But this could not be the final resting place of the liberals' doctrine of God. In order to stress the immanence of God and yet not fall into pantheism, liberalism talked of *panentheism,* "God in all things." This would salvage the doctrine of the divine immanence which was so important to religious liberalism and yet hopefully save it from a pantheism which would be fatal to Christian theology.

A second very important drift away from the historical understanding of the doctrine of God was the impact of ethical theology on Christian theology. It was the philosopher Kant who really introduced the concept of ethical theology, and this was given a great impetus by the philosopher Johann Fichte (1762-1814), a close follower of Kant. The result was a sentimentalizing of the concept of God. God as heavenly Father is also a God of sentimental morality.

Such a God could not severely punish the wicked in this life; nor was it ethical for Jesus Christ to bear the sins and judgment for the world; nor was it ethical to punish men forever in hell. Hence, when liberal theology became so ethically concerned and so sentimental in its doctrine of the fatherhood of God, all the sternness and moral fiber of the historic, orthodox understanding of God became undermined.

Unitarianism has had a long history in Christianity and was known in the early Church as Monarchism. In the nineteenth century it had an articulate defender in Great Britain in the person of the famous scholar, James Martineau (1815-1900). In America, denial of trinitarianism took root in the rationalism of the 1700s and emerged as a denomination in the 1800s.[18] Its most honored leader was William E. Channing (1780-1842), and its academic center was Harvard University. Although its academic leader at Harvard was Charles W. Eliot (1869-1909), it was quite a change of events when the most famous of the modern Eliots (T. S. Eliot) turned his back upon Unitarianism because of its spiritual powerlessness and theological barrenness and turned to Anglican orthodoxy.

Another product of rethinking the doctrine of God became known as empirical theism. Empirical theists proposed to develop theology from the data of religious experience and/or the character of the universe. The most famous of such efforts in Great Britain was the work of Frederick R. Tennant (1866-1956), whose *Philosophical Theology* (1928, 1930) was considered the greatest empirical defense of Christianity in his lifetime. In America, the chief defender was Douglas C. Macintosh (1877-1948), whose basic work was *Theology as an Empirical Science*. At the same time the so-called Chicago school, or process theology, was emerging under the leadership of Charles Hartshorne, who was much inspired by the writings of Alfred North Whitehead. More recently it has had prominent spokesmen in John Cobb, Norman Pittenger, and Schubert Ogden. God is seen as having a stable part of His nature, which makes God to be God, and a second part of His nature ("consequent versus His primordial nature") which can grow in response to the universe and man. Process theology is in reaction to the supposedly static God of traditional theology, the God of the plentitude of being.[19] (But that the newer process theology has done justice to the traditional notions of God, from which it claims to so seriously distance itself, is to be seriously doubted and considered a major default in its scholarship.) Process theology is also an adaptation to the modern pragmatic, relational, and processive view of reality.

THE FORTUNES OF ESCHATOLOGY

The nineteenth and early part of the twentieth century were rich in studies in eschatology in both the conservative and liberal camps. Although not of great theological stature, the writings of J. N. Darby (1800-1882) have exerted an enormous influence upon evangelicals, fundamentalists, and even Pentecostals. His system of dispensationalism was codified with modification in *The Scofield Reference Bible* (especially the second edition), and as millions of this edition of the Scriptures were sold, the dispensational system spread. It was also institutionalized in Bible institutes and some theological seminaries where it received an even greater hearing. It is the basic eschatology of those contemporary evangelicals who see so much prophetic significance in the restoration of Israel.‡

The discussion of dispensational eschatology is only one part of a larger debate. For nearly one hundred fifty years evangelicals and orthodox theologians have fought over whether the Scriptures teach amillennialism (Christ now reigns in the church), postmillennialism (the church will win the world to Christ by the power of the Spirit; then Christ will come), or premillennialism (Christ will come personally to set up His kingdom).

The nineteenth century was also a century of universalism. Among some in the evangelical tradition, universalism was taught on the basis that if Christ died for all men, then all would be saved. Or, if Adam brought the whole race into doom, then Christ brings the whole race into salvation. Or, if all sin in Adam, all are elect in Christ.[20] Or, the only way of solving the great problem of the heathen world being lost is to include them in the Kingdom. Such was the eschatology of universalism.

Liberalism had two basic platforms in its eschatology. On the one hand, the Kingdom of God as an ethical concept and closely allied with the Social Gospel could, or might eventually, Christianize the whole world in its social, political, and economic orders. It was indeed an optimistic view of the direction of human history and Christianity's role. Although it has been debated how widespread this optimism was, that the events of the twentieth century shattered it is not. Liberal theologians were also much attracted to a doctrine of personal immortality. They considered a bodily resurrection to be a materialistic and unchristian doctrine, but they did

‡This is the groundwork for the fantastic sale of Hal Lindsey with C. C. Larson, *The Late Great Planet Earth* (Grand Rapids: Zondervan, 1970).

mightily believe in immortality, and *The Garvin Lectures* (given from 1940 to 1960) were devoted to this theme.

The movement which received the most acclaim in eschatology was that of "consistent eschatology," pioneered by Johannes Weiss (1863-1914) but made more famous by Albert Schweitzer. Schweitzer saw Jesus as essentially an eschatological fanatic who expected to see the Kingdom of God break in at any moment. Jesus' ethic was an interim ethic, namely, an ethic between His preaching and the breaking in of the Kingdom. Schweitzer's view is not held widely today, yet it did remind the liberal theologians that eschatology was a central part of New Testament theology and not part of the external rind which could be easily discarded.

Paul Althaus (1888-1966) was famous for his survey of eschatology (*Die letzen Dinge,* 7th edition, 1957) and for his view of axiological eschatology, which was very similar to C. H. Dodd's realized eschatology. Both looked at eschatological themes, motifs, or symbols as somehow being realized in the present age.

THE THEOLOGIANS OF ORTHODOXY

We have made frequent references to the fortunes and responses of evangelical and orthodox theologians in our survey; but it needs to be further emphasized that there is in the great Protestant traditions an unbroken stream of orthodox theologians, from the time of great Protestant orthodoxy of the seventeenth century until now, as much as it irks liberal theologians to admit this. There were some special efforts in the nineteenth century, worthy of specific mention, to strengthen orthodoxy. One of these movements within Anglicanism is known as the Oxford Movement (from where it originated), or the Tractarian Movement (from the *Tracts for the Times* which it published). The leader was John Henry Newman (1801-90). In 1845 he went over to the Roman Catholic Church, and the burden of carrying on an orthodox witness in the Anglican church then fell to men like E. B. Pusey (1800-82), whose commentaries were models of British biblical erudition. His understudy, H. P. Liddon (1829-90), published one of the finest defenses of the deity of Christ in all of theological literature (*The Divinity of our Lord,* 1867).

In Holland a sturdy new school of orthodoxy was prompted by Abraham Kuyper (1837-1920). Although he was raised in an orthodox, Calvinistic home, in university days he deserted that faith for the liberalism then reigning in Holland. When he went to his first parish he found only the orthodox members really knowing what and why they believed. He reverted back to the orthodoxy of his upbringing. Finding it impossible to reform the theological faculties of the universities, he started with most humble beginnings the Free University of Amsterdam. One of the most prolific writers Holland has produced, he defended his version of Calvinism by learned book and pamphlet and by decades of editorship of religious journals.

In America the most unusual defense of orthodox theology was made by the old Princeton school founded in 1812 under the leadership of Archibald Alexander (1772-1851). It had one of the most unique histories of any theological institution. It maintained for more than a hundred years the integrity of its theological stance in the Westminster Confession, and it further maintained a standard of scholarship not to be excelled. Its more famous names were the Hodges (Charles, Archibald, and Caspar), William Green in Old Testament studies, B. B. Warfield in theology, and J. Gresham Machen in New Testament studies.

P. T. Forsyth (1848-1921) was unique as a theologian in the early twentieth century and has been called the Barth before Barth.[21] He did not like either the liberal or the fundamentalist options in theology. Although trained in liberal theology, he progressed toward a more evangelical theology as he moved through life. The basic thrust of his later writings was to defend an evangelical, Christocentric, and experiential version of Christianity. He accepted a version of kenotic Christology to make the incarnation more believable and attempted to give the doctrine of authority a more Gospel-centered, experience-oriented character without giving up the priority of the divine Word. In recent years his pioneering efforts have received much appreciation.

THEOLOGY FROM 1920-60

Barth's *Commentary on Romans* (*Römerbrief,* 1919, 1921) marked the beginning of a new epoch in theology. Liberal theology had not died, for it had a strong momentum, in America in particular, which even yet has not dissipated. But Barth's work marked the beginning of the emergence of a new breed of theologians—men like Bultmann, Brunner, Heim, Tillich, Gogarten, Thielecke, Wingren, Ferré, Torrance, Weber, and the Niebuhrs.

The following are especially significant characteristics of theology in this period.

1. It was a period in which the program of religious liberalism

was seriously challenged, yet it must not be inferred that all that liberalism stood for had been repudiated. The theologians of neoorthodoxy were deeply indebted to liberalism and higher criticism. Even so, Barth could write that there had been no real progress in theology from the Reformers to neoorthodoxy. Tillich could say that as far as real theological progress was concerned, it was a wasted period. Brunner thought liberalism was a dry run into theological subjectivism. The new breed of American theologians posed a theology of the realism of sin over against the optimism of liberalism.

Particular doctrines of liberalism were severely criticized. Its doctrine of revelation could not differentiate the voice of God from the voice of man. Its Christology made Jesus a nice, romantic Galilean fashioned in our image and not in God's. Sin was not seen in its terror and enmity against God nor for its sheer quality of rebellion against the divine will. Atonement had been reduced to psychological acceptance. Justification by faith had come to mean that there was no anger nor wrath in God. The gospel of liberalism was rejected as a gospel with no wrath, a cross with no judgment, and a resurrection in which no Roman seals were broken.

2. It was a period in which the theological genius of Luther, Calvin, and the lesser Reformers was found afresh. Of course, Luther and Calvin scholars had not abated in the period of liberalism. We have only to mention the name of Karl Holl (1866-1926) to indicate the depth of Luther research that was going on in this period. But the discovery of the Reformers as religious and theological geniuses of the first order was something new. A remarkable feature of the Luther and Calvin renaissance is that Barth and Brunner, who were both Reformed theologians and with a first loyalty to Calvin, would frequently side with Luther on particular issues. To repeat an earlier theme, the neoorthodox and even existentialist theologians found in Luther and Calvin theologians with whom they could find more rapport of spirit than with the famous religious liberals of 1880 to 1920.

3. If there was one dominating theological topic, it was that of revelation. Again Barth led the way, but others followed.[22] Barth's point was that liberalism had so weakened the concept of revelation that it had become meaningless. If revelation were no more than man's best thoughts about religion or his better insights about morality or ethics, why call it divine revelation? If revelation is revelation, it is like the roaring of a lion (cf. Amos 3:8).

Even the existentialist theologians and the neo-Bultmannians or post-Bultmannians believed that revelation must be a Word given. Unless the kerygma (Gospel) is in some sense "given," that is, revealed, then faith is simply the activation of man's religious nature. If this be the case, we are then back to the dead-end theology of liberalism. As much as such writers made revelation "existential," "dialogical," or "encounter" rather than doctrinal or propositional, they at least realized that if revelation is to be a solid theological concept, it must in some sense be given, that is, originate with God.

To put it another way, liberal theology really lost the concept of the Word of God. As much as evangelicals find the neoorthodox and existential concept of revelation coming up short, it at least recovered a concept of revelation as a word from God—a concept seemingly lost in older liberalism. Without this there could be no meaningful theology.

4. The theological heritage of this period in philosophy is mixed. The French, German, and Swiss theologians were much impressed by the existentialism of Kierkegaard and Heidegger. A massive theological literature on both men exists. Strangely, in Sweden, England, and America philosophical influence in theology has come more from language philosophy, variously called logical positivism, logical empiricism, common-sense language, and language analysis.

Such theologians as Bultmann and Tillich admit the enormous influence of Heidegger on their theology. Barth, though, decided that his first attempt at systematic theology in 1927 was marked too much by Heidegger and later rejected his own work produced at that time. However, Scandinavian theologians still classify him as a follower of Heidegger as much as Barth disclaims it. Brunner admits to being more a disciple of Kierkegaard. And most theologians of the period admit profound indebtedness to the mystical, personalistic existentialism of Martin Buber.

In that existentialism bypasses the metaphysical debates of traditional philosophy, to follow existentialism was considered advantageous, for it got the theologian off the metaphysical hook which had so long bedeviled theology. Theology could be discussed existentially-descriptively rather than metaphysically, and thereby all the older contaminations of theology by metaphysics were supposedly avoided.

The God-talk theologians of America and England have claimed to be honestly facing the problem of theological language as raised by the analytic philosophers, especially the demands that language be used clearly, unambiguously, and with some responsible talk about verification. The patron saint of the later school of God-talk theologians has been the later Wittgenstein, who with his notion of language games is supposed to have admitted the validity of theological language games. In fact, some students of Wittgenstein claim that his latest work, *Philosophical Investigations,* has profound affinities with the thought of Kierkegaard.§

5. The sheer number of non-Christians in the world, the decreasing proportion of Christians in the "Christian West," and the growth of technology produced some odd reactions. One of these was death-of-God theology. Short-lived though it was, it caught major headlines for a brief period. Another was the reduction of theology solely to talk of man's love for man—a sort of neohumanitarianism built on the way Jesus was a Man for other men. Others have talked of a profound appreciation of the world ("secularity") as a recovery of the Christian doctrine of creation, in contrast to the older secularism, which stood simply for indifference to theological claims on a man's life.

Most impressive of all in this, and most frequently abused rather than correctly interpreted, was Dietrich Bonhoeffer. He saw better than any theologian of the pre-1950 period the problems facing the Christian Church in witnessing to a culture that had become totally scientific, technological, and secular in its understanding of man, culture, and human history. Bonhoeffer's view of the anonymous Christian, that is, the person who does not name the name of Christ but possesses Christian virtues, was applied by him only to those in the Christian West; but this view was used to get most of the pagan world into the Kingdom by other theologians who thought "godly" pagans were anonymous Christians.

6. As paradoxical as it may seem, the period after 1920 was a period of intensely biblical theology. Old Testament scholars led the way by taking a new look at the Old Testament. They tried to avoid the excessively Christological viewpoints of the nineteenth century or the very skeptical viewpoints of higher criticism. Instead, they came up with new, refreshing, and more positive views of the Old Testament. Theologies of the New Testament have been slower in coming, but the great, nine-volume *Theological Dictionary of the New Testament* (Gerhard Kittel and G. Friedrich, eds.) shows that

§Students of linguistic philosophy and theologians of the God-talk movement admit that Kierkegaard's views of language and logic coincide with theirs.

the New Testament scholars also came to be caught up in biblical theology. Regardless of the penchant of some of its scholars to find so much of the New Testament in pagan redeemer-myths, Jewish myths, or mystery religions, evangelicals have found the New Testament a great resource for theological and exegetical research.

7. As suggested in our discussion of the older Chicago school, a newer Chicago school has emerged. Recent process theology belongs more properly in the period after the 1950s, but in that it maintained an unbroken continuity no matter how small the thread became, it has emerged as a major theological option.

In all of this the evangelical wonders how much is new, how much is orthodox, and how much is more of the older liberalism. We shall indicate only briefly where we think no change has been made with the older liberalism and its critical view of Scripture and orthodox theology:

1. There has been no return to the Reformation view of the Bible as the sole, authoritative, infallible rule of faith and practice. The Bible is taken as normative, but not in the historic sense of its divine authority.

2. The liberal view that revelation was primarily insight or experience and neither propositional, doctrinal, nor dogmatic has been qualified but has not been completely repudiated. This comes out clearly in John Baillie's book, *The Idea of Revelation in Recent Thought;* in Brunner's endless chatter that revelation is encounter; and in Bultmann's existential version of revelation.

3. The liberal view that the essence of Christianity is primarily in experience, or in the existential encounter, rather than in the great Word of God and the great work of God in Christ frequently is recited, although in different settings. Gerhard Ebeling clearly reflects this view in his book, *The Nature of Faith.*

4. Finally, the universalism in liberal theology has not really been challenged. Although Barth denies universalism in word, universalism is the implication of his theology. Bultmann and Tillich are universalists, or at least according to their theology nobody can "get damned around here." Brunner is staunchest in maintaining that unless salvation and damnation are still relevant categories, life has become vapid. We are reminded of T. S. Eliot, who told Paul Elmore More that if there is no hell, More has made God into Santa Claus and the seriousness of life into a parlor game.

Notes

1. Out of the many books on the Enlightenment I suggest Peter Gay, *The Enlightenment: An Interpretation: The Rise of Modern Paganism* (New York: Knopf, 1967). For the impact on Protestant orthodoxy, see Bernard Ramm, *The Evangelical Heritage* (Waco: Word, 1973), chapter 5.

2. For a work showing how studies of this period spilled over into theology and biblical studies, see Gilbert Highet, *The Classical Tradition* (New York: Oxford, 1949).

3. The following books not only contain information about Schleiermacher, but each has a survey of the Enlightenment and conditions which led up to the theology of the nineteenth century. In view of the sheer glut of materials, all bibliographical references in this essay are only suggestive. H. R. Mackintosh, *Types of Modern Theology: Schleiermacher to Barth* (London: Nisbet, 1937), sections 2 and 3; Karl Barth, *Protestant Theology in the Nineteenth Century* (Valley Forge: Judson, 1973), chap. 11; Claude Welch, *Protestant Thought in the Nineteenth Century* (New Haven: Yale, 1972), chap. 3; James C. Livingstone, *Modern Christian Thought from the Enlightenment to Vatican II* (New York: Macmillan, 1971), chap. 4; Paul Tillich, *Perspectives on Nineteenth and Twentieth Century Protestant Theology* (London: SCM, 1967), chap. 3.

4. Quoted in Mackintosh, p. 48.

5. For a simple, straightforward explanation of how Hegel attempted to save Christianity for modern man, see Rudolph Siebert, "Hegel and Theology," *The Ecumenist* (November-December 1973) 12:1-6. For a discussion of Hegel and the Hegelians, see Livingstone, chap. 6; Barth, Marheineke, chap. 14; Hegel, chap. 10; Feuerbach, chap. 18; Welch, chap. 4; Tillich, chap. 3; Mackintosh, chap. 4.

6. See Mackintosh, section 6.

7. For a compact survey of American theology, see Sydney E. Ahlstrom, *Theology in America* (New York: Bobbs-Merrill, 1967), pp. 23-91. He also has an excellent select bibliography, pp. 93-110. For Bushnell, see pp. 62-64 and chap. 7.

8. These ideas come out clearest in Ritschl's small book *Unterricht in der christlichen Religion* (1875, 1886).

9. In our own book, *The Christian View of Science and Scripture* (Grand Rapids: Eerdmans, 1955), we have surveyed the debate and copiously cited the literature as well as examined the various theories propounded among evangelicals in the attempt to come to terms one way or another with uniformitarian geology and biological evolution.

10. The degree to which evolution became both a theological and a philosophical assumption in liberalism is detailed in Kenneth Cauthen, *The Impact of American Religious Liberalism* (New York: Harper & Row, 1962).

11. The classic of the period was N. P. Williams, *The Ideas of the Fall and Original Sin* (Bampton Lectures for 1924).

12. See Richard H. Grützmacher and Gerhard Muras, *Textbuch zur Deutschen Systematischen Theologie*, vol. 1, 4th ed. (Gütersloh: C. Bertelsmann Verlag), chap. 15 (Beck, Cremer, Kähler, Schlatter, Heim, Piper). Welch, chap. 9; Tillich, chap. 5; Barth, chap. 25.

13. *Theopneustia* (1840, 1842). Many English editions.

14. Philadelphia: Westminster, 1968.

15. See "The Holy Spirit and Inspiration," in *Lux Mundi,* ed. Charles Gore (New York: U. S. Book Co., n.d.), pp. 263-302.

16. We have only touched upon the ferment in the Christology of this period. See further, John Stewart Lawton, *Conflict in Christology: A Study of British and American Christology from 1889-1914* (London: SCM, 1947) and Herbert M. Relton, *A Study in Christology* (London: SCM, 1917).

17. See Mackintosh, pp. 50ff.

18. See the survey article by Ahlstrom, p. 38 ff., and chap. 3 on William Ellery Channing.

19. The classic work on the concept of the plenitude of being is that of Arthur O. Lovejoy, *The Great Chain of Being* (New York: Harper & Row, 1936).

20. See the long, thorough article by James Edwin Odgers, "Universalism," in *Hastings Encyclopedia of Religion and Ethics,* 12: 529-35.
21. Forsyth was a prolific writer, but see John H. Rodgers, *The Theology of P. T. Forsyth* (Naperville, Ill.: Allenson, 1965) and Samuel Mikolaski, ed., *The Creative Theology of P. T. Forsyth* (Grand Rapids: Eerdmans, 1969).
22. An evangelical theology of revelation is given in Bernard Ramm, *Special Revelation and the Word of God* (Grand Rapids: Eerdmans, 1961). H. D. McDonald has given us an excellent historical survey in his two books: *Ideas of Revelation* (London: Macmillan, 1959) and *Theories of Revelation* (London: Allen & Unwin, 1963). In German we have Hans Waldenfels, *Offenbarung* (Munich: Max Hueber Verlag, 1969). John Baillie, *The Idea of Revelation in Recent Thought* (New York: Columbia, 1956) is too short to compete with the above references.

Selected Reading List

Ahlstrom, Sydney E. *Theology in America.* Indianapolis: Bobbs-Merrill, 1967.

Barth, Karl. *Protestant Theology in the Nineteenth Century.* Valley Forge: Judson, 1973.

Blaikie, Robert J. *Secular Christianity and "God Who Acts."* Grand Rapids: Eerdmans, 1970.

Conn, Harvie M. *Contemporary World Theology.* Philadelphia: Presby. & Ref., 1973.

Daniélou, J.; Couratin, A. H.; and Kent, John. *Historical Theology.* Pelican Guide to Modern Theology, vol. 2. Baltimore: Penguin, 1969.

Hamilton, Kenneth. *Revolt Against Heaven.* Grand Rapids: Eerdmans, 1965.

————. *What's New In Religion?* Grand Rapids: Eerdmans, 1968.

Henry, Carl F. H. *Frontiers in Modern Theology.* Chicago: Moody, 1964.

Hughes, Philip Edgcumbe, ed. *Creative Minds in Contemporary Theology.* Grand Rapids: Eerdmans, 1966.

Mackintosh, H. R. *Types of Modern Theology.* London: Nisbet, 1937.

Macquarrie, John. *Twentieth-Century Religious Thought.* London: SCM, 1963.

Marty, Martin E., and Peerman, Dean G., eds. *A Handbook of Christian Theologians.* Cleveland: World, 1965.

Nicholls, William. *Systematic and Philosophical Theology.* Pelican Guide to Modern Theology, vol. 1. Baltimore: Penguin Books, 1969.

Ramm, Bernard. *The Evangelical Heritage.* Waco: Word, 1973.

————. *A Handbook of Contemporary Theology.* Grand Rapids: Eerdmans, 1966.

Reymond, Robert L. *Introductory Studies in Contemporary Theology.* Philadelphia: Presby. & Ref., 1968.

Tillich, Paul. *Perspectives on 19th and 20th Century Protestant Theology.* New York: Harper & Row, 1967.

PACESETTERS FOR THE RADICAL THEOLOGIANS OF THE SIXTIES AND SEVENTIES

    I. Rudolf Bultmann
       A. The Wholly Other
       B. Demythologization
       C. Asking the right questions
       D. From inauthenticity to authenticity
       E. Critique
   II. Pierre Teilhard de Chardin
       A. Teilhard's goal
       B. The evolutive process
       C. The immanent goal
       D. Christ-omega
  III. Dietrich Bonhoeffer
       A. Bonhoeffer as theologian
       B. The center of his faith
       C. The world come of age
       D. Religionless Christianity
       E. Holy worldliness
  IV. Paul Tillich
       A. The principle of correlation
       B. Dialectics
       C. Man
       D. God
       E. Jesus as the Christ
       F. Critique

They are all bringing certain Philosophies to Christianity - admittedly.

Why, What is their concern. To make it understandable.

Does it really distort the Christian message. for all, for some, is it valid for those people who can understand it - Can you give

2

Pacesetters for the Radical Theologians of the Sixties and Seventies

by
VERNON C. GROUNDS

If contemporary theology is like a rushing, muddy river, as indeed it is, a pertinent question naturally arises: How did it ever become so turbulent and turbid? A related question also obtrudes itself: What were the tributaries somewhere upstream which poured themselves into this now swirling flood? An exhaustive answer to these questions would require a study that reaches back into the remotest depths of human civilization and ransacks the vast resources of specialized scholarship. But we are at least entitled to say that in the more recent past the potent influences of four men have converged to swell this river. Our task, therefore, is to consider briefly the distinctive input which individually Rudolf Bultmann, Pierre Teilhard de Chardin, Dietrich Bonhoeffer, and Paul Tillich have made to the onflowing tide of present-day theology.

VERNON C. GROUNDS, B.A., B.D., Ph.D., is president emeritus of Conservative Baptist Theological Seminary, Denver, Colorado. He is author of *Evangelicalism and Social Responsibility* (Herald, 1969) and *Revolution and the Christian Faith* (Lippincott, 1971). Dr. Grounds has contributed to several symposia and encyclopedias. His analyses of theological trends have appeared in *Christian Heritage*. He is also a regular contributor for a wide variety of periodicals.

RUDOLF BULTMANN

Born on August 20, 1884, at Wiefeldstede in Oldenburg, Germany, Rudolf Bultmann has spent his entire career in the academic world. He taught at Marburg from 1912 to 1916; then he was assistant professor at Breslau until 1920. Very briefly he held the rank of full professor at Giessen, returning to Marburg in 1921, where he remained until his retirement in 1951. Though not a political activist, he supported the Confessing Church during the Hitler era.

An encyclopedic scholar, he moves with competence and distinction, not to say critical creativity, in the fields of Judaism, Old Testament, biblical criticism, New Testament studies, classical culture, historical theology, modern science, contemporary theology, and world religions. Let Schubert M. Ogden give an appraisal of his importance.

> Rudolf Bultmann is one of the most significant figures on the contemporary theological scene. By whatever criteria one judges such significance—whether quantitative or qualitative, whether with reference to specific areas of concern (i.e., "historical," "systematic," or "practical" theology) or to theological inquiry as a whole—his contribution is unchallengeably among the most important of our time. In the course of a long and productive scholarly career, which already spans half a century and still continues with unabated power, he has come to be one of the most decisive influences on the direction of Protestant theology in the twentieth century. The basic reason for this, undoubtedly, is that to an extent that seems to distinguish him among his contemporaries he has become a part of all that he has met theologically, and thus embodies in his own achievement virtually all of the important motives in the long tradition of German theology in which he stands. Of his work, as perhaps of no other, it can be said that it represents an integral and creative restatement of the cumulative wisdom of classical Protestant theology in its several decisive phases.[1]

THE WHOLLY OTHER

The Bultmann corpus is an impressive body of books and articles, much of it devoted to a highly technical exegesis of the New Testament. How best, then, can we understand this multifaceted contribution to present-day theology? Does it have a controlling purpose, and, if so, what is that? Running the risk of oversimplification, we can say that Bultmann's primary passion is to communicate the kerygma, or the Christian message, to the twentieth-century world. In order to carry out this task, he engages, negatively, in a demythologization of the biblical sources, while, positively, he sets forth an existential analysis of the Gospel proclamation. Thomas Oden helpfully elucidates the relationship between these two aspects of Bultmann's task.

> Demythologization is distinguished from existential analysis (*Daseinsanalyse*) in that the former deals with the special problem of trying to perceive the New Testament proclamation in the context of the mythical world picture of the first century, and to indicate how this world picture is not necessary to the particular understanding of existence expressed therein. Existential analysis of the New Testament proclamation, however, involves the positive task of taking these first-century conceptualities, language, and meanings and translating them into terms that are familiar and understandable to modern man and that correspond to the actual situation of human existence.[2]

But why is demythologization necessary? Why, moreover, must the New Testament be subjected to an existential analysis? As we ponder these questions, Ogden can again be of help to us. He calls attention to the well-known passage from the preface to the second edition of Karl Barth's *Epistle to the Romans*.

> If I have a "system" it consists in the fact that I keep in mind as persistently as possible what Kierkegaard called the "infinite qualitative difference" between time and eternity in both its negative and its positive meaning. "God is in heaven and you are on earth." The relation of *this* God to *this* man, the relation of *this* man to *this* God, is for me at once the theme of the Bible and the essence of philosophy. The philosophers speak of this crisis of human knowing as the primal source, while the Bible sees at this parting of the ways Jesus Christ.

Ogden then asserts that this system, repudiated by Barth in his later years, is precisely the system to which Bultmann tenaciously adheres: an "affirmation of the 'infinite qualitative difference' between time and eternity in its several negative and positive implications." And Ogden concludes his incisive orientation with these words, mostly italicized.

> Indeed, we may lay it down as a rule that *one ought never to suppose he has correctly understood anything that Bultmann says, as regards either the method or the content of his theology, until he is able to see it as permitted or required by this basic dialectic.*[3]

The bearing of this "infinite qualitative difference" on Christian faith is incalculably decisive, Ogden argues. An analogy may prove illuminating. I am a self, and at my deepest center is a reality qualitatively different from my psyche or my body or my world. Its existence can never be identified with any physical process within my organism nor with any action I perform nor word that I speak. My self, though inextricably related to my body, my psyche, my world, nevertheless qualitatively transcends its environment. My self, in fact, transcends my own subjective world as well as its objective world, revealing itself indirectly by the decisions which determine its network of relationships and activities. Analogically, Ogden points out, God is the reality who infinitely transcends everything and who, paradoxically, is at the same time related to everything. Yet because He is the wholly Other, nothing in nature or history—nothing, for instance, that man is or does—can directly reveal God. In Bultmann's own words, "God is the *Creator,* i.e., he is not immanent in the ordinances of the world, and nothing that encounters us as a phenomenon within the world is *directly* divine."[4] Hence as cosmic Self, He remains *Deus absconditus* except as He indirectly discloses something of Himself. To quote Ogden once more,

> Just as man in his finite "historicity" transcends the whole sphere of the subject-object correlation, so also does God as infinite Thou or "Existent" transcend all that falls within the macrocosmic counterpart of this same sphere.[5]

One may believe that God has been at work in an event, but one cannot demonstrate God's reality by an appeal to that event any more than an appeal to some human action will demonstrate to a disciple of B. F. Skinner that a self has been responsible for a specific behavior. In short, the reality of God is as undemonstrable as the reality of the human self. Since God is Spirit, Bultmann assumes, He simply does not disclose Himself miraculously in space-time. History, like nature, is a closed continuum of causes and effects, with even human motives susceptible to causal explanation. Bultmann, consequently, makes a significant assertion:

> This closedness means that the continuum of historical happenings cannot be rent by the interference of supernatural, transcendent powers and that therefore there is no "miracle" in this sense of the word. Such a miracle would be an event whose cause did not lie within history. While, for example, the Old Testament narrative speaks of an interference by God in history, historical science cannot demonstrate such an act of God, but merely perceives that there are

those who believe in it. To be sure, as historical science, it may not assert that such a faith is an illusion and that God has not acted in history. But it itself as science cannot perceive such an act and reckon on the basis of it; it can only leave every man free to determine whether he wants to see an act of God in a historical event that it itself understands in terms of that event's immanent historical causes.[6]

DEMYTHOLOGIZATION

It follows, therefore, that revelation comes in symbols which must be decoded. To use Bultmann's term, they must be *demythologized.*

Besides the theological reason for demythologization, there is an apologetic reason. Modern man thinks scientifically, in strictly causal categories. Spirits, demons, miracles, the devil, a virgin birth, the Saviour's literal descent into hell and His equally literal ascension into heaven, a supernatural Being returning in clouds of the sky as if the universe were a structure of three levels like flats in an apartment house—to demand that modern man accept all this as anything but myth is to demand a *sacrificium intellectus,* which prevents people today from taking the kerygma seriously. Who, to state the issue sharply, can utilize the achievements of science and deny its presuppositions?

> It is impossible to make use of electric light and of the radio, when sick to take advantage of all the resources of medical and clinical research, and at the same time to believe in the world of spirits and of miracles as we find it set forth in the New Testament. Anyone who claims to be able personally to do so must recognize that, if he presents this as the attitude which is required of Christian believers, he is making Christian preaching incomprehensible and impossible of acceptance in the modern world.[7]

So, when a grossly misguided apologetic insists on faith in the facticity of the biblical myths rather than on faith in their underlying meaning, it is substituting a false stumbling block for the true *scandalon.* What demythologizing does, then, is "eliminate a false stumbling-block and bring into sharp focus the real stumbling-block, the word of the cross."[8] Or, as Bultmann writes in another context, "This stumbling-block is that the Word of God calls man out of all man-made security."[9] Apologetically, then, no less than theologically, demythologization is imperative if twentieth-century culture is to be confronted with the kerygma in all its authentic offensiveness and redemptive power.

Myth, though, needs to be defined; and Bultmann proposes a

rather simple definition which applies to myth per se, whether in
Judaism, Gnosticism, Christianity, or any other religion.

> Mythology is that form of imagery in which that which is not of this
> world, that which is divine, is represented as though it were of this
> world and human; "the beyond" is represented as "the here and
> now." For example, the transcendence of God is expressed in terms
> of distance in space. When this kind of imagery is used, worship is
> readily understood as an action in which, by the use of material
> means, non-material powers are communicated to man.[10]

With myth thus defined, that polysyllabic term, *demythologization,* may now be explicated. Essentially, Bultmann declares,
"It is a method of hermeneutics," which seeks to extract the kernel
of insightful significance from the shell of an antiquated world view.

> This method of interpretation of the New Testament which tries to
> recover the deeper meaning behind the mythological conceptions I
> call *de-mythologizing*—an unsatisfactory word, to be sure. Its aim is
> not to eliminate the mythological statements but to interpret them.[11]

Bultmann insists that demythologization does not necessitate a
root-and-branch rejection of Christianity. On the contrary! It rejects
only a prescientific cosmology. Bultmann argues, "The world-view
of the Scripture is mythological and is therefore unacceptable to
modern man whose thinking has been shaped by science and is
therefore no longer mythological."[12]

ASKING THE RIGHT QUESTIONS

Once the mythological materials in Scripture have been demythologized, what remains? A revelation that is meaningful to the
modern mind, a revelation of a new possibility in human existence.

> Revelation means *that opening up of what is hidden which is abso-
> lutely necessary and decisive for man if he is to achieve "salvation"
> or authenticity;* i.e., revelation here is the disclosure of *God* to
> man . . . an occurrence that puts man in a new situation.[13]

Revelation, then, offers a new self-understanding and with it the
challenging hope of a new self-possibility.

Simple as this message may sound, its elucidation requires the
collaborative labor of both philosophy and theology, with their vast
apparatus of learning. But why philosophy? Why not, as with
Barth, the exegesis and systematization of revelational data
—demythologized, to be sure, but precisely on that account accept-

able to the modern mind? The answer to that question depends on one's view of philosophy, and Bultmann's view makes philosophy a necessary propaedeutic to theology. Hence, replying to the criticism of Gerhardt Kuhlmann that he has done little more than baptize Martin Heidegger's anthropology, Bultmann advances his own view of the relationship between philosophy and theology.

> *Every* theology is dependent for the clarification of its concepts upon a pretheological understanding of man that, as a rule, is determined by some philosophical tradition. . . . Even preaching is guided by a specific understanding of man, even if it does not need to make this understanding conceptually explicit. Theology, however, does have to make it explicit, since its task is to stand guard over preaching's purity and understandability. It can fulfill its task only if it inquires after concepts that express the being of man in the most appropriate and "neutral" way possible. And if it does not ask philosophy for these, this is a mere fake. For then it is either uncritically dependent upon some older philosophical tradition or else itself engages in philosophical work—in which case the results are usually inferior enough![14]

But why is a pretheological understanding of man necessary? For a most compelling reason. It is impossible to approach any text "without asking questions of it," and simultaneously bringing to bear upon the interrogative process certain concepts which we already hold. If, accordingly, we approach the Bible asking for an answer to the question of man's existence, we must be sure, Bultmann contends, that we are operating with "an adequate hermeneutical principle, the right way to ask the right questions," and we can discover this principle "only by objective, critical reflection."[15]

The right pretheological conceptions are available—providentially, Bultmann might be tempted to say—in the ontological analysis of Martin Heidegger, who penetratingly dissects the formal structures of human life. Indeed, there is a remarkable correspondence between Heidegger's anthropology and the New Testament delineation of the natural man—man before faith, man as a fallen being, experiencing care and anxiety and dread, haunted by the inescapability of death and nothingness, struggling to achieve self-security out of the bankrupt resources of his own self-sufficiency, and so existing in bondage and inauthenticity. Man's root trouble is his willful misunderstanding of himself, his refusal to face the truth about his own existence. This is Heidegger's analysis and Paul's as well.

The anthropologies of Heidegger and Paul diverge radically, however, in their teaching as to the process of human self-actualization. Heidegger, on the one hand, calls man into a new life of authenticity by the exercise of sheer resolve. Here is Bultmann's summary of the position espoused by his philosophical mentor:

> To be a man . . . is something that uniquely belongs to the individual; and the being of man is a "possibility of being," i.e., the man who is involved in care for himself chooses his own unique possibility. This choice is a genuine resolve only when it is a carrying out of the "resolution" that grows out of man's seeing in death his properest possibility and letting himself be thrown back by death into the now—of understanding the now from the standpoint of death and thus resolving in the situation.[16]

Heidegger's authentic man is, in the end, a resolute Stoic.

Paul, on the other hand, calls man out of his false and frustrating self-misunderstanding into a new and fulfilling self-understanding revealed in Jesus Christ. If man chooses to respond in faith to the biblical message, he will perceive himself as a being totally dependent on God, gaining his frantically sought-after security by a committal of his life to God's inscrutable and unpredictable power, existing in freedom and openness and love, and so existing in authenticity.

This is Bultmann's description of the life which follows when a human being, fallen and frustrated, apprehends a new self-understanding and in decisive self-surrender begins to actualize his new self-possibility:

> Because man thereby no longer belongs to himself (I Cor. 6:19), he is free from care, free from anxiety about death, free from legal prescriptions and human conventions and standards of value. In short, he is free from himself as he actually is as he comes out of his past; he is a new creation in Christ (II Cor. 5:17). As a man of faith, he has passed from death to life (John 5:24). But—and this is the paradox—his freedom is never a static quality; it never loses the character of a gift that never becomes a secure possession, but must rather constantly be laid hold of anew as a gift. But in what does this constantly new apprehension consist? In nothing other than the constantly renewed attitude of faith, i.e., in that openness for what God demands and sends that can never be taken for granted, but must always be realized anew.[17]

FROM INAUTHENTICITY TO AUTHENTICITY

But the utterly crucial factor in this transition from inauthenticity to authenticity has not yet been mentioned, and that fact is the revelation of human authenticity in Jesus Christ. Bultmann, as we have noticed, highlights this indispensable factor by affirming in italics that revelation means the *"opening up of what is hidden which is absolutely necessary and decisive for man if he is to achieve 'salvation' or authenticity."*[18] And this "opening up" occurs when the Church proclaims God's action in the death and resurrection of Jesus Christ. Accordingly, "the preaching itself belongs to the salvation occurrence."[19] We are brought into a saving encounter with Jesus Christ "through the preaching of the Church, which proclaims him as the grace of God made manifest."[20]

Undeniably the cross, which the Church proclaims, is a "mythological event," yet through this event—and through this event alone—God works to save man from his life of inauthenticity.

> The cross as saving event is not an isolated event which happened to a mythical person, whom we know under the name of Christ; this event has in its significance a "cosmic dimension." And its decisive significance, in the sense that it effects a revolution in history, is summed up in its particular character as eschatological event; this means that it is not simply an event in the past, to which we look back retrospectively; it is the eschatological event in time and beyond time, inasmuch as when understood in its true significance, when understood through faith, it is always present reality.[21]

And this significance Bultmann expounds more fully, distinguishing "mythological happening" from "saving event."

> Considered as saving event, the cross of Christ is not, then, a mythological happening; it is a truly historical happening, which has its origin in a merely historical event, the crucifixion of Jesus of Nazareth. The true historical significance of this event is that it is the judgment passed upon the world, the judgment passed upon men which sets them free. And in so far as this is true, Christ was crucified "for us." Not in the sense of a theory of "satisfaction," or of vicarious sacrifice. The fact of mere history discloses its significance as the event that brings salvation, not to a mythological interpretation, but to a genuinely historical interpretation; for it is only a truly historical understanding which grasps the meaning of a merely historical happening in terms of the importance of that which it signifies. The mythological form of speech has in reality no other purpose than that of finding expression for the significance of the merely historical

event. What the merely historical event of the cross means, when its significance is rightly grasped, is that it has created a new historical situation; the proclamation of the cross as saving event challenges the hearer to make up his mind whether he is willing to make that significance his own, whether, that is, he is willing to be crucified with Christ.[22]

As for the resurrection, which the New Testament never isolates from the cross, that too is a "salvation event" presented under the guise of a "mythological happening." Thus, Bultmann points out:

> The cross cannot be separated from the *resurrection;* i.e., precisely he who accepts as valid for himself the judgment that is spoken in the cross, who, as Paul puts it, lets himself be crucified with Christ, experiences the cross as liberation and redemption, and is able to believe that, by giving Jesus up to the cross, God thereby led him into life—a life in which all share who let themselves be crucified with him.[23]

This relationship between Christ's crucifixion, His resurrection, and the possibility of a new life is explicitly stated by Bultmann.

> The resurrection is not a mythological event which can be adduced in order to make credible the significance of the cross; this too has to be *believed in*, just in the same way as the significance of the cross has to be accepted by faith. Belief in the resurrection is simply and exactly the same as belief in the cross as "salvation event" (*Heilsereignis*), in the cross as the cross of Christ.[24]

The actual historicity of the Man Jesus is, therefore, curiously incidental; so as well is the fiercely debated issue of His divinity. In a sense, while Bultmann appreciates why traditionally these matters have been regarded as the hallmarks of Christianity, he treats them with relative indifference. A founder of the form-criticism school, he espouses a radical devaluation of gospel history in his book *Die Geschichte der synoptischen Tradition*. What is left when the "forms" are analyzed, those congealed segments of biographical material which the early church created for propaganda purposes? Virtually nothing.

> As a result of this investigation it appears that the outline of the life of Jesus, as it is given by Mark and taken over by Matthew and Luke, is an editorial creation, and that as a consequence our actual knowledge

of the course of Jesus' life is restricted to what little can be discovered in the individual scenes constituting the older tradition.[25]

Moreover, as for the dogma of Christ's divinity painstakingly deduced by the Church from the New Testament data, that also must be reinterpreted in the light of a valid hermeneutic:

> In the New Testament, or at least in the greater part of it, declarations concerning the divinity or deity of Jesus Christ are, simply as a matter of fact, declarations intended to express not his nature but his significance for faith; their purpose is to confess that what he says and what he is do not derive their origin from anything within this world; they are not human thoughts or events of this world; on the contrary in them God speaks to us, works upon us and for us. Christ is the power and the wisdom of God; he has become to us the wisdom of God, righteousness, sanctification and redemption (I Cor. 1:30). I would, then, give it as my opinion that in so far as declarations of this kind are adopted in the form of propositions in which Christ is set before us as an *object* for our discernment, they must be subjected to critical evaluation.[26]

CRITIQUE

Bultmann's demythologized, Heideggerian version of Christianity, though it embraces insights which are of inestimable value, has been subjected to whithering criticism. And one criticism in particular cuts to the very heart of his reinterpretation of the kerygma. What compelling reasons convince a scholar of Bultmann's stature that God, the inscrutable and unpredictable Source and Sustainer of reality, has acted redemptively in a Man whose historicity is very dubious and whose alleged significance comes to us through a mythological fog that only sophisticated scholarship can penetrate? Why accept this Man as the saving model of authenticity? Oden reminds us, consequently, that an unanswerable question arises from the head-on collision between philosophy and theology—or at least theology as Bultmann understands it.

> Although the New Testament hardly provides us with an existential analysis of the nature of man, it does proclaim an event of redemption that addresses man in his ontic situation with a new and actual possibility of truly human existence. *Since it understands that man's new moral possibility is given in an event, the saving act of God, it also understands that without this event man's situation is one of despair, an assertion that philosophy rejects.* How can the New Testament maintain this, in contrast to the whole weight of the philosophical tradition?[27]

Bultmann has no reply to such devastating inquiries except a sheer fideism:

> If we still ask these questions, we are obviously not yet rightly prepared. For they indicate that we still consider the Bible as an ordinary book which we may study like other books in order to profit by it. If we ask for plain convincing reasons why God speaks actually here, in the Bible, then we have not yet understood what God's sovereignty means. For it is due to his sovereign will, that he has spoken and speaks here. The Bible does not approach us at all like other books, nor like other "religious voices of the nations," as catering for our interest. It claims from the outset to be God's word. We did not come across the Bible in the course of our cultural studies, as we came across, for example, Plato or the Bhagavad-Gita. We came to know it through the Christian church, which put it before us with its authoritative claim. The church's preaching, founded on the Scriptures, passes on the word of the Scriptures. It says: God speaks to you *here!* In his majesty he has chosen *this* place! We cannot question whether this place is the right one; we must listen to the call that summons us.[28]

But if one does not hear God speaking through Scripture, what then? History and logic are powerless to persuade. Bultmann on his premises cannot appeal to any internal testimony of the Holy Spirit—another mythological concept! Hence, if modern man will not or cannot resort to a most unscientific voluntarism, his sole alternative is skepticism or atheism. Thus Bultmann becomes a John the Baptist for the God-is-dead movement.

PIERRE TEILHARD DE CHARDIN

Born in 1881 at Sarcenat in the Auvergne district of central France, Pierre Teilhard de Chardin became a Jesuit priest who gained an international reputation as a paleontologist. After receiving his doctorate in geology from the Sorbonne, he carried on research in China for many years, later traveling in Southeast Asia and Africa. A philosopher as well as a scientist, a mystic whose prose is soaringly poetic, he engaged in speculation on a cosmic scale, projecting a vision of reality which reconceptualizes traditional Christian dogmas in terms of an all-inclusive evolutionism. Though the Church refused him permission to publish any of the books which set forth his iconoclastic theorizing, he obeyed its authority and remained its loyal son throughout his life. As he explained in a letter to his friend Henri de Lubac, "Only in the

Roman 'trunk' do I see the biological support sufficiently vast and differentiated to carry out the enduring transformation of humanity which we await.''[29] Following his death in 1955, however, some fifteen volumes of his writings were published in rapid succession; these have called forth an ever increasing plethora of books and articles which seek to interpret Teilhardism.

TEILHARD'S GOAL

The impact of this creative genius has been extraordinary. On the one hand, Bernard Towers pays tribute to his originality and creativity in the field of science.

> A Christian priest of rare spiritual insight, he was also a scientist of great eminence. His geological and palaeontological studies, published in the journals of learned societies in Europe, Asia and America, constitute the kind of lasting contribution to science that marks a distinguished scholar. The honours which he received from, and the esteem in which he was held by, his scientific colleagues are matters of record. But he was not only a highly skilled and dedicated research worker, whose labours served to push forward the boundaries of knowledge "inch by inch." This is the normal way in which science advances, by the steady, competent work of those who have mastered the necessary skills. But as well as being a master in his scientific field, he was also one of those relatively rare people, the pioneers of science. He was, in fact, a pioneer of great intellectual daring and originality, whose ideas are likely to modify profoundly, and to advance enormously, our understanding of the nature of science and of its relation to other aspects of living.[30]

On the other hand, the Very Rev. Father Arrupe, General of the Society of Jesus, in a press conference on June 14, 1965, had this to say regarding Teilhard's theological contribution:

> Père Teilhard is one of the great masters of contemporary thought, and his success is not to be wondered at. He carried through, in fact, a great attempt to reconcile the world of science with the world of faith. Starting from the evidence provided by scientific investigation, he used a phenomenological method now popular with contemporary thinkers, and completed his system by a spiritual teaching: in this, not only does the person of Christ stand at the centre of the world's evolution, as St. Paul meant when he spoke of the Christ "in whom all things hold together." It is impossible not to recognize how rich a contribution to our time has been made by the message of Père Teilhard.[31]

It is impossible, moreover, to understand the development of avant-garde theology among both Catholics and Protestants in recent years without an appreciation of the work done by this priest-paleontologist.

Teilhard's central and controlling conviction can be quite simply stated: if the Gospel is to win the allegiance of the twentieth-century world, it must be reconceptualized in keeping with the most advanced knowledge.

> After two thousand years, so many of our views have been modified that, in religion, we have to slough off the old skin. The formulas we have been using have become too narrow and unyielding. We find them irksome and they have ceased to move us. If we are to go on living we must make a fresh start. By constant repetition of dogma in the same form and by developing it only abstractly, we are losing ourselves in the clouds, where we are completely out of touch with what agitates the world, with what it seeks, and with what feeds its vigour. From the religious point of view we are living cut off from the world, both intellectually and emotionally.[32]

Only a reconceptualized Christianity, he repeatedly contends, will make sense to the modern mind.

> We who are Christians know that the Saviour has already been born. But now that we have this completely new phase of mankind, should he not be *reborn,* in a way adapted to our present needs? . . . We find something too narrow and something lacking in the Gospel as it is now presented. Our soul needs stronger meat. The trial through which we are passing is not a crisis of weakness and spiritual frigidity, but one of metamorphosis and growth. Wider horizons are not tighter control, that . . . is the only thing that can effectively bring our generation back to the paths of truth.[33]

Concerned, then, to demonstrate that the ancient faith is in deepest harmony with the truths discovered by an evolution-oriented science, he once offered this prayer:

> In my own small way, Lord, I would wish to be the apostle, and (if I may be so bold) the evangelist of *your Christ in the universe.* . . . *To bring Christ, in virtue of interconnexions that are specifically organic, to the very heart of the realities that are considered the most fraught with danger, the most philosophically naturalistic, the most pagan*—that is my gospel and there lies my mission.[34]

In working to help God answer his prayer, Teilhard tirelessly seeks to reformulate "old Christianity" in order that, with the relevance of a seemingly new religion, it will magnetize even contemporary pagans to Jesus Christ. Reassuringly, he therefore remarks, "The new religion will be exactly the same as our old Christianity, but with a new life drawn from the legitimate evolution of its dogmas as they come into contact with new ideas."[35] Hence in Teilhard's new Christianity the concepts of evolution, God, and Christ are daringly intermeshed. Let us examine, then, these three fundamentals of Teilhardism.

THE EVOLUTIVE PROCESS

He holds, to start with, that reality is a temporal process, operating under the dynamic and direction of evolution.

> Taken at this degree of generalisation (in other words where all experimental reality in the universe forms part of a *process,* that is to say, is *born*) evolution has long ago ceased to be a hypothesis and become a *general condition of knowledge* (an additional *dimension*) which henceforth all hypotheses must satisfy.[36]

He also holds to the organic interrelatedness of everything that exists: being, inextricably interrelated from its lowest primordial levels to its highest ultimate reaches, is one enormous fabric with all its threads woven together. Energy, he likewise holds, is the essence of being, and being is psychic through and through. Reality, he therefore hypothecates, has a within as well as a without. Hence Teilhard speaks indiscriminately about interiority, mentality, and consciousness from man on down through to the cell. Energy, he further postulates, is of two kinds, radial and tangential, and in its processive churning through space-time it has undergone and keeps on undergoing amazing transformations.

This evolutive process Teilhard characterizes as orthogenesis, a straight-line development toward a predetermined goal. At various "thresholds," or "critical points," he thinks, major breakthroughs occur as qualitative changes take place and new properties are precipitated, all of this brought about by the concomitant activities of "complexification" and "centering." So cosmogenesis leads to biogenesis, and biogenesis leads to noogenesis, and noogenesis is leading to Christogenesis as energy or matter is being more and more Christicized; and Christogenesis will eventually terminate in the Omega point. This process, Teilhard assumes, was guided from within by Christ through its divergent phases until the level of hominization was reached; at that critical point Christ became incarnate and is now directing orthogenesis through its convergent phase until Christicized reality attains the Omega point, the Future-Universal which is Hyper-Personal. Concerning the nature and significance of this cosmic goal, Teilhard waxes rhapsodic.

> If we pursue the perspectives of science as they relate to the humanization process to their logical and final conclusion, we then discover the climax of anthropogenesis to be the existence of an ultimate centre or focus of personality and consciousness which is indispensable for the orientation of the historical growth of spirit and for its synthesis. Now this *Omega point* (as I have called it), is it not the ideal centre from which to see radiating the Christ whom we worship—a Christ whose supernatural lordship is accompanied, as we are aware, by a predominating physical power over the natural spheres of the world? *In quo omnia constant.* Marvellous coincidence, indeed, of the data of faith with the processes of reason itself! What at first appeared to be a threat instead turns out to be a splendid confirmation. Far from coming into opposition with Christian dogma, the vastly increased importance assumed by man in nature results (when considered exhaustively) in traditional Christology being given a new lease of relevance and a new vitality.[37]

This breathtaking vision, it must be borne in mind, rests on the premise that evolution is an indisputable fact. Teilhard has no patience with an obscurantism which insists that it is only a theory. For him it is the master key, providentially forged by modern science, that unlocks the secrets of nature and history.

> Appearing locally, in the wake of zoology, evolution, after making gradual progress through the neighbouring realms, has finally *invaded everything....* Let us be done once and for all, therefore, with the naive conception of the "evolutionary hypothesis"; it has long been out-of-date. No, taken sufficiently broadly, evolution is no longer, and has not been for a long time, a hypothesis—nor merely a simple method. It is in fact a new and common dimension of the universe, and consequently affects the totality of elements and relations of the universe. Not a hypothesis, therefore, but a condition which all hypotheses must henceforth fulfill.[38]

More fully, but with equal dogmatism, he spotlights this premise which is foundational to the edifice of his Weltanschauung.

> What modern natural scientists most fundamentally hold to—what they cling to as an unshakable conviction, a conviction that has continuously grown beneath their surface arguments—is the fact of a *physical connexion* between living beings. Living beings *hold*

together biologically. They have organic command of their successive appearances. . . . The successive growths of life can be the *substance of a history*. . . Every being in our universe is by its material organization part and parcel of a whole past. It is in essence a history. And by its history, by this chain of antecedents which have prepared and introduced it, it is joined with no severance to the milieu within which it appears to us. The smallest exception to this rule would upset the entire edifice of our experience. . . . *Reduced to its essence,* transformism is not a hypothesis. It is the particular expression, applied to the case of life, of the law which conditions our whole knowledge of the sensible universe: the law that we can understand nothing, in the domain of matter, except as part of a sequence or collection.[39]

THE IMMANENT GOD

As for the existence of Deity, it is neither negated nor verified, in Teilhard's opinion, by orthogenesis or any other evolutionary hypothesis. The question of Deity's existence stands exactly where it stood before the time of Charles Darwin. Thus, in *The Vision of the Past,* Teilhard writes:

Just as the materialistic biologist thinks he has gotten rid of the soul in demonstrating the physicochemical mechanisms in the living cell, so certain zoologists imagine that they have dispensed with the need for a First Cause because they have discovered a bit more of the general structure of his work. It is time to put aside a problem so badly formulated. No scientific theory of evolution strictly speaking proves anything for or against God. It merely states the fact of a linked series in reality. It shows us an anatomy, not a final reason, of life. . . . The decision as to whether the course of evolution is intelligible by itself, or whether it demands a progressive and continuous creative act of a First Mover, is a question for metaphysics. Evolution, one must keep repeating, does not impose any particular philosophy.[40]

But evolution has modified the traditional doctrine of God, in one respect at any rate: it assumes that God did not create punctiliarly, at some moment in the mists of the past; rather, as the active élan of the cosmic process, He is continually creating. Teilhard, therefore, urges us to think of creation not "as an instantaneous act, but in the manner of a process or synthesizing action. . . . Creation has never ceased. Its act is a great continuous movement spread out over the totality of time. It is still going on."[41]

In another respect, too, evolution has modified the traditional view of God. It conceives Him not as static perfection but as active

and undoubtedly changing. So in a typically difficult passage, one
which climaxes in adoring devotion, Teilhard speaks about his own
mind-staggering view of God.

By one of those strange inhibitory effects that prevent us from seeing
what is staring us in the face, I did not realize that as God "metamor-
phosized" the world from the depths of matter to the heights of spirit,
so, and in the same degree, the world in return must "endomorphize"
God. Under the influence of the unitive operation that discloses him
to us, God in some way "transforms himself" as he incorporates us.
Thus what now seems to me to be the essential act and concern of
hominized evolution is not simply to see God and allow oneself to be
enveloped and penetrated by him . . . but at the same time (if not first
of all) to disclose (or even in a sense to complete) him ever more fully.
Around us and in us, through the encounter between his attraction
and our thought, God is in process of changing. Through the rise of
"the quantity of cosmic union," his radiance grows brighter and his
colour richer. Here at last we find, here we have the expression of, the
great event, the great tidings. . . Lord of consistence and union, you
whose *mark of recognition and essence* are the power to increase
indefinitely, without distortion or rupture, in step with the mysterious
matter in whose heart you reside and of all whose movements you are
the ultimate master—Lord of my childhood and Lord of my end
—God, for himself ever complete, and yet, for us, over and endlessly
being born.[42]

"God is in process of changing." Explicitly Teilhard makes this
pronouncement. In other texts he alludes to "the fulfillment of God"
who "consummates himself only in uniting," and adds, "God is
entirely self-sufficient, and nevertheless creation brings to him
something vitally necessary." In still another passage he declares:

Truly it is not the notion of the contingency of the created but the
sense of the mutual completion of God and the world that makes
Christianity live. . . . God, the eternal being in himself, is everywhere,
we might say, in process of formation for us.

Then he further affirms the notion that the raison d'etre of
creation was a divine necessity.

In the world viewed as the object of "creation," classical
metaphysics accustoms us to see a sort of extrinsic production,
issuing from the supreme *efficiency* of God through an overflow of
benevolence. *Invincibly*—and *precisely* in order to be able to act and
to love fully at one and the same time—I am now led to see therein (in

conformity with the spirit of St. Paul) a mysterious product of completion and fulfillment for the Absolute Being Himself.[43]

So at this juncture the criticism of Claude Trestmontant seems to be entirely justified:

> In order to avoid the Charybdis of a universe created in a purely contingent and arbitrary way, Teilhard falls into the Scylla of a well-known mythology. According to it, God fulfills Himself in creating the world. God engages in a struggle with the Many (the ancient chaos) in order to find Himself again, richer and pacified, at the terminus of this world. This is an old gnostic idea which is found in Boehme, Hegel and Schelling.[44]

Entirely justified, too, is the comment of biologist D. Gareth Jones: "Anything suggestive of an unchanging God who is in some sense over against the processes of this present world can find no place in Teilhard's theology."[45]

Thus the traditional view of God has been radically challenged by evolution. No longer adequate, it cries out for drastic reconceptualization. And John Baptist Walker, a popularizer of such reconceptualization, counsels Christian theology to take as its "starting-point the work of Teilhard de Chardin," and begin to think adventuresomely in terms "of an evolutionary God." What are the implications of such a thinking or rethinking?

> Our ancestors looked back to a time "in the beginning" when God expressed himself by creating an unchanging universe. If we now accept the fact that this universe is in reality evolving, then this can only mean, in consequence, that God's *expression* of himself is undergoing evolutionary change. The transcendent and unchanging Father is immanent and present in his changing creation, shaping and moulding it until it shall finally proclaim his glory to the fullest extent of which it is capable. Then, as Paul tells us, "God will be all in all". . . . It would also be wrong to imagine that evolution is sustained and directed by God from the outside, as though he were a celestial puppet-master holding all the strings. Yet this is precisely what we do if we rely upon special divine interventions as explanations of those facts of earth that human knowledge is at present unable to fathom.[46]

This changing, nonintervening, totally immanent God is scarcely identifiable with the God Self-revealed in Jesus Christ. To reconceptualize is one thing; to metamorphosize totally the traditional view is to destroy while alleging to preserve.

CHRIST-OMEGA

Let us notice, finally, how Teilhard, in the light of his evolutive assumptions, reconceptualizes the traditional view of Jesus Christ. That he worships this Person with a burning ardor is movingly apparent from his unabashed and repeated confessions of love and trust. Lyrically, for example, he bears this testimony to Christ.

> And then comes the question of Christ himself—who is he? Turn to the most weighty and most unmistakable passages in the Scriptures. Question the Church about her essential beliefs; and this is what you will learn: Christ is not something added to the world as an extra, he is not an embellishment, a king as we now crown kings, the owner of a great estate. . . . He is the alpha and the omega, the principle and the end, the foundation stone and the key-stone, the Plenitude and the Plenifier. He is the one who consummates all things and gives them their consistence. It is towards him and through him, the inner life and light of the world, that the universal convergence of all created spirit is effected in sweat and tears. He is the single centre, precious and consistent, who glitters at the summit that is to crown the world, at the opposite pole from those dim and eternally shrinking regions into which our science ventures when it descends the road of matter and the past.[47]

Thus what orthogenesis does, Teilhard claims, is open up the way for a deeper apprehension of Christology. "By showing us the summit that crowns the world, evolution makes Christ possible—just as Christ, by giving meaning and direction to the world, makes evolution possible."[48] It is a tragic mistake, consequently, to imagine that evolution and Christology are in conflict. Instead, they require and supplement each other.

> Not only does the Christological tradition through experience show itself capable of tolerating an evolutionary structure of the world; but even more, contrary to all previews, it is at the heart of this new organic and unitary milieu, in favor of this particular orientation of space linked with time, that it develops most freely and fully. It is there that it assumes its true form. . . . Christianity and evolution are not two irreconcilable visions, but two perspectives destined to fit together and complement each other.[49]

Rather than searching after some new deity, therefore, Teilhard insists that Jesus Christ has all the essential qualifications for an "evolutive God."

> A hitherto unknown form of religion—one that no one could yet have

imagined or described, for lack of a universe large enough and organic enough to contain it—is burgeoning in men's hearts, from a seed sown by the idea of evolution. . . . Since his appearance Christ has never ceased to emerge from every crisis of history more present, more urgent, more assertive than ever. What, then, does he lack to be able to appear once more to our new world as the "new God" we look for? 1. He must no longer be limited, *constitutionally,* in his operation to no more than the "redemption" of our planet. 2. We now realize that everything in our universe follows a single axis of co-reflexion: we must, therefore, avoid that subtle confusion of "super-natural" and "extra-natural," so that Christ will no longer be offered to our adoration as a peak distinct from and in rivalry with the summit to which the slope of anthropology, extended biologically, ultimately leads.[50]

Most of the historic doctrines of Christology Teilhard bypasses with not so much as a fleeting glance or with at best a hasty nod. Typically, arguing that suffering is an integral element in the cosmic process, he offers this comment:

Following the classical view, suffering is above all a punishment, an expiation; it is efficacious as a sacrifice; it originates from sin and makes reparation for sin. Suffering is good as a means of self-mastery, self-conquest, self-liberation. In contrast, following the ideas and tendencies of a truly cosmic outlook, suffering is above all the consequence and price of a labor of development. It is efficacious as effort. Physical and moral evil originate from a process of becoming; everything which evolves experiences suffering and moral failure. . . . The Cross is the symbol of the pain and toil of evolution, rather than the symbol of expiation.[51] *(the act by which atonement is made)*

Significantly enough, though, the second coming looms large in his thought. For as he reconceptualizes the meaning of the Parousia, Teilhard manages to pull together the multiple threads of his theorizing:

Christ's first coming to earth was only feasible—and nobody will dispute this—after the human species, in the setting of the general process of evolution, had been anatomically constituted and from the social standpoint had attained in some degree a collective consciousness. If this much be granted, why not go a step further and ask whether in the case of his second and last coming *also,* Christ defers his return until the human community has realized to the full its *natural* potentialities, and thereby becomes qualified to receive through him its supernatural consummation? Indeed, if the historical development of spirit is bound by definite physical rules, must not this be equally the case—*a fortiori,* even—where its further unfolding and completion are concerned?[52]

Pondering Teilhard's Christology, as well as his other reinterpretations of traditional faith, one concludes that Dietrich von Hildebrand has not been overly severe in his criticisms:

> It was only after reading several of Teilhard's works, . . . that I fully realized the catastrophic implications of his philosophical ideas, and the absolute incompatibility of his theology-fiction (as Etienne Gilson calls it) with Christian revelation . . .
> Teilhard's Christ is no longer Jesus, the God-man, the epiphany of God, the Redeemer; instead he is the initiator of a purely natural evolutionary process and, simultaneously, its end—the Christ-Omega. An unprejudiced mind cannot but ask: Why should this "cosmic force" be called Christ?
> In Teilhard's theology, the stress is laid on the progress of the earth, the evolution leading to Christ-Omega. There is no place for salvation through Christ's death on the Cross, because man's destiny is part of the pancosmic evolution. Teilhard has written: "Yes, the moral and social development of humanity is indeed the authentic and natural consequence of organic evolution." For such a man, original sin, redemption and sanctification can no longer have any real meaning. Note that Teilhard does not seem quite aware of this incompatibility: "Sometimes I am a bit afraid, when I think of the transposition to which I must submit my mind concerning the vulgar notions of creation, inspiration, miracle, original sin, resurrection, etc., in order to be able to accept them."[53]

Teilhard's anxiety is well-grounded. For while he can manage to rationalize his continued profession of faith in the "vulgar notions" of traditional Christianity by a kind of speculative legerdemain, many of his less adroit admirers and disciples are unable to mimic his dazzling performance. Hence they eventually conclude that even Teilhard's reconceptualized faith is a "vulgar notion" that an honest modern must totally abandon.

DIETRICH BONHOEFFER

Born February 4, 1906, in Breslau, Germany, Dietrich Bonhoeffer was the son of a prominent psychiatrist. His mother was a loving, cheerful, artistic woman. Reared in bourgeois comfort and culture, the boy decided to enter the ministry despite strong paternal objections. After study at Tübingen and Berlin, he secured a licentiate degree when he was only twenty-one with his thesis, "The

Communion of Saints," which Karl Barth called "a theological miracle." In 1930 he began to teach at the University of Berlin, leaving there, however, to spend a year at Union Theological Seminary in New York City as a Sloan Fellow. He was then appointed Youth Secretary of the World Alliance for Promoting International Friendship through the Churches.

With Hitler's seizure of power in 1933, Bonhoeffer became a leader in the Confessional Church. In 1935 he was asked to direct its seminary which started in Zingst and soon moved to Finkenwalde. Though urged to remain in the United States where he had influential friends, Bonhoeffer elected to cast in his lot with his own people and especially with the resistance movement. Following an abortive attempt to assassinate *der Feuhrer*, Bonhoeffer was arrested on April 5, 1943, and sent to the military prison, Tegel, in Berlin. He was later removed to Prinz-Albrecht-Strasse, shipped next to Buchenwald, and finally to Flossenburg, where he was hanged on April 9, 1945, a week before Hitler committed suicide.

Something of Bonhoeffer's spirit, his candor, his faith, his struggle against doubt and despair during his years in Nazi hands, is shown in his moving poem, *"Wer Bin Ich?"*

> Who am I? They often tell me
> I stepped from my cell's confinement
> Calmly, cheerfully, firmly,
> Like a squire from his country house.
> Who am I? They often tell me
> I used to speak to my warders
> Freely and friendly and clearly,
> As though they were mine to command.
> Who am I? They also tell me
> I bore the days of misfortune
> Equably, smilingly, proudly
> Like one accustomed to win.
>
> Am I then really all that which other men tell of?
> Or am I only what I myself know of myself?
> Restless and longing and sick, like a bird in a cage,
> Struggling for breath, as though hands were
> compressing my throat,
> Yearning for colours, for flowers, for the voices of birds,
> Thirsting for words of kindness, for neighbourliness,
> Tossing in expectation of great events,
> Powerlessly trembling for friends at an infinite distance,

Weary and empty at praying, at thinking, at making,
Faint, and ready to say farewell to it all?

Who am I? This or the other?
Am I one person today and tomorrow another?
Am I both at once? A hypocrite before others,
And before myself a contemptibly woebegone weakling?
Or is something within me still like a beaten army,
Fleeing in disorder from victory already achieved?

Who am I? They mock me, these lonely questions of mine.
Whoever I am, Thou knowest O God, I am thine![54]

Shortly after Bonhoeffer's execution, one of his American admirers, Reinhold Niebuhr, wrote about him feelingly and prophetically:

> The story of Bonhoeffer is worth recording. It belongs to the modern Acts of the Apostles . . . Bonhoeffer was a brilliant young theologian who combined a deep piety with a high degree of intellectual sophistication . . . less known than Niemöller, he will become better known. Not only his martyr's death but also his actions and precepts contain within them the hope of a revitalized Protestant faith in Germany.[55]

Dietrich Bonhoeffer has indeed become better known, one of the best known of twentieth-century theologians, exerting a decisive influence on the emergence of radical Christianity.

Bonhoeffer as Theologian

It is difficult to know how we can succinctly present and justly assess Bonhoeffer's work, truncated as it was by his tragic death at the age of thirty-nine. Thus in his definitive study, *Dietrich Bonhoeffer: Theologian of Reality,* André Dumas has this to say: "Bonhoeffer is a Barthian who is sensitive to the questions raised by liberal theology that Bultmann has never stopped asking, and so he is the key man in dealing with the present theological situation."[56] That assessment of Bonhoeffer by a discerning scholar—"the key man in dealing with the present theological situation"—highlights his significance and at the same time indicates how formidable an assignment it is to do him justice. Because Bonhoeffer did not live to explain those cryptic and fragmentary letters, written at Tegel in a situation of excruciating pressure, one shares Karl Barth's uncertainty as to what exactly his young friend may have meant in many passages:

What is the "world come of age"? What does "non-religious interpretation" mean? What am I to understand by "positivism of revelation"? I know everything, or at least a great deal of what the experts make of it up to Heinrich Ott. But to this day I do not know what Bonhoeffer himself meant or wanted by it, and I am even inclined to doubt a little whether Systematic Theology (I am also thinking of his *Ethics*) was his strongest field. . . . Even if I should be mistaken, I should still re-affirm that his letters from prison represent only one (in this case the last) of the stations in his intellectual and spiritual journey, a journey that was very turbulent from the beginning even though that was not its aim; that he might have been capable of the most astonishing evolution in quite a different direction; and that we do him an injustice when we suddenly place him in some line with Tillich and Bultmann and interpret him in relation to those passages (or as his own prophet based on these passages), whether in the sense of a very bourgeois liberalism or, as H. Müller sees it, as the precursor of the ideology of the D.D.R., or, in R. Prenter's interpretation, as a new Lutheran Church Father.[57]

One appreciates, moreover, the near bewilderment which Dumas, a topflight Bonhoeffer authority, admits to be his own reaction.

It is somewhat disconcerting to see what those who enter into conversation with Bonhoeffer make of him, and what strange amalgams result from such encounters, sometimes with Luther, sometimes with Feuerbach, Freud and Nietzsche, and sometimes even with St. Thomas Aquinas, Teilhard de Chardin and Karl Rahner! Barth's question is unavoidable: did this "impulsive young thinker" really have a systematic viewpoint if his readers can organize his thought into so many contradictory systems?[58]

Perhaps the wisest approach, then, will be to sketch Bonhoeffer's basic theological approach before focusing on some of his more controversial concepts, briefly elucidating those concepts without indulging in eisegesis insofar as that proves possible.

Let it be said at the outset that there seems to be little reason for assuming, as is rather frequently done, a discontinuity between Bonhoeffer's earlier work and the speculations he advanced while in Tegel. Continuity, rather than discontinuity, marks his thought throughout the three periods into which his closest friend, Eberhard Bethge, initially divided Bonhoeffer's career: the university period, 1927-33; the period of the Confessional Church, 1933-40; the period of political activity and of imprisonment, 1940-45.

THE CENTER OF HIS FAITH

Bonhoeffer agrees with Barth that God discloses Himself only in and through Jesus Christ. Nothing could be more explicit than his answer to the question, "Who is God?"

> Not in the first place an abstract belief in God, in his omnipotence etc. That is not a genuine experience of God, but a partial extension of the world. Encounter with Jesus Christ. The experience that a transformation of all human life is given in the fact that "Jesus is there only for others." His "being there for others" is the experience of transcendence. It is only this "being there for others," maintained till death, that is the ground of his omnipotence, omniscience, and omnipresence. Faith is participation in this being of Jesus (incarnation, cross, and resurrection). Our relation to God is not a "religious" relationship to the highest, most powerful, and best Being imaginable—that is not authentic transcendence—but our relation to God is a new life in "existence for others," through participation in the being of Jesus. The transcendental is not infinite and unattainable tasks, but the neighbour who is within reach in any given situation.[59]

Again, in one of his last letters to Bethge, Bonhoeffer reaffirms the Christocentricity of his faith:

> It's your birthday in a week's time. Once again I've taken up the readings and meditated on them. The key to everything is the "in him." All that we may rightly expect from God, and ask him for, is to be found in Jesus Christ. The God of Jesus Christ has nothing to do with what God, as we imagine him, could do and ought to do. If we are to learn what God promises, and what he fulfils, we must persevere in quiet meditation on the life, sayings, deeds, sufferings, and death of Jesus. It is certain that we may always live close to God and in the light of his presence, and that such living is an entirely new life for us; that nothing is then impossible for us, because all things are possible with God; that no earthly power can touch us without his will, and that danger and distress can only drive us closer to him. It is certain that we can claim nothing for ourselves, and may yet pray for everything; it is certain that our joy is hidden in suffering, and our life in death; it is certain that in all this we are in a fellowship that sustains us. In Jesus God has said Yes and Amen to it all, and that Yes and Amen is the firm ground on which we stand.[60]

Bonhoeffer further agrees with Barth that God's self-disclosure must control our understanding of ontology and epistemology. He emphasizes God not as He may be *a se,* but as He is *pro nobis,* God as He freely enters into relationship with man.

> In revelation it is a question less of God's freedom on the far side from us, i.e., his eternal isolation and aseity, than of his forth-proceeding, his *given* Word, his bond in which he has bound himself to historical man, having placed himself at man's disposal. God is not free *of* man but *for* man. Christ is the Word of his freedom. God *is there*, which is to say: not in eternal non-objectivity but. . . "haveable," graspable in his Word within the Church.[61]

In James Woelfel's opinion, Bonhoeffer makes this view of divine self-disclosure and self-humiliation absolutely central: Christology is the very heart of his theology.

> *Finitum capax infiniti* could well be the theological motto of Bonhoeffer's whole theological development. His writings show him pushing this "material" doctrine of the Incarnation in an ever more concrete direction with creative passion and rigor. Here is the key to Bonhoeffer's whole theological method, including the final "non-religious interpretation of biblical concepts": God is God become man, the man Jesus Christ, and that is all we can concern ourselves with as men. The only majesty, sovereignty, glory, and freedom of God which we know are what he has revealed in Jesus Christ. God is God-turned-toward-man in the Incarnation. He is "haveable," "graspable" in the concrete, historical affairs of men, not "eternal non-objectivity," related to the world only formally and tangentially through bare acts.[62]

Hence Christology likewise determines Bonhoeffer's doctrine of the Church. Drafting the outline of a book shortly before his death, he writes:

> The church is the church only when it exists for others. To make a start, it should give away all its property to those in need. The clergy must live solely on the free-will offerings of their congregations, or possibly engage in some secular calling. The church must share in the secular problems of ordinary human life, not dominating, but helping and serving. It must tell men of every calling what it means to live in Christ, to exist for others. In particular, our own church will have to take the field against the vices of *hubris*, power-worship, envy, and humbug, as the roots of all evil. It will have to speak of moderation, purity, trust, loyalty, constancy, patience, discipline, humility, contentment, and modesty. It must not under-estimate the importance of human example (which has its origin in the humanity of Jesus and is so important in Paul's teaching); it is not abstract argument, but example, that gives its word emphasis and power.[63]

This Christological approach to the whole range of theology and ethics, a complex and dialectical perspective, obviously requires a much fuller treatment than is here being attempted. Yet even this superficial treatment may facilitate a better understanding of Bonhoeffer's more radical ideas. What, specifically, are they?

THE WORLD COME OF AGE

One is that the world in our twentieth century has come of age. Philosophically and technologically it is now *eine mündige Welt*, a mature or adult world, a world which man can run autonomously without the need of either divine truth or divine grace. It is the stage of human development described by the renowned scientist F. von Weizacker in his book *The World View of Physics*, which Bonhoeffer mentions explicitly as one text he had been reading in prison. At this stage of history the God-hypothesis is no longer required to account for reality; it functions, therefore, as, in Woelfel's phrase, "an evershrinking stopgap"; and hence too it functions only privatistically in the purely personal and psychic areas of human life. Weizacker says,

> Every scientist must certainly set himself the goal of making the hypothesis "God" superfluous in his field. God and the faded, half-religious concepts which have often been substituted for him in recent times, always designate, as scientific hypotheses for the explanation of particular facts, only the incomplete points in science, and therefore with the advance of knowledge they find themselves in continuous and dishonourable retreat.[64]

One hears echo of Weizacker in Bonhoeffer's letter of June 8, 1944, addressed to Bethge and smuggled out by a friendly guard.

> Man has learnt to deal with himself in all questions of importance without recourse to the "working hypothesis" called "God." In questions of science, art, and ethics this has become an understood thing at which one now hardly dares to tilt. But for the last hundred years or so it has also become increasingly true of religious questions; it is becoming evident that everything gets along without "God"—and, in fact, just as well as before. As in the scientific field, so in human affairs generally, "God" is being pushed more and more out of life, losing more and more ground.[65]

The world come of age, Bonhoeffer realizes, a world that is godless, proves to be nihilistic. It is a world without idols; a world that worships nothing; a world completely devoid of religious illusions, even the inverted religion of Marxism; a world that refuses to

bow down before man in an act of self-deification. Bluntly Bonhoeffer declares: "We have experienced too clearly the frailty and
invalidity of all things, of all men, and of ourselves for us still to be
able to deify them."[66] Yet this world come of age is, as Bonhoeffer
sees it, not a world of despair, chaos, and violence, a world which
provides opportunities for evangelism in keeping with the pious
dictum, "Man's extremity is God's opportunity." While Bonhoeffer is neither optimistic nor utopian about *eine mündige Welt,* he
refuses to deny that a self-sufficient secularism may be creative and
healthy, possessing its own virtues and values. Bethge defends him
against the charge of a naive overconfidence in the possible
achievements of a godless society:

> Bonhoeffer never pointed to an optimistic analysis of man as becom-
> ing better and better. . . . The main notion for Bonhoeffer is "responsi-
> bility," the unreversible capability and duty of adults individually to
> answer the questions of life in their own particular fields and within
> their own autonomous structures. This includes, to be sure, the joy
> which follows when human beings grow into their own manhood, but
> it also includes the integration of historical determinations, guilts,
> failures, even when they turn childish, immature, or tyrannical.[67]

Whatever one's appraisal of *eine mündige Welt,* Christianity
has no option but to adjust its witness gratefully to this emerging
phenomenon of Western history. To oppose it in the name of faith,
Bonhoeffer warns, is to do faith a grave disservice.

> The attack by Christian apologetic on the adulthood of the world I
> consider to be in the first place pointless, in the second place ignoble,
> and in the third place unchristian. Pointless, because it seems to me
> like an attempt to put a grown-up man back into adolescence, i.e. to
> make him dependent on things on which he is, in fact, no longer
> dependent, and thrusting him into problems that are, in fact, no longer
> problems to him. Ignoble, because it amounts to an attempt to exploit
> man's weakness for purposes that are alien to him and to which he has
> not freely assented. Unchristian, because it confuses Christ with one
> particular stage in man's religiousness, i.e. with a human law.[68]

Not only is opposition to the world's maturity an apologetic
blunder; it is likewise proof of spiritual blindness, a failure to perceive God's will and purpose in the course of human affairs:

> We cannot be honest unless we recognize that we have to live in the
> world *etsi deus non daretur.* And this is just what we do recognize
> —before God! God himself compels us to recognize it. So our coming

of age leads us to a true recognition of our situation before God. God would have us know that we must live as men who manage our lives without him. The God who is with us is the God who forsakes us (Mark 15:34). The God who lets us live in the world without the working hypothesis of God is the God before whom we stand continually. Before God and with God we live without God. God lets himself be pushed out of the world on to the cross.[69]

RELIGIONLESS CHRISTIANITY

Another of Bonhoeffer's troubling concepts is that of religionless Christianity. Suppose we set down a major passage which brings out this arresting paradox.

What is bothering me incessantly is the question what Christianity really is, or indeed who Christ really is, for us today. The time when people could be told everything by means of words, whether theological or pious, is over, and so is the time of inwardness and conscience—and that means the time of religion in general. We are moving towards a completely religionless time; people as they are now simply cannot be religious any more. Even those who honestly describe themselves as "religious" do not in the least act up to it, and so they presumably mean something quite different by "religious." Our whole nineteen-hundred-year-old Christian preaching and theology rest on the "religious *a priori*" of mankind. "Christianity" has always been a form—perhaps the true form—of "religion." But if one day it becomes clear that this *a priori* does not exist at all, but was a historically conditioned and transient form of human self-expression, and if therefore man becomes radically religionless—and I think that that is already more or less the case (else how is it, for example, that this war, in contrast to all previous ones, is not calling forth any "religious" reaction?)—what does that mean for "Christianity"?[70]

Exactly what, we wonder, does Bonhoeffer have in mind when he refers to religionless Christianity?

One clue is his insistence that he himself is not religious. In a June 1942 letter to Bethge, he expresses a growing disdain for "all religiosity":

Again and again I am driven to think about my activities which are now concerned so much with the secular field. . . . I feel the resistance growing in me against all religiosity, sometimes reaching the level of an instinctive horror—surely, this is not good either. Yet I am not a religious nature at all. But all the time I am forced to think of God, of Christ, of genuineness, life, freedom, charity—that matters for me. What causes me uneasiness is just the religious clothing. Do you *religion as man recieving*

understand? This is no new concept at all, no new insights, but because I believe an idea will come to burst upon me I let things run and do not offer resistance. In this sense I understand my present activity in the secular sector.[71]

Notice that, despite this vigorously expressed disdain of religion per se, Bonhoeffer confesses that "all the time" he is thinking of "God, of Christ, of genuineness, life, freedom, charity," matters which he evidently identifies as nonreligious! A year and a half later, in November 1943, he voices an even stronger repugnance for religion.

Don't be alarmed; I shall not come out of here a *homo religiosus!* On the contrary, my fear and distrust of "religiosity" have become greater than ever here. The fact that the Israelites *never* uttered the name of God always makes me think, and I can understand it better as I go on.[72]

This antireligious attitude, however, exists simultaneously with his own profoundly devout discipline of Scripture reading and prayer; his love of liturgy, particularly hymns; and his sustaining sense of God's presence. Hence the ambiguity of his references to religion is glaringly patent, contradicted, it would seem, by the whole orientation of his life.

That ambiguity lessens, though it by no means completely disappears, when we probe deeper into Bonhoeffer's thinking with respect to this complicated issue. He concurs with the New Testament and Karl Barth in viewing religion as the supreme manifestation of human disobedience and idolatry. For religion is, first, a matter of speculative metaphysics; an attempt, as in German idealism, to deduce a kind of Supreme Being from finite reason, arguing that man with his capacity for God is really one with God in the depths of his psyche. Man is thus elevated to deity, while God is identified with humanity. Religion, so construed, is a metaphysical affair which devotes itself to an explanation of reality, a matter of hairsplitting and logic-chopping over the nature of whatever is. Second, religion is individualistic or privatistic; it concerns itself almost exclusively with inwardness, the subjective, the emotional, and the moralistic. Third, religion, limited as a rule to the spiritual, the otherworldly, posttemporal dimensions of human experience, is segmental. It does not embrace the whole man and all of life; it does not demand a total response from its devotees. Fourth, religion tends to be magical, viewing God as a deus ex machina who intervenes in moments of crisis, answering prayer, solving problems, providing miraculous escape-hatches for an elect in-group. It thus likewise tends to minimize man's responsibility and discourages his self-activity, inculcating a childish dependency hard to distinguish from slavish servility. Finally, religion with its in-group of the elect invariably fosters an attitude of pharisaic superiority, it assumes an aristocracy of true believers separate from the lost world except for occasional evangelistic forays into that God-forsaken territory. It is this interpretation, then, which motivates Bonhoeffer to affirm that, as a matter of inelectable destiny, "We are moving towards a completely religionless time; people as they are now simply cannot be religious any more."[73]

Once more, however, we wonder whether we understand such a statement correctly. If religion is ritualistic ecclesiasticism, pietistic world-denial, and an idolatrous ideology which serves as a tool for the preservation of the status quo, who will bemoan its obliteration? But if the religious premise is man's need for God self-revealed in Jesus Christ, then no matter how mature man becomes, the disappearance of religion will spell the frustration of human fulfillment.

So, to intensify the ambiguity, there are times when Bonhoeffer acknowledges and praises true religion. After sharing in a service at the Riverside Church in New York City, he muses: "Do people not know that one can get on as well, even better, without 'religion'—if only there were not God himself and his Word?"[74] Ah! "God himself and his Word" are here, as with Barth, exempt from the category of religiosity. Perhaps what Bonhoeffer desires, therefore, is a reinterpretation of Christianity which will bring it into alignment with God and his Word. He intimates that, at any rate, in setting himself against Rudolf Bultmann's demythologization.

> I expect you remember Bultmann's essay on the demythologization of the New Testament? My view of it today would be, not that he went "too far," as most people thought, but that he didn't go far enough. It's not only the "mythological" concepts, such as miracle, ascension, and so on (which are not in principle separable from the concepts of God, faith, etc.), but "religious" concepts generally, which are problematic. You can't, as Bultmann supposes, separate God and miracle, but you must be able to interpret and proclaim *both* in a "non-religious" sense. Bultmann's approach is fundamentally still a

liberal one (i.e. abridging the gospel), whereas I'm trying to think theologically.[75]

And this intimation is reinforced by an apparently unequivocal assertion.

> Here is the decisive difference between Christianity and all religions. Man's religiosity makes him look in his distress to the power of God in the world: God is the *deus ex machina*. The Bible directs man to God's powerlessness and suffering; only the suffering God can help. To that extent we may say that the development towards the world's coming of age outlined above, which has done away with a false conception of God, opens up a way of seeing the God of the Bible, who wins power and space in the world by his weakness. This will probably be the starting-point for our "secular interpretation."[76]

Does Bonhoeffer demand, consequently, the religion which the Bible demands, traditional religiosity transformed into true religion by a total human response to God's revelation in Jesus Christ? As he puts it in one of his earlier writings, *Act and Being:*

> It must be plainly said that within the communion of Christ faith takes shape in religion, that therefore religion is here called faith, that, as I look on Christ, I may and must say for my consolation "I believe"—only to add, of course, as I turn to look on myself, "help Thou my unbelief." All praying, all searching for God in his Word, all clinging to his promise, all entreaty for his grace, all hoping in the sight of the Cross, all this for reflexion is "religion," "faith-wishfulness"; but in the communion of Christ, while it is still the work of man, it is God-given faith, faith willed by God, wherein by God's mercy he may really be found.[77]

Yet, as later on in prison he ponders the possibility of a religion-less Christianity, he has his misgivings:

> In what way are we "religionless-secular" Christians, in what way are we the ἐκ-κλησία, those who are called forth, not regarding ourselves from a religious point of view as specially favoured, but rather as belonging wholly to the world? In that case Christ is no longer an object of religion, but something quite different, really the Lord of the world. But what does that mean? What is the place of worship and prayer in a religionless situation? Does the secret disci-pline, or alternatively the difference (which I have suggested to you before) between penultimate and ultimate, take on a new importance here?[78]

Does he realize the probable outcome of his ambiguous position? William Kuhns doubts it.

> Bonhoeffer himself hardly perceived the extremes to which his questions would drive him. He probably saw, if somewhat vaguely, that to overthrow the area of "religious understanding" meant to topple the usual manifestations of God to men—in other words, to leave Christians without the older ways of "sensing God." The result was almost inevitable, a recognition of "Christian atheism," a realization that to discover God in nature, in the "unknown" that science stands on the brink of knowing, or in man's deepest failings is not really to discover God at all. Such efforts to perceive God in the "unknown" result in a false and unnecessary religious delusion. A "Christian atheism" would challenge such efforts. Whether Bonhoeffer actually anticipated such a movement there is no way of knowing; the prison letters suggest that he would have welcomed it, provided, of course, it kept the proper christological perspective.[79]

André Dumas, on the other hand, is sure that Bonhoeffer would not have sanctioned the extreme conclusions drawn from his writings:

> The expression "the death of God" does not occur as such in Bonhoeffer's writings. He speaks of the world "without God," *etsi Deus non daretur,* using Anselm's expression, where the *etsi* (as though God were not given) is combined with the *coram Deo* (before God) of Lutheran faith. He also speaks of a suffering, powerless God being "pushed out" of the world while preserving the act of his presence in God's annihilation on the cross. If "the death of God" is meant to signify simply his effacement, his withdrawal and his absence, it does not do justice to the fullness of Bonhoeffer's paradoxes, since it would lead either to secularization or mystical silence, both of which are foreign to the Old Testament and therefore to Bonhoeffer himself.[80]

Perhaps Paul van Buren, William Hamilton, and Thomas J. J. Altizer may very plausibly claim that they are Bonhoeffer's legitimate heirs.

HOLY WORLDLINESS

Holy worldliness is still another of Bonhoeffer's controversial concepts, as he places in juxtaposition an adjective and a noun which traditional Christianity has struggled to keep hermetically sealed off from each other. In his *Ethics,* for instance, he alludes to what Kuhn calls "a new style of Christian holiness."[81]

A life in genuine worldliness is possible only through the proclamation of Christ crucified; true worldly living is not possible or real in contradiction to the proclamation or side by side with it, that is to say, in any kind of autonomy of the secular sphere; it is possible only "in, with and under" the proclamation of Christ.[82]

While controversial, this notion of a Christomorphic worldliness is really ambiguous. Bonhoeffer is pleading against the background of his Christology that the natural life, human life here and now, be valued and enjoyed to the full because God shows His valuation of it in Jesus Christ. He argues,

Natural life must not be understood simply as a preliminary to life with Christ. It is only from Christ Himself that it receives its validation. Christ Himself entered into the natural life, and it is only through the incarnation of Christ that the natural life becomes the penultimate which is directed towards the ultimate. Only through the incarnation of Christ do we have the right to call others to the natural life and to live the natural life ourselves.[83]

God's valuation of the present world is dramatically shown again in the resurrection of Jesus Christ, which adumbrates the future transformation of existence here and now rather than functioning solely as a guarantee of life beyond the grave. The people who comprise the Christian community, Bonhoeffer declares, do not consider themselves

superior to the world, but persevere together in the midst of the world, in its depths, in its trivialities and bondages. They persevere because in this kind of existence they now demonstrate their loyalty in their own curious way, and they steadfastly keep their eyes on that strange place in this world where they perceive in utter amazement God's breaking through the curse, his unfathomable "Yes!" to the world. Here at the very center of this dying, disrupted, and desirous world something becomes evident to those who can believe—believe in the resurrection of Jesus Christ. . . . It is just in this occurrence that the old earth is affirmed and that God is hailed as Lord of the earth. . . . God's kingdom is the kingdom of the resurrection on earth.[84]

Thus Christians are human beings who do not seek to escape from the much maligned secular life by a world-denying pietism or mysticism. They are, per contra, authentically worldly. In Bonhoeffer's words:

By this-worldliness I mean living unreservedly in life's duties, problems, successes and failures, experiences and perplexities. In so doing we throw ourselves completely into the arms of God, taking seriously, not our own sufferings, but those of God in the world —watching with Christ in Gethsemane. That, I think, is faith; that is *metanoia;* and that is how one becomes a man and a Christian (cf. Jer. 45!).[85]

Shocking, then, as it may sound to pious ears, a biblically informed faith, taking Luther as its paradigm, will use the help of secularity to secure a better Christianity and will use Christianity to secure a better secularity!

Luther was protesting against a Christianity which was striving for independence and detaching itself from the reality of Christ. He protested with the help of the secular and in the name of a better Christianity. So, too, today, when Christianity is employed as a polemical weapon against the secular, this must be done in the name of a better secularity and above all it must not lead back to a static predominance of the spiritual sphere as an end in itself.[86]

For in the end the Christian aspires merely to be a man, not a saint, not a particular human type, but a man with everything that genuine manhood implies from an incarnational standpoint.

During the last year or so I've come to know and understand more and more the profound this-worldliness of Christianity. The Christian is not a *homo religiosus,* but simply a man, as Jesus was a man—in contrast, shall we say, to John the Baptist. I don't mean the shallow and banal this-worldliness of the enlightened, the busy, the comfortable, or the lascivious, but the profound this-worldliness, characterized by discipline and the constant knowledge of death and resurrection. I think Luther lived a this-worldly life in this sense.[87]

And when a Christian lives as a man, loving the earth, loving his neighbors regardless of their secularism, and loving God, his experience is a polyphony.

What I mean is that God wants us to love him eternally with our whole hearts—not in such a way as to injure or weaken our earthly love, but to provide a kind of *cantus firmus* to which the other melodies of life provide the counterpoint. . . . Where the *cantus firmus* is clear and plain, the counterpoint can be developed to its limits. The two are "undivided and yet distinct," in the words of the Chalcedonian Definition, like Christ in his divine and human natures. May not the attraction and importance of polyphony in music consist in its being a musical reflection of this Christological fact and therefore of our *vita christiana?* . . . Only a polyphony of this kind can give life a wholeness and at the same time assure us that nothing calamitous can happen as long as the *cantus firmus* is kept going.[88]

One more passage must be added to round out Bonhoeffer's concept of holy worldliness. For with all of his emphasis on the present life, he does not ignore the world to come. He never allows the temporal to negate the reality of the eternal; neither does he allow the eternal to negate the value of the temporal.

> I believe that we ought so to love and trust God in our *lives,* and in all the good things that he sends us, that when the time comes (but not before!) we may go to him with love, trust, and joy. But, to put it plainly, for a man in his wife's arms to be hankering after the other world is, in mild terms, a piece of bad taste, and not God's will. We ought to find and love God in what he actually gives us; if it pleases him to allow us to enjoy some overwhelming earthly happiness, we mustn't try to be more pious than God himself and allow our happiness to be corrupted by presumption and arrogance, and by unbridled religious fantasy which is never satisfied with what God gives. God will see to it that the man who finds him in his earthly happiness and thanks him for it does not lack reminder that earthly things are transient, that it is good for him to attune his heart to what is eternal, and that sooner or later there will be times when he can say in all sincerity, "I wish I were home." But everything has its time, and the main thing is that we keep step with God, and do not keep pressing on a few steps ahead—nor keep dawdling a step behind. It's presumptuous to want to have everything at once—matrimonial bliss, the cross, and the heavenly Jerusalem, where they neither marry nor are given in marriage.[89]

If this is holy worldliness, then, please God, may it begin to dominate Christian thought and life.

These three controversial concepts, which embody the quintessence of Bonhoeffer's radicalism, reveal why he has been a tantalizing problem to his interpreters. As Dumas remarks, he raises questions which he leaves unanswered—or which, to be charitable, he did not live long enough to answer. Correspondingly, these concepts reveal why this paradoxical thinker has exerted so divergent and ambivalent an influence. How shall we appraise justly a theologian whom Christian radicals applaud while evangelical Christians find their piety deepened by his *The Cost of Discipleship* and *Life Together?*

PAUL TILLICH

If any one man has decisively shaped the development of contemporary theology, that man is Paul Tillich. Reinhold Niebuhr describes him as "the Origen of our period, seeking to relate the Gospel message to the disciplines of our culture and whole history of culture."[90] Walter M. Horton calls him "one of the principle architects of the new theological structure that has been erected on the ruins of idealistic liberalism."[91] John Herman Randall, Jr., applauds him as "the ablest Protestant theologian of the present day."[92] And eulogistically, Theodore M. Greene sums up the sweep and depth of the herculean work performed by this most "enlightening and therapeutic theologian of our time."

> He analyzes our conscious problems and our unconscious needs more profoundly, and he shows us how these problems can be solved and these needs satisfied more constructively, than any recent or contemporary thinker. His critique of historical Christianity would, if taken seriously, provoke revolutionary changes in the Church and in present-day theology. No less significant is his diagnosis of our secular culture and his affirmative answer to the recurrent question: How can we, with complete integrity, reinterpret religion and, through such reinterpretation, recapture the spiritual and cultural vitality which modern secularism has so largely lost?[93]

In brief, then, the course of contemporary theologizing cannot be understood apart from an understanding of Paul Tillich's massive influence.

The son of a Lutheran minister, he was born on August 20, 1886, in Starzeddel, Germany. His life can be divided into four periods: (1) the early years until 1900; (2) the prewar years from 1900 to 1914; (3) the postwar years in Germany from 1914 to 1933; (4) the American years, ending with his death on October 22, 1965. After serving as an army chaplain in World War I, Tillich was a professor of philosophy and theology at Berlin, Marburg, Dresden, and Frankfurt. Driven from Germany by the Nazi takeover, he emigrated to the United States at the age of forty-seven, mastered English, and taught successively at Union Theological Seminary, Harvard University, and the University of Chicago.

THE PRINCIPLE OF CORRELATION

Tillich's self-imposed task was to communicate the abiding truth of the Christian message in terms that would be intelligible and challenging to modern culture. Thus in the last chapter of his book, *Theology of Culture,* he asks:

> How shall the message (which is presupposed) be focused for the people of our time? In other words, we are concerned here with the question: *How* can the Gospel be communicated? We are asking: How do we make the message heard and seen, and then either rejected or accepted? The question *cannot* be: How do we communicate the Gospel so that others will accept it? For this there is no method. To communicate the Gospel means putting it before the people so that they are able to decide for or against it.[94]

Effective communication necessitates, as with Bultmann, the removal of "the wrong stumbling block in order to bring people face to face with the right stumbling block and enable them to make a genuine decision."[95] And, of course, the wrong stumbling block is literalistic supernaturalism, blind to the need for a breaking of the biblical myths and a decoding of the biblical message. Karl Barth's revelational Christomonism must therefore be repudiated, and, as an option to that updated yet outdated orthodoxy, a new theological structure must be erected which will synthesize human wisdom and experience with biblical religion, employing the full resources of science, history, literature, art, and depth psychology, as well as classical and modern philosophy, especially the existentialism of Kierkegaard and Heidegger. Tillich's compendious system, Guyton Hammond tells us, discovers and expounds "continuities and relationships among diverse regions of reality and diverse areas of human thought and action," interpreting man's existence synthetically, "as the fulfillment of the drive of nature (indeed of all being) towards individualization and self-relatedness."[96] Leonard Wheat shares Hammond's opinion but speaks much more in detail about "the great synthesis" which as a Halle student Tillich hoped could be effected "between Christianity and liberalism."

> Synthesis—this is the challenge that fires Tillich's imagination. His response, one which could only come from a prodigious imagination, is a four-level synthesis: (1) disciplinary, (2) ontological, (3) historical, and (4) personal life. The foundation level is the broad disciplinary synthesis of theology and philosophy. This supports what might loosely be termed an ontological synthesis, which combines the two absolutes, God and being. The ontological synthesis leads to a historical one. It is a merger of theology's eschatological history—Eden, sin, and the Kingdom of God (or salvation)—and the dialectical

histories of Hegel and Marx. On this same level are subsidiary synthe-
ses of Eden and essence, sin and estrangement (existence), and the
Kingdom of God and utopia (Hegel's Germanic monarchy, Marx's
world communism, and so on). The top level is a "life" synthesis, in
the sense of a personal life. Here the theological story of the Son's
going out from and returning to the Father ("separation and return")
is correlated with philosophy's dialectical movement of affirmation,
negation, and negation of the negation (Yes-No-Yes).[97]

Understandably, then, Tillich chooses to operate "on the
boundary" between religion and culture ("Religion," he writes, "is
the substance of culture and culture the form of religion"), theology
and philosophy, faith and doubt, Christianity and world religion,
Protestantism and Catholicism, American empiricism and European existentialism.[98] Autobiographically, Tillich reflects on his
stance of always having a foot in each of two traditionally antagonis-
tic camps.

> The "boundary" concept is an apt symbol for my whole personal and
> spiritual development. Almost everywhere it has been my fate to
> stand between two existential possibilities, not entirely at home in
> either and not able to reject one or the other completely.[99]

Understandably, too, his method is that of correlation, showing
how the symbols of the Christian message provide answers to the
questions raised by contemporary analyses of the human situation.
This method, Tillich explains,

> makes an analysis of the human situation out of which the existential
> questions arise, and it demonstrates that the symbols used in the
> Christian message are the answers to these questions. . . . These
> answers are contained in the revelatory events on which Christianity
> is based, and they are taken by systematic theology from the sources,
> through the medium, under the norm. Their content cannot be de-
> rived from the questions, that is, from an analysis of human exis-
> tence. . . . There is a mutual dependence between questions and
> answers. In respect of content the Christian answers are dependent
> on the revelatory events in which they appear; in respect of form they
> are dependent on the structure of the questions which they answer.[100]

It is his insistence that the answers to man's problems cannot
be derived from the questions, that is, from an analysis of human
existence. They are spoken *to* human existence beyond. This, consequently, is the essence of Tillich's method: "The questions of
human existence are answered by divine revelation."[101]

Thus (1) the problem of human reason finds its answer in revelation; (2) the problem of being finds its answer in the Christian concept of God; (3) the problem of existence finds its answer in Jesus as the Christ; (4) the problem of life finds its answer in the Christian concept of the Holy Spirit; (5) the problem of history finds its answer in the Christian concept of the Kingdom of God.

DIALECTICS

Not quite so understandable, however, is another key element in the Tillichian technique of theological systematization—dialectics, a baptized employment of a thesis/antithesis/synthesis formulation reminiscent, needless to comment, of Hegel and Marx. The dialectical approach as explicated by Tillich, is this:

> One element of a concept drives to another. Taken in this sense, dialectics determine all life-processes and must be applied in biology, psychology, and sociology. The description of tensions in living organisms, neurotic conflicts, and class struggles is dialectical. Life itself is dialectical. If applied symbolically to the divine life, God as the living God must be described in dialectical statements. He has the character of all life, namely, to go beyond and return to himself.[102]

What is the range of this triadic movement? Tillich holds it to be all-encompassing, a principle which governs reality in toto. That is why we encounter this kind of formulation at every turn in Tillich's speculation:

Affirmation/Negation/Negation of Negation
Innocence/Sin/Salvation
Ultimate/Concrete/Concrete Ultimacy
Heteronomy/Autonomy/Theonomy
Union/Estrangement/Reunion
God/Man/Godmanhood
Supernaturalism/Atheism/God beyond God

Wheat helps us again to penetrate beneath the imposing surface of Tillich's theology and discover its essentials. He observes,

> Dialectics is the workhorse of the system. This means the Hegel-Marx dialectics of thesis-antithesis-synthesis, not Barth's nonsequential and unresolved oppositions. Cleverly disguised dialectical formulations permeate every corner of the system. Estrangement is thus identifiable as the antithesis of an ontological dialectic moving from (a) the thesis of *potential* human unity, or essence, to (b) the *actual* separation of man from man, or existence, toward (c) *ac-*

tualized potentiality, where man realizes himself as God, and where essence=existence. Again, in the symbolic conglomeration that passes for an analysis of "reason and revelation," everything revolves around the dialectic of union, separation, and reunion. "Subjective reason" (individuals) and "objective reason" (humanity) start out essentially united as "ontological reason" (thesis), then are existentially separated in three "conflicts in reason" (antithesis), and finally are brought back together through the "revelation" that the "depth" of both forms of reason is God (synthesis). The many and the one are merely two sides—human and divine—of the Tillichian God.[103]

Wheat's inventory of the dialectical formulations in this vast system covers page after page in his devastating critique, *Paul Tillich's Dialectical Humanism,* entirely justifying the conclusion that Tillich seems afflicted with an overwhelming passion for dialectics: "Thesis, antithesis, and synthesis permeate his thought."[104] To grasp this fact is to be prepared to discover and keep on discovering that the most intractably irreconcilable antitheses are by some subtle logic amalgamated with one another in this all-inclusive synthesis.

MAN

We are now ready to sketch Tillich's profoundly original reinterpretation of the Christian message—and only a sketch is here possible, like a simple pencil drawing that intimates the grandeur of a Rocky Mountain landscape without aspiring to recreate its heights and vastnesses.

Man, the being who wonders about Being, must be our starting point, man the questioner who seeks answers to the mystery of his own being. Tillich argues, accordingly, that man occupies

> a pre-eminent position in ontology, not as an outstanding object among other objects, but as that being who asks the ontological question and in whose self-awareness the ontological answer can be found. The old tradition—expressed equally by mythology and mysticism, by poetry and metaphysics—that the principles which constitute the universe must be sought in man is indirectly and involuntarily confirmed, even by the behavioristic self-restriction. "Philosophers of life" and "Existentialists" have reminded us in our time of this truth on which ontology depends.[105]

Man, the being who inquires concerning the mystery of his own being and all being, experiences the unconditional, the holy, the absolute. In so affirming, Tillich is following Rudolph Otto with his stress on the *mysterium tremendum* as *sui generis,* incapable of subsumption under any other category. Tillich, therefore, postulates this ontological principle as basic to the philosophy of religion: *"Man is immediately aware of something unconditional which is the prius of the separation and interaction of subject and object, theoretically as well as practically."*[106]

Man's awareness of "something unconditional" has a concomitant and inescapable corollary, the experience of ultimate concern, or "unconditional demand." Out of this springs those concerns which are unique to human experience:

> Man, like every living being, is concerned about many things, above all about those which condition his very existence, such as food and shelter. But man, in contrast to other living beings, has spiritual concerns—cognitive, aesthetic, social, political. Some of them are urgent, often extremely urgent, and each of them as well as the vital concerns can claim ultimacy for a human life or the life of a social group. If it claims ultimacy, it demands the total surrender of him who accepts this claim, and it promises total fulfillment even if all other claims have to be subjected to it or rejected in its name. . . . it is also the promise of ultimate fulfillment which is accepted in the act of faith. The content of this promise is not necessarily defined. It can be expressed in indefinite symbols or in concrete symbols which cannot be taken literally, like the "greatness" of one's nation in which one participates even if one has died for it, or the conquest of mankind by the "saving race," etc. In each of these cases it is "ultimate fulfillment" that is promised, and it is exclusion from such fulfillment which is threatened if the unconditional demand is not obeyed.[107]

The concept of ultimate concern Tillich regards as an abstract translation of Mark 12:29, the command highlighted by Jesus; and this concept, Tillich affirms, "transcends the cleavage between subjectivity and objectivity."[108] It is the negative and formal principle of his entire theology, paralleled by the positive and material principle of the New Being.

GOD

But ultimate concern, the "dominating center" of personal life, implies God. Indeed, Tillich informs us that "the fundamental symbol of our ultimate concern is God." Again, defining faith as "the state of being grasped by an ultimate concern," he goes on to remark that "God is the name for the content of the concern."[109]

If God is to be known, however, revelation is imperative. But the concept of revelation like all other aspects of theology, Tillich charges, has been grossly misunderstood and distorted by traditional Protestantism. In its most elementary definition, "revelation is the manifestation of what concerns us ultimately. . . . the manifestation of the depth of reason and the ground of being." It points, rather, to the reality which underlies all human experience. Thus it is not a matter of words and propositions but of events which break into human existence and disclose ultimate being. Discussing "the many words from the Lord which are recorded in the Old Testament," Tillich reduces them to revelatory events.

> They are not promises of an omnipotent ruler replacing political or military strength. They are not lessons handed down by an omniscient teacher, replacing sound judgments. They are not advices of a heavenly counselor, replacing intelligent human counsel. But they are manifestations of something ultimate breaking into our existence.

At all costs, then, revelation must not be identified with the very words of Scripture. Even and especially in the case of the final revelation in Jesus as the Christ, there lurks the danger of that identification. But "if *Jesus as the Christ* is called the Logos, Logos *points to a revelatory reality, not to revelatory words.* . . . Taken seriously, the doctrine of the Logos prevents the elaboration of *a theology of the spoken or the written word, which is the Protestant pitfall.*"[110]

Not limited to words, revelation is not limited, either, to the Hebrew-Christian Scripture. On the contrary, since everything participates in being, everything can serve as a medium of revelation. According to Dr. Bernard Martin,

> Revelation occurs when anything becomes transparent to its own depth, to being-itself as distinguished from the structure of being. Natural objects, historical events, groups, and individual persons —all have been, and may be, media of revelation. . . . Nothing, however—neither natural objects nor historical events nor groups nor persons nor words—can be a medium of revelation unless it appears in a "miraculous" constellation which shakes the mind and serves as a sign-event, and unless it is existentially received in a state of ecstasy.[111]

Neither is revelation limited to any one religion. It occurs in all religion; it likewise occurs apart from religion. "Prophetic criticism, and promise," Tillich avers, "are active in the whole history of the church. . . . They are active in religious revolutions and foundations outside Christianity, as in the religion of Zoroaster, in some of the Greek mysteries, in Islam, and in many smaller reform movements."[112] Disclosing as it does the very ground of being, revelation comes necessarily in symbols and myths, which Tillich actually refers to as "the center of my theological doctrine of knowledge." Tillich, therefore, admits, "No definition of the contents of revelation is possible." He adds, similarly, "The revelation is *not* definitely definable, although the one pole of the revelatory correlation—namely, Jesus as the Christ—is final, definite, and beyond change."[113] So where does this leave us? We are left wandering in a semantic bog without a revelation that imparts definable doctrine. For Martin discerns that the so-called divine revelation of God is

> in no sense supernatural. Both "ecstasy" and "miracle" are natural events. Events which are called miracles are extraordinary only in the sense of being experienced as particularly weighted with the sense of the depth and mystery of existence.

And Martin adds that what we have in the end is

> nothing more than symbols and rites and myths; and since we are given no clear-cut criteria by which to distinguish the true (or valid) among these from their opposites, how can we know with certainty that those of the Christian revelation are among the former?[114]

Assuming, nevertheless, that God, the ultimate concern behind and beyond other idolatrously absolutized concerns, breaks through in revelatory event, what is disclosed concerning the nature of the unconditioned Being? One fact stands out in blinding clarity. God is certainly not the God of traditional theism, that one-sided and lopsided concept which "must be transcended."

> The God of theological theism is a being beside others and as such a part of the whole of reality. . . . But every statement subjects him to them. He is seen as a self which has a world, an ego which is related to a thou, a cause which is separated from its effect, as having a definite space and an endless time. He is being, not being-itself. As such he is bound to a subject-object structure of reality; he is an object for us as subjects.[115]

Not a being per se, "God is being-itself," Tillich contends, the "God above God,"

the basic and universal symbol for what concerns us ultimately. . . .
Everything we say about being-itself, the ground and abyss of being,
must be symbolic. . . . Therefore it cannot be used in its literal sense.
To say anything about God in the literal sense of the words used
means to say something false about Him. The symbolic . . . is the only
true way of speaking about God.[116]

Thus aside from this one nonsymbolic statement, "God is
being-itself," every statement about God must be symbolic. But
symbols, obviously, must be interpreted and deliteralized coura-
geously. The symbol of person, for instance, is permissible with
respect to God; it is, in fact, indispensable. Yet this symbol can
easily be misconstrued and degraded into a gross anthropomorphism.

> The concept of a "Personal God," interfering with natural events
> makes God a natural object beside others, an object among objects, a
> being among beings, maybe the highest, but nevertheless *a* being.
> This, indeed, is the destruction, not only of the physical system, but
> even more the destruction of any meaningful idea of God. It is the
> impure mixture of mythological elements (which are justified in their
> place, namely, in the concrete religious life) and of rational elements
> (which *are* justified in their place, namely, in the theological interpre-
> tation of religious experience). No criticism of this distorted idea of
> God can be sharp enough.[117]

God, furthermore, as being-itself, transcends the being/non-
being dichotomy, dialectically embracing and conquering nonbeing.

> If one is asked how nonbeing is related to being-itself, one can only
> answer metaphorically: being "embraces" itself and nonbeing. Being
> has nonbeing "within" itself as that which is eternally present and
> eternally overcome in the process of the divine life. The ground of
> everything that is, is not a dead identity without movement and
> becoming; it is living creativity. Creatively it affirms itself, eternally
> conquering its own nonbeing.[118]

Hence in view of God's indefinable and dialectical nature as
being-itself, to speak of His existence is to indulge in absurdity. As
being-itself, "God does not exist. He is beyond essence and existence. Therefore, to argue that God exists," Tillich dogmatizes, "is
to deny him."[119] In Tillich's opinion, "a God about whose existence
or non-existence you can argue is a thing beside others within the
universe of existing things."[120] Regardless, then, of how heretical it

may sound, the statement that God does not exist is both warranted and required.

Whatever else may be said concerning Tillich's view of God, it is plainly a repudiation of what that name has historically denoted. Tillich, who avows that "the antisupernaturalistic attitude" is fundamental to all his thinking, sets himself unequivocally to the destruction of the traditional concept.

> Self-transcending realism requires the criticism of *all* forms of supra-naturalism—supra-naturalism in the sense of a theology that imagines a supra-natural world beside or above the natural one, a world in which the unconditional finds a local habitation, thus making God a transcendent object, the creation an act at the beginning of time, the consummation a future state of things. To criticize such a *conditioning of the unconditional,* even if it leads to atheistic consequences, is more religious, because it is more aware of the *unconditional character of the divine,* than a theism that bans God into the supra-natural realm.[121]

JESUS AS THE CHRIST

Tillich's desupernaturalized concept of God dovetails with his reinterpretation of Christology. The revelation and the salvation mediated by Jesus as the Christ are possible because of "an eternal unity of God and man within the divine life."[122] But this unity was compromised, not dissolved (as if indeed it could be!) by sin; for sin, if we may "use a concept which everybody understands," is "estrangement from oneself, from the other man, from the ground out of which we come and to which we go."[123]

The Man Jesus, however, remaining transparent or open to being-itself, did not succumb to the estranging forces of human existence. He rose above the alienating contradictions which are, with His exception, the common experience of humanity: He somehow maintained an unbroken oneness with God. Tillich dwells at length, consequently, on the victory of Jesus over all negativities —concupiscence, unbelief, hubris, even death. Maintaining unbroken His unity with God, Jesus also maintained unbroken His unity with man.

> His loneliness and his frustrated attempts to be received by those to whom he came do not suddenly end in a final success; they are taken into the divine acceptance of that which rejects God, into the vertical line of the uniting love which is effective where the horizontal line from being to being is barred. Out of his unity with God he has unity

with those who are separated from him and from one another by finite self-relatedness and existential self-seclusion.[124]

Thus, as Tillich interprets, or actually reinterprets, the Gospel,

> The New Being is manifest in the Christ because in Him the separation never overcame the unity between Him and God, between Him and mankind, and between Him and Himself. . . . In Him we look at a human life that maintained the union in spite of everything that drove Him into separation.[125]

Tillich reiterates and elaborates this interpretation in his *Systematic Theology*, where Jesus as the Christ, the symbol of New Being, becomes the positive and material principle of the Tillichian system:

> In all its concrete details the biblical picture of Jesus as the Christ confirms his character as the bearer of the New Being or as the one in whom the conflict between the essential unity of God and man and man's existential estrangement is overcome. Point by point, not only in the Gospel records but also in the Epistles, this picture of Jesus as the Christ contradicts the marks of estrangement which we have elaborated in the analysis of man's existential predicament.[126]

Notice, though, that it is the *picture* of Jesus *as the Christ* which is revelatory and salvific. And this picture, Tillich contends, is "the concrete absolute" which furnishes us with the final revelation.

> The paradoxical Christian claim is that this picture has unconditional and universal validity, that it is not subject to the attacks of positivistic or cynical relativism, that it is not absolutistic, whether in the traditional or the revolutionary sense, and that it cannot be achieved either by the critical or by the pragmatic compromise. It is unique and beyond all these conflicting elements and methods of existential reason.[127]

Yet Tillich admits that the historicity of Jesus is extremely dubious. He does not hesitate, as a matter of fact, to impugn the veracity of almost the entire gospel record.

> The only factual element in it having the immediate certainty of faith is the surrender of him who is called the Christ to the ultimate consequence of existence, namely, death under the conditions of estrangement. Everything else is a matter of historical probability, elaborated out of legendary interpretation.[128]

How final, then, is this picture, the historicity of which Tillich elsewhere confesses to be "a very faint probability"?[129] Evidently the historicity of Jesus does not constitute a life-and-death problem for Tillich. He relates that in 1911, after interacting with Albert Schweitzer's *The Quest of the Historical Jesus,* he read a paper to a group of theological friends in which, to quote his own words,

> I raised and attempted to answer the question, how the Christian doctrine might be understood, if the non-existence of the historical Jesus should become historically probable. Even today I maintain the radicalness of this question over against compromises, which I encountered at an earlier time, and are now attempted again by Emil Brunner. The foundation of Christian belief is not the Historical Jesus, but the biblical picture of Christ.[130]

So Martin is right in asking whether this historically vague and debatable picture of Jesus as the Christ, a picture which fails to include many major elements of the New Testament account, entitles us to believe that Jesus is the Messiah, the New Being, "the ultimate criterion of every healing and saving process." Martin's conclusion seems irrefutable.

> Surely, this is nothing more than an existential commitment of a Christian theologian. Those uncommitted to the Christian revelation as Tillich defines it might find equal saving power in the contemplation of the life and death of a Socrates, a Rabbi Akiba, or a Mahatma Gandhi—to mention only a few.[131]

CRITIQUE

Many other areas of Tillich's theology ought to be explored in depth: his views of the Trinity, man, demonism, *chronos* and *kairos,* symbolism, deliteralizing (a term which he prefers to demythologizing); his argument that justification applies to doubt no less than sin; and his denial of absolute truth in the name of the Protestant principle.

But enough of his theologizing has been presented to make any student of this system appreciate the relevance of Nels Ferré's probing criticism:

> Tillich, to be sure, uses both the words "transcendent" and "transcendental," but his consistent stress on (1) there being no Being above or besides other beings, (2) his doctrine of eternity as the unification and purification of meaning, (3) his declaration that, regardless of historic, explanatory power, love is finally indefinable, and (4) his total stress on symbolism in relation to being and the abyss

makes questionable any genuine Christian doctrine of incarnation. This is certainly true in the classic Christian sense of (1) a supernaturally transcendent realm of being, (2) a genuine creation from beyond this cosmic realm, and (3) a goal-centered historical process with personal destinies beyond physical death, into which the incarnation came as its center of meaning, judgment, and salvation.[132]

And Ferré proceeds to ask some very searching questions which strike at the heart of Tillich's great synthesis, exposing its irreconcilability with biblical faith.

If Tillich can be counted ontologically as thoroughly within the Christian perspective, he must be ranked as one of our greatest Christian thinkers. Unfortunately, there are grave doubts on this point. . . . Does he actually operate within the transcendental perspective, rather than within the transcendent? His refusal to accept the great, immemorial Christian perspective of supernaturalism at least seems to convince us of this, whatever his use of occasional words may be. Is God *in fact,* the Creator of process, *and in this sense,* above, before, and behind it? Is He personal Spirit in the sense of a separate consciousness and an eternal being, beyond all created beings, and therefore other than and beside all else, however different in kind? Is supernaturalism, *defined in this sense,* to be taken as normative, including secondarily all truth of naturalism, or are both to be transcended in terms of some formal realm of meaning, or in terms of some relation of being and the abyss to which we can refer finally only in terms of myth and symbol?[133]

An impressive intellectual achievement, this correlation of theology and philosophy gives us a concept of God which has no relationship except in name with the living God of the Bible: Tillich's God is a God to whom we cannot pray and with whom we cannot fellowship. We cannot, in fact, even properly allude to being-itself as He, since being-itself lies beyond all predication. This system, which rules out biblical Trinitarianism, rules out as well a veritable incarnation, advancing a Christology which is a peculiar species of adoptionism. Since it postulates no historical Fall and equates sin with estrangement rather than rebellion, its soteriology ignores a substitutionary sacrifice which obtains the sinner's justification. This system transforms unbelievers into unconscious believers by imputing to every human being some ultimate concern. It places no more value on faith than it does on doubt since being-itself embraces all men equally, accepting them though they are unacceptable. It repudiates on the ground of Tillich's Protestant principle any claim to absolute truth and offers us a deliteralized Bible which, instead of supplying revelational data that can be propositionally formulated, turns out to be a farrago of symbols and myths. This system holds out no prospect of personal immortality and so brings us to death with the same bleak hopelessness that marked Tillich's own end. His wife Hannah relates that in the hospital, as he was terminally ill,

> He wanted to know what happens to his centered self after death; there would be no memory of his person as a person. I tried to tell him that his thought-images would be there, that his thoughts, having changed the substance of our cosmos, would enter the circle of the spiritual powers, which created the images of the world. He spoke about the Tibetan Book of the Dead. "Go after the clear light," I said, "the clear light will guide you, not any self-centered immortality." We talked about the Buddha powers which have the same spiritual unity—if you look through a many faceted crystal you seem to see many Buddha images, but if you forgo the crystal, there is one Buddha spirit and as much as you are the spirit you will be joined with it.[134]

Her comment, as she reflects upon his death, is this:

> I had not brought anything to the hospital since he had been ill, except his Bibles—a small Greek New Testament, a German Bible, which had been his from his first year of life, and an English version. I had hoped to read from the Bible to him when he became restless, if he wished me to, but he had only touched the Greek version with his frail hand. He did not wish to see the other Bibles or to have the Bible read to him. I was glad. He belonged to the world, to the cosmos, not to one book.[135]

With no presumptuous intention of exercising God's prerogative of judgment, we seem entitled to conclude that Tillich does not, for all his eminence, belong to the faith set forth in that one Book, the Bible. His great synthesis has been variously designated a system of gnosticism, naturalism, pantheism, and atheism; and all these designations are more or less accurate. Thus Wheat is surely justified in arguing,

> No matter what the theological and philosophical inputs at each level, the output—Tillich's synthesis—is always humanism. T + P = H is the rigid formula. . . . Here is Tillich's thought in a nutshell. He who frees himself from the tyranny of the false God, the God of theism, finds God in man.[136]

Assume the correctness of Wheat's assessment and the pieces

of the Tillichian puzzle fall into place—only the pattern which emerges is not that of Christian supernaturalism. Tillich, therefore, "through his attacks on the God of theism helped prepare the way for a later generation of theologians" and also "undoubtedly helped nourish the God is Dead theology."[137]

Notes

1. Schubert M. Ogden, ed., "Introduction," *Existence and Faith: Shorter Writings of Rudolf Bultmann* (New York: Meridian, 1960), p. 9.
2. Thomas C. Oden, *Radical Obedience* (Philadelphia: Westminster, 1964), p. 47.
3. Quoted by Ogden, p. 14.
4. Rudolf Bultmann, "The Task of Theology in the Present Situation," in *Existence and Faith*, p. 160.
5. Ogden, p. 16.
6. Rudolf Bultmann, "Is Exegesis Without Presuppositions Possible?" in *Existence and Faith*, p. 292.
7. Quoted by Giovanni Miegge, *Gospel and Myth in the Thought of Rudolf Bultmann* (Richmond: John Knox, 1960), p. 8.
8. Rudolf Bultmann, *Jesus Christ and Mythology* (New York: Scribner, 1958), p. 36.
9. Ibid., p. 39.
10. Quoted by Miegge, p. 91.
11. Bultmann, *Jesus Christ and Mythology*, p. 18.
12. Ibid., p. 36.
13. Rudolf Bultmann, "The Concept of Revelation in the New Testament," in *Existence and Faith*, p. 59.
14. Rudolf Bultmann, "The Historicity of Man and Faith," in *Existence and Faith*, p. 98.
15. Bultmann, *Jesus Christ and Mythology*, pp. 53-54.
16. Bultmann, "The Historicity of Man and Faith," p. 102.
17. Rudolf Bultmann, "Man Between the Times According to the New Testament," in *Existence and Faith*, p. 255.
18. Bultmann, "The Concept of Revelation in the New Testament," p. 59.
19. Rudolf Bultmann, "Jesus and Paul," in *Existence and Faith*, p. 200.
20. Quoted by Miegge, p. 87.
21. Ibid., p. 43.
22. Ibid., pp. 43-44.
23. Bultmann, "Jesus and Paul," p. 197.
24. Quoted by Miegge, p. 46.
25. Rudolf Bultmann, "The New Approach to the Synoptic Problem," in *Existence and Faith*, p. 39.
26. Quoted by Miegge, p. 86.
27. Oden, p. 79.
28. Rudolf Bultmann, "How Does God Speak to Us Through the Bible?", in *Existence and Faith*, p. 168.
29. Quoted by Christopher F. Mooney, "Teilhard de Chardin and Christian Spirituality," in *Process Theology*, ed. Ewert H. Cousins (New York: Newman, 1971), p. 317.
30. Bernard Towers, "Introduction" in Bernard Delfgaauw, *Evolution: The Theory of Teilhard de Chardin* (New York: Harper & Row, 1961), p. 9.
31. Quoted by Emile Rideau, *Teilhard de Chardin: A Guide to His Thought*, trans. Rene Hague (London: Collins, 1967), pp. 659-60.
32. Ibid., pp. 574-75, n. 198.

33. Ibid., p. 317.
34. Ibid., p. 331.
35. Ibid., p. 644.
36. Quoted by Ian G. Barbour, "Teilhard's Process Metaphysics," in *Process Theology,* p. 325.
37. Quoted by N. M. Wildiers, "Cosmology and Christology," in *Process Theology,* pp. 274-75.
38. Quoted by Rideau, p. 388, n. 9.
39. Ibid., pp. 386-87, n. 9.
40. Quoted by Michael H. Murray, *The Thought of Teilhard de Chardin* (New York: Seabury, 1966), p. 30.
41. Quoted by Barbour, pp. 336-37.
42. Quoted by Rideau, p. 502.
43. Quoted by Barbour, pp. 341-42.
44. Ibid., p. 342.
45. D. Gareth Jones, *Teilhard de Chardin: An Analysis and Assessment* (Grand Rapids: Eerdmans, 1970), p. 63.
46. John Baptist Walker, *New Theology for Plain Christians* (Denville, N. J.: Dimension, 1970), pp. 8-9.
47. Quoted by W. J. P. Boyd, "Teilhard de Chardin and Modern Protestant Theology," in *Teilhard Reassessed,* ed. Anthony Hanson (London: Darton, Longman & Todd, 1970), p. 124.
48. Quoted by Rideau, p. 635, n. 180.
49. Henri de Lubac, *Teilhard Explained,* trans. Anthony Buono (New York: Paulist, 1966), p. 61.
50. Quoted by Rideau, pp. 642-43.
51. Quoted by Barbour, p. 344.
52. Quoted by Wildiers, p. 280.
53. Dietrich von Hildebrand, "Teilhard de Chardin: Catholicism's False Prophet," *Triumph* (May-June 1967).
54. Sabine Leibholz-Bonhoeffer, *The Bonhoeffers: Portrait of a Family* (London: Sidgwick & Jackson, 1971), p. 194.
55. Quoted by William Kuhns, *In Pursuit of Dietrich Bonhoeffer* (Dayton, Ohio: Pflaum, 1967), p. 265.
56. André Dumas, *Dietrich Bonhoeffer: Theologian of Reality* (New York: Macmillan, 1968), p. 270.
57. Quoted by ibid., p. 242.
58. Dumas, p. 276.
59. Dietrich Bonhoeffer, *Letters and Papers from Prison,* ed. Eberhard Bethge (New York: Macmillan, 1972), p. 381.
60. Ibid., p. 391.
61. Quoted by James W. Woelfel, *Bonhoeffer's Theology: Classical and Revolutionary* (Nashville, Tenn.: Abingdon, 1970), p. 138.
62. Woelfel, pp. 141-42.
63. Bonhoeffer, pp. 382-83.
64. Quoted by Woelfel, pp. 31-32.
65. Bonhoeffer, pp. 325-26.
66. Quoted by Woelfel, p. 35.
67. Ibid., p. 306, n. 49.
68. Bonhoeffer, p. 327.
69. Ibid., p. 360.
70. Ibid., pp. 279-80.

71. Quoted by Woelfel, pp. 105-6.
72. Bonhoeffer, p. 135.
73. Ibid., p. 279.
74. Quoted by Woelfel, p. 105.
75. Bonhoeffer, p. 285.
76. Ibid., p. 361
77. Quoted by Woelfel, p. 126.
78. Bonhoeffer, pp. 280-81.
79. Kuhns, p. 185.
80. Dumas, p. 191, n. 53.
81. Kuhns, p. 155.
82. Quoted by Kuhns, p. 155.
83. Quoted by Woelfel, p. 249.
84. Ibid., p. 172.
85. Bonhoeffer, p. 370.
86. Quoted by Kuhns, p. 156.
87. Bonhoeffer, p. 369.
88. Ibid., p. 303.
89. Ibid., pp. 168-69.
90. Reinhold Niebuhr, "Biblical Thought and Ontological Speculation in Tillich's Theology," in *The Theology of Paul Tillich*, ed. Charles W. Kegly and Robert W. Bretall (New York: Macmillan, 1952), p. 217.
91. Walter M. Horton, "Tillich's Role in Contemporary Theology," in *The Theology of Paul Tillich*, p. 26.
92. John Herman Randall, Jr., "The Ontology of Paul Tillich," in *The Theology of Paul Tillich*, p. 161.
93. Theodore M. Greene, "Paul Tillich and Our Secular Culture," *The Theology of Paul Tillich*, p. 50.
94. Paul Tillich, *The Theology of Culture* (New York: Oxford, 1959), p. 201.
95. Ibid., p. 213.
96. Guyton B. Hammond, *Man in Estrangement* (Nashville, Tenn.: Vanderbilt U., 1956), p. 180.
97. Leonard E. Wheat, *Paul Tillich's Dialectical Humanism: Unmasking the God above God* (Baltimore: Johns Hopkins, 1970), p. 87; cf. p. 104.
98. Paul Tillich, *The Protestant Era* (Chicago: U. of Chicago, 1948), p. 57.
99. Quoted by Arne Unhjem, *Dynamics of Doubt, A Preface to Tillich* (Philadelphia: Fortress, 1966), p. 1.
100. Paul Tillich, *Systematic Theology* (Chicago: U. of Chicago, 1951), 1:26-27.
101. Ibid., p. 64.
102. Paul Tillich, *Systematic Theology* (Chicago: U. of Chicago, 1957), 2:90.
103. Wheat, pp. 189-90.
104. Ibid., p. 192.
105. Tillich, *Systematic Theology*, 1:24.
106. Tillich, *Theology of Culture*, p. 22.
107. Paul Tillich, *Dynamics of Faith* (New York: Harper, 1957), pp. 1-2.
108. Tillich, *Systematic Theology*, 1:12.
109. See Wheat, pp. 114-15.
110. Quoted by R. Allan Killen, *The Ontological Theology of Paul Tillich* (Kampen, Holland: Kok, 1956), pp. 64-68.
111. Bernard Martin, *Paul Tillich's Doctrine of Man* (Digwell Place, Welwyn, Herts: Nisbet, 1966), p. 63.

112. Quoted by Killen, p. 74.
113. Paul Tillich, "Reply to Interpretation and Criticism," in *The Theology of Paul Tillich*, pp. 332-33.
114. Martin, pp. 74, 77.
115. Tillich, *The Protestant Era*, pp. 184-85.
116. Quoted by Wheat, p. 39.
117. Tillich, *Theology of Culture*, p. 130.
118. Hammond, p. 99.
119. Tillich, *Systematic Theology*, 1:205.
120. Tillich, *Theology of Culture*, p. 5.
121. Quoted by Wheat, p. 38.
122. Quoted by Hammond, p. 137.
123. Tillich, *Theology of Culture*, p. 210.
124. Quoted by Hammond, p. 165.
125. Quoted by Wheat, p. 178.
126. Tillich, *Systematic Theology*, 2:125-26.
127. Quoted by Martin, p. 67.
128. Ibid., p. 166.
129. Quoted by Killen, p. 151.
130. Ibid., p. 197, n. 17.
131. Martin, p. 179.
132. Nels F. S. Ferré, "Tillich's View of the Church," in *The Theology of Paul Tillich*, p. 251.
133. Ibid., p. 262.
134. Hannah Tillich, *From Time to Time* (New York: Stein & Day, 1973), p. 222.
135. Ibid., p. 224.
136. Wheat, pp. 87, 111.
137. Ibid., pp. 52, 269.

Selected Reading

RUDOLF BULTMANN

Bultmann, Rudolf. *Faith and Understanding*. New York: Harper & Row, 1969.

————. *The Gospel of John*. Oxford: Basil Blackwell, 1961.

————. *The History of the Synoptic Tradition*. New York: Harper & Row, 1963.

————. *Jesus Christ and Mythology*. New York: Scribner's, 1958.

————. *Kerygma and Myth: A Theological Debate*. Ed. Hans W. Bartsch. New York: Harper & Row, 1961.

————. *The Presence of Eternity*. New York: Harper, 1957.

————. *The Theology of the New Testament*. 2 vols. New York: Scribner, 1951, 1955.

Jaspers, Karl and Bultmann, Rudolf. *Myth and Christianity*. New York: Noonday, 1958.

PIERRE TEILHARD DE CHARDIN

Crespy, Georges. *From Science to Theology*. New York: Abingdon, 1968.

Delfgaauw, Bernard. *Evolution: The Theory of Teilhard de Chardin*. New York: Harper & Row, 1961.

de Lubac, Henri. *The Religion of Teilhard de Chardin*. New York: Desche, 1967.

Murray, H. *The Thought of Teilhard de Chardin: An Introduction*. New York: Seabury, 1966.

Rideau, Emile. *Teilhard de Chardin: A Guide to His Thought*. London: Collins, 1967.

Smulders, Piet. *The Design of Teilhard de Chardin*. Westminster, Md.: Newman, 1967.

Teilhard de Chardin, Pierre. *The Divine Milieu*. New York: Harper & Row, 1960.

————. *The Future of Man*. London: Fontana, 1964.

————. *Hymn of the Universe*. New York: Harper & Row, 1965.

————. *Man's Place in Nature*. New York: Harper & Row, 1966.

————. *The Phenomenon of Man*. New York: Harper & Row, 1965.

————. *Science and Christ*. New York: Harper & Row, 1968.

————. *The Vision of the Past*. New York: Harper & Row, 1966.

DIETRICH BONHOEFFER

Bethge, Eberhard. *Dietrich Bonhoeffer: Man of Vision, Man of Courage*. New York: Harper & Row, 1970.

Bonhoeffer, Dietrich, *Act and Being*. New York: Harper & Row, 1956.

————. *Christ the Center*. New York: Harper & Row, 1960.

————. *The Cost of Discipleship*. London: SCM, 1948.

————. *Ethics*. New York: Macmillan, 1962.

————. *Letters and Papers from Prison*. Ed. Eberhard Bethge. New York: Macmillan, 1972.

————. *Life Together*. New York: Harper & Row, 1954.

————. *No Rusty Swords*. New York: Harper & Row, 1947.

————. *Sanctorum Communio*. London: Collins, 1963.

————. *The Way to Freedom*. New York: Harper & Row, 1966.

Bosanquet, Mary. *The Life and Death of Dietrich Bonhoeffer*. New York: Harper & Row, 1968.

Dumas, André. *Dietrich Bonhoeffer: Theologian of Reality*. New York: Macmillan, 1968.

Hamilton, Kenneth. *Life in One's Stride*. Grand Rapids: Eerdmans, 1968.

Kuhns, William. *In Pursuit of Dietrich Bonhoeffer*. Dayton, Ohio: Pflaum, 1967.

Ott, Heinrich. *Reality and Faith: The Ideological Legacy of Dietrich Bonhoeffer*. Philadelphia: Fortress, 1972.

Smith, R. Gregor, ed. *World Come of Age*. Philadelphia: Fortress, 1967.

Woelfel, James W. *Bonhoeffer's Theology: Classical and Revolutionary*. Nashville: Abingdon, 1970.

PAUL TILLICH

Brown, D. Mackenzie. *Ultimate Concern: Tillich in Dialogue*. New York: Harper & Row, 1965.

Hamilton, Kenneth. *The System and the Gospel: A Critique of Paul Tillich*. Grand Rapids: Eerdmans, 1963.

Leibrecht, Walter. *Religion and Culture: Essays in Honor of Paul Tillich*. New York: Harper, 1959.

McKelway, Alexander J. *The Systematic Theology of Paul Tillich: A Review and Analysis*. Richmond: John Knox, 1964.

Tillich, Paul. *Biblical Religion and the Search for Ultimate Reality*. Chicago: U. of Chicago, 1955.

———. *A Complete History of Christian Thought*. Ed. Carl E. Braaten. New York: Harper & Row, 1968.

———. *The Courage to Be*. New Haven, Conn.: Yale, 1952.

———. *The Eternal Now*. New York: Scribner, 1963.

———. *Morality and Beyond*. New York: Harper & Row, 1963.

———. *The Religious Situation*. New York: Henry Holt, 1932.

———. *Systematic Theology*. 3 vols. Chicago: U. of Chicago, 1951, 1957, 1963.

THE MEANING AND USE
OF RELIGIOUS LANGUAGE

I. Religious language in theology based on Continental thought
   A. Pre-Kantian orthodox theology replaced by anti-metaphysical theology
   B. Twentieth-century antirational theology
   C. Hermeneutical theology
II. Religious language in the English-speaking world
   A. Logical positivism rejects religious language as cognitive
   B. John Wisdom's "therapeutical" analysis
   C. Wide interest in metatheology developed
III. The noncognitivist position
   A. R. M. Hare's notion of a "blik"
   B. Noncognitivism as metatheological skepticism
IV. The verificationist and falsificationist criteria of meaning
   A. Should something "count against" a believer's assertion?
      1. Meaninglessness and truth or falsity conditions
      2. Genuineness and truth or falsity conditions
   B. Heimbeck's appeal to the falsification test
V. The linguistic analysis of religious language
   A. Three sources of doubt about theological assertions
   B. Nondefinitional, nonempirical cognitive meaning
      1. Theological statements concern the mysterious
      2. Wittgensteinian fideism and language games
   C. An empiricist critique of Wittgensteinian conceptual relativism
   D. The empiricist confusion of meaning and referent
   E. The valuable aspect of the empiricist critique

VI. The interpretative or "seeing as—" approach
    A. Wittgenstein's analysis of "seeing as—"
    B. Ferré and theology as a conceptual synthesis
        1. Ferré's position explained
        2. Ferré's position evaluated
    C. Hick's hypothesis of eschatological verification
        1. Hick's position explained
        2. Hick's position evaluated
    D. Circularity of the validation of the theological model
    E. The "transcendent" God becomes "intra-experiential"
VII. A nonexperiential basis for religious language
    A. The supreme object of religious worship necessarily exists
        1. Necessary statements as arbitrary linguistic conventions
        2. Some necessary statements reflective of the state of affairs in all possible worlds
    B. The ontological argument for God in the logical framework of possible worlds
    C. Logically and conditionally necessary assertions about the infinite God

3

The Meaning and Use of
Religious Language

by
STANLEY OBITTS

There are two main approaches being taken at present to the multifaceted problem of the meaning and use of religious language. One approach derives from continental European philosophy; the other is the product of British philosophy. Of course, theologians have been concerned with human talk about God ever since Thomas Aquinas explicitly restricted all predications about God's nature to those which are analogical. But in the past thirty or so years, the religious language problem has become of central importance in theology, for philosophical reasons quite different from those prompted by Aquinas's Aristotelianism. Moreover, the religious language question and the reason for its centrality in the European-based hermeneutical theology is entirely different from the situation in English-speaking philosophical theology and philosophy of religion. We shall begin by looking at the theology whose roots lie in Continental thought.

RELIGIOUS LANGUAGE IN THEOLOGY BASED ON CONTINENTAL THOUGHT

PRE-KANTIAN ORTHODOX THEOLOGY REPLACED BY ANTIMETAPHYSICAL THEOLOGY

The metaphysical structure of orthodox theology had justified universally valid, commonsense assertions about God and other

STANLEY R. OBITTS, B.A., B.D., Ph.D., is professor of philosophy at Westmont College and is a frequent contributor to scholarly journals.

supernatural entities and states of affairs. In particular, the nature, work, and words of God were understood as expressible in doctrinal formulations whose references were to a reality as objective as that to which ordinary, and even scientific, descriptions referred. This was the conviction of both the Lutheran and Reformed theologians of the seventeenth and eighteenth centuries. But Kant's banishment of metaphysics to the realm of the unknowable gradually gave rise to an antimetaphysical theology which continued to affirm God's existence but no longer felt epistemologically confident to describe God and His revelation in universally valid statements. As Kant had advised, all objects of thought were said to be knowable only in relation to the knowing subject rather than objectively. In Kant's terminology, not being able to know the nature of things "in themselves," the knower grasps them phenomenally, that is, as they figure in his experience. No longer, then, could Scripture be assumed to contain truths revealed by God about His nature, plan for man, the origin of the world, or anything else beyond the scope of human experience. Biblical declarations no less than other religious utterances and theological formulations could concern only the appearances, the effects, and the relations of the supernatural world to and upon man.

Lutheran theologians, especially, faced with the challenge of Kantian epistemology, wasted no time in discovering a distinctly antimetaphysical trend in their mentor's thought. Luther's repudiation of the rational knowledge of God "in himself" by the medieval scholastics, and his insistence that the God known in the process of salvation as He is *pro me, pro nobis* is the only God compatible with the *sola fide*, was developed into a full-fledged antimetaphysical theology by the father of religious liberalism, Friedrich Schleiermacher. On his basic thesis Schleiermacher never wavered, namely, " 'Christian doctrines are accounts of the Christian religious affections set forth in speech.' "[1] In other words, the referent of theology is anthropological, not theological. God in His transcendence is beyond the scope of theological formulations.

TWENTIETH-CENTURY ANTIRATIONAL THEOLOGY

It is not until the twentieth century that Kantian antimetaphysical theology can be found in a Calvinist whose influence is comparable to that of Schleiermacher. In Karl Barth's implacable hostility to natural theology, there is even more than an antimetaphysic for epistemological reasons. There is also an antirationalism, which gains sustenance from Kierkegaard's unrelenting overemphasis upon irresoluble paradox in all human thought and experience, particularly if it be Christian. Barth's biblicistic fideism, which has become popular among some quasi-evangelical theologians, breaks apart any natural cognitive relationship between God and man. Objectifying, universally valid conceptualizations of God are totally out of the question. Any awareness man has of God is through self-interpreting, self-authenticating, propositionally incommunicable divine self-disclosures.

Couched in the I-Thou and I-It distinction of Martin Buber, this disjunction between the God of reason and the God of Christian faith is no less radical. Brunner, attempting to soften the impersonalism of God implied in Barth's stress upon God's utter transcendence of the human mind, placed the cognitive relationship between God and man in a temporal, I-Thou encounter by man of God as an eternal, ever present Thou. But such an encounter, mediated for Brunner through the Word of God, takes place *in* Christian faith, with the resulting knowledge of God completely different from knowledge of Him prior to faith.*

This is not belied by theologians such as Harold E. Hatt who argue that an encounter includes, not just produces, interpretation. While describing an encounter experience with God as dependent upon or mediated by propositional knowledge about Him, Hatt still limits that knowledge to an "existential, personal" kind. Thus, a sufficient condition of man's acquiring knowledge of God is still an encounter as such. It is true that Hatt goes so far as to stipulate, "There is no sense of 'I' and 'Thou' involvement until there is interpretation, since prior to interpretation 'I' and 'Thou' are indistinguishable." And bringing this stipulation to bear on Scripture, he declares, "Our sense of relation with God and our interpretation of this in terms of the resources we have in the Bible and in the various forms of the proclamation of the church are inseparably involved in our encounter with God."[2] But the difficulty which Hatt overlooks here is that if these resources are not reliable, then they would not actually provide the knowledge necessary for the correct interpretation. Without the correct interpretation, as he admits, the encounter could be false. However, he is not troubled by the possible unrelia-

---

*"The word 'Christian' suggests the way in which rational knowledge is corrected by the knowledge of faith. . . . In the case of the idea of God it is not merely a case of correction, but of a complete substitution of the one for the other," declares Brunner (*Revelation and Reason* [Philadelphia: Westminster, 1946], p. 383).

bility of the biblical resources, because for him the "basis of trust" is "existential knowledge," not "propositional knowledge" revealed and, therefore, infallible.[3] So it appears that the logic of his position, in spite of his claim to the contrary, is that the authentication of the biblical interpretation is the encounter experience, but not vice versa.

Barthian antirationalism is even more pronounced in the thinking of T. F. Torrance, whose penchant for characterizing theology as rational and scientific cannot be taken at face value. As he sees it, "the interior logic of our knowledge of God" is incompatible with "the logico-verbal atoms of our thought and speech that are already schematized to this world, for the truth of God as it is in Christ Jesus breaks through all our linguistic and logical forms." For theology to be "faithful to what God has revealed and done in Jesus Christ," therefore, it must, "epistemologically speaking," engage in "an eschatological suspension of logical form" in order to be amenable to "what is radically new."[4]

W. D. Hudson correctly comments that Torrance is not simply saying, "The fruitful paradoxes are those which are *not* self-contradictory." When Torrance avers, "The Truth of God as it is in Christ Jesus breaks through *all our linguistic and logical forms*" (italics Hudson's), Hudson construes this to mean more than, "What at first sight appear to be self-contradictory statements about God may turn out on closer inspection to be not self-contradictory." Rather he understands Torrance to be saying, "In the very nature of the case, if God is to be spoken about at all, he must be spoken about in self-contradictory terms." Such a view, Hudson appropriately remarks, "would make nonsense of God-talk."[5]

HERMENEUTICAL THEOLOGY

Focusing specifically upon the meaning and use of religious language as these antimetaphysical, antirational theologians construe it, we learn that their view stems from the continental European view of language. That view is as different from its counterpart in the English-speaking (and Scandinavian) world as the methodological assumptions of the natural sciences are different from those of the *Geisteswissenschaften* (the social sciences and humanities). A grasp of what the European thinkers mean by "hermeneutic" is crucial to understanding their view of the meaning and use of religious language.

Schleiermacher was the first to call for a "general hermeneutics" in place of the philological hermeneutics. Instead of formulating rules for exegeting historical texts as a hermeneutician, he saw the need to systematically work up principles for the interpretation of any text. What is more important, he conceived this enterprise as the examination of understanding itself,[6] which begins with the interpreter identifying himself with the author of the text.[7]

At the turn of this century, Wilhelm Dilthey gave hermeneutics the task of providing the framework for all the social sciences and humanities, that is, all the *Geisteswissenschaften*. In order to understand the expressions of the human spirit, in Scripture or elsewhere, the method of the natural sciences is fruitless. What is needed is a historical understanding dependent upon knowing personally what is implied in being human, he maintained. In his words, "We explain nature; man we must understand."[8]

In 1927 Martin Heidegger, in *Being and Time,* gave a new twist to Dilthey's notion of *hermeneutic* by defining it as the phenomenological analysis of being human (he called it a "hermeneutic of *Dasein*"). Since being a human involves interpreting and understanding, Heidegger felt that a phenomenological analysis of man's being from this standpoint is the proper subject of hermeneutics. Thus, he wants to turn hermeneutics into an ontology of understanding, rather than limiting it to the study of textual interpretation or of the methodology of the *Geisteswissenschaften*.

Later Heidegger came to stress the role of man as a respondent to the call of being, a call which expresses itself in language. For instance, he writes, "Language is in its essence neither expression nor an activity of man. *Language* speaks."[9] Or again he says, "The human is in its essence linguistic."[10] Man's way of being is linguistic; to understand himself he depends upon the hermeneutical function which language itself has. To interpret language is to dialogue with a text so that the being of the text will declare itself. As might be expected, Heidegger feels that it is in poetry where this hermeneutical function of language is most forcefully encountered. The poet is the speaker, the "hermeneut," between the gods and man.

The formative impact of Heidegger upon Bultmann's theory of demythologizing the New Testament as a process of transforming one's self-understanding is incontestable. Specifically, there are three foci of this influence, as R. E. Palmer sees it:

(1) There is the distinction between language used as mere information to be interpreted objectively as fact, and language filled with personal import and the power to command obedience. . . .

(2) There is the idea that God (Being) confronts man as *Word*, as language. . . .
(3) There is also the concept that *kerygma* as Word in words speaks to existential self-understanding.[11]

Since 1960 a student of Heidegger and Bultmann named Hans-Georg Gadamer has increasingly come to dominate the scene, with a hermeneutic geared less to existentialism than simply to language and its subject matter. Gadamer has brought hermeneutics fully into a linguistic phase. He declares, "Being that can be understood is language." "Language is the universal medium in which understanding itself occurs."[12] Hermeneutics he describes as "an encounter with Being through language" because he thinks the reality of being human is determined by man's linguistic nature. Hence, hermeneutics must grapple with such philosophical issues as the relationship of language to being, understanding, history, existence, and reality. Gadamer thinks of himself as making an "ontological turn" in hermeneutics because of this interest in the ontological nature of understanding.

This concept of language as the disclosure of our lifeworld brought into theology has spawned the new hermeneutic, under the leadership of Gerhard Ebeling and Ernst Fuchs. They view hermeneutics not so much as a matter of bringing out one's self-understanding under the influence of that to which the proclaimed Word of God refers, á la Bultmann, as a linguistic matter; rather they are more interested in the word event. Ebeling puts it this way: Hermeneutics is concerned with "how a word [word event] that has taken place comes to be understood." The "object of hermeneutics is the word event as such."[13] He is disagreeing with the Bultmannian program of engaging in the hermeneutical task in order to make the Bible more effective today by penetrating through the mythology to the real message. For Ebeling the goal of hermeneutics, as it deals with its object the word event, is to enable the word itself to mediate understanding. In his words, "The primary phenomenon in the realm of understanding is not understanding *of* language, but understanding *through* language." But it is language with which he is concerned, nonetheless, for he asserts on the next page: "Hermeneutics as the theory of understanding must therefore be the theory of words."[14]

It is obvious that the meaning and use of religious language in this framework has nothing to do with scientific explanation. The interpretation of religious language here is a matter of understanding, not in terms of empirical factors but in terms of philosophical issues, namely, the a priori presuppositions for all knowledge, empirical or otherwise. The new hermeneutic approaches the questions of the a priori structure of the world from the standpoint of a conceptual ontology. Analytical philosophy, on the other hand, looks for the solution to the a priori structure of the world of experience (it is interested in no other world) by understanding the use of language from the standpoint of its semantical system (the logical positivists, especially Rudolph Carnap) or language games as forms of life (Ludwig Wittgenstein), matters which Heidegger designated "pre-ontological."

RELIGIOUS LANGUAGE IN THE ENGLISH-SPEAKING WORLD

In the English-speaking world the problem of the meaning and use of religious language has a special urgency because logical empiricism and the philosophical methods of logical, conceptual, and linguistic analysis have brought the truth claims and language of religion under a new type of examination. As a result, the logical status of religious discourse and the very conceptual possibility of religious knowledge have become central issues in philosophy of religion and philosophical theology. The antimetaphysical thrust of much of what is written from this perspective, then, is not Kantian, as is the case with the theologians reviewed earlier, but derives from British empiricism, logical positivism, and analytic philosophy.

As determined by these schools of thought, the problem of religious language in the English-speaking world is perhaps most easily grasped at the outset by seeing it within the context of the following three literary events: first, A. J. Ayer's influential preachment of logical positivism in *Language, Truth and Logic;* second, John Wisdom's attempt in the well-known article "Gods"[15] to counter Ayer's theological skepticism by use of the later Wittgenstein; and third, the announcement by the appearance in 1955 of the widely read *New Essays in Philosophical Theology,* edited by Antony Flew and Alasdair MacIntyre, that Ordinary Language Philosophy considered the logical analysis of the nature of religious language to be worthy of its attention.

LOGICAL POSITIVISM REJECTS RELIGIOUS LANGUAGE AS COGNITIVE

Ayer was the first logical positivist to focus provocatively the verificationist criterion of the meaning of factual statements upon theological affirmations. And, in no uncertain terms, Ayer limited the source of the meaning of all cognitively meaningful statements to sensory experience. As modified in the Introduction of the second edition of *Language, Truth and Logic*, this meant that a nonanalytic, literally meaningful statement should be either directly or indirectly verifiable as follows:

> A statement is directly verifiable if it is either itself an observation-statement, or is such that in conjunction with one or more observation-statements it entails at least one observation-statement which is not deducible from these other premises alone. . . . A statement is indirectly verifiable if it satisfies the following conditions: first, that in conjunction with certain other premises it entails one or more directly verifiable statements which are not deducible from these other premises alone; and, secondly, that these other premises do not include any statement that is not either analytic, or directly verifiable, or capable of being independently established as indirectly verifiable.[16]

Nor did he hesitate to draw the implications of this for the believer in God:

> The theist . . . may believe that his experiences are cognitive experiences, but, unless he can formulate his "knowledge" in propositions that are empirically verifiable, we may be sure that he is deceiving himself. It follows that those philosophers who fill their books with assertions that they intuitively "know" this or that . . . religious "truth" are merely providing material for the psychoanalyst.[17]

By reducing the logic of religious belief to a matter of the psychological cause of a person's believing the way he does, Ayer was overlooking the philosophical fact that beliefs are supported by evidence. The assumption he makes of the impossibility of adequately evidencing religious belief does not provide a basis for his further assumption that the expression of religious belief has meaning only with reference to the psychological cause of the belief.

JOHN WISDOM'S "THERAPEUTICAL" ANALYSIS

A closer look at the actual use of religious language could have prevented Ayer from jumping to the conclusion he did. At least this is the thinking behind John Wisdom's famous parable of the invisible gardener in the essay called "Gods." In concert with the later Wittgenstein, Wisdom felt that the meaning an assertion carries is to be ascertained by examining the manner in which it is actually used.

Moreover, he did not preclude the possibility that a religious sentence could be cognitive and even rational without satisfying the empirical criteria of meaning that was adopted by the logical positivists. Admitting the conceptual confusion frequently expressed in the language of religious belief, Wisdom advised a "therapeutical" analysis of such language. The purpose of this analysis is to become clear about exactly what kind of evidence religious beliefs are assumed to have by those who express them linguistically.

In his parable of the invisible gardener, Wisdom presents two views of a neglected garden. Two observers argue over the experimental difference the postulation of an invisible gardener would make. Wisdom concludes that such a postulation would make no experimental difference whatever. The believer in an invisible gardener is not expecting any change in the data observed which the skeptic is not also expecting. Nonetheless, explains Wisdom, a rational argument can still be conducted by the two viewers of the garden. As long as each viewer calls attention to the pattern of relations among the parts of the garden with which he is impressed, there will continue a cognitively meaningful discussion. To discern, think, and talk about patterns in what is experienced is essential to human understanding. The implication Wisdom drew for the logic of language about God is that it is cognitive and rational to the extent to which it refers to patterns observed in the flow of this-worldly events.[18]

One should not suppose that Wisdom considered any or all sentences about a transcendent God to be, as a matter of fact, true. But he did at least reason in favor of the possibility of their being either true or false. Ayer, it will be recalled, had withdrawn this possibility by branding theological assertions as cognitively without meaning.

WIDE INTEREST IN METATHEOLOGY DEVELOPED

The appearance of Wisdom's essay triggered a gradually increasing concern with what came to be designated "metatheology," that is, the logical analysis of religious language. Distinguishing between statements purporting to be about God and other theological entities, on the one hand, and, on the other hand, sentences containing the word *God* and the names of other theological subjects, metatheology deals with the latter. It seeks to determine if and how such sentences actually perform the linguistic function of being theological statements, that is, whether they can be used in a cognitively significant fashion. Rather than talking about God, it talks about the kind of meaning talk about God has.

The respectability metatheology had gained within philosophical and theological circles became obvious with the 1955 publication by editors Antony Flew and Alasdair MacIntyre of the influential *New Essays in Philosophical Theology.* (The choice of this title involved a redefinition of philosophical theology to mean metatheology.) From that time through the 1960s and, to a lesser extent, on into the present decade, the literature has been full of various attempts at clarifying the conceptualization of religious discourse. The extent of interest in this problem can be gauged by noting that a bibliography of the topic published in 1969 contains nine pages of entries.[19]

As intimated, the primary issue of the debate has been whether theological sentences, particularly those containing the word *God,* have cognitive meaning. That is, as determined by the empiricistic context in which the debate has been conducted, the issue is whether religious utterances have factual significance in the sense of constituting claims about an independently existing world, natural or supernatural, empirical or transempirical, which are either true or false. While there has been a general agreement that this is the central issue, there has never developed a consensus of opinion on its resolution. Just as there were cognitivists and noncognitivists at the beginning of the debate, so there are now.

THE NONCOGNITIVIST POSITION

Few of the noncognitivists have gone so far as Ayer did by peremptorily denying any meaning to theological assertions. Recognizing that such assertions are in widespread use, they have sought to discern the meaning which might inhere in that use. Some analysts have concluded that there are no cognitive meanings of any kind discernable in the actual use of religious language. Various other uses, and thus meanings, were allegedly found, however. R. B. Braithwaite, for instance, contended that "the primary use of religious assertions is to announce allegiance to a set of moral principles."[20] Other analysts of God talk have felt able to accord it cognitive significance but restrict that significance to assertions about man's outlook on life rather than about an infinite Person. A major representative of this reductionist approach, at one time, at least, was R. M. Hare.

R. M. HARE'S NOTION OF A "BLIK"

In response to the criticism that the believer in Wisdom's Garden Parable was left without any cognitive meaning in his affirmation of an invisible gardener, Hare proposed another illustrative parable. It concerns a lunatic who is "convinced that all dons want to murder him." No matter how many friendly dons he meets who try to assuage his fears, the lunatic is unmoved, for he takes their gestures of kindness as instances of "diabolical cunning" in which the dons are seeking to throw him off his guard. Now, if nothing the dons do or say can dissuade the lunatic from fearing for his life at their hands, then what is for him an unfalsifiable belief that the dons have murderous intentions might be said, by the critic of Wisdom's Garden Parable, to have no relevance to the real world. Being unfalsifiable, his conviction is neither true nor false, and hence, asserts nothing about any state of affairs. In that case, Hare points out, the lunatic would not actually be deluded, i.e., his belief about the dons entails no factual assertion, either true or false. Hence, the fact that the dons continue to regard him as a lunatic and to feel uneasy with him around is inexplicable. In order to account for their view of the lunatic, one must admit that an unfalsifiable belief is not necessarily without factual significance, even though by virtue of its unfalsifiability it cannot be ranked as an assertion.

What is it, then? Hare calls it a "blik." The lunatic has one blik and the dons another. Hume has shown us, according to Hare, "that our whole commerce with the world depends upon our 'blik' about the world." Moreover, Hume has made it clear that "differences between 'bliks' about the world cannot be settled by observation of what happens in the world." For instance, it is obviously inappropriate to seek for confirmation or disconfirmation of the following religious blik found in the Psalms: "'The earth is weak and all the inhabiters thereof: I bear up the pillars of it.'" Such a belief is not a scientific explanation of anything. But it does express the view that the world does not operate by pure chance. Thus, for those espousing this blik the scientific search for explanations is worthwhile, even though no assertion is entailed by it which contradicts an affirmation of the opposing blik about chance. Either blik is "compatible with anything happening or not happening." The difference lies in the impossibility of explaining, predicting, or planning anything if the belief in chance is held. A similar difference exists in the belief in God and the disbelief in Him, avers Hare.[21]

NONCOGNITIVISM AS METATHEOLOGICAL SKEPTICISM

A theologian who adopted a reductionist interpretation of religious utterances similar to that of the philosopher Hare was Paul van Buren, for whom affirmations of faith, far from being factual claims, are "to be interpreted, by means of the modified verification principle, as statements which express, describe, or commend a particular way of seeing the world, other men, and oneself, and the way of life appropriate to such a perspective."[22] But whether they give religious language solely noncognitive meaning or give it a reduced cognitive meaning, these thinkers are of one accord in not finding its function to include the conveyance of information about an infinite God or other supernatural entities, states of affairs, or events. For this reason these functional analysts may be classified as taking the noncognitivist position.

It should be noted that they are not necessarily repudiating the truth of any particular theological statement. The adequacy of the substantiation of knowledge claims about God was an irrelevant question because of the unavailability of sentences for stating putative theological facts. In other words, these metatheological skeptics were neither theists, atheists, nor agnostics, for to be such would be to assume the possibility of making truth-claims about God and other theological subjects. As Antony Flew put it in his development of John Wisdom's parable of the invisible gardener:

> When the Sceptic in the parable asked the Believer, "Just how does what you call an invisible, intangible, eternally elusive gardener differ from an imaginary gardener or even from no gardener at all?" he was suggesting that the Believer's earlier statement had been so eroded by qualification that it was no longer an assertion at all.[23]

The point Flew wanted to make, of course, is that religious believers apparently are content to make assertions from which they gradually retrench when presented with falsifying evidence, until the whole meaning of the original assertions changes into one for which evidence can count neither for nor against. The man who thinks he is talking rationally about God is unaware that "Someone may dissipate his assertion completely without noticing that he has done so. A fine brash hypothesis may thus be killed by inches, the death by a thousand qualifications."[24]

The theologian or other user of religious language purportedly intending to make statements which are true or false might deny that he so qualifies his assertions to the place where they cease being cognitively significant. But he will not convince the metatheological skeptic unless he can satisfy the verificationist or falsificationist criterion of meaning which is presupposed by both parties to this dispute.

THE VERIFICATIONIST AND FALSIFICATIONIST CRITERIA OF MEANING

Since those criteria of meaning are the points at issue, the theologian dare not rest the entire case for the cognitivity of his language upon what he takes to be experiential confirmation of his knowledge claims. Furthermore, there are many empirically non-verifiable affirmations concerning transcendent beings, events, and states of affairs which the religious believer makes. In fact, there are so many that it is impossible for him to counter, by a few experiential confirmations of some of his statements, the accusation that other of his statements are actually pseudostatements by virtue of their apparent lack of verifiability or falsifiability.

Nor can the theologian who accepts the verificationist criterion of meaning underlying this accusation hope to strengthen his case by pointing out the existence of similar difficulties in the confirmation of historical knowledge, knowledge of the future, knowledge of other minds, and inductive knowledge of the external world. For instance, the theologian might argue that the verifiability criterion applied to statements about past events makes those statements noncognitive. Assuming that, nonetheless, historical claims are acceptably made, he would then demand the same right for theological claims. Unfortunately for the theologian's argument here, the viability of the verificationist criterion of meaning entails the unintelligibility of historical knowledge no less than of theological knowledge. In both instances, *ex hypothesi,* no means is available for the determination of that which counts as evidence for or against a knowledge claim about an historical event, even one which heretofore has been considered well evidenced.[25]

SHOULD SOMETHING "COUNT AGAINST" A BELIEVER'S ASSERTION?

Be that as it may, a closer scrutiny of the demand Flew makes of cognitive meaning being determined by the state of affairs counting as falsifying evidence for an assertion may disarm his thrust. He declares, "One way of trying to understand" a religious believer's statement is "to attempt to find what he would regard as counting against, or as being incompatible with, its truth."[26]

Meaninglessness and truth or falsity conditions. Since the need expressed here is the understanding of the believer's affirmation, Flew is actually concerned with the meaning, rather than the truth or falsity of the affirmation. In asking the believer about what situation would get him to withdraw his assertion, Flew is trying to ascertain the meaning which the believer intended for his utterance to bear. If so, then Flew is confusing the meaningfulness of a statement with its truth or falsity when he claims that the meaning of the believer's utterance is cognitively vacuous by virtue of the believer's inability to specify its truth or falsity conditions. Granted, meaningless sentences are neither true nor false. But in a meaning situation, the respondent's inability to decide upon the truth or falsity of a statement, even when this is the result of the agent using the sentence in such a way as not to delineate the conditions of truth or falsity, has no bearing on whether the agent loaded or was capable of loading his meaning bearer (that is, his utterance) with cognitive meaning. Another way of putting this is to say that a person can conceivably have evidence or grounds for his assertion even though he cannot, for whatever reason, specify the criteria for that evidence.

We have not hereby repudiated the commonly accepted definition of knowledge as true, justified belief. The challenge, *How* do you know? is entirely appropriate to one making a knowledge claim. Equally so is the more basic challenge, What do you mean; what fact or state of affairs do you point to; and how will what you indicate disclose itself? Yet the American philosopher C. I. Lewis is no doubt on target when he points out,

> If only such mental states as clearly include the answer to these questions should be accounted knowledge, then cognition, instead of being a pervasive phenomenon of human life, would be one which is highly exceptional. Particularly so if such answers should be required to be explicit and complete: in that case knowledge would probably be nonexistent.

Indeed, we may wish to go further with Lewis and remind those, like Flew, who bring the falsification criterion of meaning so demandingly to the declarations of the religious believer that, "Almost one can say that the surer we are of what we know, the less clear we are as to precisely what we mean and just how we know it." "Even in the best and clearest cases of knowledge . . . [we] can go a little way in explication . . . , but to go further would become progressively more difficult." The most that can be asked is that one who is making an authentic knowledge claim be able to provide an explication of it "when the need . . . is genuine, and after reflection, and up to a certain point." That is, in spite of the practical difficulty of justifying most of what we take to be true belief, we must remember that designating something knowledge is still to place upon it a normative rather than a descriptive category. As Lewis phrases it, "Yet if in the analysis of knowledge we characteristically substitute for the relatively vague and inexplicit believing attitude an ideal explanation of it, this procedure has its warrant."[27] What is unwarranted, we might go on to say, is Flew's failure to recognize that not all ideals, including those in epistemology, will ever be fully actualized, and that this does not imply an epistemological collapse.

Genuineness and truth or falsity conditions. So much, then, for the kind of skeptical attack upon religious language in which the nonspecifiability of the truth or falsity conditions of a proposition is confusedly taken to entail its meaninglessness. Suppose, next, without mixing in the question of their meaningfulness, the genuineness of religious utterances as factual assertions be denied. This is certainly part of what Flew wishes to say. In his more recent comments on the matter he makes this clear: "If statements about God are supposed to be statements of fact, as they obviously are, and if nothing which might conceivably occur in the world could show them to be false, then, surely, neither their truth nor their falsity could possibly be directly relevant to that world and what happens in it."[28] The logic behind this, according to Flew, is inexorable: "Just as any choice that is a choice must be between alternatives, and must make some difference: so any assertion which is an assertion must involve a corresponding denial, a denial, that is, of the negation of what is asserted."[29] This he calls the "falsification test," which must be passed by any candidate for the rank of "assertion." For him, God talk will never qualify, as we can discover for ourselves. Simply apply the test: "Ask, while politely conceding that it may well be in fact true, what would have to have happened, to be happening, or to be going to happen, to show any particular candidate assertion to be false." Flew, focusing specifically upon Thomistic Christians here, feels that their attempt to cut through the conceptual break between man's mind and God's transcendent nature by predicating analogues of God and His creation according to the analogy of proportionality is a failure. Unless something "positive" is said about God as defined by the falsification test, the Thomist must confess agnosticism.[30]

Obviously, there are three moves open to the religious believer in the face of this kind of challenge to the genuineness of his alleged assertions about God. One alternative is to admit failure of his utterances about God to pass the falsification test and to argue, instead, that they never were intended to be cognitively significant. We have seen above that Braithwaite and Hare would opt for this approach.

The second alternative is to claim that the falsification test, while acceptable in itself, does not apply to God talk. John Hick adopts this alternative. Consider his answer to a paraphrase of Flew's question: Hick asks, "But is there any *logical* terminus any definite quantum of unfavorable evidence in face of which it would be demonstrably irrational to maintain theistic belief?" To this he replies, "It does not appear that there is or could be any such agreed limit. It seems, on the contrary, that theism is to this extent compatible with whatever may occur."[31]

With particular reference to the Christian belief in the existence of a loving God in a world full of natural and moral evil, Hick confesses, "There is something unusual, perhaps even unique, about such a belief," and, thus, about the logic of the affirmations of the belief.[32] In the first edition of *Faith and Knowledge,* Hick more firmly assumes the falsifiability criterion as he disassociates it from Christian faith. In spite of "the believer's experience" becoming "less and less compatible with theism . . . there is no ascertainable point at which in logic it ought to succumb." No set of experiences "would constitute a logically conclusive verification or refutation of theism." In his opinion, "The only experience that could conclusively *refute* belief in a loving God would be the obverse of a Beatific Vision, namely a satanic vision, a direct confrontation with an all-powerful and wholly evil being whose existence precluded the possibility that a God should exist as described by Christianity."[33]

The third alternative move in response to Flew's falsification challenge is to grant the viability of the falsification test and appeal to its verdict in order to eradicate any doubt about the religious belief being expressible in genuine, or "positive," assertions. The advantage of this route is that it disarms the skeptic in his own lair, without surrendering hostage to fortune by gratuitously admitting with Hick to the uniqueness of the logic of religious belief.

HEIMBECK'S APPEAL TO THE FALSIFICATION TEST

R. S. Heimbeck persuasively argues the merits of this third

approach. The context for his argument is the following procedure for verifying statements affirming the existence of anything including God:

> Try to verify any attributive statement which presupposes the existential statement you are interested in verifying, and if that attributive statement is verified (or can be verified) then *ipso facto* the existential statement presupposed by it is verified (or can be verified).

Underlying this procedure is the principle, "If there is anything which counts for a given statement, the fact of its counting for that statement argues at the same time for the genuineness over against the spuriousness of the statement." Applying this to assertions of God's existence, Heimbeck infers,

> If there were only one attributive G[od]-statement with existential import which was conclusively verifiable (even in principle only), then this fact alone would be sufficient proof that the statement that God exists was conclusively verifiable in principle.
>
> The statements made by "God loves all human beings" and "God raised Jesus of Nazareth from the dead" are normal G-statements with existential import; if verification procedures for these G-statements can be specified, then *ipso facto* verification procedures can be specified for the statement that God exists.[34]

This position explicitly denies that God's existence must be established before a genuine use of a God sentence is being made and before it is at all possible to verify the God statement conveyed by a God sentence. His view, explains Heimbeck, is that "one verifies the statement made by some such 'G'-sentence as 'God loves all human beings' *and* establishes the genuineness of that G-statement *and* proves the existential presupposition of that G-statement all in one movement, all concurrently." He cannot conceive how any existential statement can be established apart from "the establishing of some attributive statement."[35]

The disproof of God's existence, however, is not so easy, he admits. Yet it is not impossible. It would be impossible if the case were, as Flew assumes, that singular existential statements, while conclusively verifiable, are not conclusively falsifiable. But singular existential statements, for example, the one made by the sentence "God exists," are conclusively falsifiable when they contain time and place indicators. Granted, God in concept is invisible, intangible, and otherwise empirically elusive, but no more so than an electric current. The statement made by the sentence, "'There is an electric current in that wire now'" is conclusively falsifiable, nonetheless, as long as the empirical expectations associated with the truth of the statement do not obtain. Although the electric current itself is not an object of direct sensory experience, the shocks and sparks produced by its presence in a wire are. The absence of all such empirically discernable manifestations of electric current would conclusively falsify the assertion, "'There is an electric current in that wire now.'"[36]

Suppose, then, that the statement made by "God exists" were entailed by the claim, "'God was in Christ reconciling the world unto himself'" (2 Co 5:19). And suppose, further, that the latter claim suggests certain empirical expectations about Jesus' appearance on the scene, His behavior, His personality, His teachings, His death, and even, by authority, His resurrection. Then the total lack of fulfillment of such empirical expectations would conclusively falsify the statement made by "'God was in Christ.'" It would not, of course, falsify all meanings of the claim made by the sentence "God exists." Statements involving time and space are the only ones conclusively falsifiable by sensory experience. God's transcendent existence is not necessarily precluded by the lack of evidence of His immanent existence.

Nevertheless, affirmations of God's transcendent existence, although not conclusively falsifiable, are disverifiable, Heimbeck hastens to point out. By the disverifiability of statements, he means that without jeopardizing their cognitive meaningfulness, "They can be shown to be groundless and hence outside the scope of serious consideration."[37] Applying this characteristic of singular existential statements to the one conveyed in the sentence "God exists transcendently," he declares,

> If any evidence is advanced in behalf of the transcendent existence of God, we know what it would take to disqualify it. And if after much searching no evidence in behalf of it turns up, the very failure of an extensive attempt to discover positive evidence defeats the purpose of the assertion. A sentence which states a disverifiable assertion is still a cognitively significant sentence, however. The fact that God's transcendent existence cannot be conclusively falsified does not help the cause of Flew's scepticism, therefore, since the claim for God's transcendent existence is in principle both verifiable and disverifiable.[38]

THE LINGUISTIC ANALYSIS OF RELIGIOUS LANGUAGE

The above kind of *logical* analysis of the relation of the cognitivity of an utterance about God to its verifiability and falsifiability or, at least, disverifiability, is in response to the type of challenge made by Flew in which the verifiability criterion of cognitive meaning is assumed. Thus it will not entirely put at rest the doubts about the cognitivity of God talk which the *linguistic* analyst has, as he probes the actual usage to which such talk is put. We shall need now to see if the cognitivity of religious language fares as well in the context of linguistic analysis philosophy as we have seen it do in the initially worrisome context of logical empiricism. This is not to imply the identity of the religious language problem with the cognitivity issue. But in order to keep the crosscurrents of logic and epistemology, upon which the problem of religious language has been tossed, manageable within the confines set for this essay, it is necessary to limit our focus to the issue which has historically proven central as the controversy has developed.

THREE SOURCES OF DOUBT ABOUT THEOLOGICAL ASSERTIONS

The linguistic analyst in doubt about the cognitivity of theological assertions because of their alleged unverifiability might argue that his doubt is confirmed by three further problems. These problems arise when the claim is made that knowledge may be had of such inferred entities as the mind of another, the future, the past, or the material world as opposed to one's momentary perception of that world. In the first of a series of articles entitled "Other Minds," which initially appeared in the journal *Mind*, John Wisdom delineates three sources of "philosophical doubt" about knowing these kinds of objects, with particular reference to knowing other minds.

The first source of doubt is "the infinity of the criteria" as to whether what is affirmed is true. When evidence is being gathered for the substantiation of the knowledge claim—whether about historical events; the future; external objects; other minds; or theological objects, such as God—the endless number of possibly relevant items of evidence render it impossible to state without hesitation that sufficient evidence is in for a final decision to be made on the matter. Typical of the linguistic analyst who uses what we ordinarily say to determine whether a locution is cognitively meaningful, Wisdom opines that unless all the evidence is in, we do not "unhesitatingly say" of the collection of evidence in hand, " 'With these enough are present.'" For example, in response to the question "'Is this love or infatuation?'" one might say, "'I don't know with Annabel, I can never know with anyone; How I'll feel tomorrow, How she'll feel tomorrow, Whether it's really love.'"[39]

Second, there is the doubt which arises "from conflict among the criteria for S's being P." Wittgenstein's example of questions expressing such doubt, cited by Wisdom, are these: "'Can you play chess without the queen?'" "'Is a tomato a fruit or a vegetable?'" Wisdom's own example is, "Can you unintentionally keep a promise?"[40]

Third, the uncertainty about whether or not we have knowledge can stem from the knower's being limited, in the case of knowing the mind of another person, to outward signs of the inward states of that mind. Wisdom phrases it thus: "The doubt may arise from hesitation at the jump from the criteria . . . to S is P, e.g., from the outer (bodily) to the inner (spiritual), from the present to the past, from the actual to the potential, from possibilities of sensation to physical things."[41] For example, we are uncertain about whether another person is angry, because we have nothing more than his behavior from which to judge. If he were intending to deceive me into thinking he is angry when his real emotion is something else, I realize that he will probably succeed. In other words, bodily behavior is evidence for an assertion about a different type of object than a mental state.

Coupled with the verificationist criterion of cognitive meaning, these sources of philosophical doubt delineated by Wisdom lie behind most metatheological skepticism. This is particularly true of the third kind of uncertainty mentioned by Wisdom, namely, the kind raised by the difference in logical type between the empirical statements of the evidence for a theological conclusion and that nonempirical conclusion itself.

NONDEFINITIONAL, NONEMPIRICAL COGNITIVE MEANING

Not all evaluators of the logic of theological affirmations follow the logical empiricists in limiting cognitive meaning either to definitions and tautologies or to empirical statements. As presaged by Wisdom's approach in "Gods," some linguistic analysts claim to discern a third kind of cognitive meaning in religious statements. Michael B. Foster, in *Mystery and Philosophy,* is a leading early protagonist of this view.

Theological statements concern the mysterious. Although he does not wish to disassociate his philosophical method from that common to the linguistic analysts, Foster takes exception to their stress on clarity of expression and their tendency to identify all thinking with problem solving. He wants to make room for "oracular utterance" as a vehicle for communicating truth. A statement can be mysterious and still be true. This implies the legitimacy of "another kind of thinking which depends on the revealing of a mystery." Foster develops a distinction made by E. L. Mascall, in an unpublished paper, between a puzzle, on the one hand, and Gabriel Marcel's well-known differentiation between mysteries and problems, on the other hand.[42] Foster distinguishes between a problem, which can be solved; a mystery, which cannot be solved despite the temptation to try; and a puzzle, which is only apparently mysterious and is amenable to being solved through clarification of present knowledge. The analytic philosopher mistakenly construes mysteries to be puzzles and appoints himself the puzzle solver. But the Christian theologian is dealing with mysteries, not puzzles. That is, the intellectual objects of interest to him are mysterious things. He thinks in an understanding way about what will always remain mysterious because beyond man's comprehension, explains Foster.[43] Indeed, he goes on to say, "Belief in a divine Revelation seems to involve something like a repentance in the sphere of the intellect." "When Zechariah says 'Be silent all flesh before the Lord,' this is not wholly different from Wittgenstein's 'Whereof one cannot speak, thereof one must be silent.'"[44]

Wittgensteinian fideism and language games. A similar position is being argued at present by D. Z. Phillips, who has been carrying on a running battle with Antony Flew and the presently most forceful proponent of Flew's brand of skepticism, Kai Nielsen.[45] Phillips is sensitive to Flew's challenge, "One way of trying to understand (or perhaps it will be to expose)" the utterance of someone about whom "we are sceptical as to whether he is really asserting anything at all . . . is to attempt to find out what he would regard as counting against, or as being incompatible with, its truth."[46] Phillips's sensitivity reveals his desire to retain some degree of cognitivity in religious statements. But his understanding is explicitly molded by the later Wittgenstein's notion of "language games" as "forms of life," in this case religious language games and the religious form of life. Phillips finds the use to which religious believers put their affirmations to be expressions of "religious pictures" which are "unshakeable beliefs in the sense that they form the framework within which those who live by them assess themselves and the events that befall them." The belief in the Last

Judgment, or in immortality, or in God are examples of such pictures. It is "what gave rise" to such beliefs that is important.
"*Believing* them has little in common with any kind of conjecture."
Rather "it has to do with living by them, drawing sustenance by
them . . . etc.," explains Phillips.[47]

It is wrong, therefore, Phillips argues, to treat, say, the belief in
life after death as a prediction the way Flew does. The "religious and
ethical significance" of the belief is to be found in the picture the
believer has of his family being reunited after death. This picture is
"not a prediction for which he has evidence, but a vision in terms of
which much of his own life is lived out." For the believer, "the
picture . . . is the measure of assessment."[48]

The modification which Phillips construes a religious context
to place upon religious assertions is clearly akin to the thinking of the
later Wittgenstein. In his lectures on religious belief, Wittgenstein
drew a distinction between the logic of evidential substantiation
adopted in religious controversies and that used in "normal controversies." In his typically aphoristic manner he comments upon
religious controversies thus:

> They are, in a way, quite inconclusive.
> The point is that if there were evidence, this would in fact destroy
> the whole business.
> Anything that I normally call evidence wouldn't in the slightest
> influence me.
>
> * * * * * *
>
> That is partly why you don't get in religious controversies, the
> form of controversy where one person is *sure* of the thing, and the
> other says: "Well, possibly."
> You might be surprised that there hasn't been opposed to those
> who believe in Resurrection those who say "Well, possibly."
> Here believing obviously plays much more this role: suppose we
> said that a certain picture might play the role of constantly admonish-
> ing me, or I always think of it. Here, an enormous difference would be
> between those people for whom the picture is constantly in the
> foreground, and the others who just didn't use it at all.
> Those who said: "Well, possibly it may happen and possibly it
> may not" would be on an entirely different plane.
> This is partly why one would be reluctant to say: "These people
> rigorously hold the opinion (or view) that there is a Last Judgment."
> "Opinion" sounds queer.

It is for this reason that different words are used: "dogma," "faith."

We don't talk about hypothesis, or about high probability. Nor about knowing.

In a religious discourse we use such expressions as: "I believe that so and so will happen," and use them differently to the way in which we use them in science.

* * * * * *

Anyone who reads the Epistles will find it said: not only that it [Christianity] is not reasonable, but that it is folly.

Not only is it not reasonable, but it doesn't pretend to be.

Why shouldn't one form of life culminate in an utterance of belief in a Last Judgment? But I couldn't either say "Yes" or "No" to the statement that there will be such a thing. No "Perhaps," nor "I'm not sure."[49]

We have cited Wittgenstein at length in order to make unmistakably clear the Wittgensteinian flavor of Phillips' attempt to counter the thrust from such skeptics as Flew and Nielsen that if a religious assertion is a genuine assertion then "it will necessarily be equivalent to a denial of the negation of that assertion."[50] Says Phillips,

From a consideration of the kind of force characteristic religious pictures have, we can see that to ask whether they are true as if they were would-be empirical propositions is to ask the wrong question. It is of the utmost philosophical importance to recognise that for the believers these pictures constitute truths, truths which form the essence of life's meaning for them. To ask someone whether he thinks these beliefs are true is not to ask him to produce evidence for them, but rather to ask him whether he can live by them. . . . If the answer is in the affirmative then no doubt there will be factual consequences for him. If a man does believe that death has no dominion over the unity of the family . . . he will make decisions and react in ways very unlike the man who holds ideas [to the contrary].[51]

AN EMPIRICIST CRITIQUE OF WITTGENSTEINIAN CONCEPTUAL RELATIVISM

It is clear that both Wittgenstein and Phillips, no less than Flew, are still operating under the assumption that truth or falsity is a quality which properly belongs only to an empirical statement. They simply make a gift to the logical empiricist of that point. Then they proceed to figure out a way in which religious language can be meaningful nonetheless. It is for this reason that Kai Nielsen picks up Flew's cudgel and hammers relentlessly on Phillips' Wittgensteinian fideism because of what Nielsen shows to be the propositional meaninglessness entailed by its "conceptual relativism."

Whereas the logical empiricists such as Ayer and Flew, in their earlier writings, had equated the meaning of the statement with its method of verification, Nielsen, learning from the criticism of the verification principle, separates the issues of meaning and verification. Moreover, he does not demand that in order for a statement to be considered as having factual content it be conclusively verifiable or conclusively falsifiable. Nor will he accept the phenomenalists' dictum that a physical-object statement is actually a statement about sense impressions. Further, he repudiates the typical logical empiricist view that descriptive definitions have to be ostensive (that is, that the definition of an object term is the pointing to a sensory experience to which the term referred), or else that its verbal definition has to be reducible to an ostensive one.†

But a theory of meaning expansive enough to accommodate terms for abstract and theoretical concepts does not open the door to a meaningful use of the word *God,* warns Nielsen. *God* is supposedly an object term, that is, it putatively refers to the "Creator." While cognizant that the meaning of a term is usually not its referent, Nielsen still wonders how the meaning of any object term can be ascertained unless its referent is known. Herewith lies our "puzzlement," he feels.

> We seem to have no way of identifying the referent of "God." Since whatever it is, it is not something literally observable . . . or something we could become directly aware of like a pain or an anxiety, it is not clear what, if anything, is actually being referred to or could be referred to by "God" given its present use in the language.[52]

This kind of empiricist critique of religious language, more critical of its assumptions than the earlier versions mentioned above, must be taken the more seriously. Assuming that the statements made by "God exists" and "God loves me" are intended by re-

†By 1966 Flew can be found making a similar qualification. He admits that words like "'justice,' 'space,' or 'function'" are "philosophically above reproach," for, "though they are not words for corporeal things, they are not words for incorporeal things either. Their meaning derives from their use . . . and without any sort of direct or indirect pointing to objects of a special kind." Because "God" putatively refers to an incorporeal individual, thereby implying an ostensive definition, Flew continues to deny it cognitive status (*God and Philosophy* [London: Hutchinson, 1966], pp. 31-32).

ligious believers as true, substantive statements of fact, we must face squarely the problems posed by the referent of the term *God* in these statements. First, there is the difficulty of identifying the referent of *God* when it is taken to be incorporeal and transcendent. Second, as the medieval theologians were particularly concerned to point out, the referent of the word *God* can be described only in negative terms, for example, *infinite* or *unlimited,* or else in analogical terms. Third, the faithful make God the subject of assertions for which there does not appear to be any state of affairs which, not conclusively but only tentatively, would falsify them; for example, in the face of a series of the cruelest of misfortunes the believer will still proclaim his faith that God loves him.

THE EMPIRICIST CONFUSION OF MEANING AND REFERENT

It certainly does seem reasonable, at least initially, to be skeptical about the meaning of God talk in light of the difficulties in identifying its referents; in making positive, univocal predications about the referent; and in learning what would count against the assertions made about it. However, T. E. Hill has made a point about the relation between the referents and the meanings of statements which needs to be kept in mind at this juncture:

> A fact of special importance that the dependence of reference on meaning helps to explain is that the referents of expressions are, with rare exceptions, not the meanings of these expressions. When someone says, "The cat is on the green mat," the reference of the sentence, if it has one, is a certain situation involving a cat and a mat, not the meaning of the sentence.

Or, to come conversely at the same point about the ineraseable distinction between reference and meaning and the dependence of the former upon the latter, he declares:

> One can pick out referents without getting meanings and give examples of what is meant without grasping just what the examples are examples of. To know what the referents of bearers of intentional meanings are is to come very close to apprehending these meanings but, in itself, it is not yet fully to grasp these meanings.[53]

THE VALUABLE ASPECT OF THE EMPIRICIST CRITIQUE

Without examining in detail the merits of the three oft stated problems listed above for defining the referent of the term *God,* the overall thrust of the concern expressed in these problems we may

accept as valid.[54] The overstatement of these problems with which
one is frequently treated does not belie the underlying urgency of an
empirical critique of theological affirmations. One need not assent to
the verifiability theory of meaning of Carnap and Ayer in order to
agree with this. Neither must one limit the meaning of an expression to its truth conditions as Gustav Bergmann does by spec-
ifying that a particular term is "to occur in a statement only if its
referent is immediately apprehended—in perception, memory, or
imagination—by a speaker, and . . . an undefined predicate is to
occur in a statement only if at least one exemplification of it is known
to the speaker."[55]

Granted that experiential applicability is helpful in discerning
the meaning of an expression, the meaningfulness of an expression
is not determined thereby, nor is the meaning itself its experiential
applicability. If this were not the case, then reports of one's intentions, feelings, and so forth, nontautologous statements like "No
two objects can occupy the same place at the same time,"
philosophical claims such as "Generalizations cannot be reduced to
singular statements" or "There are other minds," and evaluations,
would all have to be classified as without meaning. Moreover, as
Hill points out about verifiability criteria in general, "They obscure
the fact that confirmation conditions depend upon meanings rather
than meanings upon confirmation conditions, and accordingly that
even when sensory and observational confirmation conditions are
relevant to meanings, confirmation conditions can often not be
determined until meanings are known."[56]

We are not, therefore, intending to join those who equate verification and meaning when we confess a sensitivity to the empirical
critique of religious language. Assuming that the theologian is much
of the time not evaluating life but describing factual situations for
which truth conditions are relevant, the nature and extent of possible patterns of experience germane to the discovery of the truth or
falsity of such descriptions must be determined. As Hill correctly
points out, there is one insight which those advocating the verifiability criteria have had which we do well to remember, namely, "The
meanings of sentences belonging to that limited class of sentences
the truth or falsity of which can be confirmed by sensory and
observational experiences consist in part of possible patterns of
experience the fulfillment of which would help to confirm the truth
or falsity of these sentences."[57]

THE INTERPRETATIVE OR "SEEING AS—" APPROACH

The rise of neoorthodoxy has brought to popularity an appeal to a nonmystical, self-authenticating, self-interpreting, direct awareness of God, which is regarded as affording an ostensive definition of Him. This "I-Thou" encounter, as Martin Buber called it, does not, however, permit the believer to objectify and rationally conceptualize, and linguistically categorize God. Karal Barth, who brought this view into prominence,‡ was dead set against any scientific or historical verification of God's presence to man. In his view, God is the "Subject that remains indissolubly Subject," the "wholly other," the utterly transcendent.§ The encounter theologians have been severely criticized for the logical problems posed by anyone's claim to know that it was God he encountered.[58] But an attempt has been made in recent years to circumvent these criticisms by appealing to the interpretative element in all experience.‖ We shall examine two important examples provided by Frederick Ferré and John Hick.

WITTGENSTEIN'S ANALYSIS OF "SEEING AS . . ."

In order to understand this move it will be necessary to look at another part of the later Wittgenstein's thinking, namely, the notion of "seeing as. . . ." At one point in the *Philosophical Investigations,* Wittgenstein does a conceptual analysis of two uses of the word *see.* He discovers a "difference of category between the two 'objects' of sight corresponding to the different uses of the word 'see' in 'I see two faces' and 'I see a likeness between these two

‡According to Wolfhart Pannenberg, the concept of God's revelation as self-disclosure rather than the "communication of some 'truths' by supernatural means, by inspiration, for example," a concept "almost universal" in its acceptance "in contemporary Protestant theology," "goes back to German Idealism, especially to Hegel," and was "mediated to Barth particularly through Marheineke." Pannenberg also admits that the contemporary equation of the concept of revelation with God's self-disclosure is not to be found in the Old Testament and New Testament expressions translated by "'to reveal' and 'revelation.'" What those words meant was "the making known of the most varied sorts of information through inspiration or as the 'appearance' of God or of Jesus," he explains. (*Jesus–God and Man,* trans. L. L. Wilkins and D. A. Priebe [London: SCM, 1968], pp. 127-28).

§While Barth in his later years came to speak of the "humanity" of God, one should not assume that he thereby withdrew his extreme emphasis upon God's otherness. See John Macquarrie, *Twentieth-Century Religious Thought* (N.Y.: Harper & Row, 1963), pp. 322-24.

‖By "interpretative element" is meant the analytic notion, not that associated with the *Geisteswissenschaften.* For a comparison, see Karl-Otto Apel, *Analytic Philosophy of Language and the 'Geisteswissenschaften,'* trans. Harold Holstelilie (Dordrecht, Holland: D. Reidel, 1967), pp. 37-57.

faces.'" The fact that a person could accurately draw the two faces without noticing a likeness between them which someone else can see indicates coincidentally no change in the object perceived by the two people, and a change. The change is called "'noticing an aspect.'"

Now suppose that one were looking at a line drawing which sometimes he saw as a rabbit and sometimes as a duck's head, with the long bill of the duck where the rabbit's long ears were before. About this illustration Wittgenstein, in his rather cryptic fashion, says the following:

> The change of aspect. "But surely you would say that the picture is altogether different now!"
>
> But what is different: my impression? my point of view?—Can I say? I *describe* the alteration like a perception; quite as if the object had altered before my eyes.
>
> "Now I am seeing *this*," I might say (pointing to another picture, for example). This has the form of a report of a new perception.
>
> The expression of a change of aspect is the expression of a *new* perception and at the same time of the perception's being unchanged.
>
> * * * * * *
>
> And above all do *not* say "After all my visual impression isn't the *drawing;* it is *this*—which I can't shew to anyone."—Of course it is not the drawing, but neither is it anything of the same category, which I carry within myself.
>
> * * * * * *
>
> If you put the "organization" of a visual impression on a level with colours and shapes, you are proceeding from the idea of the visual impression as an inner object. Of course this makes this object into a chimera. . . .
>
> * * * * * *
>
> If I saw the duck-rabbit as a rabbit, then I saw: these shapes and colours (I give them in detail)—and I saw besides something like this: and here I point to a number of different pictures of rabbits.— This shews the difference between the concepts.
>
> "Seeing as . . ." is not part of perception. And for that reason it is like seeing and again not like.[59]

In one use of the word *see,* then, the viewer can look at exactly the same object and yet see it as two different objects without being able to show that difference to someone else by drawing it, etc. This is why Wittgenstein decides "'Seeing as . . .' is not part of perception." "Seeing as . . ." is the result of the interpretation of perception.

We have already observed John Wisdom's pregnant employment of this analysis by Wittgenstein in the former's garden parable. Instead of perceiving just a single object, two people are depicted as viewing an entire garden, one seeing it as being tended by an invisible gardener, and one seeing it as unattended. It would be possible, of course, to expand the object viewed to include the world as a whole or all of one's experiences considered together. Many are currently doing this who have followed Wisdom's lead in making a functional analysis of the meaningfulness of theistic discourse. They do it by finding the cognitive import of that discourse to derive from the believer's seeing the totality of his experiences as revelatory of God. For those thinkers with metaphysical sensitivities, the "seeing as . . ." approach typically develops into the view that metaphysical theories are analogies. Dorothy Emmet, a longtime protagonist of this view of metaphysics, explains metaphysical theories thus:

> As analogies of being, they seek to say something about "reality" transcending experience, in terms of relations found within experience. As co-ordinating analogies, they seek to relate diverse types of experience by extension of a key idea derived from some predominant intellectual or spiritual relation.[60]

FERRÉ AND THEOLOGY AS A CONCEPTUAL SYNTHESIS

Ferré's position explained. A noteworthy instance of this understanding of metaphysics used to complement a functional analysis of religious language is to be found in the thinking of Frederick Ferré. That he was moving in this direction at the beginning of his career can be detected in the final pages of the published version of his doctoral dissertation, *Language, Logic and God.* There he maintains metaphysics to be *"conceptual synthesis."* For him this means, "A metaphysical system is a construct of concepts designed to provide coherence for all 'the facts' on the basis of a theoretical model drawn from among 'the facts.'"[61] Relating this to theological statements he decides that such statements semantically function as metaphysical statements:

> Theological speech projects a model of immense responsive significance, drawn from "the facts," as the key to its conceptual synthesis. This model, for theism, is made up of the "spiritual" characteristics of personality. . . . For Christianity . . . the conceptual model consists in the creative, self-giving, personal love of Jesus Christ. In this model is found the only literal meaning which these terms, like "creative," "personal," and "love," can have in the Christian vocabulary.[62]

But how can it be determined that a conceptual synthesis coherently modeled upon the love of Jesus Christ is true to reality? Since the terms of the system are relative to the key metaphor, namely, Jesus' love, they are not literal descriptions of reality. Ferré correctly recognizes, "If words are drawn from human experience and used concerning 'ultimate reality,' it will not be appropriate to expect a 'picturing' relationship between language and referent." However, all he feels prepared to say in this book by way of solution to the question of the correspondence of theological assertions to reality is that in addition to their being coherent among themselves their truth is indicated if they are capable of "illuminating our experience."[63]

More recently, he has elaborated on this solution. He declares that "whatever definiteness of content" theistic affirmations have is given in "the language through which the 'gross anthropomorphic predicates' of theism's ultimate images are expressed." This can be seen to be the case, according to Ferré, because theistic religions historically have been willing to withdraw all of the following conceptual elements before giving up their ultimate imagery: "'theory,'" including theories about God's nature, man's nature, and the universe; "'historical'" statements; "'empirical hypotheses'"; and "'injunctions'" concerning ethics and ritual.[64]

What is basic, never to be given up, is "the vision of God" which carries the religious system along. This "'vision,'" or "'way of seeing'" has "a direct and powerful impact on what one is likely to notice or believe, even though 'the vision' itself is not knowledge in any standard sense." Indeed, Ferré goes on to admit that religious language is essentially heuristic in function. That is, "It may contribute to cognitive inquiry without itself being subject to the same rules of inquiry."[65]

How is this done if "theistic imagery may not appropriately be treated as constituting or warranting limited, falsifiable empirical hypotheses"? The answer is, "In all logical respects . . . anthropomorphic theistic imagery can function on its speculative side as a vivid metaphysical model." That is,

it can give conceptual definiteness to the ultimate nature of things by picturing all of reality as constituting either creature or Creator, each with specifiable characteristics; it can suggest patterns and unity in the totality of things in terms of its representation of the various relations between the entities so pictured; and it can give a sense of intelligibility, an aura of meaning and familiarity, by virtue of the appeal to personal purpose, volitional power, and moral principle as the ultimate explanatory categories.

The advantages of this explication of theistic imagery is, he believes, the avoidance of any confusion with "either falsifiable empirical propositions or with empty linguistic conventions."†[66]

Still, the truth question demands attention. Aware of this, Ferré spends some time grappling with it. For a starter he defines that which is conceptually true to be that which is conceptually "reliable." This is construed to mean, "The truth of a thought is finally to be defined by its capacity not to need correction, not to fail us in performing the logical function we appropriately expect of it." The "'correspondence of thought to reality'" is "nothing more than a special case of conceptual reliability," we are told. Indeed, reality is whatever "we *count on* not to let us down."

So it seems that Ferré remains wedded to a coherence theory of truth. The truth quality of a theistic model is "derivative." It is true *"to the extent that some theory judged appropriate for its articulation can itself qualify as conceptually reliable."* This latter reliability is ascertained by appealing to the criteria of the appropriateness, adequacy, and coherence of the theory in explaining one's thoughts and experiences. Ferré does not wish to go so far in his rejection of the correspondence theory of truth as to deny that "the referent of our metaphysical models ('ultimate reality') may somehow 'resemble' one of our best-accredited conceptual means of giving conceptual definiteness to it." Yet, he feels, "the loose nature of the appropriate criteria of 'success' prevents us from insisting that there is but one *single* 'best-accredited' way of thinking about this referent."[67]

Ferré's position evaluated. By resting the cognitive significance of theistic religious language upon a conceptual model whose truth can be no more than derived from the usefulness of an explanatory system, Ferré eliminates any basis for the absolute authority which Protestant theologians traditionally have given the theistic descriptions in Scripture. No matter how pragmatically successful a coherent account of life viewed as being most meaningful from the standpoint of the "love of Jesus" may be, the

†Ferré, after disassociating his position from Ian Ramsey's "similar-sounding suggestions," reveals that "a more nearly similar treatment of the status of theistic models may be found in Dorothy Emmet, *The Nature of Metaphysical Thinking . . .* whose influence will be obvious in the passages that follow" (*Basic Modern Philosophy of Religion* [New York: Scribner, 1967], p. 373, n. 2).

question of the extent to which such an account reflects reality must be answered. Unless an answer is forthcoming, the heuristic role of theological assertions cannot be known to be descriptive. In that event, they must be reduced to having a Kantian-like regulative office or, at best, be given the status of symbolizations of religious bliks, à la Hare.

Certainly if God has revealed truths about Himself, the world, and man, as orthodox theologians maintain, then, contrary to Ferré, there is, at least theoretically, "but one single 'best-accredited' way of thinking" about the referent of the theistic model. Moreover, such a revelation would permit the rejection of competing "world models," or "organizing images," regardless of the appropriateness, coherence, and adequacy of the systems these models might generate. Ferré has no mechanism available for deciding between two or more mutually exclusive but equally appropriate, coherent, and adequate metaphysical systems.

A partially different criticism is lodged by Anders Jeffner. Noting that Ferré introduces the nonempirical component of his system by appealing to metaphysical " 'facts,' " which are the products of conceptual activity as the thinker or believer attempts to explain the entirety of his experiences, Jeffner presses Ferré on the matter of the starting point. The starting point seems to be the existence of ambiguous objects of experience. Examples are human nature, human history, the world of sensory experience, to name a few. How these objects are to be accounted for, Ferré is assuming, "cannot be solved by an appeal to facts." But says Jeffner, for Ferré's "argument to work we must also assume that these ambiguous objects are objects with an uncertain *Gestalt* and not a changing *Gestalt.*"

Because Ferré fails to observe this distinction he has no way of substantiating his claim that "one of the possible interpretations may be the correct one." Even supposing Ferré had taken the stronger alternative of carefully limiting his assumption to one in which "the objects giving rise to a religious interpretation are objects with an uncertain *Gestalt,*" still, alleges Jeffner, "it is very difficult to see what reasons can be given for it, and to neglect this point is a serious gap in the argument."[68]

HICK'S HYPOTHESIS OF ESCHATOLOGICAL VERIFICATION

Hick's position explained. John Hick, like Ferré, links the significance of God talk to the interpretative element in all experience. But he tries to establish the veridicality of the believer's "seeing as—" by assuming at the outset that the metaphysical "facts" are immediately experienced and by devising at the conclusion a means of appealing to the verification principle.

In Barthian fashion, John Hick stresses both the impossibility of knowledge of God's transcendent being and the possibility of apprehending God's self-disclosure in Christ. But Hick does this in a way that is designed to meet the verifiability criterion on its own terms. Granting the experiential verifiability of factual truth claims, and taking religious statements about God's self-disclosure to be factual, Hick proposes the hypothesis of eschatological verification to account for the meaningfulness of those religious statements.‡ He admits that Jesus' teachings about His infinite Father can hardly be accorded the logical status of commonsense, empirical truthclaims. However, following Barth by limiting man's knowledge of God to what was revealed in Christ, Hick posits the possibility of an "indirect verification," rather than the normal "observational verification" of "God's self-revelation to men in Christ." That indirect verification would be the establishment of the authority of Christ as God's Revealer by "an experience of the reign of the Son in the Kingdom of the Father." Specifically, this experience, as promised in the New Testament, is one of participating, as "'children of God,'" in "eternal life" and becoming aware in that eschatological Kingdom of what the New Testament expresses in "visual symbols when it says that the Lamb will be in the midst of the throne of the Kingdom."

According to Hick, this latter "element completes the circle of verification, linking the future fulfillment situation directly with that which is to be verified, namely, the authority of the Christ who is the source and basis of Christian faith." Although Hick recognizes that such "an experience of the promised Kingdom of God, with Christ reigning as Lord of the New Age, could not constitute a logical certification of his claims," he does argue that in the light of the impossibility of logically demonstrating any matters of fact, the evidence from an eschatological verification of the promised King-

‡While Hick's eschatological verification argument has received considerable attention, Ian Crombie had presented essentially the same argument in his contribution to the series of essays entitled "Theology and Falsification" in Flew and MacIntyre's *New Essays in Philosophical Theology,* pp. 108-130. It also appears in Crombie, "The Possibility of Theological Statement" in Basil Mitchell, ed., *Faith and Logic* (London: Allen & Unwin, 1957), pp. 31-83.

dom of God is entirely adequate to remove all rational doubt about the truth of Christianity.[69]

Hick's position evaluated. This attempt by Hick to conceive of "an experienced situation that points unambiguously to the reality of God"[70] has had its critics. Terence Penelhum has put his finger upon a fundamental weakness of the argument.[71] He grants the validity of Hick's notion of eschatological verification of the believer's claims for meeting Flew's challenge that the believer admits no state of affairs or event as refuting his position. He also concedes for the sake of the argument the concept of survival of bodily death, which Hick employs. Yet Penelhum does not think that Hick has provided evidence for anything more than the belief, "'In the end, the universe is a good rather than a bad one to live in.'" The identity of a transcendent Being, different in kind from the natural realm is no less difficult to discover in any future existence than in the present one.

Having "fulfilled the verificationist demand for some structure of verification-falsification," Hick has still made no headway "against the problem of transcendence," alleges Penelhum. "Eschatological expectations" should be distinguishable from "secular ones" in order to show how "religious assertions relate to God as their subject as well as to the world within which he is said to show his love." To achieve this "we must show that the expectations contain meaningful references to the deity and not merely to improved circumstances for his creatures." In other words, unless our "religious expectations" have a "concrete content" which "we can elucidate in terms of our experience here and now," then "it is merely fraudulent to answer the verification criticisms by reference to religious expectations," concludes Penelhum.[72]

CIRCULARITY OF THE VALIDATION OF THE THEOLOGICAL MODEL

Hick's partial failure to beat the empiricist critique of religious language on its own terms points up the stark fact that the real problem which must be solved by anyone for whom the world of experience is theologically significant is not experiential verification. It is rather the problem Aquinas posed concerning the use of finite concepts about an infinite God. Without initial meaning religious expectations could never be verified, for the identity of the predicted event or situation would remain unknown. And without a means of verification, the interpretation of one's experiences now as mediating God's presence—an interpretation which eschatological verification supposedly validates—becomes pointless.

These representative attempts by Ferré and Hick to establish the cognitive meaningfulness of religious language by means of a functional analysis supplemented with a metaphoric view of metaphysics are assuredly not antimetaphysical in intent. But they are attempts firmly bound within the same empiricism of the critique which they are trying to overcome. The analogical manner of their God talk argues from patterns perceived in the world of experience to that which is not experienced. The model giving content to religious utterances is something experienced here and now which enables the believer to interpret the entirety of his experiences here and now *as* revelatory of God. God Himself is not experienced, nor is a divinely authorized interpretation of one's experiences available. Theological assertions are all analogical because they express an analogical way of thinking.

Yet the point of univocity which any analogy must possess to keep from breaking into an equivocation is never specified. Indeed, it cannot be, for the validation of the metaphysical or theological model is said to rest upon its usefulness as a synoptic starting point for an overall interpretation of one's experiences. But since the validation of that overall interpretation itself, granting its internal coherence, is, again, its usefulness in our giving meaning to life, the validation process is circular. No way of transcending the world of experience is provided by the approach now under scrutiny. Positive, univocal discourse about a transcendent God becomes impossible. But so also do analogical predications as construed in the traditional sense of the application of a common concept or term in different senses to a finite and an infinite object.

THE "TRANSCENDENT" GOD BECOMES "INTRA-EXPERIENTIAL"

The kind of analogy being adopted by the "seeing as—" philosophical theologians would be called "existential" or "intra-experiential" by Emmet. Her description of that perspective on metaphysical analogy points up the difficulty the traditional notion of a transcendent God gives it. She begins her characterization of it thus:

> A metaphysical analogy might express [and, she thinks, properly does express] a relation to an object in part experienced and in part not experienced, describing it in concepts drawn from intra-experiential relations. In this case it would be necessary to under-

stand "transcendent" not as meaning "beyond" or "outside" any possible experience. . . . We should need to understand the word "transcendent" as standing for that which is "other" than our minds—"being" or "existence" apart from our interpretations. But this would not preclude our interpretations from arising within some situation in which we are related to that which is "other" than our minds. . . . Such analogies must of necessity be indirect attempts to say something about being [itself] through our judgments concerning the relationships in which we find ourselves.

In order to make viable this notion of metaphysical analogy she realizes the need

to show that there must be relationships in which we stand to that which is other than our ideas, and that the nature of that other or others could be suggested indirectly by drawing analogies between the feelings and the judgments evoked in such relationships, in order to suggest possible characterizations in that which evokes them.[73]

This task of so describing the " 'transcendent,' " that is, "that which is what it is" apart from our interpretations, she deems worthwhile to undertake even though "we have no direct apprehension of [its] intrinsic properties" but "only indirect apprehensions, arising out of relations in which we stand to it."[74]

The concept of a transcendent God, by nature beyond or outside human experience, has been jettisoned, therefore, because the lack of any direct, nonanalogical relation to it prevents any experiential knowledge about it arising. In its place is put a "transcendent" which is continuous with what we do experience, even though, not having experienced it, we must think of it as existing apart from our minds and, thus, apart from our interpretations of what we have experienced. It comes as no surprise, then, to read John Hick concluding his treatment of faith and verification with such comments as the following:

Within Christianity it is possible to talk about the infinite God, incomprehensible though he still remains, because he has become finitely incarnate in Jesus of Nazareth. That is to say, God is identified as the Being about whom Jesus taught and whose attitude to mankind was expressed in Jesus' deeds . . . the starting point and basis of the Christian use of the word "God" remains the historical figure of Jesus. . . . Under his impact we come (in some degree and at some times) to experience life in a distinctively new way, as living in the presence of the God whose love was revealed in the words and actions of Jesus.[75]

In fact, Hick declares a few pages earlier, "the believer can already have [regardless of an eschatological verification], on the basis of his religious experience, a warrant as to the reality of God." The believer thereby "may know God in a way which requires no further verification."[76]

This restriction of the logically basic knowledge and definition of God to the experience of life as being lived in the presence of the God disclosed in Jesus' loving ways is tantamount to rendering meaningless such expressions as "the infinite God" with which Hick began the passage quoted. If the believer can know conclusively, here and now, on the basis of his religious experience, the existence and nature of God, then that God would have to be continuous with the realm of human experience. If God still be called "transcendent" it would have to be in Emmet's sense, that is, "As standing for that which is 'other' than our minds—'being' or 'existence' apart from our interpretations" but still "within some situation in which we are related to" it within experience. In other words, the traditional concept of a transcendent God is relinquished; metatheological skepticism concerning it remains unchallenged.

A Nonexperiential Basis for Religious Language

But perhaps our conceptualization and its linguistic symbolization about God need not be limited to definitions derived from the religious dimension in human experience of the world. Let us look more closely at the *actual use* to which the Christian theist puts the proposition which is logically prior for his system, namely, "God exists."

The supreme object of religious worship necessarily exists

Whatever else the statement "God exists" means, it surely includes an intended reference to the supreme object of religious worship.§ Realizing this, J. N. Findlay rightly affirms such an object for the believer to be one whose "non-existence must be wholly

---

§Charles Hartshorne is strongly in favor of construing the meaning of religious language in terms of an analysis of the conceptual assumption of worship. He writes, "I have enough faith in the wisdom of belief to think that the sharper we make the implications of worship, the better it will be for the future of religion. . . . The theistic question . . . is not one more question. . . . It is, on the fundamental level, and when all its implications are taken into account, the sole question. Linguistic analysis which fails to grasp this is not . . . analysis of the basic metaphysical idea. Whether and how we conceive the God of worship, in His necessary, eternal aspect, this is all that is left when empirical accidents of the world, including language, are set aside" (*The Logic of Perfection* [LaSalle, Ill.: Open Court, 1962], pp. 131-32).

unthinkable in any circumstances'' and one who possesses his attributes in no ''merely adventitious or contingent manner.'' To be a
fully adequate object of religious worship, as linguistic descriptions
of that Being are actually used, its ''qualities must be intrinsically
incapable of belonging to anything except in so far as they belong
primarily to the object of our worship,'' explains Findlay in his
well-known article, ''Can God's Existence Be Disproved?''[77]

If Findlay's explication of the meaning of the term *God* as used
in the statement conveyed by the sentence ''God exists'' be correct,
then the logical status of that statement is such that two implications
may be drawn:

1. God's existence, and, thus, the truth of the statement of His
   existence, is a necessary condition for the contingent existence
   of anything, and thus, for the truth of any contingent statement.
2. The statement of God's existence is itself necessarily true. In
   other words, no contingent state of affairs can conceivably
   verify or falsify the statement ''God exists'' as used by the
   religious believer.

Necessary statements as arbitrary linguistic conventions.
Anyone familiar with Findlay's argument knows that he would not,
at the time he wrote this article at least, have concurred with the
above implications, if they are taken to entail God's existence and
the cognitive meaningfulness of the assertion of His existence. For
Findlay and most analytic philosophers, ''The outcome of the whole
medieval and Kantian criticism of the Ontological Proof'' is the
proper unwillingness of the ''modern mind'' to feel ''the faintest
axiomatic force in principles which trace contingent things back to
some necessarily existent source.'' Neither is it any longer difficult
''to conceive that things should display various excellent qualities
without deriving them from a source which manifests them supremely,'' he reports approvingly. Why? Because ''necessity in
propositions merely reflects our use of words, the arbitrary conventions of our language.'' Hence, to speak of God's existence as
necessary is meaningful only ''if we had made up our minds to speak
theistically *whatever the empirical circumstances might turn out to
be.*''[78] All of which brings us back to the criterion of cognitive
meaningfulness which we have earlier seen Flew enunciating,
namely, ''If there is nothing which a putative assertion denies, then
there is nothing which it asserts either: and so it is not really an
assertion.''[79]

But is the modern mind, regardless of the Humean and Kantian skepticism which may or may not underlie it, adequately reflective of the logical rules of language if, as Findlay, Flew, and the majority of analytic philosophers assume, it considers logically necessary propositions to be vacuous metaphysically?[80] What is actually meant by classifying a proposition, for example, the one conveyed by the sentence "God exists," as necessarily true? Is necessity in propositions simply a matter of "the arbitrary conventions of our language," as Findlay has just said?

Some necessary statements reflective of the state of affairs in all possible worlds. Naturally, every rationalist would vehemently reply to the last question in the negative. But even among analytic philosophers there are those repudiating the linguistic theory of logical necessity. A *locus classicus* is the work of Arthur Pap, particularly *Semantics and Necessary Truth*. The position maintained there traces any logically necessary relationship between statements to the *meanings* conveyed by the statements. Thus, logical necessity would not be dependent upon claims about language usage.[81]

But perhaps it is possible to go even further away from the "arbitrary conventions of our language" view of logical necessity than is possible through Pap's tracing of necessity to the meanings of statements. Hopefully the state of affairs in any possible world could unqualifiedly be involved, without any contingent state of affairs being needed for verification, and without appealing to the usual rationalist arguments (not that they are inherently weak, but it is better in reasoning with analytic philosophers to make as few reflective or speculative metaphysical assumptions as possible.)

According to R. C. Sleigh, Jr., there are three "intuitions" on the concept of necessity which can be discerned running through the modern discussion of that issue. The first is an epistemological intuition which, distinguishing between sensory experience as one mode of knowledge and logical necessity as another, considers either as capable of justifying our belief in a proposition. The second intuition is "metaphysical or, perhaps, semantical" and holds that a necessarily true proposition is one expressed through a sentence which is true solely by virtue of the meanings of its constituent words. So far a logical empiricist would agree with Sleigh's comment that these two intuitions are really just two ways of looking at the same thing. If experience is not the source of the justification of a proposition, then what else could be its source of justification except the understanding of the meaning of the terms of the sentence expressing it? Is not that which is true by the first intuition also true by the second, as well as the converse?

Before answering in the affirmative too hastily, however, one should be aware of a third intuition, says Sleigh. While the truth of some propositions is considered to be dependent upon the actual states of affairs which obtain in the world, the truth of others "(i.e. the necessary ones)" is independent of those states of affairs. "This suggests the idea," he infers, "that a necessary truth is a proposition that is true in all possible worlds," a concept which "has played a significant role in recent developments."

In order to illustrate the conception of necessity which is not simply a mode of a proposition *de dicto* but rather is *de re,* Sleigh cites the following:

"(1) It is necessary that 9 is greater than 7.

(2) It is not necessary that the number of planets is greater than 7.

(3) The number of planets is necessarily greater than 7."

He then observes that while in the case of the first two sentences necessity is being predicated affirmatively or negatively of a proposition, in the third case "necessity seems to be affirmed not of a proposition but rather of the connection between a certain object —the number of planets (at present 9)—and a certain property—the property of being greater than 7." Alternatively, he thinks we might wish to "read (3) as predicating the property of being necessarily greater than 7 of a certain object."[82] If Sleigh's explication be acceptable, then, without having come so far as declaring with the rationalist that the "real is rational and the rational is real," we are in a position to claim that the logical necessity of the assertion of God's existence and the contingence of all else upon Him *could* entail His existence.‖ That is, this assertion could be true in the sense that its justification is the inconceivability of its being false in any possible world.

The ontological argument for God in the logical framework of possible worlds

Within the analytic tradition, the most noteworthy attempt to

‖ Alvin Plantinga, for instance, argues for *de re* necessity in the context of the notion of possible worlds in "World and Essence" (*The Philosophical Review* 89 [1970]: 461-92. See also his *The Nature of Necessity* [Fair Lawn, N.J.: Oxford, 1974]).

argue for the necessary existence of God is Norman Malcolm's famous defense of Anselm's ontological argument.[83] While his defense has been criticized in the literature since its appearance in 1960, as someone has pointed out, the critics cannot seem to agree wherein precisely he might be at fault. However, it is Alvin Plantinga who is most concerned to establish the necessity of God's existence in the logical framework of possible worlds which Sleigh is describing.

Relying on some recent developments in the semantics of quantified modal logic, Plantinga has retracted his uniformly negative appraisal of Malcolm's reconstruction of Anselm's ontological argument in (Plantinga's) *God and Other Minds* and is now maintaining that at least one version of it is sound.[84] In other words, not only does he recognize, unlike Kant, that Anselm "claims to have an *argument* for the necessity of at least one existential proposition," but also he takes a version of it to be incontrovertibly true.[85]

His argument runs as follows:

> We suppose . . . that there is a maximal degree of greatness. We add the supposition that this maximal degree of greatness is enjoyed, in a given world, only by a being that has the maximal degree of excellence in every world. The maximal degree of excellence, furthermore, contains omniscience, omnipotence, and moral perfection. So the being who occupies this degree of greatness (supposing for the moment that there is only one) has the properties of omnipotence, omniscience and moral perfection in *W,* the world in which it attains this maximal degree of greatness, and in every other [possible] world as well. Now a being has the property of omnipotence, for example, in a given world, only if it exists in that world. This being, therefore, if there is such a possible being, exists in every world and in every world has the maximal degree of excellence. . . . Given this conception of God it is evident . . . that if it is possible at all that God exists, then it is necessarily true that he does.[86]

The point of this kind of reasoning is not that it indubitably proves the existence of God to everyone who becomes aware of the argument. An argument may be both logically valid and true, that is, sound, and yet not constitute a proof for a given person. For an argument to prove something to someone it must be persuasive. George Mavrodes calls the kind of argument which is taken to be a proof a "convincing" argument. An argument is convincing for a person when it is cogent and when that person "knows that each of its premises is true without having to infer any of them from its conclusions or from any other statement or statements that he knows only by an inference from that conclusion," explains Mavrodes.[87] He does not know of an argument for God's existence which has been accepted as a proof by everyone. Not ruling out the possibility of such an argument being formulated, however, he notes that there will have to be found "some set of propositions that everyone knows and that entail, by logical relations that are also known to everyone, that God exists."[88]

Of course, not every item of knowledge is shared universally. If someone knows something, for instance, a set of propositions which entail God's existence, there is no reason for that person to refrain from drawing the appropriate conclusion. The fact that certain other people will not grant the premises to be true does not necessarily mean that they are untrue. Suppose that someone claimed to know the existence of a maximally great being was not impossible. For such a person Plantinga's type of argument could readily become a proof of a maximally great being's existence. If, furthermore, that person believed in the existence of God, then the proof would become an item of natural theology for him.

Nevertheless, it might still be maintained that an a priori proof of a maximally great being whose excellence includes omniscience, omnipotence, and moral perfection is one proof whose crucial premise should be expected to be universally acceptable. Since not everyone accepts "the existence of a maximally great being is possible" as a premise, the cogency, for anyone, of an argument built upon it should be questioned. Surely there is enough of a point to this line of attack upon a modal ontological argument (or any other type of ontological argument) to prevent one from describing Plantinga's argument as proof of God's existence in the sense of "proof" now being discussed.

Plantinga himself recognizes the validity of placing this kind of restriction upon the epistemological pretensions of his argument. He is aware that not everyone is going to grant his "central premise," that is, "that the existence of a maximally great being is *possible*." "Still," he counters, "there is nothing *contrary to reason* or *irrational* in accepting this premise" either. What he does wish to assert about the argument is "that it establishes, not the *truth* of theism, but its rational acceptability." Thus, he is no doubt justified in thinking of it as accomplishing "at least one of the aims of the tradition of natural theology."[89]

LOGICALLY AND CONDITIONALLY NECESSARY ASSERTIONS ABOUT
THE INFINITE GOD

If, indeed, there is even one form of an ontological argument for
God which establishes the "rational acceptability" of theism (and
Plantinga's version has so far not been shown not to be successful),
then our own problem is solved. Our problem is not the demonstration of God's existence but the provision for giving a content to the
conception of God expressed in necessarily true propositions which
are neither "senseless" nor "impossible." The God whom the
believer worships is one about whom he makes what he takes to be
such necessarily true assertions as those expressed in the sentences
"God exists," "God is omnipotent," "God is morally perfect."
Although the truth of these statements is not dependent upon any
contingent state of affairs, by virtue of their being true in all possible
states of affairs, they are not vacuous. No factually true proposition
could verify or falsify them. Yet it would not be possible, as with
those thinkers holding to the verificationist criterion, to say of any of
these assertions, "It is not really an assertion." Nor is it needful to
restrict our assertions about the transcendent God, as with the
"seeing as—" or interpretation theologians, to claims about a religious dimension of the experienced world.

Moreover, because the contingency of everything else which
exists is a contingency upon God, if God be necessarily existent,
then the arguments for God's existence and aspects of His nature
from the contingency of the world, and, by implication, from certain
essential aspects of the contingent world, are confirmed and supplemented by the ontological argument. For instance, the world as a
set of dependent beings whose existence could be caused by another
being, or the world as a set of dependent beings with the particular
membership it has, require, on the principle of sufficient reason, that
not every being be dependent, that is, that an independent being, not
a member of the set, exist as the causal explanation of the set's
existence and membership.[90] The kind of being argued for here is
not, of course, logically necessary, as in the case of the ontological
argument. Bruce Reichenbach succinctly puts it thus: the cosmological argument "contends for the logically contingent, conditionally
necessary existence of a necessary being, a being which, if it exists,
cannot not exist."[91] Propositions about such a being are conditionally necessary, not logically necessary, for they are not independent
of all states of affairs in the world, as are logically necessary propositions. The two kinds of necessary propositions about God, assuming

both be granted (Reichenbach still regards all logically necessary propositions as tautologous, but we have seen some reasons to doubt whether this can be true in all cases), would then complement each other. This would allow an argument concluding to a conditionally necessary proposition about God to supplement an argument concluding to a logically necessary proposition about Him, resulting in a corresponding extension of the range of concepts applicable to God.

Referring finite concepts to an infinite God should not, therefore, pose such a problem for the empirically oriented modern mind in its understanding of, and talking about, God as has been frequently held. Concepts understandable to a finite mind but not instantiated in the finite world—for example, necessary existence, omnipotence, moral perfection—can refer to attributes of the infinite God which must necessarily be predicated of Him. And not just in case God must be thought of as the cause of those perfections which we apprehend in a mode appropriate to our finitude by virtue of the analogous being God and finite beings share, as Aquinas has it, but because it is undeniable any other way.#[92] That is, given the instantiation of these attributes, which the religious worshiper does hold, then the impossibility of their not being instantiated in any possible world leads the religious-language user to regard these attributes as predicable of God's essential nature. The logical status of all religious utterances consistent with those predications is thereby identified and established as cognitively meaningful. (What the logical status is of statements containing or reporting alleged revelations from or of God inconsistent with those predications is not clear.)

However, at least one evangelical philosopher of religion, Norman Geisler, opts for Aquinas on this point: "Once it is shown by causality *that* God is, then Aquinas can unpack *what* God is from the analogy implied in this causal relation" (*Philosophy of Religion* [Grand Rapids: Zondervan, 1974], p. 283).

Notes

1. Frederich Schleiermacher, *The Christian Faith*, trans. H. R. Mackintosh and J. S. Stewart from the 2d Ger. ed. (Edinburgh: T. & T. Clark, 1928), p. 76.
2. Harold E. Hatt, *Encountering Truth* (Nashville, Tenn.: Abingdon, 1966), p. 194.
3. Ibid., p. 196.
4. T. F. Torrance, *Theological Science* (London: Oxford, 1969), pp. 279-80.
5. W. D. Hudson, *A Philosophical Approach to Religion* (N.Y.: Harper & Row, 1974),pp. 160-61. For a development of this kind of criticism of Torrance, see Frederick Ferré, *Language, Logic and God* (N.Y.: Harper & Row,) pp. 89-93.
6. H. Kimmerle, ed., *Hermeneutik* (Heidelberg: Abhandlungen der Heidelberger Akademie der Wissenschaften, 1959), p. 79.

7. Ibid., pp. 32, 88.
8. Wilhelm Dilthey, *Gesammelte Schriften* (Stuttgart: B. G. Teubner, 1958), 5: 144.
9. Martin Heidegger, *Unterwegs zur Sprache* (Pfullingen: Neske, 1959), p. 19.
10. Ibid., p. 30.
11. R. E. Palmer, *Hermeneutics* (Evanston, Ill.:Northwestern U., 1969), pp. 49-50.
12. Hans-Georg Gadamer, *Wahrheit und Methode* (Tübingen: J. C. B. Mohr, 1960), p. 366.
13. Gerhard Ebeling, *Word and Faith*, trans. James Leitch (Philadelphia: Fortress, 1963), pp. 313, 319.
14. Ibid., pp. 318-19.
15. John Wisdom, "Gods," *Proceedings of the Aristotelian Society*, n. s., 45 (1944-45): 185-206. Reprinted in Antony Flew, ed., *Logic and Language*, first series (London: Oxford, 1951).
16. A. J. Ayer, *Language, Truth and Logic*, 2d ed. (New York: Dover, 1936), p. 13.
17. A. J. Ayer, *Language, Truth and Logic*, rev. ed. (London: Gollancz, 1946), p. 120.
18. Wisdom, p. 154.
19. See Raeburne S. Heimbeck, *Theology and Meaning* (London: Allen & Unwin, 1969), pp. 261-69.
20. R. B. Braithwaite, *An Empiricist's View of the Nature of Religious Belief* (Cambridge: Cambridge U., 1955), p. 19.
21. R. M. Hare, "Theology and Falsification," in *New Essays in Philosophical Theology*, ed. Antony Flew and Alasdair MacIntyre (London: SCM, 1955), pp. 100-102.
22. Paul van Buren, *The Secular Meaning of the Gospel* (London: SCM, 1963), p. 156.
23. Flew and MacIntyre, p. 98.
24. Ibid., p. 97.
25. See Ayer, 2d ed., pp. 18-19.
26. Flew and MacIntyre, p. 98.
27. C. I. Lewis, *An Analysis of Knowledge and Valuation* (Chicago: Open Court, 1947), quoted by Charles Landesman, ed., *The Foundations of Knowledge* (Englewood Cliffs, N.J.: Prentice-Hall, 1970), pp. 18-19.
28. Antony Flew, *God and Philosophy* (London: Hutchinson, 1966), p. 22.
29. Ibid., p. 29.
30. Ibid., pp. 39-40.
31. John Hick, *Faith and Knowledge*, 2d ed. (London: Macmillan, 1967), p. 167.
32. Ibid., p. 168.
33. John Hick, *Faith and Knowledge* (Ithaca, N.Y.: Cornell U., 1957), p. 156.
34. Heimbeck, p. 114.
35. Ibid., p. 115.
36. Ibid., p. 121.
37. Ibid., p. 117.
38. Ibid., p. 122.
39. John Wisdom, *Other Minds*, 2d ed. (Oxford: Blackwell, 1965), p. 1, n. 1.
40. Ibid., p. 2.
41. Ibid.
42. See Gabriel Marcel, *The Philosophy of Existentialism*, trans. Manya Harari, 4th ed. (New York: Citadel, 1964), pp. 13-23.
43. Michael B. Foster, *Mystery and Philosophy* (London: SCM, 1957), pp. 14-19.
44. Ibid., p. 28.
45. A similar Wittgensteinian approach is taken by W. Donald Hudson, *A Philosophical Approach to Religion* (New York: Barnes & Noble, 1974).
46. Flew and MacIntyre, p. 98.
47. D. Z. Phillips, *Death and Immortality* (London: Macmillan, 1970), p. 68.
48. Ibid.

49. Cyril Barrett, ed., *L. Wittgenstein: Lectures and Conversations on Aesthetics, Psychology and Religious Belief* (Berkeley: U. of Cal., 1966), pp. 56-58.
50. Flew and MacIntyre, p. 98.
51. Phillips, p. 71.
52. Kai Nielsen, *Contemporary Critiques of Religion* (New York: Herder & Herder, 1971), p. 38.
53. T. E. Hill, *The Concept of Meaning* (New York: Humanities Press, 1971), pp. 176, 178.
54. *E.g.*, Flew, *God and Philosophy*, pp. 28-41.
55. Gustav Bergman, *The Metaphysics of Logical Positivism* (New York: Longman, Green, 1964), p. 158.
56. Hill, pp. 200-201.
57. Ibid., p. 203.
58. See, e.g., Ronald Hepburn, *Christianity and Paradox* (London: Watts, 1958); and Stanley Obitts, "Religious Certainty and Infallibility" in *Toward a Theology for the Future*, ed. David Wells and Clark Pinnock (Carol Stream, Ill.: Creation House, 1971), pp. 275-92.
59. L. Wittgenstein, *Philosophical Investigations*, trans. G. E. M. Anscombe, 2d ed. (New York: Macmillan, 1958), pp. 193e-97e.
60. Dorothy Emmet, *The Nature of Metaphysical Thinking* (London: Macmillan, 1957), p. 215.
61. Ferré, p. 161.
62. Ibid., p. 164.
63. Ibid., pp. 164-65.
64. Frederick Ferré, *Basic Modern Philosophy of Religion* (New York: Scribner, 1967), pp. 362-63.
65. Ibid., p. 366.
66. Ibid., pp. 379-80.
67. Ibid., p. 402.
68. Anders Jeffner, *The Study of Religious Language* (London: SCM, 1972), p. 116. For a further development of this criticism see J. S. K. Ward, "Existence, Transcendence and God," *Religious Studies* 3 (1968):466.
69. John Hick, *Philosophy of Religion*, 2d ed. (Englewood Cliffs, N. J.: Prentice-Hall, 1973), pp. 93-95.
70. Ibid., p. 92.
71. Several critics are listed in a footnote by Hick, *Philosophy of Religion*, p. 90.
72. Terence Penelhum, *Religion and Rationality* (New York: Random House, 1971), pp. 137-40.
73. Emmet, pp. 13-14.
74. Ibid., p. 17.
75. John Hick, *Faith and Knowledge*, 2d ed., pp. 198-99.
76. Ibid., p. 194.
77. J. N. Findlay, "Can God's Existence Be Disproved?" *Mind* 57 (1948), reprinted in Flew and MacIntyre, pp. 47-56.
78. Ibid.
79. Flew and MacIntyre, p. 98.
80. See Bowman L. Clarke, "Linguistic Analysis and Religion," *The Monist* 47, no. 3 (Spring 1963): 379-80.
81. Arthur Pap, *Semantics and Necessary Truth* (New Haven, Conn.: Yale, 1958), pp. 179-81.
82. R. C. Sleigh, Jr., *Necessary Truth* (Englewood Cliffs, N. J.: Prentice-Hall, 1972), pp. 1-3.
83. Norman Malcolm, "Anselm's Ontological Arguments," *The Philosophical Review* 69 (1960): 41-62.
84. Alvin Plantinga, *God and Other Minds* (Ithaca, N. Y.: Cornell U., 1967), pp. 26-94.

85. Unpublished lecture entitled "God and Possible Worlds," delivered at The Council for Philosophical Studies Conference in the Philosophy of Religion, Summer, 1973, Calvin College, p. 1. See also Alvin Plantinga, *God, Freedom, and Evil* (New York: Harper & Row, 1974), pp. 85-112.
86. Ibid., p. 112.
87. George Mavrodes, *Belief in God* (New York: Random House, 1970), p. 34.
88. Ibid., p. 46.
89. Plantinga, *God, Freedom, and Evil,* p. 112.
90. See William Rowe, "Criticisms of the Cosmological Argument," *The Monist* 54, no. 3 (July 1970): 441-59.
91. Bruce Reichenbach, "Divine Necessity and the Cosmological Argument," *The Monist* 54, no. 3 (July 1970): 415. See also his *The Cosmological Argument* (Springfield, Ill.: Charles C. Thomas, 1972), especially chap. 6.
92. Battista Mondin, *The Principle of Analogy in Protestant and Catholic Theology* (The Hague: Martinus Nijhoff, 1963), pp. 85-102.

Selected Reading

Brown, Stuart C. *Do Religious Claims Make Sense.* London: SCM, 1969.

Burrill, Donald R., ed. *The Cosmological Arguments.* Garden City, N. Y.: Doubleday, 1967.

Campbell, James I. *The Language of Religion.* New York: Bruce, 1971.

Clarke, Bowman L. "The Language of Revealed Theology." *The Journal of Bible and Religion* 32, no. 4 (October 1964): 334-41.

Ferré, Frederick. *Language, Logic and God.* New York: Harper & Row, 1961.

Flew, Antony, and MacIntyre, Alasdair, eds. *New Essays in Philosophical Theology.* London: SCM, 1955.

Geisler, Norman. *Philosophy of Religion.* Grand Rapids: Zondervan, 1974.

Gill, Jerry H. "Wittgenstein and Religious Language." *Theology Today* 21 (1964): 59-72.

————. *The Possibility of Religious Knowledge.* Grand Rapids: Eerdmans, 1971.

Hartshorne, Charles. *The Logic of Perfection.* LaSalle, Ill.: Open Court, 1962.

Heidegger, Martin. "The Problem of a Non-Objectifying Thinking and Speaking in Contemporary Theology." In *Philosophy and Religion,* ed. Jerry A. Gill, pp. 59-65. Minneapolis: Burgess, 1968.

Heimbeck, Raeburne S. *Theology and Meaning.* London: Allen & Unwin, 1969.

Helm, Paul. *The Varieties of Belief.* New York: Humanities Press, 1973.

Hepburn, Ronald W. *Christianity and Paradox.* London: Watts, 1958.

Hick, John. *Faith and Knowledge.* 2d ed. London: Macmillan, 1967.

————. "Theology and Verification." *Theology Today* 17 (1960): 12-31.

Hick, John H. and McGill, Arthur C., eds. *The Many-faced Argument: Recent Studies on the Ontological Argument for the Existence of God*. New York: Macmillan, 1967.

High, Dallas M., ed. *New Essays on Religious Language*. New York: Oxford U., 1969.

Holmes, Arthur F. "Three Levels of Meaning in God-Language." *Journal of the Evangelical Theological Society*, 16:2 (Spring 1973): 83-94.

Hudson, Donald. *Ludwig Wittgenstein: The Bearing of his Philosophy upon Religious Belief*. Richmond: John Knox, 1968.

Jeffner, Anders. *The Study of Religious Language*. London: SCM, 1972.

McKinnon, Alastair. "Unfalsifiability and Religious Belief." *Canadian Journal of Theology* 12 (1966): 118-25.

Malcolm, Norman. "Anselm's Ontological Argument." *The Philosophical Review* 69 (1960): 41-62.

Mascall, E. L. *Words and Images*. New York: Longmans, Green, 1957.

Mavrodes, George I. *Belief in God*. New York: Random House, 1970.

———. "God and Verification," *Canadian Journal of Theology* 10 (1954): 187-91.

Mondin, Battista. *The Principle of Analogy in Protestant and Catholic Theology*. The Hague: Martinus Nijhoff, 1963.

Nielsen, Kai. *Contemporary Critiques of Religion*. New York: Herder & Herder, 1971.

Palmer, Richard E., *Hermeneutics*. Evanston, Ill.: Northwestern U., 1969.

Penelhum, Terence. *Religion and Rationality*. New York: Random House, 1971.

Plantinga, Alvin. *God, Freedom, and Evil*. New York: Harper & Row, 1974.

———. *The Nature of Necessity*. Fair Lawn, New Jersey: Oxford U., 1974.

Plantinga, Alvin, ed. *The Ontological Argument*. New York: Doubleday, 1965.

Ramm, Bernard. *Special Revelation and the Word of God*. Grand Rapids: Eerdmans, 1961.

Ramsay, Ian T. *Religious Language*. London: SCM, 1967.

Reichenbach, Bruce. *The Cosmological Argument*. Springfield, Ill.: Thomas, 1972.

Richmond, James, *Theology and Metaphysics*. London: SCM, 1970.

Robinson, James M., and Cobb, John B., Jr., eds. *The Later Heidegger and Theology*. New York: Harper & Row, 1963.

———. *The New Hermeneutic*. New York: Harper & Row, 1964.

Ross, James F. "Analogy as a Rule of Meaning for Religious Language." *International Philosophical Quarterly* 1 (1961): 468-502.

Santoni, Ronald E., ed. *Religious Language and the Problem of Religious Knowledge*. Bloomington, Ind.: Indiana U., 1968.

Sleigh, R. C., Jr., ed. *Necessary Truth*. Englewood Cliffs, New Jersey: Prentice-Hall, 1972.

Sumner, L. W., and Woods, J., eds. *Necessary Truth: A Book of Readings*. New York: Random House, 1969.

Spiegelberg, Herbert. *The Phenomenological Movement,* 2d ed. The Hague: Martinus Nijhoff, 1969.

Talk of God. Royal Institute of Philosophy Lectures, vol. 2 (1968). New York: St. Martin's, 1969.

Trethowan, Ian Lloyd. "In Defense of Theism—A Reply to Kai Nielsen." *Religious Studies* 2 (1966): 37-48.

Wisdom, J. O. "Metamorphoses of the Verifiability Theory of Meaning." *Mind* N.S. 72 (1963): 335-47.

Wittgenstein, Ludwig. *Lectures and Conversations on Aesthetics, Psychology and Religious Belief*. Ed. Cyril Barrett. Oxford: Blackwell, 1966.

———. *Philosophical Investigations*. Trans. G. E. M. Onscombe. New York: Macmillan, 1953.

SECULAR THEOLOGY

4

Secular Theology

by
HAROLD B. KUHN

INTRODUCTION

The development of what is popularly called secular theology parallels the radical secularization of life which came to fullness in the late 1950s. Following the close of World War II, a younger group of theologians appeared on the American scene to whom the dominant themes of God's transcendence and of man's dilemmas of anxiety, despair, and sin seemed no longer relevant to the mood of the sixties. The movement of theology during this period was largely reactive—to the waning liberalism and more especially to dialectical theology (neoorthodoxy) with its emphasis upon existential despair and faith in a God thought of as being totally other than man.

Numerous general causes lay behind the emergence of specifically secular forms of theology. On the one hand, the tremendous successes in the field of technology signaled man's growing ability to control many aspects of his existence. On the other hand, this technology had a paradoxical inability to cope with hidden and dark elements in human existence. The latter produced a feeling of alienation and desperation on the part of the younger group of theologians.

Coupled with this sense of frustration was a growing feeling that conventional Christianity was irrelevant to the emerging age. It had,

HAROLD B. KUHN, A.B., S.T.B., S.T.M., Ph.D., is chairman of the Division of Theology and Philosophy of Religion at Asbury Theological Seminary. His columns analyzing current religious thought regularly appear in *Christianity Today*.

157

so the newer theologians felt, manifested a series of crucial weaknesses. It could neither prevent World War II, nor control the events of the postwar era. Especially was the organized church criticized for succumbing to the mentality of the Cold War rather than pointing the way to a public mentality which was felt to be more in accord with the realities of the times. Again, it was maintained by the newer theologians that postwar theology had failed to give men and women of the fifties any firm footing for belief in a God concerned with the human enterprise.

Along with this, there came a blurring of the line between sacred and secular, a line which many felt to have been wrongly drawn. Younger theologians were not slow to see that professing Christians had become more and more assimilated into the secular culture and secularity of the time. Taking a cue from this, the theologians of the sixties sought a way out in terms of a more thorough secularization of life, a secularization which was to be overt rather than covert. It is almost as if these thinkers had decided to say to their elders: So you conform at nearly every point to the secularity of the times; we will take your cue and carry the process to its logical conclusion!

It seemed to these recent theologians that conventional Christianity showed a general indifference toward God, together with an increasing preoccupation with worldly affairs. This suggested, as a general conclusion, that God as traditionally understood had no relevance to modern man. They saw, no doubt quite correctly, that theologians in the liberal tradition accepted scientific judgments as superior to the insights of revealed Christianity. It seemed that these theologians had become conditioned to listen whenever science spoke. This was expressed by a tendency to accommodate doctrinal pronouncements to scientific terminology. In the meantime, Rudolf Bultmann and his academic followers had contributed to the movement toward "worldliness" in theology by their removal of Christian truth from objective verification and by the separation of religious expression from the normal usages of language.

Although the younger theologians contended that historic Christianity had failed to meet the basic problems of modern life, it would be more accurate to say (and some of the younger theologians themselves recognized this) that historic Christianity had been abandoned by major religious bodies. Thus, Christianity was applied to the issues and problems of modern life in a deformed and defective manner. It is true that the secularization and relativizing of life was retarded by the strength of some movements in orthodoxy and by some of the features of neoorthodoxy. But the major voices of the newer theology of the sixties marshalled their forces to project secular versions of Christianity as the only religious force capable of meeting the inevitable trends of today's life.

It should be noted that within the more liberal circles of postwar Christendom there were voices raised in protest against the secularizing of Christian theology. Outstanding among these who expressed concern was Professor Georgia Harkness, whose volume *The Modern Rival of Christian Faith* pointed up in careful fashion the sharp and enduring antithesis between secularism and essential Christianity. While showing an appreciation for the this-worldly, Miss Harkness sounded an able warning of trouble ahead for theology. Especially relevant was her concern that good ends not be accepted as a guarantee of the validity of any world view.[1]

Her warning went largely unheeded, and by the midsixties the advocates of a "worldly," or secularized version, of Christianity had gained the public ear and were finding acceptance in major institutions of theological education. Their popularity was enhanced by the appearance of paperbacks whose publishers had access to the public eye and mind. (Mention of some of these volumes will be made later.) The movement toward secularity in theology awaited only a radical catalyst to open a smooth path for its acceptance. Such a catalytic agent appeared in the midsixties in the death-of-God movement.

At this point, some definitions may serve to make clear what the secular forms of theology sought to accomplish. The term *secular* has both a general and a specific meaning. In general, it suggests a concentration upon the things and concerns of this present world from a base which rejects the entire order of objects and usages usually regarded as spiritual or sacred. In a more specific sense, the term suggests an outlook upon life which operates without any reference to God or to divine claims upon human life. It is this sense of the term with which the late Georgia Harkness was so deeply concerned. The secular man need not be a formal atheist; he is more accurately described as a practical atheist who lives as if there were no God. Man and human concerns lie at the heart of his thinking and striving.

The term *secularism* is more directly concerned with the theoretical in human life. It may be defined as a system of belief *and* action which rejects all forms of public religion, both of faith and of worship. It consciously avoids any expression of the religious element and finds its referent solely in this-worldly concerns and is thus usually understood to indicate a form of sociopolitical philosophy. Its major rejection is that of the element of transcendence, the supernatural.

The word *secularize* has several common meanings. In the broadest sense, it indicates a process by which things, persons, or institutions are separated from religious use or religious influence. The objective is that of making everything worldly, or unspiritual. There is an historical use of the term, in which it connoted the transfer of property or economic resources from ecclesiastical use or control to civil use and possession. This occurred, for example, when Henry VIII "secularized" church lands by separating them from churches, abbeys, monasteries, or other religious institutions and transferring the title to such lands to civil rulers or private citizens. Napoleon accomplished the same for much of the lands held by religious institutions in central Europe. A more specialized use of the term is that descriptive of the change of status of a clerical person from the "regular" (that is, one belonging to an order with a *regula,* or rule) to an ordinary, or "secular," priest not bound by monastic or other vows.

It will be seen that the secularization of theology, or the building of *secular* theologies, implies the radical severance of theology from its historic concern with things sacred. In addition, of course, it involves a restatement of theology in terms devoid of transcendent dimensions or supernatural conceptions. This necessitates a twofold procedure. First, there is a structured divesting of historic Christian supernaturalism of its essential qualities; and second, there is the erection of a pattern of theological premises based exclusively upon this-worldly concerns and considerations.

Such a theology will take its cues from secular society and will make no demands upon its followers for nonconformity. Rather, it will affirm the values of the world. Its formulators are usually reluctant to sever entirely their systems from the Protestant tradition, preferring to describe their product as "worldly Christianity." Secular theology is and must be pragmatic and socially revolutionary. The latter is a requirement of the deeper need to be innovative in order to live; for thrusts into theology upon the basis of religious concerns only would hardly attract public attention, particularly at the levels of sophistication to which it would need to address itself.

Before turning to the mainline architects of the secular theology, it seems best to give attention to the left-wing movement toward secularization known as the death-of-God theology. The "God is dead" theologians appeared as meteors in the religious sky, and while their views did not sustain themselves over a long period of time, their work did serve to prepare the public mind for revolutionary formulations of theology within less unconventional limits.

THE DEATH-OF-GOD THEOLOGY

The theological climate in America underwent a profound alteration in the mid-1960s as a result of the bold declaration by several younger theologians, "God is dead!" Major voices heard in this connection were Thomas J. J. Altizer, William Hamilton, Gabriel Vahanian, and Paul van Buren. As a part of the movement toward the secularization of theology, this theological form carried the secular claim into the marketplace, this being the result of its strongly journalistic quality. Some have indeed termed it a "paperback theology," alluding to its rapid rise to popularity and its equally rapid decline in public appeal.

It should not, however, be concluded that death-of-God theology was frivolous, nor that its advocates were merely headline-seeking eccentrics. Rather, it was a serious attempt to project a system which had deep historical roots, and which embodied serious assumptions concerning man and his world. True, the negations of the architects of this theological form were the first to catch the public eye and to capture the attention of leading journalists. No doubt the very statement "God is dead" was designed to shock the reading public and to gain notoriety for the popular features of a more serious movement.

The boldest of the thinkers proclaiming God's demise was Thomas J. J. Altizer, who at the time was a professor at Emory University. He did not invent the phrase "God is dead," for nearly a century earlier Friedrich Nietzsche in his *Thus Spake Zarathustra* had made the same announcement. Atheists and agnostics have expressed or implied the same from time immemorial, but only occasionally and at crisis points in the career of human thought is it given formal expression. And what Nietzsche did for his century, Professor Altizer did for ours.

It is significant that many elements in Friedrich Nietzsche's thought, notably that of Eternal Recurrence, are embodied in that of Thomas Altizer. Both have maintained, each in his own way, that all of reality undergoes constant destruction and re-creation through an irresistible, ongoing dialectic. Thus, they deny all forms of traditional ontology and allow for no sovereign and unconditioned Being but only a "God" who at some point in the dialectic wills His own self-annihilation.

Another assumption underlying the death-of-God theology is that of the essential identity of the divine and the human. Thus "God" would be subject to the same principles of change—of growth and decay—as are operative within all of the created world. The divine would on this basis be a committed part of the historical flux. This stands in vivid contrast to the biblical understanding of God as radically distinct from both creature and creation. The God who transcends the world and is its sovereign Lord is a scandal to Professor Altizer. He holds that after nineteen centuries man has discovered that such a God no longer exists.

When Altizer's volume *The Gospel of Christian Atheism* appeared in 1966, some were inclined to disbelieve that he maintained that God had actually *died*—that he was speaking of an ontological dying of Deity. In reply, he insists, "God has died in our time, in our history, in our existence."[2] He maintains that such men as Nietzsche grasped this in the nineteenth century and that it is the task of theologians in this century to bring it home to the masses in general and the Christian masses in particular. He goes a step further and suggests that the traditional view of God as separate from the created universe was a merely temporary form of thinking, a projection of the kind of alienation which man has felt within himself and which needs now to be overcome.

It is significant that Altizer appeals to New Testament motifs in support of his view of the actual death of God. Thus he makes a great deal of the passage in Philippians which deals with the self-emptying *(kenosis)* of Christ and the broader theme of the incarnation, as models for his view of the merging of a no-longer-living God with the world.[3] In the incarnation, he suggests, God personally annihilated himself by dissolving the distinction between himself and man.

This position involves a radical departure from the usual understanding of revelation. He frankly declares that the historic Christian understanding of authority as rooted in the Scriptures can no longer be regarded as valid. He suggests in *The Gospel of Christian Atheism* that the application of "the root radical principle" now requires a "whole new form of faith." This "faith" involves the acceptance of his view of organic development in God, by which He can assume radically new forms or even will Himself into annihilation. Thus Altizer can say that to the new form of radical theology, God must be "a perpetual and forward-moving process of self-negation, pure negativity, or kenotic metamorphosis."[4]

Altizer goes further. He maintains that the view of historic Christianity at this point is inconsistent. If one maintains that God in Christ emptied Himself of what Altizer calls "his original sacrality" in the incarnation, then one cannot consistently speak of a God who is unchangeable in his being and distinct from the world of flux. Altizer holds that if God can act in the world and its affairs, He must be One "who negates himself, gradually but decisively annihilating his own original Totality."[5]

Central to his view that God has experienced an ontological death is the assertion that He experienced that death in Christ. Altizer maintains that the *kenosis,* or self-emptying process which the incarnation involved, was an irreversible process. Note his words: "I repudiate the idea that God became man in Christ and then in some sense annulled His humanity by returning to a spiritual realm."[6] This disallows, of course, the resurrection of our Lord and His subsequent ascension and session at God's right hand.

It follows that Altizer's view of the incarnation is a radical departure from that of historic Christianity. To him, the Deity accepted self-annihilation at the cross and in Christ set in motion an entirely new form of divine activity by which redemptive forces came into operation that hitherto were not known. Thus, in Christ there come to all men new resources which were somehow unavailable to them as long as God "lived," being withheld from man so long as He remained transcendent.

Incarnation thus becomes an event of metamorphosis, in which God permanently divested Himself of transcendence, power, authority—in short of all of the qualities attributed to Him in the Christian Scriptures. In an evolving process, God passed ontologically into Christ to project some sort of new and redemptive relationship into the life of man. In His dissolution there is also dissolved all that has been historically thought concerning Him, except that which may be clearly affirmed concerning Christ. Incarnation, then, becomes a progressive movement of Deity into temporal concreteness, a movement which may be said to be dialectical in that there may be both advancing and regressive movements.[7]

In other words, incarnation as *a death of God* implies a voluntary shedding of divine transcendence and spirituality and a divine entry into immanence and fleshliness. Altizer considers this to be a movement forward, and one which embodies within itself some final goal. That is to say, there is movement toward an eschatological and ultimate transformation of all things. Altizer rejects, to be sure, any eschatology whose thrust is a future beyond this world. He has no place in his system for a *jenseits,* or "other world" beyond this one, in which either human or divine purposes are realized. Rather, eschatological goals are to be realized in man's common life here and now, in a liberated and liberating fullness, "a totality of life and energy here and now in the world."[8]

Something also needs to be said concerning Professor Altizer's use of oriental motifs in the building of his system. Here and there in his earlier writings he made reference to Eastern mysticism, especially in its relation to the language of Western religious experience. He admired Nietzsche's symbolic use of the name of Zarathustra, noting that the "new" Zarathustra was intended by Nietzsche to introduce Eastern modes of thought. The purpose was to reverse the forms of Western consciousness and to point the way to new modes for the affirmation of life which would deliver Western man from perverse forms of individualistic consciousness.[9]

Zarathustra's affirmation of the present world, expressed in his inebriate song in Part 4 of *Thus Spake Zarathustra,* afforded a sort of aesthetic rationale for the doctrine of Eternal Recurrence.[10] This may, however, have been a temporary point of emphasis for Altizer, for in his later work *The Descent into Hell,* he attempts to develop a more conventional eschatology for the godless man in terms of what he calls the New Jerusalem.

In his "new vision" of a world without God, Professor Altizer suggests that there must come a reversal of our Western ways of conceiving God and of understanding religious forms. A new world can be erected, he thinks, only as we negate all of our usual conceptions of Deity. This negation can best be effected through the acceptance of oriental ways of thinking, which will eliminate all finalistic views of God. He regards these finalistic views as rigid forms holding Western man in thrall. Our way of thinking, he alleges, shuts the door to seeing God as "the All" and to our sharing in the "eschatological All."

Altizer sees such terms as *Nirvana, Tao,* and *Ātmān-Brāhmān* as expressions of a universal totality toward which we must, with the assistance of Eastern thought, move if the eschatological New Jerusalem is to be ours. Oriental modes of thinking will, he thinks, eliminate man's moral alienation by involving the nontranscendent All in the human Fall. He views the absence of the category of the transcendent in Eastern thought not as a deficiency in Oriental ways of thinking but as an evidence of the nonuniversalism of Christianity. The West is thus held to have lost, through its adherence to particularistic modes of conceiving things, a true understanding of the primordial and undifferentiated consciousness which underlies the Eastern concept of *Nirvana*.[11] Thus, only by the assistance of the Oriental way of viewing reality can Western man shed his misleading view of an unchanging and transcendent Totality, and come to perceive through new eyes the form of consciousness which marks the New Jerusalem, or the "eschatological Christ"— distinguished, of course, from the historical Jesus.

Nirvana, as a concept, is regarded as the most effective instrument for delivering Western man from the narrow conceptualizing of the self and for returning him to the new realization of the universally conceptualized All. This suggests that it is the Buddhist vision which can wrench Western man from his particularistic self-ishness and lead him to a new form of compassion. The Buddha is regarded by Altizer as an earlier form of Christ; and to recognize the Buddha as a primordial "Christ" will, Altizer believes, help to liberate Western man from the false claims of the historic Christ and the historic Christian past. The "primordial Christ" will, he suggests, not only deliver us from the thraldom of a divine Christ, but also confer upon us a new vision of reality which can accompany our walk in the dark arena of life.[12]

It is clear that Professor Altizer is not interested in Orientalism merely as a genial alternative to Western forms of thinking. Rather he envisions it, especially with reference to the teachings of the Buddha, as an agent for a potential transformation of the Western Christian consciousness. The goal is, he believes, a mental climate structured along radically different lines from what we now find in the West, which will enable man to live in relative confidence in a world in which God has allegedly died a voluntary, ontological death.

William Hamilton identifies himself with the death-of-God theologians, but writes in a somewhat less concrete and systematized way of God's supposed demise than does Altizer. He accepts as self-evident that the understanding of God typical of both historical theology and the neoorthodox tradition is unacceptable to today's man. But he is not willing to remain among those who stand in distress before the loss of faith which is observable all about us and who deplore the temporary "silence" of God.

Against any belief in the merely short-term absence of God from man's experience, he asserts that we must not expect at any time the reappearance of the Christian God. Unlike Altizer, he does not pinpoint the dying of God at any particular point in history, but contents himself with seeing it as "a historical-cultural event in Europe and America over the last two hundred years."[13] He is concerned to bring the individual to a personal awareness of what has in fact already occurred in history. This "death" has expressed itself primarily in the substitution of nontheistic explanations for the problems confronting human life for explanations derived from historic Christian revelation. Hamilton believes that this is an irreversible trend; man must therefore come to terms with the historical-cultural death of God.

Thus he affirms God's death; and any reliance upon Him to meet any need appears to him to be futile. As a replacement, Hamilton commends the acceptance of "the secular world as normative intellectually and ethically good."[14] Thus he seeks to point the way to a reformulation of the thought of today's persons, loaded down as many are with traditional Christian formulations, in a manner which omits reference to the God of Christianity. Some of the concepts —and convictions—of today's men and women are not, he admits, susceptible to any kind of restatement. More important, Hamilton asserts that it is impossible to isolate any aspect of the self or of the experience of the self which points either to a real existence of God or to a need for God.

Professor Hamilton believes that current studies of man have laid to rest all supposed validity for the belief in a religious *a priori,* a religious givenness in man. God is no longer necessary to deliver man from restlessness, despair, or self-righteousness; indeed, there is no God to do so. Man, having come of age, should not ask God to do for him what either the world or his own intrinsic resources can do for him. Thus, he says, we must be sufficiently mature to trust the world "to be our need fulfiller and problem solver, and God, if he is to be for us at all, must come in some other role."[15]

Hamilton makes a great deal of the motif of "waiting" for God, presumably for some new appearance of evidence for His existence. In this, he rather clearly echoes the motif of Samuel Beckett's famous play, *Waiting for Godot.* In Hamilton's approach there is a distinctly negative quality, although he tries to offer some positive "picture of faith." By this he means that even though the typical Protestant—for whom he believes himself to be speaking—believes that God (and with Him, all forms of theism) is dead, yet that Protestant is seeking in the affairs and usages of *this world* that which he has lost.

Thus, the movement is twofold: today's "Christian" is at the same time turning his attention "toward the world and away from religion."[16] Denial of historic theology is balanced off, thinks Hamilton, by affirmation of the world. And he suggests that it is in the exploration of this dialectic that he "joins the death of God movement."[17] He sees the motif of hope—of waiting—as distinguishing death-of-God theologies from classical forms of atheism.

Hamilton sums up his understanding of the movement in the following terms: we must affirm God's death, since we can no longer speak with confidence of Him. We must wait for Him to reappear in a style which is credible to us in our technological age. As we await Him in our godlessness, we can take refuge in a world which can offer us a provisional definition of faith and can sustain life in the lonely interim.

Hamilton differs, of course, from Altizer in that the latter is concerned to explore what he feels to be the cosmic events which issued in the demise of God; while Hamilton is content to accept what he feels to be true, namely, that somehow God no longer lives. He is thus willing to accept the death-of-God premise and leave the antecedents to be explained by others. His more immediate concern is that of marking out the path of the appropriate life-style for what he terms the post-Oedipal phase of human experience. Now that the Father has been killed, he thinks, the intelligent Protestant must take up the classical role of Orestes, whose task is to destroy the faithless "mother who represents security, warmth, religion, authority, but who has become corrupt and an evil bearer of all that she is supposed to represent."[18] The mother must now be killed in order that the real meaning of religious devotion may be discovered. And this discovery must be made, not in devotion to the sacred, but in service to the earthly city.

Gabriel Vahanian is also regarded as one of the death-of-God theologians; but he does not offer a systematic scheme for God's demise as does Altizer, nor does he propose a creative future for the typical Protestant as does Hamilton. Much of Vahanian's work is devoted to tracing in the Christian tradition the elements which have contributed to the death of God and to investigating the lessons which Christians of the present era may draw from this.

In his work *No Other God,* Vahanian announces: "Without God, no Jesus: this is the corollary of the New Testament's without Jesus no God."[19] This implies that the "death of God" makes it impossible to return to the Jesus of history. Thus no such appeal to Jesus as some (for example, Altizer) make can offer a viable replacement for the God who has died. As Jesus was human and thus could not possess a divine nature, so only through the human can what Hamilton called metaphorically "God's holiness" be expressed in our world in our time. Vahanian is deeply concerned that the church not retreat into any form of eschatological existence either by withdrawal from the world or by expending its efforts in creating alternate structures to those providing the driving force in society. His plea is for a form of Christianity which recognizes the loss of God and which, as a consequence, exerts its influence in and through the worldly. Only through such a plan of action, thinks Vahanian, can the church justify its existence in what he confidently affirms to be the post-Christian era.[20]

Paul van Buren is usually regarded as part of the death-of-God movement, although his approach differs considerably from those of other admitted exponents of this theology, notably, Professor Altizer. Rather than attempting to discover and elaborate some cosmic and metaphysical rationale for God's death, he concerns himself with the linguistic aspect of the question. He begins with the proposition that it is today meaningless to speak of God at all; the laws of human language have rendered the very word *God* inoperative.

He bases his case for the proposition, "The *word* 'God' is dead," upon what he terms the "verification principle," by which he means that the function of a statement must determine its meaning.[21] He contends that the statement "God exists" is meaningless to the person whose attitude and approach is that of secularism, for it does not fit the standards of empirical verification. On similar grounds, Professor van Buren insists that a statement such as "God is at work in history" represents a begging of the question and must be ruled out. The crux of his argument is that real knowledge and significant meaning can be derived solely from data which are empirically verifiable. The knowledge and meaning which are indicated by God language do not meet this criterion.

Van Buren does recognize that some respectable thinkers view certain faith statements as cognitively valid. But as one committed to modern analytic philosophy, he freely admits that his mode of thinking rules out both any religious *a priori* and an acceptance of what he terms "simple literal theism."[22] He also maintains that his method of linguistic analysis is a legitimate (perhaps the *only* legitimate) one for the articulation of a religion of secularity, which is demanded by the end of the era of God talk (see chap. 3). This method must be frankly empirical and as such can and must afford a new "language of faith" for the man and woman trained to think in the categories of modern technology.

In his quest for the secular meaning of the Gospel, van Buren turns to the person of Jesus. While recognizing that the older quest for the historical Jesus ended in an impasse, he is hopeful for the results of the renewed quest undertaken by such scholars as Günther Bornkamm and Gerhard Ebeling. He himself sees the "Easter event" as crucial for our understanding of Jesus.[23] This event seems to him to account for the new faith and the new freedom which the disciples manifested—a freedom which they are said to have acquired from Jesus by a process of contagion.

Statements of faith such as are found in the New Testament are held to issue from a particular way of viewing the world. This means that as men's perspectives upon the world change, the verbal expressions of faith must also change. Van Buren sees his task as one of discovering what may be asserted within the limits of the terms which carry meaning for today's man. Basically a linguistic theologian, Professor van Buren does not rely upon any metaphysical "death of God" (or rather, any "death of a metaphysical God"). Like Altizer and Hamilton, he holds that little has been lost in the loss of God to modern man. Unlike them, he finds God's disappearance to occur primarily in the realm of the thinking and language of modern secular man.

It is possible to question whether van Buren has even accepted the ontological existence of a deity at all. For van Buren "God" seems to have been a construct of the imaginative powers of men who needed a referent for elements of the unexplained in their environment. Thus God talk would only make sense among men and women who had not yet come of age.[24] The inconsistency in van Buren's theological formulation lies in his insistence on the one hand upon the actual improbability of God's existence and on the other hand upon commitment to Jesus—the Jesus of the Easter event.

Perhaps enough has been said concerning death-of-God theology, or better, the death-of-God theologies. Their formulators were concerned with the secular as something of a by-product of their central contention—that God has died in our time. Altizer had for his central thrust the ontological or metaphysical death of God in the course of the incarnation and subsequent death of Jesus. Van Buren was interested primarily in God talk—its earlier role among those who had not yet come of age and the manner in which recent events have rendered it at best meaningless and at worst a detriment. William Hamilton and Gabriel Vahanian seem to stand somewhere between the positions held respectively by Altizer and van Buren.

It is frequently asked why the death-of-God theologies vanished from the scene almost as rapidly as they appeared. With respect to Altizer's contention that a transcendent God had emptied Himself into a Jesus who had then died and was not raised from the dead, it was too lacking in theological content to be interesting. Indeed, it was not altogether new, for the second- and third-century Modalists advocated views remarkably similar to his. Van Buren's view of an alleged death of God which is said to follow an outmoding of God language seems to many but a pale copy of the more thorough work of Rudolf Bultmann in his demythologizing of biblical language and terminology (see chap. 2).

Finally, attempts to erect systems of theology upon the supposed ruins of a revelation which is rejected run counter to what has been deeply felt by the Christian community. More important still, such systems have an opponent which they refuse to see or to acknowledge—namely, the dynamic which is inherent in the inspired Word, the dynamic of the Holy Spirit, who was the agent of its inspiration.

Death-of-God theologies, which are really antitheologies, did serve to stimulate other quests for alternatives to historic Christian faith. In this sense they served as catalysts to shatter dominant theological patterns, notably the pattern of neoorthodoxy. And in this role, they gave impetus to new attempts at nonevangelical formulations.

"MAN COME OF AGE"—DIETRICH BONHOEFFER

Dietrich Bonhoeffer caught the imagination of the Christian world by his courageous stand against Hitler's regime and his resultant imprisonment and execution. However, it is not accurate to call Bonhoeffer a Christian martyr: he was a Christian who became a martyr for a patriotic and political cause. This does not detract from the heroism with which he witnessed to his convictions; nor does it give endorsement to some of the theological positions which he assumed, particularly during the last year of his life.

There is an earlier and a later Bonhoeffer. The earlier works from his hand were well reasoned and well structured. One thinks especially of *The Cost of Discipleship* and *No Rusty Swords* as typical of these. On the other hand, he made statements in his diaries and letters, collected and published under the title *Letters and Papers From Prison,* which seem to have been projected only as a basis for discussion. They were quite evidently the result of the frightful pressures under which he existed from day to day in the prison at Tegel.

His most frequently quoted statement speaks of mankind having now "come of age." Consequently, either we no longer need God, or we must learn to live without God.[25] This implies that we must now rely only upon our own resources, upon that which our environment and our society afford us. These and related expressions spread like wildfire in the sixties and were adopted by younger theologians as cornerstones for the erection of entire theological structures. In retrospect, one is amazed at the ability of a few slogans, accepted uncritically, to galvanize a generation of theologians into system building.

One wonders also how a prisoner of the Nazis could speak of the era of nightmarish holocaust, with its gas ovens and crematories, as one in which man had reached maturity. It is possible that he spoke metaphorically and really meant that mankind, regardless of readiness for acting responsibly, was at that moment thrust upon its own resources. But in either case, it seems at this distance that the theologians who seized upon Bonhoeffer's later statements as clues to an entire theology ought to have taken into account his situation as a prisoner of the Nazis.

But it cannot be denied that Bonhoeffer furnished major slogans for the secular theologians. "Man must now get along without God," they declaimed. "Mankind can no longer turn to God either for answers to its questions or for supernatural assistance in its moral and spiritual emergencies," was the watchcry. Nor did any large measure of Bonhoeffer's anguish enter into the proclamations of the theologians of secularity. Rather, to the query, Are you ready for the bearing of the challenge and able to carry its responsibilities? the secular theologians manfully replied, "We are ready, and we are able!"

All but forgotten were the voices emphasizing man's basic

alienation from God, from himself, and from society. Forgotten for the moment, too, were the perils of depersonalization and standardization of life in a technological society. Leaders in the religious life of the nation were ready to accept and affirm worldliness as a norm and life in modern, urban society as conducive to human fulfillment in the best and highest sense. This implied not only that language about God was of questionable meaningfulness, but that the very existence of God was problematic—so problematic that modern man could no longer look upon God as relevant to his life or as a viable resource for his living.

This is not to say that Bonhoeffer was a systematic thinker; to the contrary, he was frequently inconsistent with himself. John A. Phillips points out that his later writings appear to be retractions of what he had written earlier. But it is from these later writings that the rationale for the secular forms of theology was drawn.

In addition to the motif of "man come of age," the secular theologians have made much of Bonhoeffer's statements concerning a proposed "religionless Christianity."[26] The more precise designation of what he meant by this phrase is regarded to be "the non-religious interpretation of biblical concepts."[27] Interpreters have considered this notion, shortened to the form "religionless Christianity," to be the major thrust of his writings from prison —writings which were produced under the greatest pressure and which were not subject to revision and clarification. But whether or not Bonhoeffer would have wished to have seen this slogan regarded as typical of his whole thinking, it has been virtually so. However, his writings do have a certain woolliness about them which made misinterpretation easily possible.

In his letter of April 30, 1944, written from the prison in Tegel, he declares: "We are proceeding towards a completely religionless time; men simply, in the condition they are now in, cannot be religious any more."[28] To be sure, one must take into account what Bonhoeffer meant by the term "religious." He felt that mankind, and especially mankind under Christendom, had been mistaken in supposing that it possessed any special capacity or set of capacities which may be specifically labeled as religious—that there is such a thing as a religious *a priori*. He assumed that those who profess to be religious in the traditional sense are really maintaining that religion is man's quest for God. Bonhoeffer drew from this the conclusion that such "religiousness" would render revelation unnecessary. Thus he held that for the present age, true Christianity must reject all of the forms and expressions which belong to mere religiousness; and, by moving beyond religion, lay hold of a Christ who can "become the Lord even of those with no religion."[29]

It is small wonder that expressions such as these were misunderstood. Bonhoeffer's dialectical method was obscure; and it was easier for the secular theologians to derive slogans from his statements than to follow them through to understand what he really meant to say. And in the shuffle, Bonhoeffer's call for "the nonreligious interpretation of biblical concepts" became lost. What has survived is his presumed call to a nonreligious interpretation of the entire phenomenon of Christianity, one in which the transcendent dimension becomes lost. His careful work, found in his earlier writings, emphasizing the centrality of Christ has been set aside in favor of the more spectacular and titillating emphases upon worldliness which mark the later writings, particularly the *Letters*.

Nor was his emphasis upon worldliness the same as that which came to characterize the forms of secular theology professing to extend his theological emphasis. To Bonhoeffer worldliness meant primarily a worldly discipleship in which life was lived responsibly "under the aspect of God as the ultimate reality."[30] Through the responsible disciple, the reality of God as found in Jesus Christ is expressed in the world. In belonging to Christ, one may stand completely in the world as a witness to Christ's reality in a role of selfless deputyship. Both self and action must be devoted to God, and from that devotion will spring the responsible quality of discipleship.

The theologians who, professing to take their cue from Bonhoeffer, elaborated a "theology of worldliness" failed to take time and effort to understand the deeper meaning of his advocacy of a worldly discipleship. Seizing upon his rejection of a view of God as a stopgap invoked to fill up the incompleteness of human knowledge, (that is, a "God of the gaps"), they failed to understand him when he spoke of the "polyphony of life," by which every aspect of life, whether painful or agreeable, is a part of a unity as it is related to God. This implies that to Bonhoeffer, *worldliness* signified a rigorous and disciplined attempt to live in the world as Christ's deputy.

It is significant that the most radical theologians of the sixties claimed to ground some or much of their work in Bonhoeffer. As mentioned earlier, most of them have limited their references to the *Letters and Papers from Prison*. They seized upon the ambiguous statements which mark these writings, and failed or refused to acknowledge many of his major positions. To him, God was the living God, incarnate in Jesus Christ who brought the reality of the beyond into our common life. They failed somehow to recognize his emphasis upon the church, which through faith and obedience is to be transformed into an agent of authentic mission in the world.

Had he lived until our own day, no doubt Bonhoeffer would have revised much of what appears in the *Letters,* particularly those written in April, May, and June of 1944. Quite probably he would have scarcely recognized the image of himself which the theologians of secularity have presented. Certainly he would not have agreed with the gloomy lamenting of those who adopted, as a point of departure for "doing theology," the nonexistence of God. Nor would he have consented without protest to being interpreted as "all things to all theologians."

At the same time, Bonhoeffer did make statements which were ambiguous in the extreme, and which left an opening for misapplication. His untimely death prevented the elaboration of the many-sidedness of his thought and of the wide range of topics which engaged his mind, particularly in the days of his enforced physical inactivity. The fact remains, however, that the secular theologians found inspiration and impetus from his statements, although not without what seems to many an outrageous prooftexting of them. It is the themes which were thus drawn from him which were germinal to the work, not only of the death-of-God theologians, but also of the more moderate architects of the secular theologies which have engaged the attention of the Christian public since about 1960.

"HONEST TO GOD"—JOHN A. T. ROBINSON

The genial Bishop of Woolwich, concerned as he was that God was no longer real for today's secular person, drew inspiration especially from Rudolf Bultmann and Dietrich Bonhoeffer. With Bultmann, he contends that the Christian Scriptures are inextricably bound up with a hopelessly antiquated view of "a three-decker universe."[31] Even though the thought of a God "up there" may have been replaced by a metaphysical conceptualizing of a God "out there," Bishop Robinson holds that today's man cannot utilize *any* spatial or quasi-spatial placing of God without embarrassment. He would prefer, if it were possible, that contemporary man might "live with" some such localization of God (in a figurative sense) while at the same time continuing to think as a scientifically oriented person.

He feels, however, that this would be asking too much of

today's man, to whom the concept of a God who is localized *anywhere* is "more of a stumbling-block than an aid to belief in the Gospel."[32] His proposal is that we may well need to suspend the use of traditional theological language for a generation or two and, in its place, offer modern men and women a perception of God as being here on earth, in the midst of our common life.

Basic to his "revolutionary theism" is the contention that no supposed arguments for God's existence will avail to tell us what God, as ultimate reality, actually is. Our problem will therefore be that of locating and identifying that ultimate reality. With Paul Tillich, he rejects the traditional supernatural formulation of Christianity in terms of a God as sovereign Being who transcends the world and governs it according to His purposes. In other words, he is willing to surrender the view of God as a self-existent entity and to join hands with the naturalistic philosopher who holds that the term *God* is interchangeable with the term *universe*.[33]

The question arises whether in this view it is not superfluous to speak of God at all. In other words, it is the historically held propositional truth of Christianity that is at stake. Or, to say it another way, Bishop Robinson believes that the words in which truth has been expressed in the past are no longer acceptable. But, he is saying, truth persists, and the faithful theologian must be honest with himself in recognizing that traditional ways of saying Christian things do not give the appearance of plausibility to the outsider. Thus honesty demands a kind of Christian radicalism in the manner in which the Evangel is expressed.

Immediately upon the publication of *Honest to God* the question was raised whether Robinson ought in honesty to remain in the church at all. In reply he suggested that Jesus Himself had shocked adherents of the established religion of His day by moving outside the institutional structures which had hardened into something other than that which God had intended.[34] Robinson proposed instead a kind of Christian radicalism, which he defined in terms of the primeval meaning of the term as found in the Latin *radix,* meaning "root." He would challenge an adventuresome few to go to the root of the issues involved and to be men "of roots."[35]

In this verbal usage, Robinson gave to the secular theologians a term which they came to use and cherish. They termed their forms of theological formulations "radical theologies," and the type of Christian expression which they developed they liked to call "Radical Christianity." The aim, as stated by the secular theologians beginning with Bishop Robinson, was the expression of what is permanent in historic Christian faith in terms congenial to men and women whose thought categories were those of the new knowledge.

There was a carefully considered strategy in Robinson's mind as he released his epoch-making volume. It was that of dealing with the honest seeker after religious answers from *within* the Church, rather than compelling him to look for them outside the Christian orbit.[36] What he may have failed to see, at least in the beginning, was that his *Honest to God* was quite as much an airing of his own doubts as an affirmation of the faith to which he claimed allegiance.

Robinson's theological mentors were primarily three: first, Rudolf Bultmann, with his emphasis upon "demythologizing" the Christian message to make it acceptable to modern men and women; second, Dietrich Bonhoeffer, particularly in his emphases upon "man come of age" and "religionless Christianity"; and third, Paul Tillich, with his emphasis upon God as the object of "ultimate concern" and as being the "Ground of our being."[37] This afforded him a wide field within which to range, and he utilized it skillfully. The result is a kind of intricate, theological interweaving.

Basic to his formulation is the view that traditional images of God, based upon antiquated world views and fantasy, must go and must be replaced by one congenial to the depth psychologists. It is at this point that he finds Paul Tillich helpful, for in place of a God "up there" or "out there," Tillich would locate God somewhere within the depths of human personality. This position would involve abandonment of Christian supernaturalism (Robinson, following Tillich, calls it *supranaturalism)* and the replacement of traditional theism with the change of symbolism implied by the new category of "depth."[38] This would, he felt, correct the situation to which Bonhoeffer called attention, in which God is regarded simply as a deus ex machina.[39]

The "depths" of human personality, to which both Tillich and Bonhoeffer make reference, are regarded by Robinson to be not only the last available locus for the "divine" but as well the intimate and private world in which all, in their quiet moments, try to find refuge and solace. It is as if even those who suppose themselves to be totally secular will, if rightly instructed, discover God at hand and available.

This represents the surrender of God's self-existence and transcendence. Professor E. L. Mascall of the University of London calls attention to the fact that the motif of depth is scarcely new and that Robinson might have discovered it in the *Confessions* of St. Augustine rather than in Tillich.[40] It needs to be noted in this connection that Robinson does not feel that he is abandoning Christian transcendence. Rather, he suggests, he is aiming to "validate the idea of transcendence for modern man."[41]

Just what he believes God to be is not wholly clear from his writings. But he comes near to affording a definition in his volume, *Exploration into God*. His words are:

> If one had to find a label to replace that of traditional "theism," I would fall back on . . . "panentheism." This is defined by the Oxford Dictionary of the Christian Church as "the belief that the Being of God includes and penetrates the whole universe, so that every part of it exists in him, but (as against pantheism) that his Being is more than, and is not exhausted by, the universe.[42]

This is a rather clear reflection of the language of process theology. In *Honest to God*, he quotes with approval Norman Pittenger, one of the architects of this theological form, and suggests further that something of this kind of definition has been a part of "popular Christianity."[43]

In the same connection, he does raise the question whether to sacrifice divine transcendence would mean the abandonment of Christianity. To save the day, he suggests, it will be necessary to show that popular ideas of transcendence may be abandoned without the loss of what is vital to the Christian understanding of things. As an alternative to popular views of transcendence, he suggests that a view which preserves the essence of the matter would be the following: theological statements, properly drawn, do not analyze or describe "the highest Being" but afford "an analysis of the depths of *all* experience 'interpreted by love.'"[44]

In other words, Robinson proposes that the Christian world reject all conceptualizations of God, presumably including that derived from our understanding of Jesus Christ.[45] At stake here is the question of whether we may regard God in rational terms at all, or whether any attempt so to regard Him is idolatry, the creating of a deity in our own image. He uses what he believes to be the New Testament language concerning Jesus Christ as an argument against the "supranaturalistic view of Christ."[46] By picking and choosing passages and versions, he asserts, "Jesus never claims to be God, personally."[47] By sleight-of-hand statements (as it seems to this writer) he drains from the words of the New Testament that which has usually been regarded as their major thrust and leaves us with a Jesus who "by being utterly transparent to him" (God) somehow reveals Him.[48]

The appeal here, as was the case in the formulation of Altizer, is to the kenotic theory of Christology—the self-emptying of our Lord.[49] Robinson gives to the passage in Philippians 2 a turn of meaning which is, to say the least, open to question. His contention is that our Lord, in becoming man, emptied Himself of Himself until He was literally nothing "in himself" so that He could be a *Bringer* of God to man.[50] And as intrinsically *nothing,* so Bishop Robinson writes, "he discloses and lays bare the Ground of man's being as love."[51]

In defense of this view, he quotes the well-known statement of Dietrich Bonhoeffer, that in Christ God permitted Himself to be "edged out of the world and on to the cross."[52] Robinson appeals to Bonhoeffer's slogan, that Jesus is "the man for others," to support his view that He was not God incarnate, but one "in whom Love has completely taken over" and who is thus man's pioneer in the matter of the uniting the self with the "Ground of being."[53]

This is a radical reinterpretation of Christology, a restatement of what the Christian has always understood Jesus Christ to be which in reality drains that understanding of all supernatural and transcendent elements. Robinson's view is totally opposed to the historical conception of Jesus Christ as the eternal Son, who for us men was made flesh and lived among us—without at the same time ceasing to be God. This has been the faith of the church, and it is this which was not only stated in the New Testament but also defended in the early councils of the church.[54] It is at this point that the radical disagreement between Robinson and historic Christianity becomes most evident.

It is here also that the essentially secular quality of Robinson's thinking becomes apparent. Not only does he propose to strip Christianity down to the bare essentials and rid the Christian movement of what he regards to be excess baggage; he proposes in reality to drain it of its essential content. For he not only seeks to divest Jesus Christ of all that has been historically thought concerning His otherness from man (that is, His deity); but as well, he seeks to reduce human redemption to a matter of pursuing the example of a "man for others" in becoming one with the Ground of our being. It is this which Robinson terms a secular form of both atonement and resurrection.[55]

As a sequel to this, Robinson develops what he calls a "worldly holiness." Underlying his understanding at this point is his view of worship and prayer as basically human activities. He has little patience with any view of the life of devotion which calls for periods of withdrawal from life's busyness for a replenishment of spiritual energies. Thus he would reject emphasis upon the interior life and its cultivation. Here he follows the alleged emphasis of Bonhoeffer.

In reinterpreting the role of prayer, Robinson plays down the personal aspect, by which one "goes into his closet." He suggests that in the solution of problems about which Christians have traditionally prayed, the better way is to work these problems through by participation in them. Now, it cannot be denied that in many cases problems do yield best to treatment by those who identify themselves sympathetically with both the problem and the persons involved. One asks, however, whether most of us do not need prayer to enable us to do this—to afford us perspective on issues, and more important, to find God's providential assistance in resolving them.

In his treatment of prayer, Robinson has criticisms and suggestions which are very much to the point. Prayer can be a substitute for action, an exercise in escape from responsibility. Prayer ought to issue in an openness of the one who prays, toward God and toward others. But to equate prayer with action, and to define it exclusively in terms of openness without recognition of the One to whom we must be open, gives the evangelical great concern.[56] Similarly, worship should serve to sensitize us to the world's needs and to the deep hurts which those about us carry. But worship which does not spring from a relation of awesome devotion in the presence of a transcendent One will, it is to be feared, be little more than a humanistic exercise.

Robinson seems in his discussion of "worldly holiness" to be a prisoner to one of the foibles of Bonhoeffer. The fuzziness of the definition of *religion,* with which both men begin, and the ill-defined proposition of "religionless Christianity" lead Robinson to conclusions which are questionable at best. Granted, all sorts of evasions and hypocrisies may grow out of self-centered uses of prayer and worship. But it is questionable whether the radical humanizing of these is an acceptable Christian answer to the problem.

The evangelical who looks carefully at the volume *Honest to God* will without doubt conclude that its writer has indeed attempted to be fearlessly honest in facing the intellectual and religious difficulties confronting modern men. He will appreciate the personal honesty of the bishop as he reveals much of his own spiritual pilgrimage. But he will also, we think, feel profoundly that Robinson overestimates the adequacy of the values of modern science and the society which they engender. After all, values need to be validated; and it is highly questionable whether they carry within themselves the authentication which *Honest to God* assumes.

Man in our age has frequently found in technological modes of thought that which feeds his own pride, only to discover later that technology turns back upon him. Far from affording him a firm ground of assurance, the values of the secular age tend to produce public and private anxiety on a wide scale. This seems to suggest not only that man needs a God who exists as sovereign Lord of the universe, but that God still is in the business of bringing down the lofty and the prideful from their seats. For this, Robinson's version of secularism has no eyes and no ears. But the old German proverb "He who does not hear must feel" seems still to hold good. We may today be on the verge of learning much the hard way.

"THE SECULAR CITY" — HARVEY G. COX

None of the secular theologians made greater use of the paperback market than did Harvey Cox, the Victor S. Thomas Professor of Divinity at Harvard University. His volume *The Secular City,* which appeared in 1965, was an instant best seller and gained an immediate readership. The work had the advantage of a lucid style and a warm geniality. The metaphor underlying the work was appealing; the technopolis, or city emerging from the age of technology, was made the symbol of an age and of a quality of life which is emerging all about us.

Professor Cox opens with the assertion that the city is both the symbol and the agency of secularization—of turning the attention of man away from what has formerly been regarded as sacred toward the affairs of this world and this time. This he equates with what Dietrich Bonhoeffer called "man's coming of age."[57] To Cox, the modern city is the cutting edge of an era in which religious concerns have little or no place and in which men and women no longer look for guidance or meaning in religion. Assuming that religion is a product of social and economic patterns, he sees technopolitan existence as producing a mentality to which religious matters and concerns are superfluous. The city is the agency for secularization in our time.

One cannot understand Cox's thinking without a grasp of his

understanding of the process of secularization and the forces which produced it. Beginning with primitive man, who is assumed to have regarded all of nature and indeed all of his environment as "sacred," he traces the course of desacralization. Understanding secularization to be a process by which man is liberated "from religious and metaphysical tutelage," he lists a series of events, symbolized by biblical concepts and actions, which removed the "religious tinge" from human life.[58]

To his view, the concept of creation served to "disenchant" nature by separating nature from God. The account of the Exodus seems to him to indicate a process of desacralization of politics, by which Pharaoh was shown to be divested of divine qualities and by which the perceptions of Israel were altered. With exceptions (in the form of backslidings), Israel then no longer regarded rulers as exercising any divine right; God had withdrawn from politics and had left political responsibility with man.[59] Similarly, Cox feels that the events at Mt. Sinai brought a "deconsecration of values" in the light of which no set of religious values can be said to possess intrinsic and permanently binding force.

Of major importance is Professor Cox's view that the Judeo-Christian tradition has led the way in the process of secularization. Man has been left on his own through the desacralization of nature, politics, and values; but he has yet to work his way through what Cox calls "massive residues of magical and superstitious world-views."[60] These are elements which have been held over from earlier cultural periods, chief among which is man's "fascination with other worlds—astrological, metaphysical or religious."[61] He believes that the Christian community is to serve as an "exorcist" to rid men and women of bondage to these demonic distortions.

Cox links together his view of the mission of the Christian heritage to desacralize human life with Bonhoeffer's view of "man come of age," adding to the latter's assertion a confident expectation that Christianity, as Cox understands it, will finally eliminate the element of the religious from the mind of modern man. He is not an avowed adherent of the death-of-God theology (-ies); but with respect to God's supposed demise his view has closer affinities with the views of van Buren than with the metaphysical position of Altizer. That is to say, he feels that language by which God is understood as One to lean upon for help or to be invoked to solve personal problems is no longer persuasive to technopolitan man.

Thus it is the concept of God as One who serves to explain metaphysical mysteries which has died, not a violent death, but a death by irrelevance.

Since with Professor Cox, as well as with Bishop Robinson (and Paul Tillich) God can no longer be localized "up there" or "out there," then where is He? Dr. Cox would answer that He is exactly where He should be—right here on earth. He feels that whenever religion in general, or Christianity in particular, has polarized God and the world, regarding God to be good and the world evil, it has taken a wrong turn. He opposes any view of transcendence, which places God over and above the world, or any view which would locate Him somewhere in a cloistered retreat. It is this world in which God is to be found, for the secular world is seen to be the proper sphere for His work of liberation.

The "secular city" is to Cox the arena within which all liberating and renewing activity among men and women is to be found. To him the word *secular* is both up-to-date and praiseworthy. The removal of all significant areas of human life from bondage to the "sacred" presents mankind (and especially urban mankind) with a unique historical opportunity to find emancipation and fulfillment. It is within the experience of technopolitan man that "the hiddenness of God" may come to disclosure.[62] This disclosure may come in terms of creative social change or in the production of team relationships in which men and women may find God in interpersonal I-You encounters.

It is time to ask the question, In what ways is the theological form proposed by Harvey Cox to be understood as secular? First of all, he rejects any "two-level" perception of the world—any dualism of supernatural *vs.* natural, or of grace *vs.* nature. Any return to such dualistic ways of thinking is regarded as a regression to a pattern of dependency. Rather, he sees the role of theology in the coming urbanized society as one of freeing man from all dependence upon either religious or metaphysical understandings of God. He calls technopolitan man to "accept the full weight of this world's problems as the gift of its Maker."[63] Thus, the this-worldly is to be the focus of interest, and any so-called spiritual realm is to be viewed with suspicion. Any recourse to such a realm is alleged to represent a return to bondage to "principalities and powers."[64]

Again, the secularity of his system appears in his summons to the reader (presumably the Christian reader) to join him in the affirmation of "technopolitan man in his pragmatism and in his profanity.''[65] By "profanity" he does not mean the use of the divine names as expletives. Rather he has in mind the classical understanding of the term, by which *pro-fano* suggested those things which were left before the temple as the worshiper entered. Thus the "profanity" of the dweller of the secular city would be an attitude which rejects the dualism of sacred vs. secular and understands all things in terms of the priority and legitimacy of the nonsacred.

The life-style of the man and woman of the technopolis would thus be one of urbane worldliness unmixed with religious or metaphysical concerns. Each would be free to develop whatever pattern of life seems most likely to lead "to the maturation of persons."[66] Presumably the binding force of what have been historically regarded as moral norms will no longer be felt; for in the secular city, freedom, supported by almost total privacy, will be the order of the day. The church, if it is to minister to persons of secular life-style, must itself "assume a secular style."[67]

The rationale for this, as Professor Cox suggests in *God's Revolution and Man's Responsibility,* is that in the incarnation God voluntarily secularized Himself by laying aside "his religiousness, his divine attributes and taking upon himself the form of a servant."[68] This is, to be sure, a novel interpretation of our Lord's coming into the world, particularly in the light of the statements in the gospels to the effect that He was in a vital sense not of this world. It neglects the rather wide variety of biblical statements concerning our Lord's deity and the manner in which His teachings and His mandates challenged the earthbound thinking of His contemporaries.

One looks in vain in the pages of *The Secular City* for any expression of vital concern for the transcendent element in man —the element which from time immemorial he has intuited as surviving death and projecting itself (or being projected) into a life beyond the frontiers of this world. While one cannot read too much into silence, it seems clear from the context of Cox's thinking that he is not particularly concerned with this. Supporting evidence for this can be found in the fact that he nowhere suggests that any well-adjusted citizen of the secular city would concern himself with this question.

It seems clear, rather, that to Cox man's ultimate duty is that of partnership with God in living creatively within the technopolitan context. He seems to feel that the eschatological idea formerly expressed in terms of the Kingdom of God must now be considered to be assimilated into the concept of the secular city. Here, it seems, God wishes man to be interested not in Him but in other people. Thus the futuristic thrust of historic Christianity has been absorbed into thinking concerning the present.

God talk must, to this view, be held no longer within the framework of religious or metaphysical concerns but in terms of the language of politics. (Here he means the language of the *polis,* or city; *politics* would thus concern itself with the affairs of the secular metropolis as man's best achievement.) Professor Cox writes, "In secular society politics does what metaphysics once did. It brings unity and meaning to human life and thought."[69] Quoting Gerhard Ebeling, he suggests, "Worldly talk of God is godly talk of the world."[70]

Such talk must be, he thinks, in the language of action. It occurs at the vocal level as we talk of man as God's active partner in human affairs. But it also occurs as we stand in the picket line or work in other ways for the betterment of mankind. Thus in speaking of human affairs and human concerns, we are really as Christians addressing secular man in God language.

All of this has profound implications for Christian experience. Cox insists that man is not to become fascinated with God Himself. As for Jesus Christ, Cox sees no future in any theological formulation based upon God's act in sending His Son. He quotes with approval Bonhoeffer's affirmation, "In Jesus God is teaching man to get along without Him, to become mature, freed from infantile dependencies, fully human."[71] Nothing is said concerning repentance, concerning faith in the Lord Jesus Christ, concerning the new birth, or concerning the gift of eternal life.

It is at this point that Harvey Cox's secularism comes into direct and final conflict with historic Christianity. Between his perception of the Christian message and the historic Evangel there is an irreconcilable difference. Making the secular metropolis the paradigm for whatever doctrine of the Kingdom of God modern man can accept, he rules out the whole dimension in man which requires a Saviour.

A GENIAL CRITIQUE—JOHN MACQUARRIE

The most pertinent criticisms of a movement frequently come from those who are in some measure a part of it. John Macquarrie is variously classified as a secular theologian and as a process theologian. Actually he is not easy to classify, but he has made sufficient identification with the secular style in theology to deserve to be heard as one evaluating it. His most detailed assessment is found in his work *God and Secularity* (volume 3 of the series New Directions in Theology).

Within the context of a basic appreciation, Macquarrie offers a shrewd analysis of the secularizing movement in today's theology. Following a sketch of the background of secularization, especially in the use of Bonhoeffer's "latest and most fragmentary utterances," he traces the general intellectual history of many of the secular theologians, noting that many of them are "disillusioned Barthians."[72] These, he suggests, are in revolt against the neoorthodox understanding of God's transcendence.

Chapter 3, entitled "The Secular Outlook," offers a careful statement of the basic qualities and objectives of secular theologies. Rather than define secularism, he prefers to describe the mind-set of the secular man. This mind-set centers in the view that only this world exists or is worthy of our attention. The interests of secular man include the whole range of cultural phenomena as they express purely human endeavor. He creates his own values and gladly accepts the task of working out his own salvation—or any salvation which he may need.

Macquarrie's conclusion at this point is that Christianity would forfeit its very heart if it were to come to terms in any full sense with the secularist. In a rather definitive statement, he asserts that Professor van Buren, in *The Secular Meaning of the Gospel,* has capitulated to the secular mind to a degree which would abolish Christian faith.[73] He maintains, further, that the secular theologians operate from the base of a false and artificial severance between sacred and secular. He also challenges Cox's view that it was primarily the Judeo-Christian heritage which served to secularize our Western outlook, pointing out that this secularization has come from a complex of causes, notably from Hellenism.[74] He criticizes Cox's extravagant praise of secularity, placing him among those who have pushed the case for secularization so far as to deny Christian faith.

Macquarrie asserts that the church best serves the world not by surrendering to it but by a dialectic of acceptance and rejection. This involves acceptance of what is valid and rejecting the false claims for, and unrealistic forms of, human autonomy. He offers a stern critique of "religionless Christianity," especially its ambiguous and doctrinaire character. Recognizing some of the secularists' objections to religion, he challenges them to offer a viable equivalent for such concepts as sin and grace and warns them against the latent and subtle pride concealed within their premises.[75]

Professor Macquarrie seems to opt for process theology as affording the most viable link between God and today's mentality and as affording the best bridge to the secular mind. He sees it as superior in this regard to either existentialism or empiricism. He does credit some of the secular theologians with a measure of success in making contact with the contemporary mentality, and he implies that they do well to utilize the insights of what he terms an "existential-ontological theism." He feels this has a view of God which "concedes all the legitimate interests of the modern secular outlook."[76]

While taking seriously the warnings of the secular theologians against idolatrous constructs of Deity, Macquarrie commits himself firmly to the belief in a form of deity which is worshiped rather than understood speculatively.[77] In his final chapter, he proposes a synthesis of theism and secularity in which justice is done to the latter by "developing those doctrines of the faith which specifically link God with the material world."[78]

In conclusion it may be said that Professor Macquarrie is an irenic theologian who seeks to find a middle way between historic theism and the claims of the world around us usually regarded to be secular. His critique of the avowed secular theologies is penetrating. His own version of theology represents a blend of process theology with the right-wing forms of secular theology. He seems to find the task of harmonizing this view of Deity with what evangelicals consider essential tenets of the Christian faith to be a difficult one—as indeed it seems to be.

In Conclusion

The secularization of Christianity is one of the facts with which evangelical Christianity must reckon, not only as typical of the sixties, but as a continuing trend. It has always been the case with Christian theology that those who formulate it must relate the essential features of the Evangel to the changing intellectual framework of their time. To fail to do so is to fail to make contact with the very persons whom they hope to reach. But there are built-in perils in every attempt to come to terms with contemporary idiom, and these are multiplied when that idiom is rooted in this-worldly usages to the near exclusion of supernatural and transcendent elements.

If evangelicals have at times oversimplified their approach to the world, the secular theologians also have worked from too narrow a base. And if evangelicals have at times failed to recognize the degree to which they were participants in the intellectual perspectives of their time, so also the secular theologians have not only taken their own relation to the climate of their times for granted, but have regarded it as religiously normative.

Secularism and *secularization* are, as we have attempted to show, terms which have been poorly defined and indiscriminately applied. It has been noted also that the secular theologians have been, to a large degree, persons in revolt against existing forms of theology, particularly against the dialectical theology commonly known as neoorthodoxy. Reactions tend always to be extreme and very frequently impulsively uncritical.

In light of the foregoing, the following evaluations of the movement toward the secularization of Christian theology are in order.

The secular theologians are to be commended for their desire to render the Christian message understandable to the men and women whose intellectual outlook is derived largely or wholly from the secularity of our time. Twentieth-century man needs to hear Good News just as truly as did his counterpart in the first or the twelfth or the sixteenth century. No presentation of the Gospel can be effective if the one presenting it talks only to himself or to those within the Christian tradition.

Likewise, they have a sensitivity both to mood and to language as these relate to the quality of the public mentality. Paul van Buren has given the largest amount of attention to the development of the linguistic and verbal aspects of the secularization of Christianity. Orthodox faith would do well to take note of the criticisms which secular theologians level at its occasional lack of precision in expression and coherence in articulation.

The secular theologians experience some major difficulties in their treatment of the question of transcendence and of the supernatural. It is highly significant that van Buren, after his earlier rejection of transcendence as a category for the understanding of religious faith, has expressed serious second thoughts at this point. In the spring of 1974 he began talking about both God and transcendence. In speaking of the kind of theology needed now, he raises the question, "Is not theology set in the more fundamental context of something utterly final and transcendent?"[79] Hard social realities have quite evidently brought him to a position of advocating a theology which will bring a dimension of transcendent hope into our human situation. It does not weaken the force of his turnabout that he still seeks for the transcendent in the secular. It is significant that he has now weighed in the balances and found wanting the older form of secularism which he once welcomed in the sixties.

The robust optimism which has marked much of the work of the secular theologians seems to many to have ignored many factors which demand serious and even anguished attention. Some of the many voices in the protest movements in the late sixties held that the secular scene, with its cheeriness and its welcoming of technology, was actually destructive to human dignity. Young protesters, predominantly from middle-class homes, were far from certain that the pattern of urban or suburban life was something to be celebrated.

The praise of the technopolis, typical of Harvey Cox's idealization of the secular city as a bearer of the religion of secularity, seemed and still seems to many to fail to reckon with many of the persistent negative qualities of urban life. Anonymity, a mark of the urban scene, all too frequently leads to intense alienation and loneliness. Freedom of choice (for example, the multifaceted opportunities for entertainment) may only mock the person whose income barely meets the soaring costs of rent, food, and transportation. Social life in the metropolis may be supportive and fascinating to the person who is effectively rooted in one of the social subgroups; but to the one who is caught between small-town and urban life-styles, it may only increase frustration.

It is true that there are liberating influences within urbanism; but it seems quite possible that these are not primarily the result of the increase of mere freedom. Rather, urban living leads to new forms of social groupings, some wholesome, some not so wholesome—but they are still forms, substitutions of new forms of social compulsion for old. And it is far from certain that the absence of religious faith in the newer structures is really adequate and satisfying. The rise of the occult, of the offbeat in religious sectarian movements, and of ecstatic forms of Christianity suggest the inadequacy of much of the technopolitan life-style.

The widespread and doctrinaire transition of interest from the otherworldly to the this-worldly, with its revolutionary consequences, seems to many a departure not only from historic theology but from deep-seated sentiments in the human consciousness. While some periods of history have succeeded temporarily in suppressing interest in the world beyond, it may be questioned whether this can be successful over any long period of time. Some might want to argue whether or not traditional theology has been adequate to sustain plausibility in its claim to reveal a *jenseits* which ought to condition and shape life in the here and now. Nevertheless, the sentiment for life after death and the feeling that what one does here may have crucial effects in an afterlife are too fundamental to human nature to permit acceptance for long of the exclusive claims which the secular theologies make for this-worldliness.

Nor are the proposals for a worldly Christianity made by some of the radical theologians likely to be, in the long run, either satisfying or self-sustaining. Robinson's proposal for a worldly holiness is far too ambiguous to offer much challenge to the spiritually earnest, while its denaturing of prayer and worship may ultimately remove the motif of holiness (or wholeness) from our sight. Life must, it is true, be lived in the world; but to remove from the Christian thrust the biblical emphasis upon separateness from sin and the scriptural injunctions to "set your affection on things above" (Col 3:2) may ultimately cause such a Christianity to appear superfluous.

If historic Christianity may at times have constructed idols, and the charge contains some merit, it needs to be noted that the secular theologians are not free from this temptation. To some Harvey Cox comes very near to absolutizing the concept of the city so that it becomes an idolatrous construct. In a larger sense, the use of slogans, typical of many of the theologians of secularity, bears a constant tendency in this direction. And the "instant Christianity" which is offered under the label "religionless" may prove to be not only a kind of spurious grown-upness which is gained overnight but a kind of verbal and ideational idol in itself.

One wonders whether the optimistic judgments rendered upon man, his secular life, and social change by some of the theologians of secularity are not ambiguous and parochial. Here, as in all of life's transactions, means and ends tend to become confused. Further, the assumption that God is at work unambiguously in all of man's social and political life seems, in the light of the New Testament understanding of things, to neglect the entire range of issues involved in "the principalities and powers." May not the demonic be as prevalent in the citadel of secularity, the city, as well as elsewhere?

Finally, the secular theologians are ambiguous (and, it seems to some, reckless) in their treatment of Jesus Christ. There is an uncritical acceptance of the separation of Jesus from Christ, which has been part of the conventional wisdom of classic liberalism and for which there is little justification in the New Testament. Nor has it been particularly helpful to hear that we should think of the Gospel records as kerygma rather than accounts of historical fact. The fact remains that the New Testament records, taken as they stand, clearly identify Jesus of Nazareth as the promised Messiah and the incarnate Son of God. With all of the talk of a "secular Christ" with no ontological relation to the Jesus of Nazareth *and* of Golgotha, there is little evidence that such a construct can be savior in any vital sense. And few thinking persons are convinced that because there were those prior to the advent of our Lord who claimed to be Christs, we are in error in identifying Jesus with the Christ of revelation.

One semiredeeming feature does emerge in the appearance of secular theologies, and in particular, the left-wing form known as death-of-God theology. Altizer seemed unable to establish his metaphysical view of God's death without having recourse to Jesus. True, his understanding of our Lord may have been defective; we are certain that it was. But the point to be observed is, *Jesus Christ will be preached.* As in the days of St. Paul, some preached Him for the wrong reasons. But under divine inspiration Paul rejoiced that in any event, He was proclaimed. And though the secular theologians fail to understand either the personal character or the redemptive role of our Lord, they have been unable to erect their systems without reference to Him. He remains the inevitable Christ; He will be heard.

Notes

1. Georgia Harkness, *The Modern Rival of Christian Faith* (New York: Abingdon-Cokesbury, 1952), p. 13.
2. Quoted on the blurb of Thomas J. J. Altizer and William Hamilton, *Radical Theology and the Death of God* (New York: Bobbs-Merrill, 1966).
3. Thomas J. J. Altizer, *The Gospel of Christian Atheism* (Philadelphia: Westminster, 1966), pp. 62ff.
4. Ibid., p. 84.
5. Ibid., p. 89.
6. *The Altizer-Montgomery Dialogue* (Chicago: Inter-Varsity, 1967), p. 9.
7. Altizer, pp. 43ff.
8. *Altizer-Montgomery Dialogue*, p. 17.
9. Altizer, p. 149.
10. Ibid., pp. 154-55.
11. Thomas J. J. Altizer, *The Descent Into Hell* (Philadelphia: Lippincott, 1970), pp. 177, 179, 185, 193.
12. Ibid., pp. 197, 202.
13. Jackson Lee Ice and John J. Carey, eds., *The Death of God Debate* (Philadelphia: Westminster, 1967), pp. 226-27.

14. Altizer and Hamilton, p. 46.
15. Ibid., p. 40.
16. Ibid., p. 37.
17. Ibid., p. 41.
18. Ibid., p. 43.
19. Gabriel Vahanian, *No Other God* (New York: George Braziller, 1966), p. xii.
20. Gabriel Vahanian, *The Death of God* (New York: George Braziller, 1961), pp. 228-29.
21. Paul M. van Buren, *The Secular Meaning of the Gospel* (New York: Macmillan, 1963), p. 103.
22. Ibid., p. 100.
23. Ibid., pp. 132ff.
24. Ibid., pp. 66, 68, 77, 84.
25. Dietrich Bonhoeffer, *Letters and Papers from Prison*, rev. ed. (New York: Macmillan, 1967), pp. 178ff.
26. John A. Phillips, *Christ for Us in the Theology of Dietrich Bonhoeffer*, 1st Am. ed. (New York: Harper & Row, 1967), p. 20.
27. Ibid., p. 199.
28. Bonhoeffer, p. 152.
29. See Phillips, p. 152; see also pp. 188, 196.
30. William Blair Gould, *The Worldly Christian: Bonhoeffer on Discipleship* (Philadelphia: Fortress, 1967), p. 61.
31. John A. T. Robinson, *Honest to God* (Philadelphia: Westminster, 1963), p. 11.
32. Ibid., p. 16.
33. Ibid., p. 32.
34. David L. Edwards, ed., *The Honest to God Debate* (Philadelphia: Westminster, 1963), p. 27.
35. Ibid., p. 28.
36. Robinson, pp. 25-26.
37. Edwards, pp. 34-35.
38. Robinson, pp. 45ff.
39. Ibid., p. 37.
40. Edwards, p. 94.
41. Robinson, p. 44.
42. John A. T. Robinson, *Exploration into God* (Stanford, Calif.: Stanford U., 1967), pp. 15-16.
43. Robinson, *Honest to God*, p. 40.
44. Ibid., p. 49.
45. Ibid., p. 124; J. M. Morrison, *Honesty and God* (Edinburgh: St. Andrew, 1966), p. 55.
46. Robinson, *Honest to God*, pp. 70-71.
47. Ibid., p. 73.
48. Ibid.
49. See p. 74.
50. Robinson, *Honest to God*, p. 74.
51. Ibid., p. 75.
52. Ibid., p. 75; Bonhoeffer, p. 196.
53. Robinson, *Honest to God*, p. 76.
54. See van Buren, pp. 159ff.
55. Robinson, *Honest to God*, pp. 64-83.
56. Ibid., pp. 97, 102.
57. Harvey G. Cox, *The Secular City* (New York: Macmillan, 1965), p. 2.

58. Ibid., p. 17.
59. Ibid., pp. 25ff.
60. Ibid., p. 150.
61. Ibid., p. 154.
62. Ibid., p. 258.
63. Ibid., pp. 83-84.
64. Ibid., pp. 128-29.
65. Ibid., p. 83.
66. Ibid., pp. 83-84.
67. Harvey G. Cox, *God's Revolution and Man's Responsibility* (Valley Forge, Pa.: Judson, 1965), p. 104.
68. Ibid., pp. 104-5.
69. Cox, *The Secular City*, p. 254.
70. Ibid., p. 255.
71. Ibid., p. 258.
72. John Macquarrie, *New Directions in Theology Today*, vol. 3, *God and Secularity* (Philadelphia: Westminster), pp. 30, 52.
73. Ibid., p. 49.
74. Ibid., pp. 53ff.
75. Ibid., p. 81.
76. Ibid., pp. 98-99.
77. Ibid., p. 114.
78. Ibid., p. 131.
79. Paul M. van Buren, "Theology Now?," *The Christian Century*, 91 (May 29, 1974): 585.

Selected Reading

Altizer, Thomas J. J. *The Descent Into Hell*. Philadelphia: Lippincott, 1970.

————. *The Gospel of Christian Atheism*. Philadelphia: Westminster, 1966.

Altizer, Thomas J. J., and Hamilton, William. *Radical Theology and the Death of God*. New York: Bobbs-Merrill, 1966.

The Altizer-Montgomery Dialogue. Chicago: Inter-Varsity, 1967.

Bonhoeffer, Dietrich. *Letters and Papers From Prison*. Rev. ed. New York: Macmillan, 1967.

Callahan, Daniel, ed. *The Secular City Debate*. New York: Macmillan, 1966.

Clarke, O. Fielding. *For Christ's Sake: A Reply to "Honest to God."* 3d Am. ed. New York: Morehouse-Barlow, 1963.

Cox, Harvey G. *God's Revolution and Man's Responsibility*. Valley Forge, Pa.: Judson, 1965.

————. *The Secular City*. New York: Macmillan, 1965.

Edwards, David L., ed. *The Honest to God Debate*. Philadelphia: Westminster, 1963.

Kliever, Lonnie D., and Hayes, John H. *Radical Christianity.* Anderson, S. C.: Droke House, 1968.

Macquarrie, John. *New Directions in Theology Today,* vol. 3, *God and Secularity.* Philadelphia: Westminster, 1967.

Mascall, E. L. *The Secularization of Christianity.* New York: Holt, Rinehart & Winston, 1965.

Ogletree, Thomas W. *The Death of God Controversy.* New York: Abingdon, 1966.

Phillips, John A. *Christ for Us in the Theology of Dietrich Bonhoeffer.* New York: Harper & Row, 1967.

Robinson, John A. T. *Honest to God.* Philadelphia: Westminster, 1963.

Vahanian, Gabriel. *The Death of God.* New York: George Braziller, 1961.

———. *No Other God.* New York: George Braziller, 1966.

Van Buren, Paul M. *The Secular Meaning of the Gospel.* New York: Macmillan, 1963.

THEOLOGY OF HOPE

5

Theology of Hope

by
DAVID P. SCAER

INTRODUCTION

Christianity had been hit by what seemed to many to be such a mortal blow by the God-is-dead theologians in the 1960s, that any prediction for significant theological recovery at that time would have been unfounded at best. But in the middle of the 1970s, hardly a decade later, the names of the morbid heralders of God's demise have been removed from the marquee, and quite unnoticed at that. Replacing Paul van Buren, William Hamilton, Gabriel Vahanian, John Robinson, and Thomas Altizer have come new notables, the theologians of hope. Sometimes also called futurology, theology of hope is a way of looking at theology and theological concerns from the perspective of the future rather than the past or present. Past and present have value only with reference to the future. Reality is not-yet; it is future oriented. The question of God's existence can be answered only in the future, for God is subject to time as it pushes into the future. Three prominent leaders of the new movement are German theologians Jürgen Moltmann (Reformed), Wolfhart Pannenberg (Lutheran), and Johannes Metz (Roman Catholic).

The theology of hope has been articulated in the United States by two Lutheran theologians, Carl Braaten and Robert Jenson,

---

DAVID P. SCAER, B.A., M.Div., Th.D., is professor of systematic theology at Concordia Theological Seminary, Fort Wayne, Indiana, and editor of *Concordia Theological Quarterly*. He is author of the following books: *What Do You Think of Jesus?* (Concordia, 1973), *Getting into the Story of Concord: History of the Book of Concord* (Concordia, 1978), and *A Latin Ecclesiastical Glossary* (Concordia, 1978).

whose works have done much to popularize the new movement. In
Brazil Rubem A. Alves, with a few revisions of his own, has done
much to convert the theology of hope into a program for action.
Roman Catholic theology has not remained untouched. Metz combined the ideas of incarnation with future and history. In addition,
other Roman Catholic theologians, prominent in their own right,
have adopted much of the new thinking. The avant-garde Dutch
theologian, Edward Schillebeeckx, has amalgamated the theology
of hope into the Roman Catholic framework of hierarchy and sacramental theology. The theology of hope, with its eventual call for an
activistic ethic, might finally prove to be more successful in the
utilitarian mind set of American theology than in the reflective
thought of Europe, where it was spawned. The translation of many
of the German writings into English is still not complete, so the full
impact in American theology has not yet been felt. Its
philosophical-theological basis might prove too ethereal, but its call
to action might be heard.

Unlike other theological movements which can be exhausted
by and divided into the traditional categories of exegetical, dogmati-
cal, and historical theology, the theology of hope embraces more
than what is generally recognized as strictly theology. Its secular
orientation permits it to be combined with any number of subjects,
including politics and biology.[1] At the heart of theology of hope
there is a basic philosophical instability which not only attempts but
requires future satisfaction in an indefinite number of possible com-
binations. The definitionless future is one of its hallmarks. For
example, the theology of hope has already expressed itself in political terms as the theology of revolution.[2] There is really no aspect of
secular life that would a priori be excluded from its grasp.

The theology of hope sees an outline for its plan in the eschatological thrusts of the Old and New Testaments and attempts to
make them applicable to the church's understanding of itself and its
mission in the world. Because it understands reality from the perspective of eschatology, the movement is also called futuristic
theology. With its forceful launch into the future in its quest for
reality, it sees itself as an immediate reaction to the melancholy and
personal subjectivism of the neoorthodoxy which had ruled in Germany since Karl Barth came to prominence in the post-World War I
days and which gradually took hold in the United States. Theology is
not so narrow as to be limited to an I-Thou relationship; it is to be
expanded to envelop the entire world. The Latin word for *world* is

saeculum. Since this theology addresses the world as world, it wants to be considered a *secular* theology and hence an inheritor of the tradition of the God-is-dead theologians, who were the more radical secular theologians of the 1960s.

With its pilgrim theme of marching into the future, the movement is a protest against any form of Constantinian Christianity, which attempts to find religion's ultimate answer in the present society instead of the future. No existing ecclesiastical structures are necessarily permanent; and all structures, ecclesiastical or political, may be destroyed or changed as the future advances. There are no sacred cows. In some Roman Catholic thought, this concept is modified to allow the church structures to remain, but in a servant position toward the changing world structures. This has not been without appeal to many Protestants.

To the world of religion, the theology of hope is the public refusal to accept the finality of the verdict of the God-is-dead theologians of the 1960s. That verdict's irrevocable quality, spelled out so positively and dogmatically, was simply unacceptable to theologians who still saw themselves playing a role in the church and the world. The futuristic theologians have walked away from the grave dug for God and shut their ears to the funeral dirge. The black crepe has been stored away. It was not that theologians of hope ignored the evidence of the God buriers or that they denied that a secular age had indeed come, but they hoped to use the negative evidence to produce more hopeful and positive results. The humanism of the God-is-dead theologians became the seedbed in which the theology of hope would take root.

The God-is-dead theologians asserted that in the secular age, religious questions were no longer relevant. The theologians of hope declared that all questions, religious and secular, were open. The question about God was relevant not in spite of the secular age but because of it. This does not mean that any of the theologians of hope accepted that it was possible to give certain and definite answers to these questions. From their futuristic perspective they did not and indeed could not accept a unique, historical revelation in the past. Providing such permanent answers is not really possible. In contrast to the secular theologians of the 1960s, who categorically stated that questions about God were no longer important, the theologians of hope said the questions were important even though answers as final conclusions could not be provided. Even when answers were provided, they went through the metamorphosis of the impending future and became questions again.

The advocates of hope did not disagree with the God-is-dead theologians in their concept that the world, especially the world as history, was the only sphere that existed and hence the only basis for revelation. But instead of accepting what seemed to some to be the inevitable conclusion that God no longer existed in the world, they opened the question again on the basis that history had not reached completion. The question of God must be answered historically, and the question of history can be answered only in the future. It was not that the evidence of the 1960s was disputed or the judgment about God's death was itself judged to be an absolute error. The only desire was to obtain a stay of execution so that history as evidence could be reviewed from the future. Future means possibilities. Perhaps God would be alive in the future. The possibility must be kept open. Nothing, including God's existence, can be ruled impossible from the present perspective. The men who opened up again the question of God's existence are called the theologians of *hope* because they kept this flicker of hope alive for theology.

THE CIRCUMSTANCES SURROUNDING ITS RISE

The individual-centered, subjectivistic, and introverted theology of neoorthodoxy might have been adequate in reflecting the general political and mental depression which followed the great European wars in this century; but it soon became inadequate in handling the quietly growing world optimism dawning in the second half of the twentieth century. The nuclear Armageddon between the Soviet Union and the United States, predicted in the late 1940s, typologically symbolized by the Berlin blockade and airlift, and expected by Western Europe, never materialized. A relatively stable political situation, coupled with comparatively prosperous economies in the East and West, gave birth to a mind-set entirely different from the suspicious and hesitant attitudes of the immediate postwar climate.

The Nazi war-crimes trials may have served to call an entire nation vicariously before the court of world opinion, but the children of the war generation did not share the remorse of their parents. Original sin might be inherited, but here was a case where war guilt was not being passed down from one generation to another. The self-contained and self-directed attitude of the melancholy Dane, Sören Kierkegaard, as it was fed to the Europeans and then to the

Americans through the theology of Karl Barth and his disciples, suddenly seemed curiously out of step with a world that was succeeding in picking itself up out of the ashes. This was not the age of the uncontained optimism that greeted the turn of this epoch, dubbed then as the Christian century. It was, rather, an age constructed on the ruins of two world wars. With the past and its structures so devastatingly destroyed, it saw its only possible redemptive solutions in the future. Viewing the past from a negative perspective provided a kind of reverse thrust toward the future. Things can look so hopeless that hope becomes the only possible alternative left. After World War I there was an attempt at partial political reconstruction; but after World War II in Germany, for example, there was the deliberate attempt to sweep the Nazi past under the rug. It was a case of the past looking so bad that only the future looked good.

The political situation was not alone in undergoing change; for scientifically, mankind was making some astounding strides in this period. After the holocaustic destruction of World War II, man's scientific performance was giving hope for a greater future. While arsenals full of bombs did make apocalyptic destruction a historical possibility, this was counterbalanced by some positive advances. Russians and Americans climbed over one another to get as far out into space as possible, with the moon as the ultimate goal of the first phase. Space exploration had more symbolical than real value for the spirit of man. As Europeans were experiencing a constantly improving economy, a new, significant opening to a future in space was being forged. At a time when the earth's frontiers were vanishing and the new world of America had aged like the old world in Europe, a new frontier and world were found in space. Perhaps a future could provide answers for mankind that the past had not. A new age of scientific enlightenment could be reborn, taking for its substance not the smoking ashes of an older order, but something loosely defined as "out there."

These scientific advancements were not without their drawbacks. Social tensions between nations and classes were becoming keenly felt, especially in the third-world nations. This emerging group of nations avoided permanent political alliances with the two major world powers and began to demand what they thought was their share of this world's goods. This was a wrinkle on the face of the world politic not envisioned in the post-war power struggle. Because of the rapid, global communication systems, the have-nots were becoming aware of what the haves really had and wanted some of it. Marxism's philosophy of equal distribution of material goods provided an attractive solution to these new problems. In addition, it was sufficiently future-oriented to provide an inner philosophical structure for a world that wanted to look forward because the past had proven to be a failure.

Whatever societal and cultural structures remained in Europe and America after World War II were seriously threatened again in the second half of the 1960s by student unrest. This unrest reflected the general impatience of the times.

Perhaps it was inevitable that theologians would sooner or later be caught up in the new, futuristic world spirit without regarding its ephemeral nature. Through the forties and fifties and into the sixties they seemed content with an introverted theology on a course bent for its own destruction. Theologians were still reflecting the older, postwar world view and had failed to read the blossoming signs of optimism. In New Testament studies, Bultmann and his followers had virtually eliminated what little history had been bequeathed them by the nineteenth century historical researchers. The God-is-dead theologians had read the signs of the times, pronounced that God had been dead for some time, and proceeded to bury Him—so they thought. To do the job well, they buried Him with as many philosophical and theological funerals as possible. It was a case of overkill and overburial.

But just as God was being buried, some were thinking that all this was somewhat premature. Could not the church share in the world's progress? Could the church, which had viewed itself as the preserver of God's voice on earth, continue with the proclamation that the divine Proclaimer was Himself dead?

The matter had repercussions in the lives of the churches. Church leaders began to face the damaging statistics within their own organizations and were startled. Church institutions which had enjoyed phenomenal periods of growth in the nineteenth and early twentieth centuries were now marking their ledgers with red ink. Decline in church membership was paralleled by a less effective mission program in foreign lands. No longer was it probable that Christianity would be spread in every land by Gospel preaching and that this would be the Christian century. On the contrary, it was the century of a world come of age, the secular age. Universal conversion, which had seemed a possibility at the beginning of the century, was more remote than ever. In proportion to the total world population, Christians were in a shrinking minority. This was not going to be the golden age of Christian triumphalism. The ecumenical movement, created to gather the united forces of Christendom in one massive array to speak the ultimate word to the world, was coming apart at the seams. It was becoming an organization for survival, not conquest. To make matters worse, there was no ecumenical prairie fire at the grassroots.

As church leaders were facing a decline in church membership, phenomenal population growth, especially in non-Christian areas, made the picture look even bleaker. While the former American president might have been overenthusiastic in his remark that man's arrival on the moon was the greatest day since the creation of the world, the feat did point out by comparison the church's weak performance. The world was advancing, and the church was in retreat. Part of the effort of the Bultmannian era was to proclaim the Gospel to modern man on man's own terms, even if the original message had to be adjusted. The hard fact is that this plan failed. The church had tried to make its message relevant to the world; but the world was listening less and less, if it was listening at all, to the pared-down and restructured message.

The theology of hope is fully cognizant of the critical symptoms of the current ecclesiastical sickness and attempts to reverse the trend. The situation demands a theological revolution to save the patient from the sickness unto death. The theology of hope offers a cure. The theme for the movement can be summarized in the words *future* and *hope*. Present and past have their value only in their service to the future. Neoorthodoxy claimed that God could be known only in special revelation transmitted from a transcendent realm and not from the world. The God-is-dead theologians agreed with Barth that the world could not and did not reveal God, but they shut off the Barthian pipeline to heaven. With heaven and earth blocked so they could give no answers, the theologians of hope look to the future to answer the question of God's existence.

Not only does the question of God's existence have to be answered differently, but man also must be approached from another perspective. Preaching readjusted to modern man had shown itself to be ineffective as an instrument for the church's survival. The solution for this dilemma is sought in directing the church's energies away from the individual to society's structures. No longer is the church's prime target the individual and his conversion to faith in Jesus, even in the neoorthodox sense of a divine-human encounter. For the theology of hope, the church's chief task is involvement in the fabric of society. This involvement means changing governmental structures, economic divisions, organizations, and whatever else is recognized as part of society. The change of structures, especially political ones, is envisioned as the new mission of the church to the world. This will bring about eschatology, now viewed as the new and only reality. The conversion of structures instead of individuals means that political theology replaces pastoral theology as the core of practical theology. Hope, not faith, becomes the individual response to the overarching reality of the future. The base is the future; the attitude is hope; and change is the indispensable mark of sanctification.

No longer does religion have to answer the question of God as the first question but as the last. And all questions, including those about God and man, must remain unanswered, because they are controlled by the future. Asserting any definition about God would be ipso facto placing a limitation on God. It would deny His future and circumscribe His freedom. For the same reason man or his relationship to God cannot be defined. Man too is molded and shaped by the future as it constantly unfolds in his history.

Very fittingly, the call to arms for the theology of hope is the words of the glorified Lord from the most futuristic book of either testament, and without coincidence the last of the entire Bible, the book of Revelation: "Behold I make all things new." The Bible is read from cover to cover, but now from the back to the front. In these words from the Apocalypse, many in the sixties and seventies wanting to be associated with the theology of hope heard its marching orders. The theology of hope pulled up the church's anchor in past and present reality and set its sails deliberately in the direction of an uncertain future. Past certainty and present values have to be reexamined and reestablished in and by a future that is by definition free and uncertain. From now on, all plateaus of certainty are to be abandoned for an endless change of challenges which never take final shape. Life is now to be defined syntactically by a series of questions whose answers always become new questions.

ERNST BLOCH: THE PHILOSOPHER BEHIND IT

Philosophically the theology of hope found its origins in the ideas of Ernst Bloch, a German professor, who emigrated in 1961 from the German Democratic Republic to the German Federal Republic, where he joined the faculty of the University of Tübingen.

Ernst Bloch's philosophy of the "not yet" can be traced back through Karl Marx to Hegel. In the nineteenth century Hegel had introduced a philosophy involving a movement of inherent forward thrust. A thesis required necessarily an antithesis and together these two opposing principles produced a third compromising principle known as a synthesis. This synthesis became in turn a thesis for a repetition of a new thesis-antithesis-synthesis. This is a continuous process.

Although Hegel's philosophy was only superficially trinitarian in any Christian sense, some Christian theologians did adopt it into their religious systems. Others, however, adopted the philosophy without any reference to God at all. Thus, without difficulty, Marx added an economic dimension to Hegel's three-part scheme and proceeded to dispose of God. This Marxist by-product is known as dialectical materialism, a philosophy which attempts to shape society economically by political revolution.

Both Marx and Bloch are recognized as representatives of left-wing Hegelianism; however, no simple identification can be made between the philosophies of Bloch and Marx as the latter developed politically into Communism. For example, Ernst Bloch does not see his mission as that of an apostle for the political policies of the eastern European nations. Nor does he see the establishment of the proletariat as the final, glorious kingdom, a thought so basic to Marxism.

In comparison, Bloch's idea of a future which knows no real end or consummation is more radical than Marx's and is perhaps more in keeping with the original thought of Hegel. Marx shares with Christianity a recognition of an ultimate plateau in time, when time itself reaches a predetermined destiny and set goal. Then the "saints," as they are understood according to each system, will be glorified. For Marx, the goal is a heaven on earth, with the time clock implanted right into matter and history; for Christianity, earth is assumed into heaven, with God determining the moment of glorification. For Bloch and the theologians of hope dependent upon him, the clock of history has itself an infinite future and keeps running. The future is infinite.

In spite of the differences between Bloch and Marx, both are agreed that matter provides the dynamic for man in his history. The concept of a transcendental God controlling the shape and destiny of history plays no role in their thought. This thought of a nontranscendental God is adopted into the theology of hope. Both Marx and

Bloch hold that matter is the basis for the future development of mankind; but development for Bloch leads in no predetermined direction. This also is basic to the theology of hope. Answers to reality, for Bloch, are all found in the future. This might be fatalism, but hardly a predetermined form of it.

As an etymological base for his philosophy, Bloch traced the word *matter* back to the Latin word for mother, *mater*. Matter is *mater,* the mother, of the future. Such etymological derivation is fanciful linguistics and hardly provides a firm basis for any philosophical system. Still, it points up the essential place given to matter in his system. Bloch's concepts of materialism and future are both incorporated into the theology of hope.

Bloch summarizes his futuristic philosophy in a grammatical scheme written as an algebraic formula: S is not yet P, subject is not yet predicate. Using syntactical or grammatical terminology, he states that the subject of every sentence or thought comes to completion only in the predicate. Thus Hegel's thesis-antithesis-synthesis philosophy is converted into grammatical terminology. In a more complex way, his philosophy may be summarized by the German phrase, *Ontologie des Noch-Nicht Seins,* which can be translated, "Ontology of being-that-is-not-yet." All this really means is that life, with all that goes with it, finds its fundamental meaning in the future. The present is necessarily inadequate because it has not been answered by the future. Reality is by definition incomplete and remains so. Man's attitude to life should be formulated not by what has been or what is but rather by what will be. Even the past has no fixed, permanent value in itself, but only receives consideration because of how the future values it. This future value is constantly reestimated as more of the future breaks into the present. The past is not thought of as providing a foundation for an understanding of the present and future. There can be no forward projection of past categories but only a reverse projection of future categories. The future through history is the controlling factor for man. The meaning to life is not found in man's past but in the future, which remains unknown. Man's family tree is turned upside down. Man's value is determined not by his progenitors but by his progeny. The goal is not the recovery of the past in the sense of renaissance, but the future which is reflected in man's present and past. Where the past serves as the basis for a philosophical understanding of man, definite and fixed categories of the understanding are possible. But a future with an undetermined destiny provides limitless possibilities.

In Bloch's philosophy, unlike that of Christianity and Marxism, a directionless future became the most recognizable feature. The concept of future provides limitless answers to present and past questions. In any secular philosophy or system of Christian thought which found for itself an orientation in the past, outlines for the future could be at least tentatively drawn. In the new futuristic philosophy, all categories and projections remain elastic and provisional, except, of course, for the overarching category of the future. All present categories are expendable in the light of the future which offers an undetermined number of categories. These also may become expendable as the future breaks in upon them.

Without much difficulty this type of philosophy could be converted into theological terms, which Bloch himself did. A philosophy which saw all questions answerable in and by the future could easily be called a philosophy of hope. Man's inner desires as he faced the future could be called hope, a concept which was imbedded in the fiber of the Old and New Testaments and not unknown to the history of Christian thought. But in traditional Christianity, hope is preceded by a faith which not only includes a future redemption but which anchors itself in God's past activity in history. This history is determinative for God's future actions as a firm promise and is inherently complete. The real ground of Christian faith is what God has done once and for all, especially in Jesus Christ, and not what God is going to do. Foreign to Christianity is the concept that hope is the basis of itself.

In spite of the essentially different understanding of *hope* in Christianity and the thought of Bloch, an overlay of the two systems is at least superficially possible. But the apparent parallel does not erase the fact that in Bloch's thought, faith is incorporated in hope and finds its real security in the future and not in the past. Similarity in language does not in this case assure similarity in substance.

Dialogue with contemporary philosophy cannot be avoided by responsible theologians. Christianity's apologetic task requires it to give a theological response to the contemporary cultural climate. Paul Tillich viewed the theological task of the church as providing answers to philosophical questions, and to a certain extent he was right. But one of the bad side-effects of theology's conversations with philosophy has been that Christianity too frequently has unwittingly incorporated philosophy's questions into its own answers.

Theology's conversation with the contemporary philosophy has made the development of Christian thought possible, but theology is always faced with the herculean task of cleaning out its own temples by tossing over the tables of the merchants of philosophical thought.

So there is nothing really new in the challenge that Christianity faces in the influential thought of Ernst Bloch as it appears in the theology of hope. What is new is that this philosopher, with an outlook on life which is by his own confession materialistic and atheistic, has a positive appreciation of the Bible and has worked biblical themes into his philosophy. Hence, the amalgamation of these philosophical ideas into theology was easier because the philosophy had already borrowed from theology. The typical pattern is for the theologian to go hat in hand to the philosophers asking for an audience. Bloch has partially inverted this caricature. The Bible, for the atheistic philosopher Bloch, is recognized as the supreme expression of man's radical hope. There he finds man portrayed as a creature of promise, oriented to the future. He even sees a basis for his philosophy in the name *Yahweh,* the Old Testament tetragram for *God,* and replaces the usual translation of "I am that I am" with the possible but not generally accepted translation, "I will be who I will be."

With theology grinding to a halt in the mid-1960s, it is not difficult to see the immediate and sudden attraction that Ernst Bloch would have for some theologians. To some he seemed almost too good to be true. He had provided a philosophical skeleton for the theologians, both Protestant and Catholic, to flesh out. It was a task done with relish, so that hardly ten years later there exists in Christianity a vibrant and impressive theology of hope hanging on the materialistic bones of Ernst Bloch's philosophy. Christian theology was revitalized after it had ground to a halt in the individualism of Karl Barth and the seek-and-destroy exegetical method of Rudolf Bultmann. For the ground of its certainty, Christianity did not have to look in the individualistic revelation of neoorthodoxy, but could see itself and its piety as a part of the entire world process.

The vision was tempting. What appeared attractive to some was that the two great lights in the movement, Jürgen Moltmann and Wolfhart Pannenberg, were doing exegetical and doctrinal theology in a style resembling the more traditional procedures of past and forgotten generations. Exegetically, they were taking a holistic approach to the Bible. But following Bloch, they made the whole world, and not the isolated individual or the Church, the target of their futuristic philosophy, now totally immersed in biblical con-cepts. However, in adopting Bloch's materialism, theology also surrendered its bases in a historical past and a transcendental sphere for the uncertain heritage of the future.

JÜRGEN MOLTMANN: THEOLOGIAN OF THE FUTURE

Moltmann and Pannenberg are the prominent names in the theology of hope. To distinguish these theologians from each other, Moltmann can be called the theologian of the future and Pannenberg the theologian of history. Pannenberg might prove to be the more profound, but Moltmann has continued to occupy the spotlight in the world of theological literature.

As fate had brought Bultmann to Marburg, where the existentialist philosopher Martin Heidegger was at work, so the paths of the Marxist philosopher Ernst Bloch and the Protestant theologian Jürgen Moltmann crossed at the University of Tübingen in the 1960s.[3] The political climate in the Black Forest region of Germany was ideal for the grafting of the new philosophy into theology. The division of the two Germanies by the Berlin Wall in 1961, with its personal and political tragedies, was a nonrepealable verdict that the two states would develop separately. With the flood of refugees from the East reduced to a trickle, the emotionally charged issue of political Communism gradually subsided so that an intellectual assessment of theoretical Marxism became increasingly possible. In a situation where the cold war was cooling off, theoretical debate and exchange with the Marxists could begin, less hampered by such hard political realities as a refugee problem.

In the 1960s the Christian-Marxist dialogue was taking place at Tübingen. It should not be forgotten that Karl Marx was not a Russian but a German and that the German university was aptly suited for such intellectual and philosophical exchange. During this time German universities were the scenes of political unrest among the student bodies. This unrest had a Marxist tinge to it and was found not only in Tübingen but at Heidelberg, Münster, and, strangely, in West Berlin, that island of freedom in the midst of a political sea of extreme Marxism, the German Democratic Republic. Students studying in the Protestant theological faculties of these universities were leaders in these political upheavals.

In the early 1960s Jürgen Moltmann published his *Theologie der Hoffnung*, and by 1968 it had gone through eight printings. From the fifth printing in 1965 came the English translation, which made its debut in the United States in 1967 as *The Theology of Hope*. For this reason Moltmann is called the theologian of hope. Moltmann was quickly on the American lecture circuit, and his lectures were printed as essays in 1969 in *Religion, Revolution and the Future*. The essays provided the clear philosophical outline that was not totally apparent in *The Theology of Hope*. The influence of Bloch in his thought was quite clear. Moltmann did not merely restore eschatology to the rightful place in theology from which it had fallen during the age of neoorthodoxy, but he made eschatology the key to understanding all theology.

In his *Theology of Hope* Jürgen Moltmann went through the Bible with a cover-to-cover thoroughness to identify the ideas of future and hope. The approach was refreshing in contrast to the here-and-now humdrum of the existential theologians who had long overstayed their welcome on the religious stage of the first half of the century. Neoorthodox theologians had given the impression that they had little interest in the past or the future. The present reality was the theater where the truth was played. If Jesus Christ is risen, He is risen for me here and now. If He is to return for judgment, it is more important to realize that Jesus Christ is exercising His judgment now in my life. In this approach, with its emphasis on "this is the day of repentance and salvation," overconcern with the problem of historical truthfulness or of a real future was seen as destroying the significance of the present moment. To existentially oriented theologians, all history and all the future eventually dissolve into the present moment of faith.

In contrast to this mood, and much to his credit, Moltmann takes a realistic view of history which offers a real future. Past and future are not dissolved into an eternal present. There is more to reality than just the present. In developing his futuristic theology, Moltmann does have the considerable weight of biblical history on his side, and he makes ready use of it. Luther interpreted the Bible from the principle of justification by faith, and he saw it shining through on every page. For Moltmann, the hermeneutical principle is eschatology, and hope is the major theme of the Bible. In emphasizing the future, he has developed a legitimate biblical thought which lay deeply buried in nineteenth- and twentieth-century ethical and existential theology. Prior to and contemporary with Moltmann's systematic presentation of an eschatological theology, many scholars of the New Testament were giving more attention to

Jesus as an apocalyptic Preacher. Albert Schweitzer at the beginning of this century pioneered in this exegetical emphasis.

Without getting into the debate now of whether Moltmann's principle of hope is philosophically or exegetically based, we may say that he rightly recognized the Old Testament God as the God who promises. The present does not exhaust the meaning of His promises, but the future demonstrates that God is faithful in keeping His promises.[4] The promises serve to tie the believer down not to the present but to the future.

The name *Yahweh* is preferred to the name *Elohim* in understanding God. *Yahweh* is recognized as the God of the nomadic tribes of Israel going through Sinai, always going before His people and leading them into the future. Therefore the Exodus-Sinai tradition of the Jews is seen as the fundamental pattern of God's future activity of leading. The past promise and fulfillment projects God's people into the future. Even when God's promise is fulfilled, the promise is not destroyed because of its fulfillment; but rather through the fulfillment, the original promise takes on greater dimensions. The past constantly serves the future. Even the appearances of God in past history are significant not because of their meaning for the present but because of future expectation. Of the various Old Testament offices, the prophet is all-important because it interprets past and present in the light of the future.

In planning for the future of Israel, *Yahweh* reserves for Himself the right of annulling His own covenants and agreements. Nothing is sacredly fixed in the mind of *Yahweh*. He exists under the condition of perfect freedom. There are no divine absolutes even in regard to His essence. Absolutizing God is scored as a Hellenistic understanding of God. The terminology of the latter prophets in Israel, especially Jeremiah, with such phrases as the "new David," "new covenant," "new Israel," and "new Zion," is incorporated into the theology of hope and is seen as an example of Israel's eschatological awareness even at the close of the Old Testament.

The New Testament is read with the same eschatological interpretation as the Old. Again God is not the Absolute, but the God who demonstrates His faithfulness by bringing His promises into the future. The present is the way station on the path to the future. No longer are the gospels considered legends, as they were for Bultmann; but they are recollections of persons who have been caught up by the eschatological hope. Paul develops the future of Abraham into a universal eschatology. The Old Testament, with its proclamation of the future, opens for the church new possibilities.

The resurrection of Jesus Christ is not important because it is part of a past history, but its importance lies in making history possible. It is the beginning of the general resurrection. Moltmann interprets the resurrection of Jesus eschatologically and not historically.[5] It is part of the future projected backward into time and forms the base of history without becoming part of that history. We are reminded that for Karl Barth also, the resurrection stands precariously on the rim of history.

Whatever difficulties those holding to a physical resurrection had with Karl Barth's view are hardly more resolved by Moltmann's understanding of the resurrection. The question of the historicity of the resurrection of Jesus Christ is not valid in Moltmann's system, since such a factual historical question demands a once-and-for-all, static answer of yes or no. For him, the truthfulness of any historical question, including the resurrection, must be understood from the future. He argues like this: "What happened between the cross and the Easter appearances is then an eschatological event which has its goal in future revelation and universal fulfillment."[6] Traditionally it has been expressed that Christ's resurrection is the historical and theological basis of the final resurrection. Moltmann reverses this and makes the final resurrection the basis of Jesus' resurrection. Rather than standing at the open tomb and looking forward, we are to project ourselves into the final resurrection. From that vantage, the resurrection of Jesus can be legitimatized. Since that part of the future has not dawned, there can be no historical certainty about His resurrection.[7] Moltmann asserts that the New Testament versions of Jesus' resurrection are clothed in Jewish apocalyptic of which Jesus Himself was a preacher. Describing Jesus in such apocalyptic language further enhances the idea that Jesus was an appearance in history of God's future. While Moltmann has a more positive appreciation of history than the neoorthodox theologians, yet as long as history is only eschatologically verifiable, it remains just as elusive.

Eschatology also provides the key to his understanding of God and man. For Moltmann, God and man exist in a condition of perfect freedom without any restrictions. Since man is to be understood from the future, he is not capable of an autonomous, fixed definition. Man can be understood only with reference to a restless, constantly unfolding history in relation to the future of God. God and history are inextricably joined. Humanity in its totality is in a state of becoming and has not yet acquired a fixed nature. In conventional theological terms, anthropology is understood in the light of theology, that is, the doctrine about God, and theology in the light of eschatology. This eschatology constantly approaches man in his history. As long as the individual exempts himself from this historical process culminating in an uncertain future, he is guilty of self-deification by concentrating on himself. This is called a theology of glory. The solution to this perversion is man's finding his true destiny in associating himself with God, who discloses Himself wherever humanity is despised and brutalized. Moltmann calls this the theology of the cross.[8] Man shares in this theology of the cross by accepting life's challenges as future moments breaking into the present. In this way God is found. Rather than saying that man has a nature, it is preferable to say that man has a history which reaches for the future in a series of constant challenges.

Moltmann's view of anthropology has consequences for his understanding of the incarnation. No longer can incarnation be understood as God's assuming one particular human nature; but rather, it is God's participation in the history of the rejection and humiliation associated with Jesus' death. Jesus represents true humanity in the midst of inhumanity. Incarnation means God's sharing in mankind's suffering to remove this inhumanity. This radical kenotic Christology is reminiscent of the God-is-dead theologians, who held that in Jesus God died in the world in such a way that He gave up His existence. But in contrast to the finality of this extreme radical position, Moltmann sees a future for God as a real possibility. Incarnation is not a from-heaven-to-earth occurrence, since there is no transcendental sphere for Moltmann; but it is an appearance of something new in history offering a promise to mankind of what it will become.

With his idea of definitionless future, Moltmann cannot present a clear, explicit picture of mankind's future. It must, however, in some sense involve suffering for mankind and eventual sharing in God's future. Man's inhumanity will not allow for this participation now. This remains as the hope of the future.

Sin must also be interpreted from this future perspective. If hope is the proper attitude to be taken to the future, then hopelessness is the overarching category in understanding sin. Hopelessness, according to Moltmann, can take two forms, *praesumptio* and *desperatio*.[9] *Praesumptio* is that sinful attitude in man which attempts to usher the future and its benefits into the present without waiting for God to act. The attempt to do this is work-righteousness, to use a common cliché. *Desperatio* involves adopting the premature opinion that God will not act in the future at all. It is an apathy, an indifference to life. Psychologically, it results in anxiety.

Hopelessness, whatever the form, must be overcome so that man may realize the image of God within himself. This image is defined as the capability of transcending the present life into the future and having a foretaste of the eschatological life. Man in the image of God is defined not in relation to a past, creative act of God, but in relation to God's future. There is no restoration of what man used to be; instead man looks forward to a participation in a better future, whose outlines cannot now be drawn.

Two strictures can be raised against Moltmann's views of man and future because of inherent contradictions. His call to associate with the downtrodden to overcome inhumanity presupposes that Moltmann does in fact have a fixed definition of humanity. In spite of all his explicit disclaimers, he must have some sort of fixed notion of what *human* means, otherwise there is no meaning to his concept of *inhuman*. How can one participate in God's future revealed in history by associating with man in his inhumanity, if he has no way of recognizing this?

Second, any attempt then to remove the present conditions of inhumanity now does in effect realize eschatology by ushering in the future humanity, at least partially. But it is this attitude that Moltmann himself labels as *praesumptio*. His theology of the cross may under a more careful analysis be a theology of glory with triumphalism. Moltmann explicitly rejects any apotheistic anthropology, which turns men into God.[10] But how does this square with his concept of new humanity with a boundless future? Establishing any kind of limitations is judged as idolatry. In a limitless future, why should the category of God be put off-limits for man?

With Moltmann's promise of a new humanity within the plane of history, it seems inevitable that his theology will evolve into a type of optimistic humanism not totally unlike that of the Enlightenment. There is no safeguard that glory will not become the dominant theme. Some associated with Moltmann's theology have already taken up this suggestion. On the other hand, if Moltmann allows suffering to be the mark of God's participation in history, is it really possible any longer to call his theology of the future a theology of hope? Some of these views are further developed in his system of ethics.

Moltmann's prominence as a theologian might finally come from his ethical program rather than from his Marxist-related theology. Both Moltmann and Marx share a common Hegelian heritage, not only in principle, but also in their ethical systems. Moltmann, in an essay with the self-explanatory title "God in Revolution," lays down an ethic which finds its focus in changing the structures of society.

Contrast this to the older theology, where the emphasis was placed on an individual ethical response which included personal conversion and a life of good works. To bring about this type of sanctified life in the individual, the Church used the preached Word to bring about an internal change within the individual. The church saw its purpose as bringing the person into its fellowship and keeping him there. The individual Christian would then affect his society.

Moltmann offers a program in which the church confronts society directly, and not through the medium of the converted individual. Basic to this ethical program is his view of the world, with no fixed norms or structures. Replacing fixed structures are what are known as functional forms. God has not laid down authoritarian forms in the past which must be maintained. Rather, man with the freedom promised him in the future sets down forms which are to be utilized in realizing the future. The future and not the past provides the ethical norm. Future means freedom, and freedom includes relativity, in this case ethical relativity. Christ's death has opened for mankind messianic possibilities which have entered the stream of history. This ethical freedom, oriented toward the future, is exercised by criticism and protest, creative imagination and action. The church exercises ethical freedom by putting itself on the side of the oppressed and humiliated in the world. This kind of activity initiates the dialectical progress in history. The similarity between Moltmann's program and Marx's can be best demonstrated by Moltmann's own words:

> By undermining and demolishing all barriers—whether of religion, race, education, or class—the community of Christians proves that it is the community of Christ. This could indeed become the new identifying mark of the church in our world, that it is composed, not of equal and like-minded men, but of dissimilar men, indeed of former enemies. . . . The way toward this goal of new humane community

involving all nations and languages is, however, a revolutionary way.[11]

Several points in this program must be singled out. Reconciliation is a historical process taking place across cultural boundaries, including those of religion. It seems impossible to avoid the idea that Moltmann's theology is universalistic, with the final salvation understood purely as an act within history. The Church's end goal is the establishment of a kind of universal reign of God, quite apart from individual commitment to God.

Moltmann seems aware of the similarity between his program and Marx's, as he attempts to dissociate himself from an absolute comparison. But it is not from an understanding of the commandment prohibiting stealing that a distinction is made, but from a principle of humanity. Moltmann sees the financial exploiter bringing more harm to himself, by destroying his own humanity, than to the exploited. This is hardly the Marxist attitude, by which only the exploited deserves sympathy. But ultimately there is little difference between them in that both Moltmann and Marx see salvation as something being reached in history and not in an afterlife. Reconciliation is not a transcendental act of God Himself, but a historical act between men. With Moltmann's view of history, with the future as the only plane of reality, this concept of salvation is the only one possible.

The church is instrumental in attaining this salvation by siding with the world's oppressed. Salvation becomes a movement toward economic equalization. The church can no longer look upon itself as the favored recipient of God's activity in the world where the redeemed are gathered; but the church's existence is made subservient to the world's. Redemption takes place between opposing classes. To borrow the language of traditional theology, the kingdom of grace is subsumed under the kingdom of power in order to realize the eschatological kingdom of glory. From this final kingdom, no one is excluded. When the exploiters, the damners, are reconciled with the exploited, the damned, salvation will have occurred.

In order to bring this about, Moltmann does not rule out the possible use of revolution with violence: "The problem of violence and non-violence is an illusory problem. There is only the question of the justified and unjustified use of force and the question of whether the means are proportionate to the ends."[12] This kind of open-ended ethic, for which there is no fixed law or legal precedent, is a natural concomitant of his view of the future, in which absolute freedom is the only norm. If God and Christ receive their value for us from the future, then our actions should also be judged by what they accomplish in the future. The application of commandments can have no part in such a system. If the redemptive action brings about the reconciliatory results, then such action is recognized as justified. Ultimately it is a matter of the end justifying the means. Participation in revolution always involves the idea that the revolution is not the final one, but one in a process of revolutions. Moltmann's nonfinalized revolution is distinct from Marx's finalized revolution which results in the perfect state.

In Moltmann's thought, God does not stand at the beginning of theological thought but at the end of history, as a future possibility. The order for Moltmann is history, eschatology, and finally God. Passing over the option of the God who is in us, above us, and between us, Moltmann prefers to speak of the God who is in front of us. This does not mean there is no divine involvement now. There is an anticipation of God now as the future takes control of the present, but He is not yet present in the form of His eternal presence. A new dialectic of being caught between His being and His being-not-yet, which is the pain and power of history, is introduced. "Caught between the experiences of His presence and of His absence, we are seeking His future, which will solve this ambiguity that the present cannot solve."[13] Instead of speaking of God now, Moltmann speaks of the coming of God.

His views of God are also reflected in his understanding of Jesus' deity, also called His dignity.[14] When God's purposes in the future are finally realized, then Jesus, as the Bearer of God's future in the present, will have outlined His purpose, and His dignity will be surrendered. Jesus can be called God because He embodies the future. The coming of the future will terminate this function.

While Moltmann does not make the church the only recipient of salvation, the church plays a unique role in the world's salvation. The church is not qualitatively different from the world, but it serves as the vanguard of the new humanity that is being freed from inhumanity. The church participates in the world's groaning as the world moves forward to the eschatological goal. Thus the church has a sacramental role of proclaiming for the world a hope to be realized in the future. This concept of messianic eschatology proclaimed by the church is a description of the process of world history itself. Since

God and future are combined, the future assumes the creative function for time and history. This future brings new creative possibilities which continually bring into being new realities. Thus eschatology gives real meaning to present events. The church's proclamation of the divine is the proclamation of the historical.

Moltmann's concept of giving eschatological value to present events might simply be a reintroduction into the theology of Platonism, eschatologically interpreted. Events and objects in our sphere of existence receive their ultimate meaning from a transcendental future, which is as far removed from us as Plato's world of ideas. Moltmann's historical monism finally becomes a dualism, with the past and present on one side and the future as the ultimate reality on the other.

Moltmann is able from his basic premises to present a cogent, if not orthodox, doctrine of the Trinity, which finds its originating point in the cross of Jesus and its completion in the Spirit working in history. Since Moltmann recognizes eschatologically interpreted history as the sole reality, the Trinity must be understood economically and not ontologically. The distinction between what God is in Himself *(opera ad intra)* and what God does in the world *(opera ad extra)* is simply not valid for Moltmann. God's essence is confined to God's history. There can be no God out there. Basic for Moltmann's concept of the Trinitarian unity is participation of three persons, not in absolute deity, but in the unity of the abandonment revealed by the cross. The Father abandons, and the Son is abandoned; and from this cross the Spirit proceeds as the "Spirit of abandonment and love who raises up abandoned men."[15] Hegelian influence is quite evident here.

What is more important is that Moltmann offers a Trinitarian doctrine without ever having settled the question of the existence of God, a question which safely and continually is avoided. The substance of the Trinity does not involve the eternal substance of Deity but the historical event of the cross, which expresses itself in a Trinitarian sense.

Because of his assertion that God's existence is to be understood only on a historical plane, it could be logically concluded by some that Moltmann is in reality an atheist or pantheist. For those who find this judgment too premature, these words should give some food for thought: "This also means that God's being is historical and that he exists in history. The 'story of God' then is the story of the history of man."[16] (See also chap. 6.)

WOLFHART PANNENBERG: THEOLOGIAN OF HISTORY

Wolfhart Pannenberg, who holds a teaching post in systematic theology at the University of Munich, presents his theology from the category of history. With the appearance of his *Jesus–God and Man* in 1968, he became an influence in the English-speaking world. A more popular type of theology appeared with the two-volume publication of his essays, *Basic Questions to Theology,* in 1970 and 1971.

Because he sees history as the key to revelation, Pannenberg can be called the theologian of history. For him history is the principle of verifying the future. Pannenberg comes to his conclusions out of a reaction to Karl Barth's transcendentalism, with its concept of revelation in the Word. Barth's position had been that the revelatory Word is so self-sufficient that history and hence historical questions are irrelevant and are not really important in finding the revelation of God. For Pannenberg, all history is God's revelation. History is so clear in its revelatory functions that its interpretation can be made without the aid of a supernatural revelation. The revelatory truth is necessarily inherent in all history and quite plain to all observers.[17] Failure to grasp the revelation within history is the fault of the individual and his investigation and not of history itself. Pannenberg's view does not really take into account any kind of spiritual blindness in man as a basic cause of failure to interpret the historical revelation. Thus he avoids the question of original sin and, by skirting the issue, denies its debilitating effects.

Where Barth made no use of anything resembling a rigorous historical investigation, Pannenberg introduces it with an honest vengeance, without any preconceived notion of what will or must be found in history. History is an adequate vehicle of revelation, independent of any prior philosophical or theological ideas on the part of the seeker. Applying this principle of historical investigation to Christology, Pannenberg approaches the study of the person of Jesus from the horizontal plane of history and not in terms of a vertical revelation from heaven. Christology is a result of historical and not theological investigation. Revelation is seen as coming not directly from God but indirectly, through history. History possesses its own inherent capacity to be interpreted by whoever has the eyes to see it. No supernatural intervention is needed or provided to comprehend the significance of history.

Two corollaries follow this approach of viewing revelation from the perspective of history. First, since history is understood in its totality and not in isolated events, even in the sense of connecting these events, the historical revelation is universal.[18] No one historical event is inherently superior to another. Thus, the traditional Christian division between a natural revelation communicated in the created world and special revelation uniquely given through Israel and Jesus Christ cannot be maintained. Pannenberg does not recognize a revelation of the Law in nature and a revelation of Law and Gospel in the history connected with Jesus Christ. In Pannenberg's theology of history, the line between these two categories is erased so that God's redemptive purposes are universally revealed in and throughout all history.[19] There is no one special, unique, divinely controlled history in which God's redemptive purposes are clearly revealed. Second, since the historical revelation is universal, it can be understood only in its totality. Unlike traditional Christian thought, with its once-and-for-all revelation in Jesus Christ, revelation for Pannenberg is not restricted to a past event in history, but it continues to happen as history unfolds itself. The historical revelation comes to completion only at the end of history. For Pannenberg, the question of historical truth and hence revelation will be answered only by the future. Absolute historical certainty is simply not a possibility in the present. Since the future alone provides absolute answers, Pannenberg is classified with Moltmann as a theologian of hope.

Though history is a revelation of God, history itself does not give a direct revelation of God, even through Israel or Jesus.[20] Individual historical events point inwardly to God's revelation in themselves, but Pannenberg is careful to disassociate himself from any concept of pantheism. However, a verdict of panentheism, the enclosure of God in the world in the sense of interpenetration and inseparability might not be totally inappropriate.

Revelation finds its basis in history itself and not in reports about history. Therefore, the Law in the Old Testament and the proclaimed Gospel in the New Testament are not in themselves the revelation, but point back to the revelation in history. However, Law and Gospel do have a function in regard to revelation's process. The Law points back to Yahweh's revelation to Israel, and the Gospel to the events constituting God's revelation in Jesus Christ. They also serve a prophetic function in preparing the way for God's continued and future revelation in history. With their apocalyptic hopes, the histories of Israel and Jesus help shape future history. The event, and not God Himself, is apprehended from history.

God cannot possibly be known from any one event in history. It is through reflection on the historical event that one learns something about God. Since the historical process in its totality is revelatory, the revelation attached to any one event is fragmentary. Each event must be integrated into the whole, and the whole can be known only at the end. Pannenberg does not intend to deny that revelation exists now but rather to assert that history in its entirety is the vehicle of divine revelation.

We turn now to Pannenberg's method of harmonizing the idea of universal history as revelatory with the concept of a unique, historical significance attached to Israel. The uniqueness of Israel's religion is not due to the fact that Israel was the recipient of special revelation but that it had acquired a special consciousness of history, which recognized God's participation in that history.[21] Pannenberg says Israel saw history as the one reality and, through time, learned that this reality will be completed only at the end. Jewish genealogies going back to Adam, together with lively apocalyptic expectations, tie history into a unified whole. Other religions concentrated on disconnected and unrelated theophanies.

Pannenberg's appraisal of Israel's superior intellectual abilities in reading history seems to militate against the concept of God's sovereign election of Israel. In the Bible, Israel is pictured as spiritually ignorant. Pannenberg's favorable assessment of Israel really amounts to ascribing to Israel a kind of work-righteousness in intellectual dress. Such a view of revelation can logically result only in universalism.

Pannenberg's concept of Jesus as the final revelation must also be squared with the idea of universal revelation in history. This problem is resolved by considering Jesus as God's self-revelation in the sense that He is the anticipation of history's end. Jesus was the appearance in time, not of a preexistent Being, but of history's future horizon.[22] He stepped backward out of the future of history into present and past, and by this action unified history in Himself. Jesus performs the function for the Christian church that the apocalyptic performed for Israel. It was the Jewish apocalyptic that provided the basis for Jesus' mission.

Jesus, in His anticipation of the future, is part of God's self-definition, as God is defined under the category of the future. The doctrine of the *homoousion*, defined by the Nicene Christology as the Son's sharing in the Father's deity, is redefined as Jesus' sharing in God's total self-revelation at the end of the history.

Essential to the understanding of Jesus is His resurrection, which is viewed as the authentication of His apocalyptic message. His resurrection actualizes the end of history within history itself. Here Pannenberg's view is close to Moltmann's, as both interpret the resurrection as an eschatological event in history. The resurrection itself stands outside of history. The focal point in Christology is switched from incarnation to resurrection. The traditional concept of incarnation, emphasizing the appearance of a preexistent Deity on earth is not the basic principle for understanding Pannenberg's Christology.[23] For Pannenberg, it was the God of the future and not the past who entered history. The resurrection was the appearance of the God of the future. The historic Jesus is understood as an apocalyptic Preacher who gave men a chance to share in the future by preparing them for it.[24] Without this preparation, men would be overwhelmed by the future. Through historical investigation, we may recognize Jesus as the apocalyptic Preacher.

In spite of his disclaimer to philosophical presuppositions, Pannenberg does have a philosophical view of history. In arriving at his concept of universal history, he does not collect history's individual parts to arrive at the whole, but he approaches history with a previous acceptance of its wholeness. Individual historical events are to be constantly interpreted and reinterpreted in the light of the whole of history as it unfolds and, where necessary, adjusted. New events continue to shape the whole picture of history as they appear, and in turn these events are interpreted in light of history's totality. Through a growing tradition of hope and remembrance, isolated events are woven into one fabric of history.

Pannenberg's revelatory history is event interpreted within the context of tradition. For example, the resurrection of Jesus appears within the context of Jewish apocalyptic. The event is reinterpreted in different situations and, where necessary, adjusted. As another example, the fourth gospel is considered a deliberate attempt to reinterpret for Hellenism God's revelation in the historical Jesus. As the word of revelatory history is transmitted, it is intermingled with the tradition of interpretation. In this process there is an interaction between history and the tradition, each acting to shape and form the other. History remains the revelatory moment, and the tradition of its interpretation must be constantly judged by history.

Essential to this historical tradition is the prophetic word of promise that arises in history and shapes it.[25] This prophetic word is itself transformed in its transmission through history. The interpreting word is never final but can be corrected by additional events. The interpreting word can never be finalized, because history is not completed. Events now have revelatory significance as they anticipate the end of history; but they do not have final revelatory significance, as this would violate the scheme of looking at history in its totality. The interpretation of any event is provisional in light of future events.

The revelatory event of God in Jesus is not open to correction, as are other events, because it is an appearance of the end in the present. The finality of God's revelation in Jesus does not mean that it is the last chronologically. Other historical events have and will follow it, but they do not share in the eschatological uniqueness revealed in Jesus. Jesus is God's future in the midst, and in this futuristic sense Pannenberg speaks of incarnation.

A distinguishing mark in Pannenberg's approach is his nearly total confidence that historical research will discover revelatory significance in history. Objective historical research has a religious purpose, not because of any religious *a priori* inherent in the process of historical research, but because such research is capable of discovering God in history. Such a position stands in contrast to those of Martin Kähler and Karl Barth, who abandoned the field of history in their search for God. Bultmann used the tools of investigation in the study of history but separated the results of his historical research from faith's acclamation of God.

Pannenberg rejects all attempts to sidestep history and sees it as the only vehicle and final judge of revelation. Existentialism, supernaturalism, or any form of fideism cannot serve as refuges in which to escape the difficult historical questions concerning Christianity and its foundations. In the face of secular questions of truth, Christianity's truthfulness, including its assertion about God, is to be judged according to secular criteria and not by a special category of theology where an expected and sometimes contrived faith answer, *deus ex machina,* will save the day for theology regardless of the success of the secular opponents. Fearlessly Pannenberg takes the debate over Christianity's historical claims right out into the open, with the ever present possibility that the claims will fall. But if history is the only vehicle of revelation, then the risk cannot be avoided.

Even if faith is not the foundation of Christianity's veracity, this does not mean that faith is unimportant or without function for Pannenberg. But he does not equate faith with the results of historical investigation. Underlying Pannenberg's entire system is the proposition that the historical events have a truthfulness prior to any apprehension of them by faith. He revives the Reformation distinction that *notitia* with *assensus,* knowledge with assent, necessarily precedes *fiducia,* faith as trust.[26] Faith is different than knowledge, but can never exist without it. Faith is never uninformed by knowledge. Thus, faith as a basis of salvation must be rejected as subjectivism.

Pannenberg carefully distinguishes between historical certainty and the certainty of faith. Historical investigation does not result in absolute certainty; faith does. History and faith are related, but not identical. Interpreting history as revelation involves an uncertainty built into the process of investigation. This uncertainty comes from viewing historical events as part of a now incomplete historical totality. In the interpretative process, the evaluation of past events can be and is corrected and adjusted. This interpretative process includes the promise which will itself determine future history and interpretations of it. Therefore, historical investigation with interpretation can never reach the level of certainty but only of probability.

Pannenberg cannot rule out the possibility that our knowledge of Jesus and His eschatological significance will be ruled improbable by the probes of historical research. In Pannenberg's system, there are no absolute certainties and impossibilities but only probabilities and improbabilities. Nothing can be ruled out as a certain impossibility, because this would negate his principle that the future is open, with unlimited possibilities. The final question of the truth is now unanswerable. He frankly admits that the whole foundation of Christianity could stand in danger of collapse if the results of historical research so indicated. Pannenberg is ruthlessly honest in the application of this kind of historical investigation and, regardless of any possible negative and destructive results, will not back away from it. He looks to no heaven for any salvation in determining the truth. History and history alone will provide the answers.

While asserting the probabilities of historical investigation, he is nevertheless willing to assert a certainty of faith which relies on the distinctive eschatological significance of the Christ event. Faith relies on the results of historical investigation but acquires a certain independence of history by putting its trust in the God revealed in history rather than in the individual events themselves. Such faith is never autonomous, because it continually goes back to history to find God. Even where historical investigation calls into question interpretations upon which faith is built, faith anticipates future historical investigation which will vindicate it.[27] It is not a faith built on an absolute certainty of historical investigation but a faith in God's continued revelations in history. Since the results of historical investigation are always provisional in the light of the future, faith finds its focal point in the future and not in the past. For the present, faith must content itself for the ground of its certainty with its understanding of Jesus, which has proven itself satisfactory in daily experience.

Pannenberg has promised more historical support for faith than did neoorthodoxy, but in the final analysis he has not really succeeded in his task, because the results of all historical investigation are open to change. Pannenberg's view that the Christ event is an appearance of the future in history is a theological but not really a historical assertion. Thus, there seems to be an inherent self-contradiction in his entire system of thought.

JOHANNES METZ: A ROMAN CATHOLIC INTERPRETATION

The influence of the theology of hope has not been confined to Protestant Christianity but has also found expression in Roman Catholicism. In the first half of this century, a French Jesuit, Pierre Teilhard de Chardin, combined ideas of theology, philosophy, and biology and offered his theory of cosmic evolution, describing mankind's progression toward omega point. Teilhard even suggested that the incarnation was the appearance in time of what mankind would become at the end of time. This Jesuit, with his fundamental dependency on a unique evolutionary world-view, does not belong to the theologians of hope, with their historical orientation; but with his eschatological emphasis and his concept of progress, he certainly belongs in the vanguard of recent thought, and he helped prepare theological thinking for the theology of hope, especially in Roman Catholicism.

Any expression of the theology of hope in Roman Catholicism would most naturally take into consideration the church as an institution. The ideas of future and of the church as institution would have to be combined to be true to both Catholicism and the fundamental concepts of theology of hope. An inroad for the theology of hope into the Roman Catholic Church was provided by Vatican II, some of whose decrees expressed a belief in the basic unity of God.

with the world through the Church. Here is one example of such thinking: "In Christ, the church is as the sacrament, that is, the sign and instrument of the inner unity with God and of the unity of the whole mankind."[28] The world as world is defined as part of the church's responsibilities. The renowned Dutch Catholic theologian, Edward Schillebeeckx, popularized the pronouncements of Vatican II by reinterpreting them from the perspective of the theology of hope in his *The Mission of the Church*.

Closer, however, to the originating center of the theology of hope in the Roman Catholic Church is Johannes B. Metz. Metz, like his Protestant counterparts Moltmann and Pannenberg, is German born and holds doctorates in philosophy and theology. He is professor of fundamental theology at the Catholic Faculty of the University of Münster. His *Theology of the World* is a collection of some of his essays in translation. In contrast to other leaders in the movement, Metz could be dubbed the theologian of politics. Theology is to serve as critic of the socio-political structures.[29] Within this theological obligation, the church performs the role of a servant over against the world.

The starting point for Metz's theology is the incarnation, which is regarded as God's acceptance of the world as world. Metz deplores the Enlightenment and all movements related to it for separating church and world into separate spheres. Any church-centered theology is labeled ascetic. Metz sees his role as helping the church and world realize that they are cut from the same piece of cloth, that is, the world. The world serves as the common ground of unity for church and world.[30] The incarnation of the Logos means that the Christian spirit is embedded in the flesh of the world, and all subsequent history is a process in which the Christian Logos is the inherent principle. The irreversible secularization of the world does not mean that Christianity is disappearing but that it is becoming historically effective. The secularity of the world is interpreted not as defeat but as victory for Christianity. The secular theologians of the previous decade look at the same secular evidence as did Metz. The former proclaim that God is dead and the latter that Christianity is victorious. The evidence is admittedly the same, only the verdict is different.

Metz sees the incarnation as an objective act in history. For him it is a definite certainty, a position not possible for Moltmann and Pannenberg. However, he shares with them the view that universal history is caught up in the plan of salvation. Whatever might have been transcendental in the past condescends through the incarnation into history in such a way that whatever may have been considered before as transcendental is now part of the future. Because of God's participation in history, history is viewed as a totality permeated by the incarnation and not subdivided into the categories of general and special histories. God's participation in history through the incarnation of the Logos is the sign and promise that God has accepted the world eschatologically.[31] Future salvation takes its substance from the world. Through the incarnation, God becomes the principle of history and not merely a principle within history. God's appearance in the world is not in the guise of divinity, but He lets the world appear as world. The attempt to isolate the element of divinity in secularization is improper. The historical process reenacts the Christ event as it enfolds itself in the world. Incarnation is not a qualitatively different act in history, but it generates and provides the momentum to the historical process.

The challenge for the church, as Metz sees it, is to recognize the Christian element enfolding itself in the process of universal history. This history is not proceeding to an other-worldly, heavenly Jerusalem outside of history. Rather, history finds its goal always coming into being in the historical moment of faith. Metz shares with Moltmann and Pannenberg the concept of an evasive history always appearing on the horizon but never fully arriving.

Since history for Metz is incarnational, the church as an institution orients its task toward the political institutions. This churchly activity is called political theology.[32] This attitude is set in deliberate opposition to the I-Thou theology of the existentially oriented neoorthodox theology. Neoorthodoxy is judged as personalistic and the unenviable heritage of the Enlightenment. In serving as critic of political institutions, the church finds her true identity. In this criticism, the form of the church's message is shaped by the historical process. Thus the church participates in world history culminating in the future.

In Metz's view, salvation is already present in the historical process and does not have to be introduced as a foreign element. The church has an obligation to recognize her mission as an agent for institutional transformation in the world. To do this the church calls the world's attention to its own secular character so that the world can be the world. In performing this task of transformation, the church is to avoid identity with the structures of any one political institution. To do so would be totalitarianism. The church in this critical activity and responsibility can cooperate with explicitly non-Christian groups.[33]

Metz occupies a conservative place in the spectrum of theology of hope. He feels the incarnation and the church have firm places within history and serve as guideposts for God's future actions in history. As long as the church as church remains an institution, there is a visible stabilizing force in Metz's theology which is lacking in other expressions of the theology of hope. Total revolution in the political order is impossible as long as the church as a political institution remains part of the process. But like others in this movement, he does tie the fate of God, man, and the church to the changing exigencies of history.

Political involvement is part of the historical fabric of the Roman Catholic church. This church has never repudiated that all earthly and spiritual powers have their source in the Roman pontiff. With this history in view, Metz's political theology might be only a contemporary expression of Rome's historical self-understanding at a time when her political influence is not very high. Since Metz does not and perhaps cannot theologically dispose of ecclesiastical structures, his political theology might prove more usable; but to create this theology, he has sacrificed much of the traditional understanding of a transcendent God and has subsumed the church into the category of the world. He has provided an interesting union between church and world; but many will find that his views hardly do justice to the biblical view, where church and world are opponents of each other.

RUBEM ALVES: ONE STEP FURTHER

The very nature of theology of hope is to be open to corrections and reformulations of all kinds.[34] To have a once-and-for-all theology of hope would deny its major tenet of the limitless possibilities offered by the future.

A Brazilian who studied in America, Rubem A. Alves, finds Moltmann's approach of waiting for the future too conservative. Instead of waiting for the future to take hold of man in the present—a stance which Alves calls messianic humanism—man should grasp the future for himself. This Alves calls humanistic messianism. It is also what Moltmann calls *praesumptio*, a kind of work-righteousness, an attitude presumptuous enough to set directions for itself in history. Man right now, according to Alves, has the messianic capabilities of realizing the future without waiting for

God. For Moltmann, man is part of the historical process, but between man and history God functions as a Mediator.

Alves does not surrender the concept that history is the category under which man works; but instead of man following God's directives in history, he sees God following man's directives as he participates in history. Man becomes the captain of his own destiny. Structures, including capitalism, must be overthrown if man is to recover the dominant hand in controlling his own history. No longer is there any hint of the fatalistic attitude of awaiting whatever history will have to offer; man is to take history into his own hands. The guiding ethic is love, defined as removing obstacles preventing man from realizing his own freedom.

Alves's views are expounded in his book fittingly entitled *A Theology of Human Hope*. God becomes the power of humanization, which frees man historically even when all objective and subjective possibilities in history have been exhausted. Man's oppression becomes God's crucifixion, and man's political language becomes resurrection. For Alves, there is no uniqueness attached to Jesus.

Regardless of the radicalness of Alves's program, his conclusions were easily drawn from Moltmann in spite of the limits that Moltmann outlined for himself. Theology of hope attempted to reintroduce the question of God into theology in the aftermath of God-is-dead theology. But in fact, it has only returned to eliminating God. For Alves's book, Harvey Cox, the prominent secular theologian, provided a complimentary foreword in which he points to the similarities in both their views. With Alves, the theology of hope has come full circle and has repeated the verdict of the God-is-dead theologians.

CONCLUSION

In large part, theology of hope sprang up as an answer to the God question, which had been answered negatively by the God-is-dead theologians in the 1960s. If this new theology had not reintroduced the God question, nonconservative theology might have hastened to extinction in the last part of the twentieth century. For one hundred years theology has moved in the direction of minimalism. Creation was replaced by evolution; a divine Jesus was replaced by a human Jesus who did no miracles and who blundered intellectually and morally; and then, finally, the very history of Jesus was questioned.

Yet until the 1960s theology had not dared to discard God, although atheists have always felt they had more than ample arguments to dispose of Him. What was new in the 1960s was that Christian theologians openly admitted that they made use of the arguments of the atheists. Using the theological tradition going back to the eighteenth-century Enlightenment, they saw the handwriting on the wall and officially proclaimed that God was dead. Of course, there were differences of opinions about what this meant and when it had happened. Conservative theologians since the publication of Darwin's theories had warned the church that a kind of domino theory was at work and would result in a loss of God. This prophecy did come true in the God-is-dead theology.

Many wondered where theology would go after this extreme. No one had proclaimed that the church was dead quite yet. Such a step would be more radical than proclaiming God's death. The past and present were searched to find God, and the reports came back negative. Only the option of the future remained viable for the continuing search for God. Moltmann and Pannenberg, who had developed their futuristic thought in the 1950s and early 1960s, had a ready-made theological audience, people who were frustrated and waiting for a way out of the dilemma. The theology of hope is safe from historical and philosophical scrutiny, since the evidence for its position is ultimately in the future. All sorts of unprovable theological assertions can be made, because everything is open to chance and correction in the future. It is a perpetually over-the-next-hill theology.

Theology of hope has given a false and deceptive solution to the pessimism of God-is-dead theology, a solution more cruel because it refuses to say yes or no. The entire theology-of-hope movement effectively primed the theological pump, but the water now in the theological well is only the water the theologians of hope themselves have poured down. Theology of hope proclaims that the transcendental sphere of a majestic God is still nonexistent and that this world with its history is the only realm of reality. This is really no advance over the theology of the 1960s. As long as history is not complete, there are no certain historical answers and hence no certain answers about God. All possibilities must remain open.

If God is really dead, man can prepare himself for his atheistic existence and make the best of it. Theology of hope leaves the question of God's existence open as a future possibility. God is not dead, but listed as missing in action. No one has used the word *agnostic* in referring to this approach, but it might not be inappropriate. Theology of hope hardly takes an agnostic approach to what can be learned from history by each person; on the contrary, it is very optimistic about man's innate abilities to read history and to come to conclusions. But it is agnostic about the conclusions, including the conclusions about God. The God-is-dead theologians effectively buried the corpse of God. The theologians of hope tell us that they cannot find His corpse. Americans have just lived through the trauma of the POW and MIA problems in Viet Nam. The POW problem is solved. The MIA is not. Many families want to hear one way or another so that they can get on with the job of living. Theology of hope leaves us in a similar position theologically.

As mentioned above, the theology of hope has a built-in instability. This instability has only two possible consequences. Either theology of hope will lurch ahead with the same false, optimistic humanism born in the eighteenth century that contributed to the European collapse in the twentieth century; or else it will write its question marks so boldly that many people will wish that God were dead. Sometimes wishing becomes believing.

From either angle, the theology of hope is hopeless. The only answer is the reintroduction of a Christianity which hopes in God's future redemption but establishes this hope on past events of which it is confidently certain. The theologians of hope rightly saw that there is more to existence than the present. They set their sails toward the future, but unfortunately they failed to take their bearings from the compass of the past. Without a fixed course charted from the past, the theology of hope has no real future in which to sail; and there is no haven or harbor where it will ever drop its anchor.

Friedrich Schleiermacher is considered the father of modern liberal theology. In the early nineteenth century he called the consciousness of man the basis of religion and of God's existence. First there was consciousness, then self-consciousness, and then God-consciousness. Though the terminology is different, Carl Braaten's argument for a religion of hope seems to be basically no different from Schleiermacher's religion of consciousness. "Where there is life, there is hope, and where there is hope, there is religion, and where religion receives the promise of God for the fulfillment of life through the person of Jesus, there is Christianity."[35] In the final analysis, man is left alone, whether it be with his own consciousness or with life.

Notes

1. Kenneth Cauthen, *Christian Biopolitics* (Nashville: Abingdon, 1971).
2. Jürgen Moltmann, "The Revolution of Freedom: Christians and Marxists Struggle for Freedom," in *Religion, Revolution and the Future*, trans. M. Douglas Meeks (New York: Scribner, 1969), pp. 63-82.
3. Carl E. Braaten, "Ernst Bloch's Philosophy of Hope," in *The Futurist Option* (New York: Newman, 1970), pp. 59-78.
4. Jürgen Moltmann, *The Theology of Hope*, trans. James W. Leitsch (New York: Harper & Row, 1967), pp. 216-17.
5. Moltmann, "Resurrection as Hope," in *Religion, Revolution and the Future*, pp. 42-62; *Theology of Hope*, p. 219.
6. Moltmann, *Theology of Hope*, p. 201.
7. Jürgen Moltmann, "God and Resurrection," in *Hope and Planning*, trans. Margaret Clarkson (New York: Harper & Row, 1971), pp. 31-55.
8. Moltmann, "Understanding of History in Christian Social Ethics," in *Hope and Planning*, p. 106.
9. Moltmann, *Theology of Hope*, pp. 22-26.
10. G. Clark Chapman, Jr., "Moltmann's Vision of Man," *Anglican Theological Review* 51 (July 1974): 28.
11. Moltmann, "God in Revolution," in *Religion, Revolution and the Future*, p. 141.
12. Ibid., p. 143.
13. Jürgen Moltmann, "Hope and History," in *Religion, Revolution and the Future*, p. 209.
14. Ibid., p. 213.
15. Jürgen Moltmann, "The 'Crucified God': God and the Trinity Today," in *New Questions on God*, ed. Johannes B. Metz (New York: Herder & Herder, 1972), p. 34.
16. Ibid., p. 35.
17. Wolfhart Pannenberg, "Redemptive Event and History," in *Basic Questions in Theology: Collected Essays*, trans. George H. Kehm (Philadelphia: Fortress, 1970, 1971), 1:22-23.
18. Ibid., pp. 45-50.
19. Ibid., p. 78.
20. Wolfhart Pannenberg, et.al., eds., *Revelation as History*, trans. David Granskou (New York: Macmillan, 1968), pp. 16-17.
21. Pannenberg, "Redemptive Event and History," in *Basic Questions in Theology*, 1:18.
22. Wolfhart Pannenberg, "The Revelation of God in Jesus," in *New Frontiers in Theology*, vol. 3, *Theology as History*, ed. James M. Robinson and John B. Cobb, Jr. (New York: Harper & Row, 1967), p. 130.
23. Wolfhart Pannenberg, *Jesus—God and Man*, trans. Lewis L. Wilkins and Duane Priebe (Philadelphia: Westminster, 1968), pp. 150-58.
24. Wolfhart Pannenberg, "Appearance as the Arrival of the Future," in *Theology and the Kingdom of God*, ed. Richard John Neuhaus (Philadelphia: Westminster, 1969), pp. 132-33.
25. Wolfhart Pannenberg, "Response to the Discussion," in *Theology as History*, pp. 256-58.
26. Wolfhart Pannenberg, "Insight and Faith," in *Basic Questions in Theology*, 2:30-31.
27. Pannenberg, "Response to the Discussion," p. 274.
28. As quoted in Edward Schillebeeckx, *Mission of the Church*, trans. N. D. Smith (New York: Seabury, 1973), p. 43.
29. Johannes B. Metz, *Theology of the World*, trans. William Glen-Doeppel (New York: Herder & Herder, 1969), pp. 107-24.
30. Ibid., pp. 13-50.
31. Ibid., pp. 26-27.
32. Ibid., p. 110.

33. Ibid., p. 123.
34. Wolfhart Pannenberg, "Postscript," in *The Theology of Wolfhart Pannenberg*, by E. Frank Tupper (Philadelphia: Westminster, 1973), p. 305.
35. Carl E. Braaten and Robert W. Jenson, *The Futurist Option* (New York: Newman, 1970), p. 83.

Selected Reading

Alves, Rubem A. *A Theology of Human Hope*. Washington: Corpus, 1969.

Benz, Ernst. *Evolution and Christian Hope: Man's Concept of the Future from the Early Fathers to Teilhard de Chardin*. Trans. Frank G. Heinz. Garden City, N. Y.: Doubleday, 1966.

Braaten, Carl E., and Jenson, Robert W. *The Futurist Option*. New York: Newman, 1970.

Cauthen, Kenneth. *Christian Biopolitics: A Credo and Strategy for the Future*. Nashville: Abingdon, 1971.

Jenson, Robert W. *Story and Promise: A Brief Theology of the Gospel about Jesus*. Philadelphia: Fortress, 1973.

Marty, Martin E., and Peerman, Dean G., eds. *New Theology No. 5*. New York: Macmillan, 1969.

Metz, Johannes B. *Theology of the World*. Trans. William Glen-Doeppel. New York: Herder & Herder, 1969.

Metz, Johannes B., ed. *Faith and the World of Politics*. Concilium, vol. 36. New York: Paulist, 1968.

———. *New Questions on God*. Concilium, vol. 76. New York: Herder & Herder, 1972.

Moltmann, Jürgen. *The Gospel of Liberation*. Trans. H. Wayne Pipkin. Waco, Texas: Word, 1973.

———. *Hope and Planning*. Trans. Margaret Clarkson. New York: Harper & Row, 1971.

———. *Religion, Revolution and the Future*. Trans. M. Douglas Meeks. New York: Scribner, 1969.

———. *The Theology of Hope*. Trans. James W. Leitsch. New York: Harper & Row, 1967.

Pannenberg, Wolfhart. *The Apostles Creed: In Light of Today's Questions*. Trans. Margaret Kohl. Philadelphia: Westminster, 1972.

———. "Appearance as the Arrival of the Future." In *Theology and the Kingdom of God*, ed. John Richard Neuhaus. Philadelphia: Westminster, 1969.

———. "Insight and Faith." In *Basic Questions in Theology: Collected Essays*, trans. George Kehm, vol. 2. Philadelphia: Fortress, 1971.

———. *Jesus–God and Man*. Trans. Lewis L. Wilkins and Duane A. Priebe. Philadelphia: Westminster, 1968.

————. "Redemptive Event and History." In *Basic Questions in Theology: Collected Essays,* trans. George Kehm, vol. 1. Philadelphia: Fortress, 1970.

————. *What Is Man? Contemporary Anthropology in Theological Perspective.* Trans. Duane A. Priebe. Philadelphia: Fortress, 1970.

Schillebeeckx, Edward. *The Mission of the Church.* Trans. N. D. Smith. New York: Seabury, 1973.

Wilken, Robert L. *The Myth of Christian Beginnings.* Garden City, N. Y.: Doubleday, 1971.

PROCESS THEOLOGY

I. The background of process theology
II. The process theology of Whitehead
   A. The general character of Whitehead's process philosophy
      1. The scientific background
      2. The metaphysical character
      3. The atomic nature
      4. Platonic affinity
      5. Empirical base
      6. A process metaphysics
   B. Specific nature of Whiteheadian process philosophy
      1. Process and permanence
      2. Actual entities
      3. Eternal objects
   C. Whitehead's bipolar view of God
      1. God: His primordial nature
      2. God: His consequent nature
      3. God: His superject nature
      4. God and evil
      5. God and creativity
      6. God and negative prehensions
III. The process theology of Charles Hartshorne and John Cobb
   A. Basic similarities between Whitehead's and Hartshorne's systems
      1. A similar bipolar metaphysical model
      2. The contrast between bipolar and monopolar concepts of God
   B. Some distinctive differences between Whitehead and Hartshorne
      1. The methodological difference between Whitehead and Hartshorne
      2. Hartshorne's statement of the ontological argument
      3. Hartshorne's defense of his ontological argument
      4. The metaphysical differences between Whitehead and Hartshorne
   C. John Cobb's modifications of Whitehead and Hartshorne

6

Process Theology

by

NORMAN L. GEISLER

A major movement, perhaps the major movement, in contemporary theology is process theology. Forms of process metaphysics stressing God's immanence in an evolving world were proposed in the first third of this century. However, its immediate influence was checked by two antimetaphysical movements emerging at the same time: (1) Barthian theology and related forms of neoorthodoxy stressed God's transcendence and the gulf between the God of philosophy and the God of revelation; (2) logical positivism and ensuing discussions about the significance of God-talk called into question not only the truth claims of religious language but even its very meaning. Nevertheless, in this period of eclipse, interest in process metaphysics and a process concept of Deity was kept alive by the expositions of Charles Hartshorne.

In the 1960s and 1970s the processive view of reality has emerged again as a leading contender for the preferred model upon which to expound Christian theology. The list of authors publishing books and articles in this period favoring this view is impressive: Bernard Meland; John B. Cobb, Jr.; Schubert M. Ogden; Norman Pittenger; Daniel Day Williams; Leslie Dewart; E. Baltazar; Eugene

NORMAN L. GEISLER, B.A., M.A., Th.B., Ph.D., is professor of systematic theology at Dallas Theological Seminary. Some of his recent books are *Christian Ethic of Love* (Zondervan, 1973), *Philosophy of Religion* (Zondervan, 1974), *From God to Us* (Moody, 1974), *Christian Apologetics* (Baker, 1976), and *The Root of Evil* (Zondervan, 1978).

Fontinell; and Gregory Baum. This list also testifies to the appeal that process theology has for both Protestant and Catholic theologians. Indeed, some have proposed that process theology might well provide the model for an ecumenical theology. To understand this current trend in theology, we must first examine its philosophical background.

THE BACKGROUND OF PROCESS THEOLOGY

Process philosophy is not new. The ancient Greek philosopher Heraclitus (Fl. 500 B.C.) declared that a man "could not step twice in the same river; for other and yet other waters are ever flowing on." Although Heraclitus himself believed there was an unchanging Logos beneath and beyond the changing world that measured and made the change possible, a later disciple carried the position to its logical extreme.[1] Cratylus, the fifth-century Sophist, believed that no one even steps into the same river once. Change is so pervasive that there is no river there at all. So skeptical was Cratylus of his own process existence that reportedly he would merely wiggle his finger when asked whether or not he existed. There are other precursors of contemporary process philosophy among the ancients. The bipolar model of God is derived from Plato and others like Diogenes before him, who held that God is to the World as the soul is to the body. This same analogy, with some significant modifications, is used by the contemporary process theologian Charles Hartshorne.

There are many modern philosophers who contributed to the development of process philosophy. Only the most significant and influential names will be mentioned here. Hegel (d. 1831), under the influence of a Christian linear view of history and a dialectic that developed from a post-Kantian synthesis of thesis and antithesis in human experience, set forth a kind of dialectical pantheism, although he disclaims the label. God is in historical process. In fact, history is the footprints of God in the sands of time. God is unfolding Himself in the phenomena of the world in a continual process. Herbert Spencer (1820-1903) expanded the Darwinian biological hypothesis into a philosophy of cosmic evolution. It is in the wake of Spencerian process evolution that Henri Bergson wrote his influential *Creative Evolution* (1907). Bergson explained the evolutionary process of the world by an *Elan Vital,* a vital impetus, or life force, that accounts for the discontinuous "leaps" that lead to progress in biological development. In a later work, Bergson identified this *Élan Vital* with God, who is "undertaking to create creators, . . .

beings worthy of His love."[2] This identification of process and God is a significant moment in the history of process theology. The most influential formulation of process theology, however, is found in Alfred North Whitehead (1861-1947).

THE PROCESS THEOLOGY OF WHITEHEAD

Perhaps the earliest precursor of process theology is Samuel Alexander's *Space, Time, and Deity* (1920).[3] But the systematic honors belong definitely to Alfred North Whitehead. From a background in mathematics and philosophy of science and a grappling with the problems of space, time, and relativity,[4] Whitehead's thought gradually matured into a complete process metaphysics found in his classic *Process and Reality* (1929).[5] It is primarily from this work, as elucidated by *Adventures of Ideas* (1933)[6] and *Modes of Thought* (1938),[7] that we take our exposition of Whitehead's system.

Whitehead's view of God has many names. Some call it pan-en-theism (God-in-the-world) in distinction from classical pantheism, in which God *is* the world. In some respects it is a developmental pantheism, as Hegel's view is a developmental pantheism. Some label it finite godism or a quasi theism or neoclassical theism. Still others refer to Whitehead's philosophy as an organism because of the organic interconnection of God in the process of all things. But it seems that the most appropriate description is bipolarism, because God is viewed as bipolar, or dipolar.

THE GENERAL CHARACTER OF WHITEHEAD'S PROCESS PHILOSOPHY

The chief characteristic of Whitehead's philosophy is that of process: reality is not static and substantial but dynamic and in process. The real, including God, is not composed of unchanging essences but of changing activities. Whitehead's system as a whole may be characterized as follows:

The scientific background. Whitehead candidly admits that his process metaphysics arose out of the needs posed by his mathematics and in opposition to mechanistic physics.

> In fact by reason of my own studies in mathematics and mathematical physics, I did in fact arrive at my convictions in this way. Mathematical physics presumes in the first place an electromagnetic field of activity pervading space and time. The laws which condition this field are nothing else than the conditions observed by the general activity of the flux of the world, as it individualises itself in the events.[8]

So Whitehead's metaphysical position may be viewed as a broadening of his cosmology, which arose out of his attempt to build a philosophy of science as a foundation for the physical sciences.[9]

The metaphysical character. For Whitehead, "Science does not diminish the need of a metaphysics. . . . Science only renders the metaphysical need more urgent."[10] He further contends, "No science can be more secure than the unconscious metaphysics which tacitly it presupposes."[11] That is, Whitehead's concern is more than cosmological. Cosmology "is the effort to frame a scheme of the general character of the present stage of the universe."[12] Metaphysics, on the other hand, is a more general scheme of things that must be true of every stage or epoch of the world.[13] Whitehead believes, "All reasoning, apart from some metaphysical reference, is vicious."[14]

The atomic nature. The Whiteheadian metaphysic views reality as "incurably atomic." "Thus the ultimate metaphysical truth is atomism. The creatures are atomic." By these "atoms" Whitehead does not mean hard pellets of material stuff but what he calls "actual entities," or "actual occasions." These "atoms" are "drops of experience," or the "final facts" of the real world. He says, "continuity concerns what is potential; whereas actuality is incurably atomic."[15] That is, ultimate reality is made of many things actually which have oneness only potentially.

Platonic affinity. Whitehead clearly acknowledges his debt to Plato. He admits that *Process and Reality* presents a Platonic point of view, which he explains by saying,

> I mean that if we had to render Plato's general point of view with the least changes made necessary by the intervening two thousand years of human experience in social organization, in aesthetic attainments, in science, and in religion, we should have to set about the construction of a philosophy of organism.

He does not pretend to be exegeting Plato's writings, though at times he does speak of his philosophy as an interpretation of Plato. Indeed, he alludes to his own view as a "platonic realism."[16]

Empirical base. Whitehead's realism is empirically based. For, he says,

> The true method of discovery is like the flight of an aeroplane. It starts from the ground of particular observation; it makes a flight in the thin air of imaginative generalization; and it again lands for renewed observation rendered acute by rational interpretation.

In this sense Whitehead stands in the line of British empiricists. He wrote, "The endeavour to interpret experience in accordance with the overpowering deliverance of commonsense must bring us back to some restatement of platonic realism."[17]

A process metaphysics. Above all, Whitehead's philosophy is definitely Heraclitian. For Whitehead, "the ancient doctrine that 'no one crosses the same river twice' is extended. No thinker thinks twice; and, to put the matter more generally, no subject experiences twice." For "It is fundamental to the metaphysical doctrine of the philosophy of organism, that the notion of an actual entity as the unchanging subject of change is completely abandoned." In other words, process is the rule of the world. "There is a becoming of continuity, but no continuity of becoming." Whitehead wrote clearly,

> That "all things flow" is the first vague generalization which the unsystematized, barely analyzed, intuition of men has produced . . . it appears as one of the first generalizations of Greek philosophy in the form of the saying of Heraclitus. . . . Without doubt, if we are to go back to that ultimate, integral experience, unwarped by the sophistications of theory, that experience whose elucidations is the final aim of philosophy, the flux of things is one ultimate generalization around which we must weave our philosophical system.* [18]

SPECIFIC NATURE OF WHITEHEADIAN PROCESS PHILOSOPHY

Whitehead's pluralism may be described as a Platonic pluralism in process, with a distinctive empirical and realistic basis. However, Whitehead did not emphasize process to the total neglect of permanence: both elements are plainly presented.

Process and permanence. Briefly stated, the permanent element in the metaphysical makeup of the temporal world is the *potential* element (for example, eternal objects) and the process element is the *actual* element (for example, actual entities). He wrote, "Continuity concerns what is potential; whereas actuality is incurably atomic."[19] For Whitehead, "One all-pervasive fact, inherent in the very character of what is real is the transition of things, the passage one to another."[20] In other words, "It belongs to the nature of a 'being' that it is a potential for every 'becoming.' This is the 'principle of relativity.'" Or to state a kindred principle, "How an actual entity *becomes* constitutes *what* that actual entity *is* . . . .

---

*Whitehead does allow for personal identity or a "nexus," or "society," of actual entities but not for individual actual entities such as is God Himself (see n. 52).

Its 'being' is constituted by its 'becoming.' This is the 'principle of progress.'"[21]

On the other hand, Whitehead recognized the need for permanence in his metaphysical system.

"Permanence can be snatched only out of flux; and the passing moment can find its adequate intensity only by its submission to permanence. Those who would disjoin the two elements can find no interpretation of patent facts." Whitehead finds this permanence on two levels.

1. In the temporal world permanence is found in what he calls "eternal objects," or "forms of definiteness," which are something like platonic forms except that they are constituently connected with the sensible world (whereas Plato's forms were not). So, "In the philosophy of organism it is not 'substance' which is permanent, but 'form.'"

2. On the nontemporal, or eternal, level the element of permanence is found in the primordial nature of God.[22]

In the temporal world, however, it is actual entities and eternal objects which constitute respectively the processive and permanent sides of the Whiteheadian metaphysic. An elaboration of each, then, is crucial to an understanding of Whitehead's kind of process philosophy.

Actual entities. The most fundamental realities in Whitehead's system—indeed, the only actualities—are actual entities. They "are the final real things of which the world is made up."† [23] For, "every actual occasion exhibits itself as a process: it is a becomingness." Each actual entity is an "event" whose outcome is a "unit of experience."[24] That is, "In the becoming of an actual entity, the *potential* unity of many entities—actual and non-actual—acquires the *real* unity of the one actual entity; so that the actual entity is the real concrescence of many potentials." Since they are a process, in a real sense their birth is their death. In fact, there is a sense in which they never exist.

> This conception of an actual entity in the fluent world is little more than an expansion of a sentence in the *Timaeus:* "But that which is conceived by opinion with the help of sensation and without reason, is always in the process of becoming and perishing and never really is."

† Actual entities are not to be confused with persons (*Process and Reality,* p. 531) or with molecules (ibid., p. 114) or with electrons (ibid., p. 140). All of these are societies, or groups, of actual entities (ibid., pp. 136-37).

That is to say, "events become and perish. In their becoming they are immediate and they vanish into the past. They are gone; they have perished; they are no more and have passed into not-being."[25] However, when Whitehead agrees with Plato's phrase "Always becoming and never really are," he is quick to note that for Plato (in the *Sophist)* "Not-being is itself a form of being." What Whitehead means is that the process is ongoing. Events appear (they "are") and then they "perish" (they "are not"). "Thus we should balance Aristotle's. . . doctrine of becoming by a doctrine of perishing," he writes. "When they perish, occasions pass from the immediacy of being into the not-being of immediacy. But that does not mean they are nothing. They remain 'stubborn fact.'" As may be apparent from this discussion, the doctrine of the perishing of actual entities assumes a major role in the philosophy of Whitehead, as he clearly confesses.[26]

However, what an actual entity loses subjectively by perishing it gains in objectivity. "Forms suffer changing relations; actual entities 'perpetually perish' subjectively, but are immortal objectivity. Actuality in perishing acquires objectivity, while it loses subjective immediacy." That is to say, "It loses the final causation which is its internal principle of unrest, and it acquires efficient causation." So, it is only by perishing as a subject that an actual entity becomes immortal as an object. Once an actual entity has become objectively immortal, it can act as an efficient cause for other actual entities that are in the process of "concrescence," or coming to be. For all efficient causality moves from the past to the present like tradition. Final causality, on the contrary, operates in the present. It is the "subjective aim" of the actual entity that controls the process of its own becoming. The "subjective aim is this subject determining its own self-creation." This it does by determining its own "subjective form," that is, by determining *how* it will prehend its data.[27]

By "prehension" Whitehead means "a process of 'feeling' the many data, so as to absorb them into the unity of one individual 'satisfaction.'"[28]

> Thus a prehension involves three factors. There is the occasion of experience within which the prehension is a detail of activity; there is the datum whose relevance provokes the origination of this prehension; this datum is the prehended object; there is the subjective form, which is the affective tone determining the effectiveness of that prehension in that occasion of experience. How the experience constitutes itself depends on its complex of subjective forms.[29]

Further,

> There are two species of prehensions, the "positive species" and the
> "negative species." An actual entity has a perfectly definite bond
> with each item in the universe. This determinate bond is its prehen-
> sion of that item. A negative prehension is the definite exclusion of
> that item from positive contribution to the subject's own real internal
> constitution. This doctrine involves the position that a negative pre-
> hension expresses a bond. A positive prehension is the definite inclu-
> sion of that item into positive contribution to the subject's own real
> internal constitution.

Then too, "prehensions whose data involve actual entities [objec-
tively immortal]—are termed 'physical prehensions'; and prehensions of eternal objects are termed 'conceptual prehensions.'" For
all actual entities are dipolar, involving both of these aspects.[30]

Most important to the Whiteheadian concept of an actual entity
is what he terms the "ontological principle." "The ontological
principle declares that every decision is referable to one or more
actual entities, because in separation from actual entities there is
nothing, merely nonentity." To state it another way, "everything
must be somewhere; and here 'somewhere' means 'some actual
entity.'" "This ontological principle means that actual entities are
the only reasons; so that to search for a reason is to search for one or
more actual entities." Succinctly stated, it means "no actual entity,
then no reason." For, "it is a contradiction in terms to assume that
some explanatory fact can float into the actual world out of nonentity."

So it is the ontological principle which affirms,

> There is no going behind actual entities to find anything more real.
> They differ among themselves: God is an actual entity, and so is the
> most trivial puff of existence in far-off empty space. But, though there
> are gradations of importance, and diversities of function, yet in the
> principles which actuality exemplifies all are on the same level. The
> final facts are, all alike, actual entities; and these actual entities are
> drops of experience, complex and interdependent.[31]

Eternal objects. If actuality is the element of process in the
temporal world, then potentiality is the element of permanence.
This potential element Whitehead calls "eternal objects" or
"platonic forms," which ingress into actual entities. "Thus the
metaphysical status of an eternal object is that of a possibility for an
actuality." They are like what other philosophers have called uni-

versals; that is, they are abstract in themselves, even though they cannot be understood in complete abstraction from the actual world. But since they are manifest only in the concrete, they are called "sense objects," such as sounds, colors, and scents.[32] By this it is meant that they are the "forms of definiteness" or "pure potentials for the specific determination of fact." That is, "the definiteness of the actual arises from the exclusiveness of eternal objects in their function as determinants." In point of fact, Whitehead says,

> There is no character belonging to the actual apart from its exclusive determination by selected eternal objects. The definiteness of the actual arises from the exclusiveness of eternal objects in their function as determinants. If the actual entity be *this,* then by the nature of the case it is not *that* or *that.*[33]

Since a given actual entity may be definite in more than one way, it may then possess more than one form of definiteness or eternal object. And even though there are no novel eternal objects, nor can one change, nevertheless "it varies from one occasion to another in respect to the difference of its modes of ingression." That is, while "any eternal object is just itself in whatever mode of realisation it is involved," yet there may be "more than one grade of realisation." Eternal objects in themselves are simple, although they may form complex groups and relationships, called "propositions." "There can be no distortion of the individual essence without thereby producing a different eternal object."[34] It is because eternal objects are simple that they may be negatively prehended in toto. And, furthermore, it is only because they are potential, they may also be prehended negatively, for "the actualities *have* to be felt (prehended positively), while the pure potentials *can* be dismissed (prehended negatively)." In "their function as objects this is the great distinction between an actual entity and an eternal object. The one is a stubborn matter of fact; and the other never loses its 'accent' of potentiality."[35]

WHITEHEAD'S BIPOLAR VIEW OF GOD

Now that the Whiteheadian system has been discussed in general, we are prepared to discuss his view of God. God, like all other actual entities, is bipolar. He has an eternal (potential) pole and a temporal (actual) pole. The former is called God's *primordial* nature and the latter His *consequent* nature.

God: His primordial nature. Even though eternal objects are forms of definiteness for actual entities, they are in themselves indefinite and unordered. They are pure potentials, and pure potentials cannot order and relate themselves: only an actual entity can do that. But since some eternal objects are not in the realm of the temporal world (that is, those which have not ingressed or have not been realized in some temporal actual entity), Whitehead finds it necessary to introduce a nontemporal actual entity.[36] Such is God in His primordial nature. He wrote,

> In what sense can unrealized abstract form (eternal objects) be relevant? What is the basis of relevance? "Relevance" must express some real fact of togetherness among forms. The ontological principle can be expressed as: all real togetherness is togetherness in the formal constitution of an actuality. So if there be a relevance of what in the temporal world is unrealized, the relevance must express a fact of togetherness in the formal constitution of a non-temporal actuality (God in His primordial nature).

That is, "By reason of the actuality of this primordial valuation of pure potentials [that is, God], each eternal object has a definite, effective relevance to each concrescent process," for "apart from such ordering, there would be a complete disjunction of eternal objects unrealized in the temporal world." As Orderer of eternal objects, God in His primordial nature is like a backstage director who organizes and lines up the actors, making them "relevant" for their moment of "ingression" on the stage of the temporal world. Without such ordering, there would be chaos among the unrealized ("backstage") eternal objects.[37]

One should not be misled, however, to think of God's primordial nature as distinct from the order of eternal objects; they are, in fact, the same. For, "Viewed as primordial, he is the unlimited conceptual realization of the absolute wealth of potentiality. In this aspect, he is not *before* all creation, but *with* all creation." This is why, for Whitehead, God is a finite but "primordial creature," who "does not create eternal objects; for his nature requires them in the same degree that they require him."[38]

God: His consequent nature. Neither should the references to God in His primordial nature lead one to think that there is no other aspect to God, for like "all actual entities, the nature of God is dipolar." This other pole is called God's consequent nature. Whitehead's metaphysics contains at least two reasons for positing the consequent nature of God:

1. First, every actual entity, including God, must be dipolar, for it

needs a physical pole (consequent nature) to complete the vision of its conceptual pole (primordial nature). That is, since God's primordial nature is "deficient" and "unconscious," it needs the consequent nature to realize its own subjective aim, or self-creative urge. So "the perfection of God's subjective aim, derived from the completeness of his primordial nature, issues into the character of his consequent nature."

2. Second, God's consequent nature is necessary because of the principle of relativity, which holds that every entity in the universe must be relative to every other entity. Since God in His primordial nature is relevant only to eternal objects, there must be another "side" to God which can be related to other actual entities. "Thus by reason of the relativity of all things, there is a reaction of the world on God." So, as the primordial pole shows God's relevance to eternal objects, the consequent pole reveals his relation to actual entities, and the latter is necessary to complete the former.[39]

God: His superject nature. The consequent nature of God as enriched or satisfied by its prehensions in the temporal world is sometimes referred to as God's *superject* nature. It is the repository of all achieved value in the universe and is available for prehension by other actual entities. It is the storehouse of all that God has accomplished in the world and contains the permanent and progressive achievement of good as envisioned by God in His primordial nature.[40]

God and evil. As a matter of fact, it is by virtue of God's consequent nature (His immanence in the temporal world) that He saves the world from chaos, "as it passes into the immediacy of his own life" by "a tenderness which loses nothing that can be saved." This process of preservation by God's consequent nature (also God's superject nature) is a perpetual one—never reaching a final, static goal. It is in this light, too, that evil is explained as a necessary incompatibility (or inconsistency) with a given concrescence and which, therefore, cannot be salvaged in the becoming of that particular actual entity, even though in the total process, under "God's tender care," nothing is to be lost but is to be "saved by its relation to the completed whole."[41]

God and creativity. There is a multiplicity of actual entities, which need eternal objects, which in turn require God's primordial nature to explain their definiteness, and which actual entities de-

mand God's consequent nature to explain how they can be prehended by Him. However, since each actual entity is separate and
even causally independent from every other actual entity, it is only
natural to inquire what it is that provides this "definite bond"
between all actual entities and yet manages to explain how each is
distinct. In other words, how does Whitehead relate his pluralistic
subjects one to the other on the one hand and yet avoid a monism on
the other hand? Whitehead's answers to these two questions are,
respectively, "creativity" and "negative prehensions."

For Whitehead, creativity "is that ultimate principle by which
the many, which are the universe disjunctively, become the one
actual occasion, which is the universe conjunctively." Creativity is
shared by all actual entities, including God. In fact "every actual
entity, including God, is a creature transcended by the creativity
which it qualified." However, creativity is said to be "without a
character of its own in exactly the same sense in which the Aristotelian 'matter' is without a character of its own." The general
activity of creativity "is not an entity in the sense in which occasions
or eternal objects are entities." Rather, it is a general metaphysical
character which underlies all occasions. It is like Spinoza's one
infinite substance. Its attributes are its character of individualization
into a multiplicity of modes. As Whitehead puts it:

> In all philosophic theory there is an ultimate which is actual in virtue
> of its accidents. It is only then capable of characterization through its
> accidental embodiments, and apart from these accidents is devoid of
> actuality. In the philosophy of organism this ultimate is termed
> "creativity"; and God is its primordial, non-temporal accident.

"Accordingly no value is to be ascribed to the underlying activity
[creativity] as divorced from the matter-of-fact events of the real
world."[42]

Creativity is a kind of "substance" which is real only in virtue
of its "accidents." It is the potential unity which binds together the
actual plurality of the world. It is in this sense that Whitehead often
compares creativity to the "receptacle" of Plato's *Timaeus*, which
imposes a common relationship on all that happens, that is, "whose
sole function is the imposition of a unity upon the events of Nature."
Whitehead says, "another illustration is to be found in the *Sophist*,
where Plato states that 'not-being' is a form of 'being.'" By this he
means that creativity in itself is not an actual entity but only a real
potentiality.

It can thus be termed a "real potentiality." The "potentiality" refers to the passive capacity, the term "real" refers to the creative activity, where the Platonic definition of "real" in the *Sophist* is referred to. This basic situation, this actual world, this primary phase, this real potentiality—however you characterize it—as a whole is active with its inherent creativity, but in its details it provides the passive objects which derive their activity from the creativity of the whole. The creativity is the actualization of potentiality, and the process of actualization is an occasion of experiencing. Thus viewed in abstraction objects are passive, but viewed in conjunction they carry the creativity which drives the world. The process of creation is the form of unity of the Universe.[43]

That is, creativity is the real potentiality that binds the many actualities of the universe into the form of their novel unity. In fact, "creativity is the principle of novelty," which introduces new patterns of definiteness by making a disjunctive many into a new one. And by providing new unity diverse from any entity in the many which it unifies, creativity is the ground for novelty in the universe.[44]

God and negative prehensions. Not only is creativity the principle of potential unity but, through negative prehension, it is the principle of actual separation. That is, negative prehension "constitutes the machinery" by which creativity operates. For "this element of 'exclusive limitation' is the definiteness essential for the synthetic unity of an actual entity." In other words, unless some things were eliminated (by negative prehension) from a given process of concrescence, that actual entity would become everything, which would be monism. It is only by a definite exclusion of other actual entities from a particular actual entity that a pluralism can be maintained. So, "in this process, the negative prehensions which effect the elimination are not negligible." In fact, they are absolutely essential. As Whitehead notes,

> The importance of negative prehensions arises from the fact, that (i) actual entities form a system, in the sense of entering into each other's constitutions, (ii) that by the ontological principle every entity is felt by some actual entity, (iii) that, as a consequence of (i) and (ii), every entity in the actual world of a concrescent actuality has some gradation of real relevance to that concrescence, (iv) that, in consequence of (iii), the negative prehension of an entity is a positive fact with its emotional subjective form, (v) there is a mutual sensitivity of the subjective forms of prehensions, so that they are not indifferent to

each other, (vi) the concrescence issues in one concrete feeling, the satisfaction.

Negative prehensions are a "positive fact" in the coming to be of an actual entity because what is definitely excluded is at least as important as what is definitely included. For example, what is cut away from a block of marble is in the end as important for the formation of the unity as is what remains. Perhaps this is why Whitehead said, "the negative judgment is the peak of mentality."[45]

Of course, negative prehensions are not intended by Whitehead to eliminate the need for positive prehension, for while "negative prehensions may eliminate its distinctive importance," nevertheless, "in some way, by some trace of causal feeling, the remote actual entity is prehended positively." But the significant role played by negative prehension is seen not only in the fact that it can eliminate the "distinctive importance" of a positive prehension, dismiss "other feelings," and contribute their own subjective form to the process, but because "this element of 'exclusive limitation' is the definiteness essential for the synthetic unity of an actual entity."[46]

God, however, has no negative prehensions of eternal objects. All potentials are included in His vision for reality; no potentiality is absent from the unity of God's subjective aim. Thus it is that all things are *one* potentially, although they are *many* actually. Reality is potentially monistic but actually pluralistic. And God in His primordial and consequent poles corresponds respectively to these two aspects of reality. He is a dipolar combination of the eternal and unchanging potential and of changing temporal actuality; of infinite vision and finite realization; of abstract conceptualization and concrete materialization in the real world.

THE PROCESS THEOLOGY OF CHARLES HARTSHORNE AND JOHN COBB

Process theology has taken two main directions since Whitehead, the empirical and the rational. The former emphasis is found in Bernard Loomer, Bernard Meland, and Henry Weiman; and the latter is championed by Charles Hartshorne. Hartshorne is perhaps the most significant post-Whiteheadian process theologian in the rational stream, followed by John Cobb and Schubert Ogden. His defense of dipolar theism by way of modal logic and the ontological argument is already classic. It will not be necessary here to repeat in detail the basic elements of process that Hartshorne holds in common with Whitehead. A basic sketch will suffice. Of more concern to us are the differences between Whitehead and Hartshorne that grow out of the distinctive contributions Hartshorne made in attempting to work out problems in Whitehead.

BASIC SIMILARITIES BETWEEN WHITEHEAD'S AND HARTSHORNE'S SYSTEMS

Both Whitehead and Hartshorne have the same basic metaphysical model of God—a bipolar one. God is conceived by them in the following way.

A similar bipolar metaphysical model. There is an actual pole and a potential pole in God. The potential pole is the order of all that can be, and the actual pole is the order of all that is. The former is God's "mind," and the latter is His "body."[47] That is, the potential pole is God's conceptual vision and the actual pole is the physical realization of that vision. And since the actual world is in constant process, this pole is perishable; whereas the potential pole is imperishable. The potential pole is both absolute and eternal, but the actual pole is relative and temporal. What is more, the primordial (potential) pole is infinite (that is, indefinite) whereas the consequent (actual) pole is finite. So then God is actually finite but potentially infinite. He comprises the pole of changeless possibility and the pole of changing actuality. In this respect both Whitehead and Hartshorne are united in their expression of bipolar theism.

The contrast between bipolar and monopolar concepts of God. Both Whitehead and Hartshorne are united in rejecting traditional theism, represented by men like Anselm, Augustine, and Aquinas. In the traditional view God is *Creator* of the world; in process theology God is only *Director* of world process. For theism God created the world *ex nihilo,* but in bipolarism God is forming the world *ex hulās* (out of "matter" eternally there at the other pole). Hence, the theistic God is in sovereign control *over* the world, whereas the process God is working in cooperation *with* the world. In the former case God is *independent* of the world; in the latter the world and God are *interdependent.* That is, the theistic God is not dependent on the world as the world is dependent on Him; but the bipolar God and world are mutually dependent. The world can change in relation to a theistic God; but, unlike the process God, He does not change in relation to the world.[48] And from the process point of view, traditional monopolar theism presents a changeless, inflexible, impersonal, and even unworshipable Being.[49] In any event, the process God is by contrast clearly changeably and reciprocally related with the actual world process. With this both Whitehead and Hartshorne are in basic agreement. And with regard to perfections, the theistic God has all perfections eternally and *concurrently;* whereas the God of panentheism attains perfections *successively* and endlessly.

SOME DISTINCTIVE DIFFERENCES BETWEEN WHITEHEAD AND HARTSHORNE

The differences between Hartshorne and Whitehead are both methodological and metaphysical. That is, they differ in both their approaches to and views of God.

The methodological difference between Whitehead and Hartshorne. Despite the fact that their views of God are similar, the methodologies of Whitehead and Hartshorne are almost entirely diverse. As we said earlier, Whitehead's methodology is basically *empirical;* by contrast, Hartshorne's approach is highly *rational.* The former begins with *descriptive generalizations,* but the latter starts with *analytic concepts.* Similarly, the one is *scientific* whereas the other is *logical.* Whitehead's methodological starting point is *hypothetical,* based only on empirical necessity or adequacy; Hartshorne's point of departure is *categorical* and based on logical necessity. Hence, like a scientific hypothesis, Whitehead's system can be falsified by *empirical inadequacy.* But Hartshorne's metaphysics can be falsified only by showing a *contradiction* in it. Conversely, Whitehead's test for truth includes empirical adequacy, whereas Hartshorne's involves only logical consistency. The former method is broadly *a posteriori* but the latter is *a priori.* And in keeping with their overall methodology, Whitehead's argument for God is a form of the *teleological* argument and Hartshorne's is definitely an *ontological* argument.

Hartshorne's statement of the ontological argument. Professor Hartshorne was stoutly defending the ontological argument some twenty years before Norman Malcolm revived contemporary interest in it.‡ We may summarize Hartshorne's reasoning in this fashion:[50]

1. The existence of a necessary Being is either
   a. impossible, and hence there is no example of it;

‡Hartshorne's *Man's Vision of God* was first published in 1941 and Norman Malcolm's article was first published in the *Philosophical Review* 49 (1960).

   b. possible, but there is no example of it;

   c. possible, and there is an example of it.

2. But premise 1b is meaningless (like square circles), for a necessary Being cannot be a merely possible being.

3. And premise 1a is not eliminated by the ontological argument as such, but the meaningfulness of the term "necessary Being" is justifiable assumption which is later defended.

Leaving the basic logic of the ontological argument, Hartshorne proceeded to give the fuller elaboration of it, including his promised defense of the meaningfulness of the concept of a necessary being. The argument may be stated in this form.

1. All thought must refer to something beyond itself which is at least possible, because of the following:

   a. Wherever there is meaning, there must be something meant.

   b. The only thoughts which are less than possible are contradictory ones.

   c. Meaning must refer to something more than its own contents or inner consistency, otherwise it is meaningless.

   d. Total illusion is impossible; illusion presupposes a backdrop of reality. Confusion is possible about specific reality but not about reality in general. (Hartshorne further defends this point in answers to objections.)

2. The necessary existence of a necessary being is at least possible.

   a. There is nothing contradictory in the concept of a being that cannot *not* be.

   b. The only way to reject this is to plead a special meaning to the word *possible*. For in the usual logical sense of the word *possible* there is no contradiction in the concept of a necessary being.

3. With a necessary being, an at-least-possible existence is indistinguishable from a possible-and-actual existence. A necessary being cannot have a merely possible existence (if a necessary being *can* be, then it *must* be), because of the following:

   a. God by definition is an independent Existence and, hence, He cannot be produced by another as merely possible beings can be.

   b. God is everlasting, and so He could not have come into being as merely possible beings can come into existence.

4. Therefore, a necessary being necessarily has both a possible and an actual existence.

Hartshorne's defense of his ontological argument. Professor Hartshorne anticipated and replied to many different objections to his ontological argument. Space permits discussing only a couple significant points.

Hartshorne argues that the ontological argument proves more than the mere self-consistency of the idea of a necessary being, for all meaning has an external referent which is either possible or actual. And God by definition cannot be merely a possible being. Therefore, the following result.

1. All meaning implicitly affirms God in reference to either of these:
   a. What He *has* done (called His consequent nature—God's immanence).
   b. What He *can* do (called His primordial nature—God's transcendence).
2. Without God as the universal ground of meaning, there would be no meaning for universals (that is, nothing can have objective meaning unless there is a realm which is objectively meaningful).
3. We can be confused as to whether specific things exist but not as to whether God—who is the content of existence itself—exists.
4. The only way to oppose the ontological argument is to make an absolute disjunction between meaning and reality. But this kind of disjunction is meaningless (meaning and reality must meet at some point; that point we call "God").

Hartshorne also replies to the objection that the ontological argument produces God out of pure thought. Mere thought does not produce reality; but necessary thought does, he contends. There can be no absolute disjunction between thought and reality. Thinking is a real experience, and we do think of God as possible. Hartshorne concludes, therefore, that all thoughts are experiences of what is at least possible. We do have thoughts about a Being which must be (that is, a necessary Being). But a necessary being cannot be a merely possible being. Therefore, a necessary being must be more than merely possible (namely, it must be actual).

To summarize his thought, we have only to exclude impossibility or meaninglessness to establish God's actuality. That is, either *God* is a meaningless term or there exists a divine Being. Or, to restate the argument, either the existence of a necessary being is less than an idea (that is, contradictory and impossible); merely an idea but not a reality; or more than a mere idea, namely, a reality. But it is not less than an idea, for it is a noncontradictory concept. Neither is it merely an idea, for it is contradictory to speak of a necessary being as merely possible (if a necessary being exists at all, it must exist necessarily; there is no other way it can exist). Therefore, the existence of a necessary being is more than a mere idea; it is a reality.

It is clear that Hartshorne's method is very unlike that of Whitehead, despite the similarity in their metaphysical views of God. Nonetheless, there are some dissimilarities in their basic metaphysics. It is to these we now turn our attention.

The metaphysical differences between Whitehead and Hartshorne. There are a number of significant differences between Whitehead's and Hartshorne's concepts of God. Since we have already documented Whitehead's views, we will refer to them here only by way of contrast, in order to explain how Hartshorne differs from him. One of the most important differences is found in the fact that Whitehead considers God an actual entity, whereas Hartshorne views God as a series or society of actual entities.[51] At this point Hartshorne calls upon an anthropomorphic analogy. God as Cosmic Mind is resident in the world as His body, which comprises a whole society of actual entities.

This brings us to another difference. In viewing God as a single actual entity rather than a society or series, Whitehead was able to claim a univocal relation between God as the primary actual entity and all other actual entities. God is not an exception to metaphysical principles; He is their chief exemplification. By contrast, Hartshorne maintains that God is as modally different from the world as necessary being is from contingent being. Thus, if there is more of an analogy between God and the world, then there would not be a univocal understanding of both.

There is also a marked difference between Whitehead and Hartshorne in their views on how God grounds the world. For the former, the world is based on God's subjective aim—the vision of the conceptual pole for this particular world. For Hartshorne, however, the world is based in God as the logically necessary ground of all contingency. Whitehead's God is seen as the ground for this particular world, but Hartshorne's God is the universal ground for all possible worlds. In fact, Whitehead's God is a universal subject; Hartshorne's is the universal object—the objective referent point for all meaning. Hence, for Whitehead only actual entities can be reasons or causes; but for Hartshorne, God as a series or society of actual entities is the cause of the world. And coupled with this is the fact that Whitehead's God is only concretely necessary to explain this particular world, whereas Hartshorne's God is universally and logically necessary to explain this and all possible worlds. Herein lie the essential differences between their views of God.

JOHN COBB'S MODIFICATIONS OF WHITEHEAD AND HARTSHORNE

John Cobb offers two significant changes for bipolar theism while he nevertheless wishes to remain in the overall tradition of Whitehead. First, Cobb rejects the disjunction of two separate poles in God entailed in the Whiteheadian scheme. God, like man, is a unity and acts as a unity and not in just one pole as such. For example, God's subjective aim, or vision, for all is not to be associated only with His primordial pole but also with His consequent pole.[52]

Second, Cobb denies that "the initial phase of the subjective aim need be derived exclusively from God." This is aimed at resolving the problem of determinism, if God alone provides the initial subjective aim of every actual entity. "The subjective aim of the new occasion must be formed," writes Cobb, "by some synthesis or adaptation of these aims for which it [the actual entity] is itself finally responsible."[53]

Like Hartshorne and unlike Whitehead, Cobb views God as a living Person and not as an actual entity, for several reasons. First, in view of God's unity and of process in His consequent nature, it appears to Cobb that, "God's causal efficacy for the world is like the efficacy of completed occasions for subsequent occasions and not like that of phases of the becoming of a single occasion for its successors."[54] Further, if God were a single entity He would never know satisfaction, but if He is a Person then He would realize satisfaction like any other person does. Also, if God is a Person or society of entities, then His prehension of all earlier entities is identical with His prehension of His own past. Hence, He remains self-identical. And since we lose our past primarily because of unconsciousness, God can remember everything because He never experiences the loss of identity with persons. Finally, even though God's vision of eternal objects be viewed as a succession of acts, it still remains a single unchanging and eternal act, because absolute identity obtains from moment to moment.

With these modifications of Whitehead, Cobb hopes to maintain, in the tradition of Hartshorne, the essence of process theology while avoiding some of the problems latent in Whitehead's statement of it. Particularly does Cobb wish to solve the problems of the nature of God and of determinism. With regard to the latter, Cobb is very careful to observe that God's role in initiating the subjective aim of each actual entity is influential but not determinitive. However, Cobb, like Whitehead, finds it necessary to posit "creativity" to ground everything, including God. It is "that apart from which nothing can be . . . the actuality of every actual entity."[55]

THE CONTRIBUTIONS OF NELSON PIKE AND SCHUBERT M. OGDEN TO PROCESS THEOLOGY

Whitehead and Hartshorne have developed a highly philosophical basis for process theology. Nelson Pike and Schubert M. Ogden have worked out some biblical and theological dimensions supportive of process thought. Pike singles out in particular the traditional concept of God as timeless or eternal as against the process view of a temporal God. Ogden, on the other hand, develops a series of Kantian-like antinomies in traditional theism in order to show by contrast the viability of a more relational process theology.

PIKE'S OBJECTIONS TO A TRADITIONAL TIMELESS GOD

Professor Nelson Pike stakes out serious problems with the traditional view of God as timeless, or eternal. These may be best understood in contrast to the argument for a timeless God given by Thomas Aquinas. The argument has two major steps. First, Aquinas argues that God is immutable in His essence, and that eternality is derived from immutability. He offers three arguments for God's immutability.

The first argument is based on God's pure actuality as follows:[56]

1. Everything that changes has potentiality, for change is a passing from a state of potentiality (for a change) to a state of actuality (of having undergone that change).
2. But there can be no potentiality in God; He is pure actuality (if God had potency in His being He would not be the necessary Being that He is).
3. Therefore, God cannot change in His being; He is unchanging, or immutable.

The second argument for God's immutability follows from His simplicity:

1. Whatever changes is composed of what changes and what does not change (for there must be continuity in change, otherwise

there is not one thing that changes but a series of annihilations and recreations of new things).
2. But there can be no composition in God at all; He is an absolutely simple Being (if God were composed, He would not be God but a creature).
3. Therefore, God cannot change in His being; He is immutable.

The third argument of Aquinas for God's immutability is from God's absolute perfections:

1. Whatever changes acquires something new that it did not have before the change.
2. But God cannot acquire anything new; He is already absolutely perfect and could not be more perfect (if He could be more perfect, then He would not be God).
3. Hence, God cannot change in perfection or nature; His nature is immutable.

Once Aquinas has established God's immutability he proceeds to demonstrate His eternality, or timelessness, in the following manner:[57]

1. Whatever changes is temporal (that is, is in time):
   a. Whatever changes has a successive series of different states.
   b. Time is a computation built on successively different states.
2. But God is immutable and cannot change (as was shown earlier).
3. Therefore, God is not temporal; He is eternal, or timeless.

And for Aquinas eternality is not the same as endless time.[58] They are only accidentally similar in that both are without end. But they are essentially different in that eternality is an essential whole, or unity; whereas time is broken up in endless parts. Both involve a "now," but the eternal now is immovable and innumerable, while the temporal now is movable and enumerable. God, then, is an essentially different Being from all creatures; He is both immutable and eternal by nature. It is this traditional view of God that comes in for particular criticism from Nelson Pike.

Pike lays out six criticisms of this traditional view of God's timelessness. First, timelessness would eliminate God's *foreknowledge*.[59] The Bible presents God as foreknowing the future (see Ro 8:29; 1 Pe 1:2). But there is no future for a timeless God; everything is an eternal *now* with Him. An eternal God does not *fore*-see; He already *sees* everything in one single and eternal now.

Hence, if we are to accept the biblical view of God, then we must reject the Greek view of God as timeless, which was incorporated into Christian theology by traditional theists such as Augustine, Anselm, and Aquinas.

Second, according to Pike, the traditional doctrine of God's timelessness conflicts with the doctrine of *Creation*. For a timeless God cannot act in time but only in eternity. But the Bible presents this world as a creation in time, that is, as a temporal world with a beginning in time. Therefore, a timeless God could not create a temporal world. Again, the influence of Greek philosophy by way of scholastic theology has seemingly corrupted the Christian view of God as temporal and changing.

The third charge Pike levels at the concept of a timeless God is that it would eliminate His *personality*. For whatever cannot respond intellectually, emotionally, and volitionally to persons is less than significantly personal. This is what is meant by being personal. But this is precisely what a timeless Being cannot do. For timelessness implies immutability, and an immutable Being cannot change His mind, feelings, or will. In fact, He cannot change in any way. But an unmovable, unchangeable, impassible Being that cannot be touched with the feelings of our human infirmities is certainly less than significantly personal.

The fourth problem seen by Pike with the traditional notion of a timeless God is that of *worshipability*. It would seem that a supreme but temporal God who could respond to a person's needs would be more worthy of worship than One that cannot change. Why pray to a Being who cannot be moved by one's petitionary pleadings? An eternal and unchangeable God is less worthy of worship—if worthy at all—than a temporal God who can responsively interact with human needs.

Fifth, Professor Pike contends that timelessness is incompatible with the *incarnation* of God in Christ. In the incarnation, the Eternal entered into and lived in the temporal world. But in the traditional view, the eternal and changeless cannot become temporal and changing. The two are essentially different and, hence, "never the twain shall meet." The incarnation of God in human flesh is seemingly impossible within the framework of traditional theism.

Sixth, a timeless God does not accord with the basic biblical and credal language about God. The Bible repeatedly speaks of God as changing His mind in answer to prayer (Jos 10) or upon the repentance of men (Jon 3) or because of human wickedness (Gen 6). Further, Pike would agree with Oscar Cullmann[60] that the biblical language favors a temporal view of God, in, for example, phrases like "from everlasting to everlasting, thou art God" (Ps 90:2). The Hebrew word *'olām* and the Greek word *aiōnios,* usually translated "everlasting" or "eternal," mean "age-lasting" and denote an endless time (cf. the phrase "day and night forever" in Revelation 20:10). Indeed, the New Testament phrase for eternity is literally, "unto the ages of the ages" *(aniōnas tōn aiōnōn).* With these biblical usages the early creeds of Christendom concur, Pike argues.[61]

In summation, Pike writes, "I shall conclude that the doctrine of timelessness should not be included in a system of Christian theology." Plato is the source of the doctrine of timelessness, "But Plato was not a Christian—nor can I think of any reason," Pike continues, "why a Christian should accept Plato's judgment on this matter."[62] The probable reasons for Christians introducing timelessness are, according to Pike, that platonic philosophy was stylish and the doctrine offered some appeal to systematic theology. But the first reason is entirely inadequate, and the second one backfires into the six problems mentioned above. In view of this, Christians should discard the timeless and immutable concept of God for a temporal and changing concept.

SCHUBERT M. OGDEN'S CONTRIBUTION TO PROCESS THEOLOGY

Whitehead developed process theology out of a scientific and mathematical background. Hartshorne approached it from a logical and rational vantage point, and Pike from a liberal biblical and theological perspective. But Schubert M. Ogden arrived at the need for a process God out of a Bultmannian existential background. Like Bultmann and Heidegger before him, Ogden believes that an existential "preunderstanding" of history is necessary. That is, one cannot understand the world (objective) properly unless he has a prior understanding of his own existence in the world (subjective). Ogden believes that existential philosophy and theology have the same goal; but whereas the latter speaks only religiously (á la Barth), the former speaks ontologically. As Bultmann showed, modern secularity and science have forced the demythologization of the Bible. The net result of this demythologization is two parties: God and man, as Bultmann showed. Heidegger has adequately analyzed man, but he did not analyze God. Ogden feels Hartshorne is the key to analyzing God. His choice of Hartshorne is based on several factors. First, Hartshorne's process theology avoids the antinomies implicit in traditional theism (see below). Second, Hartshorne provides the necessary theocentric counterpart of Bultmann's anthropocentricism without opposing his existential epistemology.

Ogden's dipolar God. Ogden develops the dipolar model of God around the poles of God's absoluteness and His relatedness. God is both absolute and relative.

1. God is relative. As relative, God is related to all that is. In opposition to classical theism:

> We must cease, finally, to ask in what sense, if any, that which is absolute can be understood as personal and ask, rather, how that which, by analogy with ourselves, is genuinely and eminently personal can also be conceived as absolute.[63]

The world itself, made up of many actual entities, is the body of God. And God is related to it as "I" am incarnate in my body, namely, by direct internal relations.[64] Thus God's sphere of interaction is the universe itself.

In accordance with Whitehead's principle of relativity, every actual entity is related to every other one by either a positive or a negative prehension. There is no vacuum; all is one organism. God is related to all by "sympathetic participation," which synthesizes in each new occasion the whole of achieved actuality.[65]

It follows that God gives value to our lives in two ways. First, He is responsible for the concrescence of actual entities which constitute our bodies. He is responsible for the structure and order of the actual world. He is what "calls forth and justifies our original and inalienable truth in life's worth." God alone makes it possible to avoid absurdity. Life is worthwhile because God exists. Second, God gives our lives eternal value. It is to Him that actual entities return and become immortal as eternal objects. God makes an "imperishable difference," and in Him our lives "find their ultimate justification."[66]

Since the world is God's body, His own reality as an actual entity is dependent on the world. This dependence does not refer to God's existence as such, which is necessary. It does not refer to *that* God is; His dependence refers only to *what* God is. His nature is dependent on "what actual state of the infinite number of states possible for him is in fact actualized."[67] Hence, God's body is contingent; and yet it is necessary for Him to have a body, which is in fact eternal.

262 Tensions in Contemporary Theology

2. God is absolute. Ogden understands God's absoluteness by means of analogy. That is, he takes univocal notions and applies them to God in an eminent sense.[68] However, absoluteness is not conceived by Ogden in the classical sense of "infinite." A dipolar God is absolute in terms of relativity, that is, by "relative absoluteness." First, God is absolute by His inclusion in all beings, for to experience is to experience God.[69] Second, God is absolute in relation by virtue of His internal relatedness to every actual entity in the universe, each of which God loves equally with "no gradations of intimacy."[70] God's perfection lies in His continual openness to change. His perfection is not concurrent, as in classical theism, but is successive. God is not statically completed perfection but a "dynamic maximum of possibilities."[71] Third, God is absolute in knowledge in the sense that at every state of the process, all that exists is within His sphere of relation.[72] Fourth, God is absolute in His temporality. God is "the eminently temporal one." His perfections are ever increasing.

> This is so . . . because anything we do to advance the real good either in ourselves or of one another is done quite literally to "the glory of God," as an imperishable contribution to his ever-growing perfection, which is, indeed, "the true life of all."[73]

In summary, God is absolute in that His "being related to all others is itself relative to nothing, but the absolute ground of any and all real relationships."[74] His absoluteness is an absolute relatedness to all else; hence, His perfection is a perfect relativity with all the value in the temporal world.

3. God is necessary. For Ogden, God's existence is experientially necessary. He agrees with Hartshorne that it is impossible to deny that meaning has a necessary ground. That is, experience itself, since it is always of God, is possible only if God exists. Ogden develops the necessity of God in a type of moral argument. He speaks of the inescapability of faith and of the impossibility of atheism. The argument may be summarized as follows:[75]

1. All judgments imply meaning, value, and purpose in the universe.
2. It is self-defeating to deny the possibility of making judgments.
3. Hence, there must be meaning, value and purpose in the universe.
4. But meaning requires a ground and value and a value-giver.

5. Therefore, there exists a ground of meaning and giver of value (God).

There seems to be a teleological element in Ogden's argument; but he rejects the teleological argument as such, because it leads to a God who is "wholly other" than the world. Whereas, for Ogden:

> The true theistic view, I maintain, is that God is nothing external to the world's order but is that order itself fully understood—analogous to the way in which the human self or person is not anything merely additional to the unified behavior of its body but is what enables us to understand and account for such unified behavior.[76]

Ogden's rejection of classical theism: three antinomies. There are for Ogden three insoluable contradictions in the traditional theistic notion of God as a timeless, changeless, and unrelated Being. These are the antinomies of creation, of service, and of relationship.

1. The antinomy of *creation* is a paradox involving the contingency of the created world and the necessity of God's nature. Briefly stated: "God creates the world freely, as the contingent or nonnecessary world of our experience discloses it to be." However, "God's act of creation is one with his own eternal essence, which is in every respect necessary." This leads to the "hopeless contradiction of a wholly necessary creation of a wholly contingent world."[77] In other words, if God's will is one with His necessary essence, then a wholly contingent creation would be as necessary as the essence of God—which is impossible. Classical theism must be corrected to avoid this contradiction. Ogden's neoclassical theism would avoid antinomy by the relative necessity (as against absolute) with which he conceives God.

2. In the antinomy of *service,* the contradiction is between God's absolutely complete perfections and man's service "for" God. It may be stated thus: "The end of man is to serve or glorify God through obedience to his will and commandments."[78] On the other hand, God as pure act is eternally and "statically completed perfection" that can be neither increased nor diminished by anything. Hence, no service is significantly "for" God. A God of process who becomes increasingly perfect through human achievement would, of course, avoid this dilemma; but, if our service does not really affect God, then what difference does it make if we serve Him?

3. The antinomy of *relationship,* the most often repeated antinomy, involves a divine isolationism from the world. Briefly

stated, the God of classical theism is the changeless and independent Cause of all other things, but all genuine relationship involves mutual dependence. However, since God by His very nature cannot have dependent and changing relationships, it follows that He cannot be genuinely related to the world. As Aquinas put it, "In God there is no real relation to creatures, but a relation only in idea, inasmuch as creatures are referred to Him."[79] Such a God, Ogden believes, is monopolarly isolated from the real world and from significant personal interaction. Such is not the God of the Bible nor of Whitehead-Hartshorne theology. Therefore, classical theism must give way to neoclassical bipolarism, concludes Ogden.

The Process Christology of Norman Pittenger

Pierre Teilhard de Chardin was a pioneer in process Christology. Ten years before Whitehead published *Process and Reality* (1927) Teilhard had spoken of the cosmic growth of the mystical body of Christ,§[80] a view expressed more fully in *The Phenomenon of Man* in the late thirties. His process Christology is unique; it stands alone. The direct line of influence in contemporary process Christology is from Whitehead through Hartshorne to Meland and Norman Pittenger. Since the latter has given a full expression of it, we will concentrate our attention on his position.

Whitehead's most illustrious protégé, Charles Hartshorne, provided an important impetus to contemporary process Christology with a provocative article in 1947.[81] In it he argued that God's absoluteness is not a mere absoluteness in itself but an absoluteness in relation to the universe. That is, God's essence is love, or giving; His perfection is to be Himself in relation to all else. According to Pittenger, Hartshorne's view caused him to rethink his own Christology, which has become increasingly dominated by process thought.[82]

Pittenger became acquainted with Hartshorne's view in 1938, three years before his first major work on Christology, *Christ and the Christian Faith* (1941), was published.[83] Although Hartshorne is not used in this early work, Pittenger did use other process precursors like von Hagel, Samuel Alexander, Bergson, and Whitehead.

The deity of christ defined

Pittenger acknowledges no essential change in the main thesis

§This section was written by Teilhard in 1917.

of his Christology over the years.[84] From first to last he defines the deity of Christ in terms of God's *activity* in Christ. He claims to be first to so define Christ's divinity, even before D. M. Baillie's famous *God was in Christ* (1948). The deity of Christ means "that which is act of God in him, that which is act of God through him; or, better expressed, it is God acting in and through him." Christ is "God's act for men, in men, to men, and as man." Thus He is not only human "he is also divine, since his life as a total human act is supremely the instrument for God's action among men." Hence, in Jesus of Nazareth "the divine causation is involved here to a degree which is not true of other instances of human causation."[85] Even in his latest work, Pittenger was not willing to give up his difference-in-degree Christology for a more radical difference-in-kind Christology. The latter, Pittenger considered, is a subtle form of Docetism.[86]

The reasons for defining the deity of Christ in terms of divine *activity* in Christ rather than a divine *essence* is made clear. Since the Whitehead-Hartshorne process philosophy is the only viable metaphysics today, "all this makes it more important that some attempt be made to work out a Christological statement which has 'points of contact' with the 'process' thinkers, especially when (as in the case of Hartshorne for example) they are already so 'available' for this purpose." Indeed, Pittenger confessed to be an avowed proponent of such a process theology: "I believe that Professor Hartshorne has correctly expressed the basic idea which must govern any conception of God that can really claim to be Christian."[87]

GOD'S IMMANENCE AND RELATABILITY TO THE WHOLE UNIVERSE

The basic idea of process theology is the relatability of God to the whole universe. Traditional theism, according to Pittenger, sacrifices the immanent God for a transcendent other. But according to Pittenger, God is not related in an external way to the universe; rather, He is at work in and through it. Pittenger agrees with the definition of panentheism in the *Oxford Dictionary of the Christian Church* (1957) that "the being of God includes and penetrates the whole universe, so that every part of it exists in him, but (as against pantheism) that his being is more than, and not exhausted by, the universe."[88] In contrast to some neoorthodox theologians, Pittenger believes that God is immanently manifest in the whole cosmos and not merely in history. Nature is more than simple recur-

rence without theistic significance. God is no intruder from the
outside; He is manifest in the whole cosmic process.[89]

There are three ways in which God is involved in the world:
first, He provides the initial subjective aim for each creature; second, He provides the lure toward fulfillment, or self-realization, for
each creature (which is persuasive but not coercive); finally, God
acts in the world through the fact of mutual prehension, that is, the
divine love operates in and through the mutual grasping of creatures
for one another. "Thus every occasion, in its own quality and in its
own degree, is an incarnation of the divine dynamic which we call by
the name God." Hence, God's transcendence does not mean "re-
moteness or outside-ness; it can and must mean inexhaustibility of
resource, indefatigability of act, and (in Christian faith at least)
indefeasibility in achievement."[90]

GOD'S ACTIVITY IN THE INCARNATION

God is not only manifest generally in all of creation and human
history, but He is specially evident in the incarnation of Christ.
Pittenger dislikes the terms *absolute* and *final* as applied to the
incarnation; rather, he prefers speaking of it as "important" and
even "decisive." Christ differs only in degree, not in kind, from
other men. But this is to an important degree, in fact, "a very great
degree of intensity." Pittenger rejects the enhypostasis view of the
incarnation, that the only one person in Christ is the one in God, too.
Christ is merely the *organon*, the fully human and personal instrument of God's activity. Further, "It is impossible to demonstrate
from the available material that Jesus was absolutely sinless," because the Gospel record may reflect some occasional lack of proper
love, and because we know nothing of much of His life. Pittenger is
content with the fact that the general impression of Christ is "of a
man who can properly be described as embodying love-in-action."
However, there is no ideal love in Christ. What is more, "there is no
ideal perfection; even in God himself, the Unsurpassable Lover." It
is sufficient for Pittenger that Christ is a very significant and prime
manifestation of God's loving activity in and through a man. So
there are three essentials in Pittenger's Christology:

> First, there is the firm conviction that in some fashion we meet God in
> the event of Jesus Christ. Secondly, there is the equally firm convic-
> tion that God is thus met in a genuinely historical, conditional, and
> entirely human being. Third, there is the assurance that God met in
> that man, and the man in whom God met, are in relationship . . . of

personal union rather than after some model which suggests a less
secure and abiding togetherness of God and man.[91]

Pittenger acknowledges that his Christology does not satisfy
the demands of orthodoxy in a commonly accepted sense of the
term. Nonetheless, he considers that to be a mere *verbal* orthodoxy
as opposed to his more *vital* orthodoxy.[92] He agrees with Maurice
Wiles that "true continuity with the age of the Fathers is to be sought
not so much in the repetition of their doctrinal conclusions or even in
the building upon them, but rather in the continuation of their
doctrinal aims."[93] This, he implies, could mean that we "abandon
all talk about the one *ousia* and three *hypostases*."[94] In view of this
distinction one is not surprised to read of his defense of a modalistic
Trinity as "orthodox" as well.[95]

Pittenger understands one of the important contributions of
process Christology to be its ability to explain the suffering and
impassibility of God in Christ. Since God is supremely related in and
through all things, He "contains suffering, in accordance with the
suffering of the world." And in a special way is "the Christian idea
of a suffering deity—symbolized by the cross, together with the
doctrine of the Incarnation."[96] The God of traditional theism is
immutable and, hence, impassible. He cannot, as the process God
can, really enter into the suffering of the world. In view of this,
Pittenger believes that it is necessary to accept a process theology in
order to explain the basic tenets of Christian belief.

An Evaluation of Process Theology

No one has the right to criticize a view who has not first
understood it and learned something from it. The reader will have to
judge the former, but this writer can attest to the latter. There are a
number of very significant insights to be gained from an understanding of contemporary process theology.

Some positive contributions of process theology

In view of the foregoing discussion, there are at least eight
significant contributions of which we will take brief note.

The unavoidability of metaphysics. If the Christian is to make
sense out of his beliefs and the data of Scripture, he must develop a
philosophical framework by which they can be understood. The sine
qua non of Christian theology is an attempt to render the credible
intelligible. Without a metaphysics rooted in and growing out of the
biblical revelation, Christian theology cannot be done. For theology

involves a "putting together," or systematization, of the various teachings of Scripture into a meaningful and unified whole. At the very minimum, a comprehensive theology must be internally consistent; it cannot contain contradictory assertions. And in addition, a complete theology must be coherently inclusive of the facts of human experience and of the world process as a whole. The fact that, despite the contemporary linguistic veto, many contemporary theologians have found it necessary to do metaphysics is testimony to its indispensibility.

Evangelical theologians cannot avoid metaphysics. First, the biblical teaching about God and the world contains and implies a basically theistic view of the universe, without which the Bible would tell us nothing consistent about reality. Second, the Christian is urged by Scripture to use his mind, think, defend, and expound the faith—all of which launch him into a systematic theology;[97] and a systematic theology implies a certain metaphysical view of God and the universe. Third, if for no other reason, the Christian must engage in good metaphysics in order to counteract bad metaphysics. As C. S. Lewis stated it, "Good philosophy must exist, if for no other reason, because bad philosophy needs to be answered."[98]

The reality of God's relationship with the world. Process theology has rightly stressed the necessity of a metaphysics that allows God a free and real interaction with the world. Such is the God of the Bible, and such must be the God of any biblically oriented theism. A God who cannot act or interact with the world would be less than significantly personal. Prayer and service possess little meaning unless there is a real, personal relationship between God and men. The God of the Bible and of Christian experience is responsive to human needs and actions. There is no existential appeal in an impersonal and unrelatable Being. The doctrine of God's relationality is a biblical and vital teaching which is neglected or lost in some expressions of traditional theism. Process theology is to be thanked for reviving this important emphasis.

The need to account for all the biblical data on God. It is with no little embarrassment that orthodox Christianity is challenged by liberal process theology to take the biblical picture of God more seriously. The Scriptures do indeed speak of God as "foreknowing," as "repenting," as acting in time. Biblical words for God depict Him as everlasting and endless rather than simply as eternal and above time. And even if this language is taken as richly anthropomorphic, it must be accounted for in one's total understanding of Scripture.

Why does the Bible so often speak this way? What is the purpose of these models of God? Process theology has pointed up the need to approach with utmost seriousness the presentation of God in Scripture.

The necessity of analogical God-talk.[99] Whitehead tried to preserve univocal language about God. But as will be shown below, he was not successful in so doing. Schubert Ogden clearly saw the need to speak analogically about God. For Hartshorne, God is modally different from the world; He is infinite and it is finite. God is necessary, and the world is contingent. Hence, whenever we predicate something of both God and the world, it must be affirmed according to the mode of each, which is different. Ogden distinctly saw that this was the way of analogy. Our univocally conceived concepts can be applied only analogically of God in His transcendence. There is no universal agreement among process thinkers on the basis or test for the meaningfulness of religious language. But it is safe to say that the needs of the process metaphysical system, as indeed the needs of any system that retains some meaningful sense of transcendence, point in the direction of some nonliteral God-talk. For there is no way that the language of finite experience can be applied in a straightforward and literal way to a transcendent God.

The inadequacy of purely essentialistic Greek categories of expression. Process theology is also to be commended for its liberating influence vis-a-vis Greek essentialism. God cannot be understood exclusively in terms of unchanging substance, essence, or being. The God of the Judeo-Christian Scriptures is a God of ceaseless activity. He is actively sustaining creation; He is active in history and is manifest in nature. God cannot be understood properly if conceived solely after the model of a platonic super-form or an Aristotelian unmoved Mover. Greek essentialism is deadening if it is superimposed rigidly on the living God of Abraham, Isaac, and Jacob. The personal God of Scripture cannot be so essentialized. Whatever help Greek categories and terms may provide for Christian theology, one must always guard against the lurking danger of stultifying God by dressing Him in the straitjacket of a purely Greek structure. Any biblically and experientially adequate concept of God must include the dynamic and personal.

The importance of a natural revelation. Unlike some neoorthodox theologians, the process people have not lost sight of God's revelation in nature. God is manifest in His created world, as the Scriptures repeatedly stress.[100] The heavens declare His glory; the visible work speaks of His invisible deity. God is manifest in more than the history of the incarnation. The cosmos is a great temple of God's glory. It is significant in this regard that contemporary process theology (á la Teilhard) has not totally negated the importance of the Logos doctrine. Christ is supreme over the whole created world; He is "the . . . Light, which lightens every man, coming into the world" (Jn 1:9, Weymouth). By His creative power the entire universe is "held together."[101] Process theology has not betrayed one puff of existence to the secularistic scientists. God is working in all and through all. This is indeed the biblical picture of God and the only one adequate to a total theistic Weltanschauung.

Insights into the incarnation of God in Christ. Whatever one may decide as to the intramural debate between Thomists and Scotists on the need for an incarnation, it seems safe to conclude that the insights of process theology can be helpful in preserving the true humanity of Christ and the passibility of God the Son. The temptation of Christ was not a charade, nor was His suffering a sham. Jesus Christ, who was "God of very God," did agonize, suffer, and die. In the incarnation there is a real relationship of God and humanity. Christ is really "touched with the feeling of our infirmities" (Heb 4:15, KJV).

Furthermore, it seems that process theology has provided some crucial insights into some otherwise very difficult biblical statements. In what sense did the sinless Son of God become "perfect" (Heb 2:10, KJV) through the incarnation? Indeed, how can we explain the sense in which we "complete what is lacking in Christ's affliction for the sake of his body" (Col 1:24, RSV)? And what do we make of the fact that Christ's mystical body "is growing into a holy temple in the Lord" (Eph 2:21, NASB)? These passages can take on a new and important significance if we understand the body of Christ in terms of the superject nature of God. Perhaps it is here in the consequent nature of God (that is, the "body" of Christ) as enriched by interaction with the entire creation, where there is stored all the value achieved by God in His involvement in the history of the universe. This concept of permanent and stored value can be of great value in Christian theodicy as well, by displaying the modus operandi through which God is really gaining on evil and preserving value that will guarantee evil's ultimate doom.[102]

The basis for explaining novelty and creativity. Some Christians have taken too literally the statement of Ecclesiastes, "There is nothing new under the sun" (Ec 1:9, NASB). The context is that in man's search for happiness apart from God, there is nothing new; there is simply the same, old, cyclical futility. But the Scriptures repeatedly stress that God is at work doing new things. He established a new covenant, is building a new creation, and will one day construct a new heaven and new earth.[103] God did assume new relationships in creation and is involved in ever new relationships in the preservation of creation, the incarnation of Christ, and in the redemptive process. Further, beauty is an expression of God. God is active in the projects of human creativity. "Every good gift and every perfect gift is from above" (Ja 1:17, KJV), including the gifts of creativity and beauty. Process thought enables us to overcome the rigid concept that men do nothing more than think God's thoughts *after Him*. It enables us to see that there is a real sense in which creativity and novelty are a means of expressing God's thoughts *for Him*. Man as a subcreator becomes the instrument of divine creativity, just as man as ambassador of Christ becomes the channel of redemption to men. Process thought enables us to explain how God's creativity is infinitely extended through novelty in human creativity.

These eight suggestions are not intended to be exhaustive; they are merely suggestive of the many ways that process theology has contributed constructively to contemporary theology. Needless to say, there are some serious problems with process theology as a total system. We turn our attention briefly to these now.

SOME CRITICISMS OF PROCESS THEOLOGY

Their understanding and appreciation of traditional theism is lacking. It is not uncommon for process theologians to caricature traditional theism to the point of inaccuracy and incorrectness. For example, to define Aquinas's God of pure act as "statically completed perfection" is both misleading and wrong.[104] It is wrong because God is not static but dynamically active in creation and conservation of the world; and it is misleading because it leaves the impression that God has potential for perfection that has been completely actualized. For Aquinas, God has no potentials in His being at all; God is *pure* act. This does not mean God never engages in activity. On the contrary, God never ceases to be actively supporting creation. And even in eternity there flowed the ceaseless and changeless activity of eternal love among the members of the Trinity.

Another common misconception is that in traditional theism

God sustains no real relationship between Himself and the world. On the contrary, the God of Augustinian-Thomistic theism does sustain a real relationship with the world; however, God does not change in the relationship. Rather, it is the world and the relationship that changes. Even Aquinas admitted that since the creation is really subject to God, "it follows that God is Lord not in idea only, but *in reality*"[105] (italics added). Aquinas denied that God was really related to creatures in the sense that relationship is understood to affect some change in the *nature* of God. This does not mean that the *person(s)* of God cannot and does not enter into changing relationships. Indeed, as Walter Stokes has capably shown, it is definitely part of traditional theism that God has more than a rational relation with the universe; He enters into intimate, personal relations in love.[106] Space will not permit analysis of other misleading charges that the God of traditional theism is conceived after the "substance-philosophy" of Aquinas.[107] It will suffice to say that this misses what Aquinas meant by pure act, or *esse*.[108]

Process criticism of traditional theism is indecisive. A careful study of the *Summa Theologiae* will reveal that most criticisms of traditional theism were adequately anticipated by Aquinas over seven hundred years ago.[109] Let us briefly respond to the criticisms.

1. Pike objects that timelessness eliminates foreknowledge. This is true; but traditional theism does not view this as a disadvantage, for several reasons. First, if God is timeless, or eternal, then theism can avoid the implicit dualism in supposing time is an everlasting reality already there outside God that He did not create. Second, timelessness explains how God can know future contingents, namely, because they are present to Him in eternity. Third, an eternal God avoids determinism. For if everything is *now* to God, then He is not *pre*determining things contrary to the way people will choose. Fourth, an eternal God best fits the biblical description of God as Creator of the temporal world (Col 1:16), who is the I AM (Ex 3:14), and the one who "made the ages" (Heb 1:2, Rotherham). As the creed says, God existed "before all ages." A timeless God is not Greek and pagan; He is biblical and Christian. He knows past, present, and future in one eternal now. But even though He knows all *in* one eternal now, nevertheless He knows the past *as* past and what is future to us *as* future.

2. Pike objects that timelessness conflicts with creation. This criticism misses a very fundamental difference between God's being, which is eternal, and His creative activity, which is not. The

theistic God can *be* beyond time and yet *act* in the temporal world. God's being is eternal, but His creative activity is temporal. Furthermore, it is misleading to speak of God as creating *in* time, as though time were already there, outside God. More properly, it is a creation *of* time, or better, of a temporal world. There was no time before time, only eternity. Time is a concomitant of creation. That is to say, time began with the creation of the temporal world. There was no time before time; time began with the creation of a world of successive progress.

3. Pike objects that timelessness conflicts with personality in God. In affirming that an unchangeable and eternal Being would be less than significantly personal, Pike overlooks an important distinction in traditional Christian theism, namely, that between *nature,* or essence, and *personhood.* The fact that God is unchanging by nature does not hinder Him from entering into real, personal interaction with a changing world. God is love, and love is essentially personal. And as a loving Person, God can love and be loved in accordance with the unchanging consistency of His very nature as love. This kind of loving Person may be more than what is ordinarily meant by *person,* but He is certainly not less than significantly personal. It is gross anthropomorphism to charge otherwise.

4. Pike objects that timelessness conflicts with worshipability of God. The reply to the previous objection is likewise the answer to this one. Contrary to Pike's understanding, the God of Christian theism can respond personally to man's needs and prayers. Hence, it is meaningful to worship Him. In fact, one could reverse the criticism and argue that anyone less than the infinitely and ultimately perfect Being the Christian believes to be God would not be worthy of worship. The God of traditional theism is ultimately perfect, and only what is really ultimate in perfection is worthy of an ultimate commitment demanded in Christian worship. One could conclude, then, that only the God as conceived by traditional theism is a worthy Object of worship.[110]

5. Pike objects that timelessness is incompatible with the incarnation. Here again there is a confusion of *nature* and *person.* As Aquinas pointed out, it was not the infinite and unchanging *nature* of God that became finite and changing in the incarnation. Rather it was the second *Person,* who possesses that infinite nature, who also assumed a second and finite nature. God did not literally become man, nor did the Infinite actually become finite. This makes good poetry, but poor theology. Rather, there are two separate and dis-

tinct natures which are united in one Person. In the Trinity, there are three Whos (Persons) and one What (essence); in Christ there are two Whats and one Who, the same Who (Person) that is one of the Persons in the Trinity. The failure to clearly distinguish person and nature leads to paradox and contradiction which are avoided in the orthodox distinction between *ousia* and *hypostasis,* between *substantia* and *persona.*

6. Pike objects that timelessness is contrary to biblical language about God. The fact that the Bible speaks of God in temporal and changing terms is unquestioned. But it is special pleading to assume ipso facto that God is temporal and changing, for the Bible also speaks of God as not changing: "I, the LORD, do not change" (Mal 3:6, NASB); "in order that by two unchangeable things, in which it is impossible for God to lie" (Heb 6:18, NASB); "for he [God] is not a man, that he should repent" (1 SA 15:29, KJV); thou changest them like a raiment, and they pass away; but thou art the same" (Ps 102:26-27, RSV); "every good and perfect gift is from above, coming down from the Father of lights with whom there is no variation or shadow due to change" (Ja 1:17, RSV). Now the question is this: Which way describes God's *nature,* and which way describes His *activities?* In the light of biblical usages and systematic consistency, it seems more reasonable to understand that God is really unchanging in nature but changing only in activity, because of His relations to the changing conditions in creation. For example, God *acts* in wrath when the condition of man's rejection prevails, and He *acts* in mercy when this condition is changed to repentance. But in both cases there is a changeless consistency in His nature as holy-love. The difference in *activity* does not signal a change in the *attributes* of God. It indicates rather a change in the creatures who are the recipients of God's activity, which activity is wholly in accord with His unchanging nature.

7. In his antinomy of creation, Ogden also makes a kind of category mistake by assuming that a necessary Being must necessarily create. This would eliminate traditional theism's view that God exercised free choice to create. However, Ogden's conclusion is not at all necessary. As Aquinas pointed out, the only thing a necessary Being must will necessarily is His own necessity. There is no necessity placed upon God to will anything else necessarily.[111] Hence, it is entirely consistent that creation would flow freely from a necessary Being.

Further, there is again a confusion between nature and person, an implicit essentializing of personhood. It is only the nature of God that is essentially unchanging; the person(s) of God is free to enter into changing relationships with others. Of course, there are the "limits" of His unlimited love on what He can will to do; but there is no contradiction in affirming personal freedom, within the realm of unchangingly consistent love, as flowing freely from God to creation. In brief, God must *be* unchanging love by nature; but there is not thereby any obligation placed on Him to *do* anything by way of creation, unless He freely chooses to do so. It is a misapplication of the platonic principle of plenitude to the Christian doctrine of creation that has led to confusion on this point. That the "good is diffusive of itself," namely, that God as good must overflow in His goodness by acts of creation, is not a Christian principle. The Christian use of this must be significantly qualified, namely, that God is *desirous* of sharing Himself but is in no way coerced or in need of doing so. The Good (God) is sufficient in Himself. It was not necessary for God to *do* any creating; it is only necessary that He *be* God. What He desired to do beyond this is entirely a matter of His free choice.

8. Neither is Ogden's antinomy of service valid. The traditional view of God does not eliminate the meaningfulness of service for God. Theists have noted,

> Time, history and freedom make a difference because through them God reveals Himself as waiting for man's free return of self. These factors have meaning because God wills to be a lover waiting upon man's free return of love. . . . And that gift [of God's love] increases as man's return gift of self increases.

That is, "time does make a difference, for it is only in time that man completes God's love." It follows then that "man's free decisions are seen to share truly in God's creative activity and produce real novelty that really matters." In this sense, "it is possible to understand that God's creative activity is a call to the creature to create itself." That is, God's sovereign and free love is a call to man to respond freely to it. God has determined that man be self-determining, that is, that man decide to accept or reject that divine love.[112] Hence, time and man's choices in it do make a significant difference—an eternal one.

9. Ogden's antinomy of relationship is the most oft-repeated criticism of traditional theism by process theology. We have already replied that there are real relationships between God and creation.

As personal, God can and does enter into real and changing relationships. However, change does not occur in God's nature but in creatures with whom He is relating. Further, a real relationship does not demand mutual *dependence* but only reciprocity. God does not *need* man's love, but He does *desire* it; and the mutual desire is sufficient for the real and reciprocal relationship. Herein lies a reconciliation of Pittenger's objection to Nygren's concept of agape as a one-way giving without receiving in return. Love is one-way in the sense that God does not *need* man's love for any essential enrichment. On the other hand, love can be two-way for God in the sense that He *desires* man's positive response even though He does not need it. And God's desire for us to return His love can be *relationally* enriching (with regard to His personhood) without being *essentially* enriching (with respect to His nature).

Although these criticisms by process thought miss the mark, they do point up clearly that Christian theism cannot avoid the stress on the personal and relational. Essences as such do not love; only persons can love. Nonetheless, process theology offers no decisive criticisms of the traditional and biblical claim that God is unchanging and eternal in essence. Indeed, as will be seen below, that there is an unchanging basis for all change is still a viable metaphysical option for Christian theology.

Their assumption that God must be either static or bipolar is unjustified. Process theologians assume that God must be viewed *either* as essentially unchanging *or else* as relationally changing, but not both. But this disjunction is unwarranted, as has already been indicated. God can be unchanging in His *essence* and yet involved in changing activity which flows from His *person(s)*. In other words, God does not need another pole in His being in order to explain His interaction with creation; relationality flows from personality, and God is personal. The immutability, eternality, and actual infinity of God can be preserved without sacrificing His relatability to a changing, temporal, and finite world.

Likewise, the choice is not between an immutable, static God of theism and the panentheistic God who is involved in growth and enrichment via involvement with the world. The theistic God cannot grow *essentially,* but He can be enriched *relationally.* That is, He cannot attain any new *attributes* by interaction with the world, but He can and does acquire new relationships and *activities*. This is particularly evident in the incarnation, where God the Son learned, grew, suffered, and even died. And Christ, by relational enrichment with His mystical body, is experiencing further redemptive "growth" (Eph 2:21). Further, as Logos to the cosmos, He experiences the relational movement of cosmic process in sustaining the universe (Col 1:17). And in His mystical body He is "completing" His suffering (Col 1:24, RSV). In view of these kinds of relational enrichment experienced by the *person(s)* of God, eternally distinct from His essence, it is unnecessary to posit in His nature a finite, changing, and temporal pole.

Their concept of God has serious philosophical problems. First, let us speak to the concept of a bipolar God in general, that is, a God with a potential pole and an actual pole. How can God actualize His own potentiality? How can potency actualize its own being? Visions are not realities; the conceptualization is not materialization. Panentheists ask us to believe that the potential pole somehow generates the actual pole. This makes no more sense than to affirm that the mere potential for learning in itself guarantees that one will be knowledgeable. Steel has the potency to be a skyscraper, but it cannot actualize itself. A man may have the dream of great success, but this potency does not thereby actualize the dream into reality. Indeed, it makes much more sense to say, as traditional theists like Aquinas have, that no potency can actualize itself; only an act can actualize. Hence, anything passing from potency to actuality must ultimately depend on what is pure actuality (namely, God).

A bipolar process God would be no more than a big creature that needs grounding. And it will not salvage the process God to invoke creativity in order to ground Him. For in this event, two new problems emerge. First, creativity is thereby given a reality status that only actual entities have in the Whiteheadian system, for only actual entities can be reasons, causes, or grounds of explanation. Second, if creativity is an ontological ground for God, then it becomes, in effect, "the God beyond God." Creativity so used becomes the ultimate ground for all changing beings, including the process God. In this case creativity is serving the function that pure and unchanging act, or *Esse,* does in Aquinas.[113] In brief, in order to make sense out of the process God we must posit the theistic God to explain Him!

There are a number of other problems within the Whiteheadian view of God.

1. How can God be the source of all creativity in the universe, when He is Himself grounded in it? How can a creature of creativity be the source of it?

2. How can change be conceived in any other way except continual annihilation and recreation, if nothing endures? How can something continue to come from nothing, being from nonbeing, unless there is an unchanging Being beyond the process of change (which occurs even with the process God) that grounds the change?
3. How can God be univocally conceived with other actual entities when *God alone,* in contrast to all other actual entities, has no past, envisions all eternal objects, is nontemporal, and never perishes? With all this important difference, how can Whitehead claim God is not an exception to the metaphysical principles of all other actual entities?
4. Further, how can there be more than one agent in the universe, when God provides everything with its initial, subjective aim? That is, how can determinism be avoided?
5. How can anything other than God have intrinsic value, when everything is for His satisfaction, that is, for the fulfillment of His subjective aim?
6. How can God be distinct from the world when the world *is* His consequent nature? How can God be both the order of the world and yet the Orderer of it?

Hartshorne and Cobb avoid some of the problems in Whitehead's view of God by positing that God is not a single, actual entity (as Whitehead argued) but a routing, or series of actual entities. But this move has some serious problems of its own. First, a mere series, or route of entities, each potentially independent of the others, makes order and endurance an extremely precarious problem. For as Whitehead observed, if "there is a world, and if there be order, there must be an ordering entity." How can God know and love the actual world when He knows only the intensity of His own subjective aim for the world? That is, how can God be meaningfully related to the world if it is the result of an unconscious drive?[114]

Their theodicy is a highly inadequate way to explain evil. The objections to a panentheistic theodicy are numerous.[115]
1. In view of the apparent fixity of natural laws and the persistence of evil, what guarantee is there that a limited God can ever achieve a better world?
2. Further, why does a God who cannot overcome given evil even engage in such an apparently wasteful attempt?
3. How can God absorb evil into His nature without embibing a strange, dualistic combination of opposites?

4. How can God achieve a better world via human cooperation when most men seem almost totally unaware of His purposes?

5. How can a limited God who does not control the actual events of this world provide any real assurance that there will be a growth in value?

6. Of what value is it to individual men today to promise a serial appearance of maximal value over the next billions of years?

7. How can men give "absolute admiration to a God who stores value that is unexperienced by any actual entity and when there is no assurance that this preservation will bring progress?

8. How can the God of panentheism be considered morally worthy when He allows the sum total of human misery in order to enrich His own aesthetic value? Is all this misery justified for beauty's sake?

9. How can anyone worship a God so ghastly that He neither controls what happens in the world nor can He call the whole thing off? Is not such a God so paralyzed as to be perilous?

10. How can the panentheist avoid slurring the nature of God when he holds that God is engaging in a character-building activity at our expense in His efforts to overcome evil?

11. How can they avoid making individual evil illusory when they claim that victory over evil is really God's vicarious triumph over evil in us?

It is worthy of mention that none of these objections applies to the God of traditional theism. In fact, an all-powerful God could and an all-good God would triumph over evil; the theistic God is the only adequate solution to these problems. We may conclude that if the God of the Bible does not exist, evil is without an adequate solution.

Their view of Christ is unbiblical and unorthodox. Despite the learned attempts of Pittenger and others, it is both theologically inadequate and biblically unfounded to describe Christ as anything less than perfect God and perfect Man in one eternal Person, the second Person of the blessed Godhead. It is a gross misrepresentation of Scripture to represent the incarnation as merely God *in* Christ. Rather, Christ *is* God. He claimed for Himself the attributes of God (Mk 2:10; 14:62; Jn 5:23, 25; 8:58; 10:30); He accepted worship on several occasions (Mt 28:17; Jn 9:38); He was acclaimed to be God by His immediate followers (Jn 1:1; 20:28; Col 2:9; Heb 1:8), and the Christian church has from earliest times acknowledged His full deity.

Their God is not the God of the Judeo-Christian Scriptures.

Perhaps we may summarize many of the criticisms of the panentheistic God by noting that He is not the God of the Bible. First, as
has already been noted, the God of Scripture is immutable (cf. 1 Sa
15:29; Mal 3:6; Ja 1:17). Second, the God of Holy Writ created *ex
nihilo* and not *ex hulās* (Gen 1:1; Jn 17:5; Ro 4:17; Col 1:17; Heb 1:2;
11:3). Third, the God of Scripture knows the future and both planned
and controls the course of human events (Dan 4:25; Ro 8:29; Eph
1:4-10). Fourth, the biblical God is infinite in power and perfections
(1 Ki 8:27; Job 42:2; Ps 71:15; 147:5). Fifth, the God of Scripture is
fully intelligent and personal (Eph 1:9, 11; 1 Jn 4:16). Sixth, the
theistic God is eternal (Ex 3:14; Ps 90:2; 1 Ti 1:17; 6:16). By contrast,
the panentheistic God of process theology is finite, mutable, deficient in power and perfection, and temporal. Such is not the biblical
God of Abraham, Isaac, and Jacob.

Their basic presuppositions are mistaken. First, their whole
system is built on an anthropomorphic, bipolar model of the relation
between body and soul. It is a classic error of creating God in man's
own image, which image is in turn extrapolated from an organistic
model of nature. Second, they replace the unchanging *attributes* of
God with His changing *activities.* That is, essence is reduced to
activity. There is moving without anything moving; becoming but no
being that comes to be. Third, basic to process thought is a failure to
understand the dynamic nature of *esse* as expressed in the theism of
Aquinas. God for Aquinas is not static but is pure act, engaged in
ceaseless activity. Finally, there seems to be a misdirected desire to
make God's perfection subject to man's moral efforts. In this connection we call attention to the depraved tendency of man-centered
philosophy that desires both to tame God and tone down His
sovereignty so as to make Him domestically harmless. The result is
disastrous for a truly biblical and supernatural theism.

In summation, process theology provides some significant insights into the activity of God, His personal interaction with men,
and the incarnation of Christ which may be appropriated and
adapted to a biblical theism. However, the attempt to use these
insights to negate the teachings of traditional biblical theism has
proven both unacceptable and unnecessary. Indeed, when these
insights are incorporated into the context of a biblically based systematic theology they shed significant light on God's activity and
His interpersonal interaction with a changing world. God's essence
is not in process, but His world is, and He is in the process of
constant and changing interaction with His world. Although some

insights of contemporary process theology are helpful in explaining God's relational interaction with the changing conditions of creation, only traditional theism provides a strong and adequate way of expressing the fact that God is essentially unchanging.

Notes

1. Heraclitus, Fragment 41, in *Early Greek Philosophy,* ed. Milton C. Nahm (New York: Appleton-Century-Crofts, 1964), pp. 70, 68.
2. Henri Bergson, *Two Sources of Morality and Religion,* trans. R. Ashley Audra and Cloudesley Brereton (New York: Holt, 1935).
3. Samuel Alexander, *Space, Time, and Deity* (New York: Dover, 1966). First published in 1920 from the 1916-18 Gifford Lectures.
4. Alfred North Whitehead, "Space, Time, and Relativity" (1915) in *Whitehead: The Interpretation of Science,* ed. A. H. Johnson (New York: Bobbs-Merrill, 1961).
5. Alfred North Whitehead, *Process and Reality* (New York: Macmillan, 1929).
6. Alfred North Whitehead, *Adventures of Ideas* (New York: Macmillan, 1933).
7. Alfred North Whitehead, *Modes of Thought* (New York: Macmillan, 1938).
8. Alfred North Whitehead, *Science and the Modern World* (New York: Macmillan, 1956).
9. This is the view proposed by Nathaniel Lawarence, *Whitehead's Philosophical Development* (Berkeley: U. of Calif., 1956), pp. xiv-xvi.
10. Alfred North Whitehead, *The Aims of Education and other Essays* (New York: Macmillan, 1951).
11. Whitehead, *Adventures of Ideas,* pp. 19⁻-98; cf. *Science and the Modern World,* pp. 154-55.
12. Alfred North Whitehead, *The Function of Reason* (Princeton: Princeton U., 1929), p. 61.
13. Alfred North Whitehead, *Science and Philosophy* (New York: Philosophical Library, 1948), pp. 126-27.
14. Whitehead, *Adventures of Ideas,* p. 198.
15. Whitehead, *Process and Reality,* pp. 95, 53, 32, 28, 95.
16. Ibid., pp. 63, 70, 129, 68.
17. Ibid., pp. 7, 132-34, 79.
18. Ibid., pp. 43, 53, 317.
19. Ibid., p. 95.
20. Whitehead, *Science and the Modern World,* p. 88.
21. Whitehead, *Process and Reality,* pp. 33, 34, 35.
22. Ibid., pp. 513, 32, 70, 44, 73.
23. Ibid., p. 28.
24. Whitehead, *Science and the Modern World,* pp. 158, 159.
25. Whitehead, *Process and Reality,* pp. 129, 126.
26. Whitehead, *Adventures of Ideas,* pp. 304, 305.
27. Whitehead, *Process and Reality,* pp. 44, 45, 209, 334, 134, 320-21, 37, 108, 130, 29, 35.
28. Ibid., p. 65.
29. Whitehead, *Adventures of Ideas,* p. 227.
30. Whitehead, *Process and Reality,* pp. 66, 35, 366.
31. Ibid., pp. 68, 73, 37, 28.
32. Whitehead, *Science and the Modern World,* pp. 144 (cf. *Process and Reality,* pp. 70, 392), 68-69.
33. Whitehead, *Process and Reality,* pp. 32, 367.
34. Whitehead, *Science and the Modern World,* pp. 144, 155, 150.
35. Whitehead, *Process and Reality,* p. 366.

36. Ibid., pp. 44, 46, 521. For an excellent treatment of this point see George E. Connelly, "Whitehead and the Actuality of God in His Primordial Nature," *The Modern Schoolman* 41 (May 1964): 309-22.

37. Whitehead, *Process and Reality*, pp. 48, 64, 392, 169.

38. Ibid., pp. 521, 70, 134, 46, 392.

39. Ibid., pp. 527, 33, 135, 523.

40. Ibid., p. 135.

41. Ibid., pp. 169, 525, 529, 518.

42. Ibid., pp. 95, 66, 31, 340, 135, 47 (cf. *Science and the Modern World*, pp. 68, 159, 99).

43. Whitehead, *Adventures of Ideas*, pp. 192, 241, 130-231; cf. *Science and the Modern World*, p. 147.

44. Whitehead, *Process and Reality*, pp. 31-32.

45. Ibid., pp. 362, 72, 346, 66, 7.

46. Ibid., pp. 366, 35, 39, 66, 346, 72.

47. See Charles Hartshorne, *Man's Vision of God and the Logic of Theism* (Chicago: Wilet, Clark, 1941; Archon Books, 1964) and *The Logic of Perfection and Other Essays in Neoclassical Metaphysics* (LaSalle, Ill.: Open Court, 1965).

48. Thomas Aquinas *Summa Theologiae* 1. 13. 7, *Basic Writings of Saint Thomas Aquinas*, vol. 1, ed. Anton C. Pegis (New York: Random House, 1945).

49. See Nelson Pike's criticisms below (Nn. 61-62).

50. This summary is adapted from Norman Geisler, *Philosophy of Religion* (Grand Rapids: Zondervan, 1974), pp. 151-55.

51. Hartshorne, *The Logic of Perfection*, pp. 64-67, 93-94; cf. John B. Cobb, *A Christian Natural Theology* (Philadelphia: Westminster, 1965), p. 189.

52. Cobb, p. 178.

53. Ibid., p. 178.

54. Ibid., p. 189.

55. Ibid., pp. 204, 210.

56. Aquinas 1. 9. 2.

57. Ibid., 1. 10. 1, 2.

58. Ibid., 1. 10. 4.

59. Nelson Pike, *God and Timelessness* (New York: Schocken, 1970).

60. Oscar Cullmann, *Christ and Time* (Philadelphia: Westminster, 1964).

61. Pike, pp. 180-87.

62. Ibid., pp. 190, 189.

63. Schubert Ogden, "Beyond Supernaturalism," *Religion in Life* 32, no. 1 (Winter 1963): 15.

64. Schubert Ogden, *The Reality of God and Other Essays* (New York: Harper & Row, 1961), p. 58.

65. Schubert Ogden, "Love Unbounded: The Doctrine of God," *Perkins School of Theology Journal* 19, no. 3 (Spring 1966): 13.

66. Schubert Ogden, "How Does God Function in Human Life?" *Christianity and Crisis* 27, no. 8 (May 15, 1967): 106-7.

67. Ogden, *The Reality of God*, p. 10.

68. Ibid., p. 59.

69. Ibid., p. 124.

70. Ibid., p. 10.

71. Schubert Ogden, "Theology and Philosophy: A New Phase in the Discussion," *Journal of Religion* 44, no. 1 (January 1964): 7.

72. CF. Charles Hartshorne, "God as Absolute, Yet Related to All," *Review of Metaphysics* 1, no. 1 (September 1947): 24.

73. Ogden, *The Reality of God*, p. 59.

74. Ogden, "Love Unbounded," p. 14.
75. Ogden, *The Reality of God*, p. 124.
76. Schubert Ogden, "God and Philosophy: A Discussion with Antony Flew," a review of Antony Flew, *God and Philosophy*, in *Journal of Religion* 38, no. 2 (April 1968): 175.
77. Ogden, *The Reality of God*, p. 17.
78. Ibid., p. 17.
79. Ibid., p. 18; cf. Aquinas 1. 13. 7.
80. See Pierre Teilhard de Chardin, *Hymn of the Universe*, ed. N. M. Wildiers (New York: Harper & Row, 1965), p. 14.
81. Hartshorne, "God as Absolute, Yet Related to All," pp. 24-51.
82. Norman Pittenger, *The Word Incarnate: A Study of the Doctrine of the Person of Christ* (New York: Harper, 1959), p. 146.
83. Norman Pittenger, *Christ and the Christian Faith* (New York: Round Table, 1941), pp. 52, 55, 98.
84. Norman Pittenger, *Christology Reconsidered* (London: SCM, 1970), p. 149.
85. Pittenger, *Christ and the Christian Faith*, pp. 45, 47, 87.
86. Pittenger, *Christology Reconsidered*, pp. 3, 110, 126.
87. Pittenger, *The Word Incarnate*, pp. 172, 149.
88. See F. L. Cross, ed., *Oxford Dictionary of the Christian Church* (London: Oxford, 1957), p. 1010.
89. Pittenger, *The Word Incarnate*, p. 154.
90. Pittenger, *Christology Reconsidered*, pp. 139-41.
91. Ibid., pp. 88, 110, 131-32, 44, 55, 56, 61, 7.
92. Pittenger, *The Word Incarnate*, pp. xiv, xv.
93. Maurice Wiles, *Christ for Us Today* (London: CUP, 1967), p. 173.
94. Pittenger, *Christology Reconsidered*, p. 4.
95. Pittenger, *Christ and the Christian Faith*, pp. 139, 143-44.
96. Pittenger, *The Word Incarnate*, p. 149.
97. Cf. Mt 22:37; Phil 1:27; 1 Pe 3:15.
98. C. S. Lewis, "Learning in War-Time," in *The Weight of Glory* (London: Macmillan, 1949), p. 50.
99. See Norman Geisler, "Analogy: The Only Answer to the Problem of Religious Language," *Journal of the Evangelical Theological Society* 16, no. 3 (Summer 1973): 167-79.
100. See Ps 19; Ac 14, 17; Ro 1, 2.
101. Col 1:17; Jn 1:9.
102. On this point see Norman Geisler, *Philosophy of Religion*, pp. 368-69.
103. Jer 31:31; Rev 3:14; 21:1.
104. Ogden, *The Reality of God*, p. 17.
105. Aquinas, 1. 13. 7, 5.
106. Walter Stokes, "A Whiteheadian Reflection on God's Relation to the World" in *Process Theology*, ed. Ewert Cousins (New York: Newman, 1971) p. 149.
107. See Pittenger, "Process Thought: A Contemporary Trend in Theology" in *Process Theology*, p. 26.
108. See Etienne Gilson, *God and Philosophy* (New Haven, Conn.: Yale, 1941)
109. Aquinas 1. 9-14.
110. See J. N. Findlay's article in *Ontological Argument*, ed. Alvin Plantinga (Garden City, N. Y.: Anchor, 1965), pp. 11-12.
111. Aquinas 1. 19. 3.
112. See Stokes, p. 149.
113. See Larry Azar, "Esse in the Philosophy of Whitehead," *New Scholasticism* 37 (October 1963): 462-71.

114. Whitehead, *Process and Reality*, p. 248.
115. These criticisms are adapted from those of E. H. Madden and P. H. Hare, *Evil and the Concept of God* (Springfield, Ill.: Charles C. Thomas, 1968), chap. 6.

Selected Reading

Alexander, Samuel. *Space, Time, and Deity.* New York: Dover, 1966.

Bergson, Henri. *Creative Evolution.* Trans. Arthur Mitchell. New York: Holt, 1911.

Bretall, Robert, ed. *The Empirical Theology of Henry Nelson Wieman.* New York: Macmillan, 1963.

Brown, Delwin, et. al., eds. *Process Philosophy and Christian Thought.* Indianapolis: Bobbs-Merrill, 1971.

Cobb, John B. *A Christian Natural Theology: Based on the Thought of Alfred North Whitehead.* Philadelphia: Westminster, 1965.

Cousins, Ewert, ed. *Process Theology.* New York: Newman, 1971.

Hartshorne, Charles. *The Logic of Perfection and Other Essays in Neoclassical Metaphysics.* LaSalle, Ill.: Open Court, 1962.

———. *The Divine Relativity.* New Haven, Conn.: Yale, 1948.

———. *A Natural Theology for Our Time.* LaSalle, Ill.: Open Court, 1967.

Meland, Bernard E., ed. *The Future of Empirical Theology.* Chicago: U. of Chicago, 1969.

Ogden, Schubert. *The Reality of God and Other Essays.* New York: Harper & Row, 1966.

Pike, Nelson. *God and Timelessness.* New York: Schocken, 1970.

Pittenger, W. Norman. *Process Thought and Christian Faith.* New York: Macmillan, 1968.

———. *Christology Reconsidered.* London: SCM, 1970.

Reese, William, and Freeman, E., eds. *Process and Divinity: The Hartshorne Festschrift.* LaSalle, Ill.: Open Court, 1964.

Teilhard de Chardin, Pierre. *The Phenomenon of Man.* New York: Harper & Row, 1965.

Whitehead, Alfred North. *Adventures of Ideas.* New York: Macmillan, 1933.

———. *Modes of Thought.* New York: Macmillan, 1938.

———. *Process and Reality.* New York: Macmillan, 1929.

———. *Religion in the Making.* New York: Macmillan, 1926.

Wieman, Henry Nelson. *The Source of Human Good.* Chicago: U. of Chicago, 1946.

Williams, Daniel Day. *What Present-Day Theologians are Thinking.* New York: Harper & Row, 1967.

RECENT ROMAN CATHOLIC THEOLOGY

7

Recent Roman Catholic Theology

by
DAVID F. WELLS

The Second Vatican Council, held in Rome between 1962 and 1965, was an event of such magnitude that its full implications for Catholic theology are still being assessed a decade later.

Among Protestants, this council has frequently been considered as a watershed not only dividing Catholic thought of the sixties into two parts but also separating its whole modern development into two phases. Before the council, it is said, Roman Catholic theology was fixed, static, untroubled; after the council, it became fluid, unpredictable, and uncontrollable. The inherited teaching, elaborated and accumulated over the centuries, dissipated over night. Suddenly, it became difficult to say what Catholics did or did not believe and still more difficult to see what they ought to believe.

While there is an element of truth in this assessment, the council was not the abrupt innovation it appeared to be; that was merely the way some people saw it. In fact, it was more the culmination of a process of adjustment and intellectual reorganization that had been going on in the Roman Catholic church for a considerable time. If we were to look back far enough, we might even say that the changes which occurred in the council and those which followed it were really the long-delayed reaction to the shifting intellectual climate, not merely of this century but also of the last.

DAVID F. WELLS, B.D., Th.M., Ph.D., is professor of historical and systematic theology at Gordon-Conwell Theological Seminary. He has written *Revolution in Rome* (Inter-Varsity, 1972), *The Search for Salvation* (Inter-Varsity, 1978), and has coedited *The Evangelicals: What They Believe, Who They Are, Where They Are Changing* (Abingdon, 1975).

There are few religions that have not made adjustments of one kind or another to the tide of secularism that has swept through Western culture. Least affected has been Islam, which, following its expulsion from Spain in 1492, has tended ῑo stand apart from the intellectual developments of Europe just as the Arab nations, until very recently, have stood outside Western technology and industrial development. Judaism, on the other hand, has been deeply affected by the zeitgeist. In America itself, one need only to see the growth of Reform over Orthodox Judaism to gauge the extent to which the old truths have been reinterpreted in rationalistic and often Americanized terms. Likewise, in much of Protestantism the pressures of science and philosophy, the development of biblical criticism, and the corrosiveness of a humanistic culture have combined to assault supernaturally oriented faith.

The changes which have been accepted in other faiths—sometimes accepted only with the greatest reluctance and pain—are now intruding upon the Roman Catholic mind. Once the church, in all of the majestic splendor of its divine endowments, stood as the guardian of the faithful. It was the bulwark against all the assaults which were made on Catholics. This is no longer true. For the single most important change which took place in the 1960s in the Catholic tradition was the erosion of ecclesiastical authority, both in practice and theory. Catholic faithful, religious and priests, are now exposed to the acids of modernity in a way that they never were before. As a result, they are frequently reliving the experiences which took place in Protestantism a century ago.

The Beginnings of Change

That these changes, both in mentality and belief, might have come at the same time that they did in Protestantism was at least a possibility. In the second half of the nineteenth century the Roman Catholic church was troubled by a series of dissident movements, whose interconnections were sometimes obscure but whose combined effect was beyond doubt. These movements—Liberal Catholicism, Action Française, Sillon, Americanism, Modernism—differed in their intents, goals, and methods but shared a common discomfort both with the high orthodoxy formulated by luminaries such as Franzelin, Billot, Deneffe, and Semmelroth and, in certain instances, with the political posture of the church. Thus, for example, one of the rallying points for all Liberal Catholics was the call, made by Döllinger in Europe and Lord Acton in England, for a separation of church and state.

To Catholics still steeped in the notions of medieval theocracy, this proposal seemed to strike at the very heart of the church's authority. In the colorful expression of Pope Pius IX, political power was thought to be as necessary to the proper functioning of the papacy as robes were to Jesus Christ; there would, in other words, be something indecent and humiliating about a pope denuded of these powers. The Liberals, consequently, were castigated as treacherous subversives; and long before they had their hoped-for opportunity to refurbish the church's message in the going philosophical vernacular, Pius IX issued his condemnation, *Syllabus Errorum* (1864). It was, in fact, a broadside fired at the main drift of modern life and ended with the celebrated saying that it is an error to imagine that "the Roman Pontiff can, and ought to, reconcile himself to, and agree with, progress, liberalism and modern civilization."[1]

As fierce as this condemnation was, it failed to still the fears of a minority of Catholic thinkers that the church, by so deliberately repudiating modern culture and intellectual life, had cut itself off from any useful role in the world. Between 1890 and 1907 a group of dissidents who came to be known as Modernists reopened the whole discussion. Their concerns were more obviously theological and their conclusions more decidedly radical.

In Europe, Alfred Loisy argued for a different view of biblical inspiration, one that undercut the traditional view.[2] His articles cost him his professorship in Paris, but he did not yield his belief that Catholic orthodoxy could be integrated with the prevailing views on biblical criticism. Unknown to the world at this time was the fact that long before, as a seminary student, Loisy had lost his faith. His willingness to barter Catholic orthodoxy was not, therefore, the painful matter that it might have been for others. Perhaps this was best seen in his *L' Evangile et l' Eglise* (1902), a response to Adolf von Harnack's best seller, *What is Christianity?* Initially hailed as a brilliant piece of demolition, Loisy's book produced jubilation in Catholic circles until it was realized that the very principles that he had used to overturn Harnack, could also be used to overturn Catholicism. He had developed the thesis that Christian faith needs social, cultic, and symbolic forms for its expression. Liberal Protestants had pursued this idea with respect to the New Testament letters arguing that the simple Jesus had become acutely Hellenized,

Christianity being interpreted by the means of Greek philosophy. However, according to Loisy, they had not seen that even the thought forms of Jesus were but the frail, fallible vehicles of His faith. A remnant of traditional piety, Loisy said, was spoiling the scholarship of liberal Protestants! Thus, borrowing popular apocalyptic language, Jesus mistakenly predicted the coming of the Kingdom, but what arrived was the (Catholic) church. If Loisy had thereby found a justification for Catholicism it was at the cost of an orthodox Christology, and Roman authorities promptly assailed his book as sacrilegious.

But the same irreverence with regard to the inherited orthodoxy was also evident among other thinkers. LeRoy argued that dogma, far from being absolute and unchanging, was merely the product of a relative, human mind. Dogma is an interim report on the way the church sees truth at any one moment; but like all interim reports, it is subject to revision. More recently, this has been the contention of Hans Küng and others.

In England, George Tyrrell assailed the idea of papal infallibility and the traditional authority of the church. Newman's idea of development was pivotal for Tyrrell.[3] According to Newman, biblical truth is somewhat like a telescope, segments of which were present but concealed in apostolic times and remain so until the church begins to pull them out through intuition as much as by logic, thereby exposing the Bible's "implicit" teaching. Tyrrell argued that a fresh assimilation of philosophical ideas was again necessary to draw out the contemporary significance of the faith Jesus epitomized. For some reason the church had allowed doctrinal development to reach a pinnacle in medieval scholasticism, and this subsequently came to be regarded as the last word, the essence of divine, unchanging truth, in matters theological. Tyrrell argued that this was a grievous error. In the United States the same points were made with acerbic brilliance by William Sullivan.[4]

These voices, impatient with the iron grip of traditional authority, became increasingly shrill and demanding. Although their ideas have often found a new lease on life in the post-Vatican II phase, they are not the most obvious forerunners of the contemporary movement; their intemperance disqualifies them emotionally, if not intellectually. But there were those in the movement, such as Baron Friedrich von Hügel and Maurice Blondel, who were modernists (the former more than the latter) but who at the same time were responsible churchmen for whom submission to the holy office was not the moral disgrace that it was for Loisy and Tyrrell. It is to von Hügel and Blondel that we look for the nearest anticipation of those ideas that are currently being made fruitful by Bernard Lonergan, Karl Rahner, Yves Congar, and even Hans Küng.

Whatever organization the Modernist movement had was due largely to the work of von Hügel. His philosophy was concerned with balancing a mystical and a historical element against the institutional element to determine the place the church should play in personal faith. The whole development of Catholic faith from apostolic times to the present must be considered, he said, rather than the one phase Scholasticism; and this must be undergirded by a personal sense of God's presence in the world. After the Modernists were condemned, von Hügel came to see how dangerous had been their stress on the immanence of God, that is, their identification of God's being with the world's processes. This was one of several important criticisms made of Modernist views in the encyclical by which they were condemned, *Pascendi dominici gregis* (1907).

Blondel was by nature, training, and instincts a philosopher whose early association with the Modernist movement was in the role of critic rather than supporter. He was drawn into this role by the publication of Loisy's *L' Evangile et l' Eglise,* which he described as "an unhappy book." Nevertheless, it was Blondel who provided the philosophical framework within which Modernist ideas evolved. In England, his books were avidly read by Tyrrell and von Hügel, who became ardent supporters and disseminators of his ideas. Indeed, Tyrrell spoke of himself as a convinced Blondellian even though he had arrived at these same conclusions by a different route.

The immense, contorted edifice of Blondel's thought, especially as seen in *L'Action,* almost defies analysis. The French is so painful, it is practically beyond translation. An apologetic work aimed at both the dilettante and the nihilist, Blondel's study seeks to show that volition, the process of making and implementing choices, is impossible unless it is assumed that within man there is a divine élan underlying all of his faculties. With this hidden dynamic, the will is in perpetual if unknowing contact. It was this general notion of the pervasiveness of the divine in human life: or of human personality being a crucible, or receptacle, for the divine; or of God being by, with, and under human personality, that was developed by most of the modernists, though in different ways. It was this idea which Schleiermacher on the Protestant side had espoused. Thus, God is to be found not merely in the Catholic faithful but among all men of good will, whose varying religious ideas are but the feeble and often misguided attempts to explain what is intuitively but truly felt within.

Both Tyrrell and Paul Sabatier noted that what following the Modernists had was among the younger clergy; there was little popular support for the Modernists. The majority of Catholics were relieved when Pope Pius X struck down these dissidents in one of the harshest of all encyclicals, *Pascendi*. The leaders were excommunicated, seminary faculties were purged, libraries were weeded, and in 1910 an oath against Modernism was instituted, which became obligatory for all those entering the priesthood. This oath remained in force until Pope Paul VI lifted it a decade ago.

Once again the Roman Catholic church had looked modern culture in the eye and decided that accommodation required a price that was too high. However, this was not to be the last word on the subject. The Christian church as a whole has always to assess anew the accepted *dicta,* the prevailing philosophical and scientific notions in every age, judging where there is and is not compatibility with Christian faith.

So it was that in the 1940s a group of theologians, principally Jean Danièlou, Yves Congar, Marie Dominique Chenu, Karl Rahner, and Hans Urs von Balthazar once again reopened the subject of the relationship between the received orthodoxy and contemporary culture. They did so with caution, tact, and with every indication that they would submit to church authority as they pursued their ideas. A corrective was needed; but Pope Pius XII's encyclical *Humani Generis* (1950) was so mild in its wording, it can hardly even be seen as a rebuke. The work of the new theologians was not imperiled and still less consigned to the graveyard of heresy. After a further decade of study, their conclusions seemed sufficiently safe and fruitful to be given papal approval. Pope John XXIII, in his address which inaugurated the Second Vatican Council, stated that the council had not been called merely to repeat what fathers and theologians had already taught; all of that, he said, "is presumed to be well known and familiar to all." Instead, he asked for a doctrinal breakthrough, and the means he proposed was studying the church's teaching "through the methods of research and through the literary forms of modern thought." His justification for this was that the "substance of the ancient doctrine of the deposit of faith is one thing, and the way in which it is presented is another."[5]

Prior to this speech, Pope Pius XII had warned against the dangers of trying to disentangle the kernel of divine truth from its cultural, linguistic, and historical wrappings.[6] His successor, however, nudged the council toward this end. His implied argument was that there is a distinction between truth in itself and truth as it is perceived by actual people, with particular life-histories, in specific circumstances and cultural settings. The perception of truth is not the same thing as truth in itself.

The problem raised by John was by no means new; but in an age that is acutely agnostic, it has taken on a new sharpness. Accepting that truth and man's understanding of it are not identical, can similarities be found; and if so, under what circumstances? The problem is that outside of the notion of propositional revelation, truth is never seen in its naked form, for it is always transmitted through human personality. And human personality, with its cultural assumptions, its psychological setting and composition, its warping and twisting, always colors the truth which has been perceived. Even if it is possible to discern in another person where the distinction lies between naked truth and his perception of it, it is never possible to do so in one's own case. Even when one has separated truth from the perception, one has really recovered only one's perception of that truth and never truth in its nakedness.

It is this kind of ambiguity which has opened a veritable Pandora's box in Catholic thinking. Some thinkers have assumed that this distinction merely necessitates the constant rephrasing of dogma in contemporary, philosophical jargon, but others have drawn more radical conclusions. Hans Küng, for example, led an attack on all forms of infallibility—biblical, ecclesiastical, conciliar, and papal—as a result of this distinction.[7] Naked and infallible truth derives only from God, he argued, and all these infallibilities have to be false because of the blurring, perverting influence of the processes of cognition. What is presented as binding and infallible is at best merely theological wisdom having the power of suggestion, perhaps of guidance, but never of coercion.

The new climate in Catholic thinking evident in the 1960s was not, then, the sudden innovation which it may have appeared to be. Rather, it was the result of a long process of reflection occasioned often by the inescapable contact between Catholic thinkers and the prevailing intellectual ethos. The church has instinctively recoiled from these contacts, but during the last thirty years in particular, theologians have had greater opportunity and have felt more desire to rephrase the meaning of faith in a way that would not violate secular and humanistic assumptions so brutally. It is this process which radicals and reformers argued was indispensable to the future survival of Catholicism; but it is a method which conservatives fear will subvert the old faith, making future survival all the more difficult. As a strategy for survival it has not been a stunning success, for the Catholic church continues to decline in its numbers and finances as do most Protestant bodies. Whether this is the proper way to do theology is a question that Catholics themselves will have to decide, and they will hopefully address it at the level of a truth question. For whether a religious strategy works or not is no criterion as to whether that religion is true or not.

A New Approach to Theology

It is as natural as it is mistaken for a Protestant to think that theology means the same thing to a Catholic as it does to a Protestant. "Catholic theology" and "Protestant theology" as systems of belief are not rough equivalents. Apart from the differences in belief which distinguish Protestants from Catholics, there are also differences in the very conception of theology itself. It is important to discern where these differences lie.

The role which the professional theologian plays in Catholicism is quite different from that played by his counterpart in Protestantism. The Catholic theologian is part of a much larger and more complex ecclesiastical matrix. Unlike the Protestant, he must guard his relationship not merely to his own conscience but also to the ecclesiastical hierarchy. Therefore, the work of a Catholic theologian often lacks the individualistic touch of his Protestant counterpart. It must always be seen as a legitimate extension of what has been said in the past. Novelty has been equated in the past with heresy. Whereas Protestant theology tends to crest in individuals—Barth, Bultmann, Moltmann—Catholic theology reaches its pinnacles in "schools," or movements, in which the individual thinkers are spokesmen rather than lonely pioneers. The movement is more important than the individual, for private judgment, or the appearance of private judgment, has been avoided from the Reformation to the present. As a result, Catholic theologians are less lonely than Protestant thinkers, but they are also less exalted and less influential.

Catholic theology is the work of interpretation which Catholic theologians do. But what are they interpreting? Traditionally, theologians have been interpreting, first, the created world from which they acquired by unaided reason the knowledge of God's existence and self-evident truths of the natural world such as causation, first principles, the laws of logic, and natural law in general. Second, they have been interpreting revelation as it has been mediated through Scripture and tradition. This latter study has usually been called "positive theology." Further pursuit of the interrelations between the truths derived from Scripture and tradition, their mutual connections and logical consequences, has often been referred to as "speculative theology." Defined in these ways, theology found a comfortable niche in the structure of medieval life at a time when society as a whole was subject to a theocratic vision at the center of which was God's earthly agent, the church. Theology was the queen of the sciences, and philosophy was but its handmaiden. The crowning work of interpretation was theology, through which man in all his activities and the world in all of its parts were united into a single, interlocking life-view.

But all of that has now changed. Following the revolutionary work of Newton, modern science has refused to work within the dogmatic shackles Scholastic theologians wanted to place on it. Western culture as a whole has become predominantly more humanistic and secular, vastly increasing the realm of the natural at the expense of the supernatural. As the fields of learning have been forced into divisions and subdivisions in order to make the newly acquired knowledge manageable, the possibility that there will again be anyone who will be able convincingly to address the whole spectrum of existence has disappeared.

Consequently, Scholasticism is frequently viewed today as unserviceable, even as ridiculous and arrogant. By comparison, the scope of the new theology is far more modest. Its practitioners are content to speak across a much narrower front. Despite the fact that Scholastic orthodoxy as explicated by Aquinas has been upheld as the quintessence of theological truth by over one hundred encyclicals, contemporary scholars are attempting to make a new start. Instead of merely perpetuating the older ideas, they are making herculean efforts to "get back to the sources," a process often known as *ressourcement*. They are trying to rediscover the Christianity of the first five centuries before it was shrouded in the Dark Ages and before it emerged in its Aristotelian finery in the Schoolmen. In this, Catholic theologians were greatly aided in the 1960s by two movements which began independently but subsequently coalesced: the so-called revivals in biblical studies and in patristic studies.

The renaissance in biblical interest is particularly associated with the Pontifical Biblical Institute in Rome and with a branch of this institution in Jerusalem. It was founded by Pope Pius X as an integral part of the Gregorian University, with the goal in mind of combatting the erroneous interpretations of Scripture which the Modernists fostered. In 1928, however, it was given its autonomy; and when Bea was appointed rector in 1930, it was plain that a new attitude toward biblical studies was imminent. The fruit was not long in coming, for in 1943 Pope Pius XII issued his famous encyclical, *Divino Afflante Spiritu*. Among other things, the encyclical allowed moderate form criticism, although it outlawed in advance the kind of extremes to which Bultmann and his followers were to go. Similarly, the moderate use of critical methods was allowed by Vatican II.[8] It is this which underlay the new attitude toward Scripture that was apparent in the journals during the 1960s.

The new interest in patristic studies began at the same time as the flowering of interest in biblical studies, and, in fact, the two have worked together in tandem. This was evident, for example, in one of the most important studies to appear on the eve of the Council, Congar's *Vraie et Fausse Reforme dans l' Eglise*. He argued that true reform in the church is characterized by a return to the basic sources of Christian life, both biblical and patristic. This was one of four marks of a genuine reform, the other three being that it is charitable, communal (involving the whole church, not merely the hierarchy), and patient (allowing time for the whole organism to respond, not merely being imposed from above). If Christian identity through the ages is to be preserved, he went on, continuity with the past must be demonstrated; but the preservation of this identity does not mean that the outward forms of past expressions of Christianity must be slavishly imitated. A new cultural environment needs a new theological expression. It was this idea that Pope John reiterated at the council, as did his successor Pope Paul VI. especially in his encyclical *Ecclesiam Suam*.

This means that Catholic theologians are not merely interested in finding out what the Bible teaches and then repeating it. Although Scripture contains revelation and is therefore revelatory, it is not so uniquely. For the council stated that tradition also is able to hand on the revelatory Word of God. The most important statement in the documents reads accordingly:

> Hence there exist a close connection and communication between sacred tradition and sacred Scripture. For both of them, flowing from the same divine wellspring, in a certain way merge into a unity and tend toward the same end. For sacred Scripture is the word of God inasmuch as it is consigned to the writing under the inspiration of the divine Spirit. To the successors of the apostles, sacred tradition hands on in its full purity God's word, which was entrusted to the apostles by Christ the Lord and the Holy Spirit. . . . Sacred tradition and sacred Scripture form one sacred deposit of the Word of God, which is committed to the Church.[9]

The old polarization between Scripture and tradition as two independent founts of revelation is hereby overcome. Contradiction between them is impossible because they alike hand on the *same* revelation. Theoretically, at least, the possibility of playing off tradition against Scripture as some Catholics did, or Scripture against tradition as most Protestants have, is now removed. And this means that the work of interpretation to which theologians are dedicated has as its primary focus neither Scripture nor tradition but that revelation which is mediated through Scripture and tradition.

Within the council documents themselves, there are some strong suggestions that this element of revelation is, in addition to Scripture and tradition, also mediated through the religious perceptions of the whole people of God.[10] This is what Dutch theologians refer to as a "vision"; it is the sense, or inner realization, of how God is actively working in the world and in human life. This too is the proper domain of the theologian, even if it leads him into psychological and sociological analyses as it frequently did in the 1960s.

We may say, then, that Catholic theologians are trying to elicit the meaning of the Word for contemporary life, whether this Word be considered subjectively (as religious insight) or objectively (in Scripture and tradition). The focus of their attention, however, is on the first five centuries of Christian development rather than later expressions. They are aiming to develop doctrinal continuity between early Christianity and contemporary faith without violating the thought patterns or overlooking the cultural settings of either age. It is hoped that a rekindling of early Christian faith in terms native to this age and time will result.

The new endeavor is markedly anti-Scholastic, and it is this which allows for the possibility of points of contact with some of the dissident movements which have been noted in the second half of the nineteenth century and the early part of the twentieth. Thus, John Ratté has said that the Modernists

> called for a full acceptance of biblical science, and we have *Divino Afflante Spiritu*. The Italian or social wing of the church called for social democracy, and for an end to clerical aloofness, and we have *Mater et Magistra* and the indelible image of Pope John. They pointed to the achievements of Protestant theology, and we have today the phenomenon of the gradual breakdown of the barriers between Catholic and Protestant in both the scientific and interpretive study of Scripture.[11]

As significant as these parallels, however, are the following: the distinction which is now common between truth in itself and truth as it has been culturally and linguistically embodied; the notion that revelation may be communicated at least partially through the religious insights of the people of God; the recognition that genuine, saving experience of God is to be found outside of Catholicism and, indeed, outside of Christianity, perhaps even among atheists; the notion that ecclesiastical authority derives from the people's consensus rather than from ecclesiastical office; and finally, the deep suspicion in which all infallibility is held regardless of whether this is papal, ecclesiastical, conciliar, or biblical.

A New Understanding of the Role of Theologians

In seeking to describe both the antecedents to and the methodology of recent Roman Catholic theology, only professionals have been in mind. However, it is an open question as to who theologized most effectively in this period, the professionals or the laity. While it is customary to think of professionals as alone being true theologians, it may be more accurate, given the rapid and profound changes of the 1960s, to see the laity as the most important source of theology in the church.

In Western culture as a whole, there has evidently been a shift in the locus of knowledge, much of which took place in the 1960s. Formerly, intellectuals in the universities set the pace for society; they were its guides, the custodians of its collective wisdom. The most fertile ideas were often those generated in the centers of learning. Even when society resented the elitist image of the intellectual, it grudgingly allowed him this enormous power.[12] However, in the decade under consideration the relationship of the intellectual to society, of universities to culture, was seriously questioned and even altered.

Today universities are not the sole custodians of wisdom, nor are they the only organizers of knowledge. Knowledge is being communicated through channels other than the universities, and the power that knowledge exercises in society has undergone subtle changes. Especially is this true of questions such as guilt, conscience, existential meaning, sexuality, human development, and decay. These were once the coveted domain of theologians but have now been wrested from their grasp by the moviemakers. Neil Hurley writes:

> Movies are for the masses what theology is for an elite. . . . For nowhere is the distance between technics and thought so pronounced as between those who provide what *Time* once called "these celluloid fables which feed the dreams of the world" and those engaged in what Schoolman St. Anselm called "faith in search of understanding."[13]

What Aquinas and Duns Scotus were to medieval culture, Jean Luc Goddard, Schlesinger, Truffaut, and Bergman are to ours. A transition in the medium and exercise of knowledge is under way from paper to celluloid, from the written word to the cinematic image. The heady stuff of theological discourse stands about as much chance of exciting its readers today as a kindergarten teacher's lessons do of exciting her children after they have watched an hour of "Sesame Street."

The reevaluation of the role of the thinker in society has had its parallels in the church as well. Theologians were once regarded as the custodians of the divine wisdom. They were responsible for feeling out the path ahead for the church and thus were its guides. But they must now at least share this role with the laity, perhaps partly as a result of the cultural changes, but certainly in response to the new doctrine of the church which the Second Vatican Council sanctioned.

The novelty of the council's ecclesiology is probably best seen against the backdrop of the type of doctrine current during the early decades of the present century. In his influential study published in 1908, *Additamenta ad Synopsim Theologiae,* Tanquerey intended to offset modernist vices and to laud Scholastic virtues. He developed his entire discourse on the church without once referring to the laity except as those who are led and taught by the hierarchy.

His treatise is divided into two major sections, the first apologetic, the second theological: In the first he is concerned with arguing the case for the divine institution of the Catholic church, which

case he sees to be upheld in three areas. First, this belief is rationally
credible since the human mind needs both an authority in general
and the living infallibility of the magisterium in particular. Second,
this belief is historically probable since Christ instituted through the
apostles an episcopate equipped with infallibility to teach, rule, and
sanctify. This power has been passed on to successive generations
both in the episcopate in general and in the papacy in particular; so
Tanquerey's conclusion is, "Ergo sola Romana Ecclesia est vera
Ecclesia Christi" (Therefore, only the Roman church is the true
church of Christ). Third, this case is strengthened by the visible
confirmation of the church's divine institution in her character, in
particular her unity, universality, stability, and holiness.

The second major part of the treatise, dealing with the church
theologically, discusses the church's means of exercising divine
authority and power. The role of the pope, the bishops, and the
members of the church are each considered. The pope and bishops
teach and rule in their different ways, while the laity is taught and
ruled. George Tyrrell, the English Modernist, bitterly assailed this
kind of idea, complaining that the two parts of the church ("the
teaching Church" and "the taught Church") appear merely "as
master and scholar, two distant, though related personalities—the
one simply communicative, the other simply receptive."[14] But in a
private letter to von Hügel, he was to say that the laity were considered as brainless, passive sheep: "Their part is to be led, fed,
fleeced and slain for the profit of the shepherd for whose benefit
solely they exist." Further, he noted, there is the notion of the
divine teacher: "Christ is God; Peter is Christ; The Pope is Peter,
ergo he is, we dare not say God, but is Divine Teacher. . . . In
heaven's name, one asks, why doesn't he work miracles and raise
the dead?"[15]

Alongside more traditional ideas such as Tanquerey's, the
council juxtaposed something quite different. It also reiterated
Tyrrell's view that the church should be self-governed and self-
taught. Between what were originally the first and second chapters
of the *Constitution on the Church* was inserted a section entitled
"The People of God." This chapter is encountered in the finished
document *before* the discussion on hierarchy, traditional authority,
the teaching office of the church, and the papacy. Commentators
have observed almost uniformly that this means that the church can
no longer be thought to exist for the hierarchy; the hierarchy exists
for the church. And the hierarchy's mandate derives from all the

people, to whom it must be constantly responsive. Furthermore, a separate decree was written about the laity, marking the first instance in conciliar history that the laity was accorded any separate treatment. Finally, the council taught, again for the first time, that the Holy Spirit is the possession of all the people, not merely of the hierarchy.[16] The lay theologian became an immediate possibility, and one which was realized in the closing years of the 1960s.

This new development was obviously a response to the malaise which leaders perceived among the laity. In his diary written during the council sessions, Congar complained that there were some bishops who did not "seem to realize how grave a symptom of sickness is their [the laity's] depressed state and disaffection." Catholic leaders, he added, had built a church "which is self-supporting by the solidity of her own structure and could almost do without Christian people." In rectifying this dangerous clericalism, the French cardinal said, a "real theology" of the laity had emerged, not merely "an emphasis for the sake of tactics or expediency."[17]

In pursuing the question as to what Roman Catholic theology was like in the 1960s, then, the feelings, perceptions, criticisms and hopes of the laity deserve consideration. In the mid-1960s these were conveniently tabulated with respect to the American Catholic Church by Rodney Stark and Charles Glock.[18] Their work deserves consideration even if statistical surveys sometimes err in summarizing precisely what people believe. Of those church-going Catholics who were surveyed, 85 percent believed unequivocally in the existence of God, 86 percent had no doubt about Christ's divinity, 81 percent had no doubt about the virgin birth, but only 47 percent were sure that Jesus would return again. Church members were then asked to list what they considered to be essential for salvation. Fifty-one percent said belief in Jesus as Saviour was necessary, although this was not explained in any way; 65 percent mentioned baptism; 39 percent cited regular participation at the Mass; 54 percent listed prayer; 57 percent mentioned doing good works; 65 percent cited loving one's neighbor; and only 23 percent mentioned membership in a church. The phenomenon of doubt was present among Catholics, as it was among Protestants, but to a far lesser degree. Although only 49 percent said they were certain they had found the answers to the meaning of life, this figure was higher than in all the Protestant denominations surveyed. It is significant to note, however, that only 23 percent expressed any sense of having been saved in Christ, and how they understood this affirmation is not clear.

As the Second Vatican Council ended, therefore, Catholicism in the United States was distinctly traditional and conservative. Catholics seemed to be least sure about salvation than about any other single topic, and most sure about the existence of God, the person of Christ, the veracity of miracles in the Bible, and the importance of prayer. It is of interest to note that Bible reading as a devotional exercise compared poorly with prayer, no doubt reflecting the consistent discouragement which the laity received in this matter until the end of the 1960s. Fifty-three percent said they never read the Bible at all; only 2 percent said they read it daily. On the other hand, 83 percent prayed at least once a week.

Subsequent to 1968, the attitudes of the Catholic laity have apparently been affected by the new outlook which the council engendered and which began to be implemented at a local level; by the oscillations in influence which liberal and conservative forces either suffered or enjoyed; and by movements such as the charismatic which were unconventional and, in places, influential.

The impact of the charismatic movement on the Catholic church is difficult to assess, especially with reference to the type of statistics provided by Stark and Glock. The movement recently has been able to draw more support than seemed possible at the time of its beginning in the mid-1960s at Notre Dame. A recent gathering reportedly attracted twenty thousand charismatics, the majority of whom were undoubtedly Catholics. Yet given the overall figure for 1974 of over forty-eight million Catholics in the United States, those present at the Notre Dame gathering represent an insignificant minority. Of course not all Catholic charismatics were present (some have suggested that the total for the United States is around three hundred thousand). Furthermore, the figure for practicing Catholics is considerably less than forty-eight million, since this figure includes all baptized children and all adults who have once been connected with the church regardless of their habits of attendance or subsequent level of commitment. Consequently, the relative proportion of charismatic to noncharismatic Catholics is higher than these figures suggest, but it is not nearly as high as some charismatics apparently believe.

The importance of the movement is probably registering not at the level of numbers but on the plane of attitudes. The initial opposition to it which some bishops expressed has become muted; the approval accorded to it by Suenens of Belgium and other important leaders has been an encouragement. It appears to have prepared the way for greater toleration by the hierarchy of unconventional expressions of Christian faith.

The theological significance of the movement is equally hard to discern. While some charismatics speak more and more like Protestant fundamentalists, others are reverting to a purified form of Catholic orthodoxy. For example, the tongues experience has liberated some from praying to Mary, while for others it has heightened this activity. This experience seems to intensify whatever perceptions the person already has. Those who are already moving toward an evangelical simplicity find that their transition becomes more rapid, while those who are already moving back into a pristine Catholic orthodoxy become more convinced of the wisdom of such a course.

Whatever importance the charismatic movement has, it is clear that since the 1960s it has been part of a church that on the lay level has been both conservative and traditional. Roman Catholic lay people, unlike their scholars and theologians, were not attuned to the intellectual developments of Europe. America is a conservative country when judged by European standards, and it was this conservatism that proved constantly frustrating to those whose antennae were directed to Europe. James Hitchcock, in a scathing critique of Catholic radicalism, underscored this point, complaining:

> "The faithful" or "the people" are regularly invoked by conservatives, reformers and radicals with virtually no effort to discover precisely who the faithful are. Most bishops and religious revolutionaries probably do not wish to know who the faithful are, since precise definition would rob the term of its authoritarian usefulness. . . . The conservatism of most laity, which dawned on reformers only rather slowly, has posed a fundamental dilemma for the whole reform movement. For if the imposed, elitist authority of the hierarchy is to be repudiated, it must be repudiated for the sake of greater freedom. Yet Catholic revolutionaries, like secular revolutionaries, have discovered that the desires and "felt needs" of "the people" by no means always correspond to the programs of the reformers.[19]

The attitudes and values of both priests and bishops were often in sharp contrast to those of the laity. In a study conducted by the National Opinion Research Center of the University of Chicago,[20] it was discovered that by the end of the 1960s, while there was still a strong element of orthodox belief among priests, it was counterbalanced by new and more liberal ideas. The differences between priests and bishops were also significant. On matters of faith and morals, bishops were generally more traditional and conservative than priests; but on issues of race, welfare, and ecumenism, they were more liberal.

Perhaps the most interesting set of statistics concerns the priests' attitude toward the church. Despite the avalanche of change that has seemingly rolled over the church in recent years, 84 percent still believe that its basic values have been unaffected. Yet when it comes to the traditional roles of the church, especially its formerly unchallenged authority to teach, it becomes clear that deep and pervasive changes have taken place. Only 45 percent define faith as believing what the church teaches, 65 percent think that openness to the Spirit is more important than obedience to the church, and 52 percent foresee the possibility that conscience might have to be followed instead of obedience to the church. In one instance, at least, the exercise of papal authority actually stimulated disobedience to the official teaching. Before the publication of Pope Paul VI's encyclical *Humanae Vitae,* which reiterated the traditional teaching that all means of artificial contraception are wrong, 40 percent of priests were in agreement with this teaching; after the publication of the encyclical, only 29 percent supported the pope's position.

Catholic priests during the 1960s did hold orthodox views in some matters. For example, 87 percent believed that the Catholic church is the one true church established by Christ, with Peter and his successors as its head; and 88 percent believed that Christ died for our sins, although this figure is somewhat nullified by the fact that only 54 percent believed in His divinity. At the same time, however, new attitudes were developing alongside the old. God, 60 percent believed, is to be found through interpersonal relations; His Word, 58 percent thought, comes through such contemporary prophets as Mahatma Gandhi and Martin Luther King.

On sexual issues there was again a mingling of old and new attitudes. On the one hand, premarital sex was approved by only 7 percent; but, on the other hand, the official teaching on birth control found little support, and there was a far more permissive attitude toward masturbation than in the past. Of those surveyed, 43 percent saw this as a normal part of growth for an adolescent and as an acceptable practice for adults under stress.

Bishops were more theologically conservative than priests.

Bishops who affirmed that the Catholic church is the one true church represented 97 percent of the total, as opposed to 87 percent of priests. The same pattern was evident with respect to affirming the divinity of Christ, where the figures were 73 percent and 54 percent; that He died for our sins, 96 percent and 88 percent; that the sacraments are channels of grace, 86 percent and 66 percent; and that faith should be defined as believing what the church teaches, 69 percent and 45 percent. On social matters, however, the roles were reversed. Affirming the need for a national guaranteed income were 68 percent of bishops and only 52 percent of priests. With respect to urban riots by Blacks, 67 percent of bishops but only 55 percent of priests found these "understandable." On ecumenism, 79 percent of bishops had taken part in such a gathering whereas the figure for priests was only 53 percent.

What the Catholics believed during the 1960s, then, varied a great deal depending apparently upon three main factors: first, it is clear that the church as a whole was more conservative at the beginning of the decade than it was toward the end; second, there was a significant difference in the values held by laity and priests, especially toward the end of the period, the former tending to be more conservative and the latter more liberal; third, there was a greater tendency toward more liberal views among those who were younger, say in the twenties and thirties, than among those who were older, say in their fifties, sixties, and seventies.

NEW THEOLOGICAL EMPHASES

During the 1960s, Catholic theology at a professional level was in a state of ferment and turmoil hardly reflected among the laity. The disappearance of Scholasticism, the closer cooperation with both Protestant and Eastern Orthodox thinkers, and the gathering momentum of *ressourcement*, were the contributing factors. Unlike the Protestant situation, Catholic theology was not so much dominated by individual thinkers as by schools, and these schools cannot be classified as they are in Protestantism. The distinctions between them do not arise from different theologies as much as from different emphases, different priorities, and varying approaches. The 1960s was a time of plowing, and it is still not clear what the harvest will be like. Therefore, in trying to ascertain what constituted Catholic theology in this period, it seems wise to avoid approaching it either through its individual thinkers or the schools of which they were spokesmen but, instead, to slice through several key concepts.

Inasmuch as the whole range of ideas cannot be examined, the choices that have been made may appear rather arbitrary, for it is difficult to find solid justification for choosing one concept and rejecting another. The reason for this selection, therefore, is to eliminate the illusion that the whole corpus of theological notions has been surveyed. The discussion therefore seeks merely to find out what that theology looked like in a few particular instances. Three themes offer themselves most naturally to this analysis: secular culture, God, and the sacraments.

The church and secular culture

Precisely what role Roman Catholic Christians should have in an age assuredly secular has broken upon the church with new vigor. No longer applicable are the old ideas of theocracy or old distinctions between God and the world, the sacred and the profane.

Secularism, according to Protestant theologian Langdon Gilkey, is "the cultural *Geist* within which all forms of thought, including the theological, must operate if they are to be relevant and creative." He goes on to say that secularism is not so much a clearly defined philosophy as it is a mood, a "prerational basis" of thought existing "on the level of what are called presuppositions and thus is expressed *in* the variant forms of a given culture's life rather than being one of these forms."[21]

And what are these assumptions? Gilkey and others seem agreed that where they are operative, a thinker will posit no absolute and enduring truth that stands outside or above the human situation; instead, he will work from within the flux of the human experience, allowing it to set his questions and frame the bounds of his answers. He will assume, further, that human life, even if it is not self-caused, is at least self-interpreting. His knowledge, as a result, will never transcend the domain of human experience nor will it ever appeal to an authority outside that domain.

From a Catholic point of view, the impact of secularism on Christian thought was felt in the political realm with quite as much pain as in the intellectual.

It was only a century ago that Pope Pius IX, in his *Syllabus Errorum,* stated that it is an error to think that any civil government has "indirect and negative power over religious affairs." He went on to declare that it is also an error to imagine "that every man is free to embrace and profess the religion he shall believe true." Catholicism is alone true, and every state has the obligation of supporting it.

No state is at liberty either to separate itself from its marriage partner or to infringe upon the rights of the church. It does not follow, of course, that in a state where Protestantism predominates, government might favor it over Catholicism; for it is also an error to think that through this form of Christian faith "it is possible to please God equally as in the Catholic Church."[22]

In November, 1885, Leo XIII in his encyclical *Immortale Dei* also lamented the growth of secularism as it related to the church's political influence. He criticized freedom of thought, for then "all government is nothing more nor less than the will of the people, and the people, being under the power of itself alone [rather than of God through the church], is alone its own ruler." The result is that the authority of God is ignored, and the state feels no duty toward Him. It "believes that it is not obliged to make public profession of any religion; or to inquire which of the very many religions is the only one true; or to prefer one religion to all the rest; or to show to any form of religion special favor." This lamentable "indifferentism," Leo XIII argued, can be traced back to the Protestant Reformation, which introduced the fatal principle of "private judgment."[23]

In June 1941, Pope Pius XII argued that the state cannot have a purely human foundation. By the same token, it must not "obstruct the liberty of that body which continues the work of Jesus Christ in this world, the Church."[24]

By the 1960s, however, the impact of secular thinking was forcing scholars to debate the whole issue afresh. What was at stake became evident in the opposing views that were articulated by Chenu and Danièlou.[25] Although both had been associated with the *"Nouvelle Théologie"* of the 1940s, Danièlou had subsequently become increasingly more conservative, especially in the 1960s. What was at issue was whether the form of Christianization begun by Constantine in the fourth century and continued in the Middle Ages should live on unmodified, or whether an entirely different civilization should be sought. Danièlou argued for the benefits of the Constantinian order; Chenu for its drawbacks. Christendom, the former argued, was the proper context for personal Christian faith. Wherever the sacred influence is found it must, therefore, be defended as a means to this end. Chenu, on the other hand, rejoiced in the disintegration of Christendom and the corresponding "emancipation" of its institutions, political structures, and culture. These should not be subjugated to ecclesiastical authority but allowed to develop in terms of their own inner life.

Whether the world should be evangelized was not in debate, for both agreed that it should; nor yet, whether Christian faith should influence secular institutions, for that too was agreed. The point at stake was whether faith ought to have institutional and cultural buttressing, or whether it can live a naked existence—in short, whether Christianity ever needs Christendom. Should Christians be merely an ephemeral presence in the world, or should their existence be given cultural and institutional recognition? Or, to put the matter in the words of Rahner: should Christians now emigrate from the "Holy Land" of Christian, Western culture and go into a phase of diaspora (dispersion) among the secular institutions and within the secular values of our time?

These two ways of Catholic life, one of which represents a moderate orthodoxy and the other a serious attempt to be a Christian within secular assumptions, stem as much as anything from Vatican II itself. The document in which these issues were discussed, *"Gaudium et Spes,"* is more compatible with a secular outlook than any other. Although the theme is "The Church in the Modern World," the document clearly interprets *church* very loosely. Indeed, it prefers the word *community,* for what is in view is not primarily the hierarchy but the people. This is important because it enables Catholics to think of themselves not so much as parts of a huge, international organization but simply as autonomous nomads of faith. Furthermore, the entire discussion of political, economic, ethical, and cultural problems is undertaken without ever appealing to divine or ecclesiastical authority. Values are derived from within the human situation itself. Thus, at the beginning of the constitution it is stated, "The pivotal point of our total presentation will be man himself, whole and entire, body and soul, heart and conscience, mind and will."[26] The human heart provides a point of contact between the churched and unchurched, and it is to this authority that appeal is made. Whereas the church may see in this a thread that ultimately leads to God, thoroughgoing secularists might be forgiven for seeing only a thread. In the "solar night of agnosticism" which now prevails, what is at the end of the thread is quite irrelevant.

The tensions which the thrust of secularism posed for Catholic thinkers is probably best exhibited in the United States by the contrasts between two lodestars of the left, John Courtney Murray and Daniel Berrigan.[27] Murray was at the height of his influence in the 1950s but was nevertheless still highly regarded at the Second

Vatican Council. For Murray, who is living in a country that unlike Spain or Portugal is religiously pluralistic, it is unthinkable to demand of Congress that it support Catholicism and subvert Protestantism. He has been quite willing, as many European Catholics have not, to accept democracy. The responsibility of the Catholic, he has argued, is to understand the multiple compromises and concessions by which democracy functions and adapt to these. The Christian is to be courteous, if persuasive, leaven in the dough of the System; he cannot dictate to it.

Father Murray's influence rapidly faded with the dawning of social discontent in the early 1960s. During the Eisenhower years, with their decency, quiet, and order, it was not difficult to identify Catholic interests with the process of democracy; but all this changed when deep disillusionment set in over the Vietnam War. Then the establishment became obnoxious to many, and the complacency of the Eisenhower years an unmitigated disaster. A sharp polarization set in between the interests of Catholic faith as seen by Daniel Berrigan and others and the whole American way of life. Murray supported "the System"; Berrigan opposed it. Murray talked of creative compromise; Berrigan rejected all compromise as derogatory to the Gospel. Murray supported democracy; Berrigan began to hint at the necessity of violence in overcoming societal corruption.

The differences between Murray and Berrigan can, and perhaps should, be viewed from two different perspectives, the historical and the theoretical. First, which thinker is more in line with the tradition represented by Popes Leo XIII and Pius XII, or is this teaching applicable only to Catholic countries? Second, which thinker has best captured the spirit of *"Gaudium et Spes"* and is evolving principles of action from within the situation itself by an examination of needs, problems, fears, and sins, rather than by appealing to authority which is external or metaphysical?

In the long run, the historical question will probably lose its significance, for Catholic thinkers are no longer so concerned about justifying their thoughts in this manner. The issue, therefore, turns on the second question; and in the absence of authoritative teaching, it is no easy matter to discern who has best pierced the armor of self-deception and overt manipulation that often protects the inner workings of the political process even from its principal actors. It is clear, however, that the new approach to these problems proposed in the council document, an approach which is not incompatible

with that of secularism, opened up some painful ambiguities and
divisions within the Catholic church in the 1960s.

THE CHURCH AND GOD

Vast changes have occurred in the way the God question is
posed today and in the way God-talk is undertaken. The issue
concerns the way in which we think and speak about God, for human
experience at this point is shot through with contradiction and
ambiguity. In the sixties, theology tended to reflect this experiential
ambiguity rather than the rational certainties of the older orthodoxy.

There are basically three approaches that can be taken in deriving a doctrine of God: the philosophical, the empirical, and the
experiential. According to the first, what is said about God arises out
of the process of explicating logical principles. In Catholic thought it
is probably best exemplified by Thomas Aquinas, who approached
God not through the revelation of His Son but through a philosophical network of truths. In the *Summa Theologiae,* this network
reduces itself to the famous "five ways," which not only "prove"
the existence of God from the world's contingency but also make
metaphysical assertions about God, such as His self-sufficiency as
the unmoved Mover and the uncaused Cause. The argument rests
heavily on the twin assumptions of natural revelation and the rational continuity between God and man, so that the latter through his
rational processes actually is revelational of the former in His being.
Modern theology in general has shown a restiveness with both ideas.

The second approach, the empirical, sees the life, teaching, and
death of Jesus as providing a definitive statement on what God is
like. Beginning with the theology of the New Testament, it seeks to
extrapolate a doctrine that will not only encompass all the biblical
data but also provide a satisfactory explanation of the experience of
redemption. Given the whole impetus of *ressourcement* in Catholicism, this would seem like a viable substitute for the rejected
Scholasticism. As it turns out, however, Catholic theologians have
in many ways followed their Protestant counterparts in arguing that
the theology of the Bible is not so much the result of divine inspiration as it is the summary of the authors' religious experiences.
Traditionally the former is infallible, whereas by common consent
the latter is not. Consequently, the empirical approach fades away,
leaving only two basic choices, the philosophical and the experiential. By and large theologians have chosen the latter.

In this third approach, God can be distilled from human experience. Within the everyday processes of living, thinking, loving, serving, and communicating, "whiffs of transcendence" can be detected which point back to that Power in whom we all live, move, and have our being. The biblical perception of this is by no means discarded nor, for that matter, is the church's collective experience of God down through the ages; but it needs to be recognized that every faith expression, such as we have in the Bible, is conditioned by the frailty, relativity, sins, and limitations of the author. God alone is infallible, Küng contended in his *Infallible? An Inquiry,* and no human, be he pope, theologian, or apostle, can ever participate in this infallibility. Thus it is to our own experience that we must look even if this is understood against a broader canvass of the experience of others.

Nowhere has this new approach been more influentially treated than in the Dutch *De Nieuwe Katechismus,*[28] which appeared in Europe in 1966 and was translated for American use in the following year. Although it is written in nontechnical language, the catechism provides an apt summary of the thinking represented, for example, in the four-volume symposium entitled *Mysterium Salutis* and the series of books under the general title *Unser Glaube,* both of which were published more or less simultaneously with the catechism and were recognized as important theological statements.

Systematic theologies such as Thomas Aquinas' *Summa* have customarily begun with a discussion of the possibility, methodology, range, and limitations of theology and then moved into a discussion of God, how He can be known, and what can be known about Him. The Dutch catechism, however, begins not with God, but with man and with his perennial question as to "what is the meaning of the fact that we exist."[29] The question is inescapable, it is said, for "all our work and all our family affairs, all that we do be it pleasant or tiresome" persistently reiterates it. What we do to live "is a tender, strong and urgent request put to existence."[30]

Human experience, the catechism states, does not provide the answer; indeed, the more we examine it, the more hollow and insubstantial it appears. Its feebleness contrasts with the idea of omnipotence, its humanness with that of the divine, its finitude with that of the infinite. Yet the transition from knowledge about man to knowledge about God cannot be made by reason, as Thomas Aquinas thought. "Experience shows that in general, men must first be familiar with God through faith before they can accept the rational evidence."[31] And what is faith? In essence it "is a leap," but, the catechism adds, "not an irresponsible one."[32] Reason can take a man only so far. The analogy drawn is between faith and falling in love. Using our minds is appropriate in choosing a life partner in order to ensure that there is some compatibility of personality, outlook, and interest; but to have found a person with whom we are compatible does not necessarily result in being in love with that person. Similarly, faith is an added dimension which it is beyond the capacity of reason to produce and according to which God says, "I ask of you the gift of yourself, if you really wish to know who I am."[33] In this important respect, commitment precedes the knowledge of the God; to that extent, the catechism is correct in describing faith as a "leap."

The leap, it is argued, is not irresponsible, because it does not take place in a total absence of knowledge. This knowledge varies depending upon whether one approaches God from the direction of "the nations" (Hinduism, Buddhism, Chinese Universism, Islam, Humanism, or Marxism) or of "Israel." With respect to the former, there is undoubtedly error mingled in with whatever knowledge of God is possessed; but we have to see that wherever truth exists, it inevitably comes from the Holy Spirit. "Humanity's groping quest for God is animated by God's quest for man." And these gleams of truth in other religions "can help Christians to gain a deeper and more vital conviction of Jesus' truth."[34] But it is in the latter, the people of Israel, that God has sought out man in a unique manner, especially in the coming of His Son. In His Son He has disclosed Himself, and through His Son He is best apprehended.

> The way to Jesus is not irrational. Nonetheless the final step is an act of confidence. And even this is not done indeliberately. But it is a way of knowing which is something more than pure reasoning. It is something deeper. For no matter how highly one esteems the analytical work of the intellect, this is not what is deepest and most total in man, nor even in his knowledge. There is a level of our being which is deeper than the intellect, more personal than feelings, more human than the subconscious. It is the level on which the unity of the two great aspects of our being, knowledge and love, exists. There man's effort to lay hold of truth is inseparable from his striving after goodness. In this primal unity, knowledge is not a cold light and love is not a blind urge. Knowledge is full of love, and love itself has vision. . . . To this core of our being Jesus addresses himself when demanding faith.[35]

What is wholly true is also wholly good; thus the level at which Jesus addresses us is, in addition to being mystical, also moral. And the assent which we return, not merely with the mind but also the whole being, is "a judgment of value."

The presence of Jesus is felt at the ground level of our existence through the work of the Spirit. The presence of this Spirit, His Spirit, makes Jesus once again visible to the world through the life of the church, its sacraments and preaching, its joys, sorrows, its living and dying. "His risen life in the world is reflected visibly in the life of men."[36]

The life of man, therefore, is where the existence of God is felt and where He is seen to be the answer to that void, that hollow insubstantiality which human existence presents by itself. Man should no longer pursue those Olympian insights by which Aristotelian philosophers imagined they had penetrated the heavens; God cannot be found there, nor can He be found in this way. Rather, God addresses us at a different level of our being, requiring of us commitment before further disclosing Himself. And not only does He address Christians in this way, but also those in other religions and even atheists, those who have also responded to Him, but faultily. Thus God is known through human relations, through human feelings, hopes, ideals, joys, and sufferings. Consequently, the church really is, as the Second Vatican Council put it, "the sacrament of salvation to the world."

THE CHURCH AND THE SACRAMENTS

Following the Protestant Reformation in the early sixteenth century, and in direct response to it, the Council of Trent was called for the purpose of formulating Catholic doctrine and rectifying ecclesiastical abuses. Among the many issues addressed were the sacraments, for the Reformers had assailed these doctrines unmercifully. In his tract entitled *The Babylonian Captivity of the Church* (1520), Luther had argued that it was the whole sacramental system which had led the church into bondage in much the same way the Old Testament people of God had been carried off into Babylon. He reduced the traditional seven sacraments to three—penance (which he later discarded), baptism, and the Lord's Supper—and he went on to change their conception. He insisted that a sacrament, particularly the Lord's Supper, is something God gives to man, not what man offers to God. The emphasis on the mechanical and outward act of taking the sacrament to the exclusion of personal faith in the Giver of the sacrament, and the offering of the bread and wine as means of propitiating God through the resacrificing of Christ, were both rejected. Calvin reiterated these same criticisms. As popularly conceived and practiced, the Mass, he said, detracted from the uniqueness of Christ's sacrifice, substituted a human priesthood for a divine one through Christ, and obscured the benefits of the atonement by teaching that salvation arises not from God's gift to man but out of man's dedication to God.

The Council of Trent, however, unflinchingly reaffirmed the traditional doctrines. It anathematized those who added to or subtracted from the accepted seven sacraments: baptism, confirmation, the Eucharist, penance, extreme unction, holy orders, and matrimony. These are necessary for salvation because "the grace of justification" cannot be received "through faith alone."[37] These sacraments are efficacious because they are not merely signs, or representations of God's grace, but they actually convey the grace which they signify. And this grace is given "always and to all men" through the ministration of the sacraments. Those who say "that faith alone in the divine promise suffices for the obtaining of grace" are anathema.

With respect to the Eucharist itself, the council affirmed again the idea of transubstantiation, namely that after the bread and wine have been consecrated, "our Lord Jesus Christ, true God and man, is truly, really, and substantially contained under the species of those sensible things." It assailed those "contentious and wicked men" who had denied that the bread and wine actually became Christ's flesh and blood by turning Jesus' words of institution (Mt 26:26-28; Mk 14:22-24; Lk 22:19-20) into "fictitious and imaginary tropes."[38]

Thus were the battle lines drawn up and sustained for three full centuries. With respect to Catholic thinking on the sacraments during the 1960s, however, two developments proved to be determinative: the liturgical movement and the Second Vatican Council itself.

The liturgical movement, beginning in the mid-nineteenth century, was originally inspired by the thought of recapturing earlier Christian worship. Led by Dom Luis Guéranger, liturgical innovators sought to recapture the splendor of medieval worship. If Guéranger's intentions were good, his execution, it is generally believed, was deficient; for medieval worship was by no means the most pristine, original, and primitive form of the Latin rite. His work, however, did inspire others; and in 1903, Pius X furthered the movement by restoring both the Gregorian chant and the singing of psalms, insisting on more lay participation in worship and encouraging more frequent attendance at communion. Pius XII's famous encyclical, *Mediator Dei et Hominum* (1947), summed up these intentions by saying that the faithful are not to attend merely as "outsiders or mute onlookers" but are to be active participants in the worship. Laity are to act as priests inasmuch as they join with the priest in the Mass, not offering up to God the body and blood of Christ but their own flesh and selves as a spiritual sacrifice. The emphasis on the internal act of worship, over against the rather external, mechanical, and rote participation, was underscored although not to the denigration of outward and public worship. Careful and guarded encouragement was given to the desire to find more simple and primitive forms of worship.

The Second Vatican Council recapitulated, especially in the *Constitution on the Sacred Liturgy,* the gains of the liturgical movement but plowed fresh soil with regard to the sacraments themselves. The council appears both to have spiritualized the sacraments and to have enlarged their number. However, in order to circumvent the anathema of Trent on those who prefer more than seven sacraments, a distinction was drawn between sacraments and sacramentals. [39]

At the center of the sacramental system is Christ. This means that the emphasis has shifted from the outward act of participating in the administration of a sacrament by the faithful to their inward attitude of faith toward Him who gives Himself in the sacrament. Their participation in the act and their priestly function through it is thereby underscored. The presence of Christ is mediated principally through the Eucharist, which is still the heart of the system. The council did, however, address itself to the issue of transubstantiation somewhat ambiguously by saying that Christ "is present in the sacrifice of the Mass, not only in the person of his minister."[40] What content is to be put into the word "present" and how this presence is to be explained is the vital but unanswered question.

Around the Eucharist are clustered the other traditional sacraments, three of which are church oriented (baptism, confirmation, and holy orders) and three of which are more personal (marriage, penance, and extreme unction). These are sacraments because they mediate Christ, who is "the fountain from which all sacraments and sacramentals draw their power,"[41] but they are not the only means by which this presence comes to men. Alongside these are other rites which achieve the same purpose, such as those for the consecration of virgins, renewal of vows, and the burial of the dead.

Throughout the *Constitution on the Sacred Liturgy,* this emphasis on Christ's presence is heard like a persistent drumbeat in the words "the paschal mystery." It is made all the more real by the transition from worship in Latin to the vernacular. This, however, does not exhaust the notion of the sacrament; for if the reality of Christ constitutes the center of the sacrament, then it is also proper to speak of the church as "a kind of sacrament or sign of intimate union with God." For the church both points to and mediates the presence of that Christ by whom she has been called and consecrated. Thus the *Constitution on the Church* treats the whole people of God sacramentally, as they share in the priesthood of Christ, participate in the Eucharist, and finally are "used by Him as an instrument for the redemption of all." The saving intentions of God are declared, exhibited and mediated by this people.

The atmosphere which the council created in its pastoral emphasis upon Christ, its broadening of the notion of sacrament, and its insistence on the active participation of the laity set an entirely new mood during the 1960s. Innovative liturgies, folk Masses, and congregational participation, as well as a de-emphasis on the significance of the traditional seven sacraments were the immediate outcome. Some saw this as inestimable gain, others as great loss.

Among theologians a new attitude toward the sacraments was in evidence even before the council convened, and certainly this was so afterwards. Two of the most interesting studies along this line, although not the only ones, were written by Edward Schillebeeckx and entitled *Christus, Sacrament van de Godsontmoeting* (1960) and *Christus' Tegenwoordigheid in de Eucharistie* (1967).[42]

Schillebeeckx's first study has been hailed for its reworking of the sacraments into more biblical and patristic categories than formerly, but they are also more heavily dependent on philosophical existentialism. The central concept is that of "encounter," by which Schillebeeckx distinguishes between our knowledge of persons and our knowledge of things, mechanisms, and the physical world. It is his complaint that the grace of the sacraments has all too frequently been treated objectively, as if it were a thing, that which was inherent in and a part of the physical elements. What has been overlooked is that the sacraments do not operate in this physical, external, depersonalized way. They mediate an encounter with God, which takes place in the intimacy and immediacy of our inner being. For this reason, Christ should be seen as the primordial and basic sacrament. The divine in Jesus performed through His human life saving acts which were sacramental. "Consequently, if the human love and all the human acts of Jesus possess a divine saving power, then the realization in human shape of this saving power necessarily includes as one of its aspects the manifestation of salvation: includes, in other words, sacramentality."[43] The physical "element" of His humanity mediated the redemptive presence of God then as it does now. All of the other sacraments, therefore, are related to Christ as the cluster of petals is to its center.

In his second study, Schillebeeckx related these ideas to the Eucharist in particular. His theology is now bolder and more critical of Tridentine orthodoxy. It was strengthened in the seven intervening years by the growth of progressive ideas and by the council itself. Schillebeeckx is now sharply critical not only of the Tridentine formulation but also of the Aristotelian philosophy which lay behind it. He seeks to show that the latter has been wholly discredited by modern physics, which makes it imperative for the church to reformulate its faith in categories which are not derived from Aristotelianism.

Perhaps the most interesting idea advanced by the Dutch theologian concerns transubstantiation. Bread and wine, he argues, were symbols of human cultivation and of life. In the eucharistic context they symbolize Christian community and Christ's risen, saving life. Christians are invited to share their own lives and participate in this, the taking of the sacrament being the occasion when all of this occurs. What is changed, therefore, is not so much the constitution of the bread as its *meaning;* it becomes the form, or indication, of "Christ's giving of himself to the Father and to men." Thus, he concludes that in "this commemorative meal, bread and wine become the subject of a new *establishment of meaning,* not by men, but by the living Lord *in* the Church, through which they become the *sign* of the real presence of Christ giving himself to us."[44]

To the Reformers, the sacraments in Catholicism were offensive because they undergirded the idea that man is justified by what he does, in particular by his positive response to God's grace. It is not always clear that the latter aspect has changed in contemporary Catholicism, though it is often softened by the personalistic terms in which it emerges. On the former aspect, however, many of the older differences have dissolved. Whereas the priesthood of all believers was once denied, now it is largely affirmed; whereas the congregation was often discouraged from actively participating in the worship, now it has assumed a responsive role; whereas transubstantiation was once the most distinctive aspect of the Catholic Eucharist, it now has been relegated, at least by some, to the nether regions of deliberate ambiguity or discarded altogether.

CRITIQUE

The sixties saw such turmoil, so many deep, pervasive changes, with such spectacular collisions in Catholicism, that it is difficult to avoid the conclusion that an intellectual revolution is now under way. But this is a peculiarly Protestant way of viewing things; 84 percent of priests apparently still believe that the basic values of Catholicism remain unaffected by all of these changes. What these values are, however, is for an outsider difficult to discern. They are not exactly what the Council of Trent said they were, nor do they always coincide with what was widely believed even in the first three or four decades of this century. At what point development becomes revolution and whether continuity can be preserved through change are issues which Catholics have had to confront frequently in the past and have to confront today. Despite their sensitivity on this point, it does not seem inappropriate to speak of a "New Catholicism." But how "new" can Catholicism become before it ceases to be Catholic? Within the Catholic church today that is the issue which outranks all others in importance.

If, however, we are to accept Catholic belief for what it is, there are still a number of questions that need to be singled out for comment.

The most obvious issue, to many evangelicals, is the transition from theology to anthropology, from thinking about the world as God sees it to thinking about it as man experiences it. It is a transition that makes contemporary Roman Catholicism more compatible with the way in which modern people think than it would have been formerly. Secularism operates on the assumption that there are no answers from the outside, that human experience must be allowed to frame its own questions and human ingenuity to answer them; this attitude does find some echoes, however muted and qualified, in contemporary Catholic thought.

This shift in vantage point, however, is not necessarily wrong. Depending on how it is developed, it could result in an apologetic strategy of some usefulness. Whether this happens or not will obviously depend on how it is pursued, especially with reference to some of the key biblical issues like sin, revelation, grace, and atonement. But it is worth recalling that John Calvin, at the threshold of his *Institutes of the Christian Religion,* argued that knowledge of ourselves is inextricably related to knowledge of God, and that the former should lead naturally into the latter. The connection between these two forms of knowledge he describes thus:

> But as these are connected together by many ties, it is not easy to determine which of the two precedes, and gives birth to the other. For, in the first place, no man can survey himself without forthwith turning his thoughts towards the God in whom he lives and moves; because it is perfectly obvious, that the endowments which we possess cannot possibly be from ourselves; nay, that our very being is nothing else than subsistence in God alone. In the second place, those blessings which unceasingly distil to us from heaven, are like streams conducting us to the fountain. Here, again, the infinitude of good which resides in God becomes more apparent from our poverty. In particular, the miserable ruin into which the revolt of the first man has plunged us, compels us to turn our eyes upwards; not only that while hungry and famishing we may thence ask what we want, but being aroused by fear may learn humility. For as there exists in man something like a world of misery, and ever since we were stript of the divine attire our naked shame discloses an immense series of disgraceful properties, every man, being stung by the consciousness of his own unhappiness, in this way necessarily obtains at least some knowledge of God. Thus, our feeling of ignorance, vanity, want, weakness, in short, depravity and corruption, reminds us (see Calvin on John iv. 10) that in the Lord, and none but He, dwell the true light of wisdom, solid virtue, exuberant goodness. We are accordingly urged by our own evil things to consider the good things of God; and, indeed, we cannot aspire to Him in earnest until we have begun to be displeased with ourselves.[45]

But there obviously are differences between the type of theology which Calvin represents and that which a growing Catholic consensus now espouses. These differences seem to lie in three main areas: the meaning of sin, of revelation, and of faith.

Even if, as an old adage has it, everyone is against sin, unanimity is not easy to find when a definition of sin's nature and effects is being sought. The Dutch *Catechism,* for example, speaks eloquently of the intrusion of sin into human life; of its transmission from generation to generation; of the inner resistance to God and His claims which it generates; and of the hurts, pains, and destruction which it works in human life. Yet, for all of that, it does not teach

—as evangelical Christianity does—that sin has shut off all fellowship with God outside of a saving trust in His Son. Instead, the
Catechism assumes that "gleams" of divine knowledge are present
throughout human experience, even in non-Christian religions.
Were it speaking merely of what is commonly known as natural
revelation there would be no problem, for natural revelation is not
salvific. It is plain, however, that this is not so. What is scattered
among the world's peoples is, indeed, a saving revelation from
which Christians can also learn.

This benevolent broad-mindedness is hard to resist, and to try
to do so is inevitably to invite the charge of bigotry. But where, one
must ask, is the offense of the cross? There is obviously no correlation between the offense of the cross and being offensive, nor
between Christian particularism and that strange necessity some
people feel to stand alone, *contra mundum*. We do not, however,
have to be afflicted with a martyr complex to see that if Christianity
is true it is true at its center, where good and evil, right and wrong are
thrown into an ultimate antithesis. That Jesus is *the* way, *the* truth,
and *the* life—not merely *a* way, truth, and life—is inescapably a part
of biblical Christianity. It cannot be softened, bartered, or eliminated without taking with it Christian faith as a whole. To live with
this as a person is hard; to live without it as a Christian is impossible.

This leads us out into a second major difference between
evangelical and Catholic theology today, namely, the whole question of revelation. It has been common to distinguish in revelation
between what has variously been called general and special, natural
and supernatural, natural and soteriological. Each of these paired
titles expresses an aspect of the difference in the two types of
revelation under consideration. As a matter of fact, God's disclosure of Himself (revelation) occurs in two stages rather than being in
two distinct types. According to the first, man as man is addressed.
God discloses His existence from the natural creation (Ps 8, 19; Ro
1:18-20) and His moral nature through man's conscience (Ro
2:14-16); thus it is a revelation which is natural and general. According to the second, He addresses man as a sinner and discloses
Himself especially in terms of His redemptive purposes. This revelation includes His acts of intervention in man's history, His sending
of the prophets, His giving of the Son, and His inspiring of Scripture;
it is a revelation designed for His own people and is, therefore,
special, supernatural, and soteriological. The revelation of God's
existence and great power is the indispensable prerequisite without

which an understanding of the incarnation is impossible; the revelation of God's morality and of man's corresponding guilt is the backdrop against which atonement makes sense and without which it becomes merely another Roman execution. Catholicism today is assuming that God's first stage in revelation, that which is natural and general, is really His second stage, that which is supernatural and soteriological. The resultant difficulty with which Catholic theologians are constantly struggling is to find a role for Jesus which is not merely different from that of other men (as revealers of God) but quite unlike theirs; for a Christianity without a unique Christ has really ceased to be Christian. It is not always clear that the theologians' efforts have been crowned with success.

Third, the new concern with existential realities, dimensions of subjective experience, and mysticism has opened up a fresh difference with evangelical Protestantism. When Luther confronted Rome in the sixteenth century, he argued that the whole element of inward trust, of faith through the promises of God, had been neglected in favor of rational assent to the church's teaching. The situation is now entirely reversed: the notion of inner commitment is present, but the rational framework within which it takes place is being denigrated. Biblical faith, it has often been said, consists of three elements: intellectual assent *(notitia)*, emotional response *(assensus)*, and volitional action *(fiducia)*. It is an error to reduce it to any two or one of these elements. Traditional Catholicism accentuated *notitia* (as it related to the church); contemporary Catholicism has largely focused upon *assensus* and *fiducia,* especially as these are understood in existential categories.

Evangelical theology has customarily thought of faith's knowledge, *notitia,* as that which comes from discovering God's revelation in Scripture. In the pages of His written Word, God has addressed man in propositional terms. Scripture is written rationally for people who are rational. This is not to say that human knowledge is wholly rational or even that God's communication of Himself comes only propositionally. Undoubtedly the Holy Spirit gives to the reader of Scripture an awareness of his own shortcomings and of the love, glory, and grace of God which, if also conveyed in the words of Scripture, is not wholly identical with the simple meaning of these words. It is a knowledge which, as it were, lies within the written revelation of Scripture, never contradicting it, never augmenting it, but merely deepening it. The salient point, however, is that Christianity is throughout the New Testament presented as something to be accepted by the mind and then acted upon by the will, if indeed we can distinguish mind and will in this way. It is never presented as merely "happening" to someone, as if he had inadvertently tripped and fallen over a log. Christianity is not subrational, even if it does encompass more than the mind.

The idea of the faith leap, however carefully it is qualified, is an unwise approach to God. In an age characterized by its irrational behavior, there may be something appealing in putting Christianity in these terms. Undoubtedly it saves the Christian from considerable toil and grief if he is no longer obliged to defend the traditional bases of faith such as a space-time Fall, a creation open to God's contemporary working in new ways (which we call miracles), the birth and death of Christ in objective time and history, and an inspired record of what these events all mean from God's perspective as well as man's. But the price to be paid for this faith leap is the loss of religious controls. Christianity "happens," even to the most unsuspecting of people like atheists, at a level of their being which is outside of their rational control and lies behind their understanding.

Who, then, is to know whether it is God or the devil who has been encountered? Put in this stark form, this question seems almost crudely beside the point, for ours is an age of great sophistication, is it not? Yet it needs to be remembered that alongside great technological achievements are to be found evidences of remarkable superstition and perversion, and that scientific brilliance is no guarantee of advanced understanding in matters of religion. On the contrary, the story of the book and movie *The Exorcist* is strangely comprehensible to our generation despite our sophistication in other areas.

This is not, of course, the only danger implicit in debunking the rational controls within which faith is nourished and protected, although it is the most dramatic. What is probably far more common is the misconception that Christ has been encountered, whereas, in fact, only a mystical experience has been had.

Mystical experience is universal; it is to be found among all peoples and in almost all religions. There are those who conclude that these experiences show that the God of Christian faith must, therefore, have been active outside of the precincts of Christianity; but this is not the only conclusion to be drawn from this phenomenon. And it is no guarantee that any particular experience, whether it is inside or outside of Catholicism, can be considered as an encounter with Christ.

Given the extraordinary diversity of views, understanding, and spirituality that exist in the Roman Catholic church today, simple evaluations and easy answers are more inappropriate than ever. Yet it must be said that, if the move to meet modern man on his own ground has some potential advantages, the price which has been paid so far has often been too high. On the other hand, the disappearance of ecclesiastical controls has exposed Catholics to a variety of influences, not all of which are bad. Indeed, there are clear signs among some of a kind of evangelical piety which is almost too good to be contained forever in the purest of evangelical denominations. This startling situation may put strains on the goodwill of some Protestants even as it encourages the naiveté of others. For both, the apostle Paul has a word. To the one he counsels that truth must always be held out in *love;* to the other he warns that it is always *truth* that we hold out, even though we do so in love (Eph 4:15).

Notes

1. Henry Bettenson, ed., *Documents of the Christian Church* (London: Oxford, 1966), p. 348.
2. See Michele Ranchetti, *The Catholic Modernists: A Study of the Religious Reform Movement 1864-1907,* trans. Isabel Quigly (London: Oxford, 1969), pp. 16-35.
3. See David F. Wells, "The Pope as Antichrist: The Substance of George Tyrrell's Polemic," *The Harvard Theological Review* 65, no. 2 (April 1972): 271-83.
4. A Modernist [William Sullivan], *Letters to His Holiness Pope Pius X* (Chicago: Open Court, 1910).
5. Walter M. Abbott, *The Documents of Vatican II* (London: Geoffrey Chapman, 1967), p. 715.
6. See G. C. Berkouwer, *The Second Vatican Council and the New Catholicism,* trans. Lewis B. Smedes (Grand Rapids: Eerdmans, 1965), pp. 57-88.
7. Hans Küng, *Infallible? An Inquiry,* trans. Edward Quinn (New York: Doubleday, 1971).
8. *Dogmatic Constitution on Divine Revelation,* sections 11, 12.
9. Ibid., sections 9, 10.
10. See David F. Wells, *Revolution in Rome* (Downers Grove: Inter-Varsity, 1972), pp. 38-51.
11. John Ratté, "The Specter of Modernism," *Commonweal* 82, no. 17 (July 23, 1965): 532.
12. See Richard Hofstadter, *Anti-Intellectualism in American Life* (New York: Random House, 1963).
13. Neil Hurley, *Theology Through Film* (New York: Harper & Row, 1970), p. ix.
14. [George Tyrrell], "Lord Halifax Demurs," *The Weekly Register* 103, no. 2680 (May 3, 1901): 550.
15. Tyrrell to von Hügel, 20 February, 1901, Von Hügel and Tyrrell Correspondence, British Museum, Additional Manuscripts 44927.
16. See Hans Küng, "The Charismatic Structure of the Church," *Concilium* 4, no. 1 (April 1965): 23-33.
17. Yves Congar, *Report from Vatican II: The Second Session of the Vatican Council* (London: Geoffrey Chapman, 1964), pp. 78-79.
18. Rodney Stark and Charles Y. Glock, *American Piety: The Nature of Religious Commitment* (Berkeley: U. of Calif., 1968), pp. 30-45, 133, 110, 112.

19. James Hitchcock, *The Decline and Fall of Radical Catholicism* (New York: Herder & Herder, 1971), pp. 97-98.
20. *The Catholic Priest in the United States: Sociological Investigations* (Washington: U. S. Catholic Conf., 1972), pp. 90-106, 120-23.
21. C. W. Christian and Glenn R. Wittig, eds., *Radical Theology: Phase Two. Essays in a Continuing Discussion* (New York: Lippincott, 1967), p. 17.
22. Bettenson, p. 383.
23. *The Great Encyclical Letters of Leo XIII* (New York: Benzinger, 1903), pp. 120-21.
24. James W. Naughton, ed., *Pius XII on World Problems* (New York: America, 1943), p. 73.
25. The literature that constitutes this debate is diverse and in French. A more complete summary with bibliographical references has been provided by Claude Geffré, "Desacralization and the Spiritual Life," in *Spirituality in the Secular City,* Concilium, vol. 19 (New York: Paulist, 1966), pp. 111-31.
26. *Pastoral Constitution on the Church in the Modern World,* section 3.
27. Cf. James Hitchcock, "The Evolution of the American Catholic Left," *American Scholar* 43, no. 1 (Winter 1973-74): 66-84.
28. *A New Catechism: Catholic Faith for Adults* (New York: Herder & Herder, 1967).
29. Ibid., p. 3.
30. Ibid., p. 5.
31. Ibid., p. 16.
32. Ibid., pp. 289-90.
33. Ibid., p. 289.
34. Ibid., p. 33.
35. Ibid., pp. 124-25.
36. Ibid., p. 193.
37. *Canons on the Sacraments in General,* session 7, canons 4-8.
38. *Decree Concerning the Most Holy Sacrament of the Eucharist,* session 13, chap. 1.
39. *Constitution on the Sacred Liturgy,* sections 59-61.
40. Ibid., section 7.
41. Ibid., section 61.
42. Edward Schillebeeckx, *Christ the Sacrament of the Encounter with God* (New York: Sheed & Ward, 1963); *The Eucharist,* trans. N. D. Smith (New York: Sheed & Ward, 1968).
43. Schillebeeckx, *Christ the Sacrament,* p. 15.
44. Schillebeeckx, *The Eucharist,* p. 137.
45. John Calvin, *Institutes of the Christian Religion,* trans. Henry Beveridge, 2 vols. (London: James Clarke, 1953), 1:1.

Selected Reading

Berkouwer, G. C. *The Second Vatican Council and the New Catholicism.* Trans. Lewis Smedes. Grand Rapids: Eerdmans, 1965.

Du Plessix Gray, Francine. *Divine Disobedience: Profiles in Catholic Radicalism.* New York: Alfred Knopf, 1970.

Hitchcock, James. *The Decline and Fall of Radical Catholicism.* New York: Herder & Herder, 1971.

Wells, David. *Revolution in Rome.* Downers Grove, Ill.: Inter-Varsity, 1972.

Wills, Gary. *Bare Ruined Choirs: Doubt, Prophecy and Radical Religion.* New York: Doubleday, 1972.

THEOLOGIES OF LIBERATION

PART ONE: AN OVERVIEW

I. Theology in context
   A. The world of liberation theologies
   B. Theological seasonings in the new mix
II. Liberation—Latin style
III. Liberation in black

8

Theologies of Liberation: An Overview

by
HARVIE M. CONN

Since 1965 the word *liberation* has moved from general usage to the technical terminology of theological descriptors. This shift is a contribution of Latin American Christianity. The theological meaning of liberation was vague until the Second General Episcopal Conference of Roman Catholic bishops (CELAM) at Medellín, Colombia, in 1968. There liberation's context was shaped, as the dominant language of development declined and the deepening Latin criticism of developmentalism grew. In the years that followed, the word occurred with increasing frequency in Roman Catholic literature. Documents by Chilean bishops display it. Themes like "salvation-liberation" and "grace-liberation," reflect it. By 1970, it had become attached to a movement, "the theology of liberation," and had spawned a number of conferences and symposia.[1] A bulletin appeared entitled *Theology of Liberation*. The fruits of those meetings appeared in a number of 1971 publications.[2] And in that year, theological reflection entered a new stage through the appearance of *Teología de la Liberación,* the work of Peruvian Gustavo Gutiérrez. Liberation was then no longer simply a linguistic "anti-development" stance. It became a call for "*a new*

HARVIE M. CONN, A.B., B.D., Th.M., Litt.D., is associate professor of missions and apologetics at Westminster Theological Seminary. During his twelve years of missionary service in Korea, he wrote three books in Korean, the most recent being *An Introduction to New Testament Studies* (Presbyterian General Assembly Theological Seminary, 1976). He is the author of *Contemporary World Theology* (Presbyterian and Reformed, 1973) and the editor of *Theological Perspectives on Church Growth* (Presbyterian and Reformed, 1977).

way to do theology.''[3] This Roman Catholic evolution of thought was paralleled by comparable studies within the Latin American Protestant community.

Liberation theology as a descriptive term has also crossed the geographical borders of its origin. James H. Cone, professor of theology at Union Theological Seminary in New York, in his second major book, *A Black Theology of Liberation* (1970), incorporates the concept of liberation into his understanding of the function of theology. In a rewriting of the traditional loci of systematic theology for the North American Black, Cone sees Christian theology as a theology of liberation, theology as "a rational study of the being of God in the world in light of the existential situation of an oppressed community, relating the forces of liberation to the essence of the gospel, which is Jesus Christ.''[4] The index of Cone's book gives no indication that at that time he had been listening to Latin America. But the liberation themes are remarkably parallel—the context of oppression functioning as the norm of theology, the struggle for redefining theology in terms of sociopolitical realities, and the fear of a theology detached from the stream of existence, its abstractness defended in the name of a pseudouniversal theology.

In August 1975, at Detroit, Michigan, a week-long conference on "Theology in the Americas: 1975" marked another turn in the development of liberation theology. Under the direction of the Chilean priest Sergio Torres, Latin American representatives of liberation theology joined their North American counterparts. The original intention of the partners in the dialogue, according to Torres, was to "prompt U.S. theologians to rethink their relationship to the dominant culture of their country and engage in critical reflection on the American experience from the viewpoint of the poor.''[5] As the planning process advanced, those goals were enriched by the reactions of the various study groups, which noted "that there was no single American experience. A theological reflection on American history cannot be complete unless one invited Christian speakers for the black community, for Mexican-Americans, the Puerto Ricans, for Asian-Americans. . . . Christian women should be invited to reflect on their struggle for emancipation in church and society.''[6] The make-up of the group that eventually participated in the conference reflected the study groups' desires. Widening circles of felt oppression were seen as spawning new liberation movements. Liberation had become a meaningful way to explore theology, and not simply for Latin America or even black America. Native Americans, Latinos, and women also sought to define or articulate their faith in terms of those same categories.[7] And still more recently, the dialogue has expanded to yet other contexts; South Africans and Irish have also initiated partnership in the discussions.

Partly out of sensitivity to that background, I did not choose to title this chapter "Latin American Theology." Liberation theology, even in its earlier stages and more so now, is too easily put down as a regional phenomenon by such language. One could just as easily lump together the rest of the chapters in this collection and call it "North Atlantic Theology." Further, as Rubem A. Alves indicates, such a geographical designation can easily hide Anglo-Saxon theologians' ethnocentrisms concerning the final normativeness of their own work: "Anglo-Saxon theologians have always claimed universality for their theologies. . . . I do not know of a single theological work from that part of the world that was humble enough to recognize its limitations."[8] In addition, the geographical designation misses the depth demanded by liberation theology. Much more is at stake in liberation theology than simply where it is done. The participants at the Detroit conference saw this, and, according to Torres, the title of the document issued by them, "The Contextualization of North American Theology," expresses a new understanding by the delegates. Says Torres: "There is no longer any attempt to 'apply' liberation theology in North America; nor is the attempt simply to discover the 'meaning' of liberation theology in the North American situation. Rather the goal is to contribute to a new theology that emerges from the historical, social and religious context of the North American experience."[9] Liberation theologians reject prefabricated theologies that bear labels reading "Made in U.S.A." and meaning, "What's good for the U.S.A. is good for the rest of world." Every theology, even North American theology, bears the marks of its own cultural upbringing, they say.

Out of sensitivity to this concern about misleading labels, I chose to title this chapter "Theologies of Liberation." Because of space limitations, the following discussion will focus more on the similarities than on the differences between the diverse expressions of liberation theology. And no attempt is made to interact with feminist theology or with theological developments within the Asian American, Latino, or Native American contexts. I hope that some future edition of this book will correct those omissions. This chapter concentrates on the Latin American formulations, with lesser attention given to the movement now popularly called black theology. But none of this procedural methodology should blind the reader to the fact that liberation theology (the singular is generally used as a concession to common usage) intends to be a pluralism. The Detroit conference stated that clearly:

> Each such theology is based on a community struggling for freedom in a concrete historical society, and while they share a common faith . . . they do not wrestle against the same enemy and hence for the time being remain somewhat distinct in their efforts. . . . It could well be that for some peoples the economic oppression is the central, over-riding element, to which all other oppressions are subordinated. These people could not be faulted if other groups, struggling out of their situation, regard racist or sexist oppression as the principal enemy.[10]

The commonness of the struggle unites the diversities of the liberation theologians' responses. But it does not remove the uniqueness of each response. All the groups, each in its own place, examine the forms of oppression that appear to them to be secondary and come to a clearer understanding of how those secondary forms are related to what they see as the principal oppression. The task in these two chapters will be to examine the methodology by which this examination is done and offer some preliminary evaluation of it for our North American liberation.

THEOLOGY IN CONTEXT

At the heart of liberation theology is the affirmation of "the contextual nature of theology,"[11] reflection on "that concrete reality in which we find ourselves," the missiological challenge that "that concrete reality presents to Christians in that continent."[12] For Gustavo Gutiérrez, that affirmation demands a theology

> which does not stop with reflecting on the world, but rather tries to be part of the process through which the world is transformed. It is theology which is open—in the protest against trampled human dignity, in the struggle against the plunder of the vast majority of people, in liberating love, and in the building of a new, just and fraternal society—to the gift of the Kingdom of God.[13]

For J. Deotis Roberts, Sr., that same affirmation is the answer to the question, Why a black theology? "We must discover the meaning which Christian theology can provide for our black experience in America," says Roberts. "Our search is timely and crucial. We must weight the claims of Christian doctrine in the framework of our black experience. Will we find it to be the answering-theology we need for the deep questions of our existence as black people?"[14]

THE WORLD OF LIBERATION THEOLOGIES

All of these comments focus on the desire of these theologians to serve human liberation. Indeed, Juan Luis Segundo, reflecting on the beginnings of the Latin American movement, says that this desire was one of the three discoveries that created it, "the realization that the Christian gospel is aimed at liberating human beings in a very real manner, that is to say, in the process of history, even if the total liberation from the last bondages will be the result of the eschatological intervention of God."[15] The Sabbath serves man, says Segundo, and theology must serve him also. Man was not made for dogmas, sacraments, and the church, but rather they were made for him.

For Latin America, says Paul Lehmann, that context of service is demanded by the dehumanization produced by what he calls "imperialist colonialism." Unlike the colonialist imperialism that shapes the protest of a Mao in China, imperialist colonialism is oppression by expansionist states in ways other than military conquest or annexation of land. It is *covert* domination. It is political, socioeconomic, and psychological control without occupying armies.[16] Latin America has discovered what José Miguez-Bonino calls "the basic fact of its dependence." Its freedom from the colonialist imperialism of Spain made possible its imperialist colonization by the Anglo-Saxon world, Miguez-Bonino says. In 1870, a legislator of the British Parliament commented, "Argentina is our least expensive colony; it even supports its own occupation army."[17] One hundred years later, Latin American lands had become monocultural suppliers of Anglo-Saxon needs, and colonization had become economic. What were the Latin American countries to the Western world? asks Miguez-Bonino. Argentina was corn and meat; Brazil was coffee; Chile was saltpeter and copper; the Central American countries were a source of bananas; Cuba was sugar; and Venezuela was oil.

In the 1950s and 1960s the full impact of Latin America's poverty and oppression came to be felt. With great expectations, the people of the Southern Hemisphere had heard the United Nations proclaim in 1950 the first "decade for development" and watched John F. Kennedy launch the Alliance for Progress in 1961. But, says Miguez-Bonino:

> Soon after the launching of the Alliance . . . the failure was already visible. The chasm between the developed and the underdeveloped world was growing wider instead of narrowing, not only because the expected minimum measure of growth was never reached, but because, applied to widely different starting points, even the same rate of growth results in ever increasing inequality. Foreign investment has taken out of Latin America far more than it has invested. The process of production, distribution, and finance has been almost totally transferred to outside agents (international monopolies). The terms of trade continue to be unfavorable. The prices paid for the use of technology—protected by licenses in the Northern world—far outweighs the benefits of its use. Production has been unable to cope with the increase of population and thus the number and condition of marginals have become worse.[18]

Cumulative frustration over the development programs began to grow. People began to make puns on the "para" in "Alianza para el Progreso." As a preposition, *para* means "for." As a verb, it means "impede." Thus the Alliance for Progress became to many the Alliance that Impedes Progress. There was more than humor in the joke, "The rich get richer and the poor get kids."

By 1964-65, various economists were raising questions regarding the development model itself. Says Alan Neely:

> To some of them it was apparent that so-called economic integration was augmenting rather than decreasing the dependence of the Latin American nations on the United States. The more strident critics talked of development as a new and more insidious form of colonialism. Then a study by Paul Baran and Paul Sweezy published in 1966 provided hard data which confirmed for many Latin Americans their worst suspicions about *el desarrollismo* [developmentalism] (1966). Baran and Sweezy were quoted widely in Latin American publications in 1966, for they offered convincing evidence of the growing monopolization of the economy by the United States and what Theotonio Dos Santos called 'the new character of dependence.'[19]

Underdevelopment was no longer being seen as the result of economic, cultural, social, and political backwardness. It was being labeled as the development of capitalism itself, what Miguez-Bonino later called "the dark side of Northern development."

Gutiérrez echoes those same judgments. Says he, developmentalism had become

> virtually synonymous with timid measures, really ineffective in the long run and counterproductive to achieving a real transformation. The poor countries are becoming ever more clearly aware that their underdevelopment is only the by-product of the development of other countries, because of the kind of relationship which exists between the rich and the poor countries. Moreover, they are realizing that their own development will come about only with a struggle to break the domination of the rich countries.[20]

How influential was the Marxist analysis of capitalism in this growing disillusionment? Gutiérrez's spiritual pilgrimage may be typical and thus shed light on the answer to this question. As he began to work, serving the poor in a very traditional, nonpolitical way, he says he discovered three things:

> I discovered that poverty was a destructive thing, something to be fought against and destroyed, not merely something which was the object of our charity. Secondly, I discovered that poverty was not accidental. The fact that these people are poor and not rich is not just a matter of choice, but the result of a structure. It was a structural question. Thirdly, I discovered that poor people were a social class. When I discovered that poverty was something to be fought against, that poverty was structural, that poor people were a class, it became crystal clear that in order to serve the poor, one had to move into political action. . . . I discovered the nature of political action, its rationality, radicality, and all-encompassing character.[21]

At that stage, Gutiérrez seems to have turned to Marxism as an instrumental tool. Marxism provided an explanation for the class struggle that Gutiérrez and others increasingly saw, not simply as the fruit of underdevelopment, but as its fountainhead. The problem was not simply underdevelopment. It was domination and dependence. The answer then was not economic integration but liberation, an anthropocentric concern that Vatican II had hinted at in an earlier stage of thinking. The structural character of the problem demanded structural answers. Marxism as an indispensable ally was a choice made existentially prior to the epistemological choice that followed it.

That existentially prior choice, says J. Andrew Kirk,

> affirms, quite succinctly, that the concrete, objective situation of the majority of humanity is so appalling, so degrading in human terms, so extensive in its practical consequences that only a global solution has any chance whatsoever of bringing these vast sectors of humanity the possibility of a new beginning to their lives. The solution, in order to be accepted, must be able to show that it has already worked (at least substantially) and that there is no other feasible alternative.[22]

For Latin America, China and Cuba were powerful object lessons that seemed to indicate that a Marxist-inspired revolution could bring tremendous social gains. Brazil stood as a testimony to the failure of every capitalist attempt to remove the discrepancy in the levels of income between the possessors and the dispossessed: after twelve years of the crudest doctrine of *laissez faire* and a spectacular rise in the gross national product, there was not the slightest difference in the share of wealth received by the average worker, except for its diminishing size.

The outcome of this kind of perspective, not its source, was a commitment from many to socialism built first and foremost on a humanitarian concern for one's neighbor, coupled with a structural analysis of the reasons for the failure of capitalism to deal with the problem of continuing abject proverty.

At the same time, that commitment and analysis have been articulated increasingly and self-consciously, using Marxist conceptions. The extent to which liberation theologians in particular are truly Marxist is subject to vigorous debate. But it cannot be debated that, to borrow José Porfirio Miranda's phrase, "We are all riding on Marx's shoulders."[23] More particularly, the liberation theologians see Marxism primarily as an instrument of social analysis rather than as a philosophy or a plan of political action. Whether these elements can be kept separate is a judgment to be saved for later in this study. At this point, I only wish to underline Marxism's usage by the majority of liberation theologians.

Cold-war rhetoric, as Gregory Baum notes, makes it hard, particularly for North Americans, to see Marxism as anything but a uniform and fixed system of ideas, institutionalized in identical ways in communist countries and parties. But it does not have those connotations among liberation theologians. Marxism, as it is incorporated, for example, in the writings of Gutiérrez, is not to "be interpreted in a literalistic fashion."[24] He and many others use a Marxist focus on the economic system to define the key factor in oppression and a Marxist understanding of class analysis as the central and indispensable element for grasping the social situation and the interests of the class that owns and controls the major industries. Asks Baum:

> Who is still interested in Marx's analysis of early industrial capitalism or his theory of surplus value? What contemporary Marxist analysis is interested in are the contradictions of modern, corporate capitalism and their link to the recurring economic crises, to the expansionist policies of the capitalist world, to the creation of dependent territories with impoverished masses, and to the spread of poverty and unemployment even in the industrialized capitalist countries. Are the disturbing events we read in the newspaper accidents of history, or are they related to the economic system that we have inherited?[25]

The existential priorities of the Latin American context also underline the differences between the Christian-Marxist "dialogue" that has been conducted in the First- and Second-World nations during the past decade and what is now going on in the Southern Hemisphere, which is part of the Third World. One dialogues against a background of developed nations, the other in the face of underdevelopment. One struggles with the problems of psychological estrangement, the other with physical existence:

> The number and quality of people varies dramatically: in the First and Second Worlds one sees a manageable number of people, who are literate, physically healthy, with some measure of social mobility; while in the Third World one still notes catastrophic population growth coupled with illiterate, ill-fed, ill-housed people—people with almost no chance to change their social relationships. Finally the experience of the inhabitants with respect to the phenomena of colonialism, imperialism and racism is different; exploiting, white superiors compose the developed world, while exploited, nonwhite inferiors make up the underdeveloped world.[26]

Out of one milieu, Christianity and Marxism dialogue about hope. Out of the other, the topics are dependence, dialectics, colonialism, and subversion. The one speaks of dialogue, which the

Latins repudiate as abstractness. The other speaks of praxis, the dialectic of action-reflection associated with a total dynamics of historical vision and social transformation.

Liberation theology's response to what its adherents see as oppression also moves on a level that is not primarily economic or political or, for that matter, even primarily Marxist. In fact, according to Paulo Freire, the Brazilian educator, liberation on these levels must be subsequent to or at least accompanied by a "consciousness raising" that touches man's psyche and motivates him toward liberation. There must be a liberation of the consciousness, Freire says, freeing people to become the agents of their own destinies.

On this level, we move beyond the vision of Marx to the psychoanalytical categories of Eric Fromm and the psychosociological commentaries of the Algerian psychiatrist Franz Fanon. We ask how man has internalized the repressive structures of society. How can this personal dimension of oppression be integrated into the question of human liberation from all dependencies and avoid the privatist trap into which liberation can easily fall? How can authentic liberation, what cannot be done by one person for another, be achieved in one whom colonialism has re-created after its own image of passive domination?

Although the references to Fanon by Freire and the liberation theologians are not frequent, Fanon's electrifying 1961 study of the Algerian and African liberation struggles is a sharp reminder of the effects of colonialism on man's definition of himself and the need for a progressive liberation of the consciousness. The psychodynamics of colonialism's sociological division of the world into "settlers" and "natives," says Fanon, paint the "native as a sort of quintessence of evil," not only lacking in values but incapable of them.[27] The colonized are dehumanized by a racial Manichaeism and reconstructed with a self-image of being spectators without history, animals without culture. Colonization defines the first as last and the last as first. "Colonialism is not satisfied merely with holding a people in its grip and emptying the native's basin of all form and content," Fanon continues. "By a kind of perverted logic, it turns to the past of the oppressed people, and distorts, disfigures, and destroys it. . . . The colonial mother protects her child from itself."[28]

Fanon's analysis was not lost on someone like Rubem Alves,

often called one of the first of the Protestant liberation theologians. Says Alves:

> One does not have to agree with Franz Fanon in order to understand the analysis he makes of the consciousness of oppressed people. Colonialism, he says, distorted them as human beings. It is a form of violence, because it robs man of any free relationship with his world and his future. The violence which this man was under became part of his own being. It created him in its own image.[29]

And Gutiérrez refers to those same studies when he states the need for liberation on a full level: "Alienation and exploitation—as well as the very struggle for liberation from them—have ramifications on the personal and psychological planes, and it would be dangerous to overlook these in the process of constructing a new society and a new man."[30]

It was especially Paulo Freire who contributed much in this area. His work focused on the creation of a liberation methodology by which the oppressed could move from a "naive awareness" of accepting things as unchangeable to a "critical awareness" that questions, challenges, and brings change; in a word, "conscientization." As Freire analyzes that process, it is not so much Marx or Fanon but Eric Fromm who offers constant help. Freire's commentary on the dehumanizing effects of oppression and the responsibility of the oppressed to struggle for their own freedom echoes Fromm repeatedly.[31] From Fromm he speaks of the "necrophilous" nature of what he calls "banking education," those pedagogical systems that transmit the values of the oppressor instead of initiating and fostering "critical awareness" in the oppressed.[32]

Against this background, liberation theology adds another dimension to that of the social and political overtones. As Gutiérrez explains:

> Man is seen as assuming conscious responsibility for his own destiny. This understanding provides a dynamic context and broadens the horizons of the desired social changes. In this perspective the unfolding of all of man's dimensions is demanded—a man who makes himself throughout his life and throughout history. The gradual conquest of true freedom leads to the creation of a new man and a qualitatively different society.[33]

It is particularly in this area of consciousness raising where black theology began its emergence as a theology of liberation.

Dehumanization is the common context that binds Latin American and black protests into one. But for Latin America the process is linked to imperialist colonialism. For the Black the link is to racism, or, to borrow the language of Fanon, Manichaean de-identification through color. Colonialism, as the context for Latin American liberation thinking, achieved dehumanization by deprivation; racism achieves it by de-identification. One destroys personal identity by devaluating people into the socially oppressed, the other by devaluating people into "non-Whites." Says Lehmann, "If the *exterior* injustice of colonialism and imperialism is the deprivation of the *opportunity* of being human in the world, the *interior* injustice of this exploitation and oppression is the deidentification that prevents the *possibility* of being human in the world."[34]

Chronologically parallel to the development of Latin American liberation theologies, black theology's context began to be shaped decisively by the 1954 decision of the United States Supreme Court that struck down the doctrine of "separate but equal" in the field of public education. A year later, on December 5, 1955, Rosa Parks was arrested in Montgomery, Alabama, for refusing to yield her seat on a bus to a white customer. A one-day black boycott of Montgomery buses grew into a protest movement that swept across the American South. Largely through the dynamic leadership of Martin Luther King, Jr., a spontaneous racial protest shifted into an awesome passive resistance movement, wedded to the church and calling for theological articulation.[35] In the maelstrom of black self-discovery, the term black theology was born. As early as 1966, it was used by the Committee on Theological Perspectives of the National Conference of Black Churchmen in the United States:

> Black Theology is a theology of black liberation. It seeks to plumb the black condition in the light of God's revelation in Jesus Christ, so that the black community can see that the gospel is commensurate with the achievement of black humanity. Black Theology is a theology of "blackness." It is the affirmation of black humanity that emancipates black people from white racism, thus providing authentic freedom for both white and black people. It affirms the humanity of white people in that it says "No" to the encroachment of white oppression.[36]

Carried on in its earlier stages as a program largely of consciousness raising, the movement under King sought to shape a new vision of black self-awareness, a new self-understanding. In the spring of 1966, Stokely Carmichael popularized that new attitude in a phrase, Black Power. Fearful that the term indicated "basically a nihilistic philosophy born out of the conviction that the Negro cannot win," King opposed it, seeing it as a call for a separate black road, the advocacy of retaliatory violence.[37]

James Cone offers his theological commentary on Black Power in his first book, *Black Theology and Black Power* (1969). To a large extent the book marks the birth of American theology in black.[38] Responding to charges of black racism in the Black Power attitude, Cone underlines King's recognition of Black Power as a "psychological call to manhood." The affirmation of black identity, the essential worth of blackness, becomes Cone's theme and that of many who respond to him. The black man, charges Cone, has been poisoned by the stereotypes that others have of him. Black Power is seen as "the power of the black man to say Yes to his own 'black being,' and to make the others accept him or be prepared for a struggle."[39] Theology is an existential tool for Cone, a tool with which he seeks to make Black Power "an expression of hope, not hope that whites will change the structure of oppression, but hope in the humanity of black people."[40] Paralleling the Latin American awareness that liberation of consciousness is a self-achievement, Cone says also, "Black people now know that freedom is not a gift from white society, but is, rather, the self-affirmation of one's existence as a person, a person with certain innate rights to say No and Yes, despite the consequences."[41]

Even in those early years, black theological reflection did not ignore the political or economic dimensions of oppression and liberation. Joseph R. Washington, Jr., offered only two alternative possibilities for understanding Black Power—either as a "flash in the pan" or as violent revolution.[42] "Washington wants a radical theology of revolution which questions the basic structures of society and desires a new political, economic and social order,"[43] says Allan Boesak. That new order would come only through unlimited violence, through "blood full of courage," writing a "bloody peace in the sky."

Washington's tone, however, has been too strident for the majority of black theologians. Most prefer, with J. Deotis Roberts, Sr., to correlate liberation with reconciliation, not revolution.[44] "Both must be given serious attention simultaneously even if liber-

ation must be primary,''[45] Roberts says. Others, like Major J.
Jones, fearful of the equation of Black Power with hatred and violence and supportive of nonviolent revolution, are criticized for
coming close to a political pietism, a one-sided focus on self-
consciousness ''which totally ignores the threats to freedom from
persons with whom and systems within which man has to live.''[46]

There is some indication of a new shift in context for black
theology that may provide another opportunity for investigating
these sociopolitical perspectives. Especially important in this connection was the 1975 Detroit conference on Theology in the
Americas, mentioned earlier. Providing communication links with
other ethnic minority and Third-World theologians, much of the
conference, says Gayraud Wilmore:

> focused on the socio-economic exploitation of minorities, the re-
> pression of human rights, and the class struggle within both the
> internal and external colonies of North and South America. Theolo-
> gians, church leaders, and grass-roots Christians wrestled together
> over the meaning of God's action in history, the need for radical
> transformation, the tensions between Marxism and Christianity, and
> the task of the churches in the praxis of liberation.[47]

Wilmore sees the conference as having

> made a decisive impact on Black theologians. . . . Recent statements
> and activities seem to point in the direction of a less exclusive intro-
> spective obsession with the American race problem than was
> characteristic of the earliest development of Black Theology. The
> Black-White dichotomy shows signs of breaking up, yielding to a
> widening perspective on human oppression which recognizes the
> importance of the class and cultural analyses of other theologians—
> especially the Latin Americans.[48]

Perhaps symptomatic of these changes is the ''Message to the
Black Church and Community'' that was adopted by the national
conference of the Black Theology Project in Atlanta in August
1977. The statement of the Project, a continuing work established
by the 1975 conference, maintains its focus on racism but amplifies
its language in socioeconomic terms. ''The root problem,'' it says,

> is human sinfulness which nurtures monopolistic capitalism, aided
> by racism and abetted by sexism. . . . Exploitative, profit-oriented
> capitalism is a way of ordering life fundamentally alien to human
> value in general and to black humanity in particular. Racism and

capitalism have set the stage for despoilation of natural and human resources all around the world. . . . The roots of our crisis are in social, economic, media and political power systems that prevent us from managing the reality of our everyday lives.[49]

Near the conclusion of the message, the issues are drawn together again: "Because of racism and imperialism, domestic and foreign, we black people are an international community of outlaws and aliens in our respective homelands and in those communities where we have chosen or been forced to reside."

The full import of the Project's message must await future developments for us to be able to judge how strongly this new context and political awareness will develop. In the meantime, we remind ourselves that at the Detroit conference, Marxism as a tool for social action received no black support either as an existential priority or an epistemological necessity. John C. Bennett, a participant, comments:

At several points during this conference I heard blacks or women say to those who have used Marxist analysis in a dominative way: "Your category of class which you claim will cover everything does not do justice to sexism or racism. You treat sexism or racism only on your own terms—in a kind of dominative relation. Although racism, sexism and class are interrelated, we are demanding that you respect the independence of each category and language system."[50]

Gregory Baum reinforces Bennett's judgments:

The Blacks felt that a class analysis is not enough: the name of the oppression under which they suffer is racism, and while racism is related to economic exploitation and class identification, it cannot be reduced to economic oppression. The Blacks complained that the holistic approach recommended by the Latin Americans subordinated and underplayed the problem of racism. It was no accident that in their talks the Latin American theologians had not paid much attention to the racial inequalities in their own countries and even less to the dominant machismo-spirit. The Blacks feared, moreover, that arguments over the economic system might divide the Black community and weaken them in the face of the white majority. For the Blacks the primary enemy is racism; and since the Latin Americans defined as principal enemy the economic imperialism of the Northern nations, especially the U.S.A., they, the Blacks, could not declare themselves in solidarity with them."[51]

The Project's message gives no evidence of changing those

perspectives on who is the primary enemy in the American context. But it does show a new, reflective openness toward the interrelation of racism and imperialism, an openness that had not been as widely voiced or as accepted a part of its context in the past.

THEOLOGICAL SEASONINGS IN THE NEW MIX

Latin liberation theology, as a new-old challenge to the "established harmonies" of theology, still remains "theological" reflection on praxis. Much of the impact on the evangelical of Miguez-Bonino's *Christians and Marxists*, in fact, comes not simply from its explicit commitment to Marxism as a tool of self-criticism but from its explicitly Christian commitment. What are some of the Christian antecedents out of which such movements build not only their discontinuity with socioeconomic ideologies of the past but their continuity with the theological past?

Within the Roman Catholic wing of Latin American liberation theology, Enrique Dussel, the historian of the movement, sees the period from 1962 to 1968 as "the time of preparation."[52] But one can find shaping influences even before that period. The first of the social encyclicals of the modern papacy, *Rerum Novarum*, was issued by Pope Leo XIII in 1891. It was an effort to seesaw between warnings against the "socialist threat" and admonitions addressed to those who use wealth destructively or selfishly. It called the rich to generosity and the poor to "tranquil resignation." Although it offered no structural challenge to the economic system, it began to face the questions. Forty years later, in his encyclical *Quadragesimo Anno*, Pope Pius XI reiterated these themes but with some important modifications. More critical of capitalism than his predecessor, Pius XI said that "the earlier blanket denunciation of socialism has been modified," and there was a recognition "that sin becomes collectivized in modern industrial life."[53]

A new breath blew with the brief pontificate of Pope John XXIII, who produced two major social encyclicals, *Mater et Magistra* (1961) and *Pacem in Terris* (1963). For a commentator like Hugo Latorre Cabal, the 1961 document

aroused the dormant conscience of the Catholic world by proclaiming that "we are all responsible for the poor of the world." In that instance he was concerned not with charity nor that occasional philanthropy which purchases good consciences with second-hand tears and weeping for ladies and gentlemen of high society, but with the question of social justice based on an active and cooperative effort which would permit all to share in the fruits of production.[54]

Pope John's call for economic aid to underdeveloped nations to overcome inequality and his sensitivity to the obligations of the well-fed to look after the undernourished were not lost on those young Latin priests to the afflicted. Said Cabal, "Among the vast, miserable, exploited areas of the world, Latin America has been most aroused by Pope John's message."[55] Pope John's 1963 message to the church, appearing after the opening sessions of Vatican II, carried an even stronger message, and its influence was apparent in the longest single conciliar document, *Gaudium et Spes* (English title "The Church in the Modern World"). Distinguishing between false philosophical *teachings* and the socioeconomic *movements* based on those teachings, it did not espouse communism and socialism, but it did not condemn them, either. "Socialism might be philosophically wrong," it said, "but if it led people to concern for social justice, then cooperation with socialists might be all right, since Catholics likewise affirm concern for social justice."[56]

Vatican II (1962-65), and especially its document, *Gaudium et Spes*, reinforced this new direction and opened the door wider to contextualized thinking in Latin America. Although oriented to the cultural realities of Europe and the conflict between Russia and the United States, Vatican II for an observer like Cabal "constituted a complete program of action in social matters that fired many Latin American priests with enthusiasm and filled them with apostolic fervor."[57] Gutiérrez calls the discussion of Vatican II on dependence and liberation "sketchy" and *Gaudium et Spes* "but a beginning. . . a rather irenic description of the human situation."[58] More temperate than Cabal, Gutiérrez nevertheless sees the texts and especially the spirit of Vatican II as "undoubtedly necessary as points of reference."[59]

It was the Medellín Conference of Latin American bishops (CELAM) in 1968 "that gave concrete form and application to Vatican II" and, although still standing midway between "developmentalism" and "the theology of liberation," began to speak in the idiom of liberation.[60] Going significantly beyond Vatican II in their understanding of the function and mission of the church in the world, the bishops toned down preparatory drafts for the Conference and offered an agenda for studies that would occupy the attention of the liberation theologians in the years to come.[61]

Denounced by the bishops were the extreme inequality among social classes; the unjust use of power by dominant, insensitive authority; the international system of dependency through its exploitative distortion of trade; and "institutionalized violence" through "a structural deficiency of industry and agriculture, or national and international economy, of culture and political life." Positively, the pedagogical theories of Paulo Freire were embraced and the liberating function of education was hailed. The oppressed must become the subjects of their own self-determination, the bishops said, liberated from those "cultural, social, economic, and political servitudes" that oppose "human development."[62] The texts were pastoral and did not present theological arguments or elaborate a systematic theology of liberation. But liberation remained a decisively Christian perspective, "an anticipation of the complete redemption of Christ." Human values were seen as converging in Christ, having an integral place in the economy of salvation. Only when men are personally converted can there be structural change; yet this conversion can only exist within new structures, the bishops concluded.

Medellín marked a new stage in the progress of liberation theology, what Dussel calls the "formulation of the 'Theology of Liberation' (1968-1972)."[63] Although Medellín's importance cannot be exaggerated, its limitations cannot be overlooked, either: "Although it adopts the dependence framework of interpretation, it is rather more descriptive than analytical and does not arrive at the mechanisms of oppression, for which it lacks adequate instruments of analysis. It is notably silent on how its ambitious aims are to be realized in society at large and in the church itself."[64]

Medellín stood at the beginning of systematic writing on the theme of liberation and a more consistent dealing with the problems it raised. In April 1972, the clearest sign of radicalization came from Santiago, Chile, from the First Latin American Encounter of Christians for Socialism. Chile furnished a conducive climate for this gathering of 450 delegates from all parts of Latin America. Chilean President Salvador Allende Gossens, an avowed Marxist elected to his country's presidency in 1970, aimed to create a socialist state by democratic means. In 1971, a group of Chilean priests, *Los Ochenta* (The Eighty), in a public message to their bishops had called for a commitment to Christ related to Marxist socialism. Said Brown about the Santiago conference:

> If the distance between Vatican II and Medellín constitutes a step, the distance between the Medellín conference of bishops and the Santiago conference of Christians for Socialism resembles a leap. Medellín was in tune with Vatican II, even if beginning to move beyond it, whereas Santiago is more self-consciously "post-conciliar." Medellín usually leans toward a "third way" between capitalism and Marxism, whereas Santiago sees no "Christian solution" as such, denounces the collapse into a "third way," and insists that Christians be involved in the liberation process in socialist terms. With a few important exceptions, . . . Medellín speaks of inequality between persons, whereas Santiago consistently links inequality to class struggle and the exploitation of the poor by the rich. Medellín presses strongly for basic reform, whereas Santiago sees no solution without revolution, not necessarily violent. Medellín hopes that love, working for justice, can provide solutions, while Santiago argues that love is not a historic force apart from engagement in class struggle. Medellín offers theoretical analyses of Marxism, while Santiago calls upon Christians to "form a strategic alliance with Marxists." At Medellín the theologians were summoned by the bishops, at Santiago they were summoned by the militant."[65]

Santiago had significance for yet another reason. It signalized the increasing evaporation of ecclesiastical restrictions that were part of the pre-Vatican II context of Latin America, and it provided a visible demonstration that Roman Catholic and Protestant alike were increasingly ready to face a common situation with common tools. The avant-garde, still largely mainline Protestant organization, *Movimiento de Iglesia y Sociedad en America Latina* (ISAL), was directly involved. Several top Protestant theologians attended the conference, and a large portion of the expenses of the gathering were quietly underwritten by a large North American mission board. The major documents were published by a Chilean Protestant publishing house (*Mundo Nueva*). "The air was dense with the dynamism and buoyancy of common purpose," says Miguez-Bonino.[66]

A common purpose had finally converged after separate development in both Catholic and Protestant camps in Latin America. But the isolated journeys were remarkably parallel in terms of history and North Atlantic sources. Within Latin Protestantism, the 1950s were to set the stage for the 1960s and what Beatriz Melano Couch calls "the awakening of reflexive consciousness."[67] Neo-orthodox supporters like the Uraguayan Methodist Pastor Emilio Castro were beginning to ask, "What is the essential message we must preach to our people today? . . . What is the meaning of Barth's thinking in relation to South American problems?"[68] Barthian theology contributed to the crisis of liberal ideology and, in the face of Latin American sociopolitical realities, made ethics a growing, central theme of Protestant thinking. The social gospel and the ideals of democracy and personal freedom were increasingly seen as inadequate to cope with unjust and oppressive structures within the continent. Protestants had begun to face the search for the concrete reality of God's justice and love in their world.

The years 1961 to 1969 represented Protestantism's "time of awakening," marking the time between the gathering of the Second Evangelical Conference of Latin Americans (II CELA) in Lima, Peru, and the third assembly in Buenos Aires, Argentina. The two conferences signaled the shift toward a new vision of social reality. Participants in II CELA manifested a general awareness of underdevelopment "and the need for structural changes in the face of oppression and a commitment to a stance on the side of freedom and justice."[69] Those at III CELA saw more clearly the roots of that underdevelopment in a "socio-economic disequilibrium of the social classes." Two CELA, according to Miguez-Bonino, was basically "developmentalistic," calling for an increase in capital investment, conditions of production, better distribution of income, and incorporation of the poor and oppressed, the "marginalized," into the mainstream of society.[70] Three CELA paralleled Medellín in its identification of the sources of underdevelopment as economic dependency on the West and on the national elite that produces exploitation. New lines of thinking were emerging at III CELA, but they were by no means uniformly accepted or even advanced without controversy.[71] Miguez-Bonino, while outlining the continuity of III CELA with traditional Protestantism, notes that there were at least three significantly new directions: "(a) The acknowledgement of the revolutionary situation and of the just demands of the oppressed. . . (b) the affirmation that the gospel refers not only to personal life (and through it to the structures) but also in the structures of society themselves. . . (c) consequently, the possibility of a revolutionary commitment of Christians."[72]

Much of the link between II CELA and III CELA came through the activities of ISAL, the Protestant-initiated organization that was born at Huampaní, Peru, in July 1961 as an outcome of II CELA. Partly an extension of the interest of the World Council of Churches in the problem of development, ISAL initially conceived of itself as a search for "the meaning that social changes have from a Christian viewpoint, and our common responsibility."[73] According to Miguez-Bonino:

> Successive meetings in 1966, 1967, and 1971 marked the rapid transformation of ISAL's conception of itself, its relation to the churches, and its role in Latin America. In the first few years (1960-1965) the analysis of the situation, which at the beginning oscillated between a developmentalist and a revolutionary approach, gained greater consistency, adopted the "sociology of dependence" (structured around the notion of neocolonialism and dependence) and made a clear revolutionary and socialist option. This ideological clarification was followed in the years 1966-1968 by a transformation in the theological perspective, veering from a predominantly Barthian theology to a "theology of God's transforming action in history" greatly indebted to Paul Lehmann and Richard Shaull."[74]

At its fourth general assembly in Ñaña, Peru (1971), other significant changes became official. Recognizing its growing intellectual, elitist character, it determined to "become a movement totally identified with and immersed in the grass-roots" inevitability of the political struggle. Its developing convictions over the rightness of the theological methodology of praxis, stimulated by the theological leadership of Rubem Alves, were formally affirmed at Ñaña. "Theology," it asserted, "cannot be done simply in dialogue *with* political praxis, but must be done *in the midst* of a political engagement. Its task is to reflect critically on the meaning of the faith in the midst of that praxis."[75] The assembly also marked a new, formal shift in its relations with the Roman Catholic Church. More and more Catholic individuals had joined it during the latter part of the 1960s. After Ñaña, the staff positions of its continental secretariats were equally divided between Catholics and Protestants. All of its national, affiliated groups had become supraconfessional.

Since 1972, the streams of Catholic and Protestant liberation theologies have merged increasingly into common themes and have faced common opposition: "Radicalized Protestants share a common language and viewpoint with their Catholic counterparts,

more than with fellow Protestants whether of the traditional
churches or the sects. Indeed, Protestant theologians and intellectuals have contributed far out of proportion to their numbers."[76]

At the same time, in both circles these radicalized Christians
represent tiny minorities of their communities facing the commonness of "captivity" and "exile," what Beatriz Melano Couch calls
the present situation of "polarization and conflict."[77] Military
coups in Uruguay (1971), Bolivia (1972), and Chile (1973) reinforced political repression and created a situation even more congenial to polarization within the churches, a "political struggle for
religious symbols."[78] Orlando Costas, using the ideological
categories introduced at Medellín, sketches the character of the
opposition:

> The Conservative forces have emphasized the role of religion as a
> moral, stabilizing force, the guardian of traditional values and a
> means of preserving law and order. . . . The Reformists have tried to
> keep a creative tension between Conservatives and Revolutionaries
> by proposing a socialist model undergirded by "Christian" ethical
> principles. In the process, however, they have fallen prey to the
> forces of reaction and conservation.[79]

Within the Roman Catholic Church, institutes at least open to
liberation theologians have been closed, "and little by little the list
increased of closures of institutions, seminaries, and groups
oriented to the theology of liberation."[80] Gatherings in Bogotá,
Colombia (November 1973),[81] and Toledo, Spain (1974), [82] were
directed against liberation theology, with partial success.

Within the Protestant fold, the tensions of III CELA have
continued and grown. Of special significance here is the surfacing
of those described by Melano Couch as "radical evangelicals." On
the fringes of the Latin American Theological Fraternity (created in
1971) and represented by voices like Samuel Escobar, René
Padilla, Orlando Costas, and others, the community of radical
evangelicals shares a deep anger over the "otherworldliness" and
abstractness of the Latin evangelical mission theology of the past
and a zeal in denouncing the structures of oppression and dependency in the present. These theologians are sharply critical of the
social class analysis used by liberation theologians and fearful of its
veiled Marxist ideology, but they fear also the ideological impact of
North Atlantic capitalism on the Southern Hemisphere. Calling for
a "functional" theology in dialogue with the concrete reality, they

propose "a theological alternative more strictly related to the classical evangelical biblical theology," but one that will make theology an instrument of transformation.[83] Conservatives remain fearful of the radical evangelicals' "leftist" tendencies, and "leftists" write them off as developmentalists and reformists. But some theologians seem to be recognizing that their contribution may be as "a kind of bridge between the conservative and the most radically engaged Protestants."[84] They represent the most significant criticism of liberation theologies.

As the 1970s have witnessed the publication of major theological works by liberation theologians both Catholic and Protestant, more and more of the European and North American sources common to both sides have emerged. Although some, like Enrique Dussel, can manage to write a chronicle of the movement in *History and the Theology of Liberation* (1976) without mentioning a single Protestant antecedent, others, like Miguez-Bonino, affirm that the North Atlantic thinkers "have had an influence on Latin American theology which should not be underestimated."[85] The fully documented 1971 study by Gutiérrez (translated in 1973 as *A Theology of Liberation*) includes references to at least twenty-three Protestant theologians, whom he quotes or cites a total of more than one hundred times. Says Alan Neely:

> Hugo Assmann appears to be less impressed by and more critical of Protestant thought than Gutiérrez. Even so, Assmann manifests a measure of appreciation for the works of Moltmann, Cullmann, H.D. Bastian, Paul Lehmann, Richard Shaull, and Harvey Cox, as well as for some fellow Latin American Protestants such as José Miguez-Bonino, Rubem Alves, Julio do Santa Ana and the work of ISAL.[86]

Fundamentally, "The theoretical sources of liberation theology are mainly two: *the European 'political theology'* . . . and . . . Moltmann's 'theology of hope.'"[87] From the work of Johann B. Metz, the Catholic professor of theology at the University of Münster, liberation theologians perceive the need for underscoring the political dimensions of faith and for a deprivatization of theology. Metz sees a need for the church to reflect critically upon the nature and extent of its complicity with the social order, "to formulate the eschatological message (of the New Testament), in the conditions of our contemporary society."[88] From Metz also comes a concept of the church as an institution of social criticism. "The positive task of political theology," Metz says, "is to determine anew the relation between religion and society, specifically under the conditions of modern society."[89] The reverse side of that task, crucial to Metz, is to assert the essentially universal catergories of theology as a negative critique in this society. Similarly, there is a stress on rescuing in Christian history and thought that "dangerous memory," the "subversive" content, the shouts of frustrated hopes.[90]

Jürgen Moltmann's underlining of the *political* transcription of eschatology opens a new avenue for those like Gutiérrez who seek to overcome the association between faith and fear of the future. The hope expounded by Moltmann is the hope Gutiérrez seeks as well. "To hope does not mean to know the future, but rather to be open, in an attitude of spiritual childhood, to accepting it as a gift," says Gutiérrez. "But this gift is accepted in the negation of injustice, in the protest against trampled human rights, and in the struggle for peace and brotherhood. Thus hope fulfills a mobilizing and liberating function in history."[91]

Reinforcing some of these emphases may perhaps be the best way to describe the contribution of Dietrich Bonhoeffer to this creative ferment. Although probably no one would want to claim that liberation theology "is highly dependent" on his thought, he has been influential.[92] Cited only a few times by Gutiérrez, Hugo Assmann, and Segundo (and hardly ever by other Roman Catholic liberation theologians), it is in his underlining of certain aspects of the theology that his voice is best heard: "In its anthropocentric point of departure, in the idea that religion should be redefined in relation to the secular context, in the repeated insistence that the Church must side with the oppressed, as well as the interpretation of Christian freedom."[93] Among Protestant theologians, his effect has been even more obvious and prolonged. Presumably introduced into the discussions as early as 1952 by Richard Shaull, himself a deep shaper of Protestant directions,[94] "no other western theologian influenced" the ISAL discussions from 1962 to 1968 "as did Bonhoeffer."[95] It was Bonhoeffer's formulations that challenged the Protestant ghetto mentality and its alleged church-world dualism. It was Bonhoeffer who aided in seeing the relationship between faith and ideology and the demands of Christian discipleship.

It is not, however, the concord between these theologies of the

North Atlantic and Latin America that needs primary emphasis in understanding the integrating themes of liberation theology. The predominant note in liberation theologies is their repeated criticism of the North Atlantic influences. And it is in their criticism that the commonness and uniqueness of the liberation theologies emerge.

Perhaps the heart of that criticism lies in the way liberation theology sees the theological task itself.[96] Political theology is recognized as a double shift from the metaphysical to the anthropological and from the inner-personal to the public-historical. But, says Miguez-Bonino, that shift has been radicalized in Latin America "by bringing it down, not merely to the language and categories of a 'general' analysis of historical existence, but to the concrete contents of our own social, cultural, political, and economic experience and to the categories that our own sociopolitical analysts have forged in order to grasp this experience."[97] Through the concept of praxis, say the liberation theologians, theological language must seek a painful concreteness that cannot be found in Europe or North America.

Therefore, Gutiérrez assaults the analysis of Metz as ultimately academic because he (Metz) is not a victim of the kind of "dependency, injustice and exploitation in which most of mankind finds itself." By failing to use the contribution of the social sciences or of "certain aspects of Marxism," Metz is said to end up with an abstract analysis of the political sphere. Further, Metz's assault on "privatized" faith misses the unique problem of Latin America. "In Latin America," says Neely "the Church has been linked hand-in-glove with government and politics. The problem, therefore, has not been privatized faith but clericalized politics."[98] Hugo Assmann is even more strident. The political theology of Metz, Assmann says, "seems afraid to name the organs of oppression openly" and perpetuates the old distinction between theology and ethics by the contention that political theology can lead to no direct connection with practice. Reluctance toward what Assmann designates an "ideology of struggle," an ideology expressing our ethical and political decision, incapacitates Metz and reinforces his mistakenly thinking there is a need to construct total certainties on theoretical bases.

Moltmann and the theology of hope fare no better against such a praxis-oriented criticism. For Gutiérrez, Moltmann's future orientation seems to have ultimately very little *concrete* influence on the present. It runs the risk of replacing a "Christianity of the Beyond" with a "Christianity of the Future" and, in the process, "neglecting a miserable and unjust present and the struggle for liberation."[99] Moltmann fails to develop vocabulary out of man's present experience, Gutiérrez says. An elaboration of these materials is provided by Miguez-Bonino, who says that Moltmann fails to understand the real challenge of liberation thought. Moltmann's social analysis is said to remain abstract, describing "the demonic circles of death . . . without giving a coherent socio-analytical account of this manifest oppression."[100] There is no consciousness in Moltmann of the need for such an analysis. Even more serious, Miguez-Bonino continues, is Moltmann's failure to give a concrete content to "identification with the oppressed." To Miguez-Bonino, Moltmann's assertion, "The crucified God is really a God without a country and without class . . . he is the God of the poor,"[101] is a contradiction. "The poor, the oppressed, the humiliated *are a class* and *live in countries*. . . . Are we really for the poor and oppressed if we fail to see them as a class, as members of oppressed societies?" Miguez-Bonino asks.[102] In this struggle of identification, the theologian may not stand "above right and left, ideologically neutral," as Moltmann is said to suggest. We must not sacralize any ideology, Miguez-Bonino says, but we "must resolutely use the best *human* politics and economics at our disposal."

Miguez-Bonino's charges drew a response from Moltmann.[103] And a number of Latin American theologians are responding again in a single volume soon to be published. But the debate at least has helped to make clear that "the theology of liberation is not so much a theology of 'hope,' used as an abstract noun, as of the historical articulation of action born of hope and generative of hope."[104] The fear remains strong among liberation theologians that Moltmann is proclaiming a hope that does not articulate and motivate the actual stages in the struggle but feeds merely on promises "already given." Ultimately, if Assmann is right, Moltmann's theology runs the risk of leaving man an inactive spectator.

Perhaps somewhat surprising to the North Atlantic commentators who too easily equate liberation thinking with the theology of revolution,[105] liberation theologians like Assmann also use their critical techniques in an assault on the theology of revolution. While recognizing that the concept of revolution was introduced by "third world" spokesmen at the WCC Geneva Conference on "Church and Society" in 1966, Assmann also notes that its development has become more and more "de-contextualized" and is now far more typical of Europe than of Latin America. In that process, it has become largely a quest for theological justification of projected action. As such it is to be deplored, Assmann says. Theology for Assmann does not begin with theoretical speculation but with critical reflection on antecedent action. A theology of revolution, therefore, that defines the revolution to come on the basis of theological categories, that seeks theoretical permission for being revolutionaries and uses theology as a theoretical instrument to provide a revolutionary ideology, cannot be acceptable to liberation theology. This does not mean, however, according to Assmann, that theology and revolution cannot be joined or related: "The theology of liberation seeks to be critical reflection on revolutionary action in both its overall aspects and its detailed circumstances, but it is not interested in discussing revolution as an abstract entity."[106]

Analyzing the antecendents and interactions of North American black theology is much more complicated than doing the same thing with the Latin American liberation theologies. For one thing, the differences between the theologians seem more pronounced on themes relating to the notion of liberation. The prolific "diplomat of black theology," James Cone, continues to produce his work oriented to topics common to Latin America—liberation, oppression, violence, and revolution. And his repeated insistence that the black experience is a source of black theology and that theology is an identification with God in the liberation of the black community comes very close to the liberation concept of praxis. But in the growing dialogue with those doing black theology, his views are not quickly accepted. J. Deotis Roberts, Sr., continues to demand that not only is liberation an essential part of the gospel, but so also is reconciliation. And he continues to say that Cone's emphasis on liberation is one-sided.[107] On the topic of sources for theology, J. Deotis Roberts, Jr., finds the dialectical method used by Cone "akin to Hegelian ideology and neo-orthodox theology. It is not the kind of thinking one finds in the African/black religious heritage."[108] Tied to this criticism of Cone's dialectical method is what the younger Roberts calls Cone's "remarkable weakness as a biblical exegete." Surprisingly, he also sees a weakness in Cone precisely in what he calls an inability "to adopt his Christo-centrism to meaningful action for the liberation of blacks. What we need is a bridge from theory to praxis. . . . Cone has yet to give his Christology an adequate political or even a pastoral shape."[109]

Even wider differences exist between black theology and liberation theology over the necessity and nature of a socioeconomic understanding of context. As mentioned already, those differences were manifested as late as 1975 at the Detroit Conference on "Theology in the Americas." A Latin delegate was quoted as remarking, "The Blacks suspect Latin theology of being too white, and the Latins suspect Black theology of being too American."[110] Latin priorities focus with often crypto-Marxist interest on the question of class analysis, whereas Blacks are concerned about any separation of a class analysis from the analysis of race in the North American context. As Herbert Edwards said at Detroit, "Latin American liberation theology, in its dialogic encounter with North American theology, must not be unaware of the ease with which one can speak universal language with the understanding that it is not really inclusive of all in the society."[111]

Unlike its relation to liberation theologies in the Latin world, the relation of Marxism-Leninism—even in its limited role as a theoretical instrument of social analysis—to the American black community has been "either altogether negligible or altogether coincidental."[112] Black radicalism, even in its de-Christianized form, from the separatist movement of Marcus Garvey to the Student Non-Violent Coordinating Committee, has historically been less political, less obsessed with ideology on the grand scale, and less committed to violence as a revolutionary strategy than Latin radicalism. It is interesting to note that C. Eric Lincoln's account of the Black Muslims contains no index reference to Marx or Marxism, an absence that is also found in *The Autobiography of Malcolm X*. Only among the Black Panthers, a group whose political influence quickly dissipated in the black community, did Marxism find any real home, and then largely as a conceptualization for the clarification of revolutionary experience, a tactical instrument for the power struggle.

Within the black church, Marxism has found even less of a home. Martin Luther King, Jr., "was simultaneously drawn to and repelled by Marx," pained by Marxism as a Christian heresy that underlined the social failure of the Christian church.[113] Even the

Black Manifesto, issued in April 1969, has had a very mixed reaction in the black church. And, although its preamble especially calls for the rejection of American capitalism and imperialism and hints at the seizure of state power and guerrilla warfare, the Manifesto's concrete proposals, outlined in its body, are far less radicalized as a strategy of action.[114] Its history "underscored the alienation of young Blacks from the doctrinaire politics of Marxism."[115] To the majority of black Christians, the evaluations of Herbert Edwards made at Detroit may still be representative:

> The black theologian, whether North or South, however, knows that ideological changes have not made any significant difference in the black situation in America. . . . When it is suggested that a "peculiar American" brand of socialism is what is needed or desired, we are too consciously aware that what has in the past made almost any economic, political or social policy or practice peculiarly "American" is the same racist spirit that informed and supported its "Peculiar Institution" for two and one half centuries.[116]

Since 1975, the dialogue between Marxism and black theology has been becoming more self-conscious. Again, the work of James Cone is a fitting symbol of that shift. His 1969 work, *Black Theology and Black Power*, contained no index references to Marx. His 1975 book, *God of the Oppressed*, contains fifteen assorted pages of interaction with Marxism, with special appreciation for Marx's insistence that thought has no independence from social existence. But even then, Cone reiterates the concerns of Edwards at Detroit: "Blacks in America and some other places believe that the problem of oppression is much more complex than Marx knew. Any analysis that fails to deal with racism, that demon embedded in white folks' being, is inadequate."[117] J. Deotis Roberts, Sr., sees Marx, with Freud, as an aid in the creation of a doctrine of man for Blacks, contributing to a deeper understanding of human nature as a social creation. The work of Marxist Ernst Bloch is commended by Roberts for "what it contributes to our understanding of human group life. His observations on Christianity are very constructive and serve as a corrective to much personal religion that does not attack social evils."[118]

Accelerated discussion with liberation theologians of the Southern Hemisphere may demand more interaction of this sort. But as yet that interhemispheric dialogue is sparse. No references to Latin American liberation theologians are found in Cone's 1975 book, and although Roberts, Sr., gives a nod to the liberation theology of Latin America for its identification with the oppressed and sees the perspective of black theology "being sharpened by" insights from the south,[119] the encounter, as Cone rightly charges, is "almost at random . . . brief and out of context."[120] On the part of the Latins, the deepest interaction with black thinking appears in the narrow but strong attention to Cone's hermeneutic by Juan Luis Segundo.[121] The widest awareness of the dialogue is represented by Allan Boesak, a South African Black. But he uses the dialogue only as a tool for working on his deeper interest in his own apartheid context, and then he is largely occupied with black theology.[122]

The absence of attention to black theology is striking in the 1978 book by Robert McAfee Brown, *Theology in a New Key*. This is especially so since by design he seeks to use Latin American themes as they speak to the conditions of North America. Perhaps the best that can be said thus far of the exchange is said in the summary provided by Richard J. Neuhaus as he compares Gutiér-rez and Cone: "Both are wrestling with the tension between what is indigenous and what is catholic. Both acknowledge the danger of liberation theology becoming captive to a political ideology that is foreign to the believing community within which any significant theological statement must be appropriated and sustained."[123]

As with Latin America, the early theoretical antecedents of black theology find "in Moltmann one of their most useful sources for citation," says G. Clarke Chapman. That picture, however, is said to have changed in the 1970s, when "there has been wide-spread reaction against reliance on any white theologian."[124] This convergence is especially clear in the work of Cone, whose work, in comparison to Moltmann, functions as much on parallel lines as on direct dependence. Says Chapman: "Both men share the basic assumption that God is presently at work in and through general history. . . . Both reject 'natural theology,' particularly in the form of civil religion which gives religious sanction to the ties and values of the nation. . . . And both insist that the future is fluid and not simply to be dictated by the past."[125] The greatest agreement is on the need for liberation, for Moltmann a "Messianism of the op-pressed" and for Cone the liberating work of Christ in the black movement today. For both, that liberation is a comprehensive to-tality, not separating sacred from secular or moral from political.

Cone recognizes in Moltmann's call for a "political hermeneutics of the gospel" "a religion of protest against the suffering and affliction of men."[126] And he sees in Moltmann's view of eschatology an analysis compatible with black theology's concern. "Hope must be related to the present, and it must serve as a means of transforming an oppressed community into a liberated—and liberating—community," Cone says. "Black Theology does not scorn Christian hope; it affirms it."[127]

At the same time, like Latin American liberation theologians, many black theologians are united by their major criticisms of the theology of hope. Specifically, these criticisms are said to take two directions. The first, not emphasized by Cone, is nevertheless widespread elsewhere. Moltmann is seen as too futuristic, "his view of revelation . . . too narrow for the openness that is desirable."[128] It is said that the black context demands a realizable eschatology in the here and now, God's will manifest in the present, not the evangelical-pietistic preoccupation of the future.[129] Too often in the racist past, some black theologians say, Blacks have been turned to the future by Whites "to write them out of history books and at the same time to refuse them access to this life." As a result, the black man has lost his past and his sense of self-presence.

It is this same motivation that lies behind the assault of many Blacks on the Christomonism of Karl Barth. J. Deotis Roberts, Sr., for example, sees this stance particularly in Cone and has been unremitting in his challenge. Specifically, he fears, as do the Latins, the otherworldliness that can be characteristic of a Barthian concept of divine transcendence. God's power then merely touches history at its tangential point without coming to grips with it and transforming it. Barth is said to offer, in Cone's application, too weak a base "for a black theological ethic to provide for an action thrust for the black church."[130] Whether Roberts does full justice to Cone's views in this area is open to to some question, at least in Cone's more recent material. Cone acknowledges his in-depth work on Barth but comments also on his frustrations with Barth after the completion of his formal theological studies. "What could Karl Barth possibly mean for black students who had come from the cotton fields of Arkansas, Louisiana and Mississippi, seeking to change the structure of their lives in a society that had defined *black*, as nonbeing?" Cone asks.[131] He chides Barth in his earlier period for playing down the human side of Christ's presence and notes that Barth never really recovered from the early theme of God's absolute transcendence.[132] He asserts, "Black truth has its own uniqueness and thus cannot be truly understood with a conceptual framework from Karl Barth or Mircea Eliade."[133]

The second area of black complaint against Moltmann's work is "that it is too alien to black experience to be of real use in the formative tasks of Black Theology."[134] For Roberts, Sr., it resembles many other "transport" theological movements. It belongs to another situation.[135] For Major J. Jones, too much of the thought of men like Moltmann, Wolfhart Pannenberg, and Ernst Bloch "is abstract and not related to what is inherent in the thought-content of the black man's aspirations for the future. Indeed, a black theology that starts with eschatology must correlate the contents of eschatological hope with the conditions of the black experience."[136]

Cone has also joined this criticism in his more recent work. His third book, *The Spirituals and the Blues* (1972), represents a major turning point in methodology. Out of his teaching experience with black students and a recognition "that black people in their sermons, prayers, and songs of the nineteenth and twentieth centuries were talking about the politics of hope long before the appearance of hope theology in Germany,"[137] he turned to the song and speech of the black community for his sources. He saw something important missing in his earlier work. His continued insistence that theology has to arise out of an oppressed community as its members seek to understand their place in the history of salvation moved him to a use of black spirituals and the significance of the blues as a reflection of that theology. His third book reflects that shift as he analyzes the theology of black music. His latest volume, *God of the Oppressed*, continues the search. There is an almost constant interaction with hymnody as a theological reflection of the black experience.[138]

In so doing, Cone is seeking much more than simply a "use" of hymnody for self-reflection. He is repudiating his indebtedness to white sources and their discussions of humanization. "The future about which they speak is too abstract and too unrelated to the history and culture of black people who have been and are being dehumanized and dehistoricized by white imperialists and colonialists," Cone says. "As a black theologian, I believe that authentic Christian hope must be defined by the oppressed's vision of the expectant future and not by philosophical abstractions."[139] Even in his use of sources, Cone is working to take seriously his own distinctive situation in the American black community. And in this mining of the theological heritage of his community, his work is more consistent than the work yet attempted by any other theologian, Latin or black.

LIBERATION—LATIN STYLE

Before outlining some of the common themes of liberation theology, let us look at the unique contributions of its more well-known representatives. Here I want to underscore the pluralism of liberation theologies.

Camilo Torres (1929-66), in one sense, does not belong to the circle of reflectors and commentators on liberation. Yet his significance for the development of the movement was great. As teacher and chaplain at the National University in Colombia, he began to articulate his call for changes in the basic economic and social structures. When opposition from the Catholic Church increased, Torres pressed his point. "Revolutionary action is a Christian, a priestly struggle," he protested. Removed from his university post and forbidden to speak further on social issues, he left the priesthood in 1965 and later that year joined a revolutionary guerrilla movement. His death in an ambush electrified the Latin world and virtually canonized him as a pioneer saint of liberation thinking. Briefly, Torres's ideas included many of the elements later to be incorporated into liberation thinking—revolutionary praxis, focus not on the church but on society, and socioeconomic analysis. But his significance is not there. He incarnated for Latin America the significance of the slogan, *conscientization*. And for that he is hailed by men like Miguez-Bonino[140] and Gustavo Gutiérrez.[141]

Still another important early figure but for different reasons is Rubem Alves (b.1933), a Brazilian by birth. His 1969 book, *A Theology of Human Hope*, was a pioneer work in its criticism of the capitalist model for Brazil, but it was a work carried on in confrontation largely with North Atlantic thought. Writing the work as a doctoral dissertation at Princeton Theological Seminary, Alves marked himself off from others who wrote later studies by his tendency to use the philosophy of language rather than sociological or political sciences as his theological coordinates.

Nevertheless, Alves's work strikes many of the themes to be heard in later materials. Critical of Moltmann's view that hope can be mediated only through the promise contained in the Bible, he turns from his portrait of God's pure futuricity as "a new form of docetism, in which God loses his present-day dimension,"[142] and finds in historical praxis and the language of the community engaged in a praxis the matrix of theological thought. Referring to the Hebrew concept of truth, he advocates a new understanding of truth, "not as an abstract realm of ideas, but as 'efficacious truth,' as 'action,' as 'the name given by a historical community to its historical deeds, which were, are, and will be efficacious in the liberation of man.' "[143]

For Alves, this methodology is epitomized in what he calls a "Messianic humanism" and its goal of the "humanization" of the conditions of life. With "humanist messianism," this new direction shares an adamant denial of "that which is," a refusal to be conformed to existing reality. With "humanist messianism," it shares a critical awareness of the present, not as an end but as a necessary means in the creation of a future of freedom for man. On the other hand, unlike "humanist messianism," it rejects the romanticism of hope without history. This form of humanization is a gift of grace, an abolition of oppression, which does not depend solely on human effort. "Messianic humanism" is the politics of God, manifested in the Exodus, Israel's consciousness not merely of having liberated itself but of having been liberated. The future that was closed because of Egypt's oppressive power and Israel's own slave consciousness is broken open by a God who is free from the determinisms of history and is active in history.

The community of believers will embrace this new language of faith, says Alves, only when it discovers that it is deeply concerned with the creation of a new future for mankind and when it deals seriously with the criticism made by political humanism. That struggle will take place not merely in the subjective world of the individual, as in existentialism's flight from history, nor in the building of a welfare state, but in politics, understood as human action carrying out a humanizing project in a historical future.[144] It will be judged by its power to open up broader horizons for hope, by the amount of freedom that it creates for human action.[145]

It is not Alves, however, who systematizes this new perspective and marks the formal beginning of liberation thinking. For that we turn to the Peruvian Gustavo Gutiérrez (b.1928) and especially his 1971 book, *A Theology of Liberation*. The work still remains one of the most comprehensive approaches to the subject, ranging over issues in dialogue with nontheological disciplines and the history of Christian thought and exegesis. More technically specific than the work of Hugo Assmann and more clearly Latin American than Alves, Gutiérrez's work moved liberation thought from the dangers of a reactionary theological negation to a positive and creative theological effort that is distinctively Latin American in style.

The starting point of Gutiérrez's concern is the church and its relation to the world in Latin America. To move from its ghetto place in culture, he says, the church needs a new understanding of its nature and mission. The Constantinian model in which the church and the Kingdom of God were practically identified has left secular reality subordinate to the church's interest, lacking autonomy. The world found its purpose and fulfillment in the church.[146] Catholic liberalism, reacting against this model, sought some freedom for society by a distinction-of-planes model, distinguishing between what is religious and what is worldly, Gutiérrez says. The layman was responsible for the world; the priesthood and the church were responsible for the religious. That model also has proven inadequate for Gutiérrez. It has left laymen taking positions contrary to the official statements of the church and the church functionally silent in the face of oppression and injustice. Vatican II opens a new way for exploration, Gutiérrez says, in its sensitivity to the church as the sacrament of universal salvation, a visible sign of the presence of the Lord in the struggle for liberation and a just society.

In this new understanding of the church and its mission, liberation functions on three levels: political liberation that expresses the aspirations of oppressed peoples and social classes; liberation as an understanding of history, with man seen as assuming conscious responsibility for his own destiny; and liberation by Christ from sin, the ultimate root of all disruption of friendship and of all injustice and oppression.[147] The levels are to be seen as parts of a single, complex process, interdependent and finding their deepest sense and full realization in the saving work of Christ. Gutiérrez's intent in all of this is to avoid the dualisms of the church's mission that were apparent in its past. There are not two histories, one sacred and one profane: "The one history in which God acts is the history of men; it is in this history where we find God. There is only one 'Christ-fulfilled' history."[148]

To achieve liberation in that integrated fashion, Gutiérrez proposes what he considers to be a "new way to do theology,"[149] theology as "critical reflection on praxis."[150] Wishing to retain "the spiritual function of theology" as a permanent dimension of theology, he rejects nevertheless the early church's model of "theology as wisdom" in which theology was preserved, a monastic model that ended up defining the spiritual as something removed from worldly concerns. In the same way, he spurns the paradigm of theology "as rational knowledge" that was prominent from the twelfth century on; but he recognizes the permanent function it performed, the correlation of faith and reason. In the light of the rediscovery of the eschatological dimension of theology and its vision of history as an opening to the future, and recognizing the stimulus of Marxism in calling on theology to reflect on the meaning of the transformation of this world, theology's goal must take on a new shape, Gutiérrez says. Retaining its spiritual dimension and its self-understanding as rational knowledge, it aims not for the discovery or refinement of doctrine as timeless truth but for the transformation of the world through reflection on praxis. Praxis is more than merely "involvement in a situation" or "practice." It bears the Marxist sense of "participation in the class struggle to bring about the creation of a new socialist society. Theology is totally internal to this praxis and deepens one's commitment within it."[151] In a critical dialogue with man's own basic principles, with the economic and sociocultural issues in the Christian community, and with society and the church, theology is formed as a constant accompaniment to the pastoral action of the church. It does not produce pastoral activity; it reflects on it.

What specific effect does this new definition of theology have on the mission of the church? It transforms the Eucharist from that rite in which the (Catholic) church ratifies its essence to a celebration of the salvific action of Christ in history, a sign of the creation of human brotherhood. Says Francis Fiorenza: "As a meal, it signifies community and brotherhood so that John's Gospel could replace it with the washing of the feet as a symbol of service of one's fellow man. As a Passover meal, it recalls the political liberation of Israel. As a memorial of the death and resurrection of Jesus it commemorates the liberation of man from sin."[152] In summary, Gutiérrez's definition of theology gathers together all the three levels of liberation and their fulfillment in the sacramental sign of redemption.

In the celebration of the Eucharist, Gutiérrez continues, the church celebrates also its need for the confrontation of any sacralization of oppressive structure, any sanctioning of injustice with the message of the gospel. In solidarity with the poor and with the oppressed, the sign of the saving act of Christ prevents us from reverting to the Constantinian model of the church. In making itself poor, the church acts out in symbol, word, and deed the redemptive values of love and liberation.

In all of this, Gutiérrez asks, what does the church do more than the Marxists? What is the Christian's contribution as a Christian? For one thing, there is a different kind of motivation—love, not hate, of the class enemy. Further, there is a call for liberation from all that oppresses, not just from the socioeconomic structures. And finally there is a different view of history, the new society formed not as a utopian craft of human construction but as the kingdom gift of God.[153]

In many ways, Hugo Assmann (b. 1933) deserves a place next to Gutiérrez as a founder of liberation theology. A former Brazilian priest, his participation in liberation struggles led to his being exiled successively from his homeland (Uruguay), Bolivia, and Chile. His career has included service as study secretary for ISAL, teaching responsiblities in the Ecumenical School of Religious Science at the Autonomous National University, Heredio, Costa Rica, and, more recently, as coordinator of the Departmento Ecumenico de Investigaciones (D.E.I.). His first full-length book, *Opresión-liberación: Desafío a los cristianos*,[154] appeared the same year as that of Gutiérrez. And, although far less comprehensive and systematic than Gutiérrez, his efforts deserve the judgment of Enrique Dussel as "together with the work of Gustavo Gutiérrez, . . . the most original in the movement,"[155] Many of the same concerns reflected in Gutiérrez are found also in Assmann—the class struggle as the liberation point of departure, the concept of praxis as the central motive in liberation, the significance of creation and salvation in the process of liberation, and the need for a new understanding of the mission of the church in that process.[156] With Gutiérrez, Assmann elaborates on those concerns with skills similar to those used in systematic theology. For Assmann, the manner of looking at the concerns of liberation theology becomes part of a polemic framework akin to what Costas calls a "guerrilla-like approach" and marks his work as more apologetic than systematic.

Miguez-Bonino sees Assmann's initial contribution in his 1971 work as an effort to respond to the already growing criticism at that time of those who see liberation thinking, with its insistence on praxis and the sociopolitical context, giving "to the historical circumstances a determinative weight in theology. This is, according to Assmann, precisely the significance of this theology. . . . The only possible point of departure is the concrete situation."[157] The ideologies hidden in the theologies of the past must be exposed, says Miguez-Bonino, interpreting Assmann. Theology must not be merely at the service of action. Rather, action is itself the truth. Truth is at the level of history, not in the realm of ideas. The task of theology is reflection of a critical sort on that praxis of history. Without it, theology itself becomes captive to ideologically enslaving sociopolitical options.

Assmann is conscious in all of this of his own limitations. As Roberto Oliveros reminds us, his purpose was not to provide an in-depth theology of cosmic vision but simply to trace the priorities with which Latin American theology must work. In particular, Assmann cites two gaps that need further work; "the Christological gap and the hermeneutic gap."[158] And he challenges us to find and elucidate more; he believes that a theology of the sacraments and a theological anthropology also need exploration.[159]

As the years pass following this initiating work of Gutiérrez and Assmann, those gaps are being filled. In the area of biblical studies, the most formative work yet seems to be that of José Porfirio Miranda, an ex-Jesuit, in his 1971 book, *Marx y la biblia* (appearing in English in 1974 under the title, *Marx and the Bible: A Critique of the Philosophy of Oppression*). Like other liberation theologians, Miranda brings to his study technical expertise in many areas and a direct engagement in Christian social action among the working class people of his native country, in his case Mexico. In that context he dedicated himself to a study of Marx's writings and came increasingly to believe: "The essential meaning of the Bible's message has been eluding us Christians and our organizations. The Bible, especially Exodus and the prophets, is the revelation of the Transcendent God, the Liberator of the oppressed who fights against the oppressors in their behalf."[160] That belief drove him to undertake specialized scriptural studies at the Biblical Institute in Rome. The result was his 1971 book. By 1973 the book had spawned a symposium, *Enjuiciamos a Marx y la Biblia*, responding to his arguments.

In many ways, Miranda's work at this early stage does not represent the same direction as that of Gutiérrez or Assmann. He seems to have worked out his own ideas independently of the Latin American ferment at which we have been looking. One finds no references to any of the major liberation thinkers in the comprehensive index to his book. Even Moltmann, a dialogue partner with so many Latins, is completely missing. Yet the thesis of this book and of those that have followed it,[161] although underscoring Miranda's indebtedness to the existentialism of Jean-Paul Sartre, places him unmistakably in the liberation orbit.

Miranda dissociates himself from "finding parallels between the Bible and Marx," intent instead on "the most rigorous and scientific exegesis."[162] With little sensitivity to the questioning of that possibility of objective exegesis by liberation thinkers, he proceeds to his central thesis, a perspective on *mispat*, social justice, the salvation of the poor as a basic datum of the Bible. The God revealed in the Bible is a God who wants justice between people—in fact, says Miranda, that is the only thing God wants. It is justice that motivates God's intervention in history. It is justice that stands behind the Old Testament rejection of private ownership of property, a concept rejected by the church Fathers and Western culture. Even the last judgment of Jesus and Paul deemphasizes the action of judging in favor of the result, justice. Through thorough, almost painstaking exegesis, he moves us to the final chapter, where he explores affinities between Christian faith and Marxist dialectics. Both aim ultimately at achieving real justice in the world, Miranda argues. They coincide "in their affirmation of the totality of evil: Sin and injustice form an all-comprehensive and all-pervasive organic structure. Paul calls this totality *kosmos*, Marx calls it 'capitalism.' "[163] Both believe that man can cease being selfish, merciless, and self-serving and can find his greatest fullness in loving his neighbor, Miranda continues. Both are opposed to the "objectivity" of a bourgeois, positivist science that separates morality as a field apart. Dialectical knowledge and biblical knowledge demand praxis. Says Fiorenza regarding Miranda's conclusion: "The result—or rather, the aim which governs his work from the very start—is to make Marx nothing less than a prophet beholden to biblical tradition."[164]

For the deeper questions of hermeneutics, Miranda cannot help. His lack of ties with liberation thinking do not allow him to ask the kind of questions posed by Miguez-Bonino: "Is it legitimate to start Biblical interpretation from a contemporary historical interpretation? What is the legitimate role and weight of social analysis and ideological interpretation? How can the freedom of the text be maintained?"[165] In this area, the most significant contributions have been coming from Juan Luis Segundo (b. 1925), a Uruguayan Jesuit, and Jon Sobrino, a Spanish Jesuit who has worked for many years in Central America.

Segundo's earliest full-length work, the five-volume *A Theology for Artisans of a New Humanity* (original edition, 1968-72), has been acclaimed by many as "a paradigm example of a systematic theology written from a liberationist perspective."[166] But that may be overdone. The work does give evidence of the hermeneutical argument that he amplified in his later work of 1975. This is especially so in the 1969 volume, *De la sociedad a la Iglesia* (a collection of essays written in the 1960s). But to call it a "paradigm example" may credit it with too much. Dussel places it in the "time of preparation," more "along the lines of Vatican II, prior to the theology of liberation."[167] Philip Berryman, supporting that judgment, notes that nowhere in the five volumes does Segundo even employ the term "liberation theology," although references to Medellín and its categories begin with volume 3 and become more frequent later. "This series was worked out in a dialogue process with laypeople in Montivideo during the years after the Council," says Berryman. "It is thus the result of a community effort over several years."[168]

It is in Segundo's 1975 book, *Liberación de la teología* (translated in English as *The Liberation of Theology* [1976]), that this elaboration of a hermeneutical methodology is finally made available in a more systematic arrangement than before. The key in that articulation is his tool, the "hermeneutical circle." In contrast to past academic theology, Segundo sees this tool as coming to grips not only with such disciplines as form criticism, archaeology, and so on, but with the social sciences as well. Further, unlike the academic theology of the past, which posed as impartial and was consequently unaware of its unconscious partiality, the hermeneutical circle demands such a partiality from its participant, a commitment to change reality and subsequently to change theology. The method demands a "continuous change in our interpretation of the Bible which is dictated by the continuing changes in our present-day reality, both individual and societal."[169]

Four steps are essential to that circle:

> *Firstly*, there is our way of experiencing reality, which leads us to ideological suspicion. *Secondly*, there is the application of our ideological suspicion to the whole ideological superstructure in general and to theology in particular. *Thirdly* there comes a new way of experiencing theological reality that leads us to exegetical suspicion, that is, to the suspicion that the prevailing interpretation of the Bible has not taken important pieces of data into account. *Fourthly* we have our new hermeneutic, that is, our new way of interpreting the fountainhead of our faith (i.e., Scripture) with the new elements at our disposal.[170]

In this process, the concept of ideology is crucial. Segundo does not believe that exegesis can be done without ideology. In fact, he says an ideology is necessary for proper hermeneutic. Specifically, he holds that there must be an ideological commitment to the oppressed that functions as a "social preunderstanding" for the interrogation of biblical texts. Here he sees a strong similarity between a faith, such as Christianity, and an ideology, such as Marxism.[171] It is from this ideological preunderstanding that his "suspicion" arises. Ideologies connected with current social conditions and the sacralization of vested interests may be unconsciously ruling our present theological ideas and pastoral practice, he says. It is those ideologies that must be exorcised through the circle. For, says Alfred T. Hennelly in analyzing Segundo:

> Faith without ideologies is a dead faith, that is, it is incapable of incarnation in history and thus totally impractical. This view undergirds a fundamental divergence he has from current European political theology; for while the latter is also critical of existing alliances with the ideologies of the *status quo*, its posture of "eschatological reserve" tends to quench the needed enthusiasm for the creation of new and more efficacious ideologies.[172]

For Segundo, the best example of a completed circle is provided by James Cone. Cone's commitment to the black community and its struggle for freedom provides his ideological suspicion of racism. That suspicion, in turn, leads to the second stage of the circle and his concern with the whole white-American superstructure. His charge that American white theology "has been basically a theology of the white oppressor" uncovers what he sees as that theology's central ideology, its pretense of "color blindness." Hennelly, summarizing Segundo's analysis, concludes:

> Cone then moves to the third point in the circle, by committing himself to uprooting the mechanisms of ideology in white theology and thus to fashioning a theology that corresponds to the perspective and aspirations of the black community. This leads directly into the fourth point, as he presents a new interpretation of Scripture based on the richer and more profound questions that have been raised.[173]

Segundo's entire book is actually, then, a nuanced attempt to perform the same task as Cone. And, as with Cone's work, it is a hermeneutic in which the ecclesiastical question is central. Hermeneutics is formed in and for the church as a minority-engaged community, undergirded by a universalistic soteriology that is structured in turn by the epistemology of Teilhard de Chardin. Space does not allow further elaboration at this stage.

Sobrino's work might easily be studied under a liberation approach to Christology.[174] But for our purposes, he holds special significance because of his careful comparison of both European and Latin theologies to the process of hermeneutics. His work on Christology is simply a utilization of that methodology in elaborated detail.

European theology, as he sees it, traces its liberating character to Kant's Enlightenment call for the freeing of reason from all authoritarianism. Its basic interest is, thus, rationality. By contrast, the Latin Americans trace their liberation source to Marx and the freeing of reality from suffering. Latin American liberation theology's basic interest is not rationality but transformation. Thus, Europe seeks solutions from philosophy, Latin America from the social sciences. The European quest is less successful, Sobrino says, for often it leaves the reality untouched and in that sense justified or at least justifiable.

These sources work out their implications in the relationship between theory and praxis. European theology is fundamentally theory or a history of theory, says Sobrino, its interest that of transmitting a body of truths or meanings. Latin thinking, by contrast, stresses the need first for a contact with reality before reflecting on the theology implied in that contact. Europeans stress the need for orthopraxis flowing from orthodoxy, Sobrino says. Latins stress orthodoxy flowing from a prior orthopraxis, Christ as "truth" insofar as He is "way."

The epistemological consequences of these approaches are far-reaching. Theology is seen as more dialectical than analogical. Unlike the Greeks, who assumed that wonder and the positive structure of reality were what moved man to know, the Latin American world is motivated by sorrow, the groans of the oppressed. Theodicy, the reconciliation of God and human suffering, is historicized and politicized. It becomes a question not of the justification of God but the justification of man in a world of injustice. "Consequently," says Hennelly in analyzing Sobrino, "the solution is not to be found in 'thinking,' about God in a way which reconciles God and suffering, but rather in the task of constructing a world according to God's will and experiencing the reality of God in this attempt."[175] Thus, for Europe "the death of God" phenomenon was the expression of the crisis of meaning within a theistic culture. For Latin America it symbolized the crisis of reality itself, "the death of man."[176]

The most fundamental difference between the two theologies for Sobrino lies in the overcoming of dualisms. In Europe this takes place on the cognitive level; in Latin America on the level of real history. "Fundamentally," Sobrino says, "Latin American theology has tried to recover the meaning of the profound biblical experiences concerning what it means to know theologically: to know the truth is to do the truth, to know Jesus is to follow Jesus, to know sin is to take away sin, to know suffering is to free the world from suffering, to know God is to go to God in justice."[177]

Sobrino's work supplements that of Segundo. In sharper lines, it uncovers basic differences between traditional and liberation approaches to theology and aims for a usable synthesis.

Assmann's regret that no liberation perspectives on Christology had yet appeared was quickly remedied in 1972 with the appearance of *Jesus Cristo Libertador*, by Leonardo Boff (b.1938), a Brazilian and Franciscan with a degree in systematic theology that was earned under Karl Rahner. Within one year, a first edition was sold out. "No theological publication in Brazil has aroused so much discussion and controversy in years," said Hans-Jurgen

Prien. "Even the daily newspapers took part."[178] Archbishop Vincente Cardinal Scherer publicly attacked the work for its humanistic leveling down of Christology and for the loss of Christology's transcendental character that was implied in it.

Part of the controversy comes from Boff's attempt to present the topic in the light of historical-critical research and his skepticism regarding the historical Jesus. His approach was completely new and challenging for the traditional Brazilian public.

A deeper source of the work's controversial character comes from Boff's description of Jesus as the Liberator and the methodology by which his portrait is sketched. Five characteristics mark Boff's approach. There is the primacy of the anthropological element over the ecclesiological, an interest not so much in the church as in the person that the church "must aid, must create and must humanize." There is the priority of utopian perspectives over factual ones, maintaining the social process is a permanent opening to continuing transformation. There is an emphasis on the critical element over the dogmatic: "A critical stance is seen as an absolute prerequisite for maintaining permanent openness to the future, since ecclesiastical traditions and institutions often become anachronistic, obsolete and a center of conservatism."[179] The primacy of the social over the personal is the fourth emphasis. In the Latin American context of "marginalization," the church must take part critically in the struggle for liberation from sinful social structures, Boff says. Finally, there is orthopraxis over orthodoxy. Here Boff calls for a return to what he terms the practice of the early church, in which "the essential element was not to reduce the message of Christ to systematic categories, but to create new ways of living and acting in the world."

Out of that methodology comes a picture of Jesus as the Liberator from human restrictions (the law). Jesus' announcement of the Kingdom of God calls for a revolution in man's thought and action, Boff argues, a complete conversion of the individual conscience, a liberation from legalism, and for fraternal love and equality. It calls also for a revolution of the world in which the human person thinks and acts, a liberation from futile conventions, authoritarianism, and all the powers that oppress and alienate man. Jesus' kingdom conduct inaugurated a new kind of human being and a new kind of humanism, Boff continues. Ours must also. His resurrection is the total liberation of human existence from its alienation, especially that of death. It inaugurates a kingdom that does not begin after death but appears in this world wherever more justice is created, wherever more love reigns, and wherever a fresh horizon is opened in understanding God's Word and His revelation in this life. Jesus as Liberator is a profound archetype of what it means to be human in such a radical way as to overcome human alienation, Boff concludes.

The list of theologians and topics has by no means been exhausted. With regret we must bypass the contributions of Juan Luis Segundo to systematic theology, of Enrique Dussel and his reconstructions of Latin American church history, and of José Comblin and his early and still wide-ranging studies. This section will close rather with some reference to the only other Protestant thinker besides Alves in our survey, the Methodist scholar José Miguez-Bonino.

Considered by many to be the dean of Latin American Protestant theologians, Miguez-Bonino represents a more moderate position in much of the dialogue, "heartily in favor of liberation" but "not . . . led to extremes on either side."[180] An Argentinian, he currently serves as dean of graduate studies at the Higher Institute of Theological Studies in Buenos Aires. He is also president of the World Council of Churches. His 1975 book, *Doing Theology in a Revolutionary Situation*, easily remains the best overview to date of the development and themes of liberation theology.

Some brief comparisons with Alves may help to sharpen our understanding of Miguez-Bonino's approach. "If Alves is the philosopher, Miguez is the ethicist of the Protestant reflection on liberation," says one commentator.[181] Both conceive of liberation in terms of the eruption of a new society that will make concrete the visible signs of the Kingdom. For Alves, this is sketched in terms of captivity and exodus, deliverance and hope. For Miguez-Bonino, the recurring themes are drawn in terms of the ethics of love and the mission of the church. The quality of life that we call liberation is justice, freedom to form a community based on one's own work and love. All confrontation with oppression is an act of love, and love is never without a future. Love's concrete historical nature expresses itself in Christian availability for the other, a commitment to the suffering inherent in all ethical action. Love, says Miguez-Bonino:

cannot, therefore, be reduced to a purely interpersonal or intersubjective dimension, but must be set in relation to the eschatological and cosmic scope of the Kingdom. This means that love is inextricably interwoven with hope and justice. The second point follows. Love is not exhausted in the area of intentionality and demonstration but it is other-directed and demands efficacy. It is not content to express and demonstrate, it intends to accomplish.[182]

Miguez-Bonino's moderate posture as a liberation theologian appears clearly in his 1976 book, *Christians and Marxists: The Mutual Challenge to Revolution*. Undoubtedly frightening to a Westerner unfamiliar with liberation theology and unprepared to identify Marxism with anything other than materialism or atheism, the book might hardly seem to represent a moderate position. But in it he does take a moderate approach. Miguez-Bonino's ultimate relationship to Marxism is not as a dupe of international Communism but as a convinced Christian believer. He makes use of the arguments from praxis and socioeconomic analysis that we have found to be common among his fellow liberationists. But his greatest contribution, and his clearly Christian one, is his attempt to substantiate his arguments from biblical revelation, and specifically from the biblical character of "truth."[183] He finds a profound "atheism" (i.e., the absolute repudiation of false gods) at the heart of the biblical disclosure of God, as found in Exodus 20:3-4*a*: "You shall have no other gods before me. You shall not make for yourself a graven image" (RSV). And out of that "atheism," he sketches God's purpose to overturn all idolatry, and especially the idolatry of religion itself when it is used to sanction injustice.[184] Positively, he turns to the God whose meaning and purpose are summed up in the concept of love, a concept always historically concrete and engaged and always demanding a protection of life, fulfillment of the law, and the practice of justice in concrete relationships.

From these considerations come Miguez-Bonino's criticism of both capitalism and Marxism and his ultimate choice of Marxism as a more workable model for change. Humanization is for capitalism an unintended by-product, for socialism an explicit goal. Solidarity is accidental for capitalism and essential for socialism. In terms of their basic ethos, "Christianity must criticize capitalism radically, in its fundamental intention, while it must criticize socialism functionally, in its failure to fulfill its purpose."[185]

Miguez-Bonino's lines of alliance with Marxism are threefold: (1) an understanding of knowledge not as theoretical contemplation of abstract truths but as a concrete engagement with reality; (2) an ethos of human solidarity, uniting people in its opposition to oppression and its search for justice; and (3) the need for a set of analytical tools, a concrete political and social program that permits us to embrace and carry forward the struggle for human liberation.[186] But even among these three, he notes divergences. And they are tied to the radical differences regarding the source and power of solidary love, the ultimate goal for man. Marxism cannot explain the real source of man's alienation, his estrangement from God. Nor can Marxism provide a mediator, one who will deliver man from the power of his innate tendency to oppress. There must be "a submission of the totality of life, including one's philosophical understanding or political allegiance, to the grace and judgment of the Lord ... nothing can be exempted from the purifying fire of submission and consecration to the Lord."[187]

Can a Christian be a Marxist? "If materialism is interpreted as a criticism of idealism," says Miguez-Bonino, then "it seems that it is not in itself inimical to the Christian faith." But if it is a totality and exclusiveness that negates in principle all reality that is not reduced to immanent terms, then it must be rejected by Christians. For we "have been grasped by the reality of the living God who is beyond history and the universe as well as active in history and the universe."[188] Can a Marxist be a Christian? Not without placing "Marxism in a different context, against a different horizon. . . . Nobody can become a Christian without repentance and conversion: not a conversion from Marx to the church, but from sin to Jesus Christ."[189]

LIBERATION IN BLACK

Black theology, in contrast to the Latin American liberation theology, offers fewer major writers to select from and is not as far down the road or as united in its reconstructions of key theological issues. If the projections of J. Deotis Roberts, Sr., can be seen as prophetic, we can expect to see detailed attention in the future to the dimensions of the black perspective as black theologians wrestle with the need for a theology that addresses the whole person, with Christology as the capstone of a theology of liberation, and with salvation being seen as the result of participation in the liberation struggle.[190] But as yet writings addressing these themes have not appeared.

Martin Luther King, Jr. (1929-68), in one sense, cannot be called a formal participant in the black theology movement. He had a system of positive theological belief.[191] But it was not that system for which he was best known. He was a practitioner who roused the conscience of the black church to passionate commitment, a model rather than a modeler of a new style of theologian. And in this role he must be regarded as more than a patron saint like Torres but less than an apologist like Assmann. For Cone, himself critical of King, the task of black theology is ultimately building "on the foundation laid by King by recognizing the theological character of the black community, a community whose being is inseparable from liberation through Jesus Christ."[192]

To that extent, King's work is a beginning point of the movement, much more than Joseph Washington's pioneer volume, *Black Religion* (1964). "While Washington is Black and a theologian," said Paul Garber, "*Black Religion* was an attack on Black folk religion in general and on King in particular, and it was a plea to Black Christians to enter into the 'mainstream' of White Christian theology. While Washington's book undoubtedly spurred debate on Black religion, from the viewpoint of Black theology, he started it off all wrong."[193] It was from King and the hermeneutical principle of his black activism that the movement began. King made a voiceless Christian community aware that oppression is contrary to the will of God and that God is working in our time to set the prisoners at liberty. King cannot be called the original black theologian, but his commitment and passionate action gave it life.

Chronologically speaking, Albert B. Cleage, Jr., based on his 1968 collection of sermons, *The Black Messiah*, could easily claim the title of pioneer in black theology. Pastor of the Shrine of the Black Madonna in Detroit, he has been called "the prophet of the black nation" for his long-standing advocacy of separatist black nationalism. But perhaps because of his radicalism and his arguments' controversial nature within the black community, scholars seem averse to labeling him a founding father. J. Deotis Roberts, Sr., says that without Cleage's 1968 book and that of James Cone in 1969, "American theology in black would not have been born,"[194] but he admits that Cleage can hardly be defended against the charge of black racism. According to Roberts, "Cleage contributes little to a worthy Christian understanding of what chosenness should mean in the black experience."[195]

That judgment results from Cleage's insistence on "the historic fact that Jesus was a black man,"[196] the member of a nation, Israel, which had become black during its sojourn in Babylon and Egypt. Thus every black person belongs to the "chosen," the black nation, says Cleage, and every effort must be made to gather them into the nation.[197] Ruthless in his approach to past understandings of Christianity, he tells his church that "almost everything you were taught about Christianity was wrong." Accepting only the Old Testament and the three synoptic gospels, he sees Jesus as part of the Zealot underground movement, whose revolutionary message of separation and liberation from Rome was corrupted by the apostle Paul and the theologians of white, Western civilization. The ethic of the Sermon on the Mount—turn the other cheek, walk the second mile— was an internal, tribal ethic for the black nation of God. The brotherhood ethic of Jesus had to do with love within that nation. Ultimately, Cleage claims God solely for the black people, what Boesak denounces as a quasi-religious nationalism that essentially denies the very nature of the Christian church.[198]

At the same time, Cleage's work had an electrifying impact in the black church. His church attracted more persons committed to Black Power than any single institution still connected to the Christian churches. His sermonic assault on the white imposition of the slavemaster's Christ was recognized as a reality of the black church's past. His call for a new black Christian consciousness actively engaged in the realm of politics and social responsibility would be echoed more calmly in the later work of others. The conservative judgment of Roberts, Sr., is that he "is correct in asserting that the black church must be concerned with this-worldly problems and not obsessed with the afterlife. He is also on target as he exalts the black church as the most powerful force at the disposal of blacks for their liberation."[199]

The Gutiérrez of black theology is James H. Cone (b. 1938). Not only does his 1969 book stand as the open door for a new direction recognized by even its black opponents, but it also marks the beginnings of the most prolific and sophisticated writing of any black theologian of his generation. No one has matched Cone either in productivity or in the challenge posed by his writings.

In many respects, Cone's emphases resemble those of Cleage, at least in Cone's earliest work. Both are, on the surface, more threatening to white readers than other black theologians. Like Cleage, Cone can appear to be one-sided, proclaiming half-truths, a pioneer writing a revolutionary theology. Both are angry men doing the necessary demolition work. Both are more sympathetic to cultural movements of black power and black pride than their black colleagues. Both are intensely committed to an understanding of the task of theology as the explication of liberation for the oppressed (although Cleage relates this theme more specifically to black nationalism under a black Messiah). Both think that, on the whole, the black church has capitulated to the demands of a white, racist society.[200] Both seem more open to the possibility of revolution or, as they might say, counterrevolution, than other black theologians. Although neither man, in spite of his rhetoric, is an advocate of armed revolution against white society, both contend that racism has already injected violence into the American culture and that the responsible Black today must be ready to defend himself and his society against that threat.[201]

At the same time, there are differences between Cleage and Cone, and they are clearly in Cone's favor. Cleage is a folk theologian, fashioning his formulations for the pulpit. Cone is an academic theologian, more sensitive to the demands of that world. Cone, unlike Cleage, is in an overall sense more pro-Black than anti-White. Even when he "is angry, there is evidence of profound reflection."[202] His attitude toward the Scriptures, unlike that of Cleage, does not totally discard ipso facto virtually all the New Testament. At the same time, there is a manipulation, but of a different sort.

Cone's 1969 judgments on black theology are formed out of an effort to provide a theological justification for Black Power. "My concern is, rather, to show that the goal and message of Black Power . . . is consistent with the gospel of Jesus Christ," he writes. "Indeed, I have even suggested that if Christ is present among the oppressed, as he promised, he must be working through the activity of Black Power. This alone is my thesis."[203]

On the basis of that thesis, Cone argues that the gospel cannot then be addressed to the need of the oppressed unless it is addressed in partisan terms. And that means American theology must be black theology because "blackness" is the mark of oppression in this society. Cone uses the term *blackness* in a twofold sense, as a physiological trait and as an ontological symbol, a condition of being, and a reality of social existence. And always there is a deliberate interplay between the two senses. "These are rarely separated," notes one commentator, in analyzing Cone, "for he well knows that the 'white liberal' reading public searches endlessly for ways to domesticate the Black Power movement into another timid reform program for all men (i.e., especially, and once again, for whites!)."[204] The black experience must remain the decisive clue to the gospel in our time and place, Cone says. Even when he expands the term, it never moves away from the oppression orbit. "Blackness," he says, embraces "all people who participate in the liberation of man from oppression."[205] His continued effort is to shun misleading distraction: "Liberation from oppression maintains its definitive role, and all diversions from this overarching concern are unmasked as regressions to the realm of theology as the tool of oppression."[206]

Out of that concreteness he defines the gospel as the black Christ providing the necessary soul for black liberation, the divine act of liberation that makes blacks free to define themselves and their own world, divine identification with the alienated. And with his second book, *A Black Theology of Liberation* (1970), he attempts an expansion of that idea by a restructuring of the traditional loci of theology. The hermeneutical center around which such things as Christology, ecclesiology, and eschatology are reconstructed is the revelation of God in Christ as the Liberator of the oppressed from social oppression and to political struggle. Through that revelation, he says, the poor recognize that their fight against poverty and injustice is not only consistent with the gospel but is itself the gospel.[207] Relying heavily on Tillich's "method of correlation," which Cone understands as a relation of the changeless gospel to changing cultural situations, he says: "There is no place in Black Theology for a colorless God in a society when people suffer precisely because of their color."[208] Thus the doctrine of God begins with an insistence on God's blackness. To say that God is Creator "means that *my being* finds its source in God. *I am black because God is black!* God as creator means that he is the ground of my blackness (being), the point of reference for meaning and purpose in the universe."[209] To speak of the omnipotence of God is to speak of God's power "to let black people stand out from whiteness and to be. . . . In this situation, divine providence is seeing divine reality in the present reality of black liberation, no more and no less."[210]

The subsequent history of the development of black theology unfolds as response and interaction with the theses of these works of Cone. His own later work represents a "dialogue" with his earlier work. He shifts his methodology in his 1972 study of black music as a theological reflection on liberation and, in his fullest work, *God of the Oppressed* (1975), he concentrates on the social basis of theology and interacts fully with his critics on the problem of the particular and the universal in theological discourse. And although critical reaction is sharp even within the community of black theologians, it is ultimately a tribute to the pathmaking work of Cone.

Cone's legacy is multidimensional. Critics will assault what they fear is his black parochialism, an exclusivism he identifies with God Himself. But they will support his attention to the black experience as a legitimate concern of Christian theology that was long overdue. Some, like Gayraud Wilmore, will question whether he has been radical enough in looking on black theology as "simply the Blackenization of the whole spectrum of traditional Christian theology, with particular emphasis upon the liberation of the oppressed." But they will still acknowledge his contribution in opening up "the possibility of a Black theology which is neither Protestant nor Catholic, but the way Black people *think, feel* and *act* with the intensity of ultimate concern about their liberation from oppression and racism."[211]

His definition of Christianity as the liberation of the oppressed, and blacks in particular, will draw fire. But the challenges generally revolve around the relation of liberation to reconciliation and do not involve a rejection in toto of the liberation theme. "Behind this dispute lies the difference between radical and more temperate outlooks in the black community," says John J. Carey.[212]

There will be a general commendation of Cone's attention to the anthropocentric dimensions of theology. He has sought to obliterate the distinction between theology and ethics, between God's concerns and man's. Whether his focus on immanence has lost its counterbalance in transcendence will be a subject of concern. Whether his focus on black theology has been too closely linked with his interest in Black Power themes will be raised. But his attention to the concreteness of black existence here and now and to theology's past tendencies, in the hands of white creators, to romanticize that existence will remain the legitimate core around which the discussion will revolve.

Cone's attention to the norm and sources of black theology will produce vigorous discussion among his discreditors. What is the relation between the Bible and the black experience? What is a legitimate hermeneutic for the black community? What paradigms of man subtly influence the "pre-understandings" that go into creating theology, and black theology in particular? How can and should the history of black experience influence the way Blacks do theology? Strong differences will emerge among Cone's contemporaries. But the questions will remain. And they are the questions that Cone demands we ask.

The theologian who has perhaps asked Cone many of these questions more fully and more critically than others is J. Deotis Roberts, Sr. (b. 1927), at one time dean of the school of theology at Virginia Union University and now on the staff of the school of religion at Howard University. *Liberation and Reconciliation: A Black Theology* (1971) represents his first comprehensive effort at providing a theology of the black experience. Far less strident in tone than Cone, he nevertheless stands with him in his presentation of liberation as a primary goal. Reconciliation must await the fruition of liberation. There can be no reconciliation as long as Whites continue to oppress Blacks, he says. To speak of reconciliation prior to liberation is to come to the peace table with a master-slave relationship, to fall into the trap of making reconciliation a white theological category for "cheap grace."

At the same time, he says that reconciliation must be part of the healing process, "a theological way of seeing the essential nature of this inter-racial society. We must not only co-exist; we must in-exist in a pluralistic society."[213] And it is at this point that he diverges from Cone. He fears that Cone is more of an advocate of Black Power and less an accurate interpreter of the biblical tradition in the black church. Cone's emphasis on God's blackness and his argument for divine identification with the cause of Blacks narrows his theological vision, he argues, and may endanger the hope of real communication between Blacks and Whites.[214]

Of concern to Roberts is what he considers to be the necessary difference between "the religion of Black Power" and black theology. The first seeks to be a theological justification, he claims, for the political, ideological, pseudo-religious elements of black nationalism. The second is the confession of faith in the God who is concerned about Blacks.[215] Roberts wants, like Cone, a theology addressed to a powerless people. But it must be a theology that "liberates the black man while it leaves the way open for reconciliation between men of goodwill, whether black or white."[216] Cross-bearing in the process of liberation and reconciliation is costly for all sides. For Blacks it demands forgiveness, for Whites repentance.

Roberts's writing since 1971 seems to be moving further and further away from the narrowness of definition with which he charges Cone. Not wanting to invest too much religious authority exclusively in the black community, and motivated partly by his own academic interests in the history of religions, he wishes to be universal in scope when he deals with the "eternal gospel, communicated through Scripture, tradition, and the witness of the Spirit in Christian Life through the ages." In fact, this universal dimension he sees as the "givenness" of revelation that some advocates of black theology are in danger of surrendering. Against these desires, he attacks Cone's Barthian Christomonism for effectively cutting off the dialogue between religions. "His Christology is so captive to the black condition," he says, "that one wonders what has become of the Universal Word, the Desire of all Nations. Black theologians as ethno-theologians must be open to the possibility that the saviour of *each* people may be Lord of all people."[217] His 1974 book, *A Black Political Theology,* begins a dialogue with Third-World theologies, motivated perhaps by those same concerns. He wants to see the black man's religious experience presented not only in its revolutionary form but as a contextual theology in indigenous shape.[218] Cone is critical and questions how far that achievement can be accomplished. But Roberts does it without any dilution of the concreteness of liberation or reconciliation as the primary focus for understanding the gospel. And his desire in doing it is to link black theological efforts with efforts going on throughout the world to "decolonize" theology. He is simply recognizing fraternal problems and fraternal efforts at solutions. Whether this prior commitment to universalism will allow a faithful building of his black theology remains to be seen.[219]

Still another moderating voice entered with Roberts in 1971 into the circle of black writing prophets. Major J. Jones (b. 1919), then president-director of Gammon Theological Seminary, joined the discussion with a focus on the concepts of black awareness and the essentials of a black theology of hope. Critical of abstractness in too much of Moltmann's work,[220] he calls for a concrete eschatology that "must correlate the contents of eschatological hope with the conditions of the black experience and an intelligible understanding of the same."[221] It must hold a promise to be redeemed within the earthly life span of those who possess such a hope, he contends, a this-world interpretation that will not put up with reality as it is but will begin to contradict it.

Involved in this eschatology of hope will be an anthropology of hope, Jones continues, an ontological analysis of man that illuminates the black man's situation as oppressive and arms him with a sense of worth, "the courage to be black."[222] Black self-affirmation must create a black self-image that sees itself as a center of power, or freedom. With Cone, he quotes favorably the judgments of Albert Camus and his concept of the rebel who says no to intolerable conditions and yes to that something in him which is "worthwhile." Self-interest must have a priority in the eschatology of the oppressed.

At the same time, Jones puts himself at a distance from Cone at a number of significant points. Although he demands that there must be a visible display of the power of God on behalf of the oppressed, he fears that "black awareness advocates have little concern for the liberation of whites" and that Cone's views move in the direction of a separatism that is counterproductive to liberation.[223] "What, essentially, is the difference between separation for black awareness and separation that is forced?" he asks. "Does separation by force do more harm than separation by choice?"[224] Similarly, he fears the identification of Jesus with physiological blackness by Cleage, or a similar identification of God. Recognizing this as a protest against "whitening" God in the name of oppression, he asks what this will ultimately achieve for the Black. "Will it make him . . . any more responsible with the use of his newly acquired black power than the white man was with his white power? Will the black man, with his black God, be a better man than the white man was with his white God?"[225] Is not the humanity of man much deeper than color? Can God acquire color without becoming identified with that which is too narrow to be fully representative of the total human family? In recoloring God, will those who do so alter the very concept of being itself?

In his second major study of the question, *Christian Ethics for Black Theology* (1974), Jones expands the ethical dimensions of a black eschatology. What is the moral requirement of the gospel in the light of the black condition of oppression and injustice? What can Jesus say to the black man in his struggle for freedom and full recognition in a prowhite society?

Critics of Jones's work, like Roberts, Sr.,[226] and Enoch Oglesby,[227] commend his effort to correlate more visibly ethics and theology in the context of the black experience. But his views on the ethical consistency of nonviolence with the ethical imperative to love are questioned even by black moderates. Charles Stith is concerned whether his support of the "not yet" can ultimately provide the impetus for a more usable future. It is too easy for a "not yet" eschatology, lacking Jones's specificity, to be manipulated into a "not now," says Stith.[228] Jones is urging Blacks to trust in the inherent redemptive efficacy of the love ethic, even independent of white response. Yet he concedes that "there might well be certain crisis conditions that the Christian might find it impossible to stand aside and let evil have its way." In such instances, the Christian turns to an "ethic of distress" in which there is a "theological" suspension of the ethical for a higher purpose. Roberts sees a major problem in this area: "Why attempt a theological ethic at all if it does not provide principles and guidelines for decision and/or behaviour when the most crucial matters are at stake? Why a black Christian ethic if we are finally left to our instincts, passions and expediency and the crisis itself to determine what we must do?"[229] Jones's second work marks a shift of black theological reflection into the "post-Black Power era." Whether it makes the shift satisfactorily must be left to future discussions.

Perhaps even more indicative of the beginnings of this "post-era" is the unique, almost maverick, work of William R. Jones, a professor at the Yale Divinity School. Jones's 1973 book, *Is God a White Racist?*, marks the first full-length reflection on the leading theoreticians of black theology, a critical reflection hailed as useful even by the conservative Roberts, Sr.[230] Without any exact parallel among Latin Americans, it underlines the less homogeneous character of the black contribution to liberation thinking. Unique among other black contributions to the discussion, it sees the major theological issue in black theology not as liberation but as a black version of the theodicy questions—What is the meaning of black suffering? Is God a white racist? More than the traditional attempt to exonerate and justify the goodness of God's purpose and works in the face of contrary evidence, black theodicy, as Jones paints it, concerns itself with the cause of suffering and, more specifically, black suffering. Even more divergent is Jones's own position in the examination. A minister of the Unitarian-Universalist "Church," Jones's own presuppositional model for the criticism is neither Western theism nor black theism but black humanism. Unlike those whose views he analyzes, Jones presumes neither the goodness nor the sovereignty of God. He works instead with the assumption of divine, not human, racism, God's sanctioning of the division of mankind into an "in group" and an "out group." God, then, in Jones's view, becomes responsible for the imbalance of suffering as He favors the "in-group," Himself a member of that group.

It is here that Jones challenges the eschatological dimensions in which the black theologians make their constructions. Given God's acts in the past and present, and given the assumption that God is the sum of His acts, Jones says, on what grounds can anyone say that His actions in the future will be different from what they were in the past and are in the present? Black theologians, he contends, can only look toward the future for black liberation to become a reality. The oppression of the past and present cannot allow them, on the basis of their presuppositions, to look anywhere else.[231]

The bulk of the book proceeds to a careful analysis of the works of Washington, Cone, Cleage, Major J. Jones, and Roberts, Sr., from these methodological givens.[232] And his own ultimate solution, after rejecting all others, is what he calls "humanocentric theism," "an explicit affirmation of the functional ultimacy of man."[233] Man is a codetermining power in the fulfillment of God's plan, he says, and that power is intrinsic to man's being. This divine endowment of man ultimately is the most authentic expression of divine sovereignty. At this point humanocentric theism and secular humanism converge. Both "affirm the principle of the functional ultimacy of man in human history and/or the arena of values," Jones says.[234]

Such radical judgments, of course, have not gone without attack. Roberts, Sr., sees Jones's theism as a hybrid alternative of humanism with a touch of theism that is both and neither: "His book is by a humanist for humanists, but not for believers in God."[235] That judgment undoubtedly represents the thinking of the vast majority of the black community. Jones's obsession with divine racism offers a framework for criticism that few, even the most extreme, could live with comfortably. His final value lies in his questioning of methodology and his attempt to analyze the liberation question as one of black theodicy.[236]

There are other black theologians whom we might add to our discussion at this point. Eulalio R. Baltazar in his 1973 book, *The Dark Center*, examines the themes of black theology from the point of view of process theology. The clearly evangelical voice of Tom Skinner touches in a more popular style on these concerns in his 1971 work, *How Black is the Gospel?* But Baltazar's ideas remain a point of view still unrepresentative of a larger community, a Filipino observation that is psychological in tone. And Skinner's book, although probably more representative of the majority in the black Christian community than any other work we have cited, never reaches the depth to which the other works go.

Notes

1. Hugo Assmann, *Practical Theology of Liberation* (London: Search, 1975), pp. 52-53.
2. *Aportes para la liberación* (Bogotá: Editorial Presencia, 1970); *Liberación* (Bogotá: Editorial Presencia, 1970), volumes I and II of the first symposium on liberation theology held in Bogotá, 1970; *Liberación en América Latina* (Bogotá: Ed. América Latina, 1971); *América Latina: Movilización popular y Fe cristiana* (Montivideo: ISAL, 1971); *Pueblo Oprimido, Señor de la historia* (Montivideo: Tierra Nueva, 1972).
3. Gustavo Gutiérrez, *A Theology of Liberation*, trans. Caridad Inda, Sr., and John Eagleson (Maryknoll, N.Y.: Orbis, 1973), p. 15.
4. James H. Cone, *A Black Theology of Liberation* (Philadelphia: Lippincott, 1970), p. 17.
5. Quoted in Gregory Baum, "The Christian Left at Detroit," *The Ecumenist* 13, no. 6 (September-October 1975): 81.
6. Ibid.
7. Sergio Torres and John Eagleson, eds., *Theology in the Americas* (Maryknoll, N.Y.: Orbis, 1976), pp. 175-212.
8. Rubem A. Alves, "Christian Realism: Ideology of the Establishment," *Christianity and Crisis* 33, no. 15 (September 17, 1973): 176.
9. Torres and Eagleson, p. 431.
10. Baum, p. 98.
11. Aharon Sapsezian, "Theology of Liberation—Liberation of Theology Educational Perspectives," *Theological Education* 9, no. 4 (Summer 1973): 254.
12. José Miguez-Bonino, "New Theological Perspectives," *Religious Education*, 66, no. 6 (1971): 405.
13. Gutiérrez, *A Theology of Liberation*, p. 15.

14. J. Deotis Roberts, Sr., "Black Consciousness in Theological Perspective," in *Quest for a Black Theology*, ed. James J. Gardiner and J. Deotis Roberts, Sr. (Philadelphia: Pilgrim, 1970), p. 67.
15. Torres and Eagleson, p. 281.
16. Paul Lehmann, *The Transfiguration of Politics* (New York: Harper & Row, 1975), pp. 110, 141-42. For a sweeping historical treatment of the background of Latin American developments, consult Enrique Dussel, *History and the Theology of Liberation* (Maryknoll, N.Y.: Orbis, 1976).
17. José Miguez-Bonino, *Doing Theology in a Revolutionary Situation*, ed. William H. Lazareth (Philadelphia: Fortress, 1975), p. 14.
18. Ibid., p. 25.
19. Alan Neely, "Liberation Theology in Latin America: Antecedents and Autochthany," *Missiology* 6, no. 3 (July 1978): 348-49.
20. Gutiérrez, *A Theology of Liberation*, p. 26.
21. Torres and Eagleson, p. 278.
22. J. Andrew Kirk, "Beyond Capitalism and Marxism: Dialogue with a Dialogue," *Theological Fraternity Bulletin* no. 1-2 (1976): 27.
23. José Porfirio Miranda, *Marx and the Bible: A Critique of the Philosophy of Oppression*, trans. John Eagleson (Maryknoll, N.Y.: Orbis, 1974), p. xiii.
24. Richard Neuhaus, "Liberation Theology and the Captivities of Jesus," in *Mission Trends No. 3*, ed. Gerald H. Anderson and Thomas Stransky (New York: Paulist; Grand Rapids: Eerdmans, 1976), p. 54.
25. Baum, p. 97.
26. Nicholas Piediscalzi and Robert G. Thobaben, eds., *From Hope to Liberation: Towards a New Marxist-Christian Dialogue* (Philadelphia: Fortress, 1974), pp. 4, 80-81.
27. Franz Fanon, *The Wretched of the Earth* (New York: Grove, 1963), p. 41.
28. Ibid., pp. 210-11. Compare the excellent summary of Fanon's emphases in Lehmann, pp. 169-79.
29. Rubem A. Alves, *A Theology of Human Hope* (Washington, D.C.: Corpus, 1969), p. 11.
30. Gutiérrez, *A Theology of Liberation*, p. 31.
31. Paulo Freire, *Pedogogy of the Oppressed* (New York: Seabury, 1970), pp. 45, 55.
32. Ibid., pp. 64-65. Compare Neely, 350-51. For a full discussion of Freire's critique of the "banking method" of education, consult the articles by Albert Rabil, Rosalyn Sherman-Lessing, and Peter Elbow in *Soundings* 61 (1963): 228-58.
33. Gutiérrez, *A Theology of Liberation*, pp. 36-57.
34. Lehmann, p. 164.
35. For the history of this stormy period, consult Lerone Bennett, Jr., *Before the Mayflower* (Baltimore: Penguin, 1962), pp. 311-59.
36. Statement of the N.C.B.C. issued June 13, 1969, in Atlanta, Georgia.
37. Martin Luther King, Jr., *Where Do We Go From Here? Chaos or Community* (London: Hodder & Stoughton, 1968), especially chapter 2. Allan Boesak argues that there were changes in King's thinking toward the end of his life that would have made him more congenial to the structural themes for change behind the slogan. See Boesak's *Farewell to Innocence* (Kampen, Netherlands: Kok, 1976), pp. 57-59.
38. J. Deotis Roberts, Sr., "Black Theology in the Making," *Review and Expositor* 70 (1973): 325.
39. James H. Cone, *Black Theology and Black Power* (New York: Seabury, 1969), p. 8.
40. Ibid., pp. 28-29. For a fuller picture of Cone's contributions, see G. Clarke Chapman, Jr., "American Theology in Black: James H. Cone," *Cross Currents* 21, no. 2 (Spring 1972): 139-57.
41. James H. Cone, *Black Theology and Black Power*, p. 29.
42. Joseph R. Washington, Jr., *Black and White Power in Subreption* (Boston: Beacon, 1969), pp. 117-23, 190.

43. Boesak, p. 61.
44. J. Deotis Roberts, Sr., *Liberation and Reconciliation: A Black Theology* (Philadelphia: Westminster, 1971), pp. 40-43.
45. J. Deotis Roberts, Sr., "Black Theological Ethics: A Bibliographical Essay," *The Journal of Religious Ethics* 3 (1975): 88. Compare Cecil W. Cone, *The Identity Crisis in Black Theology* (Nashville: AMEC, 1975), pp. 89-91.
46. Boesak, pp. 108-9.
47. Gayraud S. Wilmore, "The New Context of Black Theology in the United States," *Occasional Bulletin of Missionary Research* 2, no. 2 (October 1978): 140.
48. Ibid.
49. The Black Theology Project's "Message to the Black Church and Community," with commentary by Shawn Copeland and the keynote address by James H. Cone, appears in *Cross Currents*, 27, no. 2 (1977), 140-56.
50. Torres and Eagleson, p. 382.
51. Baum, p. 87.
52. Sergio Torres and Virginia Fabella, eds., *The Emergent Gospel: Theology from the Underside of History* (Maryknoll, N.Y.: Orbis, 1978), pp. 180-82.
53. Robert McAfee Brown, *Theology in a New Key: Responding to Liberation Themes* (Philadelphia: Westminster, 1978), pp. 28-29.
54. Hugo Latorre Cabal, *The Revolution of the Latin American Church* (Norman: U. of Oklahoma, 1978), p. 11.
55. Ibid., p. 12.
56. Brown, *Theology in a New Key*, p. 30.
57. Cabal, p. 17. For a fuller reflection of Latin American reactions to Vatican II, see Roberto Oliveros, *Liberación y Teología. Génesis y crecimiento de una reflexión (1966-1976)* (Lima: Centro de Estudios y Publicaciones, 1977), pp. 49-74.
58. Gutiérrez, *A Theology of Liberation*, pp. 33-34.
59. Ibid., p. 46.
60. Dussel, p. 113. The full texts from Medellín are available in English in *The Church in the Present-Day Transformation of Latin America in the Light of the Council. Volume II. Conclusions.* (Washington, D.C.: U.S. Cath. Conf., 1973).
61. John Drury, trans., *Between Honesty and Hope* (Maryknoll, N.Y.: Marknoll, 1970), doc. 23.
62. Francis P. Fiorenza, "Latin American Liberation Theology," *Interpretation* 28, no. 4 (October 1974): 446. Compare Oliveros, pp. 113-29.
63. Torres and Fabella, p. 182.
64. Torres and Eagleson, p. 26.
65. Brown, *Theology in a New Key*, pp. 55-56. The Santiago documents can be found in John Eagleson, ed., *Christians and Socialism* (Maryknoll, N.Y.: Orbis, 1975). Commentaries on the movement can be found in: Hugo Assmann et al., *Cristianos por el Socialismo: Exigencias de una Opción* (Montivideo: Tierra Nueva, 1973); and Pablo Richard, *Cristianos por el Socialismo: Historia y Documentación* (Salamanca: Sigueme, 1976).
66. Miguez-Bonino, *Doing Theology in a Revolutionary Situation*, p. xxii.
67. Torres and Fabella, p. 202.
68. Emilio Castro, "La situación teológica de América Latina y la teología de Karl Barth," in Torres and Fabella, p. 200.
69. Orlando Costas, *Theology of the Crossroads in Contemporary Latin America* (Amsterdam: Rodopi, 1976), p. 86.
70. José Miguez-Bonino, "Visión del cambio social y sus tareas desde las iglesias no-católicas," in *Fe Cristiana y cambio social en América Latina*, ed. Alfonso Alvarez (Salamanca: Sigueme, 1973), p. 185.
71. Costas, *Theology of the Crossroads*, pp. 102-8, chronicles the controversy in detail. Note the judgments of Beatriz Melano Couch on this polarization in Torres and Fabella, p. 208.

72. Quoted in Costas, *Theology of the Crossroads*, p. 111.
73. *Encuentro y desafío. Conclusiones y resoluciones de la Primera Consulta Evangélica Latinoamericana sobre Iglesia y Sociedad realizada en Huampaní, Perú, 23-27 de julio, 1961* (Montivideo: ISAL, 1961), p. 12.
74. Miguez-Bonino, *Doing Theology in a Revolutionary Situation*, pp. 54-55. For judgments from another theological perspective, consult Emilio A. Nuñez, "The Theology of Liberation in Latin America," *Bibliotheca Sacra* 134, no. 536 (October-December 1977): 344-48.
75. Quoted in Costas, *Theology of the Crossroads*, p. 204. Whether ISAL can achieve this basic purpose is doubted by some, including Hugo Assmann. Compare Costas, *Theology of the Crossroads*, pp. 213-15.
76. Torres and Eagleson, p. 42.
77. Torres and Fabella, p. 211.
78. Costas, *Theology of the Crossroads*, p. 81.
79. Ibid., pp. 81-82. Fears of conservative entrenchment continue to be expressed at the time of this writing as preparations are being made for the third meeting of the Latin American bishops (CELAM III) near the end of 1978 at Puebla, Mexico. Note Robert McAfee Brown, "Why Puebla Matters?" and Gustavo Gutiérrez, "The 'Preparatory Document' for Puebla: A Retreat From Commitment," *Christianity and Crisis* 38, no. 13 (September 18, 1978): 206-18; a special issue on "Puebla: Moment of Decision for the Latin American Church," *Cross Currents* 28, no. 1 (Spring 1978): 1-103.
80. Torres and Fabella, p. 186.
81. The results of this meeting were published under the title, *Liberación: diálogos en el CELAM* (Bogota: CELAM, 1974). One of these papers, by Bonaventure Kloppenburg, O.F.M., has now appeared in English under the title, *Temptations for the Theology of Liberation* (Chicago: Franciscan Herald, 1978).
82. Proceedings were published under the title, *Teología de la liberación: Conversaciones de Toledo* (Burgos, Spain: Burgense, 1974).
83. José Miguez-Bonino, "Visión del cambio social y sus tareas desde las iglesias no-católicas," p. 193. Early samples of their work can be found in: C. René Padilla, ed., *Fé cristiana y Latinoamérica hoy* (Buenos Aires: Certeza, 1974); C. René Padilla, ed., *El reino de Dios y la historía* (El Paso: Casa Bautista de Publicaciones, 1975).
84. Torres and Fabella, p. 213. In a suprising omission, the "radical evangelicals" are totally ignored (except for one footnote reference to Costas) in the history of criticism provided by Brown, *Theology in a New Key*, pp. 101-31.
85. José Miguez-Bonino, "Five Theses Towards an Understanding of the 'Theology of Liberation,' " *Expository Times* 87, no. 7 (April 1976): 198. Compare his *Doing Theology in a Revolutionary Situation*, pp. 77-78.
86. Neely, p. 357.
87. Hector Borrat, "Liberation Theology in Latin America," *Dialog* 13, no. 3 (Summer 1974): 174. Borrat's quotation subsumed the "theology of hope" under European political theology and also included the "theology of revolution." I see the influence of the "theology of revolution" as minimal and Moltmann's contribution as much more seminal than Borrat does.
88. Johann B. Metz, "Das Problem einer 'politischen Theologie' und die Bestimmung der Kirche als Institution gesellschaftskritischer Freiheit," *Concilium* 4 (1968): 403.
89. Francis P. Fiorenza, "Political Theology and Liberation Theology," in *Liberation, Revolution and Freedom*, ed. Thomas M. McFadden (New York: Seabury, 1975), p. 12. Compare Johann B. Metz, *Zur Theologie der Welt* (Mainz: Matthias-Grunenwald Verlag, 1968), p. 116.
90. Quoted in Orlando Costas, *The Church and Its Mission: A Shattering Critique from the Third World* (Wheaton: Tyndale, 1974), p. 230. Compare Hugo Assmann, *Opresión-liberación: Desafío a los cristianos* (Montivideo: Tierra Nueva, 1971), pp. 13-14.
91. Gutiérrez, *A Theology of Liberation*, p. 218.
92. Julio de Santa Ana, "The Influence of Bonhoeffer on the Theology of Liberation," *Ecumenical Review* 28 (April 1976): 188.

93. Neely, p. 359.
94. For an outline of that influence, consult Neely, pp. 362-65, and C. Peter Wagner, *Latin American Theology* (Grand Rapids: Eerdmans, 1970), pp. 53-59.
95. Santa Ana, pp. 188-89.
96. Gustavo Gutiérrez, "The Hope of Liberation," in *Mission Trends No. 3*, ed. Gerald Anderson and Thomas Stransky (Grand Rapids: Eerdmans, 1976), p. 68.
97. Miguez-Bonino, *Doing Theology in a Revolutionary Situation*, p. 79.
98. Neely, p. 356. Compare Gutiérrez, *A Theology of Liberation*, pp. 224-25.
99. Gutiérrez, *A Theology of Liberation*, p. 218.
100. Miguez-Bonino, *Doing Theology in a Revolutionary Situation*, p. 147.
101. Jürgen Moltmann, *The Crucified God* (New York: Harper & Row, 1974), p. 305.
102. Miguez-Bonino, *Doing Theology in a Revolutionary Situation*, p. 148.
103. Jürgen Moltmann, "An Open Letter to José Miguez-Bonino," *Christianity and Crisis* 36, no. 5 (March 29, 1976): 57-63.
104. Hugo Assmann, *Practical Theology of Liberation*, p. 94.
105. For a recent sample of this equation, note the charges of René de Visme Williamson, "The Theology of Liberation," *Christianity Today* 19, no. 22 (August 8, 1975): 9-10.
106. Assmann, *Practical Theology of Liberation*, p. 92. Compare Hans-Jurgen Prien, "Liberation and Development in Latin America," *Lutheran World* 20 (1973): 122-23.
107. J. Deotis Roberts, Sr., *A Black Political Theology* (Philadelphia: Westminster, 1974), p. 222.
108. J. Deotis Roberts, Jr., "A Critique of James H. Cone's God of the Oppressed," *Journal of the Interdenominational Theological Center* 3, no. 1 (Fall 1975): 60. A similar judgment is made by Cone's brother, Cecil Cone, pp. 112-13. (See note 45 for full reference.)
109. Roberts, Jr., p. 62.
110. Baum, p. 87.
111. Torres and Eagleson, p. 187.
112. Lehmann, p. 165. Compare similar judgments by Gayraud S. Wilmore, *Black Religion and Black Radicalism* (Garden City, N.Y.: Anchor/Doubleday, 1973), pp. 229-30.
113. David L. Lewis, *King: A Critical Biography* (Baltimore: Penguin, 1970), p. 20.
114. Wilmore, *Black Religion and Black Radicalism*, pp. 277-86.
115. Ibid., p. 291. A similar evaluation of the Manifesto is given by Preston N. Williams in *The Black Experience in Religion*, ed. C. Eric Lincoln (Garden City, N.Y.: Anchor/Doubleday, 1974), p. 183.
116. Torres and Eagleson, p. 189.
117. James H. Cone, *God of the Oppressed* (New York: Seabury, 1975), p. 156.
118. Roberts, Sr., *A Black Political Theology*, pp. 86, 229.
119. Ibid., pp. 26-27.
120. James H. Cone, "A Critique of J. Deotis Roberts, Sr., A Black Political Theology," *Journal of the Interdenominational Theological Center* 3, no. 1 (Fall 1975): 56.
121. Juan Luis Segundo, *The Liberation of Theology*, trans. John Drury (Maryknoll, N.Y.: Orbis, 1976), pp. 25-34.
122. Consult his *Farewell to Innocence* and his essay, "Coming In Out of the Wilderness," in Torres and Fabella, pp. 76-95.
123. Neuhaus, p. 47. (See note 24 for full reference.)
124. G. Clarke Chapman, Jr., "Black Theology and Theology of Hope: What Have They to Say To Each Other?," *Union Seminary Quarterly Review* 29, no. 2 (Winter 1974): 107.
125. Ibid., p. 108.
126. James H. Cone, *Black Theology and Black Power*, p. 37.
127. James H. Cone, *A Black Theology of Liberation*, pp. 245-46.

128. Gardiner and Roberts, Sr., p. 81. (See note 14 for full reference.)

129. Roberts, Sr., *Liberation and Reconciliation*, pp. 156-57.

130. Roberts, Sr., *A Black Political Theology*, p. 236. Compare also pages 123, 181-82. Robert A. Bennett offers his analysis of the debate in his essay, "Biblical Theology and Black Theology," *Journal of the Interdenominational Theological Center* 3, no. 2 (Spring 1976): 10-11.

131. James H. Cone, *God of the Oppressed*, p. 5.

132. Ibid., p. 117.

133. Ibid., p. 244.

134. Chapman, Jr., "Black Theology and Theology of Hope," p. 113.

135. Roberts, Sr., *Liberation and Reconciliation*, p. 156.

136. Major J. Jones, *Black Awareness: A Theology of Hope* (Nashville: Abingdon, 1971), p. 12. Compare pp. 88-89.

137. James H. Cone, *God of the Oppressed*, p. 127.

138. Ibid., p. 7.

139. James H. Cone, *The Spirituals and the Blues* (New York: Seabury, 1972), p. 106.

140. Miguez-Bonino, *Doing Theology in a Revolutionary Situation*, pp. 43-45.

141. Gutiérrez, *A Theology of Liberation*, p. 105.

142. Alves, *A Theology of Human Hope*, pp. 55-68.

143. Miguez-Bonino, *Doing Theology in a Revolutionary Situation*, p. 74.

144. Ibid., p. 77.

145. Prien, p. 129.

146. Gutiérrez, *A Theology of Liberation*, pp. 53-61.

147. Ibid., pp. 36-37, 148-87. For an analysis of these levels in Gutiérrez, see James F. Conway, *Marx and Jesus: Liberation Theology in Latin America* (New York: Carlton, 1973), pp. 142-43.

148. Miguez-Bonino, *Doing Theology in a Revolutionary Situation*, p. 71; Gutiérrez, *A Theology of Liberation*, pp. 153-68.

149. Gutiérrez, *A Theology of Liberation*, p. 15.

150. Ibid., p. 6.

151. Stephen C. Knapp, "A Preliminary Dialogue with Gutiérrez' 'A Theology of Liberation,' " in *Evangelicals and Liberation*, ed. Carl E. Armerding (Nutley, N.J.: Presby. and Ref., 1977), p. 17.

152. Fiorenza, "Latin American Liberation Theology," p. 454.

153. Gerd Decke, "Critical Review of 'A Theology of Liberation,' " *Lutheran World* 20 (1973): 204.

154. Published in Montivideo by Tierra Nueva, 1971. The English rendering of the book appears as chapter 2 in Assmann's *Practical Theology of Liberation*, pp. 43-108.

155. Torres and Fabella, p. 189.

156. These are the four divisions under which Assmann's work is analyzed by Oliveros, pp. 186-92. (See note 57 for full reference.)

157. Miguez-Bonino, *Doing Theology in a Revolutionary Situation*, p. 72.

158. Assmann, *Opresión-Liberación*, p. 139.

159. Oliveros, p. 194.

160. Miranda, *Marx and the Bible*, p. vii. (See note 23 for full reference.)

161. José Porfirio Miranda, *Being and the Messiah: The Message of St. John.* (Maryknoll, N.Y.: Orbis, 1977).

162. Miranda, *Marx and the Bible*, p. xviii.

163. Ibid., p. 283.

164. Alfredo Fierro, *The Militant Gospel* (London: SCM, 1977), p. 373. A good summary of Miranda's book is found in Christian Saade, "Marx and the Bible," *Vanguard* (November-December 1975): 9-11.

165. Miguez-Bonino, "Five Theses Towards an Understanding of the 'Theology of Liberation,' " p. 199.
166. Fiorenza, "Latin American Liberation Theology," p. 447. Similar judgments are found in Conway, pp. 155-62, and David R. Peal, "Juan Luis Segundo's 'A Theology for Artisans of a New Humanity': A Latin American Contribution to Contemporary Theological Understanding," *Perkins Journal* 30, no. 3 (Spring 1977): 4.
167. Torres and Fabella, pp. 182, 188.
168. Torres and Eagleson, p. 65.
169. Segundo, p. 8.
170. Ibid., p. 9.
171. Ibid., pp. 57-66.
172. Alfred T. Hennelly, "The Challenge of Juan Luis Segundo," *Theological Studies* 38, no. 1 (March 1977): 130.
173. Alfred T. Hennelly, "Theological Method: The Southern Exposure," *Theological Studies* 38, no. 4 (December 1977): 718.
174. His major work, *Cristología desde América Latina: Esbozo a partir del sequimiento del Jesus histórico* (Mexico City: Ediciones C.R.T., 1976), appeared in English in 1978 as *Christology at the Crossroads: A Latin American Approach*, trans. John Drury (Maryknoll, N.Y.: Orbis). For an analysis of this Christology, consult Oliveros, pp. 416-39.
175. Hennelly, "Theological Method: The Southern Exposure," p. 722.
176. Jon Sobrino, "El conocimiento teológico en la teología europa y latinoamerica," in *Liberación y cautiviero: Debates en torno al método de la teología en América Latina* (Mexico City: Comité Organizador, 1975), p. 201.
177. Ibid., p. 207.
178. Prien, pp. 126-27. A full analysis of Boff's work is found in Oliveros, pp. 414-16.
179. Hennelly, "Theological Method: The Southern Exposure," p. 712. Compare Leonardo Boff, *Jesus Christ Liberator: A Critical Christology for Our Time*, trans. Patrick Hughes (Maryknoll, N.Y.: Orbis, 1978), p. 45.
180. C. Peter Wagner, ed., *A Catolog of the C. Peter Wagner Collection of Materials on Latin American Theology of Liberation* (Pasadena: Fuller Evang. Assoc., 1974), p. 49.
181. Torres and Fabella, p. 214.
182. Miguez-Bonino, *Doing Theology in a Revolutionary Situation*, p. 114.
183. Miguez-Bonino, *Christians and Marxists: The Mutal Challenge of Revolution* (Grand Rapids: Eerdmans, 1976), pp. 29-41.
184. Ibid., pp. 65-66.
185. Kirk, p. 30. (See note 22 for full reference.)
186. Miguez-Bonino, *Christians and Marxists*, pp. 118-19.
187. Ibid., p. 126.
188. Ibid., p. 125.
189. Ibid., pp. 125-26. For an excellent analysis of Miguez-Bonino's argument, consult Thomas Finger, "Christians and Marxists ... the Debate Goes On," *Sojourners* 6, no. 4 (April 1977): 33-36; Orlando Costas, "Review: A Revolutionary Witness," *The Other Side* (July-August 1976): 40-42.
190. J. Deotis Roberts, Sr., "Contextual Theology: Liberation and Indigenization," *Christian Century* 92, no. 3 (January 28, 1976): 67-68.
191. L. Harold DeWolf, "Martin Luther King, Jr. as Theologian," *Journal of the Interdenominational Theological Center* 4, no. 2 (Spring 1977): 1-11.
192. Roberts, Sr., "Black Theology in the Making," p. 325. (See note 38 for full reference.)
193. Paul R. Garber, "Black Theology: The Latter Day Legacy of Martin Luther King, Jr.," *Journal of the Interdenominational Theological Center* 2, no. 2 (Spring 1975): 106.
194. Roberts, Sr., "Black Theology in the Making," p. 325.

195. Roberts, Sr., *Liberation and Reconciliation*, p. 56. (See note 44 for full reference.)
196. Albert Cleage, *The Black Messiah* (New York: Sheed and Ward, 1968), p. xv.
197. Ibid., p. 40.
198. Boesak, p. 95. (See note 37 for full reference.)
199. Roberts, Sr., "Black Theological Ethics," p. 93. (See note 45 for full reference.)
200. John J. Carey, "Black Theology: An Appraisal of the Internal and External Issues," *Theological Studies* 33 (1972): 691.
201. James H. Cone, *Black Theology and Black Power*, p. 143.
202. Roberts, Sr., "Black Theology in the Making," p. 324.
203. James H. Cone, *Black Theology and Black Power*, p. 48.
204. Chapman, Jr., "American Theology in Black: James H. Cone," p. 143. (See note 40 for full reference.)
205. James H. Cone, *A Black Theology of Liberation*, pp. 27, 32 n. 5.
206. Benjamin A. Reist, *Theology in Red, White and Black* (Philadelphia: Westminster, 1975), p. 89.
207. James H. Cone, *A Black Theology of Liberation*, pp. 114-16; compare James H. Cone, *God of the Oppressed*, pp. 81-82.
208. James H. Cone, *A Black Theology of Liberation*, p. 120.
209. Ibid., pp. 140-41.
210. Ibid., p. 150.
211. Wilmore, *Black Religion and Black Radicalism*, pp. 296-97. (See note 112 for full reference.)
212. Carey, p. 691.
213. Roberts, Sr., "Black Theology in the Making," p. 326.
214. Roberts, Sr., *Liberation and Reconciliation*, pp. 19-20, 106.
215. Boesak, p. 64‹ These charges are very similar to those made of Cone by his younger brother, Cecil Cone, pp. 92-122. (See note 45 for full reference.)
216. Roberts, Sr., *Liberation and Reconciliation*, p. 193.
217. J. Deotis Roberts, Sr., "Theology of Religions: the Black Religious Heritage," *Journal of the Interdenominational Theological Center* 1, no. 2 (Spring 1974): 66.
218. Roberts, Sr., "Contextual Theology: Liberation and Indigenization," pp. 64-68.
219. See the criticism of Roberts's work by Cecil Cone, pp. 136-37.
220. Major J. Jones, p. 12. (See note 136 for full reference.)
221. Ibid.
222. Ibid., pp. 63-66.
223. Ibid., p. 109. Cone, in dialogue, contends that Jones has added to this quotation from his later work and thus substantially distorted his perspective. See his *God of the Oppressed*, pp. 270-71.
224. Major J. Jones, p. 70. Boesak, pp. 107-8, responds to these charges by criticizing Jones's understanding of Black Power as a philosophy to be equated with hate and violence.
225. Major J. Jones, p. 115.
226. Roberts, Sr., "Black Theological Ethics," p. 96.
227. Enoch H. Oglesby, "Book Reviews: 'Christian Ethics for Black Theology,' " *Journal of the Interdenominational Theological Center*, 2, no. 1 (Fall 1974): 71.
228. Charles R. Stith, "Review of 'Christian Ethics for Black Theology,' " *Religion in Life* 44 (1975): 388.
229. Roberts, Sr., "Black Theological Ethics," p. 95.
230. Roberts, Sr., "Black Theology in the Making," p. 325. James H. Cone, in *God of the Oppressed*, p. 187, calls it "a fitting climax to the black power mood."
231. William R. Jones, *Is God a White Racist?* (Garden City, N.Y.: Anchor/Doubleday, 1973), pp. 12-13.

232. An excellent summary of these critiques is found in Henry James Young, "Black Theology and the Work of William R. Jones," *Religion in Life* 44, (1975): 16-21.

233. William R. Jones, p. 187.

234. Ibid., p. 194.

235. Roberts, Sr., "Black Theological Ethics," p. 94.

236. Notice the extended, two-page response to Jones in James H. Cone, *God of the Oppressed*, pp. 267-68.

For the selected reading list, see the end of the next chapter (chap. 9).

Praxis, is bib. interp. normative.

THEOLOGIES OF LIBERATION

PART TWO: TOWARD A COMMON VIEW

9

Theologies of Liberation: Toward a Common View

by
HARVIE M. CONN

THE EMERGING CONSENSUS

The richness of all the individual approaches in the preceding chapter to the themes of liberation and the insistence in each approach on the particular importance of context in shaping and defining theology make attempts to outline a common framework difficult. The designation "black theology," especially, already shows its age. Following the intramural debate makes it increasingly difficult to use the term and certainly to use it as a reference to a distinct kind of theology. Nevertheless, there does seem to be a "convergence from multiple sources," although not enough to allow comfortable use of language that speaks of an "emerging 'school' of theology."[1] What are the lines, or themes, or better yet "the indications," of this new and growing consensus?

THEOLOGY'S ORIENTATION: THE LIBERATION OF THE OPPRESSED

Liberation theologians insist that theology must start, not with theories and not with views from above, but with "the view from

HARVIE M. CONN, A.B., B.D., Th.M., Litt.D., is associate professor of missions and apologetics at Westminster Theological Seminary. During his twelve years of missionary service in Korea, he wrote three books in Korean, the most recent being *An Introduction to New Testament Studies* (Presbyterian General Assembly Theological Seminary, 1976). He is the author of *Contemporary World Theology* (Presbyterian and Reformed, 1973) and the editor of *Theological Perspectives on Church Growth* (Presbyterian and Reformed, 1977).

below." All theology is necessarily partisan. It starts "where the pain is,"[2] the sufferings of the excluded and oppressed. For the Latins, that oppression is defined largely in terms of socioeconomic categories; for the blacks in terms of racism. But for both, liberation theology is more than a sociological observation. It is a theological commitment to the poor and the disfranchised.

That commitment does not focus on the poor as objects of the gospel's concern. The poor become the subjects of the gospel, the artisans of a new humanity—shapers, not shaped. Theology, as it reflects on the gospel, acknowledges what Hugo Assmann calls "the epistemological privilege of the poor." "Their 'epistemology,' i.e., their way of knowing, is accurate to a degree that is impossible for those who see the world only from the vantage point of privileges they want to retain"[3] says Robert McAfee Brown. Christianity calls us to see the world from their perspective, say the liberation theologians, to experience the faith from within the history of racist or socioeconomic exploitation. No one may claim the title of theologian who is not personally and concretely identified with the oppressed in their struggles for liberation. No one may speak of salvation or redemption without speaking of it as liberation.

This identification, however, demands more than simply experiencing faith from within the context of blackness or socioeconomic nonexistence as a person. Liberation is a refusal to accept what exists, "a word of *confrontation* and *conflict.*"[4] It is a humanizing focus on the Kingdom as a gift of God, the process through which and in which a "new man" must emerge in the concreteness of history. It is a call for a new Exodus, a repetition within the life of the covenant community of divine emancipation from oppression, God's protest against injustice.

THEOLOGY'S DOMAIN: THE CONCRETE SITUATION AS CONTEXT

In this commitment of liberation theologians to "the view from below," there is a deep involvement with history's concreteness in the here and now. With the Latins, this involvement comes to expression in their protests against the abstractness of European theologizing. With the Blacks, the involvement results in protests against the whiteness of North American definitions of God-talk. "The strategy of liberation theology is to recover the meaning of God language within the context of history," says Carl Braaten.

"Any separation between the revelation of God and the history of mankind must be overcome."[5] Definitions of God that speak ontologically (ontology being the classical alliance of theology and metaphysics) must be seen as contemporary versions of Docetism, theology isolated from the reality of flesh and blood, White and Black, oppressor and oppressed, say the liberation theologians.

Salvation's history can no longer make distinctions between sacred history and secular history, the liberation theologians say. The history of salvation means the salvation of history. No split view of history can be allowed to isolate God's future from God's present. The mission of the church is to be defined in terms of history and historical struggles for liberation, they argue. Any theological model that locates the meaning and purpose of history above and beyond the concreteness of the historical now is idealistic, a relic of abstractional rhetoric. Even the eschatological dimensions within which theology seeks to function must be rooted in the present, they say. A black theology of hope "must hold within its content a promise to be redeemed within the earthly life span of those who possess such a hope and who discern such a promise."[6] Or, in the words of Gustavo Gutiérrez, "One must be extremely careful not to replace a Christianity of the Beyond with a Christianity of the Future." Eschatology is always immanent and incarnational.

Out of this sensitivity to contextual concreteness, Latin theologians speak of a political interpretation of the gospel. They are using the imagery of "politics" in a comprehensive sense to mean all that pertains to the building up of the city of man. Says Monika Hellwig:

> They are concerned to emphasize that the Christian gospel is not, and cannot be, merely a message about the saving of individuals out of the world but a message about the saving of the world—of that tangled and sinful complex of human relations which largely determines the possibilities of becoming of the individual. . . . The task of the churches is at all times to protest against injustice, to challenge what is inhuman (in the light of Jesus in whom the truly human is revealed), to side with the poor and the oppressed."[7]

It is that same holistic sense that also controls much black discussion. The call of J. Deotis Roberts, Sr., for "a black political theology" is a call for much more than political organization or government lobbying. It is a call for a balance between the quest for meaning and the protest against injustices. "Man in black theology is a being who exercises power on behalf of his authentic manhood,"[8] he says. In pursuing the humanization of life, he expounds the gospel as political.

In the face of this political character to life, the framework for the asking of theological questions changes. Traditional categories orbiting around God, revelation, sin, Christ, salvation, and the church are reshaped by the questions brought to them. Liberation theologians are asking what the meaning of our salvation is in terms of the contemporary experiences of racist and socioeconomic exploitation. Seeing the interdependence of the structures of human society and human beings, what is involved in the task of redeeming that world community?

THEOLOGY'S NEW PARTNER: THE SOCIAL SCIENCES

In the past, theological tools forged in the North Atlantic community have usually drawn on philosophy for their structure. Questions posed to them have come from philosophy: How can we believe in God in an age of science? How can we believe in the unchangeable God in a world of flux? But liberation theologians are driven to create tools from other disciplines in the face of different questions: How can we believe in God in a society that crushes the poor, that redefines the black into something less than a person? How can we believe in God as personal when everything in the world conspires against one's own personality? The demands of a concrete situation cause the liberation theologian to feel compelled to social analysis and to the disciplines of sociology, politics, economics, and modern history.

The difference between the two methods is profound enough to raise the charges of "the sociologization of theology."[9] Anthony Evans sees "the major mistake of many black theologians" as spending "more time exegeting theological systems, the black experience and black culture, than the Scriptures. Sociology does not make good biblical theology."[10]

Assmann's reply to such charges may help us to see more clearly how most of the Latin liberation theologians use the secular social disciplines. He sees behind discrediting objections like Evans's "the impossible postulate of a theology that did *not* take analysis of reality as made by the secular sciences as its starting point." Such a postulate is impossible, he continues, because it assumes a "scientific neutrality" to exegesis without awareness of the ideological presumptions behind much of our understanding. It is impossible, because the intrinsic value of experience is an essential ingredient of scientific investigation. It is impossible, because evangelization, the handmaid of theology, should be the historical articulation of love-in-practice. "In the Bible," says Assmann, "no message is valid unless it 'is made true' in practice."[11] In short, theology's concern with the concreteness of man's situation demands that the social sciences be brought into the analyzing apparatus as mediating instruments. "Through them," says Orlando Costas, "theology gains a concrete understanding of the world in which faith is lived, and, therefore, of the questions which it must respond to in order to enable Christians to test and strengthen the *efficacy* of their obedience."[12]

For the Latins much more than for the Blacks, this attention to the sociological dimensions of theology is oriented in varying degrees to the work of Karl Marx. Yet there seems to be no clear "party line" in their borrowing. Brown, following the remarks of Gregory Baum, sees three options open here. There are some who might take Marxism as an all-encompassing world view, a framework that demands total acceptance. For others, Marxism is not so much a total world view as a plan for political action. For still others, "and . . . for most of the liberation theologians we are considering—Marxism is chiefly an instrument of social analysis."[13] The Latin theologians' use of Marxism is a qualified acceptance of the Marxist analysis of socioeconomic structures without a commitment to a comprehensive anthropology. Reflected most clearly in the major work of José Miguez-Bonino, *Christians and Marxists*, this usage is a recognition that the Marxist economic analysis of the functioning of society offers the most coherent and rational account of the Latin American situation at present. And because of that, the Christian is committed to use it as a tool, the Latins say. Charity must be efficacious, and this can take place only with the best possible understanding of the causes of suffering and oppression. Marxism, they conclude, provides that understanding.

Whether black theologians will move more deeply into a similar usage in the future is still an open question. The 1977 statement of the Black Theology Project that was referred to in the preceding chapter would seem to indicate that some preliminary coordinations are being attempted in the more radical circles of black Christian thought. But so far their message seems to represent only a small minority of vocal opinion in the black theological community.[14]

THEOLOGY'S METHOD: REFLECTION ON PRAXIS

How can theology be liberated from its academic, ivory-tower imprisonment and returned to the center of the practice of the Christian faith? the liberation thinkers ask. How can theology speak concretely, not abstractly; prophetically, not speculatively; and polemically, not neutrally? The answer lies at the heart of the liberation methodology, its professed "new way" of doing theology, theology "as critical reflection on historical praxis."[15]

Praxis, a term borrowed from Marx and oriented by the Latins especially to a Marxist analysis of society, has much wider dimensions for liberation theology than its narrow origins. It is in danger of becoming a fad word. But it is as a tool of hermeneutics and not merely as a label that it has significance.

Meaning something quite different from the familiar "practice," praxis describes the circular traffic that is always going on between action and reflection—engagement in the world in transforming action. It is the never ending dialectical process, the liberation theologians explain, in which action forces me to reflection and reflection forces me to action again, "my participation in a process of seeking to transform society, . . . the means by which we attempt to work with God in building 'the new heavens and the new earth.' "[16] Through praxis, people seek not merely to understand the world but to change it. It "is the precondition of knowledge, even though in turn this knowledge issues forth into a new praxis."[17] It is engagement in the liberating process of transforming history, the insistence that Christians can think their faith only as they practice it.

Theology plays its role as "the second act," following praxis. It is the reflection on the struggle for liberation, on what goes on in the praxis situation. In "the first act," praxis, we commit ourselves to the renovation of society on behalf and alongside of the poor and the black, say the liberation thinkers. In "the second act," theology, we reflect on what transpires because of the first act and seek to bring our praxis into juxtaposition with the revelation of God in Christ. Theology then "is not a theory we impose on our life and world, to which we expect our life and our world to conform; it is our way of thinking, as Christians, about what is going on in that life and world."[18] It is that which comes from engagement and leads to renewed engagement.

What is new about this formulation? Has not reflection always been understood as a service to action? Replies Assmann, "In theory perhaps, it has, but not in practice." Traditional theological language has aimed "at establishing an absolute truth without any intrinsic connexion with practice, which is seen as something that comes later, as a consequent application of the 'truth' that precedes reality."[19] Liberation theology, through its praxis-oriented hermeneutics, insists that truth is in action. Past understandings of truth have left it in a world of its own, a world of thought reality, not of the reality that exists; the world of eternity, not of time. Now, in the words of Miguez-Bonino, we are to see that truth is constituted in actions, in fidelity to the oppressed and the God of the oppressed, in the present realization of the future's promises.[20] "Truth," writes Rubem A. Alves, "is the name given by the historical community to those actions which were, are, and will be effective for the liberation of man." There is no truth outside or beyond the concrete historical events in which men are involved as agents in the liberating process, says Alves. Truth then becomes not so much an attribute of ideas as a mark of action. Truth emerges in language that spells out the commitment and engagement of the Christian community for the liberating transformation of history.

Black theology, in its earlier stages, made little use of either the term *praxis* or the understanding of truth that lies behind it. Roberts, as late as 1974, although deeply conscious of theology as a reflection upon experience, can still speak of theology as "*reasoned* interpretation of the intellectual content of the Christian faith."[21] Willing to speak of black theology as "a theology of involvement," he still operates with distinctions that would be anathema to Latins—theology as a combination of the "inner felt" and the "outer known," "subjective experience" allied to "objective knowledge."[22] James H. Cone, in his earlier work, comes closer to a correlation. Operating from a Barthian view of revelation, he is quicker to recognize that "in the Bible revelation is inseparable from history and faith. . . . It is a religion which affirms that we know who God is by what he does in the historical events of man."[23] Cone sees faith as the community's response to God's act of liberation, saying yes to God and no to oppressors. But still truth may be isolable from its application. He comes several steps closer to the Latin view of praxis in his 1975 book, *God of the Oppressed.* In his first full dialogue with Marx, he endorses Marx's insistence "that thought has no independence from social existence" and claims, on that basis, that "theology arises out of life and thus reflects a people's struggle to create meaning in life."[24] But even here he does not seem to use this acknowledgment as a lever for a formulation of theology as praxis reflection. Again, he may be hindered by his obvious lack of dialogue with the Latin American liberationists.

The 1975 Detroit Conference on Theology in the Americas may mark a turning point in this area. The proposal drafted there is introduced as neither an "attempt to 'apply' liberation theology in North America; nor is the attempt simply to discover the 'meaning' of liberation theology in the North American situation. Rather, the goal is to contribute to a new theology that emerges from the historical, social and religious context of the North American experience."[25] The statement itself supports this in a section entitled "Theory and Practice." Faith is to be seen, it says, as "no longer simply 'applied' or 'completed' in action, but for its very understanding (and this is theology) faith demands that it be discovered in action." Using the praxis terminology, we are introduced to the distinctions of liberation theologians from Latin America: "Praxis is practice associated with a total dynamics of historical vision and social transformation. Through praxis, people enter into their historical destiny. Since praxis changes the world as well as the actors it becomes the starting point for a clearer vision of God in history." From this standpoint, the ongoing program of follow-up to the conference will proceed: "This program will explore this new way of knowing and its implications for theological reflection. Instead of talking about studying theology it seems better to begin 'doing theology'—that is, to discover the meaning of revelation in the midst of experience and the struggle for change and conversion."[26] How influential this intended shift in definition will be for the future cannot be evaluated here. The shift does indicate, however, that there is a new way of thinking in the black community that is moving in closer step with Latin methodological directions.

THEOLOGY'S MISSION: THE HERMENEUTIC OF SUSPICION AND HOPE

Theology as engagement in the world through reflection on praxis accents the missionary dimension of theology's commitment. Theology is missionary in its opposition to detachment and abstractness and in its participation in the struggle to turn the eschatological hope of heaven into a revolutionary transformation of society, the liberationists say. It expresses that missionary dimension in its hermeneutics of suspicion and hope. Hermeneutical suspicion as a tool seeks to uproot from our selective viewing of Scripture those unnamed, transplanted ideologies with which we rationalize self-interest, those ideals that support the oppressive status quo and resist change. "The idea of Christian brotherly love, for instance, in a society founded on serfdom remains an unrealizable and, in this sense, ideological idea," says Juan Luis Segundo, "even when the intended meaning is, in good faith, a motive in the conduct of the individual."[27] Ideologies, unlike utopias, help us rationalize keeping things as they are, say the liberationists, particularly when things are working for our benefit. And all of us are captive to ideologies. The task of hermeneutical suspicion is to confront those hidden ideologies and wrestle with the inhibitions against change that they leave with us. Since the God of the Bible is on the side of the poor, why are we undisturbed by the fact that we are among the nonpoor? Since the God of the Bible calls out for justice, why are we such complacent participants in economic or racial injustices? How does our white ideology inhibit us from identification with the humiliation of the Black? And does not the same ideology become an equal danger for persons in the oppressed community who achieve social and economic prosperity?

Says Frederick Herzog:

> Ideology critique theologically worked through means willingness to submit to God's reality, to let him break through in his shaping of human selfhood, even in the exegetical task. We always build up our little principalities where God cannot rule. Our scholarship is not exempt from it, although we hardly notice it. We do not seem to see most of our concealments. Liberation hermeneutic as ideology critique seeks to uncover them in acknowledgment of the principal unconcealment of the human condition in Jesus' selfhood. It is a constant attempt to remind ourselves that our humanity is determined by the Lord we serve.[28]

A hermeneutics of suspicion, in the language of Cone, does not ask simply whether theology is determined by social interest, but rather by *whose* social interest, the oppressed's or the oppressor's? "The Christian theologian, therefore," says Cone, "is one whose hermeneutical consciousness for an interpretation of the gospel is defined by the oppressed people's struggle of freedom, seeking to adhere to the delicate balance of social existence and divine revelation."[29]

The positive side of this hermeneutical circle is what Beatriz Melano Couch calls a hermeneutic of hope. Our missionary commitment to engagement for change raises suspicions about the innocence of our ideas and methods as we approach the Scriptures, Couch says. But once that has been done, "it hopes to let the text itself rephrase our own questions and rephrase our own conceptions about life and death, our own epistemology, our own knowledge of society, our ethics, politics, etc."[30] This process forms a dialectical circle as we move back and forth repeatedly between reality as it is described by the modern social sciences and reality as it is described by the Scriptures. And always that hermeneutical circle operates from a missionary dimension, not of immobilizing despair but liberating hope, God's no to the old and His yes to the new. A bias toward the poor, the doing of justice, the battle against racism, must be "the engagement" that changes our hermeneutical method from a struggle over words to a struggle against realities, say the liberationists.

SOME NEGATIVE ASSESSMENTS

This is that point in the chapter where, like the writers of the other chapters in this book, I enter into a criticism of the process I have been describing for so long. And anyone sensitized even to a slight degree should realize the risks we take here. Granting the validity of the liberationists' fear of ideological captivity hiding behind so much of our work, can there be some of that same destructive force hidden in the designation used to circumscribe our views in the preface of this book, "*conservative*, evangelical"? I admit such a possibility. Will my judgments now fall into the trap of an "objective" analysis, which ultimately is not neutral but pro-status quo and therefore anti-liberation? I admit this possibility also. Will my negative assessments evade the challenge of liberation theology in our own context by describing it in emotionally discrediting labels for the North American? To call some forms of it in some sense Marxist, even to say it merely relies on Marxist analysis, can have that effect in many circles. Perhaps the greatest danger of all will be to dispose of it by keeping it at a safe distance. The favellas of Rio de Janeiro are, after all, a long way from Los Angeles.

I can only say that it is not my desire to demean or ignore in any way the arguments of liberation theologians. I would rather call this section a dialogue than a criticism, a hermeneutical circle of self-criticism conducted in hope. I do not seek to disparage the movement by calling it a fad or dismissing it as naive. As I have done before, I set before myself and the reader the warnings of Hugo Assmann,[31] who cautions against making liberation theology a "consumer product to make up for your impotence; don't be spectators of our small achievements, nor project on Latin America an image of compensations; and finally, all of you, each in his own context, enter into the same struggle."[32] In that spirit, I have reversed the usual order of these procedures, entering my disclaimers first and closing the chapter with the challenges I have found to myself. I affirm liberation theology as a form of my own conscientization," the awakening of my own Christian conscience. After all, Watts is part of Los Angeles and Germantown is part of Philadelphia. I remember being beaten by police and pimps for evangelism in the brothels of Seoul, Korea, and pleading on behalf of lepers at the Ministry of National Affairs when the Korean bureaucracy took them off usable land. I have heard of the neighborhood rumors that flew on our block when we entertained a group of black brothers in our home. I have too long a distance to go to call myself, by any stretch of the imagination, a liberationist. But I have come too far already to wish to see its challenge diluted by verbalizations on paper at the end of a chapter. In that hermeneutical commitment of suspicion and hope, I write.

With Robert McAfee Brown, I reject much of the criticism that is being circulated now and also the spirit in which it is often carried on. Behind what Brown calls "defensive critiques" may lie too many ideologies that remain uncriticized in the name of liberation criticism—the charge of Marxism may be an unnamed defense of capitalism, and objections to "the epistemological privilege of the poor" may just cover a hidden presumption that affluence is respectable. Then, there are those criticisms that are characterized by oversimplification,[33] producing distortions or total rejections that give no indication of critical self-dialogue.[34] Much more usable

but still problematic are those analyses that generally make liberation theology follow the classical forms of systematic theology and
state their arguments in terms of soteriology, Christology,
ecclesiology, and eschatology.[35] Although liberation theologians
do offer themes that can be so clustered, their own methodology
follows their own agenda, not one imposed from outside. The concomitant dangers can be misrepresentation and exaggeration
through the imposition of outside categories. Anthropologists warn
against this in their helpful distinction between emic and etic judgments, the difference between criticism from "outside," using the
critic's categories of understanding, and criticism from "inside,"
using the distinctions of the system itself. Both are needed.

With Brown, I reject as an issue central to liberation theology
the question of violence.[36] This is not to say it is not of major
importance. It is only to insist that too frequently critics have misunderstood its role in the system. Hans Küng implies that liberation theologians engage in a "theological glorification of violence."[37] René de Visme Williamson simplistically sees the question as playing "a major role" in the discussion, with most theologians not bothering to distinguish between violence by public authority and counterviolence by private persons.[38] Such over-
simplifications ignore the complexity of the Latin arguments. Even
as early as Medellín, the distinctions Williamson claims are ignored
have been crucial. Assmann's assault on "the theology of revolution," discussed in the preceding chapter, surely is not "theological glorification of violence." Given this alleged equivalence of
liberation theology and glorification of violence, how can we call
the work of Dom Helder Camara, the Brazilian advocate of nonviolence, liberationist? What of Paulo Freire? Is their work margi-
nal to the liberation program?

This is not to say either that the ultimate formulations of many
liberationists in this area are finally agreeable. The lengthy treatment of Segundo on violence places too much emphasis on the
whip in the hand of Jesus at the Temple. His designation of God's
love in action as "the gospel of violence" leaves too many
frightening possibilities unblocked.[39] But it still remains true that it
is not violence per se that is advocated. It is rather a question of
what is being opposed—the institutionalized violence, "the first
violence" attributed to the power structure. It is the "repressive
violence" that is said to put down oppressed by oppressor that is

being repudiated. In that opposition to oppression, the "active nonviolence" of Helder Camara and the "guerrilla countervio-lence" of Camilo Torres are united.

Virtually the same patterns can be discerned in black discussions on violence and liberation, although the intrafraternity dialogue is much more pronounced. The extreme rhetoric of Albert Cleage and James Cone (in Cone's earlier work) gives their arguments a very militant tone. But still neither man "is an advocate of armed revolution against white society, but both contend that racism has already injected violence into the American scene and that the responsible black man today must be ready to defend himself and his family against the ever-present threats to the black man in a white society."[40] The Christian, in a context in which violence already exists, "does not decide between violence and nonviolence, evil and good. He decides between the less and greater evil. He must ponder whether revolutionary violence is less or more deplorable than the violence perpetuated by the sys·tem."[41]

In response to this position is the more cautious approach of Roberts, Major J. Jones, and Joseph R. Washington. Their main rationale seems to be theological. "They are persuaded that a Christian loyalty transcends the ethnic loyalty," says John J. Carey. "On the positive side, it is felt that the black experience can be the bearer of a new humanity, so that violence and revolution are not needed as instruments of social change."[42] Jesus really does have liberating power, even over violence. And if this is mirrored in the black tradition, they say, it can also become a reality for Whites.

With no desire to co-opt liberation language, to play games with liberation theology's language by transforming it into its opposite, I would suggest that all my real strictures boil down to what I feel is a basic failure of liberation theologies to be radical enough. In each of the general themes outlined in the previous section, I see a "flattening out" of the movement's call for engagement. Repeatedly I find myself thinking, *How really new is this new way to do theology?*

So, for example, we look at liberation theology's orientation, the liberation of the oppressed, a commitment to the poor. And we must ask if its concern for eliminating the line between the history of salvation and the salvation of history does not contribute to the very externalization of the gospel that it seeks to avoid. Alejandro Cussianovich is typical of many who make a close connection between the Kingdom of God and the liberation of the poor of the earth. "The Kingdom of God is revealed and concretized historically in the movement of all the poor, humiliated and despoiled who struggle for justice, freedom and love," says Cussianovich. "This is the historical project of liberation of those who are accounted the scum of the earth."[43] Does this holistic view of the Kingdom's relation to history give adequate expression to the depth of the evangelical idea of salvation? In a legitimate protest against the spiritualization of the poverty theme in the Scriptures, has liberation theology lost itself in the socioeconomic dimension of poverty? Can a one-dimensional focus on the poor as sinners or the humble be corrected by another one-dimensional focus on the poor as all the humiliated and despoiled of the earth? Herman Ridderbos strikes a more biblically balanced note when he suggests that the poor (the meek) "represent the socially oppressed, those who suffer from the power of injustice and are harassed by those who only consider their own advantage and influence. They are, however, at the same time those who remain faithful to God and expect their salvation from His kingdom alone."[44] In contrast to those who have fastened their hope upon this world, they expect the salvation that God has held out to His people as "the consolation of Israel" (Luke 2:25; cf. Matt. 5:4; Luke 6:24; 16:25). The idea is determined both socially and in a religious-ethical sense. The justice, or righteousness, they await is that kingly justice that will be brought to light one day for the salvation of the oppressed and the outcasts and that will be executed especially by the Messiah (see 2 Samuel 14:5-14; Jer. 23:6; 33:6).

This focus on the socioreligious character of the poor tends to be reduced by the liberationists to a universalizing externalization in which the emphasis is on social alienation. To be sure, one cannot forget Gutiérrez's emphasis on the ambiguity of all utopian hopes, Paulo Freire's on the temptation of the oppressed to imitate oppressors, or James Cone's on the task of black theology as analyzing the black man's condition in the light of God's revelation in Jesus Christ. *Reductionism*, for these reasons, does not quite convey the failing I am trying to point out. *Externalization* is a more adequate designation. Through this externalization, the remnant character of the "poor" loses its particular redemptive dimension and is assimilated into the wide category of "neighbor."

There are dangers in this kind of externalization, just as there are dangers in evangelical, middle-class internalization. One approach destroys the impact of the biblical message by spiritualizing "poverty" into an interior problem, the other by externalizing "poverty" into a social-class problem. One speaks too glibly of God's love without God's righteousness; the other sounds too often like God's righteousness without God's love. One dissolves the gospel's horizontal dimensions into a verticalism that touches earth's circle only at one tangential point of social amelioration. The other dissolves the gospel's vertical dimensions into a horizontalism that touches heaven's circle only at one tangential point of divine amelioration. Both make a simple identification of "God being on the side of the oppressed" with "the oppressed being on the side of God." For one, the results of that identification reduce the world's pain to a merely pietistic dimension. For liberation theology, the results of that identification reduce the world's pain to a merely social or economic dimension. Internalization by the evangelical falls too quickly into a spiritual captivity of the right; externalization falls too quickly into a socioeconomic captivity of the left.

With Brown, I agree that the question in all of this is never, *Shall* we take sides? But neither is it simply, With whom are we *already* siding and With whom *ought* we to be siding? It is, rather, With whom are we *already* siding and with whom *ought* we to be siding, and *how*? A middle-class, evangelical mentality can tranquilize our churches in the face of the suffering of our neighbors. A liberation mentality can make the depth of our concern superficial by inverting evangelism into activism. One flattens the whole gospel into a two-dimensional spiritualization. The other flattens it into a two-dimensional externalization.

A second set of difficulties arises as we analyze liberation theology's call for a new attention to the concreteness of our situation. Evangelical concerns have responded to the concreteness of that context with a monistic set of priorities, giving the salvation of souls top priority and concern for social justice only secondary and derived importance. In the face of the situation, Christ's work is seen as His activity within the church. And that activity of the church, in turn, touches larger human needs through individual activities by the individual Christian.[45] What critics like Robert

McAfee Brown miss in this kind of language is the proper concern of the evangelical that, whatever else, justice be done to the redemptive work of Jesus at Calvary as the Revealer and Accomplisher of the peace and righteousness of God. The evangelical speaks out of concern for the Kingdom as the coming of Christ in substitutionary atonement for the nations.

At the same time, what also must be seen is the way that the evangelical's biblical message is wrapped in a cultural cloak of privatization. Too often the evangelical readily admits an Old Testament focus "on concern for the oppressed and on righteous living within the group." But, operating from an ideological commitment to privatization, he may immediately add, "It does not command the establishment of justice in the world, nor the care of all the oppressed in the world. It gives no example for involvement in the rough-and-tumble of political life. It *does* show God's love for justice and holiness in personal living as well as in the community life of the theocracy."[46] Thus, theocentric social ethics are said to be directed principally to believers.

Liberation theologians place their emphasis on the neglected corporate dimension to sin and salvation. According to their unitary view of history and their assertion that persons cannot be saved minus their world, "Sin is not considered as an individual, private, or merely interior reality—asserted just enough to necessitate a 'spiritual' redemption which does not challenge the order in which we live. Sin is regarded as a social, historical fact."[47] The place to look for sin, they say, is in "oppressive structures, in the exploitation of man by man, in the domination and slavery of peoples, races and social classes,"[48] in white racism. In all of this, they are not seeking to deny the basic character of sin as rebellion against God. Rather they are looking at that root through its branches in the structures of society. It is not simply that the liberationists possess far too much hope in history. They have too much fear of those dualisms in the past that have abstracted the redemptive fruits of grace from the concrete, now world. Even the classic nature-grace formulations of Thomas Aquinas are suspected of this abstractness. Similarly, salvation, like sin, is seen as historical, social, and somatic. The good news of liberation must invade structurally the structural problems of racism, injustice, poverty, and inequality, they say.

But even as evangelical responses too frequently exhibit a

monistic privatization of the gospel, so liberation theologians may be falling into another kind of monism, a monistic "collectivization" of the gospel, an overemphasis on general human conditions to the exclusion of personal needs (I deliberately avoid the word *individual* as culturally conditioned). Says Carl Braaten:

> Liberation theology is right in broadening the concept of sin to include the social dimension, but its view nevertheless remains rather shallow. . . . Some of the richest pictures of sin in the Bible and the classical tradition are blurred in liberation theology. Sin provokes the wrath of God; it is slavery to Satan; it is a state of spiritual death; it is a disease of the whole person—a sickness unto death. It is a state of corruption so profound that the elimination of poverty, oppression, disease, racism, sexism, classism, capitalism, etc., does not alter the human condition of sinfulness in any fundamental way."[49]

This monism works to reduce the radical character of grace in the liberation theologians and to diminish theology's God-centered orientation. This does not mean that people such as Gutiérrez and Cone disbelieve in grace as a vehicle for humanization and sanctification. Nor do I charge them with a simplification of redemption into a system of social ethics. But given their unitary view of history and their fear of the church being led to a salvation of "cheap grace," is not God's role as the sole source of grace, God as the transcendent "Outside," diminished from a defining qualification to a modifying qualification? Roman Catholic theology, throughout its history, has compromised that *sola fide* message with its "grace, plus—" bypass. Within liberation thinking, is that "plus" not now being reinforced? In that connection, do not Braaten's questions become more urgent: "What is the gospel, then, prior to the end of the class conflict, or the race conflict, or the sex conflict? Is it only a goad to action? Is it only a goal to be achieved? . . . Is there a real presence of the gospel before the arrival of the final kingdom?"[50]

Related to this monistic correlation of gospel and context is another problem, that of gospel universalism. Among the black theologians, James Cone senses its impact enough to devote his 1975 book to it. In asking the question, I recognize that all theologies are contextually conditioned and that the nature of the Christian faith demands such contextualization.[51] These are not the problems I raise. In fact, these admissions may be one of the greatest contributions liberation theology leaves with us. I am simply asking if the insistence of the liberation theologians on context, controlled by the monism I have described, allows them to recognize in a full way the universal character of norm. And, more specifically, can they recognize Scripture as the key element in that universal characteristic of gospel norm? Is this question not ultimately the real one that needs to be asked by someone like Allan Boesak, himself a strong supporter of liberation thinking? Boesak thinks Cone makes his mistake in taking black theology out of the framework for liberation theology, and this has opened Cone to the danger of making his own situation the ultimate criterion for *all* theology. But this does not go deep enough. The problem is not solved by legitimating a particular issue within a liberation theology framework. The very framework of liberation theology is constructed precisely out of this particularism, this focus on a single issue. The problem is related to the ontological character of blackness that Cone insists upon. How does such an absolutizing block other legitimate contexts for liberation and destroy in the process liberation and context as a legitimate universal? Says Boesak:

> If black is simply determinative for oppression and liberation everywhere, if the only legitimate expression for liberation has to be black, does not Cone close the door to other theological expressions of liberation? Can the Latin American theologian concede that the *only* way to recognize God working in history is through the 'most radical deeds of black power'? Can, for instance, the American Indian liberation theology (God is Red!) share in this absolute claim for blackness?"[52]

Is this danger of absolutizing the particular to find a universal outside the Scripture not ultimately behind the dissensions at Detroit between black and Latin and their inability to agree on whether racist or socioeconomic factors were the crucial issues in contextualization? Does the monistic insistence on the historical situation in liberation theology ultimately make that, through the process of absolutizing, the only normative universal in the hermeneutics at stake here? And in so doing, is not even context flattened out by absolutizing into something other than a concrete?

A third area of dissent appears as we examine liberation theology's partnership with the social sciences and, more narrowly, the Latin orientation to Marxism for that social dimension. My problem here is not with the alleged "sociologization of theology."

With Assmann and others, I fear that too often such allegations are the result of uncriticized assumptions about the "scientific neutrality" of theology, an inability to see that even constructions based on the given of an inerrant Bible can be controlled by unbiblical presumptions regarding society and human relations. Evangelical apologetics displays a history of constant appeal to rationalistic models accredited with objectivity. The contributions of Cornelius Van Til in this very area need to be expanded. Van Til has declared a life-long war against any apologetic that pretends to objective neutrality. His own focus has been on showing the influence of philosophical preconceptions in theologizing. It would be entirely consistent with his systems-analysis method to add to his list of foes sociological and economic preconceptions as well.[53]

My problem, to use the language of liberationists, is rather that of the "antonomous ideologizing" that I see going on in their usage of tools from the social sciences. If the evangelical looks at social needs with the myths provided by capitalism intact, the liberationist does it with other myths equally intact. From the optimistic idealism that views economic growth as the only way out of poverty and individual initiative as the instrument for social justice, the evangelical has distorted the radical demands of the Kingdom of God toward neighbor-love, making them into reform of the status quo. From the pessimistic idealism that views class struggle as the only way out of poverty or identification with blackness as the instrument for racial justice, the liberation theologian has distorted the kingdom creation of a new community in Christ making it into revolution.[54] Both sides, inevitably, through their allegiance to ideologies, do not call so much for the church to be renewed as for the church to "switch sides."

The judgments of Andrew Kirk on Miguez-Bonino's support of Marxism are important for this very reason. Kirk himself writes as one committed to socialism as a viable Christian option for change. And his judgments on Marxism are, therefore, especially pertinent here. He sees a large part of Miguez-Bonino's writings as devoted to rejecting the notion of autonomy for the Christian faith. "But," he argues, "the same view of truth should be applied to Marxism as well."[55] Miguez-Bonino falls into the same error when he tries to protect for Marxism as a science whole areas of complete autonomy. Its historical analysis and projections for change are interrelated in such a way that they cannot be unraveled without each part losing its compelling force. Marxism's autonomy remains a Messianic ethic without a Messianic commitment. The Lordship of Christ extends to the use of ideological tools for discerning between concrete political or racist allegiances; but without this commitment, the Marxist tool runs out of steam. There is no commitment at the primary level; Marxism is an ideology without the intervention of a justifying ethic. Even a utopian ideology only leads to a *description* of processes and laws, not a *reason* for changing them or man. Even ideologies must be subjected to criticism in the light of our ultimate commitment, which is not to a theory of class struggle or race struggle but to the one true God who has unmistakably shown Himself to be the Redeemer-kinsman of the poor and the oppressed. This issue is blunted by liberation theologians when they too readily accept the definition of the human predicament offered by a class-oriented or race-oriented ideology that is self-insulated from the judgments of a sovereign God speaking in an absolutely authoritative Bible. Ideologies, even should we recognize them as a precommitment to praxis, cannot be excluded from Jesus' reach.

Gutiérrez has remarked many times that seeking for a "third way" between capitalism and socialism invariably ends up on the side of the status quo, giving implicit support to the oppressors rather than explicit support to the oppressed. And the general agreement of the black theologians on the priority of liberation over reconciliation may mirror the same concerns. It is not reconciliation but liberation that threatens the status quo. We can only recognize the legitimacy of these concerns and the paucity of evangelical reflection that contributes to this recapitulation of the past with new terminology. Sloganeering does not effect change.

At the same time, can an ideology that traces the origins of alienation to class or racist struggles be made to correspond to the biblical description of human history as divided into two ages, of mankind as divided into two humanities (those in Adam and those in Christ)? In the words of Andrew Kirk:

> Or, put another way, how can the old man, in the old age, be expected to sustain the momentum? There is no way of answering this one from a genuine Christian perspective without adopting the *entire* Christian response to the problem of inherent evil. With regard to the progression of evil, and man's ability to reverse it, the Bible presents a totally closed determinism. *Only* in active response to the

Cross and Resurrection of Jesus Christ can the progression to destruction of man without God be broken. In other words, faith has
something to say about the *total* conditions necessary for the new
man to take shape."[56]

I do not suggest that liberation theologians are unaware of this or
do not seek to implement it. I suggest that the autonomous character that they invest in their ideologies of suspicion does not allow
that acknowledgment to enter the dialogue at a crucial point.

We see this same problem of autonomy operative in praxis as
the liberation "first step" in methodology. By this I am not charging these theologians with holding to the argument that man can
undertake an arbitrary or isolated transformation of the world.
Their intent, as Miguez-Bonino puts it, is simply to assert "that
true knowledge can only be acquired starting from the concrete
actions of men, that theory has meaning only as it leads to a course
of action which proves significant and that action itself becomes
the test of theory."[57] Unlike the theories of Bultmann on "preunderstanding" and the "hermeneutical circle," praxis is not
something that takes place within the mind of the interpreter. It is a
"pre-commitment" to concrete action on behalf of the oppressed,
the dialectic of action-reflection out of which theology is born. The
idea of a liberating God and of man's participation in that liberating
work of God cannot be separated from historical situations or actions.[58]

In this "first step" of commitment, the problems emerge.
Granting that the process of liberation is a circle that returns to
itself; granting the part that our Christian involvement plays in that
circle; does it really touch significantly in a Christian way on the
first two stages of Segundo's four-stage circle? How do we decide,
for example, to commit ourselves or not to a particular social or
political program if one is going to avoid an ideology of another
sort? The only tools allowed us for the reflection part of praxis are
those provided by a Marxist analysis of social struggle. Is this an
unacknowledged ideology that merits the charge of autonomy? As
Kirk puts it:

> It is difficult to see how it would be possible, in practice, to commit
> oneself to a political position without knowing it and evaluating it
> beforehand. Even the act of commitment requires a choice, which if
> it is to be responsible, implies an *apriori* moral decision. A Christian
> especially ought to be very careful not to be deceived by carefully
> directed political propaganda, from wherever it may come.[59]

Further, it is true that the gospel must not and cannot be divorced from all political or racial commitment. It is also true that certain socioeconomic commitments come closer to certain features of the gospel than others. But whether they do has to be decided by the gospel, not by an autonomous sociological analysis, however it is constructed. The gospel does possess its own political program, based on its own analysis of the global reality of man. "Its 'ideological' pre-understanding, or hermeneutical key is that programme, totally unique in any contemporary debate, called the 'Kingdom of God,'"[60] says Kirk.

It is here that I question the ultimate propriety of constantly isolating Marxism as an instrumental tool of social analysis from Marxism as a systematic whole, Marxism as an anthropology of the Enlightenment. Even recognizing the attempts of the liberation theologians to isolate an instrumental use, Marxism as a tool still builds on a metaphysical definition of man as bearing within himself the power to subject to himself the whole of reality and to bring it under his own humanizing regime. The rooting of praxis in economic or social struggle still has its deeper roots in the Renaissance view of man as one who regenerates himself by his own powers. This is a manifestation of man's pretended autonomy in his own self-imposed world-vision. The sovereignty and majesty of a cosmic God are reduced in the hermeneutical circle to a "second stage." Liberation theology, while decrying His docetic abstraction from the concrete present, itself docetizes Him to such a role in the "pre-commitment" process.

Further, the autonomous levelling of what is distinctively Christian manifests itself in the priority given praxis as the source of truth. How does the Scripture function as norm in this definition? "Admitting the ideological conditioning of all theology," says Stephen C. Knapp, "can the Bible break through to tell us which ideology is better, yours or mine? . . . Haven't we simply transferred the verification question from biblical interpretation and theology to a 'scientific' analysis of reality?"[61] Does not the Bible function too minimally in pointing to the place where my praxis begins? As Kirk says:

> Human justice and injustice only makes sense, in the last analysis, in the light of the one who represents justice in his own person, God Himself. It is for this reason, that the 'righteousness of God' is of a different character to the formalist concept of justice, whether this

latter is intrinsic to the world (Marx) or extrinsic (Kant). Rather, it is to be seen in the light of He who is *the* new man. It includes, as a constitutive part, the free justification of the sinner through faith in the finished reconciling work of Jesus Christ (Rom. 3:21-26). In other words, practice of truth depends on the revelation of the truth. And the truth of revelation, because it depends upon God who reveals, is true independently of whether it is acted upon or not. Nevertheless, it demands a consistent practice, [and] will be judged by that practice."[62]

In the hermeneutical task of theology and its repudiation of ideologies for utopian perspective, still another flattening process must be examined. Deeply indebted to the theology of hope and its eschatological constructions for doing theology, liberation theologians, both Latin and black, have been unrelenting in their criticisms of the vagueness and abstractness of Moltmann's look at the future. Responding to criticism, Alves argues that their interest in the eschatological dimension does not evidence "a belief in the possibility of a perfect society but rather the belief in the nonnecessity of *this* imperfect order."[63] The concreteness of the present must not be dulled by the vagueness of a coming future, they say.

My concern is the opposite. Has the concreteness of the present for the liberation theologian dulled the specificity of Christian eschatology, flattening it into a mere "vagueness of an unqualified open future"?[64] Has the "already" of the new creation, won in Christ and awaiting its consummation "not yet," become simply a "now" without functioning lines of connection to "the God who is ahead, coming to us and pulling us toward Him?" Too often for too many Blacks, eschatology has functioned as an escape from history. Does it not now face the danger of functioning as an escape from God's future? If hope emerges only out of the present and our liberating participation in it, what will happen to the quickening power of an ultimate future Kingdom that calls us to seek here and now the doing of the Father's will as it is done in heaven (2 Pet. 3:11-13)? Liberation theology faces the danger of reducing eschatology to ethics, a danger as real as the evangelical danger of reducing eschatology to second coming diagrams and schemata hung on the front church wall. Braaten's charges need to be dealt with:

> The kingdom of God is removed to the future as a goal to be attained by the right kind of ethical action. The gospel is not thought of as a

reality in our history, prior to human action, present in the person and ministry of Jesus Christ. Whether we speak of the gospel of justification or the gospel of the kingdom of God, neither the works of personal righteousness nor the works of political liberation avail in building a staircase to heaven.[65]

The eschatological source of ethics and the ethical praxis of eschatology should not be left marooned the one without the other. Without that concrete eschatological dimension, will the concrete now lead us into new captivities? Can Cone guarantee that, isolated from the reality and anchor of Christian eschatology, his theology will not become a justification for a black bourgeoisie, indeed, a servant to it? Can we truly break away from the old now if we have no ties with the eschatological "not yet" that demands that radical transformation from us?

SOME AFFIRMATIONS

The chapter cannot be closed here, for liberation theologies are not simply threats to our faith. They are also threats—better yet, challenges—to our own hidden ideologies as conservative evangelicals. How can they serve to help refine our commitment to the gospel and all that our commitment requires? I do not suggest a heralding of Gutiérrez as our Wesley or Miguez-Bonino as our new Calvin. I ask, What do we learn from all this about ourselves and where we must go in the future? If liberation theologies can be described as arising because of the "unpaid bills of the church," what bills should we pay first?

I must begin by endorsing the need for a theology with a truly universal orientation. Our theologies have been formed out of the affluent white world, and they display that ideology. The myths of affluence, ethnocentrism, and expertise, have allowed us to categorize our results as just plain "theology" but the work of Cone and Roberts as *black* theology. The biblical concept of the Gentiles as those "outside the special revelation of God" has been ideologically transposed by us into the geographical myth of those "non-Whites in and outside the United States." The biblical demands of love-in-deed have been idealized by us into the middle class myth of sentimental love, love-in-word, love that does not take sides except in favor of the status quo.[66] The delay of the final consummation of God's justice at the return of Christ does not mean justice denied in the "already." The saints of God must still plead from under the altar, "How long, O Lord" (Rev. 6:9-10)? Those who one day will judge the nations (1 Cor. 6:2) must begin now their judgments of the inhumanity of the world's Ammons (Amos 1:13), the deportation laws of our Tyres (Amos 1:9), and the violence of our Edoms (Obad. 10). The church is not to be the launching pad for guerrilla operations, but neither is it to be the retreat where the pious await the parousia. Our warfare of suffering cares for the poor and the distressed. Our remembering of the prisoners is not simply a mental exercise, fulfilled by pious analogy, but a revolutionary call to prayer and ministry (Heb. 13:3). Peacemakers of the Kingdom, like good Samaritans of today, can suffer by intervention. But in suffering we are perfected. It takes the weak to deliver the strong (1 Cor. 1:27-28).

How will we achieve that universalization of the gospel in North America? We will do it by identifying with the poor and the oppressed. The language is, no doubt, threatening and ominous to many. It sounds Marxist, overbalanced, extreme, and judgmental. And, judging by the way it is often used by liberation theologians, those fears may be justified. But the thought of identifying with the oppressed need not be threatening. I seek to reflect only the language of Proverbs: "He who is kind to the poor lends to the LORD (Prov. 19:17, RSV). Or, putting it negatively, "He who oppresses a poor man insults his maker" (Prov. 14:31, RSV). I ask for no return to an Old Testament theocracy, although we should remember God's legislative concern for the oppressed in that theocracy and for the "resident alien" in Israel.[67] The mark of our covenant solidarity with God still stands. Pure and genuine religion still remains not merely keeping oneself from being corrupted by the world but also taking care of orphans and widows in their suffering (James 1:27). The Lord still requires us "to do justice, and to love kindness, and to walk humbly with [our] God" (Mic. 6:8).

Why should we identify with the poor and oppressed? Because Jesus did. In His virgin birth, His life as a refugee (Matt. 2:13-15), and then as an immigrant in Galilee (Matt 2:19-23); in His homelessness (Matt. 8:20), and dependence on charity from others; and in the shame of death's nakedness and the borrowing of an empty tomb from a rich man, He identified with the poor. His work of substitutionary atonement as the Son of God was done out of His conscious fulfillment of the Messiah's role as the suffering slave (Isa. 53), the tormented, poor Remnant of the Lord (Psalm 22). His allegiance to the poor marked His preaching and was a sign of the coming of the Messianic kingdom (Luke 4:18-21). His healing of the sick and the blind and His preaching to the poor became a validation of His Messianic claim to a doubting John the Baptist (Matt. 11:2-6). Paul can summarize His redemptive work in terms of that identification: "Though he was rich, yet for your sake he became poor" (2 Cor. 8:9, RSV).

Why should we identify with the poor and oppressed? It is the kingdom mark of those who identify with Jesus in His death and resurrection. The soldiers of the Kingdom conquer without purses or money (Luke 9:3; 10:4). Membership in the social service of the Kingdom is certified by an identification card that reads, "I was hungry and you gave me food, I was thirsty and you gave me drink... I was naked and you clothed me" (Matt. 25:35-36, RSV; see also vv. 37-40). The mark of the breaking down of walls between Jew and Gentile in the Kingdom becomes an offering gathered by Paul and his Gentile cohorts for the poor of Jerusalem (Gal. 2:9-10).[68] Faith without food shared and clothing given to cover the nakedness of a brother is "dead, being by itself" (James 2:14-17, NASB).

How these kingdom realities should be fleshed out in the life of the community is a question we must constantly ask in each *kairos* (moment of opportunity *or* time) of God. Our failure to take the risk of asking the question involves the risk of losing the genius of the Kingdom itself. "Conscientization" demands commitment, an act of solidarity with God that must create social ripples in the name of Christ the Lord.

From the liberation theologians comes also a renewing reminder that theology's domain must continue to be the context of our concrete situation. Ecclesiocentrism is theology's barrier, not its birthplace. To coin a word, *cosmocentrism* must be the domain of theology, theology functioning in the life of the church as the application of Scripture to all areas of human life and to all the ethnic diversities in which that life is expressed. We must take more seriously the challenge offered us by John Frame, who notes, "We do not know what Scripture says until we know how it relates to our world."[69] Interpretation and application are not two questions but one. And they are fused by the knowledge that to ask what Scripture says, or what it means, is always to ask a question about application.

Theology, by its very nature, is a contextual reflection, the whole life of the church caught up in the mission of God to His world. Says Orlando Costas:

> Since God's redemptive mission is oriented toward men and women in their multiple life situations, the communication of the gospel needs to be a social yet personal event. It needs to be addressed to mankind as a whole, in the totality of its historical situation, and to men and women as particular historical beings, i.e., as persons. This means: communication to all of society and to each one of its members.[70]

Externally, there must be denunciation and annunciation at the level of society's tensions and conflicts, uncertainties and hopes, failures and achievements. Internally, suspicion and hope must function in the church herself as theology confronts her organic development, her growth in the faith and in suffering service for the world, the quality of her Christian stewardship, and her self-understanding.

It is not enough to say that theology is "good" theology if it is biblically rooted. It must be that, of course. But that is only part of the process. Our exegesis, our sensitivity to the history of doctrine in the past, our understanding of the history of the church's wrestling with similar problems, must be gripped by the implications of Martin Luther's statement, "If you preach the Gospel in all aspects with the exception of the issues which deal specifically with your time, you are not preaching the Gospel at all."[71] Our model for doing theology can no longer be held captive by the same ideology of objectivism that Walter Wink sees as the bankruptcy behind the classic pattern of historico-grammatical exegesis: "By detaching the text from the stream of my existence, biblical criticism has hurled it into the abyss of an objectified past."[72] I cannot agree with Wink that the answer is a psychoanalytic approach to the text. But I find that his charges hurt my evangelical model of exegesis and theology as much as the liberal one he had in mind. Liberation theologies urge the point on me again. Has the classical model of objective exegesis pulled me away from the missiological challenge that the concrete reality of the poor presents to the world Christian rather than "conscientizing" me toward it? Do I have still more to learn from John Calvin and his methodology of *theologia pietatis*, a method that offered our world a way of doing theology radically different from the way of J. B. Lightfoot, B. F.

Westcott, and F. F. Bruce? What did Karl Barth see in Calvin's method when, in the preface to the second edition of his commentary on Romans (1921), he notes, "How energetically Calvin, having first established what stands in the text, sets himself to re-think the whole material and to wrestle with it, till the wall which separates the sixteenth century from the first becomes transparent! Paul speaks, and the man of the sixteenth century hears." I have no desire to cling to the existentialist model Barth saw as the Pauline counterpart for the twentieth century. But I no longer desire either to cling to the crypto-rationalist model of "objective" exegesis that makes our response as images of God to the world's poor an accountability primarily to "the guild of biblical scholars."[73]

With liberation theologians, I affirm also the need for new input from sociology, economics, and politics in the doing of theology and missions. To confess the concreteness of the gospel's domain is to take on obligations far more wide-ranging than we can fulfill simply by sharing four spiritual laws on a street in Nairobi or witnessing to a Black Muslim in Philadelphia. Even that simple witnessing is no longer quite so simple. How will a Black Muslim respond to our whiteness telling him, "God loves you and has a wonderful plan for your life"? Will he remember ten to twenty million Africans being captured for the slave trade? Will he remember the slave catechisms that were created by white masters to "christianize" their slaves? According to Cone, the catechisms went something like this: "Q. What did God make you for? A. To make a crop. Q. What is the meaning of 'Thou shalt not commit adultery'? A. To serve our heavenly Father, and our earthly master, obey our overseer, and not steal anything."[74] Is not the Black Muslim's very problem with the gospel that affirmation we make to him on the street corner? Theodicy is his problem, not the answer. No distortion of the gospel is intended by that testimony. But the black context does distort it. The "simple gospel" is never simple.

Even if we discard the superficialities of those liberationists who come close to flattening everything into social or economic questions, how can we neglect those social and economic dimensions? Does the failure of the "social gospel" in our past not call us to the proclamation of a gospel that is genuinely gospel and yet social in its pastoral orientation? Must we not confess as well:

Traditionally Latin American Christianity has been dominated by a mentality oriented toward the justification of the *status quo*. The faithful have been taught to separate reconciliation from the domain of justice. The rich have been permitted to 'give to the Lord' with one hand and exploit the poor with the other. The poor have been taught to accept their poverty and exploitation passively. The weak have been encouraged to be politically passive while the strong have been supported in their political aggressiveness.[75]

From where were these lessons learned, these models gotten? Did they not come in part from a missionary theology that was too deeply impressed by middle-class, pietist ideologies to see that the gospel had something to say about all of life under the crown rights of the King? Did not a notion of spirituality without discipleship in the daily social, economic, and political aspects of life mold a docetic passivism? Must we not begin again with a new sensitivity to the effects that social patterns and economic movements have on the giving and receiving of the gospel? Can we continue to isolate our missionary theology from a "theology of enough"?[76]

What are the implications of the Pauline call for "moderation" as the life-style of those who believe the Lord is near (Phil. 4:5, KJV)? Can a theology of mission emerge again from a sense of covenant accountability for the whole of creation under Christ (2 Cor. 7:2; 1 Tim. 3:3)? Should not the tyranny of self-assertion in the face of black agonies and oppressive poverty be swallowed up in the awareness that the new day of the Kingdom has come in Christ and that life must now start to manifest the beginnings of the wholeness of the restoration work of the Spirit, a work to be consummated at glory? What significance is there in Paul's identification with the poor as a confirmation of his apostolic ministry (1 Cor. 4:3-13)?

Liberation theologies also demand something from the nonpoor, what Marie Augusta Neal calls "a socio-theology of letting go." Repentance for racism and oppression must bear personal and structural "fruits worthy of repentance" (Luke 3:8, KJV), one coat for the poor if we have two, food for the hungry, and gentleness in place of brutality and exploitation. "A theology of liberation without a theology of relinquishment cannot touch us where we live and work," she says, "and so can change neither our lives nor the world in which we struggle."[77] For the nonpoor we need a theology not so much of liberation as of diminishment, of letting go. In our personal life styles, in the corporate perspectives of society, we show our solidarity with Christ in our solidarity with the poor, an army of Zacchaeuses following Jesus (Matt. 19:24; Luke 12:15-21). God's love in Christ does not abide in hearts closed to hungry brothers (1 John 3:17-18), pocktbooks closed to the poor (Matt. 19:16-22), or eyes closed to the "wrong-color" Nazareths of the world (John 1:46).

That process of diminishing, of letting go, must be the accomplishment of a new methodology for theology, theology as covenant praxis. Unlike liberation theologies and their praxis model, this one does not isolate theology as a "second step" after reflection on praxis, the "first step." Theology's mission is not a mere analytical or evaluative task, not a set of principles to be applied in specific situations. "It is rather a reflection that takes place in the concrete missionary situation, as part of the church's missionary obedience to and participation in God's mission," says Orlando Costas, "and is itself actualized in that situation."[78]

Theology, in this sense, can never be "objective." It is created out of covenant commitment to the covenant God. And that commitment is always more than propositional affirmation. The God who calls to Abram and his descendants, "I will be their God" (Gen. 17:8, KJV), makes demands that are essential to that covenant: "Now as for you, you shall keep My covenant" (Gen. 17:9, NASB). Sovereign grace bestowed creates reciprocal responses of faith, love, and obedience. In creating a response, grace testifies to divine initiation. That the response created is reciprocal testifies to the human obligation involved. In faithfulness to His covenant He liberated His people from Egypt (Exod. 6:7). And in faithfulness to the covenant the people of God must express their nature as "a kingdom of priests and a holy nation" (Exod. 19:6, NASB; see also 1 Pet. 2:9). Keeping covenant is exemplified in the doing of the covenant Giver's will. It is a call not to reflection on praxis but to reflective commitment in praxis.

Too often in the past and present, theology has lost this praxeological dimension. It has become known as an abstract discipline, not a "conscientizing" instrument, an aid for understanding some Pauline theology of the poor and not ours. Brevard Childs reminds us of its failure in precisely this area in the past.[79] Even the eschatological "now" of our stance between the "already" of Christ's first coming and the "not yet" of His second coming can be manipulated to separate the history of redemption from our place in it with Peter, Paul, and John (1 Cor. 10:11). If theology is to be biblical theology, it ends, not simply in the self-reassurance of an exegetical job well done, but in the reappraisal of those demands and solutions we originally brought to it at the initiation of our participation in the "hermeneutical spiral." In the language of Childs, "Each new generation standing in its particular moment of history searches the Scriptures in order to discern the will of God, and strives to receive guidance toward the obedient life that must be pursued within concrete issues of the world."[80]

Theology as praxis has not performed its task until it makes me ask again, in the face of my wealth and whiteness, *Who is my neighbor?* Has Amos's call for a tidal wave of justice (Amos 5:24) sent me in commitment to covenant into New York's inner city with a word of good news from God to those who prostitute themselves on Forty-second Street and Wall Street? Will James's remarkable declaration of the materially poor as the special objects of divine favor say to me, "The rich must live more simply so that the poor may simply live"? Will the Pauline exaltation of the "new man" formed out of Black and White, Gentile and Jew, open my eyes to the sinfulness of the suburban captivity of the white church and the ghetto captivity of the black? Will the psalmist's call to God not to "forget the life of Thine afflicted forever" (Psalm 74:19, NASB) be docetized into the same kind of protest against human activity that deflated William Carey's appeal for missions? Will someone say to our twentieth-century Carey, "If God wants to aid the poor, He'll do it in His own time and manner, and He doesn't need us to carry out His purposes"? Must the good Samaritan attack only the consequences of injustice, or may he also prevent the causes?

I am not arguing for the application of good theology, as if commitment could be divided into a two-step program of theory and practice. The effect of that compartmentalization may well be the creation of a pseudoautonomy for theology. I am arguing that *truth* is that word given by God in faithfulness to His covenant and lived out by man as a demand of covenant faithfulness. Frequently it is the divine nature of that truth that the Scriptures emphasize. Thus Paul can use the term *truth* to describe the deposit that he calls "the mysteries of God" (1 Cor. 4:1), the "tradition" he had "received" (1 Cor. 15:3; Gal. 1:12). But because it is covenant truth, it demands covenant response if it is to be given substance. And, focusing on this dimension, Paul can exhort us "to prove what the will of God is" by "the living and holy sacrifice" of our lives (Rom. 12:1-2, NASB), truth lived out in obedience before God in the contexts of the world's cultures. His exhortation to Titus to pursue "sound doctrine" (Titus 1:9) becomes not simply the suggestion of an academic exercise or even the cognitive creation of a heresy chart but, in terms of the passage, the expression of covenant faithfulness in a God-centered way of living (Titus 1:6-9; 2:1-8), a repentance "leading to the knowledge of the truth" (2 Tim. 2:25, NASB). By our walk we "do not the truth" (1 John 1:6, KJV). Thus, the traditional evangelical viewpoint on theology rightly confesses that "without the norm of Scripture (canon), the Christian faith runs the risk of losing itself" in the concrete situation.[81] And this new dimension of theology as praxis adds that without the concrete situation and our covenant response in it, the Christian faith runs the risk of losing itself in cultural irrelevancy, or ethnocentric passivism.

Neither must we see in this new way of doing theology some verbal manipulation that sees *praxis* as simply one more faddish word for "practice." It is reflection as well as action. It calls on us to be "letter[s] . . . known and read by all men" (2 Cor. 3:2, NASB). But it is always a call that recognizes that the only autonomy is in the sovereign God and His Word. It is the written Word of the covenant God that speaks to us and our world "for teaching, for repoof, for correction, for training in righteousness" (2 Tim. 3:16, NASB). Regardless of Miguez-Bonino's fears, our reflection is always from the Bible, God's "enshrined absolute truth." Covenant "conscientization" must have its covenant witness, whether tablets of stone or covenant word entrusted to the hands of good and faithful men who will be able to teach (2 Tim. 2:2). Theology as praxis forbids us to be in bondage to pragmatism in covenant practice without the covenant Word or to be in bondage to abstractness in the covenant Word without covenant practice.

Ultimately, then, all these elements combine to underline the missionary calling of theology. And that is a calling that is seldom articulated in academic halls or meetings of the women's missionary society. In our evangelical churches, missions functions in an exotic, back-room fashion, its perspectives on the frontier-crossing nature of the gospel emerging once a year at the annual missionary conference or with the pastor's Sunday morning prayer, "Lord, bless the missionaries." Missions is abstracted from theology by the ideology of American pragmatism and isolated into the domain of the non-North American by the geographical myth of "the religious significance of salt water." This confining of missions to other parts of the world releases us from the pain of searching for the Auca Indians of New Jersey or Montana. To use Freire's language, missions is domesticated through a "banking" concept in which we as leaders instruct *them* as learners. The consciousness-raising principle of Chinese missionary John L. Nevius, *every* believer a learner as well as a teacher, is reduced by the ideological distinctions of sending church-receiving church into us-them distinctions that Third-World churchmen now call alienating, dominating, repressive, and depersonalizing.

The opposite side appears in the theological seminaries and professional theology textbooks. There theology is abstracted from the world into isolated loci. And its learners are given a model of "using" theology that too often inhibits them from "doing" theology. Anthropology is reduced to the cognitive process of learning the history of dogma in propositional form, isolated from the personal and social demands of humanization. Ecclesiology reduces the world boundaries of the mission of God's people to church limits and effectively restricts the global, social concerns of the Word of God to questions of what the church cannot do instead of what it can do. Our models of teaching theology leave us with a message from Christ to the world that is seen as something old that needs to be protected, an ideological vision of the church as a museum used to house some treasured antiques. The gospel loses its missionary vitality, its morning-news freshness, and begins to resemble a bag of old laws and doctrines. Dynamite becomes saccharin in the world's stained coffee cups. Theology without its missionary dimension captivates rather than liberates.

Without this missionary dimension of theology, ideology critique loses its force and becomes ideology reinforcement. Hermeneutics returns to its traditional choices, the intuitive or the scientific approaches. The former studies the text "without any awareness that the writer's cultural context differs from the reader's," interpreting the text as if it had been written in the reader's own language, culture, and time. The latter, through the grammatico-historical method, recognizes that God spoke His Word to a particular people in a particular context and time, and it seeks to uncover that *kairos*. Both are destructive of the missionary dimension that needs restoration. The intuitive runs the risk of missing the real meaning God intends, substituting for it one that is ideologically conditioned by the subjective. The scientific fails to consider what Scripture may be saying to the contemporary reader, substituting for it the ideological captivity of objectivity.[82] Both approaches, if they go no further, are unable to create meaningful dialogue between the past and the present—the one because it hermetically seals off the past, the other because it seals off the present.

There is a third way to approach hermeneutics, what René Padilla calls the "contextual approach."[83] Combining the best of both "popular" and "historical" methodologies, it goes further than either. Taking seriously both the cultural contexts of the biblical text and the contemporary readers, it calls for a dialogue between the two, a dynamic interplay between text and interpreters. From the "historical" it builds on the need to study the original context and language, paying careful attention not only to the words of the text but to reading between the lines. From the "popular" it stresses the necessity of listening to God's Word in our own context and obeying it. The result is what may be called a "hermeneutical spiral," through interplay a continuous deepening of our knowledge of God in our response to His will. The imagery of a circle does not do full justice to the deepening aspect of this process, and so I choose the term *spiral*.

The process begins with a faith-commitment to living in covenant with the sovereign God in His world and in His Word. In a constant covenant dialectic of action and reflection, the spiral grows as the man of faith comes to the Scripture with an awareness of concerns flowing from his cultural and social background, his personal situation, and his acknowledged responsibility to love his neighbor as himself. These concerns will influence the questions that are put to the Scriptures as our covenant witness. What is received back, however, will not be answers only, but more questions as well. "As we address Scripture," says the Willowbank Report, "Scripture addresses us. We find that our culturally conditioned presuppositions are being challenged and our questions corrected. In fact, we are compelled to reformulate our previous questions and to ask fresh ones. So the living interaction proceeds."[84] The spiral grows out of our commitment in faith and corrects that commitment as we proceed. Ideologies are constantly questioned in the process, and we find increasingly that there are no "out of bounds" for the mission of the people of God. The more we know, the more we are called on to respond obediently. And this is because the more we obey, the more He makes Himself known.

Unless our interaction with liberation theologies takes us in this positive, growing direction, all the well-articulated criticisms we may offer are "sounding brass and tinkling cymbals." The Gutiérrezes and the Cones will still say of us, "Poor, talkative little evangelicals."

Notes

1. Monika Hellwig, "Liberation Theology: An Emerging School," *Scottish Journal of Theology* 30, no. 2 (1977): 141.
2. Frederick Herzog, *Liberation Theology* (New York: Seabury, 1972), p. 258.
3. Robert McAfee Brown, *Theology in a New Key: Responding to Liberation Themes* (Philadelphia: Westminster, 1978), p. 61.
4. Hugo Assmann, *Practical Theology of Liberation* (London: Search, 1975), p. 47.
5. Carl Braaten, *The Flaming Center* (Philadelphia: Fortress, 1977), p. 145.
6. Major J. Jones, *Black Awareness: A Theology of Hope* (Nashville: Abingdon, 1971), p. 16.
7. Hellwig, p. 142.
8. J. Deotis Roberts, Sr., *A Black Political Theology* (Philadelphia: Westminster, 1974), p. 94.
9. Assmann, *Practical Theology of Liberation*, p. 63.
10. Anthony T. Evans, *Biblical Theology and the Black Experience* (Dallas: Black Evang. Enter., 1977), p. 12.
11. Assmann, *Practical Theology of Liberation*, pp. 63-64.
12. Orlando Costas, "Liberation Theology: A Solution?," *The Mennonite* 93, no. 27 (July 11, 1978): 434.
13. Brown, p. 66.
14. A more representative reading of the Latin American interaction with Marxism oriented to the black community can be found in Osmundo Afonso Miranda, "Aspects of Latin American Revolutionary Theologies," *Journal of the Interdenominational Theological Center* 5, no. 1 (Fall 1977): 1-22.
15. Gustavo Gutiérrez, *A Theology of Liberation*, trans. Caridad Inda, Sr., and John Eagleson (Maryknoll, N.Y.: Orbis, 1973), p. 15.
16. Brown, pp. 71-72.
17. Gregory Baum, "The Christian Left at Detroit," *The Ecumenist* 13, no. 6 (September-October 1975): 85.
18. Brown, p. 72.
19. Assmann, *Practical Theology of Liberation*, p. 75.
20. José Miguez-Bonino, *Doing Theology in a Revolutionary Situation*, ed. William H. Lazareth (Philadelphia: Fortress, 1975), p. 88.
21. Roberts, Sr., p. 9.
22. James J. Gardiner and J. Deotis Roberts, Sr.,eds., *Quest for a Black Theology* (Philadelphia: Pilgrim, 1970), p. 81.
23. James H. Cone, *A Black Theology of Liberation* (Philadelphia: Lippincott, 1970), p. 93.
24. James H. Cone, *God of the Oppressed* (New York: Seabury, 1975), pp. 42-43. Compare p. 52.

25. Sergio Torres and John Eagleson, eds., *Theology in the Americas* (Maryknoll, N.Y.: Orbis, 1976), p. 431.
26. Ibid., p. 435.
27. Juan Luis Segundo, *The Liberation of Theology*, trans. John Drury (Maryknoll, N.Y.: Orbis, 1976), p. 100. Allan Boesak, in *Farewell to Innocence* (Kampen, Netherlands: Kok, 1976), pp. 80-83, discusses ideology criticism in the black community.
28. Frederick Herzog, "Liberation Hermeneutic as Ideology Critique?," *Interpretation* 28, no. 4 (October 1974), 402-3.
29. Cone, *God of the Oppressed*, p. 98.
30. Torres and Eagleson, p. 306.
31. Carl E. Armerding, ed., *Evangelicals and Liberation* (Nutley, N. J.: Presby. and Ref., 1977), pp. 60-62.
32. Hugo Assmann, "Basic Aspects of Theological Reflection in Latin America: A Critical Evaluation of the 'Theology of Liberation,' " *Risk* 9, no. 2 (1973): 28.
33. Under this category, Brown, on pages 107-9, deals with the judgments of people like Michael Novak and David Tracy. I fear now that my own earlier essay, appearing in *Teología contemporanea en el Mundo* (Grand Rapids: Subcomisión Literatura Cristiana de la Iglesia Cristiana Reformada, n.d.), pp. 80-89, may merit the same judgment. The demands of the book's format and what I still regard as a proper desire to warn against improper defects may have caused distortions that are unfair.
34. C. Peter Wagner's *Latin American Theology* (Grand Rapids: Eerdmans, 1970) is the clearest example to me of this kind of distortion. Segundo subjects it to serious criticism in *The Liberation of Theology*, pp. 134-38. Note also the strong reaction to it from a shared evangelical perspective in C. René Padilla's full analysis, "A Steep Climb Ahead for Theology in Latin America," *Evangelical Missions Quarterly* 7, no. 2 (Winter 1971): 99-106. At the same time, Brown concedes that Wagner "spells out forthrightly the criticism that certain Roman Catholic ecclesiastical authorities have more covertly launched" (p. 105). In this same category I place the recently translated work by Juan Gutiérrez González, *The New Libertarian Gospel* (Chicago: Franciscan Herald, 1977).
35. I make this judgment, with modifications, of the extremely helpful criticism of Orlando Costas in his fine book, *The Church and Its Mission: A Shattering Critique from the Third World* (Wheaton: Tyndale, 1974), pp. 250-63.
36. Brown, p. 110.
37. Hans Küng, *On Being a Christian* (New York: Doubleday, 1976), p. 570.
38. René de Visme Williamson, "The Theology of Liberation," *Christianity Today* 19, no. 22 (August 8, 1975): 10.
39. Segundo, pp. 156-65.
40. John J. Carey, "Black Theology: An Appraisal of the Internal and External Issues," *Theological Studies* 33 (1972): 692.
41. James H. Cone, *Black Theology and Black Power* (New York: Seabury, 1969), p. 143.
42. Carey, p. 693. Compare Joseph A. Johnson, Jr., "Jesus the Liberator," in Gardiner and Roberts, Sr., pp. 104-11.
43. Quoted in Brown, p. 115.
44. Herman Ridderbos, *The Coming of the Kingdom* (Philadelphia: Presby. and Ref., 1962), p. 188.
45. Good examples of this kind of approach are found in Wagner, pp. 23-32.
46. Charles C. Ryrie, "Old Testament Perspectives on Social Ethics," *Bibliotheca Sacra* 134, no. 534 (April-June 1977): 122.
47. Gutiérrez, p. 175.
48. Ibid.
49. Braaten, p. 155.
50. Ibid., p. 152.

51. I have tried to expand these same arguments in my essay, "Contextualization: A New Dimension For Cross-Cultural Hermeneutic," *Evangelical Missions Quarterly* 14, no. 1 (January 1978): 39-46.

52. Sergio Torres and Virginia Fabella, eds., *The Emergent Gospel: Theology from the Underside of History* (Maryknoll, N.Y.: Orbis, 1978), p. 88.

53. Some helpful beginnings of an analysis of sociology with clearly Christian characteristics are made by David Lyon in *Christianity and Sociology* (Downers Grove: Inter-Varsity, 1976).

54. C. René Padilla, "God's Word and Man's Myths," *Themelios* 3, no. 1 (September 1977): 3-9.

55. J. Andrew Kirk, "Beyond Capitalism and Marxism: Dialogue with a Dialogue," *Theological Fraternity Bulletin*, no. 1-2 (1976): 36.

56. Ibid., p. 34.

57. José Miguez-Bonino, *Christians and Marxists: The Mutual Challenge to Revolution* (Grand Rapids: Eerdmans, 1976), p. 93.

58. Steven G. Mackie, "Praxis as the Context for Interpretation," *Journal of Theology for Southern Africa* no. 24 (September 1978): 37-40.

59. Andrew Kirk, "The Meaning of Man in the Debate Between Christianity and Marxism," *Theological Fraternity Bulletin* no. 2 (1974): 19.

60. Ibid., p. 20.

61. Armerding, p. 25.

62. Kirk, "The Meaning of Man," p. 19.

63. Rubem A. Alves, "Christian Realism: Ideology of the Establishment," *Christianity and Crisis* 33, no. 15 (September 17, 1973) 175.

64. Costas, *The Church and Its Mission*, p. 260.

65. Braaten, pp. 300-301.

66. An amplification of this theme will be found in my essay, "The Church's Mission to All the Lost," scheduled for immediate publication in *The Reformed Review* (Spring 1979).

67. For a survey of these Old Testament perspectives, consult Ronald J. Sider, *Rich Christians in an Age of Hunger* (Downers Grove: Inter-Varsity, 1977), pp. 60-85. Also compare my chapter, "Christ and the City," in the work edited by Roger Greenway, *Discipling the City* (Grand Rapids: Baker, 1979), pp. 222-86.

68. See Keith F. Nickle, *The Collection. Studies in Biblical Theology No. 48* (Naperville, Ill.: Allenson, 1966); Harvie M. Conn, "The Money Barrier Between Sending and Receiving Churches," *Evangelical Missions Quarterly* 14, no. 4 (October 1978): 236-37.

69. John M. Frame, *Van Til: The Theologian* (Harmony, N.J.: Pilgrim, 1976), p. 25.

70. Orlando Costas, *Theology of the Crossroads in Contemporary Latin America* (Amsterdam: Rodopi, 1976), p. 9.

71. Sider, p. 58.

72. Walter Wink, *The Bible in Human Transformation* (Philadelphia: Fortress, 1973), p. 4.

73. See David C. Jones, "Who Are the Poor?," *RES Theological Forum* 6, no. 1 (February 1978): 1-11, and my reaction (Ibid., pp. 19-23).

74. Quoted in James H. Cone, *The Spirituals and the Blues* (New York: Seabury, 1972), p. 23.

75. Costas, *Theology of the Crossroads*, p. 342.

76. John V. Taylor, *Enough Is Enough* (London: SCM, 1975), pp. 40-62.

77. Marie Augusta Neal, *A Socio-Theology of Letting Go: The Role of a First World Church Facing Third World Peoples* (New York: Paulist, 1977), p. 2.

78. Costas, *Theology of the Crossroads*, p. 8.

79. Brevard Childs, *Biblical Theology in Crisis* (Philadelphia: Westminster, 1970), pp. 123-38.

80. Ibid., p. 131.
81. Costas, *The Church and Its Mission*, p. 252.
82. *The Willowbank Report–Gospel and Culture* (Wheaton: Lausanne Comm. for World Evang., 1978), pp. 10-11.
83. C. René Padilla, "Hermeneutics and Culture" (Paper read at the Willowbank Consultation on the Gospel and Culture, sponsored by the Lausanne Committee, 1978), p. 5. Publication is forthcoming from the William Carey Library, Pasadena, California.
84. *Willowbank Report*, p. 11.

Selected Reading

Anderson, Gerald H., and Stransky, Thomas, eds. *Mission Trends No. 3*. New York: Paulist; Grand Rapids: Eerdmans, 1976.

Armerding, Carl E., ed. *Evangelicals and Liberation*. Nutley, N.J.: Presby. and Ref. 1977.

Assmann, Hugo. *Practical Theology of Liberation*. London: Search, 1975.

Bennett, Lerone, Jr. *Before the Mayflower*. Baltimore: Penguin, 1962.

Boesak, Allan. *Farewell to Innocence*. Kampen, Netherlands: Kok, 1976.

Boff, Leonardo. *Jesus Christ Liberator: A Critical Christology for Our Time*. Trans. Patrick Hughes. Maryknoll, N.Y.: Orbis, 1978.

Brown, Robert McAfee. *Theology in a New Key: Responding to Liberation Themes*. Philadelphia: Westminster, 1978.

Carey, John J. "Black Theology: An Appraisal of the Internal and External Issues." *Theological Studies* 33 (1972): 684-97.

Cleage, Albert. *The Black Messiah*. New York: Sheed and Ward, 1968.

Cone, James H. *Black Theology and Black Power*. New York: Seabury, 1969.

———. *A Black Theology of Liberation*. Philadelphia: Lippincott, 1970.

———. *God of the Oppressed*. New York: Seabury, 1975.

Cone, Cecil W. *The Identity Crisis in Black Theology*. Nashville: AMEC, 1975.

Costas, Orlando. *Theology of the Crossroads in Contemporary Latin America*. Amsterdam: Rodopi, 1976.

Fiorenzia, Francis, P. "Latin American Liberation Theology." *Interpretation* 28 (1974): 441-57.

Gardiner, James J., and Roberts, J. Deotis, Sr., eds. *Quest for a Black Theology*. Philadelphia: Pilgrim, 1970.

Gutiérrez, Gustavo. *A Theology of Liberation*. Trans. Caridad Inda, Sr., and John Eagleson. Maryknoll, N.Y.: Orbis, 1973.

Hellwig, Monika. "Liberation Theology: An Emerging School." *Scottish Journal of Theology* 30 (1977): 137-51.

Herzog, Frederick. "Liberation Hermeneutic as Ideology Critique?" *Interpretation* 28 (1974): 387-403.

Jones, Major J. *Black Awareness: A Theology of Hope*. Nashville: Abingdon, 1971.

Jones, William R. *Is God a White Racist?* Garden City, N.Y.: Anchor/Doubleday, 1973.

Kirk, J. Andrew. "Beyond Capitalism and Marxism: Dialogue with a Dialogue." *Theological Fraternity Bulletin* No. 1-2 (1976): 26-38.

López Trujillo, Alfonso. *Liberation or Revolution? An Examination of the Priest's Role in the Socioeconomic Class Struggle in Latin America*. Huntington, Ind.: Our Sunday Visitor, 1977.

Mackie, Steven G. "Praxis as the Context for Interpretation." *Journal of Theology for Southern Africa* 24 (1978): 31-43.

Miguez-Bonino, José. *Christians and Marxists: The Mutual Challenge to Revolution*. Grand Rapids: Eerdmans, 1976.

————. *Doing Theology in a Revolutionary Situation*. Ed. William H. Lazareth. Philadelphia: Fortress, 1975.

Miranda, José Porfirio. *Marx and the Bible: A Critique of the Philosophy of Oppression*. Trans. John Eagleson. Maryknoll, N.Y.: Orbis, 1974.

Moltman, Jürgen. "An Open Letter to José Miguez-Bonino." *Christianity and Crisis* 36 (1976): 57-63.

Neely, Alan. "Liberation Theology in Latin America: Antecedents and Autochthony." *Missiology* 6 (1978): 343-70.

Oliveros, Robert. *Liberación y Teología. Génesis y crecimiento de una reflexión (1966-1976)*. Lima: Centro de Estudios y Publicaciones, 1977.

Piediscalzi, Nicholas, and Thobaben, Robert G., eds. *From Hope to Liberation: Towards a New Marxist-Christian Dialogue*. Philadelphia: Fortress, 1974.

Prien, Hans-Jurgen. "Liberation and Development in Latin America." *Lutheran World* 20 (1973): 114-32.

Roberts, J. Deotis, Sr. *A Black Political Theology*. Philadelphia: Westminster, 1974.

————. "Black Theological Ethics: A Bibliographical Essay." *The Journal of Religious Ethics* 3 (1975): 69-109.

————. *Liberation and Reconciliation: A Black Theology.* Philadelphia: Westminster, 1971.

Segundo, Juan Luis. *The Liberation of Theology.* Trans. John Drury. Maryknoll, N.Y.: Orbis, 1976.

Sobrino, Jon. *Christology at the Crossroads: A Latin American Approach.* Trans. John Drury. Maryknoll, N.Y.: Orbis, 1978.

Torres, Sergio, and Fabella, Virginia, eds. *The Emergent Gospel. Theology from the Underside of History.* Maryknoll, N.Y.: Orbis, 1978.

Torres, Sergio, and Eagleson, John, eds. *Theology in the Americas.* Maryknoll, N.Y.: Orbis, 1976.

Wagner, C. Peter. *Latin American Theology.* Grand Rapids: Eerdmans, 1970.

Wilmore, Gayraud S. *Black Religion and Black Radicalism.* Garden City, N.Y.: Anchor/Doubleday, 1973.

————. "The New Context of Black Theology in the United States." *Occasional Bulletin of Missionary Research* 2 (1978): 140-42.

THE CONSERVATIVE OPTION

I. Only an option?
   A. No sacrificium intellectus
   B. Unity of faith and thought
      1. "Dialogue" only a partial possibility
      2. The danger of intellectual respectability
II. Remaking the modern mind
III. Steps toward the goal
IV. "Unmasking unbelief"
   A. Criticism of presuppositions
      1. The anti-intellectual rejection of unbelief
      2. The intellectual seduction into unbelief
      3. Herman Dooyeweerd
      4. Rival religious roots
      5. Recovery of the Christian vision
      6. Contra Barth: Gerrit C. Berkouwer
      7. Cornelius Van Til
      8. Francis Schaeffer
      9. "Rationalistic" exaggerations
   B. Positive developments
V. Criticism of findings
VI. Criticism of conclusions
VII. Rebuilding from the foundations
   A. An evangelical consensus?
   B. Revelation, authority, and inspiration
   C. The doctrine of God: the Trinity
   D. Creation
   E. The Fall
   F. The person and work of Christ
   G. Sanctification and the person and work of the Holy Spirit
   H. The last things

435

10

The Conservative Option

by

HAROLD O. J. BROWN

ONLY AN OPTION?

The word option is fashionable today. Derived from the Latin *optio,* free will or free choice, *option* originally designated the power of exercising conscious, deliberate choice from among various possibilities. It carried the implication that the option is the correct choice, not merely one acceptable selection among many. In this sense it is proper to speak of conservative, evangelical theology as the Christian's option. It is necessary for him to choose it, consciously and deliberately, from among the bewildering variety of systems, trends, movements, moods, and even renamed paganism and pantheism called theologies today.

In contemporary speech, however, *option* may suggest mere taste or preference. We speak of viable options in a given situation: diverse choices, each of which one could live with. From one perspective the Christian should never hesitate to call a conservative, evangelical theology taking biblical infallibility as its fundamental principle of authority an intellectually viable option. Compared to rival views (such as liberal Protestantism, neoorthodoxy, and the more recent views discussed in this volume) that also claim to be legitimate interpretations of the Bible's message, or of the

HAROLD O. J. BROWN, A.B., S.T.B., Th.M., Ph.D., is professor of systematic theology at Trinity Evangelical Divinity School. He is the author of *The Protest of a Troubled Protestant* (Arlington House, 1969), *Christianity and the Class Struggle* (Arlington House, 1970), *The Reconstruction of the Republic* (Arlington House, 1977), and *Death Before Birth* (Thomas Nelson, 1977).

Bible's "real intention," evangelical theology need feel no embarrassment about its intellectual respectability.

No sacrificium intellectus

Being a conservative evangelical and accepting the doctrine of biblical infallibility does not require any *sacrificium intellectus* (the sacrifice of one's understanding, or intellectual integrity). Quite the contrary is true. It is, rather, other varieties of theology, ones that have enjoyed greater vogue in academic circles, that require such a sacrifice. Intellectually speaking, we should defend the viewpoint that evangelical theology is not merely a viable option but a superior one.

If we turn to the question of a doctrine, or theology that legitimately transmits and communicates "the power of God unto salvation" (Ro 1:16), we will plainly state that biblical evangelicalism is not merely *a* viable option but the only viable one. It is an "option" in the sense that we opt for it, that we deliberately, consciously choose and affirm it as the truth in the midst of a swarm of errors. Holding to an evangelical theology in the sense of a developed, internally consistent system of teaching, is not a condition of individual salvation, although faith in the Lord proclaimed by such theology is. It is only this particular *theological* choice, namely of a consistently biblical, evangelical theology, that permits our theological reflection and construction to be intellectually and spiritually consistent and faithful to our sole reliable source of theological knowledge, God's authoritative and altogether trustworthy revelation in Scripture. Just as an evangelical faith in Jesus Christ as Redeemer and Saviour is the only faith that saves, so an evangelical theology is the only variety of theology that does justice to its source in biblical revelation instead of deforming and perverting that revelation by reinterpreting it according to alien criteria or authorities.

Unity of faith and thought

Among scholars and thinkers calling themselves evangelicals and professing faith in Jesus Christ as Lord and personal Saviour as taught by the Scripture, there sometimes occurs a dangerous dichotomy between the faith that is believed for salvation and the religious-intellectual system that is developed for discourse with the academic and literary world. Van Til argues that unregenerate man cannot even understand, much less accept (prior to regeneration) the biblical picture of God's creative and redemptive work.[1] Even if one does not fully subscribe to this view, it is evident that the attempt to *inform* the unbeliever concerning the content of the biblical proclamation (as distinguished from the attempt to persuade him of its truth) suffers from a serious handicap. The unbeliever, in his conscious or unconscious rejection of the biblical message as a direct address to him, necessarily overlooks or suppresses at least some significant aspects of that message.

"Dialogue" only a partial possibility. Prior to regeneration the human mind is inherently incapable of grasping, even merely intellectually, the substance of the biblical message. Consequently, the dialogue of the believing Christian thinker with unbelieving intellectual colleagues will always operate under severe handicaps. It is, of course, possible to present the Gospel in such a manner that the difficulty of believing it is magnified unnecessarily. But it is never possible to present it in such a manner that every difficulty associated with faith is removed, particularly in the light of the fact that at least one major impediment to belief lies neither in the message itself nor in its presentation but in the heart of the unconverted hearer. There are areas of disagreement in which the nonevangelical thinker finds the evangelical presentation of the Gospel message unbelievable or even ridiculous. These areas can be reduced and misunderstandings cleared up by appropriate dialogue. What are we to say, however, when even the sensitive, intelligent, and apparently well-intentioned unbeliever continues to appear to misunderstand or to fail to grasp, rather than to reject outright, certain elements of the biblical Gospel? Even when all possible intellectual roadblocks have been cleared, some barriers will remain, apart from the grace of God and the transforming work of the Holy Spirit in the unconverted heart. The unbeliever is not prepared to see his difficulty in accepting the content of the Gospel message in these terms but will believe that certain intellectual or moral obstacles remain to be surmounted. Thus the unbeliever may well encourage his Christian colleagues in the misapprehension that by a more skillful and subtle approach to the problem, by a more delicate and discriminating sensitivity, by a more thorough command of the attendant facts and related intellectual disciplines, they could carry the dialogue through to successful persuasion. We must recognize that this is an illusion: when all major and minor intellectual obstacles have been removed, all questions fairly met, and no issues skirted, the Gospel will continue to be rejected "intellectually" as

long as it is not being accepted spiritually, that is, as long as repentance and conversion are not present.

The danger of intellectual respectability. The evangelical who is concerned to show the intellectual respectability of scriptural teachings sets himself a worthy goal; but unless he remembers that he can never fully secure the approval of unbelievers for his doctrine apart from their spiritual conversion, there may come a time when he is tempted to compromise the Bible's proclamation in order to secure greater agreement from the participants in the dialogue. The greatest scholarly accuracy and the highest intellectual attainments on the part of the evangelist or apologete will not entirely free him from intellectual disrepute as long as he submits, in the final analysis, to the authority of the Bible as the Word of God and affirms the need for personal conversion and salvation by grace through faith. In each of these doctrines there is something that offends the natural man. That offense cannot be removed, no matter how tactful or erudite the presentation, as long as the message is not altered.

The Christian who is striving to be a good workman in the academic and intellectual world will necessarily have to admit that much of what conservative, Bible-believing Christians have taken or passed off as scholarship has been deficient—sometimes embarrassingly so. He must beware of permitting his own responsible quest for academic and scholarly quality to turn him against those fellow believers, whether he call them fundamentalists, evangelicals, or obscurantists, whose intellectual performance he finds deficient. The effort to align himself with others whose academic ability is higher but whose doctrine may be weak or wrong has its dangers. It is often noted that when a conservative evangelical finds acceptance and praise in secular intellectual circles, his doctrine is gradually muted into less offensive tones. However, we should not think that intellectual respectability or recognition by nonevangelical and secular scholars is an absolute impossibility. Yet it is difficult, and holding fast to teachings rejected by the secular world or nonevangelical theology is certainly a handicap. We must beware of the subtle temptation to compromise, beginning with "cultural accretions," "adiaphora," and "nonessentials," on the grounds of thereby securing a better hearing for the Gospel, and then going on by gradual, almost unnoticed degrees to compromise and surrender one or more essentials.

Another danger inherent in the otherwise laudable attempt to communicate with the world by meeting its standards of excellence and wisdom lies in the fact that to do so may make it impossible to communicate the fundamental content and values of the faith to those entrusted to our care. The late Karl Barth, whose fundamental theological position is at variance with biblical evangelicalism, is a case in point.[2] Few who knew the man or his works, who were aware of his personal humility and his readiness to give a simple testimony to the Lord Jesus Christ as his Saviour, could deny that he gave great evidence of saving faith. Yet his theological method and the system he constructed, although certainly the most impressive theological productivity since Calvin, failed to make any lasting impression on the rest of the theological world or on his nontheological colleagues. Worse still, many of those who were his students subsequently adopted positions radically at variance with Barth's own commitment. One of the major works of so-called secular theology is by Paul van Buren, who wrote his doctoral dissertation under Barth on Calvin's view of the atonement.[3] One might hesitate to blame van Buren's secular theology on his *Doktorvater* Barth. However, as Klaus Bockmühl shows in his extremely significant monograph *Atheismus in der Christenheit (Atheism in Christendom),* the unreality of God is already implicit in Barthian neoorthodoxy despite the faith and personal piety that Barth displayed.[4] A defective theology may not destroy an individual's saving faith nor his personal relationship to Christ; but it will make it difficult or impossible for him to transmit or teach the truths of the faith to those who come after him. Much that is called modern or contemporary theology is purely a reaction, taking its strength from the "dead" orthodoxy it opposes. As soon as it appears to be victorious, it dies, or it is transformed into something that is even less recognizable as Christian teaching. Orthodoxy, by contrast, no matter how dessicated and unpalatable it may become, does hold to the fundamental, saving truths of biblical revelation. Hence it continually revives, even after its most humiliating encounters with doubt, indifference, hypocrisy, and disbelief.

REMAKING THE MODERN MIND

In the attempt to present and to hold a conservative, evangelical theology in the intellectual debate today, the Christian encounters difficulty less from individual challenges to particular doctrines or points of view, than from the fact that the whole mentality of our age is turned against the existence of a personal God, propositional revelation, and absolutes in the realm of knowledge or morality. As

Harry Blamires argues in *The Christian Mind,* the church today is afflicted with an almost complete secularization of its world of thought.[5] We may act like Christians, worship like Christians, and to a great extent even believe like Christians; but to an astonishing degree we think with the categories, values, and tools of a completely secularized mind.

We say "secularized" deliberately, for in an intellectual community with a Christian heritage, thought can hardly be innocently or neutrally secular. If thought within the realm of Christendom and Christian culture is nonreligious, it is secularized, deliberately turned toward the world and away from God and His Word. In this sense, if it is not biblical, it must necessarily be apostate. It is not by chance that the great spiritual or intellectual challenge to a Christian world and life view today, the materialistic philosophy of Marxism, was launched by a man who had turned his back on both of the great spiritual currents that molded Christian civilization, that is, Judaism and Christianity.

Not so simple

We may *be* Christians, but to an alarming degree we think like the rest of the world. This certainly is not the intellectually transforming repentance *(metanoia)* to which Jesus called us and which Paul paraphrased as the renewing of the mind *(anakainosis tou noos,* Ro 12:2). Christians today have virtually lost the habit of thinking about fundamental issues as Christians; they think as the rest of the world does, and then add a Christian comment or criticism as a footnote. Consequently, what we need is more than the refutation of certain individual errors, a task to which orthodox Christians, including classical and modern fundamentalists, have repeatedly addressed themselves with a good measure of effect. Carl F. H. Henry, in an early work, challenged his readers to undertake the task of *Remaking the Modern Mind.*[6] Henry criticized the fundamentalist mentality on the grounds that it took the theological traditions of Protestant orthodoxy, which are narrow and rightly so, and narrows them still further with sociological and cultural limitations. Henry himself has done much to broaden fundamentalism without surrendering its commitment to orthodoxy, especially during his long tenure as editor of *Christianity Today.*

However, although Carl Henry and the host of conservative thinkers associated with him in the evangelical movement succeeded in broadening fundamentalism and introducing legitimate intellectual and social concerns alongside the essential commitment to biblical doctrine and evangelization, this new breadth also threatened, according to many critics, to weaken certain of the distinctives of biblical orthodoxy. As evangelicalism has gained in recognition from the general culture, and now is interacting with and influencing the general culture, the possibility has also arisen that evangelicalism may also be adversely influenced by it. As the noted sociologist of religion Peter L. Berger has indicated in *The Noise of Solemn Assemblies,* religious groups tend to react to most issues just as would be expected on the basis of their political, economic, and sociological makeup, with scant regard for their doctrinal commitment.[7] This is, unfortunately, also true of many individuals and groups who accept biblical infallibility and seek to order their lives and attitudes in accordance with scriptural precepts. Hence, although we wish to understand and influence the surrounding non-Christian, largely secular, humanist culture, we must beware of the kind of interaction that brings with it the adulteration and ultimate loss of distinctively evangelical values. Francis A. Schaeffer, the American theologian who has made his home in the Vaudois Alps of Switzerland where the l'Abri community has grown up, has made a tremendous contribution to the task of relating the Gospel to modern secular men and women without accommodating it to suit them.

STEPS TOWARD THE GOAL

During the last third of the nineteenth century and the first half of the twentieth, the dominance of the older liberalism and of its more modern but hardly more acceptable derivatives in the seminaries was so marked that conservative Protestantism was almost everywhere forced into a defensive, even reactive position. It was first of all necessary to show that liberalism's claim to be Christian was false. The old conflict, clearly spelled out by J. Gresham Machen in *Christianity and Liberalism,*[8] remains the same today.

As the evangelical criticism of liberalism's unjustified claim to present true Christianity has become increasingly effective, the intellectual ground has been cleared for Henry's challenge—the work of remaking the modern mind. The defensive battle has been largely won, or at least the front has been stabilized so that evangelicalism is no longer in retreat. However, evangelicals now run the risk of being distracted by the vagaries of their rivals. Of course, the liberals and their modern variants, having no distinctively biblical source of authority or mandate for action, turn restlessly from one intellectual or religious fashion to another; while many evangelicals, accustomed to being in close if hostile proximity to them, seem to be following them to the neglect of the fundamental tasks that they now, for the first time in decades, have the freedom and the resources to accomplish.

To be specific, liberal theology has turned from its attempt to relate its conception of the Kingdom of God, however defective, to the world. Instead it now engages largely in a criticism of secular culture from within that culture, rather than from any biblical vantage point. Evangelicalism also, as it becomes more aware of the world, may content itself with giving an evangelical variation on what is basically a less than evangelical preoccupation. Likewise, as liberals have increasingly gone in for political rather than theological analysis of social problems, evangelicals, conscious of the narrowness of their fundamentalist past, may make the same mistake.

The first step, without which little else would have been possible, was the criticism and refutation of liberal skepticism. This has been largely accomplished. The second step was the defense and substantiation of details and specific points of biblical doctrine, particularly as it relates to biblical history. The third necessary step, the re-creation of a coherent system of thought based on biblical revelation and applicable to life in the modern world, has only begun. This is the challenge that faces Bible-believing, evangelical Protestants today: to consolidate the gains of valiant defenders of the faith from the past, and, going on from there, to present to a bewildered and desperate world a coherent theological structure, including a comprehensive world-and-life view.

"Unmasking Unbelief"

The great Dutch Christian legal scholar and philosopher Herman Dooyeweerd (b. 1894) maintains that one of the foremost tasks of the evangelist in today's world is "unmasking the unbelief that poses as scientific and scholarly objectivity."[9] It is in this critical task that evangelicals so far have been most effective.

Criticism of presuppositions

The modern doubt that afflicts the contemporary mind and contributes to the underlying rootlessness and bleakness of nominally progress-oriented Western society began against a background of orthodox Christianity. Atheism as we know it in the West is not merely lack of belief in, but rather an attack on God; only where God has been seen as real and personal can much energy be generated in the cause of rebellion against Him. Thus the virulence of modern atheism is in effect a consequence of the vigor of faith in the personal, self-revealing God of Scripture.

One important consequence of the long supremacy of Christian views in Western thought is the fact that many early rebels against biblical belief have found it expedient and even natural to cloak their rebellion in an outward conformity to the church. It is symbolic that Ludwig Feuerbach, who provided the transition between Hegel's supposed reconciliation of philosophy and religion and Marx's violent attack on religion, called his critique *The Essence of Christianity.* The attempted defense of Christianity by Hegel's contemporary, the theologian Friedrich Schleiermacher (1768-1834), embodied in his *Lectures on Religion to Its Cultured Despisers* (1799), may be described as an attempt to salvage Christian sentiment by jettisoning any claim to base it on objective truth.[10]

All such reductions of Christianity to an "essence" totally different from the historic understanding of biblical teaching concerning the nature of man, his fall into sin, and God's work of redemption, depended on largely unacknowledged or unrecognized presuppositions of an anti-Christian or antibiblical nature. To the extent that Christian theology attempted to interact with such movements without exposing and rejecting their presuppositions, it was destined to be drawn into the same morass; and this is indeed what happened.

The anti-intellectual rejection of unbelief. There has always been an element of apparent anti-intellectualism in Christianity, made explicit in Tertullian's famous gibe at Hellenistic learning: "What has Athens to do with Jerusalem, or the Stoa with the porch of Solomon?" (Of course Tertullian himself was one of the first Christian *theologians,* with an extraordinarily powerful and productive intellect.) It is proper to acknowledge that simple Christian believers, committed to the sovereign lordship of Jesus Christ and to belief in the Bible as God's inerrant Word, have frequently reacted in an unsophisticated fashion in their blanket rejection of worldly wisdom at those points where it appears to challenge biblical teaching. The fact that they cannot provide a satisfactory intellectual rationale for the rejection of untruth detracts nothing from the fact that it is better to reject untruth than to be seduced by it and thereby lose hold of vital doctrines of the Christian faith. Indeed, for nonacademic, nonintellectual Christian people who have little interest in scholarly arguments—whose loyalties, likes, and dislikes are determined, not necessarily thoughtlessly, but intuitively and without much formal reflection—an intuitive, nonintellectual repudiation of non-Christian doctrine is natural and unobjectionable enough. But we must distinguish between an unsophisticated attitude and an obscurantist attitude; by the latter we mean the position of those who deliberately exclude from their consideration of problems of Christian belief the kind of intellectual, scholarly, and logical questioning they would expect to apply to other problems they face. Clearly, a nonintellectual rejection of unbelief is natural for people who operate on a nonintellectual basis in other areas of their concern. It is neither commendable nor persuasive when adopted by Christians who do concern themselves with the things of the intellect in other areas of their lives.

The intellectual seduction into unbelief. If the educated, thoughtful, intellectual Christian is challenged not to reject unbelief categorically, on nonintellectual grounds that he would not accept in nonreligious areas, he must also beware of falling into the opposite error. Many Christians make the mistake of adopting the standards and even the opinions of secular culture except (at most) at those points where they run precisely contrary to fundamental Christian beliefs. Because the university and the intellectual culture were of Christian origin in the West, it has long been assumed that their claim to impartiality and objectivity at least implied an absence of hostility to Christian faith and life. Tacitly accepting this claim to objectivity—which more intensive examination will show has all too seldom been justified—many Christians have allowed themselves to accept a division of truth into two realms: a religious realm, where the criteria of faith and the communications of Scripture apply; and an immensely larger, nonreligious realm of secular, "objective," "scientific" knowledge, where such criteria are irrelevant. They have contented themselves with defending the fundamentals of "religious" truth, and thereby have conceded the greater part of the realm of learning to the "objective" inquiries of the secular mind.

By accepting the methods and results of such "objective" inquiry uncritically, Christians have allowed the content of Christian teaching to be whittled down and adulterated, because there can be no strict division of knowledge into religious and secular. What is accepted as true in the religious realm will have implications for many if not necessarily all areas of secular knowledge. Conversely, what is accepted in the secular realm will contain many implications for religious beliefs. The overlapping is most significant in those areas of knowledge and science that deal directly with man. Scripture teaches us that man is God's creature, made in His image, and called to a personal relationship of faith and thereby to adoption as God's child. Secular study that sees man, either methodologically or by definition, as only in nature and not before God, is bound to misunderstand him in certain very substantial ways. The misunderstanding becomes greater as the study approaches the heart or mind, those areas in which man's responsibility to and dependence on God are most acute. Thus the study of medical anatomy will be little influenced by the scientist's views concerning man's ultimate nature as God's creature, but the study of human psychology necessarily will be so influenced. The same holds true for all of the supposedly secular sciences that deal with questions of a religious dimension, that is, that touch on the origin and end of life, whether individual or of the species. It is extremely difficult to avoid contaminating with religious or metaphysical presuppositions the study of the origin of life and the generally accepted evolutionary hypothesis. And of course the conclusions reached in that area, however tentative they ought to be from the perspective of their scientific demonstrability, readily reach out to influence our religious view of man's nature, responsibility, and ultimate destiny.

Herman Dooyeweerd. A radical criticism of the innate, often unconscious presuppositions of all thought, including supposedly objective and autonomous philosophical thought, was undertaken by Herman Dooyeweerd in *A New Critique of Theoretical Thought.*[11] Dooyeweerd called for a "transcendental" criticism of theoretical thought, by which he meant an investigation of the innate "religious root" that establishes the often unrecognized presuppositions of each particular school of philosophical thought. That all thought has such an underlying religious root Dooyeweerd deduces from the fact that human thought, in its attempt to give content and meaning to the self, inevitably goes beyond the temporary horizon of objects and finite persons to make assumptions, conscious or unconscious, about a transcendent origin and end of reality. This religious root he gives the Dutch name *wetsidee,* "law-idea," usually rendered in English as "cosmonomic idea."

Rival religious roots. Fundamental to Hellenistic philosophy and religion, one of the two main sources of Western intellectual and spiritual life, was the cosmonomic idea of an essential duality between form and matter, between spirit and body. The type of think-

ing that develops out of the presupposition that the form-matter
tension is primary will of necessity move in a particular direction and
will be incompatible with the truths formulated within a basically
biblical frame of reference. The cosmonomic idea of the Bible,
according to Dooyeweerd, does not have an underlying dualism of
spirit and body, of idea and matter as its basic polarity, although
Scripture recognizes that such a duality exists. Instead, the biblical
view is historical and personal in nature, worked out around the
theme, known to us through biblical revelation, of creation, the Fall
into sin, redemption, and sanctification. This biblical framework is
not dualistic. Man's problem is not the incompatibility of spirit with
matter, the imprisonment of an essential spiritual element, the soul,
within a corrupt, material body. On the contrary, the problem is
moral in nature, resulting from our willful rebellion against the law
and authority of God. Good and evil are attributes of persons and are
not determined by the relationship between spirituality and material-
ity. In the biblical framework, *justice* can play a fundamental role
because the personal and the historic are also fundamental. This is
not possible in the essentially impersonal, ahistorical dualism of the
form-matter schema.

Historically, the biblical framework was proclaimed in an intellectual world already deeply marked by Hellenistic thinking and its
characteristically dualistic world view. The first Christians generally turned entirely away from secular thought in favor of a completely biblical orientation: hence Tertullian's sharp distinction between Athens, standing for the wisdom of the world, and Jerusalem,
the wisdom that comes from God. Several of the early church
apologetes did make an effort to express Christian convictions in
categories that the Hellenistic world could understand, but no attempt was made to find a synthesis between truths of revelation and
truths of reason. Truth and reality were seen as a coherent whole.
The truth of revelation was seen as determining all of reality, not just
the relationship between God and man.

Medieval Scholasticism, impressed by the rediscovery of classical thought and the enlargement of vision stimulated by the
Crusades, sought to reconcile revelation and human reason. It did so
by dividing the field of knowledge into a realm of grace, where
revelation is essential, and one of nature, where human reason can
arrive at valid conclusions. Although this attempted reconciliation
kept reason in a limited position, it did allow it a relative autonomy.
The Protestant Reformation reasserted not merely the superiority

but the sovereignty of revelation. In this period the Fall was seen again in all its radical impact, and man was recognized as corrupted in his intellect as well as in his moral sense.

Post-Reformation rationalism again introduced a dualism, this time the tension between freedom and determinism, a secularized version of the older scholastic dualism between grace and nature. By tacitly agreeing to work within such an intellectual framework as a condition for remaining members of the intellectual community, Christian thinkers in effect conceded the battle to their adversaries in advance. Progress is not equivalent to salvation, nor enlightenment to redemption. When Christian thinkers consent, over a wide range of issues, to accept secular analysis and values as in some way generally equivalent to and compatible with biblical ones, they lose the specificity of biblical revelation. And that is, after all, what is special about biblical religion: that it imparts to man both wisdom and salvation not accessible to unaided human inquiry and effort.

Recovery of the Christian vision. Because the human reason ever seeks to assert its proclaimed autonomy, and because the ostensibly autonomous secular reason is in constant tension and interaction with the Christian mind informed by revelation, there is a continuing tendency for the Christian mind to accommodate itself to the world. Hence those who wish to remain true to the fullness of the biblical message, involving not merely a formula for properly relating one's heart to God but a global vision of the world and life, must constantly guard against the dilution of biblical truth. This means that we must constantly reform our thinking by consciously bringing it under the Word of God and allowing that Word itself to provide the framework, the cosmonomic idea out of which we develop our thought. Other root ideas, however much they may claim to be objective or neutral, in effect absolutize something from the temporal horizon and thus are idolatrous.

Non-Christian philosophy, not recognizing the Fall, at least not in the radical sense taught by Scripture, raises the pretension of autonomy. However, while claiming autonomy (that is, freedom for itself and its intellectual enterprise), modern secular thought, locked within the dualism of freedom and determinism, is more and more led to conclude that its freedom is illusory and that we are bound under a rigid determinism, whether this determinism be seen in biochemical, behavioristic, or other terms. An impasse results in which human thought, claiming to be free, comes to the conclusion that there is no freedom. This leads to the tremendous sense of frustration, absurdity, and rebellion that characterizes so much of the modern intellectual climate, as Dooyeweerd has described it in *In the Twilight of Western Thought.**

Contra Barth: Gerrit C. Berkouwer. Although Karl Barth cannot be accepted as a reliable teacher and guide by the student who seeks to remain true to the historic Christian understanding of the inspiration and authority of Scripture, there can be no doubt that his contribution to evangelical theology is immense. First, he made a radical criticism of liberalism and its shallow optimism; then he vigorously restated and reformulated many fundamental Christian teachings. Barth stimulated a tremendous output of evangelical scholarship. The very impressiveness of Barth's work, combined with the fact that in many respects it supports the orthodox position while in other respects it reveals dangerous, even fatal, weaknesses, has motivated several of the most productive orthodox Christian thinkers. They have not only criticized him and shown his divergence from historic, biblical Christianity; but they have also tried to do on a more thoroughly biblical basis what Barth did out of his own conception of the Word of God.

Although it was not his first major work to impress the North American public, G. C. Berkouwer's *The Triumph of Grace in the Theology of Karl Barth* (English translation 1956) was a milestone in preparing the way for a more hospitable evangelical reception for Barth.[12] While main-line liberal Christians had been enthusiastic about Barth's thought in the period before and during World War II, most conservatives had looked on it as nothing more than a new and more insidious variety of modernism. The early work by Cornelius Van Til, *The New Modernism* (1946), is expressive of the general conservative hostility to Barth and his views.[13] Berkouwer (b. 1903, a colleague of Dooyeweerd's at the Free University of Amsterdam) began an ambitious project while Barth was still actively working on his own never completed *Church Dogmatics*. Berkouwer's project is of almost equal magnitude but of fundamentally different structure. His series, Studies in Dogmatics, does not begin as does Barth's *Church Dogmatics* with the doctrine of the Word of God, but with *The Providence of God* (Dutch original, 1950; English translation, 1952).[14] In so doing, he indicated his desire to stand clearly within the Reformed tradition, with its striking emphasis on

---

*In addition to his critique of thought, Dooyeweerd's social and political ideas, especially as they have been elaborated by some of his admirers, have had considerable influence in North America. However, it is only his influence on theology that interests us here.

God's election and sovereignty. Like those of Barth's magnum opus, the volumes of Berkouwer's Studies in Dogmatics have tended to increase in size, culminating for the moment in his work, *Holy Scripture*.[15] In the thirteen Studies so far published, Berkouwer has presented us with the most significant, comprehensive doctrinal structure from a conservative perspective in our century. Nevertheless, insofar as Berkouwer appears to be involved in a certain modification of the orthodox Calvinist position as exemplified in the Canons of Dordt, particularly with respect to biblical authority and the historicity of certain biblical narratives, even his impressive work does not seem entirely to fill the need for a reliably biblical, comprehensive dogmatics for our day.

Cornelius Van Til. Cornelius Van Til, the dean of Calvinist scholars in North America and a contemporary of Dooyeweerd, has also devoted much of his life's work to a reaction to Barth. As he himself says, "It occurs to me that the most effective way to set the Reformed Christian position over against that of modern theology is to set it over against the one who appears to be nearest the Reformed Faith."[16] Van Til has not been won over to Berkouwer's view, as his more recent work, *Christianity and Barthianism* (1962) makes abundantly clear.[17] In this, Van Til finds considerable support from the outstanding American philosopher in the Reformed tradition, Gordon H. Clark.[18]

Cornelius Van Til has also developed the essentially philosophical critique of Dooyeweerd in a theological direction. Accepting Rudolf Bultmann's contention that "presuppositionless exegesis is impossible," Van Til wants to build on the presuppositions of the Scriptures themselves. As his pupil Harvie M. Conn describes his method, we move from the presuppositions of the Scriptures, through the propositions of the Scriptures, to the conclusions of the Scriptures. This is of course neither neutral nor objective. But it has two tremendous arguments in its favor. Methodologically we cannot hope even to understand, much less accept, the message of the Bible if we attempt to impose alien presuppositions (for example, those of Bultmann's existentialist analysis) on it. Therefore we must allow our thinking, at least temporarily, to be shaped by Scripture's own presuppositions simply in order to understand it.

Ultimately, the Bible claims to present not merely one plausible description of the world and the ordering principles that rule in it but objective truth revealed by the Author of reality. To accept the

Bible's own presuppositions will not bring autonomy or objectivity to our thought. These remain illusory pretensions, as Dooyeweerd's analysis makes clear, for all thought has certain pretheoretical presuppositions, whether it is aware of them or not, and these inevitably determine the direction of its development and its consequences. The acceptance of biblical presuppositions will, however, preserve us from temptations to intellectual idolatry and bring us to a knowledge of "true truth." (The expression is Francis Schaeffer's. He uses it to indicate that he is speaking about what really and truly *is* true, not about some special realm of "religious" or "spiritual" truth.)[19]

The presuppositionalist critique developed by Dooyeweerd and Van Til denies the existence of any common ground between the believer and the unbeliever.[20] Even though they may use identical language—that of the Apostles' Creed, for example—the conservative, evangelical Christian and the liberal theologian necessarily mean different things. "On the third day he rose again" means something quite concrete and literal to the evangelical. But to many liberal Christian thinkers it expresses not something that took place in space, time, and history, but the way the apostles and the early Church expressed what happened subjectively to and within them in their encounter with Jesus Christ. The orthodox position, it should be understood, does not exclude the subjective faith experience of the disciples from the content of the proclamation but emphasizes the historic reality of the event, not the subjective response of the first Christians. To the evangelical, the liberal's claim to use the traditional language may appear unwarranted, outrageous, even meretricious. Yet the liberal, operating within his understanding of the nature of reality, truth, and communication, is not himself subjectively dishonest in affirming the resurrection on the third day in the language and formulas of the ancient Church even though he himself means something quite different by it. There may be an element of willful distortion of the truth in the arguments of some modern exegetes that even the apostles intended to communicate not an objective event in space, time, and history but only their subjective response to it.[21]

If one follows Van Til to his logical conclusions, the possibility of meaningful witness across differing presuppositions would appear to be negligible. The late Edward John Carnell differed sharply from Van Til at this point, and younger scholars such as John W. Montgomery and Clark H. Pinnock have developed a historical apologetic on the assumption that the clear witness of history can communicate meaningfully to the non-Christian.[22]

Francis Schaeffer. Although it is difficult to deny the theoretical persuasiveness of Van Til's critique of presuppositions, most Christian witnesses and apologists have observed that a cogently argued presentation of factual material often produces a response on the part of the non-Christian. Perhaps this is due to the fact that man, made in God's image, cannot completely obliterate his natural correspondence to his Creator. Hence there will always be something in him that remains untrue to the presuppositions of an apostate world-and-life view and longs for the message that tells him of his real place in the scheme of creation. The contemporary Christian thinker who has most creatively combined a deep awareness of Van Til's critique with effective communication across the barriers between world views is Francis A. Schaeffer. In a series of works published from 1968 onward, Schaeffer has dealt with revelation, the reality of the personal God, and the fateful breakup of the field of truth, as well as with a number of other theoretical and practical issues.[23]

It is Schaeffer who really made the concept of the divided field of truth familiar to contemporary Christians. Like Dooyeweerd, he holds that medieval Scholasticism gave a relative autonomy to nature over against grace. This creation of a supposedly autonomous, natural realm in which the human mind and its sciences could arrive at truth unaided by revelation and grace eventually led to a rejection of grace in favor of nature, or, as Schaeffer graphically puts it, "nature eats up grace." According to Schaeffer's analysis, admission of this division of the field of truth results in man's inability to find meaning in the rational, intelligible world of particulars. Seeking to escape from a closed, naturalistic universe with an unbroken but meaningless chain of natural cause and effect, man has been led by his religious needs to attempt a kind of quantum jump, a leap of faith, creating meaning for himself by believing against all the evidence. This type of leap Schaeffer rejects. He holds that while one cannot come to a saving knowledge of God from the observation of the material world, the world as God's creation and human beings as His creatures are naturally led to suppose that they and the world have meaning. Hence to listen to the Word of God in Scripture is not to make a leap of faith but to take a step that is reasonable and proper in the light of human experience and the evidence available before one puts one's trust in the Bible.

By virtue of the doctrine of creation, we know that the material world is not absolute but created; and hence we can reject pantheism, which Schaeffer correctly identifies as the great rival to revealed biblical religion. At the same time, we know that the world is not an illusion but real, although finite and subordinated to its Creator. Hence we reject the various religions and philosophies, largely of Indian origin, that teach the unreality of the world, as well, of course, as similar aberrations of Western origin, such as Christian Science.

The distinctiveness and importance of the individual person becomes not a harmful illusion, as in Eastern thought, but a natural consequence of the personal nature of the triune God, who subsists from all eternity as three coequal Persons in loving fellowship with one another. The doctrine of the Trinity, which so sharply distinguishes Christianity from the Judaism out of which it grew and which has given constant offense to rationalists through the centuries, is not simply an unnecessary complication of Gospel faith. Rather this belief stands in intimate causal relationship to all of the structures of the created world and the conditions of human life, including both creaturehood and the potentiality of adoption as children of God. Thus the rather provocative beginning of the Athanasian Creed, or *Quicumque vult,* giving faith in the Trinity as the first article of the faith that we must believe in order to be saved, is seen not as an arbitrary theological construction but as part of the very substance of reality. It is necessary to our understanding of the God who is the Author and Creator of all that is. The most sublime and mysterious Christian doctrine, that of the Trinity, is seen as the creative ground for the most immediate, existential human experience in the quest for personal identity and meaning.

Schaeffer stresses the reasonableness and importance of understanding revelation as *propositional,* that is, as expressed in content statements which (at least in part) deal with objective realities rather than merely with subjective interpretations. He also lays great stress on the biblical doctrine of the Fall into sin as a historic event in space and time. It is this historic Fall that explains the pervasiveness and power of evil as we experience it. Further, a historical Fall means that evil is neither part of God's purpose nor a necessary attribute of human nature. God is not the author of evil, nor must we ourselves remain in rebellion against Him in order to assert or maintain our individuality and authenticity. Man does not actualize himself by rebellion against God, as Paul Tillich proposed in an attempt to explain the pervasive human awareness of estrangement and fallenness without recourse to a literal Fall as described in the Bible. Thus our rebellion is real, but it is not essential to our humanness; we can be redeemed and sanctified without losing our essential personhood. Salvation, unlike Eastern views of nirvana, does not involve absorption and loss of personhood; nor does it reduce the saved human being to the bland existence among the clouds so often encountered as a caricature of the Christian's hope of heaven.

"Rationalistic" exaggerations. In their determination to defend the reasonableness of traditional Christian faith, Schaeffer, Montgomery, and Pinnock have all been criticized by Van Til and his followers as rationalistic.[24] This charge may result in part from these theologians' burning concern to free biblical Christianity from the charge that it is simply another irrational escape attempt in an impersonal, meaningless universe. Schaeffer has not worked out a positive theological system on the basis of his critique and positive presentation. Instead, he has made a tremendous practical effort to disciple individual Christians whose lives will be examples of God's reality and dependent on it for their specific direction and substance.[25] The refutation of the charge of rationalism sometimes leveled at Schaeffer should be made in terms of his own life and ministry conducted in evident dependence on the reality of the personal God of Scripture, and not on any rationalistic code of values and behavior.

POSITIVE DEVELOPMENTS

Schaeffer and those thinkers associated with him have yet to produce a fully worked-out presentation of the theology implicit in their apologetics, evangelism, and pattern of life. One Schaeffer associate, Udo Middelmann, in a little volume entitled *Pro-Existence,* attempts to work out the practical implications of man's stewardship responsibilities under God in the universe He has created.[26]

Another thinker in the conservative, Reformed position, Rousas J. Rushdoony, has presented in *The Institutes of Biblical Law* a systematic and far-reaching analysis of God's plan for individual salvation in the context of the restoration of society in a postmillennial struggle to establish the Kingship of Christ.[27] Accepting propositional revelation and biblical inerrancy, Rushdoony strongly emphasizes the graciousness of God's law and its restorative value for human society in all its manifold aspects. It is impossible to deny the impressiveness and persuasiveness of this massive work. In our opinion it is worth a place alongside the *Systematic Theology* of Charles Hodge. The integration of the political, economic, and social vision with the theological is at once a strength and a weakness of Rushdoony's approach: a strength, because it unifies what pietistically inclined evangelicalism has tended illegitimately to disrupt, the religious and secular dimensions of life; a weakness, because it can be understood and accepted only in the context of Rushdoony's postmillennial eschatology, which will not persuade the majority of conservative, evangelical Protestants.

Carl F. H. Henry's four-volume work entitled *God, Revelation, and Authority* is scheduled to begin appearing late in 1976. The projected title for volumes 1 to 3 is *God Who Speaks and Shows* and for volume 4, *God Who Stands, Stoops, and Stays.* He has done his work against the background of his far-reaching special studies in many crucial fields, including the doctrines of inspiration, Christology, and ethics, and his encyclopedic critical synthesis of the work of the most significant of his predecessors and contemporaries. We may reasonably hope that Henry will offer the comprehensive, structured kind of vision that conservative theology needs in order to go beyond mere criticism of error on the one hand and mere reiteration of credal or confessional dogmatic statements on the other.

CRITICISM OF FINDINGS

We have been discussing the massive attack on the presuppositions of modern liberal thought and theology made by recent evangelical theologians. At the same time, other evangelical biblical scholars have been continuing a detailed critique of some of the supposedly assured findings of liberal scholarship, particularly in the area of biblical introduction and interpretation. A thorough discussion of what has been accomplished in refutation of several cardinal tenets of liberal Bible scholarship would take us far beyond the scope of our immediate concern. Some of these areas include the documentary hypothesis of the origin of the Pentateuch, the late dating of Daniel, the plurality of authors in Isaiah and the late dating of his Babylonian material, contradictions and varying theologies in the synoptic tradition, the late dating and Hellenistic coloration of the Johannine corpus, and related topics. Most of the more valuable study in this area is discussed in recent works by Gleason Archer,

R. K. Harrison, Everett F. Harrison, Donald Guthrie, and F. F. Bruce.[28]

As a result of the dedicated labors of two generations of conservatively-inclined Bible scholars, it is fair to say that Christians need no longer feel intensive pressure, either in academia or in the congregation, to yield acceptance to alleged findings of biblical scholarship that discredit the plain teachings of Scripture or the historic doctrines of the Christian faith. Unfortunately, many of the major Christian communions, made anxious by the apparent threat to biblical doctrine from the world of secular learning, have already made excessive concessions and caused harm that it is difficult to undo. The first great intellectual stream that tended to relativize biblical teaching and reduce it to myth, legend, tradition, or symbol—the radically disintegrative source and form criticism of both Testaments—has been rather effectively diverted, broken up, damned, or drained by the numerous general and detailed studies to which we have alluded.

The second great movement, roughly contemporaneous with the first, also dealt with origins. However, its focus was not the origins of the documents of revelation but rather the origin of the universe and especially of life on earth. Two of the outstanding thinkers within the evangelical tradition who have tried to effect a positive synthesis between the widely accepted postulate of evolution as the mechanism explaining the diversity and development of life-forms and the theological assertions concerning Creation and the Fall are Bernard Ramm and Rachel H. King.[29] Among those who reject most or all of evolutionary theory in favor of an explicitly creationist viewpoint are a number of scientists, among whom Henry M. Morris and A. E. Wilder Smith merit attention.[30] No doubt there is much to be gained from effectively disputing the supposed findings of paleontology establishing the validity of the evolutionary theory. Although some do attempt to reconcile evolution as a mechanism with the idea of a personal Creator God, it is more difficult to harmonize the evolutionary view of human origins with some of the apparently plain biblical teachings concerning the origin of mankind and the comparison between the first and Second Adam (especially Ro 5). Hence it is relevant to include among our effective criticisms of the findings of secular and liberal science and scholarship the serious objections that have been raised to evolutionary theory.

Although none of these supposed findings sufficed to make biblical doctrine incredible, the long-term effect of constantly asserting them, even if not one was actually proved, was to weaken confidence in the reliability of the Bible. And without such confidence the whole enterprise of evangelical theology, the attempt to derive a pattern of saving faith and God-pleasing life from Scripture, naturally appears foolish. Therefore our effort to take stock of conservative theology and its viability today must take grateful note of the arduous, detailed work of those Christian scientists and scholars who have helped to shatter the illusion of incontrovertibility that many of the theories and claims of nineteenth- and twentieth-century science and scholarship presented. As a result, there are probably fewer intellectual roadblocks now than at any time in our century to accepting the traditional conviction of historic Christianity that the Bible is altogether trustworthy.

CRITICISM OF CONCLUSIONS

A natural result of the refutation in detail of many of the findings of skeptical, liberal, theological scholarship, coupled with the unmasking of its pretentions to objectivity and autonomy, is the rejection of its conclusions. As a generalization, it may be said that modern liberal theology tends to one of two errors: an unfounded optimism that makes light of the desperateness of the human predicament, or a more plausible but also unfounded conviction of the absurdity of human existence that fails to discern its ultimate meaning revealed in the Word of God. The naive optimism of much liberal Protestantism, expressed, for example, in the books of John A. T. Robinson, has been dealt with at length by the outstanding British Anglo-Catholic theolgian Eric L. Mascall in *The Secularisation of Christianity* and, on a somewhat more popular level, by the present writer in *The Protest of a Troubled Protestant*.[31]

Not all modernist theology has come to the comfortable if unwarranted conclusions of theologians such as former bishop Robinson. Whenever it has followed its skeptical and relativistic presuppositions to their logical conclusions and produced a mood of absurdity illustrated by doctrines such as the death of God, its fallacies have been exposed by such works as John W. Montgomery's *The Suicide of Christian Theology*.[32] This sense of futility and absurdity is not confined to Christian theology. It has also overtaken the culture as a whole; and from the circle around Francis Schaeffer, H. N. Rookmaaker in *Modern Art and the Death of a Culture* and Os Guinness in *The Dust of Death* have analyzed this phenomenon.[33]

Rebuilding from the Foundations

Although Augustine's accomplishments in the fifth century have been surpassed in magnitude and comprehensiveness by a number of theologians of later eras, our age so far lacks the equivalent of his *City of God*. To construct a total Christian world-and-life view will be more difficult for us today than it was in his time, for it is now necessary to coordinate the biblical vision of the plan of God not only with secular history, with its rise and fall of societies and empires, but also with the immensity of the scientific world view. It is for this reason that we should be especially grateful to evangelical thinkers such as Ramm and King for grappling from the perspective of an evangelical faith with the same cosmic issues that Pierre Teilhard de Chardin dealt with so fascinatingly if unbiblically.

An evangelical consensus?

There is as yet no comprehensive articulation of a world-and-life view from an evangelical perspective, although we have noted significant contributions in several important areas. Perhaps it is too much to expect that anyone today could produce a work of the size and clarity of Augustine's *City of God* or Calvin's *Institutes* and embrace not only the older problems which they saw but also the newer ones impressing themselves on recent generations. The evangelical community is numerically stronger than it has ever been in the past, and within it, there is considerable variety of conviction on many issues of substance. Even among that select number who accept the authority of an infallible Scripture as the only perfect rule of faith and life, there are major disagreements on divine sovereignty and election, the nature of the church, the sacraments, and eschatology, to name only four of the more obvious points in dispute. Yet, although we are far from achieving even a relative uniformity of expression, there is a growing awareness among evangelicals that all our doctrine originates not in an arbitrary intellectual construct but in the living God and in His inerrant Word. Furthermore, a good measure of our differences in questions of detail or even of substance can be explained as the result of defective vision on our part, and not seen as detracting from the solidarity, stability, and reliability of biblical doctrine nor as hindering those who earnestly seek to learn from Scripture wisdom unto salvation.

Francis Schaeffer is correct in charging that the older Christian consensus of the West deteriorated and ultimately disintegrated sometime after 1930. And this consensus is not yet on the way to restoration within Christendom as a whole. But within the framework of a nominally or formerly Christian culture, and within the structures of nominally Christian confessions and denominations, an evangelical consensus is emerging. And this consensus, because it is that of an informed, embattled, and biblically educated minority (rather than of an amorphous mass, as in an earlier era), is sharper, more detailed, and internally more consistent than the older consensus eulogized by Schaeffer. Because no individual can speak for the whole company of believing Christians in our generation, any writer's attempt to formulate and present the substance of an evangelical consensus will always remain partial and deficient. It may be that certain disputed questions are treated too lightly, that some important convictions are overlooked as trivial, and that some matters that would seem to concern only a fragment of Christendom are brought too near the center. We began by stating the necessity of making a conscious and deliberate choice for the conservative, evangelical option in theology, and by indicating the way in which many obstacles to making a right choice have, at great cost, been removed. We must in conclusion state at least several of the elements of the evangelical consensus that seem established and essential parts of the choice we make. These cardinal points may appear as guideposts for belief, as guardrails warning us not to plunge from the safe path, and even as frontier stones reminding us where we must stand and defend biblical territory against renewed encroachments by the secular mind-set.

REVELATION, AUTHORITY, AND INSPIRATION

If there is one great gain that the labors of twentieth-century evangelicals have effected, it is to give us as their inheritors the right to return with confidence to the Bible as the infallible Word of God. There are almost endless varieties of religious fancy springing from unchecked philosophical speculation, superstition, and that strange combination of the two with demonic influences and occultism. These religious phenomena and the intermingling of races, languages, religions, traditions, and cultures in our shrinking world should make us deeply aware of the fact that there is no way out of our ignorance apart from an authoritative and understandable Word from God. It should now be evident that the least sophisticated fundamentalist, with a naive and perhaps even myopic acceptance of partially understood Scripture, is less likely to make errors disastrous for his faith and salvation than the refined critic who wonders whether God can speak, whether He would use human language to do so, and whether human language is capable of expressing anything unambiguous in which we can unreservedly put our trust.

Is it possible to speak truly and reliably of the infinite God? Indeed, if and only if we speak His words after Him. In fact, we may claim that the only ultimate guarantee that any words or symbols have both meaning and objective truth is that meaning and truth have been ascribed to them by God, the ultimate Author. Thus we can say that the reliable Word of God is a necessity not only for a trustworthy knowledge about and of Him, but even for trustworthy communication on a merely human level. That God has made mankind in His own image and has spoken to mankind is the basis for human speech itself. The authority and reliability of the Word of God, whether we realize it or not, is the substratum of meaningful communication that makes it possible for lesser, fallible human communication to have a measure of clarity and reliability. The proclamations which speak God's words after Him are really the foundation not only for trustworthy communication about God and His purpose but for trustworthy communication per se.

The doctrine of revelation, then, is not only one that is directly relevant to our theology, to our doctrine and knowledge of God; it is also the ultimate foundation, even if we remain unconscious of it, of our self-awareness and of the world as real and of our ability to speak truly and meaningfully. It is not by chance that the great religious traditions that developed with no knowledge of the Word of God, such as Hinduism and Buddhism, came to teach that the world is an illusion and the self unreal. It is no accident that modern, experimental natural science grew up in a world whose thinking had been trained by God's Word. And it is no accident that as knowledge of and confidence in God's Word declines within Christendom, once nominally Christian peoples come to think of the world and themselves as unreal, absurd, unknowable, or illusory.

THE DOCTRINE OF GOD: THE TRINITY

A word presupposes a speaker, or at least a thinker. And the Word of God, not by chance, begins with the personal God, creating, speaking, taking counsel within the Trinity of divine Persons. It is not difficult to conceive of some kind of infinity. But it is **very** difficult to conceive of a Power so particular that it can speak and produce word symbols understandable by beings of our limited capacity as also having the infinite, creative might that made the universe. The paradox, the mystery of the biblical doctrine of God is not the infinity but the personhood. And God presents Himself to us, perhaps even by implication in the first chapter of Genesis, as a plurality of Persons made explicit elsewhere in Scripture as Father, Son, and Holy Spirit.

The biblical doctrine of God, then, stresses His personhood; and that personhood is trine, or triune. This is perhaps the most difficult of Christian doctrines to conceive; and yet it may not be neglected, for it is in the personal nature of God that our personhood—the fact that in our individual, existential awareness we are persons, selves—has its creative cause and its ground of meaning. Human personhood is not a painful illusion, because man is made in the image of God, who is personal. Love and the communication between those who love are not delusions in an impersonal universe but valid, if incomplete, reflections of the infinite love and utterly truthful communication eternally displayed between Father, Son, and Holy Spirit.

That God is personal means that He can have deliberation, decree, will. The course of the universe is not chance or statistic but stands in relation to the personal, intelligent will of God. One may argue, within the perplexities of the free will/determinism problem, the extent to which the course of events must reflect, may reflect, or may reject the will of God; but it is evident that their meaning depends intimately on their relationship to that will. The personhood of God and the fact that God has intelligent, sovereign will gives an altogether different teleology, or definition of goal, to human existence. Human existence will also take its character from its relationship to the personal God in terms of its conformity to or rebellion against His will.

CREATION

The fundamental importance of the doctrine of God as personal and as Trinity already suggests, as the preceding lines indicate, the doctrines of creation and of the nature of man. Yet so important are they that they require separate mention. The human rebellion against the will of God has in a way proceeded serially against the persons of the Trinity: rebellion against the Holy Spirit in the rejection of inspiration in the eighteenth and nineteenth centuries; rebellion against the Son in the rejection of a substitutionary atonement and redemption through the blood of Christ in the nineteenth and twentieth; now, rebellion against the Father in the denial of creation and even of the objective reality of the universe in the twentieth.

The doctrine of creation tells us that the universe is neither unreal nor divine. The twentieth-century secular mind vacillates between two extremes, both resulting from the rejection of the Creator and the denial of creation. The one error is to hold that the world is unreal, an illusion; this is the solution of much Asian religious thought now becoming established among the ashes of Christian civilization. The other error holds that the world is in some ultimate sense divine; it is not created but creates itself, is in some way responsible for itself and is its own ultimate judge. Man stands not above the world because he is related to its Creator, in His image, but in a sense below it, because by his intellectuality he has abstracted himself from it and made himself distinct, foreign, and harmful to it. Certain strains within the ecological movement go far beyond advocacy of responsible stewardship of God's creation, a theme which in itself is in harmony with man's biblically defined nature as His image bearer. In effect these strains reverse the creation order and make man subject to nature.

The doctrine of creation in its basic form simply tells us that God created by an act of His will, in accordance with His purpose. It does not go into detail as to how creation took place: how matter, space, and time were spun out of the eternal silence and emptiness. As such, the doctrine of creation is theoretically compatible with more than one possible mechanism for the origin of life, even human life. The evangelical doctrine of creation certainly emphasizes as essential, however the mechanism be conceived, the special creation of man at the very least, insofar as God planned it and had a purpose for man. Man is thus fundamentally creature; and, more than simply the product of God's hand, he is also person. He is not infinite as God is, but personal like God, and standing vis-à-vis God in responsibility. God creates man and speaks to man, giving him responsibilities: stewardship over the rest of creation and obedience to God. Man is a responsible creature, created by God and answerable to God (suggestive, of course, of judgment by God). This is fundamental to the biblical doctrine of creation and of man.

THE FALL

It may seem to be an arrogant anthropocentrism to list in the series begun with revelation, the Trinity, and creation a doctrine that appears to deal only with man. Yet theology is not some kind of abstract, celestial reference material concerning God, but is *man's* knowledge of God. Man as responsible creature is part of the doctrine of creation, and the Fall must be the answer to our experience of a blighted creation and twisted selves. Will in God permits purpose, and the purpose is expressed in the act of creation. Will in man, who stands over against God, permits contrary purpose, rebellion. Rebellion, even of a quantitatively and spatially insignificant element in the created universe, mars its perfection and brings everything into tension and imbalance. By giving man responsibility, God also permitted him significance, and this significance works itself out in that man's Fall is creation's blight.

Liberal theology believes that archaeology and paleontology render the concept of a literal first pair and an original sin ludicrous. It seeks to save the substance of man's rebellion, the Fall, by making it symbolic, expressive of each individual's experience, of man's self-actualization and his estrangement from God. The evangelical believes in a literal Fall in real history, in space and time, because the authoritative Word seems to permit no other reading. Yet, although he holds to a space-time Fall because the Scripture so recounts it, he gladly accepts the fact that the doctrine of the Fall means that human evil is not part of man's nature but an intrusion and a distortion. Man can be cleansed of his evil, redeemed, and sanctified, and not be dehumanized thereby. Rather he is fulfilled. The Christian doctrine of salvation is not loss of essential self but its recovery. It is not the absolute in self-denial but the ultimate in affirmation (though not self-affirmation, for the redeemed man or woman is affirmed by God, not self).

Many problems beset the biblical doctrine of a single human pair and a literal original sin, such as the dating of Adam and the putative existence of manlike.pre-Adamites. Yet many and great problems beset the naturalistic attempts to explain man and the diversity of life-forms that accompany him on this planet as the product of time plus space plus chance. Any view of man that rejects an actual, historic Fall leaves one to the unpleasant conclusion that evil, therefore, is part of man's nature—essential, not moral. It is something without which man would not be human, like finitude. Without a real, historic Fall, man is doomed to live evilly and with evil as long as he lives; for it is part of him, not something that has overcome him.

The philosophical neatness and utility of the historic space-time Fall should not blind us to the fact that it does, indeed, fly in the face of the general intellectual, scientific consensus concerning human origins. On the other hand, since the Bible whose authority we own requires us to accept it, we should not be indifferent to the fact that, however difficult it may be to postulate in our current intellectual climate, the Fall explains aspects of man's existential situation that otherwise remain bewildering mystery.

THE PERSON AND WORK OF CHRIST

Because the Fall is real and objective, there must be a real and objective redemption. In the early church it was the proclamation of the work of Christ that stimulated the theological definition of the person of Christ: fully God and fully man; two natures, one Person. And this definition has stood, from its presentation at Nicea in 325 and its expansion at Chalcedon in 451, until virtually our own day. There have, of course, been those who denied it. In the eighteenth century, Hermann Samuel Reimarus wrote anonymous tracts claiming that Jesus was merely human, and misguided at that. More recent theologians have dropped the anonymity without improving the doctrine. Most recently, however, there has been a tendency to say not that the orthodox Christology is false but that it is inappropriate. One should not ask what Christ *is* (God and Man), but what He *does* (saves us). This rather glib dismissal of convictions for which early Christians suffered and died as not untrue but *irrelevant* is justified by reference to the fact that it involves a *dynamic* rather than a static understanding of Christ. The rhetorical importation of the terminology of physics should not obscure the essential truth that Jesus the Messiah could do what He did only because He is who and what He is: the Only Begotten of the Father, very God and very Man.

Evangelical theology insists on the substitutionary and propitiatory nature of the redemptive work of Christ. That He was *our* substitute was possible because He was fully human. If the liberals have tended to overlook the one pole of the Chalcedonian formula, "of one substance with the Father according to the godhead," the traditionalists have sometimes neglected the other, "of one substance with us according to the manhood." From the biblical concept of propitiation, many have derived what they consider unacceptable conclusions concerning the vengeful nature of God, and their logic is not altogether unpersuasive. Yet the only God that we know is the God who reveals Himself in Scripture, and it is wiser to rejoice in the fact that He promises to show us mercy for Christ's sake than to express exasperation because our offenses somehow would appear to have drawn down upon us divine vengeance. We are, at all events, real and objective people, real and objective sinners. It is fair to say that unless there is something quite real and objective about the atonement, there will not be anything real and objective about the salvation that we expect from it.

SANCTIFICATION AND THE PERSON AND WORK OF THE HOLY SPIRIT

Insisting as we rightly do upon the objective nature of the atonement and the effective nature of its application to individual human beings in salvation, we sometimes appear in danger of having a doctrine that is purely historical and judicial, without any believable, human dimensions in the time and space in which we live. In the doctrine of creation we learn that the universe is the handiwork of God, who has established a certain order and certain principles in both the natural and the moral realms. Having transgressed the creation order and incurred condemnation, we find forgiveness and restoration in the atonement, the redeeming work objectively performed by one historic Person at a particular place and time in Jerusalem, under the procurator Pontius Pilate. But even as the creation order, transgressed lies for us in the past and somehow remains more theory than lived reality, so too the order of redemption, achieved by the one sacrifice, once offered (Heb 10:12) has a certain temporal fixity and separation from us in the ongoing concerns of daily life.

It is in the process of the ongoing life of the redeemed in Christ that we experience the growth in the knowledge and love of God and the increasing conformity to the image of Christ that is called sanctification. Creation is objective, the Fall is objective, the atonement is objective; and this is good, for we too are objective. But we are also in process, and sanctification, the continuing work of the Holy Spirit in our lives, is process. If evangelical theology has a strength, it is in the objective presentation of the atonement; in the presentation of creation, although less developed than Roman Catholic theology, it is also substantial. But having insisted on the objectivity of creation and redemption, each once for all, we sometimes lose the objectivity of sanctification, the process whereby, as we walk with God, we are made more conformable to His image. Evangelical theology knows that there must *be* sanctification; yet, with its awareness of the radical fallenness of man, it hesitates to say that anything so corrupted can be set apart for the purposes of God. If there is a weakness in the emerging evangelical consensus, it is doubtless at this point.

THE LAST THINGS

Objective creation, objective atonement, ongoing sanctification—where will it all end? The Christian faith clearly states that there is to be a consummation of all things, the return of Jesus Christ and a new world of glory. From the earliest disciples, Christians have lived in the eager expectation of the return of Christ. One evident aspect of the promise of the second coming is the fact that the final settlement, the establishment of justice, will come about only in the context of the personal, visible triumph of Christ and the judgment and overthrow of evil. Much is written in Scripture concerning the last days, yet perhaps nothing else that is written there is more difficult to interpret without ambiguity. Although some biblical Christians hold that the millennial reign is to be interpreted figuratively (amillennialism) and others teach that it has in effect already begun with the first advent (postmillennialism), the majority in the early Church and among contemporary evangelical Christians (the present writer among them) expect it to begin with the second advent.

It has been held by many that the prevalence of premillennialism among Christians leads to a "blocked future" (the term is Rushdoony's) in this world, to a kind of quietism and failure to seek to win the world for Christ in any respect other than by personal evangelism. On the other hand, the influence of postmillennialism in Puritan and nineteenth-century American Christianity could be and was secularized into a vision of an earthly kingdom that achieves perfection apart from God's judgment and the return of Christ. In any event, we would contend that the premillennial hope does not and should not imply quietism and resignation on the part of Christians in the complexities of this world. The premillennialist should contend as well as the postmillennialist to make the laws and structures of worldly society conform to the will and pattern of God as expressed in Scripture, although he knows that his efforts can result only in relative and localized improvements, not in any Utopia, prior to the return of Christ.

It remains the universal Christian conviction that the world must pass through a final judgment in the consummation, and that the end, like the creation and the atonement, is no mere prolongation of history but the decisive intervention of the sovereign God. Many forms of liberal Christianity have in common a vision of the world process as in some vague way being the salvation of the world. All biblical Christians know that salvation is not of or through any world process. It is of God, won for us by the incarnation, atoning death, and resurrection of His only-begotten Son, and mediated to our understanding in an intelligible, propositional, infallible revelation, the Word of God.

Notes

1. Cornelius Van Til, *The Defense of the Faith* (Philadelphia: Presby. & Ref., 1967), pp. 34-35, 78-96, 146-50, 211-13, 225-59.
2. See Harvie M. Conn, *Contemporary World Theology* (Nutley, N. J.: Presby. & Ref., 1973), pp. 22-24.
3. Paul van Buren, *The Secular Meaning of the Gospel* (New York: Macmillan, 1963); *Christ in Our Place* (Edinburgh: Oliver & Boyd, 1957).
4. Klaus Bockmühl, *Atheismus in der Christenheit* (Wuppertal: Aussaat, 1969). I am currently preparing an English translation for publication.
5. Harry Blamires, *The Christian Mind* (New York: Seabury, 1963).
6. Carl F. H. Henry, *Remaking the Modern Mind* (Grand Rapids: Eerdmans, 1946).
7. Peter L. Berger, *The Noise of Solemn Assemblies* (Garden City, N.Y.: Doubleday, 1961).
8. J. Gresham Machen, *Christianity and Liberalism* (New York: Macmillan, 1923).
9. Correspondence with Harold O. J. Brown, 1965.
10. For a helpful treatment of Schleiermacher and his influence, see Colin Brown, *Philosophy and the Christian Faith* (Chicago: Inter-Varsity, 1969).
11. Herman Dooyeweerd, *A New Critique of Theoretical Thought* (Philadelphia: Presby. & Ref., 1953). For an introduction to Dooyeweerd's philosophy, see J. M. Spier, *An Introduction to Christian Philosophy* (Philadelphia: Presby. & Ref., 1954), and Vincent Brümmer, *Transcendental Criticism and Christian Philosophy* (Franeker: T. Wever, 1961).
12. G. C. Berkouwer, *The Triumph of Grace in the Theology of Karl Barth* (Grand Rapids: Eerdmans, 1956). Somewhat similar in spirit is Colin Brown, *Karl Barth and the Christian Message* (London: Tyndale, 1967).
13. Cornelius Van Til, *The New Modernism* (Philadelphia: Presby. & Ref., 1946).
14. G. C. Berkouwer, *The Providence of God* (Grand Rapids: Eerdmans, 1952).
15. In addition to *The Providence of God,* Berkouwer has published in the Studies in Dogmatic series the volumes *Faith and Sanctification, Faith and Justification, Faith and Perseverance, The Person of Christ, General Revelation, Divine Election, Man: The Image of God, The Work of Christ, The Sacraments, Sin, The Return of Christ,* and *Holy Scripture* (Grand Rapids: Eerdmans, 1952-75).
16. Cornelius Van Til, *The Sovereignty of Grace: An Appraisal of G. C. Berkouwer's View of Dordt* (Nutley, N. J.: Presby. & Ref., 1969), p. 107, n. 1.
17. Cornelius Van Til, *Christianity and Barthianism* (Philadelphia: Presby. & Ref., 1962).
18. Gordon H. Clark, *Karl Barth's Theological Method* (Philadelphia: Presby. & Ref., 1963). Clark's philosophical contribution to the question of inspiration should be mentioned: *Religion, Reason and Revelation* (Nutley, N. J.: Craig, 1961).
19. Cf. Conn, p. ix.
20. See the dialogue in E. R. Geehan, ed., *Jerusalem and Athens* (Nutley, N. J.: Presby. & Ref., 1971), especially chaps. 19-23.

21. E.g., Willi Marxen, "The Resurrection of Jesus as a Historical and Theological Problem," in C. F. D. Moule, ed., *The Significance of the Message of the Resurrection for Faith in Jesus Christ* (London: SCM, 1968), especially Moule's introduction, pp. 6-11.
22. Gordon R. Lewis, "Van Til and Carnell, Part I," in Geehan, chap. 19.
23. Among his numerous titles, particular attention should be drawn to Francis A. Schaeffer, *The God Who Is There* (Chicago: Inter-Varsity, 1968); *Escape from Reason* (Chicago: Inter-Varsity, 1968); and *Genesis In Space and Time* (Downers Grove, Ill.: Inter-Varsity, 1972).
24. Geehan, pp. 392-403.
25. Edith Schaeffer, *L'Abri* (Wheaton, Ill.: Tyndale, 1969).
26. Udo Middelmann, *Pro-Existence* (Downers Grove, Ill.: Inter-Varsity, 1974).
27. Rousas J. Rushdoony, *The Institutes of Biblical Law* (Nutley, N. J.: Craig, 1973).
28. Gleason L. Archer, *A Survey of Old Testament Introduction* (Chicago: Moody, 1974); Roland K. Harrison, *Introduction to the Old Testament* (Grand Rapids: Eerdmans, 1969); Everett F. Harrison, *Introduction to the New Testament* (Grand Rapids: Eerdmans, 1964); Donald Guthrie, *New Testament Introduction* (Downers Grove, Ill.: Inter-Varsity, 1973); Frederick F. Bruce, *The New Testament Documents: Are They Reliable?* 5th ed. (Grand Rapids: Eerdmans, 1960), and *Second Thoughts on the Dead Sea Scrolls* (London: Paternoster, 1956).
29. Bernard Ramm, *The Christian View of Science and Scripture* (Grand Rapids, Baker, 1955); Rachel H. King, *The Creation of Death and Life* (New York: Philos. Lib., 1970).
30. A. E. Wilder Smith, *Man's Origin, Man's Destiny* (Wheaton, Ill.: Harold Shaw, 1968); Henry M. Morris, *The Twilight of Evolution* (Grand Rapids: Baker, 1964).
31. Eric L. Mascall, *The Secularisation of Christianity* (London: Darton, Longman, & Todd, 1965); Harold O. J. Brown, *The Protest of a Troubled Protestant* (New Rochelle: Arlington, 1969).
32. John W. Montgomery, *The Suicide of Christian Theology* (Minneapolis: Bethany, 1970).
33. H. R. Rookmaaker, *Modern Art and the Death of a Culture* (Downers Grove, Ill.: Inter-Varsity, 1970); Os Guinness, *The Dust of Death* (Downers Grove, Ill.: Inter-Varsity, 1973).

Selected Reading

Buswell, James Oliver. *A Systematic Theology of the Christian Religion*. Grand Rapids: Zondervan, 1963.

Clark, Gordon H. *A Christian View of Men and Things*. Grand Rapids: Eerdmans, 1952.

Henry, Carl F. H. *Frontiers in Modern Theology*. Chicago: Moody, 1966.

———. *Jesus of Nazareth: Savior and Lord*. Grand Rapids: Eerdmans, 1966.

———. *Remaking the Modern Mind*. Grand Rapids: Eerdmans, 1946.

Morris, Leon. *The Apostolic Preaching of the Cross*. Grand Rapids: Eerdmans, 1955.

———. *The Cross in the New Testament*. Grand Rapids: Eerdmans, 1965.

Packer, James I. *"Fundamentalism" and the Word of God*. Grand Rapids: Eerdmans, 1962.

———. *God Speaks to Man: Revelation and the Bible*. Philadelphia: Westminster, 1965.

———. *Knowing God*. Downers Grove, Ill.: Inter-Varsity, 1973.

Pinnock, Clark H. *Biblical Revelation–The Foundation of Christian Theology.* Chicago: Moody, 1971.

Ramm, Bernard. *The Pattern of Religious Authority.* Grand Rapids: Eerdmans, 1965.

———. *Special Revelation and the Word of God.* Grand Rapids: Eerdmans, 1961.

Van Til, Cornelius. *A Christian Theory of Knowledge.* Nutley, N. J.: Presby. & Ref., 1969.

———. *The Defense of the Faith.* Philadelphia: Presby. & Ref., 1955.

Wiley, H. Orton. *Christian Theology.* 3 vols. Kansas City, Mo.: Beacon Hill, 1964.

Index of Names

Index of Subjects

Actual entities, 242-51, 255, 261, 278
Analogy, 139-41, 269
Analytic philosophy, 111-12, 143, 168-69

Being and Being-itself, 86-87, 89-92, 94-95
Bibliology
  evangelical, 428-29, 450-51
  modernist-fundamentalist debate, 26-31
  neoorthodoxy, 39
  Tillich, 88, 95
Biblical realism, 29
Biblical theology, 38-39
Bipolar theism. *See* Process theology
"Blik," Hare's, 115, 136

Charismatic movement, Roman Catholic, 302-3
Chicago school. *See* Process theology
Christology
  Altizer, 162-64
  Boff, 369-71
  Bonhoeffer, 70-72, 79-80
  Bultmann, 54-55
  Cone, 354
  evangelical, 455-56
  liberal, 30-31
  Metz, 226-29
  Moltmann, 217
  Pannenberg, 219-22
  Pittenger, 264-67, 270, 279
  Robinson, 177-78
  Teilhard, 59-60, 64-66, 264
  Tillich, 88, 91-93
Church, doctrine of
  Bonhoeffer, 71
  Gutiérrez, 361-63
  Metz, 225-28
  Moltmann, 217
  Roman Catholic, 290, 299-301, 308-23
Consequent nature, 246-47

Conservatism. *See* Evangelicalism; Evangelical theology
Contextualization, 328-59, 377-78, 396-98, 411-12, 420-23, 427-28
Correlation, principle of, 82-85, 207-8, 377
Creation, evangelical doctrine of, 452-53
Criticism, 16, 20-21, 26-31, 446-48
Cross, 53-54, 65, 163-64

Death-of-God theology, 38, 56, 78, 90-91, 96, 159, 161-70, 174, 181-82, 190, 197-200, 203, 229-31, 431, 448
Demythologization, 46-47, 49-50, 76, 109-10, 170, 174-75, 203, 260
Desacralization, 181-82
Dialectics, 85-86, 157
Dialogue, 429-30
Dipolar theism. *See* Process theology
Divino Afflante Spiritu, 296
Dogma, development of, 290
Dutch Catechism, 311-13, 319-20

Ecclesium Suam, 296
Empirical theism, 32
Empiricism, 111-30, 139
Encounter, 107-8, 131, 182, 316
Enlightenment, 15-18, 230
Eschatological verification, 136-39
Eschatology
  Altizer, 164
  Cox, 183-84
  evangelical, 445-46, 457-58
  liberation theology, 356-58, 360, 417-18
  survey of, 33-34
  Teilhard, 65-66
  theology of hope, 197-231
Essentialism, Greek, 269
Eternal objects, 244-45
Ethics, 198, 215-17